*Paolo Portoghesi*

# Nature and Architecture

Translated by Erika G. Young

SKIRA

*Front Cover*
Axial view of a shell of the *Galeodea echinophora* species.
A free-well staircase in one of the "small towers" of Palazzo Ducale in Urbino (photo by Maria Ercadi).

*Design*
Marcello Francone

*Editing*
Giorgio Bigatti

*Layout*
Eliana Gelati

The publisher may be contacted for all iconographic sources not specifically identified

First published in Italy in 2000 by
Skira Editore S.p.A.
Palazzo Casati Stampa
via Torino 61
20123 Milano
Italy



Printed and bound in Italy. First edition

ISBN 88-8118-658-6

Distributed in North America and Latin America by Abbeville Publishing Group, 22 Cortlandt Street, New York, NY 10007, USA.
Distributed elsewhere in the world by Thames and Hudson Ltd., 181a High Holborn, London WC1V 7QX, United Kingdom.

*Thus, as has been already pointed out, thought is a material process whose content is the total response of memory, including feelings, muscular reactions and even physical sensations, that merge with and flow out of the whole response. Indeed, all man-made features of our general environment are, in this sense, extensions of the process of thought, for their shapes, forms, and general orders of movement originate basically in thought, and are incorporated within this environment, in the activity of human work, which is guided by such thought. Vice versa, everything in the general environment has, either naturally or through human activity, a shape, form, and mode of movement, the content of which "flows in" through perception, giving rise to sense impressions which leave memory traces and thus contribute to the basis of further thought.*

*In this whole movement, content that was originally in memory continually passes into and becomes an integral feature of the environment, so that... the two participate in a single total process in which analysis into separate parts (e.g. thought and thing) has ultimately no meaning.*

David Bohm

The idea behind this book is rooted in a restless adolescence, played out against the backdrop of the war. My inclination was to scour nature – discovered during contemplative holiday hiatuses - to find the answers to the origin of form.

The camera – as much a measuring instrument as a powerful extension of memory – encouraged my own tendency towards an ars analogica capable of pinpointing these similarities, not in order to identify derivations, but to rediscover that profound unity, that "secret law" mentioned by Goethe, founder of morphology, when he states that "all forms are similar, yet no two the same" and ends by calling this a "sacred enigma."

Begun many years ago, this work appeared for the first time during a slide show prepared for an exhibition organised with Paola Levi Montalcini at the Galleria Farnese. During the last decade, my analogical tendencies have led to the publication of this book which exploits recent scientific discoveries, in particular the discovery defined as "the new paradigm," to show architecture a path forward, a path along which continuity and innovation can finally be reunited, awarding to ecology the central role given to it by this "new paradigm."

An architecture which again becomes the art of living the earth under the banner of a new alliance, renouncing its role as a tool and an emblem of that thirst for supremacy and violence enunciated by Bacon when he spoke of "stalked" nature "put in chains" and considered it the task of scientists to "extort its secrets through torture." A female architecture is what is hoped for here, far from the arrogance of the widespread chaos of the twilight years of this millennium.

I found a forceful incentive to consider the similarities between nature and architecture as a reflection of the "mind" – not as something that divides man from the universe, but as a "connecting tissue" – in the writings of Gregory Bateson, an essential nutriment for me to accomplish my research: I also found this nourishment in books by John D. Barrow, David Bohm, Fritjof Capra, Geoffrey Chew, Mircea Eliade, Humberto Maturana, Francisco Varela, Benoit Mandelbrot, Ilya Prigogine, Ernst Schumaker and Enzo Tiezzi.

This book would never have seen the light if it hadn't been for that proximity to the earth concretised by my house in Calcata and my wife's love of animals and "country life." This is why my book is dedicated to Giovanna, as well as to the waters and tributaries of the river Treia, to Ulisse the olive tree, towering over our garden, and to the animals whose presence has given added meaning to our life in this special corner of the world: the donkeys Baldassare, Fantine, Macchiolina and Cibele, the shepherd dogs Tea, Saetta and Brigante, the cats Shamir, Citah and Oblomov, the goats Pelléas, Melisande and Rosamunda, the Llama Amada, Birba and Teresa and all the others.

I would like to thank Stefania Tuzi, Enrico Mattiello and Maria Ercadi for their precious help together with Maria Maddalena Alessandro, Franco Amendolaggine, Auro, Petra Bernitsa, Gianni Borgna, Gerrando Butti, Piergiulio Cantarano, Eduardo Chullen Dejo, Claudio Dall'Olio, Mario Docci, Marco Dori, Tania Grillandini, Luis Jimenez, Isabella Jodice, Sandra Latour, Luisa Laurelli, Salvo Lonardo, Piergiorgio Maoloni, Silvio Montin, Cecilia Mosconi, Ruggero Pentrella, Francesco Maria Raimondo, Oscar Savio, Rolando Scarano, Luciano Semerani, Elisa and Pietro Stoppони, Gianfranco Vannucchi, the editorial staff of Skira Marzia Branca, Eliana Gelati, Clelia Ginetti, Angelo Salvioni and Francesca Spranzi.

# Contents

*The illustrations in the introduction are dedicated to those aspects of nature that have played a fundamental role in the creation and growth of architectural imagery. The themes involved, the mountain, the tree, the flower, the human body, the skeleton, the womb, the phallus, as well as crystals, rays and weaving, do not belong to architecture alone, but to anthropology in general. They link, in a most profound way, architecture and daily life to myth and religion.*
*Architectural archetypes and the conceptual structures to which the other chapters are dedicated represent man's discovery and interiorisation of these aspects of nature, thus making him the continuator of creation.*

# Nature and Architecture

Comment enrichir ses puissances de création?
Non pas en s'abonnant à des revues
architecture, mais en partant en découvertes
dans le domaine insondable des richesses de la
nature. Là est vraiment la leçon d'architecture:
la grâce d'abord! Oui, cette souplesse, cette
exactitude, cette indiscutable réalité des
combinaisons, des engendrements harmonieux
dont la nature offre le spectacle en chaque
chose. Du dédans au déhors: la perfection
sereine. Plantes, animaux, arbres, sites, mers,
plaines ou montagnes. Même, la parfaite
harmonie des catastrophes naturelles, des
cataclysmes géologiques, etc [...]. Ouvrir les yeux!
Sortir de l'étroitesse des débats professionels. Se
donner si passionnément à l'étude de la raison
des choses que l'architecture s'en trouve
devenir spontanément la conséquence. Briser
les "écoles" (l'école "Corbu" au même titre que
l'école Vignole – je vous en supplie!). Pas de
formules, pas de "trucs", pas de tours de mains.
Nous sommes au début de la découverte
architecturale des temps modernes. Que de
toutes parts surgissent des propositions fraîches.
Dans cent ans, nous pourrons parler d'un
"style". Il n'en faut pas aujourd'hui, mais
seulement DU STYLE, c'est-à-dire de la tenue
morale dans toute œuvre créée, véritablement
créée.
Je voudrais que les architectes – non pas
seulement les étudiants – prennent leur crayon
pour dessiner une plante, une feuille, exprimer
l'esprit d'un arbre, l'harmonie d'un coquillage,
la formation des nuages, le jeu si riche des
vagues qui s'étalent sur le sable et pour
découvrir les expressions successives d'une force
intérieure. Que la main (avec la tête derrière)
se passionne à cette intime enquête.

Le Corbusier

The analogy between natural and architectural forms sometimes catches us unawares leaving profound yet fleeting impressions. Coincidences, or traces of continuity, between creation and the work of man emerge from our memory like events from the past, as if this analogy held captive a fragment of paradise lost.

Poets have always been fascinated by this similarity of form extensively exploited in metaphors and symbols.

In the third book of his *Metamorphosis*,[1] for example, when Ovid describes the Gargaphia valley sacred to Diana, rich in cypress and pine trees, he speaks of a woody gorge and remarks that here "for nature's touch ingeniously had so fairly wrought in frail sandstone and soft white pumice an arch so true it seemed the art of man, not built but born" (*Simulaverat artem / ingenio natura suo; nam pumice vivo / et levibus tofis nativum duxerat arcum*). Centuries later, Ovid is echoed by Giorgio Vasari who, in his biography of Baldassarre Peruzzi, when praising the beautiful architectural "grace" of Villa Farnesina, wrote that the building appeared "not built with walls but truly born."[2]

Nature and architecture. The first thing we should ask ourselves is whether it is appropriate to compare a part (architecture) with the whole (nature) to which it undoubtedly belongs. Like coral creating reefs in the ocean abyss, as history slowly unfurls, man leaves a resistant sediment on the earth: a mixture of objects and signs that bear witness to his passage, to his role as an agent of change on the surface of the earth and in more recent years, on what is above and below its crust. Certainly, the most significant component of this resistant sediment is architecture.

Simply speaking of nature produces a very similar problem. Being an integral part of nature ourselves, we shall never be able to talk about it *from the outside* but only *from the inside*, uncertain whether to consider something created and produced by man as being "outside" nature: this might perhaps be applicable to thought, language and spirit, but certainly not to the products of *homo faber*, which include architecture.[3] However, is not the separation between nature and spirit responsible for the Promethean attitude towards technology which promised salvation in exchange for the defeat and servitude of nature and today heralds ecological disaster?

Recent decades have witnessed the re-emergence of "archetypes" and the abandonment of the myths of palingenesis.[4] However, in order to go beyond the fashionable styles or exasperated individualism still rampant today, it is essential to re-propose the enduring validity of archetypes on a broader scale. Such validity is invested with the authority that comes from the encounter between History and Nature. It is necessary to build, to consolidate, to protect the constructed object as a part of nature, man's ally, by creating conditions that continually evolve and correspond to different (and contradictory) levels of understanding in the relationship between nature and architecture. This alliance we propose to build, based on our past catastrophic experiences and increasingly profound knowledge, would be the strongest, truest possible, and although founded on disappointments and remorse it would be rife with respect and love.

In this book, architectural archetypes will be examined according to the observations and emotions that nature inspires, leaving the reader the task of mentally rearranging material that defies rigid classification and should instead be considered a matter for fluid reflection.

In an age in which our main concern is to leave our heirs as rich a world as possible, compared to the one we inherited from our fathers, we should forgo this act of pride which considers architecture, along with many other disciplines, an "artificial second nature," an issue of our minds, a reification of the spirit, a celebration of separation seen as freedom from nature.

The least convincing effect (or consequence) of separation is the historic division between "organicity" and "abstraction" and the fact that "listening to nature" is present in certain "naturalistic" architectures rather than in other "classic" or "abstract" ones based on the intentional separation of nature and spirit.

In this book, the founding process of architecture will be studied by using its archetypes to ratify a working hypothesis based on design experience. These archetypes were almost always based on a structural and symbolic interpretation of nature to establish methods, laws and principles whose existence man perceives when faced with a variety of phenomena that he assimilates through his five senses as well as through language and thought.

In his long diatribe against imitative arts in Book X of *The Republic*, Plato reflected on a secondary architectural archetype: the bed, an object necessary for a house to be considered inhabitable.[5]

> "...there are three types of beds. One exists in the composition of ideal nature. This bed, we may say, was made by God. Or should we say by someone else?"
> "No-one else, I believe."
> "Instead, a bed is made by carpenters."
> "Yes," he replied.
> "And is the one created by a painter also a bed?"
> "So it is."
> "So a painter is a maker of beds, is God. Here are three people and all three have an understanding and a relationship with three different types of beds... And what about the carpenter? Is he not a maker of beds?"
> "Yes."
> "So! would you say that the painter is also a maker of beds, a person who truly makes beds?"
> "Certainly not."
> "But talking about beds, what is it that a painter makes?"
> "Well!" he said, "I believe we may fairly designate him as the imitator or mimic of that which others make."

"Good," I went on, "then you call him who is third in descent from nature an imitator."

If a bed is a second generation "object," whoever produces it imitates an archetype and therefore does not fall into the category of mimics. On the contrary, he is worthy of being admitted to the city of the just, which could never have survived without architects to turn collective ideas into real places.

This is certainly not the place to discuss Plato's condemnation of poetry or painting as illusionary arts, much less the problem of innate ideas. Architectural archetypes and those, such as the bed, which complement architecture, draw on the talents inherent in man's genes, on specific aspects that determine the traditions of civilisation (even in Japanese civilisation in which beds are not part of household furniture) and lastly on other talents assimilated through participation in community life. These archetypes are very similar to those Jung defined as archetypes of the collective subconscious. However, a difference does exist: by nature they are strongly rooted in matter and often involve all five of our senses even if they are immaterial.[6]

In particular, I intend to examine what it is that turns archetypes into interpretations of nature and life or even projected images of the nature of man's impulses, desires and needs and therefore the founding principles of a discipline, architecture, that by forgetting their worth has lost its incisiveness and credibility and is often reduced to being merely the concrete achievement of an individual's ability. In the field of architecture, archetypes express the collective dimension and the richest possible stratification of experiences accumulated over the years, generation after generation. Consequently, they act as an effective antidote to individualistic judgements and the exasperation of insincere processes of change.

The symbol is an excellent concept to help us understand the specific relationship between architecture and nature. It is the only one capable of helping us master the traditional difficulties experienced over the centuries when attempting to include architecture among the imitative arts, even by pushing the limits sometimes. In fact, architectural imitation is actually only partial imitation and does not involve the outward appearance of objects. However, it is an imitation that tends to assimilate the object's transcending elements, its possible use in satisfying man's needs and desires as well as its capacity for symbolism. In other words, the type of imitation that characterises architecture, as far as nature is concerned, is essentially "symbolic imitation," because the symbol (from the Greek, *symballein*, to put together) heralds a level of consciousness that is different from rational evidence, yet also expresses what cannot otherwise be expressed: that which has no clearly defined verbal "explanation." If painting and sculpture allowed primitive man to demonstrate his ability to understand and portray natural forms, architecture allowed him to accede to the realm of the subconscious by giving form to archetypes that render natural experiences ambiguously and to at-

## The Human Body

The shape of the body, its uniqueness, its identity made up of separate parts, teaches man the first rule of composition: unity in multiplicity. Whether or not reference to the human body is intentional, it is an integral part of all architectural civilisations, regardless of the period.

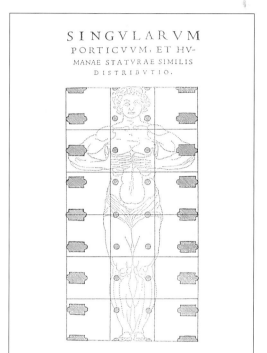

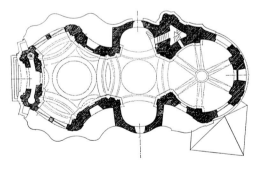

*Above: the portico of the temple of Jerusalem designed according to the proportions of the human body in a reconstruction by J.B. Villalpando (16th century) and the anthropomorphic plan of the church of Santa Marta in Agliè (1740-60). Above right: water-colour showing a public building designed by Hans Scharoun (c. 1940). Right: one of the most direct and explicit allusions to the human face, Palazzo Zuccari, Via Gregoriana, Rome (1590-98).*

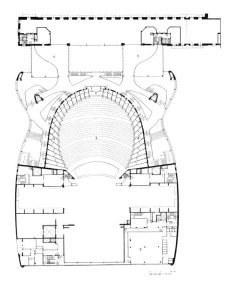

*Left: Imre Makovecz, the Catholic church in
Siofok, Hungary (1986-90).*
*The architects in the Makona Group created by
Makovecz were inspired by anthroposophic
traditions and tried to give the design of their
houses a past, so that the houses became a link
between heaven and earth.*
*Above:* Photographic Nude *by Carlo Mollino and
the plan of the Teatro Regio in Turin inspired by
the female torso and that piece of female lingerie
that goes by the name of guêpière.*

13

tempt to reproduce both form and intimate structures in such a way that this experience appears in the constructed object as being both near and far, traceable and lost.

According to research by Fischer-Barnicol and studies by Schneider, the symbol is the simplest and most profound instrument used to express a particular reality in a different medium.

"By using a symbol, a transcendent force which is literally invisible and intangible may be revealed in a material object [...]. Therefore, as an object the symbol is not identical to symbolised reality. It is none other than a means of exteriorization that permits a force, inexpressible through the senses and seemingly hidden in shadow, to reveal its presence, just like the human soul, for example, may be manifest in the body or in speech."[7]

Let us take as practical examples the house, the column and the cupola.

The house origins lie in the tree, the cave and the nests of birds, but it also relates to the archetype of prenatal life in the womb. When building a house, primitive man did not set out to imitate forms but to symbolise living conditions that were either imaginary or gleaned directly from his own experiences. Through his actions, he grafted his buildings onto nature assuming the role of continuator of Creation.

It has always been said that the column was inspired by the tree-trunk as well as by the ease with which a rolling object may be transported, but the column also corresponds to the erect position of our bodies, to the vertical expanse of mountains, to the lifting and supporting action of our arms. These and other elements reside together in the column as symbols that increase its imaginative virtuality. The distinctive trait of a symbol lies in its ability to create an "accordion" process between two images. The column-trunk is refuted by the column-body, but through the ratification of the capital-head and capital-foliage it generates a convincing metamorphic process which juxtaposes sign and significance, dynamism and ambiguity.

The introduction of cross-fade in film technique, with its overlapping and inter-permeation of images, has introduced the equivalent of the metamorphic process of symbolic imitation, permitting us to enter – so to speak – into the laboratory of visual thought.

Symbolic imitation leads into the inexhaustible and ambiguous domain of analogy and mimicry, something similar to the temple described by Baudelaire in his sonnet in which "live columns" sometimes murmur confused words, and a "forest of symbols" looks at us "familiarly"; in a mysterious and profound unity, sounds, perfumes and colours generate long overlapping echoes by "answering each other."[8]

Like echoes, analogy creates different repetitions, a resemblance that recalls the peculiar traits of family members, and this "naturally" expands the field of study and reflection. "In all those cases in which one has to group different objects or subjects and link them to similar relations," writes René Alleau, "analogy intervenes as an exploratory and unifying process capable of disclosing the general perspectives and harmonic or regulatory relations which the logic of identity alone permits neither to be perceived nor identified."[9]

If the logic of analogy occupies an important place in general symbolism, considered as a science, it is invaluable to the study of archetypes in so far as it is the primordial and universal logic behind living forms. "That which constitutes symbolic magnetism *par excellence* comes from a force which is simultaneously logical and psychological: the logic of analogy. Contrary to the logic of identity, which is a prevalently conscious act present in all abstract thought processes, the logic of analogy is characterised by its solid archaism, its unconscious thematic organisation as well as the affective and emotional charge it is capable of projecting onto all objects encountered in life."[10]

Alleau also speaks of "expression mobility" as one of the characteristic reactions of animals faced with the dilemma of survival. "Expressiveness results in the ability to modify colour, smell, behaviour and appearance, the relationship between what can and what is perceived, between signs expressed and signs understood. Direct attack or defence mechanisms are combined with indirect distraction procedures through the simulation of behaviour or signs considered offensive by prey or dangerous by predators. Analogy intervenes at all levels of mimicry." After having illustrated various forms of mimicry with the environment, he goes on to say: "the imitative expression of forms and colours, at the root of all art, is prefigurative, a prerequisite for the survival of mimetic analogy which perfects and completes an imperfect natural process."[11]

Symbolic imitation often needs to be expressed consciously, however this book often refers to unconscious imitation rooted in the unity of creation, in the fact that our way of thinking, imagining or composing draws on the same source exploited by the laws, forms and processes of nature, in short by life itself.

Not too long ago this profound unity, traces of which can be seen in both the natural and artificial worlds, seemed confined to the magical field of poetic intuition. This is no longer true, since even science now sends unexpected signals confirming this affirmation. In his poem written in 1798 and entitled *Lines written a few miles above Tintern Abbey*, William Wordsworth wrote:

> And I have felt
> A presence that disturbs me with the joy
> Of elevated thoughts: a sense sublime
> Of something far more deeply interfused,
> Whose dwelling is the light of setting suns,
> And the round ocean, and the living air
> And the Blue sky, and in the minds of man –
> A motion and a spirit that impels
> All thinking things, all objects of all thought,
> And rolls through all things [...]

## The Skeleton

The idea of the skeleton, considered the load-bearing structure of the body, is visible even in primitive huts which were made of branches and later covered with animal skins and small bushes. Not only has the wooden structure maintained this dichotomy between the load-bearing frame and the skin, but it took on new meaning when iron and reinforced concrete were used as building materials.

In brick walls, the difference between load-bearing and non-load-bearing structures is negligible due to greater plastic unity, however it is sometimes energised by ribs and buttresses. By denying the divisibility of the architectural corpus, Alberti's idea of organism is very similar to the static behaviour of an organism in which the skeleton, muscles and nerves co-operate with the *firmitas*.

*The skeleton of a snake and an elephant photographed inside the Museum of Natural History in São Paulo, Brazil.*
*Below: Aldo Rossi, a drawing for the cemetery in Modena with an intentional symbolic reference to an "osteological structure."*

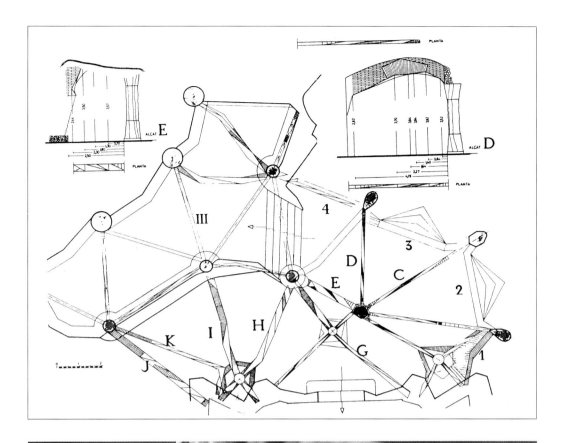

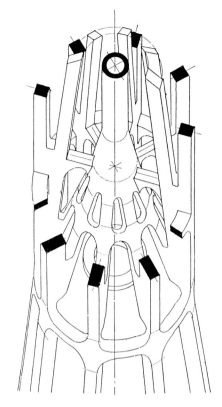

*Axonometric detail of the lantern, cupola of San Gaudenzio, Novara (Alessandro Antonelli, 1841). Left: Antoni Gaudí, detail of the roof of the crypt of Santa Coloma in Park Güell, Barcelona (1898); below left: internal view of a dissected human bone showing its trabecular structure.*

Almost two centuries later, in 1977, Gregory Bateson in a conference in the Cathedral of Saint John the Divine in New York recalled the philosophy of Lamarck. During the conference he rhetorically asked the public what structure linked the crab to the lobster, the orchid to the primrose, and all four to the speaker? Or the speaker to the audience? Or all six to an amoeba or a schizophrenic? In his attempt to provide an answer to this question Bateson pointed out that the best way to understand this common structure was to initially think of it (whatever that might mean) as a dance of interacting parts, only later constrained by all sorts of physical limitations and by the limits imposed by the characteristics of each organism. Towards the end of his presentation Bateson affirmed that if the world was interconnected, and if what he said was basically correct, then conceiving the past was common to every mind or all minds, whether one spoke of man's mind or that of the sequoia forests or sea anemone.[12]

"Linked in its mental aspects," architecture is the fruit of man's organising mind and consequently must be related to the endless other manifestations of the mind to be found in nature. This book attempts to disclose this kinship. It is also a way to affirm the aesthetic unity that "modernity" has denied. And if this aesthetic unity is denied, it is impossible to repair the damage wrought by man who considers himself an antagonist rather than an integral part of nature.

Bateson was also wont to say that man had begun to tinker with the principles of ecology, and even though he immediately exploited them commercially or politically, at least there remained in the hearts of mankind an urge to unify and therefore sanctify the entire natural world to which he belonged.[13] This observation harbours a kernel of hope and, implicitly, is an invitation for architects to again "learn from nature;" the ancient invitation that Wordsworth continued to propose:

Come forth into the light of things
Let Nature be your teacher.

Bateson's diagnosis regarding the wickedness of the mind, linked to Prigogine's theory of auto-organisation of matter and the theses of Maturana and Varela on the autopoiesis of living organisms, now provide precious tools to those who wish to view architecture in a new light, rescuing it from the dubious ambiguity of exasperated individualism.

For living creatures the processes of *analogy*, based on the concordance of functions, and of *homology*, based on the concordance of structure, are reflected in architecture that is dominated by typological processes, the growth of artificial structures and, on a larger scale, the birth and growth of the urban fabric. It will therefore come as no surprise that a book that wishes to be a journey "in search of the lost bond between architecture and nature" be full of *analogical* and *homological art*.

This comparative method calls upon a new *homological art* as well as ancient *analogical art*. Instead of partial resemblance that presumes deeper affinities and leads only to a possible increase in knowledge, this book illustrates those cases in which there is a correspondence between structures based on a common original form as well as relationships which obey a common law. Therefore "homology" will be used in the strict sense of the word as applied in descriptive geometry and biology. In 1988, an anti-conformist professor of molecular biology at the University of Lund, A. Lima-de-Faria, published a book[14] in which he strongly disputes the idea of "natural selection," typical of Neo-Darwinian theories. He put together an impressive number of illustrations demonstrating the isomorphism of mineral, plant and animal structures.

For Lima-de-Faria, molecular analysis leads to the inevitable conclusion that life had no beginning. Instead it is "a process inherent in the structure of the universe." Evolution thus becomes a physical and chemical phenomenon caused by a tendency towards self-assembly. This process is already present in elementary particles as well as in atoms and molecules. A passage in the above-cited book reads as follows: "Mesons result from the union of pairs of quarks and antiquarks. Protons, neutrons and electrons self-assemble into atoms."

Accordingly, the presence of similar models in the inorganic and organic world is considered proof of their common origin and a reflection of different evolutionary stages. In a scientific world that tends to attribute an increasingly extensive and endemic role to casual and chaotic processes, Lima-de-Faria takes a very controversial stance. He states that morphogenesis is governed by a rigid molecular order. This order is based on a limited number of original forms repeated in numerous different combinations and present in all structures of matter across all frontiers of "realms" and disciplines.

If, on the one hand, this theory lends support to faith in a new determinism, on the other, it proposes a model of absolute unity, similar to Mendeleyev's table which led to the discovery of new elements due to the empty boxes in the periodic table of the elements. This model reaffirms many aspects of classical physics and creationist theories. However, in contrast to the theories of the Neo-Darwinists, it attributes renewed importance to the permanence of fundamental structures, contradicting a viewpoint which concentrated on change and the influence of the environment. According to this concept, after the first "nanosecond" of the Big Bang, the Universe looked like a perfectly symmetrical figure. In 1982, H.R. Pagels wrote in his book *The Cosmic Code* that "all the interactions we see in the present world are the asymmetrical remnants of a once perfectly symmetrical world." This theory considers natural history as a headlong and relentless "falling" process, but does not reject the possibility of finding a remnant of "paradise lost" in primordial unity and in the magnificent simplicity of the physical and chemical processes of evolution.

The history of autoevolution thus becomes rigid and resolute. However, by continuously exploring all possibilities it also acquires the traits of freedom and unlimited differentiation.

In Lima-de-Faria's book the formal models are reviewed with the subtle complacency of this rediscovered unity and the origins of life are persuasively

## The Womb

Before the vagina and the uterus either consciously or unconsciously became the model for every "interior" and consequently for the house seen as a shelter and a return to grass roots, the areas of the earth's surface where similar forms existed were often considered sacred.

The gallery tombs (dolmen) in which the sun's rays penetrated internal spaces are not only astronomical observatories but perhaps metaphors of penetration and fertility.

In Newgrange in Ireland, the oval shape of the tumulus, the presence of a phallic pillar and two gypsum balls, but above all the spectacular vault built by overlapping stone slabs, all recall the sexual act, the primacy of Mother Earth and the beauty of empty spaces.

*Above right: a natural cave on Mary's Island off the coast of Tasmania (Australia).*
*Below right: a stone on the River Vilcanota in the Sacred Valley of the Inca (Peru).*

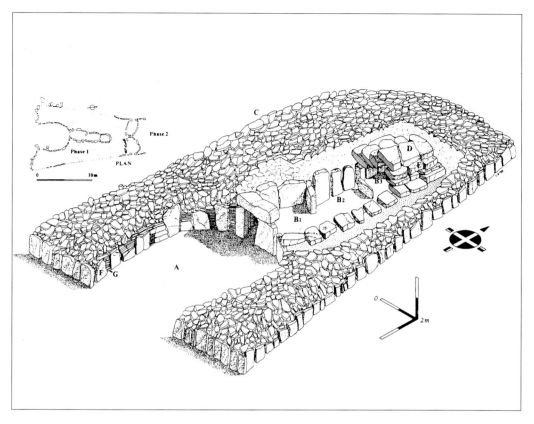

*Above: the outer door of a grotto in Matmātā, a village south of Gabés (Tunisia).*
*Axonometric projection of the courtyard tomb in Annaghmare, County Armagh, Ireland.*
*Below: Antoni Gaudí, skyward view of the courtyard of Casa Milá in Barcelona (1905-11).*

prefigured in the crystal-clear order of inorganic matter to such an extent that crystallisation may in some ways be considered a birth.

The series of Lima-de-Faria's "synoptic" tables begins with "dichotomy": one is divided into two. A calcite crystal splits into a sister form; the *Azorella selago*, a plant of the Umbelliferae family, has upper and lower ramifications in its trunk and roots and human bronchia form a mass of symmetrical figures.

This organic-inorganic mix is both diachronic and synchronic: cellular molecules assume crystalline form, a fact that occurs in begonias, the common plant that adorns our balconies and window-sills. Nestled in the plant's cells, inside a polygonal organic mesh, are octahedral calcium oxalate crystals; these crystals assume a variety of geometric shapes, sometimes simple, sometimes stellar, because small pyramidal cusps form on each face of the octahedron.

After dichotomy comes "ramification," present in electric discharges as well as in life. Ramification ranges from the "centrality" and "annular twisting" of trunks and stems prefigured by agate, to structures including veined leaves, fish bones and the nascent crystals of halite and gold, to the "floral" model of anhydride and multipointed crystals present on agate geodes as well as in the fruit of the *Durio zibethinus*. Ostensibly specific to human beings, even the labyrinthine structures of the brain and the intestines are visible when a black magnetic liquid is mixed with a non-magnetic white one and both are subject to a uniform, horizontal magnetic field. Furthermore, the crenated sutures of skull bones can be found in a mineral concretion, while the overlapping layers of ant-eater scales and pine cones resemble certain halite crystals in which numerous angular platforms jut out over the edge like the protruding balconies of a pyramidal building. Isomorphism can also be seen in the similarities between the horns of ruminators and the curved stacks of chlorite crystals, while spikes and dorsal spines may be compared to rock crystals and prehistoric animals.

When illustrating the different types of central symmetry, Lima-de-Faria explores their rotational symmetry axes, from two to three to four. When he reaches number five – the pentagonal symmetry so frequent in flowers and simple animal organisms, such as the radiolarians – his theory of analogies between the mineral and biological world seems to enter a rather critical stage, but the rigid pattern is re-established thanks to a recent discovery discussed further on in the chapter on centrality. The discovery made use of an electronic microscope with which it was possible to identify five-pointed aluminium and manganese crystals very similar to snow flakes. The diffraction of the electrons and X-rays showed a fivefold symmetry that according to the established laws of crystallography was considered impossible. These crystals were called semicrystals, but have now taken their rightful place in crystallography despite their suspect "diversity."

Having overcome the problem of fivefold symmetry, Lima-de-Faria's exemplification continues unhindered up to thirteen. It constitutes a fascinating stepping stone towards the possible completion of architectural morphologies. To some extent this book attempts to achieve this completion by citing an architectural example for each different form of radial symmetry. The theory linking the organic and inorganic worlds was foreshadowed, if not in its poetical contents, certainly by the methods used in organic architecture whose forms were inspired by both these morphological repertoires.

The drastically reduced influence of the outdoor environment on morphogenesis also applies to the world of artificial forms. Autoevolution does not exclude adaptive processes, but neither does it consider them the driving force behind forms. Consequently, it excludes the interpretation of mimetic phenomena as being the result of "natural" selection benefiting the strongest or most adaptable. If an insect looks like a leaf this is due to the fact that between animal and plant forms there may be an atomic homology with common ancestors in the field of structural configurations. Such is the case of the butterfly and the leaf when compared to the crystallisation process of halite. Likewise, the orchids of the *Ophrys* family, with which certain insects copulate "virtually," are linked not only by a superficial visual similarity, but also by a conformity of structure and chemical substances (the same pheromone secreted by the insect's sexual organs is surprisingly produced by the flower too) and this fact reflects their common formal vocation.

And what about horns? Neo-Darwinism links them to the fight for sexual supremacy by male ruminants, but forgets to explain why these horns appear on the bodies of molluscs, many of which are hermaphrodites and would be hard put to use them for the same purpose. And what about aragonite crystals that develop similar forms even if they have neither genes nor sexual activity? Even water, without the genes or DNA of living beings, behaves with the same "multiplicity in unity" as far as its forms are concerned. And how can one explain the infinite variations of snow crystal patterns, which strictly obey the laws of hexagonal symmetry, without admitting that even these flakes, capable of growing and regenerating, embody the original driving force that set the universe in motion after the Big Bang in which the persuasive evolutionary nature of symmetry triumphed?

The theory of natural selection or the survival of the strongest or the fittest has recently been challenged by a number of Japanese scientists, among them Kinji Imanishi and Mooto Kimura. They believe that this theory is influenced by western mentality, and instead see in the evolutionary process, co-operation and mutual assistance among members of a species, a theory already elaborated in 1906 by Kropotkin in his book on "mutual support."[15]

Lima-de-Faria lists an impressive series of structural homologies between the mineral, plant and animal worlds, but then in his conclusions appears to imprison them in a rigid deterministic model at both the macroscopic and microscopic level, a chemical determinism very similar to the mechanical determinism of classical physics.

The significance of these homologies changes when evaluated according

## Verticality

Phallic symbolism is generally expressed by the tower archetype, as well as the menhir and the obelisk, and those architectures in which penetration ends at a final point, such as the gallery tombs. Verticality, rather than inclination or blocked passages, is the way in which virility is celebrated with its inevitable halo of violence and elimination of empty spaces.

*Below: phallic spires of the Sangha mosque built by the native Dogon tribe (Mali).*
*Above right: adobe mosque in Mali.*
*Below right: Cornelis Anthonisz Teunissen,* The Tower of Babel *(engraving 16th century).*

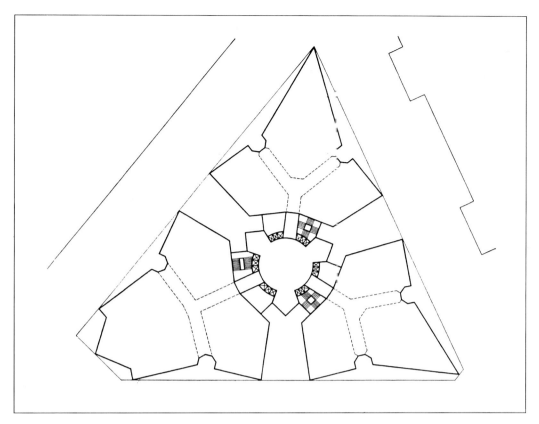

Ludwig Mies van der Rohe, project for an iron and glass building in Berlin (1920-21). The plan was inspired by maple leaves.

to Ilya Prigogine's interpretation of the relationship between science and nature. This interpretation is based on an ongoing examination that does not aim at establishing fundamental principles or uniting all natural processes according to a few "eternal" laws. In his book, *The New Alliance*,[16] he writes: "Natural sciences now describe a fragmented Universe rich in qualitative differences and potential surprises. We have discovered that dialogue with nature no longer means an external disenchanted reconnaissance of a lunar desert, but the elective local exploration of a complex and multiform nature. Recent discoveries in the fields of physics and biology, as well as this century's rapid demographic growth, are leading us towards a new naturalism."

This "re-enchantment" with nature is based on our awareness that man is an integral part of nature. The very fact that we study nature is now a part of our intrinsic activities. Freed from the imaginings of an inspired and supernatural revelation, "scientific knowledge" discovers itself to be "both the poetic ear of nature as well as its natural process: a straightforward process of production and invention in an open, productive and inventive world."[17]

In contrast, this disenchantment was determined by classical interpretations that denied evolution and diversity and raised the earth to the incorruptible perfection of the heavens. Prigogine, instead, considered the radical change in the outlook of modern science, the transition to the temporal, to the multiple, to be the exact opposite of the trend that brought Aristotle's heavens to earth: "We raise earth to the heavens. We discover the primacy of time and evolution, from elementary particles to cosmological models."[18] Freed from the fascination of narrow rationality and the myth of a "final accomplishment" to be reached by knowledge in order to consider itself mistress of the universe, natural sciences "have entered into a dialogue with nature that can no longer be dominated by theoretical considerations but only explored: a dialogue with the open world to which we belong and in whose construction we participate."[19]

This viewpoint draws man closer to nature, narrows the gap between the natural and the artificial and destroys the illusion of man's domination of the world. In this framework, architecture itself, as the product of the transformation of the earth's crust, becomes part of nature, just like the coral reefs and the shells in which invertebrates take refuge, just like the gardens built by the bower-birds for their mating rituals, just like the dams built with endless patience by beavers who eke out a "domestic space" from the playful watery currents of rivers. These homologies become the mysterious symptoms of a "wonderful simplicity" that coexists with matter's insuppressible tendency to subdivide, to differentiate, to evolve, to flow like the waters of the river described by Borges in his poem, *The Art of Poetry*:[20]

Art is that Ithaca
of green eternity, not wonders.
Art is endless like the river flowing

passing yet remaining; it mirrors the same
inconstant Heraclitus, who is the same
and yet another, like the river flowing.

One of the most innovative and significant aspects of the new relationship between science and nature is the so-called theory of chaos. Jim Yorke, the scientist who introduced the modern scientific use of the word "chaos" wrote: "We tend to think that science has explained everything when it explained that the Moon revolves around the Earth. But this idea of a universe-time-machine has nothing to do with the real world."[21]

In our everyday lives, as well as in the dictionary, chaos is defined as a synonym of disorder. Even if in ancient Greek, chaos meant "open crevice," it is immediately associated with the biblical concept of the origin of matter before Jehovah differentiated it by creating light, the heavens and the earth. However, current scientific usage attributes other meanings to the word based on the observation of the behaviour of dynamic systems and their unpredictability. For example, let us take bird feathers floating on a mountain stream. The current will sweep these feathers downstream: they will follow different trajectories at varying speeds according to the steep or flat gradient of the river, the froth of the waves, any possible reciprocal interference or unevenness as well as the presence of rocks in the river bed. The feathers' journey is determined by the water, the wind and many potential obstacles, so it is practically impossible to guess the trajectory of the feathers and the moment they will arrive at a certain point. This is therefore a determinate yet unpredictable dynamic system. We are faced with one of those phenomena (many of which, such as dripping taps, the weather, or the dynamics of animal populations, are part of our everyday life) that refuses to obey the paradigms of classical science, yet remains within a deterministic framework.

Edward Lorenz once commented that the beat of a butterfly's wings in the Brazilian forest can influence the weather to such an extent as to possibly trigger a cyclone in another part of the world. This remark spread like wildfire around the world and will probably one day end up in the text books of young school children. In some ways this sentence is similar to the one by Saint Augustine that Mies van der Rohe used to repeat to his students: "God is in little things." Undoubtedly, as the symbol of a new way of seeing and thinking, it certainly has dealt a mortal blow to one of the most stubbornly enduring myths of this dying century: the machine as a model for every physical phenomenon and all rational behaviour, a redeeming model to which even artistic creation has been subjected. "Machines... machines... machines!, this is the cry that runs like a *leitmotif* through the modern world, echoing along the highway of the future towards an objective only our imagination can envisage."[22] This prediction pronounced in 1927 by Edward Allen Jewell now seems obsolete, but its obsolescence depends more on the advent of a new mentality than the fall of ideologies and the birth of the post-industrial society. This new mentality is

## Animals

"Every archetypology," wrote Gilbert Durand, "must lead to a Bestiary and begin by reflecting on the universality and banality of the Bestiary." The symbolism attributed to animal bodies by numerous civilisations has made it possible for the architect to use symbolic imitation to communicate ideas and confirm collective values. The traits of each animal and each part of their bodies (the wing, the claw, the beak, the horns and the skin – a typical example would be the "fiercely symmetric" skin of the tiger) have sometimes been transferred to buildings for magical purposes. An example of this possible transference is the defensive action of the turtle, the liberating flight of the bird and the enveloping shape of the snail.

*Right: the condor, considered by Andean civilisations as a local divinity.*
*Below right: project for the Teatro Puccini at Torre del Lago near Pisa (Paolo Portoghesi, 1986).*
*Below: a winged shelf designed by Antoni Gaudí and the model of the project for the church of the Madonna delle Lacrime in Siracusa (Enrico Castiglioni, 1957).*

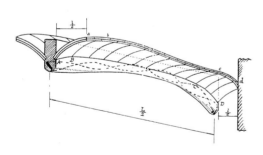

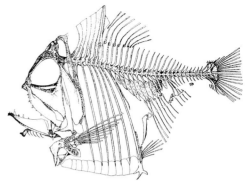

*Above from left: a tropical butterfly*
*(Callosamia Promethea)* and a bird's-eye view of
the model of the Teatro Puccini at Torre del Lago.
*Above: a fish skeleton.*
*Below: plan of the church of Kaleva in Tampere,*
*Finland (Reima Pietila, 1959-66) inspired by the*
*Christian symbol of the fish as a hidden image of*
*Christ.*

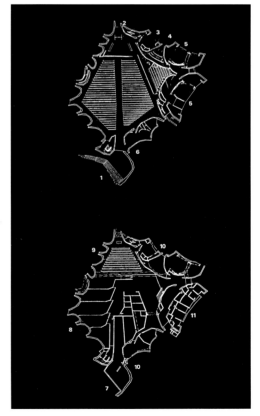

slowly replacing the one that will characterise the 20th century as one of the worst centuries in the history of the earth, despite all its successes and probable final outcome.

The widespread consequences of science's unpredictable familiarity with these complex and chaotic phenomena are almost totally omnipresent in the most varied disciplines. The fact that they are slow to invade architecture is due to the isolation set in motion by the excessive independence that architects continue to cultivate. On the other hand, attempts to establish direct analogies, such as those formulated by Charles Jencks, who considers deconstructivism (the latest attempt to revitalise machinist avant-garde language) to be the answer to the image of a "jumping universe" inspired by modern science, seem to stem from a misinterpretation of both terms of the analogy.[23]

In fact, the discovery of order nestling in chaos, in the infinite complexity of the structures generated by the self-organisation of matter, should prompt architecture to recontact nature rather than propel it towards an increasingly arbitrary disorder induced by exasperated individual desire. The discovery of chaos is the discovery of the whole, since in chaos everything is "related," everything interacts and the isolation of objects from their environment is simply an illusionary simplification. In general, the absolute freedom that inspires the deconstructivists is the refusal of any possible relationship with the exterior: it is the defence of a closed discipline which ultimately is not very different from the academic classicism to which it is only formally opposed. Certainly, the theory of chaos is based on the absence of balance, but only in so far as it is able to produce structure and complexity. The famous chemical reaction by Belousov-Zhabotinsky is proof enough.

Contrary to what chemists once believed, this reaction does not end in a final state of balance but produces a series of unpredictable transformations. Placed on a dish, its reagents create incredibly beautiful patterns such as concentric circles that overlap and unite, or intertwining spirals like the volutes of a Baroque frieze, all in continuous metamorphosis. The changes in these patterns form a spectacular whole, as if this were the work of a designer who, when decorating the dish, aimed at establishing a dynamic balance between symmetry and asymmetry. Frank Lloyd Wright obtained very similar results when designing the chinaware for the Imperial Hotel in Tokyo. Belousov's patterns go through unpredictable metamorphoses in the framework of a pattern called the "Roesseler attractor." Some of the scientists who have studied the problem think that a similar chemical reaction could have been the spark behind the first signs of life on earth. This is, however, an unusual route: a chaotic activity that spontaneously produces structure and complexity, in some ways countering entropy, whereby things slide towards dissipation and loss of structure.

The analogies and homologies between natural and architectural forms described in this book attempt to highlight the manner in which the symbolic imitation of nature, including the new horizons of knowledge, represents a fresh start to the dialogue that has accompanied the history of mankind from the very beginning and is expressed so perfectly by the universal query that Prigogine answered so clearly when he spoke of "new naturalism."

Another aspect of the current scientific revolution that might become very important in the field of architecture is the inevitable *rapprochement* of Western and Eastern civilisations and therefore the possibility of comparing and integrating architectural traditions which have remained strikingly different despite the sincere attraction that has characterised the visual culture of the West, from Art Nouveau to Expressionism. Prigogine and Stenghers wrote: "We are moving towards a new synthesis, a new naturalism that could combine Western tradition, characterised by its tendency towards experimentation and quantitative theories, with Chinese tradition centred around the concept of a spontaneously ordered world. The absolute traits of scientific theories were long considered a symbol of universal rationality. On the contrary, we believe that science will open up to universality when it no longer denies or distances itself from the anxieties and questions of society in whose bosom it has developed, when it is capable of conversing with nature and finally appreciating its multiple charms as well as dialoguing with men of all cultures and finally respecting their problems."[24]

Bridging the gap between the way in which the nature of Eastern thinking and science is perceived means assimilating their characteristic dualism, and this brings with it profound architectural implications.[25]

The complementary nature of opposites, the ability to see two aspects of every phenomenon and every object without contradicting unitary synthesis, the supremacy of evolution and movement over permanence and stasis have all been repeatedly taken into account in the Western world, particularly at the beginning of this century. One only needs to cite the physicist Niels Bohr or the architects Frank Lloyd Wright and Bruno Taut. However, by making us ponder dual concepts such as matter-energy, material-immaterial, order-chaos, dissipation-structure as well as demonstrating the infinite combinations which mediate their polarity, new science leads us to carry out a generalised revision of the traditional theories of each discipline, especially with regard to their relationship with nature. This is where certain principles of geomancy as well as the Taoist doctrine of Lao-tzu become important.[26] It certainly would be a step in the right direction if, in a renewed effort to understand the language of nature, Western culture bestowed the right of citizenship on the "dragons" and "vital spirit" (earth blood) that for centuries have inspired the Chinese attitude of respect for the earth as well as their search for harmony with the landscape.

Perhaps only the text *De re aedificatoria* clearly defines the meaning of symbolic imitation and the relationship between architecture and nature by anchoring it to the mythical concept of beauty that is also goodness, fairness and ethical and aesthetic necessity. Alberti uses Cicero's term *concinnitas* in such a way

## The Mountain

Gaston Bachelard wrote, "For those whose dreams come from nature, even the smallest hill is an inspiration." It is the cult of the mountain, regarded as a cosmic reference point (the sacred mountain), that inspires the unquenchable desire to erect artificial mountains such as the Ka'ba, the ziggurat, the pyramids, the immense temple of Borobudur, the great cupolas as well as all the skyscrapers and residential structures that imitate the landscape.

*Right: Machu Picchu, the secret city of the Incas, is situated on a plateau surrounded by mountains considered to be gods capable of governing the weather. On Huayna Picchu there is a sacred place, perhaps dedicated to the moon.*

*Above: the most sacred mountain in Asia, Mount Kailas, which even before the first texts of Buddhist mythology was traditionally identified with Mount Meru, the centre of the world, as well as the place of final ascent for the heroes of the Mahabharata. However, only Yudhisthira reached the summit and assumed divinity.*
*Right: panorama of Rome with her characteristic cupolas.*

*Left: a view of Union Beach State Park and below, a group of* trulli *in Martina Franca (Italy). Above, from top to bottom: a Hindu temple and a picture of piled stones in Machu Picchu (Peru).*

that it cannot be translated as symmetry, accord or harmony. In fact, the word involves cosmic balance in the evaluation of human works.

Alberti writes: "Beauty is a form of sympathy and consonance of the parts within a body, according to a definite number, outline and position, as dictated by the 'agreement of sounds,' the *concinnitas*, the absolute and fundamental rule in nature. This is the main object of the art of building, and the source of her dignity, charm, authority and worth. All that has been said our ancestors learned through observation of Nature herself; so they had no doubt that if they neglected these things, they would be unable to attain all that contributes to the praise and honour of the work: nor without reason they declared that Nature, as the perfect generator of forms, should be their model. And so, with utmost industry, they searched out the rules that she employed in producing things, and translated them into methods of building. By studying in Nature the patterns both for whole bodies and for their individual parts, they understood that at their very origins bodies do not consist of equal portions; with the result that some are slender, some fat, and others in-between. And observing the great difference in purpose and intention between one building and another, as we have already observed in earlier books, they concluded that, by the same token, each should be treated differently."[27]

The "rules" that presided over "producing things" are obviously the profound ties that bind the natural and the artificial worlds and constitute the only substantial reference point for the craftsman, the only "indisputable reason."

The definition of beauty as cosmic harmony is not limited to Alberti's poetics or the realm of "classicism," because the link with nature guarantees "variety" which in turn generates differences. This definition is in line with a pluralistic vision that acknowledges the fact that there are many different ways to reach a common goal.

Symbolic imitation does in fact absorb and expand the concept of "functional imitation" which tends to reduce the relationship between nature and architecture to the mere practicalities necessary to solve functional problems that are similar, from an abstract point of view, to natural ones. Architectural functionalism had enthusiastically espoused biological functionalism that defined form as the mechanical consequence of a certain function. However, new and successful developments in the field of biology now lend a precious hand to the world of architecture by reinfusing motivations that are deeper and more complex than the merely functional ones, rarely very thorough or complete.

During a conference held in 1956 for the Eranos-Kreis,[28] Adolf Portmann was crystal clear when he explained his concept of "self-presentation", a trait of both the plant and animal worlds. He argued against the theory that the shape of living things depended exclusively on the evolutionist laws of self-preservation and continuation of the species.

Portmann wrote that "light gives order to the life of man and, contrary to the isolation of our oneiric life during sleep, creates the communal universe of the

34

day; and what holds true for us, holds true for all living things, albeit in a different way." In plants, light produces the functional process of photosynthesis, but in itself this process does not explain the shape of the leaves, just as the problem of reproduction does not explain the shape of flowers. In this case, the traditional theory of natural selection, tinged with a less than scientific moralism, theorises "hyperthelia" and luxuriousness, the latter being "rhetoric" or "baroque" manifestations of nature which "by chance" abandon their simple habitat.

Adolf Portmann is a theorist of "phanerology" (in the realm of light, formative processes follow rules that are different to those that apply to areas without light). He explains how appearances as well as the organisation of the functional apparatus of living beings influence form and how these appearances follow independent rules. The similarities or disparities between the external appearance and the internal structure of an organism determine varying degrees of complexity. This can justify the following hypothesis regarding the history of life on earth: after having experimented the advantages of simple forms, life studied the sphere of complexity with increasing open-mindedness, progressively abdicating exterior and interior unity, a fact sublimely illustrated by the transparent bodies of jellyfish. Jellyfish, or, if you wish, the famous radiolarians illustrated at the end of the last century by Haeckel (in a book which was in a certain sense the bible of Art Nouveau)[29] possess a rather simple organisational form. "The whole body of these animals is a simple unitary structure. In fact, all structures follow the same laws of symmetry. This is true for the internal organs, such as the digestive system and sexual organs, as well as for the extremities, such as the outer tentacles, the oral arms and other structures of the umbrella. In living beings, a structure in which exterior and interior correspond so perfectly is often accompanied by absolute transparency, at times slightly opaque due to the milky consistency of the various layers. On the naturally transparent boundary surfaces, there may be distinct chromatic shades which blend with the symmetry of the whole organism, but it is impossible to associate them with any whatsoever conservation function."[30]

Reading this passage by Portmann, the mind easily wanders to the centrally planned Renaissance churches by Leonardo or Bramante, or the cupola of Guarini's Holy Shroud or certain modern architectural volumes by Wright, Bartning or Aalto, whose objective was absolute correspondence between the exterior and the interior. However, the analogy between architecture and living beings justifies the moralism associated with the so-called constructive truth that has demonized the "façade" without realising that it is through the façade that certain architectural objects "feel" the influence and solicitation of the urban organism by exploiting the logic of its parts, such as the road and the square.

Portmann's observations on architectural decorations are equally important. Pure functional logic cannot justify these decorations, instead their *raison d'être* lies in self-presentation, in the need to show their identity, the class to which they belong, as well as in the fact that architecture is exposed to light. Portmann goes on to say: "It is simpler to admit that the geometric or-

## The Rock

Primitive man used rocks as arms, tools and stones for building. By cutting and shaping these rocks, he learnt to recognise their different characteristics, where they are hardest and where they can crumble or flake. Crystalline rocks best illustrate the complexity as well as the regularity and rhythmic repetition that can be found in rocks. The alliance forged between man and rock marks a decisive moment in the history of mankind as a transforming agent of the earth's surface.

*Right: a rocky spur at the entrance to the Talampaya canyon in Argentina.*
*Detail of the temple base in Segesta (Italy).*

*Opposite page: a rocky formation in the Dolomites, Sella mountains (Italy); a hilltop castle near Amerzgane (Morocco).*

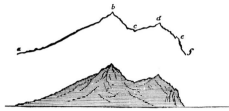

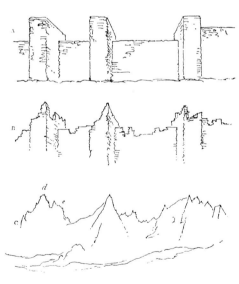

*Above, from top to bottom: John Ruskin, linear diagram of the ideal outline of an English house; analogy between the roofs of a French country house and the distant outline of mountains; analogy between the alpine peaks above Chamonix and a turreted urban wall.*

der of these drawings does not follow the same rules that govern preservation. Perhaps it would be appropriate, when trying to explain their meaning, not to dismiss these chromatic events as excretory or functional products, but to initially avoid giving them a precise meaning and concentrate on the geometric order and its relationship with the symmetric structure of the whole jellyfish. A careful examination of sea anemones has highlighted a definite relationship between coloration and the development of the various tentacle series; however, this also means that there is a link between ornamentation and the hierarchy of the tentacle series." In architecture as well as in living beings, decoration as an element of self-presentation serves to identify the parts, reveal their hierarchy and even their stages of development. "What a difference though between certain simple organisms and the human body! For the human body, the skin is used to hide an apparent 'unpresentable' disorder and the internal logic only rarely corresponds to the no less complicated logic governing the body's exterior shape. The structure of our intestines gives the impression of a logic similar to that of a hasty traveller who randomly packs his personal effects in a suitcase. So in this case, the loss of transparency (if one accepts the evolutionist model) as well as the skin that hides this complexity by creating just one structure, have freed the human body by eliminating its obligation to subjugate its internal organisation to the logic of self-presentation and vice versa."

This brief incursion into the world of biology may help architects to consider the "truth" of an architectural organism correctly or, at the very least, to view it in a less simplistic and sectorial fashion. Even theorists of organic architecture such as Frank Lloyd Wright, so careful to understand complexity, have often cited nature for its authentic and "sincere" forms as well as its ability to acclaim the gifts of matter by turning truth, sincerity and appropriateness into real dogmas. However, these theorists did not realise that for nature, appearances are no less important than their corresponding functions and that, for all their splendid independence, living organisms are made to interact with both organic and inorganic environmental reality and that this interaction is one of the reasons that determines their forms.

It was Portmann who pinpointed the architectural value of his discoveries: "For some time even modern architecture was convinced that it could turn simple conservative functions into the cornerstones of existence and consider every other necessity of life as a luxury, as something superfluous. These considerations lead to the design of real 'living machines.' If you bear in mind the changes currently taking place in the functional theories of architecture, you will note with great satisfaction (especially if one happens to be a biologist) how comfort, the joy of colour and environmental factors are all finally being recognised as vital functions of primary importance. And if you follow the controversy over the interpretation of the term 'luxury tax', the difficulties of economists to define 'luxury' will not have escaped you. A biologist will draw great satisfaction from all this since he knows only too well how the definition of a circle of 'elementary,' 'primary' needs is currently so difficult and precarious."[31]

The relationship between nature and architecture is clearly illustrated by the idea of "landscape." The history of this word (which in all Neo-Latin languages comes from the Latin, *pagus*, village) confirms how important man's presence is – the traces of his "anthropisation" upon the earth – and how it contributes an aesthetic value to landscape and therefore to the "representation" of a vast expanse of land.

Painting, literature and poetry and, to a certain extent music, when the latter more or less intentionally possesses evocative and descriptive traits, have all illustrated the significance and value of the contemplation of nature, of feeling "in harmony" with nature, but more than anything else it is through landscape paintings that contemplation portrays its profound harmony, a decoding that involves the biological legacy of the species to the full.

When we look at a landscape, it seems like the backdrop of an invisible figure, a figure that is human life itself, depicted either as reality or future potential. The landscape is therefore the scenario of a human comedy and mirrors an ideal balance that speaks to our senses of distant eras lost in the dawn of civilisation and history.

In the tierce of his *Duino Elegies*, Rilke draws a extraordinarily profound description of human love, a condition in which experiences are joined and merge together.

> No, we don't accomplish our love in a single year
> as the flowers do; an immemorial sap flows up
> through our arms when we love.
> Dear girl, this: that we loved, inside us
> not One who would someday appear
> but seething multitudes; not just a single child
> but also the fathers lying in our depths
> like fallen mountains; also the dried up riverbeds
> of ancient mothers; also the whole soundless landscape under
> the clouded or clear sky of its destiny –;
> all this, my dear, preceded you.[32]

What Rilke says of love might well be said of the sense of balance and harmony we feel when we look at a landscape in which a secret part of our genetic patrimony re-emerges. In his writings,[33] Jay Appleton, a scholar of geography, provides a convincing explanation of the psychological mechanisms that determine sensations of pleasing quiet, of involvement, of identification when we look at real or painted landscapes that have certain morphological characteristics.

By introducing the idea of "natural symbolism" in contrast to the cultural symbolism normally studied by iconology, Appleton takes as his starting point

## Geomorphism

Geomorphism represents a recent trend in architecture; it is extremely aware of its responsibilities in the systematic and negative alteration of landscape in the wake of the industrial revolution. However, man often adopts geomorphism as a defensive camouflage or out of respect for nature, viewed as a mother whose calm stability is not to be disturbed. But earth is also a building material that often generates curvilinear forms which are tender and loving, moulded by the hand of man to recall flowing water.

*Right: a view of the settlement of the Anasazi in Bruce Canyon (USA).*
*Below: a group of caves dug out of the rock face and later whitewashed like an artificial façade on the island of Santorini (archipelago of the Cyclades).*

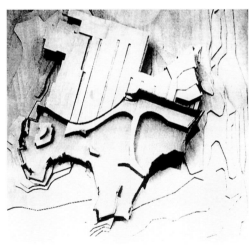

*Above from left: the façade of Casa Milá in Barcelona (Antoni Gaudí, 1905-11); Cuzco (Peru), walls gently following the outline of the underlying rock.*
*Above from right: Machu Picchu, royal tomb under the temple of the Sun; Dipoli student centre, Otaniemi, Finland (Reima Pietila, 1966).*

the considerations of those anthropologists who recently discovered in the savannah (a vegetation characterised by trees standing sufficiently far apart for grass to grow between and under their branches) the type of environment in which the first hominids established their homes.

In landscape paintings, these ancestral memories apparently influence the choice of similar situations in which the horizon is visible and vegetation outlines the natural lie of the land, highlighting the perception of space and therefore of distance. Other key concepts are introduced on the basis of this ideal model that defines our interpretation of landscape, such as the "nesting place" and the "foraging ground" as well as a couple of contradictory ideas: the balance between these two ideas is seemingly central to the ability of a certain real or painted landscape to satisfy a profound psychic need. These two ideas may be summed up as being the "refuge-prospect" and the "refuge-hazard."

While in Italian the word refuge is satisfactorily translated as *"rifugio"*, the term prospect cannot be translated by one word as it has various meanings that the Italian language renders with more than one word: view, panorama, but also expectation. This is also true for hazard which means *"azzardo"* but also risk, danger and alternative.

Appleton indicates as a common occurrence in landscape paintings the fact that a view contains this polarity between a refuge and expectation (prospect). This is a key element in understanding the relationship of identification and involvement between ourselves and the landscape, a relationship that is perceived as a tangible fact in so far as it is an opportunity for contemplation and aesthetic pleasure. Furthermore, since the idea of refuge is closely linked to architecture and to the home (and to the cave as the house's direct ancestor) it can immediately be used in the interpretation and evaluation of the relationship between constructed architecture and nature, between building and landscape, between landscape and town.

In painting, the prospect-expectation (risk) involves landscapes that stretch to infinity, that conjure up distance or a wealth of information on travel and life on earth. This is very important from an architectural point of view, not only because the presence of architecture often accentuates the sense of depth and liveability in landscapes, but also because architecture itself, especially in an urban context, lends itself to be read and interpreted in terms of prospective depth, of an illusionary concept, of an ideal invasion of space, a space that only the eye can truly cross but which gives the observer the impression of being taken on a journey or induced to read travel tales that the eye communicates to the mind. Here come to mind a cathedral's lacey profile and spires, or the stepped outline of the skyscrapers of the twenties, which seem to offer an imaginary stairway to heaven from the tentacle-like city streets.

Appleton's observations can ultimately help us understand how, especially in cities, the contrast between symbolic values is a vital ingredient of harmony, of the feeling of belonging and of an intensified perceptive experience. His considerations also illustrate how symbolic imitation, the analogy between natural and architectural symbolism and therefore the ability to make architecture a continuation-extension of nature, are necessary to attain the full array of anthropological potential inherent in architecture and town planning.

The process of symbolic imitation also permits the study of the apparently steadfast antimony between organicity and abstraction.

"It is true", writes Valéry, that man "builds absent-mindedly, ignorant and forgetful of most of the qualities of the materials he uses."[34] It is true that "man does not need all of nature but only a part." It is also true that the works of man built using "separate principles" in some ways oppose nature by violating it in order to use it. While a philosopher is "one who conceives on an ever greater scale and who needs everything," an architect, instead, may just "act" since "he can ignore or be happy with just partial knowledge." The things an architect builds by putting together natural elements are just a little less complicated than the elements themselves, but they are joined by an invisible line and very often it is easy to note a sort of complementary quality.

Paraphrasing Valéry, Elio Franzini wrote: "Even though the power of nature is 'fecund,' 'prodigious' and 'generating,' it has not invented everything."[35] It is this "open space" that houses man's creations, that Bacon called "*homo additus naturae*," a phrase which Zola taught Degas who, in turn, passed it on to Valéry. It is here that we find the "pleasure" of doing things, a pleasure that seems like the "second nature" Valéry considered to be in contrast to "the first, immediate nature."[36]

This "second nature," present in man's intelligence and architectural ability, must encompass the "imaginative paths" of the "first nature": paths which define and discover, providing a perceptible presence, a "feeling of the Universe," a human creation that "flows to and fro, from matter to idea, from the mind to the model, constantly trading off what it wants for what is possible, and what is possible for what is available."[37] It follows that art's second nature destroys the domination of *logos*, of quantity, of measure, of calculation and of the rules governing the "first nature." On the contrary, in the drama of the arts, Valéry writes that it is represented as a "theatrical" character "with many masks": "it is everything and anything, totally simple, totally complex; it avoids being considered as a whole and challenges us in the details; a resource and an obstacle, lord, servant, idol, enemy and accomplice – whether it is copied or interpreted, whether it is violated, created or re-arranged, whether it is used as matter or as an ideal. It is always close to the artist, around him, with him or against him, – and in its own true heart opposed even to itself."

After all, in Eupalinos' dialogues, doesn't Socrates choose between building and knowledge when faced with an object so ambiguous as to be simultaneously the work of man and nature? When referring to a beach described using "marine words," Socrates tells Phaedrus: "I found an object thrown up by the sea; it was white, of unblemished whiteness. Polished, hard, gentle, light, it shone in the sun, on the smooth, obscure and glittering sand; I picked it up, blew on it

## Crystals

In the chaos of degraded rock, in the heart of the mountain, the earth treasures its crystals. Here, nature apparently wishes to teach man order, clarity and obedience to the laws of creation and evolution, an obedience that should never become mechanical.

Fruit of a prefigurative mind as well as the hands of man and his tools, architecture often uses crystals as a model, even when it secretly aspires to imbue their cold haughtiness with the warmth of life, the cyclical pulsation of a living body.

*Above from right: a hexagonal crystal; the church of Santa Maria delle Grazie in Pian Calcinaio, Cortona (Francesco di Giorgio Martini, 1485). Below: royal casino on Lake Fusaro near Naples built for Ferdinand IV of Bourbon by Carlo Vanvitelli (1782).*

*Bruno Taut, a drawing of the House of Heavens (Haus des Himmels).*
*Left: a hexagonal crystal on a quartz base.*

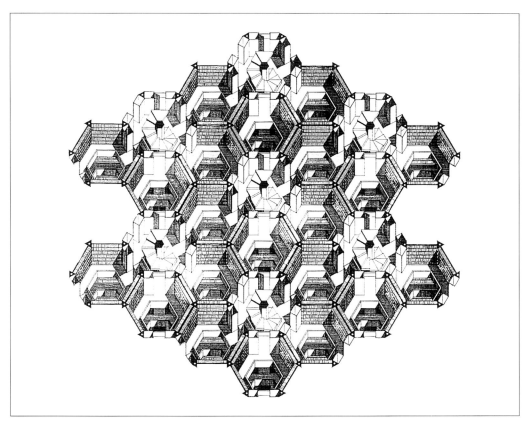

*Wenzel Hablick, a drawing from the series* Cyklus-Architektur, 1921.
*Left: reconstruction of the Library of Babel described by Jorge Luis Borges.*

45

and brushed it against my cloak; its unusual shape halted all other thoughts. Who made you? I asked myself. Different to all others yet not unshapely, are you, o nameless thing, nature's game sent to me by the Gods from amongst the rubbish repudiated tonight by the sea?"[38]

When Phaedrus asked what the object was made of, Socrates replied: "Made of the same material as its form; uncertain matter. Was it perchance a fish-bone strangely polished by the work of the fine sand under water; or perhaps ivory fashioned for an unknown reason by a foreign craftsman? Who knows? [...] A deity sunk with the ship over which it was vigilant to guarantee good luck? But who the author? A mortal obedient to an idea, his hands shaping the object in a different way by sticking, rasping, cutting or recomposing, suddenly stopping and examining the object and at last discarding it as soon as he feels it is finished? [...] Or else the work of a living being that takes no notice and concentrates on its own matter blindly forming organs, armours, shell, bones, defences, passing on the nourishment taken from its surroundings to the mysterious construction in which it lives? Perhaps it is nothing more than the fruit of infinite time [...]. A piece of rock thrown about by the never-ending work of the sea waves, rolling about, tossed and battered from all sides; if this rock is incomparably hard and refractory to roundness perhaps in time it could acquire a unique appearance. Is it also impossible that a piece of marble or shapeless stone entrusted to the perennial movement of the waters be some day discovered by another species and so acquire a likeness to Apollo? What I mean is, if a fisherman is familiar with the face of the divinity, then he will recognise it on the marble found in the sea."[39]

The analogy between natural forms and architecture was very seriously and coherently studied by John Ruskin[40], both in his book the *Seven Lamps* in which he tackles the problem of beauty and in *Modern Painters* in which he examines the problems of landscape painting by making extensive use of very powerful drawings. The chapter dedicated to the *Lamp of Beauty* starts with the description of an acquired certainty: "It was stated, at the outset of the preceding chapter, that the value of architecture depended on two distinct characters: the one, the impression it receives from human power; the other, the image it bears of the natural creation. I have endeavoured to show in what manner its majesty was attributable to a sympathy with the effort and trouble of human life (a sympathy as distinctly perceived in the gloom and mystery of form, as it is in the melancholy tones of sound). I desire now to trace that happier element of its excellence, consisting in a noble rendering of images of beauty, derived chiefly from the external appearance of organic nature."

Ruskin believed "that no form or set of forms be conceivable without there being an example somewhere in the universe" and that the origin of natural morphology be both a homage to, and a continuation of, creation.

The illustrations in the third and fourth volume of *Modern Painters* clearly reveal the way in which he saw nature in architecture and vice versa. For example the walls of a city which, when crumbling into ruin, are compared to the peaks of Mont Blanc seen from Chamonix (Book IV, part V, chap. XVI, 13, fig. 35) or the analogical relationship between the outline of the thatched roofs of a country house and that of distant mountain tops (Book IV, part V, chap. XIV, 2, fig. 30) or again, the comparative analytical observation of the branches of an ash tree with the ribs of an ogive vault.

What interests Ruskin is how artificial objects and nature share a similar beauty. His drawings seem to portray the idea that it is easier to perceive this association when objects, consumed by time and use, lose their geometric absoluteness and are considered not as isolated facts but as parts of a given environment. Other drawings in *Modern Painters* involve the "rules" that determine the shape of natural structures, rules that can be used either in architecture or in landscape painting. Plate 56 in Book V illustrates the laws of ramification and is in some ways quite prophetic. By reconstructing the geometric outline of a tree based on an equilateral triangle, Ruskin (through the author of the drawing, J. Elmslie) anticipates one of the classical examples of fractal mathematics illustrated by Mandelbrot in plate 155 of his book *The Fractal Geometry of Nature,* published in 1977.

Almost as if to corroborate the surprising analogy between Ruskin's and Mandelbrot's interests, plate 155 also illustrates the regularity of cloud formations and the way in which they form parallel arches or a set of ellipses around a circle. Even the drawings comparing the elliptical modular pattern of the gems on the branch of a small spruce to the radial ramification of thistles and oaks highlight the analogies extensively cited in relation to morphology and structural engineering. Ruskin also uses this natural-artificial parallel in his *Lectures on Architecture and Painting.* He compares the branch of an ash, whose leaves are arranged on a sloping symmetrical axis with respect to the stalk, to the diagonal pattern of the ribs of an ogive vault. Ruskin theorises the abstract interpretation of natural forms rather than their direct imitation. The importance he attributes to decoration as an integral part of architecture does, however, lead him to give privileged status to the ornate form. In his book *Seven Lamps* he wrote: "I do not mean to assert that every arrangement of line is directly suggested by a natural object; but that all beautiful lines are adaptations of those which are the commonest in external creation; that in proportion to the richness of their association, the resemblance to natural work, as a type and help, must be more closely attempted, and more clearly seen, and that beyond a certain point, and that a very low one, man cannot advance in the invention of beauty, without directly imitating natural form."

In order to clarify this concept of the use of natural forms as an arrival point in the design process, Ruskin uses examples which show how little he appreciated the tectonic aspects of architecture as against the symbolic and decorative ones. However, his observations have certain poetic touches and do give us a feeling for the period and its tastes, all elements that greatly influenced the early years of modern architecture. "Thus, in the Doric temple, the triglyph and the cornice are unimitative; or imitative only of artificial cuttings of wood. No-one

## The Shaft

Together with other images of the animal and plant world, the tree inspires in man the weave concept based on flexibility and braiding. Both these traits refer to the younger and more supple branches of the tree, the shafts of flowers and to canes, especially bamboo.
The flexible and curvilinear morphology of the trunk, the branch and the shaft is present everywhere in stone architecture as an image to be conjured up in order to overcome the restrictions of matter.

*A bamboo thicket in the garden of the Buddhist temple Saihô-ji, Kyoto.*

*Left: Loggia of Palazzo Rufolo in Ravello (11th century); above, bark of an ancient chestnut tree in Vetralla near Viterbo (Italy). Below, detail of the cloister of the cathedral in Amalfi.*

## The Branch

The tree has taught man the concept of growth
and multiplication since ramification lies at the
very heart of its nature. Ramification represents
the metamorphosis of an object that at a certain
point of its corporal growth doubles in nature,
exactly the opposite to what happens to water
courses which unite to eventually form a water
reservoir. Ramification has taught man the
power of repetition. The sequence of trunk,
branch, leaflets, leaves, rachis and venation
illustrates a law very similar to the one governing
architectural orders.

*Above right: John Ruskin, a drawing that
examines the law of ramification and illustrates
the "delicate curve" between the borders of the
foliage and the rhythmic traits of the development
process. Almost a century before everyone else,
Ruskin had seen self-similarity in the structure of
the tree, and therefore its "fractal" nature, which
would later be defined in mathematical terms by
Benoit Mandelbrot.*
*Below: Benoit Mandelbrot, drawing of a fractal
tree and study of the treelike supports of a
hexagonal frame (Frei Otto, 1976).*

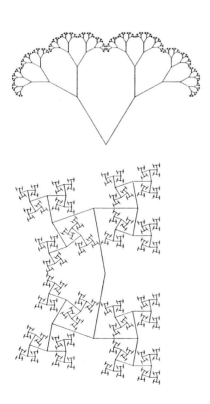

50

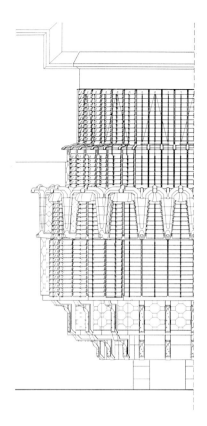

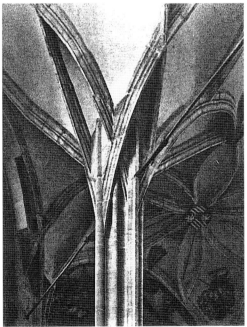

*Left: the forked ramification of a lightning bolt.*
*Above right: elevation of the rear loggia of Park*
*Güell in Barcelona (Antoni Gaudí, 1885-89);*
*treelike column in the church in Annaberg*
*(Benedikt Ried, 16th century).*

## The Tree

Gilbert Durand wrote, "Any tree, be it the one belonging to Indian traditions, the lunar tree of the Maya or Yacoute, the Kiskana tree of the Babylonians, the Yagdrasil of the Nordic tradition the solar or lunar tree of alchemists, it is always the tree that is the symbol of the entire universe, its genesis and evolution." Its vertical growth makes the tree human, symbol of that vertical microcosm, man.

The tree offers architecture the solidity of a trunk that becomes a column, upward growth and ramification: this is the law of "treeness" cited by Frank Lloyd Wright in one of his first essays.

*A tree-lined street in Acireale, Sicily.*
*Below: a model of a panoramic tower*
*(A. Al Bayati, 1988).*

52

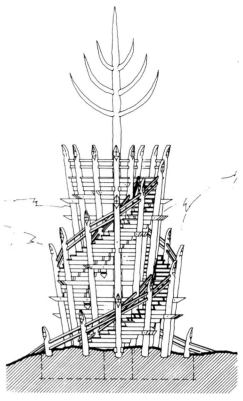

*Above left: the main lounge of the Tettuccio Baths in Montecatini (Paolo Portoghesi, 1985-87); left, skyward view of the pine-wood in Villa Pamphili, Rome.*
*Above: panoramic tower in Nagykálló, Hungary (Dezsö Ekler, 1988); a confessional in the church in Zwiefalten, Bavaria (Johann Michael Fischer, 1738-65).*

## The Inflorescence

Inflorescence is a reproductive system based on a shoot whose flowers are arranged along a vertical axis. It has a ramification system and a main axis called peduncle or rachis (A.D. Bell). In history, nearly all the various types of inflorescence have an architectural equivalent, above all in city constructions and the layout of rooms, as well as in the plastic repertoire of membranes and decoration.

*Below: the inflorescence of the* Molucella laevis*.*
*Right: the coping of the cupola in the chapel of the Holy Shroud in the Duomo in Turin (Guarino Guarini, 1668).*

54

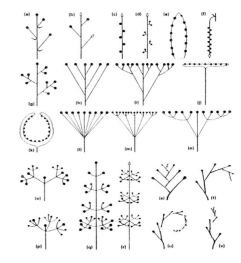

*Above from left: Frei and Ingrid Otto,* Grouped Umbrellas, *floral structure made of a plastic fabric that captures solar energy, Venice. Biennale/ Architecture 1996, German pavilion; staircase of Maison Horta in Brussels (Victor Horta, 1898-1900).*
*Above: various types of inflorescence; the "sick" flowering of an* Echium vulgaris *affected by a teratological transformation. On page 57, the serial structure is highlighted through drying up.*

## The Flower

Supreme model of centrality as well as frontality, the flower has inspired architects not only with endless decorative forms but also with distributive principles and architectural organisms based on a vertical reference axis, allowing them to affirm, through the use of different yet appropriate forms, verticality, irradiation from a point and subdivision into overlapping layers.

*Above: a drawing of the pedestrian exit from an underground parking area on the East Ring Road in Rome (Paolo Portoghesi); right, a flower of the species* Strelitzia reginae.
*Below: a drawing by Hans Scharoun for a "people's house" (c. 1940) and, right, an aerial view of the Sydney Opera House (Jørn Utzon, 1957-70).*

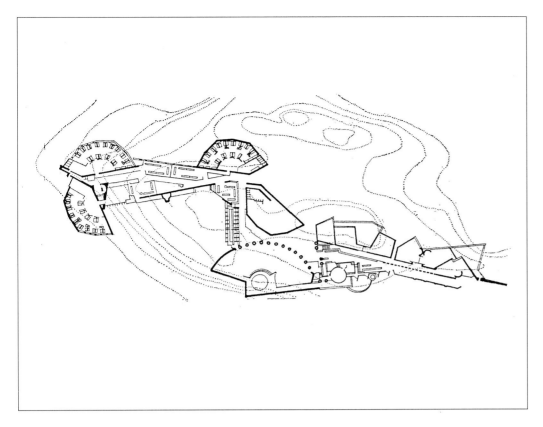

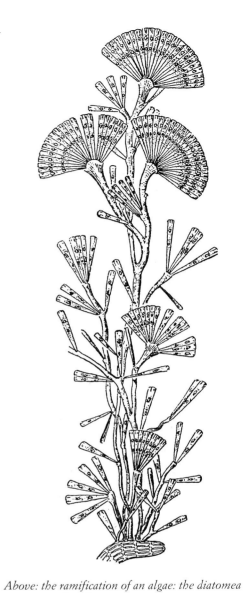

*Above: the ramification of an algae: the diatomea*
Licmorpha flagellata.
*Left, from top to bottom: a plant from the
mountain resort of Brusson, Italy (Carlo Scarpa,
1958); a mullioned window with two lights
on the corner of Palazzo Termine in Palermo
(16th century) and the image of the dried up stalk
of an* Echium vulgaris *affected by a teratological
transformation that has fused the stalks.*

would call these members beautiful. Their influence over us is in their severity and simplicity. The fluting of the column, which I doubt not was the Greek symbol of the bark of the tree, was imitative in its origin, and feebly resembled many caniculated organic structures. Beauty is instantly felt in it, but of a low order. The decoration proper was sought in the true forms of organic life, and those chiefly human. Again, the Doric capital was unimitative; but all the beauty it had was dependant on the precision of its ovolo, a natural curve of the most frequent occurence. The Ionic capital (to my mind, as an architectural invention, exceedingly base) nevertheless depended for all the beauty that it had on the adoption of a spiral line, perhaps the commonest of all that characterize the inferior orders of animal organism and habitation. Further progress could not be made without a direct imitation of the acanthus leaf. Again: the Romanesque arch is beautiful as an abstract line. Its type is always before us in that of the apparent vault of heaven, and horizon of the earth.

"The cylindrical pillar is always beautiful, for God has so moulded the stem of every tree that it is pleasant to the eyes. The pointed arch is beautiful: it is the termination of every leaf that shakes in the summer wind, and its most fortunate associations are directly borrowed from the trefoiled grass in the field, or from the stars of its flowers. Further than this, man's invention could not reach without frank imitation. His next step was to gather the flowers themselves, and wreathe them into his capitals."

The biochemist Rupert Sheldrake, a pioneer of New Science and author of three books that push the limits of the implications of his theoretical work even further, has recently elaborated the concepts of "morphic field" and of "formative causation" that could be appropriately and stimulatingly applied in the interpretation of sites and architectural works, helping the architects tune into what he defines as "the renaissance of nature."[41]

Morphogenetic fields – morphic fields with special characteristics – were introduced at the turn of the century to explain the evolution of organisms. Their function is to carry out remote-controlled actions; they are organised like nestled hierarchies or holons one inside the other (fields of organs, tissues and cells, etc.) and their role is to accompany each developing system towards its final form. According to Sheldrake, up to now the traits of these fields, characterised by their evolutionary nature, have been ignored by physicists. "The fields of a given species, such as the giraffe, have evolved; they are inherited by present giraffes from previous giraffes. They contain a kind of collective memory on which each member of the species draws, and to which it in turn contributes. The formative activity of the fields is not determined by timeless mathematical laws – although the fields can to some extent be modelled mathematically – but by the actual forms taken up by previous members of the species. The more often a pattern of development is repeated, the more probable it is that it will be followed again. The fields are the means by which the habits of the species are built up, maintained and inherited."[42]

According to this molecular theory, crystals, cells, tissues, organs and groups of organs are conditioned by "morphic fields" in which morphogenetic fields represent the relative subspecies of living organisms. The history of each of these elements influences the genesis of similar elements through a process called "morphic resonance" that does not decline with distance. In fact, "it does not involve a transfer of energy, but of information. In practice, this hypothesis explains repetition in nature through habits transmitted by morphic resonance rather than by eternal, non-material and non-energetic laws."[43]

Even if the theory of "formative causation" is far from being experimentally proven, it does justify phenomena that have not yet been convincingly explained. The field of pharmacological research is a classic example. When a new organic substance is first produced, crystallisation is difficult. Sometimes weeks or even months are needed. Subsequently there is a reduction in the time required, not only in the laboratory where the first synthesis took place, but everywhere. Up to now, the explanation given was that fragments of the first crystals easily passed from one laboratory to another as particles in the beards or on the clothes of the researchers involved and that this favoured a rapid reoccurrence of the phenomenon. This is not a very convincing explanation and has never been seriously tested.

Even more fascinating is Sheldrake's reference to records in the field of sports. He maintains that once a record is reached it fosters emulation through a sort of long-distance contagion of the means used to set it.[44]

As I mentioned earlier, the idea of a morphic field can productively be used for sites, a fact its inventor pointed out in his book on nature.[45] This is where Sheldrake's work fits in with my own efforts to apply the theory of fields to architecture, as illustrated by Rudolph Arnheim in his book *The Dynamics of Architectural Form*.[46] A convergence of problems, if not of solutions, is confirmed by the fact that we both used the same title, *The Presence of the Past*, for two undertakings carried out in very distinct, yet in some ways parallel fields: the Biennale exhibition in Venice in 1980 and Arnheim's book published in 1988.

In the sixties, the idea of fields applied to architecture permitted me to interpret the influence that Borromini's works exerted on the perception of space. It also allowed me to experiment with a compositional method based on "space as a system of sites."[47] Later on, I used a similar concept to explain how the idea of site, as well as its psychological value, can be explained by using "fields." Fields permit the site to be considered not as an island but as an entity that, on the one hand, interacts with its surroundings and, on the other, is also influenced by past events. As a result, the field is influenced by other external fields and by adding the force of its own identity to these influences; it in turn releases its own energy.

Sheldrake takes as his starting point a very pertinent citation by D.E. Lawrence: "Different places on the face of the Earth have different vital effluence, different vibration, different chemical exhalation, different polarity with

## The Stars and the Light

The movement of the stars and the planets aroused an insatiable curiosity in primitive man. He used this curiosity to focus on abstraction and impose a unitary interpretation on individual observations of nature. Many ancient sanctuaries were built based on this identification between the life of the universe and the movement of heavenly bodies. The movement of the sun, and the sense of bearing it inspires, constitutes one of architecture's supreme laws: light and shadow in perpetual metamorphosis. Horizontal orientation between the cardinal points also sparks the perception of verticality personified by the *axis mundi*.
By observing the effect of light on natural forms, architects have come to understand the concepts of chiaroscuro, transparency, luminous contrast, depth and empty spaces.

*Above right: back-lit picture of a flowering bush. Through transparency, reflection and contrast with the background, the subject acquires its "own light" and becomes itself a source of light; below right: a perforated leaf of the* Philodendron pertusam *or* Monstera deliciosa.
*Below: the star-shaped ecumenical building in Bethlehem, Palestine (design by Paolo Portoghesi).*

different stars: call it what you like. But the spirit of place is a great reality."[48]

Getting to the heart of the matter, Sheldrake asks himself what kind of fields characterise places. He writes: "They are obviously not reducible to the known fields of conventional physics, though electromagnetic fields no doubt contribute something to the quality of the place. However, it might make sense to think of the fields of places as morphic fields. Such fields are associated with self-organizing systems at all levels of complexity, and they are ordered in nestled hierarchies. If particular places do indeed have morphic fields, then these fields must be embedded within larger fields, such as the fields of river systems and mountain chains, and these in turn within the fields of islands, archipelagos and continents, and ultimately within the morphic fields of Gaia and the entire solar system."[49]

His observations on morphic resonance and self-resonance of sites are decisive for the architectural implications that ensue: "The idea of the spirits of places as morphic fields implies that particular places are subject to morphic resonance from other similar places in the past. The generic qualities of places, traditionally expressed in terms of the various types of nature spirits, will indeed have a kind of collective character and memory. Moreover, particular places will have their own memories by self-resonance with their own past. Morphic resonance takes place on the basis of similarity, and hence the patterns of activity of a place in the summer will tend to resonate most specifically with those in previous summers, and the winter patterns with the previous winter patterns and so on. Memory also plays a role in the responses of animals and of people to the particular place. Obviously when people enter the place, their memory of their previous experience in the place, or in other similar places, will tend to affect their present experience. But in addition to individual memory, through morphic resonance there will also be a component of collective memory, through which a person can tune in to the past experiences of other people in the same place."

Since architecture is undoubtedly one of the elements that contributes to defining the character and "spirit" of a place, based on this theory it could obviously contribute to artificially defining morphic fields, bearing in mind that the elaboration of these theories would be enormously helpful. In fact, equally obvious is the way in which the architect's feelings towards these morphic fields can influence the harmony between the site and its architecture, an element vital for successful acclimatisation. Chinese geomancy, which will be examined later on, is a specific area of knowledge that tends to guarantee harmony and continuity between architecture and nature based on theories very similar to Sheldrake's. Through the works and essays of architects, even Western culture has shown an intuitive understanding of the forces and energy flows that define the character and identity of a place. However, Sheldrake's theories were greeted sceptically by scientists and are yet to be experimentally tested, a process that might still invalidate them. Among other things, they reveal the need to find a solution to important phenomena in the field of architecture. An indirect confirmation of their importance comes from the paradoxical evidence of certain ascertained facts, such as the analogy between the behaviour of bacteria colonies and big computers.

These hypotheses lead to what I call "listening architecture" that stems from the site and therefore from the observation of nature and yet at the same time proposes an essentially dynamic vision of the site, quite different from the one upon which the theory of "contextualism" is based.

Naturally, listening architecture involves man and objects. Unfortunately, architects rarely meet future "inhabitants" and normally the client is a bureaucrat or a politician. An architect must naturally listen to the client, but through him, and at times despite him, he must above all listen to the recipients of his work in any way possible: this listening ranges from looking at statistics to casual conversations, from radio programmes to participation in collective ceremonies.

"All heads are interesting," wrote Elias Canetti, "if only one were inside them." And when speaking of the tasks and obligations of a writer he asked himself, "What is urgent? Is it what the writer senses in others when they seem unable to express it themselves, or is it something that he himself has felt or recognised before seeing it in others? This concordance that creates urgency must also be able to do two things: the writer must feel and think deeply and with untiring passion, he must listen to others and take them seriously."

When an architect "listens to others and takes them seriously" he leaves behind the "barbarian inventions" and "strange abuses" cited by Palladio and draws nearer to the type of architecture whose nature has almost been forgotten, an architecture that accepts itself as the varied repetition of a model, the biological repetition of a cell, the obedient achievement of a genetic legacy. In fact, listening to people also means listening to objects, because objects exist in a physical as well as a mnemonic space and our desires and dreams are full of familiar objects, either concretely experienced or imaginatively created through the careful grafting of heterogeneous objects, distant in space and time.

Listening architecture tends to connect the building to the site so that it grows upwards from the site like a plant.

Through their roots plants draw water from underground sources, taking nourishment from what "is" actually there and from what passes through or has passed through, leaving just faint traces. Vines for example: the grapes on the vines contain the salts and fluids of the geological conditions of a relatively homogeneous area. The plot of land in the best position, with more sun and wind and less hail, will produce the finest wine. The same position, the same winds and the same sun will not produce the same wine if the salts and fluids of a certain region were not part of the land: in other words, places have a common identity.

The theory of setting requires that a building be in harmony with its surroundings. However, this is a very partial theory. To be in harmony does not

## Radii

The idea of the radius, one of the basic concepts of geometry, comes from the observation of light and how it spreads over the earth. Reflecting on the way in which light is uniformly distributed by the Sun, a ray is an abstraction, yet it becomes visible and tangible when it shines through a hole. This phenomenon also occurs when the ray shines through the natural cavities in mountains due to the screening effect of the rocky peaks, and is even more apparent when applied to the holes man makes in his own walls: the doors and windows that delimit inner and outer spaces. Outward radiation from a central nucleus is one of the most common structures of the plant world, as well as being present in crystal morphology. The architect adopts the radiated structures of primitive huts and uses it as one of his main resources in the organisation of cities and roads.

*Below: Max Taut, a drawing of a flower-shaped building (1920).*
*Above right: the leaf of a palmetto.*
*Below right: a detail of the* Hibiscus *flower.*

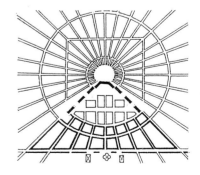

*Left: a detail of the roof of the Seagram Building in New York (William van Alen, 1930).*
*Above from top to bottom: peacock tail (Paro cristatus); quartz crystal; carrot flower (Carota officinalis); plan of Karlsruhe (J.F. von Betzendorf, 1715).*

mean that the site can be considered an island or the tile of a mosaic, because the earth as an inhabited space, the earth which man has appropriated, is a system within systems, it is a "depth" that cannot be reduced merely to its surface.

When designing a site, the site should be considered as a receiving station in which messages from a thousand other sites, near and far, cross one another. The site has its own individuality or identity even if it is always the product of other synergetic identities. The lot – a former dominant element of modern architecture – is an island, but the site is like the cell of a living being, a relational entity, a whirlpool welcoming many currents. The shears used to shape a plant cannot shape a site; any attempt to do so will reveal bleeding roots.

Every object is simultaneously a question, a possibility to draw closer to other things (the power of analogy) and a tendency towards metamorphosis. Like chemical compounds, there are things that more or less readily react with others, with or without "free valence." To turn this "listening to objects" into an architectural project, the architect must see the objects through his own eyes as well as identifying them with others. This is the only way in which the "inhabitants" of a site will discover the bond between a building and their own mnemonic experiences and imagination and quite literally "find themselves" in this new form and listen to it. The deeper and more mysterious the bonds, the more the inhabitants will draw on their imagination without relying merely on memory.

This does not mean "deforming," hiding or cheating, on the contrary, it means finding the ideogram, the elementary sign, whatever resists the vulgar naturalism of picture postcards but which, at the same time, is the reason why picture postcards represent either the occasional or the profound message that travels to and fro between mankind and sites. To listen to sites – in other words to listen to mankind through sites – has interesting analogies with psychoanalysis: one of the current ways to recuperate modern listening. "The original nature of psychoanalytical listening," wrote Barthes and Havat, "lies precisely in the exchange that links neutrality and intervention, suspension of judgement and theory: 'The rigours of unconscious desire, the logic of desire, are revealed only to those who simultaneously respect the two apparently contradictory needs of order and singularity.'" In the same way, listening to sites takes place through a minute analysis that does not privilege one aspect over another, since we must remember "that more often than not one listens to things whose meaning is only afterwards understood."

When designing a site the problem is not merely to discover its desires (often called site vocation) and connect them to those of possible new "inhabitants," but to subject the future architecture to its "morphic fields" after having identified the language of a site (in other words, the forms of expression gleaned from collective memory through long, fluctuating listening). The great advantage of this type of listening is to strike at the heart of the two traits of current architectural thinking that for most citizens contribute to its incommunicability and hostility, namely its "logocratic" nature and a tendency towards homologation: this tendency ignores all and any differences considered as elements to be eradicated in so far as they represent vestiges of the past.[50]

One aspect of the relationship between architecture and nature promoted by current architectural culture is what is commonly called "geomorphism." This recent phenomenon reflects a growing trend in aggressive attacks against the landscape, attacks that are taking place all over the civilised world on a daily basis. It also highlights modern man's guilty conscience mitigated through a sort of exorcism. As the transforming agent of the earth's surface man disguises the products he produces behind a smoke screen of pervasive vegetation and a vague superficial analogy between urban and natural spaces. Often, geomorphism as poetry (or better still as strategy) cloaks itself in highly respectable ecological motivations and technological novelties. However, its most inconsiderate forms go no further than cloaking its real nature with a mask which all too often dramatically reveals its true desire to appropriate land and avoid the legal restraints that have been approved to protect nature. However, it would be wrong to attribute this basic hypocrisy to all forms of geomorphism since it often reveals itself to be driven by a feeling of respect and a desire to attain structural harmony between architecture and nature.

There are four basic trends in present day geomorphism: "terraced slopes," "hypogeal construction," "assonant fragment" and what could be called "the artificial mountain," rooted in the archaic precedents of the pyramids and the mastaba as well as in agricultural terracing. During the sixties, Moshe Safdije experimented with these trends on the Côte d'Azur and in Montreal. The most spectacular example of these types is in the "Bay of Angels" near Nice. Certainly not hypocritical, it does propose a *habitat* more suited to termites than to man, and its analogy with hills is valid only from a great distance and on a foggy day. The terraced slope was very popular in Switzerland and was also exploited in France, Australia and the United States, but from an ecological point of view it does not solve the problem of terrain permeability and affects areas bigger than three or four storey buildings. Even when the "armed terrain" system is adopted to consolidate the surrounding land, the costs involved limit the use of this model to luxury houses alone.

The most convincing solution was adopted by Edmund Burgher for his Albany Oaks condominium in Albany, California. Here the houses are on stilts and the building volumes are treated according to the rules and materials of the Shyngle Style. Burgher also published a complete volume on the subject and is a supporter, together with Malcolm Wells, of "gentle architecture."[51] The model of hypogeal architecture, as well as the "assonant fragment," have the most historical precedents since they draw on the caverns and hypogea found all over the world and in every civilisation on earth. However, if in the past the choice to live underground was dictated by the need either to hide or protect oneself from an aggressor or from persecution (Hebrew and Christian catacombs are a fine example) or else to avoid torrid desert climates (as in the case of underground courtyard houses in China or Tunisia),[52] nowadays this same choice is influenced by a need for camouflage, a need to reduce the environmental impact to a mini-

## Transparency

In the animal and plant worlds, as well as in the sky with its clouds, fogs, storms and rainbows, transparency is exalted by contrast and over time alternates with opacity.
The perceptive architect uses the mutant moods of the environment as a learning process; by using walls and openings, empty spaces and solids, he shifts between his role as an invader of space and discloser of empty spaces and fluxes.

*Below: an example of transparency in the crown of the bud of a* Cosmos bipinnatus.
*Right: three small bell-towers on the island of Santorini (Cyclades). The holes at the top are for acoustical reasons.*

68

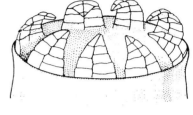

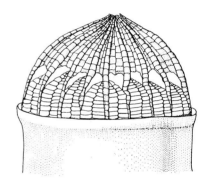

*Left, from the top: a detail of the internal loggia of a residential building in the Gallaratese district of Milan (Aldo Rossi, 1975); a separation wall made of glass tubes in the offices of the Johnson Wax company in Racine, USA (F. Lloyd Wright, 1936). Right: various types of peristomes in bryophytes of the* Bryophyta *subclass. From the top downwards:* Timmia bavarica, Octoblepharum albidum, Cinclidium stygium.

mum or to cope with energy saving problems. However, there is still a slight risk that this camouflage is based on a guilty conscience and on compromise, since the impact on the environment is not simply a visual one (and if it were, it would be part of an aesthetic evaluation and would probably be solved by designing good architecture rather than hidden architecture). The problem is much more complex and depends on the alteration of profound functional balances in which the visual factor plays only a marginal role. For example, an underground building impacts on the hydrological system, on the life of living creatures who live in the ground, on the integrity of the earth's surface, which means that excavating land is simply another form of violence.

This subterranean idea, however, has often inspired work on the landscape aimed not so much at hiding architecture as representing a desire to forge an alliance with the earth and draw closer to its cavities, a metaphor of the maternal womb and of a return to our roots. This is the idea behind Soleri's utopia, Klaus Humpert's Kurhaus in Badenweiler and certain works by William Morgan illustrated by Burgher such as the famous 1975 Dune-House or the 1979 pyramidal Hill-top house in Florida.[53] This same theme is tackled with convincing irony in many of the projects designed by Emilio Ambasz.

The "assonant fragment" model is the one with the most meanings and is indirectly analysed in this book in the review of the archetypal elements of architecture. Using this model, man does not try to hide or disguise himself. Instead, through the symbolic appropriation of the objects of his experience, he tries to find a tangible link to the natural landscape, a point of structural contact between nature and the work of his hands. Like the tree trunk that became a column and was initially introduced in construction as a supporting element in huts and later adopted symbolically through linguistic institutionalisation, the geomorphic fragment may coincide with the form of a building, with a part of the building or with the momentary visual effect of one of its defining elements. Ruskin noted the similarities between a straw roof and the rocky profile of a mountain, between the ruined towers of a walled city and the peaks of a mountain chain. In sacred architecture, pyramids and mastaba are mountains built by man while certain settlements nestle in rock cavities like natural crystals. In modern architecture, Lawrence Halprin has implanted fragments of nature into the fabric of certain American cities by creating artificial cascades, while Wright's Fallingwater takes its cue from the stone slabs in the bed of the Bear-Run River and the vertical lines of the surrounding trees.

Rarely is the harmonisation process between architecture and nature truly imitative, especially when it involves decoration. The prairie houses do not imitate the landscape of the prairies. On the contrary, they interpret its "horizontality," they obey a sort of magnetic field that "oppresses" them, not in order to limit their "presence" but to exalt it in a ribbon of erupting parallel lines, close to the earth and facing sideways for all who enter: the same stratagem that Bernini used for the elliptical spaces of Sant'Andrea al Quirinale or the square of Saint Peter's.

70

[1] Ovid, *Metamorphosis*, http://classics.mit.edu/Ovid/metam.3.third.html.

[2] Vasari, *Le vite*, Rizzoli, Milan, 1971.

[3] C. Sini, "Dialogo sulla Natura," in *Paradosso*, 1, 1992, p. 9 and R. Gasparotti, *Sui modi di dire Physis,, ibid*, p. 45.

[4] P. Portoghesi, *Dopo l'architettura moderna*, Laterza, Rome-Bari 1979 and *Post Modern*, Milan 1982.

[5] Plato, *Complete works*, http://classics.mit. edu/Plato/republic.11.x.html.

[6] C.G. Jung, *Gli archetipi dell'inconscio colletivo*, Milan 1977.

[7] M. Schneider, *Il significato della musica*, Rusconi, Milan 1979, pp. 91-95 and 35.

[8] C. Baudelaire, *Les Fleurs du mal*, http:// home.caroline.rr.com./alienfamily/flowers.htm.

[9] R. Alleau, *La science des symbols*, Paris 1976, p. 75.

[10] *Ibid.*, p. 51.

[11] *Ibid.*, p. 71.

[12] G. Bateson, *Mind and Nature*, Wildwood House, London 1979.

[13] *Ibid.*

[14] A. Lima-de-Faria, *Evolution without Selection*, Elvesier, Amsterdam 1988.

[15] P. Kropotkin, *Ethics, Origin and Development*, Harrap, London 1924.

[16] I. Prigogine, I. Stenghers, *La nuova alleanza*, Einaudi, Turin 1993.

[17] *Ibid.*, p. 228.

[18] *Ibid.*, p. 268.

[19] *Ibid.*, p. 271.

[20] J.L. Borges, *Antologia personale*, Longanesi, Milan 1981, pp. 209-210.

[21] J. Yorke, cit. in J. Briggs, *Fractals, The Patterns of Chaos*, Simon & Schuster 1992.

[22] cf., J. Briggs, *op cit.*, p. 12.

[23] cf., C. Jencks, *The Architecture of the Jumping Universe*, Academy, London 1995.

[24] cf., I. Prigogine, I. Stenghers, *op cit.*

[25] cf., D. Wade, *Crystal and Dragon*, Bideford Green Books, 1991.

[26] cf., Amos In Tiao Chang, *The Tao of Architecture*, Princeton University Press, 1956.

[27] cf., L.B. Alberti, *On the Art of Building*, The MIT Press, Cambridge (Mass.) 1992.

[28] A. Portmann, *Anfruch der Lebensforschung*, Zürich 1965.

[29] E. Haeckel, *Art Forms in Nature*, Dover Publications Inc., New York, 1974.

[30] A. Portmann, *op cit.*

[31] *Ibid.*

[32] cf., R.M. Rilke, *Duino Elegies*, W.W. Norton & Co., New York 1978.

[33] cf., J. Appleton, *The Symbolism of Habitat*, Seattle-London 1990; idem, *The Experience Landscape*, London-New York 1975; idem, *The Poetry of habitat*, Hull 1978; *Landscape in the Art and the Sciences*, Hull 1980.

[34] cf., P. Valéry, *Eupalino o dell'architettura*, Carabba, Lanciano 1932 (*Eupalinos*, or the Architect, Oxford).

[35] cf., E. Franzini, *Paul Valéry: il giardino e la grazia*, in *Il giardino, idea natura realtà*, edited by A. Tagliolini and M. Venturi Ferriolo, Guerini and Associates, Milan 1987, pp. 45-54.

[36] *Ibid.*

[37] cf., P. Valéry, *op cit.*, p. 106.

[38] *Ibid.*, p. 108.

[39] *Ibid.*, p. 109.

[40] cf., L.C. Forti, *Ruskin, un profeta per l'architettura*, Compagnia dei librai, Genoa 1983.

[41] cf., R. Sheldrake, *The Rebirth of Nature*, Park Street Press, Rochester 1991.

[42] *Ibid.*, p. 108.

[43] cf., R. Sheldrake, *A New Science of Life*, 1981 and *The Presence of the Past*, London 1989.

[44] cf., R. Sheldrake, *The Rebirth...* cit.

[45] *Ibid.*

[46] R. Arnheim, *The Dynamics of Architectural Form*, Dumont, Cologne 1980 and C. Norberg-Schulz, *Esistenza spazio, architettura*, Officina, Rome 1975 (*Existence, space and architecture*, New York 1971)

[47] cf., P. Portoghesi, "Ricerche sulla centralità," in *Controspazio*, no. 6, June 1971, p. 8.

[48] cf., R. Sheldrake, *The Rebirth...* cit., p. 173.

[49] *Ibid.*, p. 174.

[50] *Ibid.*, p. 175.

[51] cf., G. Ciucci, ed., *L'architettura italiana oggi*, Laterza, Bari 1989, p. 184.

[52] cf., M. Wells, *Gentle Architecture*, Mc Graw Hill, New York 1982; E. Burgher, *Geomorphic Architecture*, Van Ostrans Reinhold, New York 1986; D. Pearson, *Earth to Spirit*, Gaia Books 1994; V. Papìanek, *The Green Imperative*, Thames and Hudson, London 1995; M.J. Crosbie, *Green Architecture*, Rockport Publisher, Rockport 1994.

[53] cf., B. Rudofsky, *Architecture without architects*, New York 1969.

[54] cf., E. Burgher, *op cit.* p. 136.

# The Wall

*The wild and rocky peaks of the Sinai mountains rise heavenwards while further north the regularity of the horizontally stratified rocks resembles the work of man. Natural strata characterise the landscape to the south and southwest of Jerusalem in order to prepare the visitor for his encounter with the built shapes of the city. The land of the Jews is made of stony horizontal formations that bear witness to the consternation of endurance. It is interesting to note how in this context the Jewish word for "stone" also means "father," and how "place" also means "presence."*
*The world of stone is truly represented in the "Wailing Wall"; as the enactment of a place, more than any other it really does express the identity of the Jews. The Jews meet face to face in front of the wall and wait. The wall manifests no human traits nor does it console, but stands as the indestructible and firm foundation of the centre of the world. Here, arrival does not become encounter and offers no alternatives, yet remains an origin and continues to express a new beginning. Jewish architecture is not figurative form but built form.*
*The message of the temple terracing is still valid today since in Jerusalem every building must be made of local stone. The world of stone is still* inhabited landscape.

Christian Norberg-Schulz

Built by the hand of man, the wall divides space, stops us in our tracks and puts a solid obstacle in our way, yet when arranged in a certain way it can hold us like a vase holds water. The wall is the primary element of architecture, its initial archetype. It began as a combination of available materials, branches, tree-trunks and leaves and one of its first functions was to protect the fireplace from the wind, a tradition kept alive today by the native inhabitants of Tasmania as well as the members of the Adamani tribe.[1] However, the wall came into its own when earth or stones were introduced into the building process. Perhaps at first the stones lying around the building site were gathered and placed side by side; later, stones of more or less the same shape were quarried from the bosom of the earth. When stones were not available, mud was found to produce similar results when mixed and heaped in layers. The fact that stones were laid side by side and on top of one other reveals an orderly mind, yet this arrangement appears to have been inspired by natural structures that man saw and tried to imitate. The stones in polygonal walls create a network that resembles the cracks in the earth caused by floods or the sun's burning rays, while the overlapping courses of the squares seem to reproduce the horizontal and vertical fissures of sedimentary rocks.

Often in rocky landscapes it is possible to see barriers apparently made by the hand of man; slabs standing apart from the rock face and suspended in thin air between heaven and earth like walls built to encompass space. Before existing in the mind of man, potential walls existed in the earth's landscape like ambiguous elements in which natural processes prefigured artificial ones.

The wall as the product of the aggregation of similar elements is implicit in the way in which mineral crystals form and grow, especially crystals such as fluorite in which elementary aggregation is cubic. "The mechanisms according to which a crystal nucleus tends to grow are grouped into three models: separate strata, spirals or dendrite form [...]. When considering the various growth models it is useful to think of the module as a brick and the crystal as a "wall" growing in three directions."[2]

In the separate strata model, the crystal forms and grows because small cubes similar to bricks are placed side by side and on top of one another. Therefore, we can imagine a wall in which a number of bricks are already arranged in rows and columns creating a parallelepiped. Let's imagine that above the parallelepiped there is a last incomplete layer that has, so to say, some gaps. Where will the new cube, destined to make the wall grow, find its niche? It has three alternatives: to position itself so as to touch three sides of the already aggregated whole or to touch two sides or else to begin to form a new layer by touching the lowest layer with just one of its sides. Well, nature acts much like a bricklayer who chooses the first alternative if there is a niche with three sides, the second when there is a two-sided niche and the third when no other alternative remains.

"Animal skin," wrote Semper, "and tree bark are the very first kinds of tex-

*The "wall" of a hornets' nest built by the insect community by mixing oak wood with their body secretions.*
*Left: rocky formations in the Pre-Alps near Verona. The overlapping strata are lined with vertical cracks similar to an artificial bulwark.*

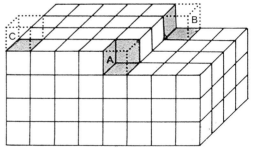

*Aggregation pattern of fluorite crystals. This aggregation method is also used for walls, as described on the opposite page.*
*Left: a wall made of regular* pietra forte *blocks, rustic on the outside but cut along the sides so that the wall has orthogonal joints (15th century). The horizontal courses are different in height so probably the stone blocks were brought roughly hewn from the quarry and then shaped on site.*

*A wall in the Sacsahuaman fortress in Cuzco, Peru (14th, 15th century).*

*Opposite page, above: a convex wall following the shape of the rock (an Inca building near Cuzco) and (right) a corn-cob grown in the Sacred Valley of the Incas. The plasticity of some of the Inca walls and their irregular layout seem to be inspired by the aggregation of corn seeds. The ashlar patterns of the walls often create central images that resemble the corn flower.*

*Opposite page, below: Machu Picchu, view of the so-called temple of the three windows and (right) the temple of the Sun.*

*An open pomegranate showing the aggregated structure of its seeds arranged in a strict quincuncial pattern.*
*Right: the cracks in this rock almost make it seem artificial.*

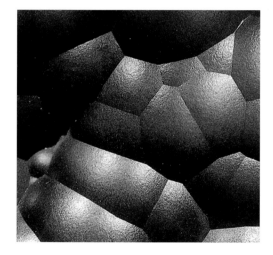

*A rounded aggregate of translucent pseudo-malachite.*
*Right: detail of the enclosure wall of the acropolis in Arpino (Italy), typical example of a polygonal construction.*

tile fabric."[5] When tents were built, primitive skins and materials were much like walls, but they did not have that stable relationship with the earth that makes the wall a permanent sign, a real transformation of the earth's surface. Woven branches are another archetype of the fence and panel wall, as well as being the original form of the weave, but they lack stability and continuity with the earth. Instead, the mud wall is an absolute continuation of the earth, since it needs to be mixed and kneaded and, in a number of ways, echoes the work of the potter who creates a receptacle that holds and contains.

The orderly arrangement of elements is a problem shared by weavers and builders, much like metre for the poet and word structure for the prose writer. A wall with parallel courses looks like a page written with lots of overlapping lines: the frontal width of the blocks might vary but their height and almost always their depth remains the same. When the bricklayer lays overlapping courses he can choose a pattern that is rarely more complex than a simple alternation between high and low courses (the so-called pseudo-isodomic arrangement).

When the elements of a wall are irregular, attempts to significantly reduce the cracks between one ashlar and another result in something that looks very similar to the fissured rocks found in the rocky outcrops of the earth's surface.

The invention of lime mortar, already in use during the 10th century B.C. in Jerusalem, gave the wall a kind of negative value. In fact, the mortar spreads out like a mesh in which the stones and bricks fill the empty spaces: this binds the structure of the wall and, together with the force of gravity, acts as an element of cohesion and resistance. The pattern produced by the assembly of these elements combines with the pattern of this continuous network which at times, especially when the colour of the mortar is different to the materials, is the first thing to catch one's eye. The relationship between object and background becomes indistinct and this is essential in order to exalt the illusive virtues of architecture.

This relationship between a binding mass and a series of submerged elements – concrete being the most common – is a recurrent theme in natural images and occurs when fluids and solids are mixed together as well as in biological tissues and composite rocks such as "breccia marble," considered by the Romans to be a precious building material.

The wall is the final product of a process that may have many phases: not always does the assembly of its elements constitute the final phase. When the bricklayer mixes mud with straw and animal excrements he adds to the mixture only the amount of material he is able to carry in his hands and usually prefers to make blocks in order to rationalise transportation and work faster. His behaviour differs little from that of many other animals: swallows who use mud to build their nests or termites who mix earth and sand with their own excrements. The need to "finish off" a surface led to the idea of covering the wall with a sort of skin: a "plaster," "uniting" elements that were initially separate and thereby satisfied a tactile and visual need.

*Villa Katsura, Kyoto. The boundary wall is made of bamboo canes.*

*Omdurman (Sudan), house built with blocks of earth mixed with straw and animal excrements. The wall is plastered with the same non-dried material.*

*Detail of the surface of an earthen wall. The blades of straw that are clearly visible act like iron in reinforced concrete. This type of wall is not very different from the nest walls of many bird species, including swallows and* furnaridae, *passerines of the tyrant flycatchers.*

Often the wall, especially a stone wall, is finished off when the ashlars are already in place, either by smoothing away the irregularities or carving mouldings or decorations. In the Tusa quarries that produced the stone masses used to build the columns of the temples in Selinunte, it is still possible to see pieces that have been detached from the surrounding rock face by unfinished annular channels. Once this excavation phase was over, the cylinders would have been cut at the base in order to transport them *in loco*.

This image is the tangible proof of an interrupted process and nostalgia invades the mind when recalling that the temple site originated here in the quarry. Once the rough blocks reached the temple, they were placed one on top of the other and only later was the vertical fluting chiselled out, possibly to emphasise the ideally unitary character of all the blocks, "to make one object out of many."

Similarly, the "rustic" wall is basically an unfinished wall with parts that have been assembled but not fashioned into their final shape, a shape which the sculptors say is achieved "by taking something away." This incompleteness, which again reveals close proximity to nature since the materials still bear traces of their original state, quickly aroused man's aesthetic interest, thanks to the seductiveness of the evolving form in a phase in which it still had free *valences*, so to speak. This same appeal can also be inspired by an impromptu sketch or by the first moulding of a sculpture, executed rapidly in order to capture and materialise an idea. Perhaps the artists themselves were the first to regret the preparation phase once the work was completed, to remember with pleasure a time in which the construction, already defined as an organism, waited for its skin to become vibrant and smooth through the use of projections and decorations. During the reign of Augustus, Roman architecture began to develop a taste for roughly hewn stone block walls; one of the best examples of this art type is the wonderful boundary walls of the Forum of Augustus, near Suburra, still visible today.

Apart from being the basis for the "rustic" style, as well as fostering mannerism, this fashion flourished during the reign of the Emperor Claudius. It can be seen in the aqueduct that bears his name, certainly the most beautiful aqueduct in Rome, but above all it reigns supreme in the so called Porta Maggiore in which relief and chiaroscuro triumph by submerging the orders in the vibrant wall mass and by turning the balance between order and panel wall into a sort of unresolvable conflict.

No less significant in its impressionist traits reminiscent of the condensed technique used in painting is the rusticated order of the houses in the port of Ostia and the construction of the temple that Agrippina dedicated to her husband, the divine Claudius, on the Caelian Hill. Under the campanile of the church of Santi Giovanni e Paolo as well as inside the monastery, it is still possible to admire the arches marked by Michelangelo's intuition of "incompleteness" almost as if the geometric form, the architect's "drawing," emerged in a hazy dreamlike form from the very core of a material resistant and refractory to the modelling force of the order yet saturated in natural qualities, qualities found on-

A wall with two brick patterns in the São Paulo Botanical Gardens in Brazil built by Carlo Linneo.
Left: Rome, remains of the temple of the divine Claudius near the church of Santi Giovanni e Paolo on the Caelian Hill. This picture shows how rustication was extended to the architectural order, one way to draw architecture closer to nature by glorifying or imitating its irregular structures.

El Yussuf, a district of Omdurman (Sudan), aerial view. The adobe houses fade into the earth on which they are built.

Landscape near Ragusa (Italy). The boundary walls are made of stones that were gathered to clear the ground and make it more fertile. They create a geometric grid and forcibly mark man's appropriation of nature as well as the obedience to nature dictated by this appropriation.
Right: a walled city in a fresco by Lorenzetti (Siena, Palazzo Comunale, 14th century).

ly in the bases Bernini designed for the Louvre and in the windows of Montecitorio in Rome.

In non-migratory agricultural cultures the wall quickly became the symbol and material sign of the "boundary," a place where the interior begins and the exterior ends in a perennial obstinate ambiguity. As a boundary between fields, the wall reifies property and rights and, like a grid, it measures the surface of the earth, highlighting its *planar nature* where this prevails and underlining its position when the latter is more variable and uneven.

Few images of walls illustrate as clearly as these outlying Ragusa and Modica, in southeast Sicily their importance as a sign of "anthropisation", of man's appropriation of the earth's surface, considered as something to be measured, divided and articulated without violating ist wholeness. Built with stones tilled from the fields, the wall becomes a humble coherent sign which, while respecting each stone's individuality, follows a common unwritten rule observed for centuries because its origins are linked to crop cultivation and harvesting.

When the wall becomes a city boundary, no longer a mere separation between the inside and outside of a house but an element of closure and defence, a limit crossed only through doors, specific places of discontinuity, then it acquires a sacred value; in other words it is "ratified," or "established by mutual consent." When the Etruscans founded a city, their ceremony called for the plough that dug the furrow for the wall to be lifted up out of the ground when

it passed the city gates because the sacred ring, symbol of inviolability, could not be broken.

At times, when bitter conflicts raged, people resorted to the walled city, but this was an exception rather than the rule. Yet even now we believe that the walled city is the city *par excellence*, the city that most resembles a living organism, the city whose symbolic form best interprets institutional reality even if the myth of the open city, open to traffic, to migrations, to the mixing of races and cultures has acquired special charisma for the advocates of modernity. In fact, walls separate rather than close, and Celestial Jerusalem with its twelve doors symbolises a universal embrace, albeit reserved only for the elect.

It was during the construction of the urban boundary of Thebes that Greek mythology tackled the problem of distinction between architecture as a purely constructive problem and architecture as an aesthetic value. Amfion and Zithos, sons of Zeus and Antiope, had conquered Thebes. Together they ruled the city, even if the true King was Amfion, since his brother preferred hunting and hard work to life at court. When it came to building the walls, Zithos carried the heavy stone slabs on his shoulders, showing himself to be stronger than any other worker. Amfion, instead, used the sound of the lyre given to him by Apollo to cast a magic spell over the stones, making them fly through the air and land on top of one other. Apart from the intrinsic affinity between music and poetry, this myth portrays two types of architects: the builder who labours side by side with his workers and the designer-poet whose work is above all a song, a picture of the natural marriage between the materials nature supplies. At another point in the book[4] I will examine how Valéry interpreted this myth in the ritual play he staged in Paris in 1932 with music by Honegger.

*Jerusalem: for the Jews, the "western wall," which comes from Herod's temple, is the "wailing wall." The faithful face it and pray. It is the symbol of the history of the people of Israel, the sufferings, frustrations and hopes that have marked the various eras. The wall is inextricably bound to the feelings it inspires in the faithful; it is the best and simplest example of human sentiments projected onto an architectural archetype.*

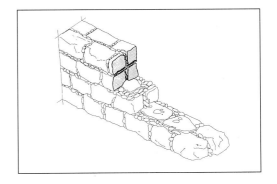

*Axonometric projection of a Tibetan wall. Note the alternation of big stone courses arranged "sister" fashion (with column rather than random joints) and the light flat tiles that horizontally bind the wall structure. The habit of building walls by rhythmically raising an arm and putting stones on top turns the structure into a sort of rhythmic dance, accompanied by a song mimicking the alternate wide or narrow courses. The song may be more or less interpreted as follows: "The great ashlars are the wall's knots/ the tiles are the skeins from which plaits are woven." The myth of Amfion is thus reflected in the humble work of Tibetan masons.*

[1] cf., V. Lips, *Vom Usprung der Dinge*, Volk und Buch, Leipzig 1951.

[2] cf., G. Tanelli, *Conoscere i minerali*, Longanesi, Milan 1988, pp. 96-97.

[3] cf., G. Semper, *Lo stile*, Laterza, Rome-Bari 1992, p. 109 and foll.

[4] cf., *infra*, the chapter on the "temple."

# The Floor, the Ground, the Tile

The horizontal plane, the perfectly flat surface, is an essential part of the experience of nature. During the very first appropriation experiences, the glade in the woods or the surface of the sea or lake on a calm day were all models of symbolic imitation used to transform the earth into a place where man could live and walk. Even when elements of the earth's surface, for example water, prevented man from advancing, in his dreams and longings he made the inaccessible, accessible.

A carefully pressed or paved surface fulfils man's dream of walking on water and makes the earth, shaped by the abstract force of the mind, an ideal place.

There are surfaces on earth that are as smooth and flat as billiard tables, for example, salt deserts, frozen lakes and certain rocky plateaux, but these are extreme cases. When we cross them, we immediately think of a room, of the idea of paving (from the Latin *pavire*), something fashioned from the earth by beating.

When toying with the idea of paving, making the earth suitable for living and walking and the dream of accessing the inaccessible represent the keys to architectural imagery. It is no surprise that men have spent hoards of precious energy in creatively imagining how to transform the floor into a decorated ornament. The most simple – the orthogonal pattern effectively transposing the Cartesian grid of abscissa and ordinates – are the playful geometric patterns so dear to Roman and Renaissance architects, the Gothic labyrinths depicting the floor as an allegory of the universe and the unexpected experience of the Duomo in Siena where the visitor walks over precious images, embarrassed by his own profanation. Decorating the floor with linear patterns often produces an effect very similar to the shadows of trees on the ground below.

The invention of the *carpet* is linked to the archetype of the floor, a warm welcoming floor made to measure for humans, a floor that defines the space of the portable house, the tent, and, later on, the prayer rug facing the Mecca, the portable mosque. It is no surprise that in *A Thousand and One Nights* the carpet is free from the forces of gravity; the floor is a visible shadow, a projection of the body, again adorned with the trappings of dreams. Like the floor, the carpet is born from the imitation of a flowered lawn instinctively sought by the body when lying down in the sun, a soft lawn that communicates the feeling of nestling against the breast of mother earth and being embraced by her.

To tell the truth, the architectural archetype is not really the floor but the "earth," the "ground." In English, the word *floor* has more than one meaning, yet the word is the perfect expression of the traits of an archetype both natural and artificial. It indicates the possession that takes place when the earth is beaten, compressed and consolidated, something that man does by simply walking and living on earth. The Campo dei Miracoli in Pisa is the best example of the genealogical link between the field and the threshing-floor, between the theatre and the square.[1]

The floor, or the ground, always has a surface and an underlying mass, one

The surface of basalt columns in the valley of
Alcantara in Sicily (Italy).
Left: a polygonal grid produced by cracks in the
clay surface of the ground during a drought.

Road surface in Ouro Preto, Brazil.
Left: Roman paving made of volcanic leucitite in
the thistle of Falerii Novi.

*The shadows cast on the ground by the trunks of beech trees on Mount Fogliano in the Cimini Mountains form an ethereal design of curved lines mirrored by the ramified pattern of the foliage. In architecture, it is not unusual for the floor design to reflect the masonry structures of the roof.*

*Ostia Antica: the mosaic pavement in the Piazza delle Corporazioni. Decorating floors satisfies man's desire to embellish this architectural image because it is the floor that "catches" man's eye the most.*

above one below. Subsoil and subterranean are words used to define "being underneath" in a relationship of absolute contiguity and protection with the earth. This is how the floor, which separates us from the realm of light, carries us into the world of shadows and chthonic forces.

Like natural ground that rises and falls creating peaks and valleys, so too the floor may rise or fall, may become a staircase or splinter into the springing steps of a ladder. Perhaps it was no chance occurrence that the Romans seized on the ancient Tunisian tradition of subterranean houses lit by a courtyard, dug at a lower level than the surrounding ground, while in the houses of Bulla Regia they focused on the floors as the defining element of their decorative program.[2]

The decoration of the floor can be carried out either with flat tiles or in a stratified and vibrant way, feigning articulated surfaces which, if real, would make the floor unusable.

In the way that walking on water is evoked by the mirror-like polish of marble floors, walking on a tightrope is conjured up by geometric patterns and visual perception, and satisfies the mysterious aspiration man has tried to achieve by using graphic trickery and perspective illusionism.

The problem of decorating floors or covering walls quickly became a theoretical problem for architects who solved it by using images culled from the observation of nature that in itself provided an incredible number of alternatives. The "modularity" of more regularly-shaped masonry provided a simple model

*Left: the Campo dei Miracoli in Pisa. Over the centuries, it has perpetuated the primitive image of the lawn upon which to sit and "inhabit" the earth.*
*Above: an oriental carpet; its image of a flowered lawn becomes tactile and ubiquitous.*

The flower of a wild carrot with its characteristic spiral structure, a structure that can also be found in sunflower seeds, pine cones, pineapples, etc. Phyllotaxis is the word used in botany to indicate the intersection sequence of leaves on a stem. To identify the types of phyllotaxis (when there is only one leaf per node) a fraction is used to measure the angle between the intersection points of the two next leaves. The phyllotactic fractions found in plants are invariably: 1/2; 1/3; 2/5; 3/8; 5/13; 8/21; 13/24.
The numerators and denominators of these fractions constitute the Fibonacci sequence, since every number is equal to the sum of the two preceding ones.
The angles that correspond to the fractions draw close to 137°30'28'', without ever reaching it. This angle, placed in the centre of a circumference, divides the latter into two segments using the golden rule. If the leaves of a plant were separated on a stem by similar angles, no one leaf would be on top of the another.
Obviously this would be advantageous for the leaf in its search for light.

86

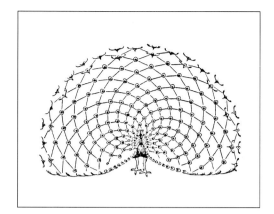

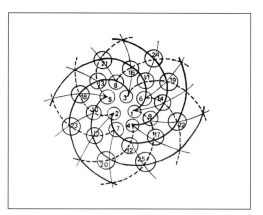

*Above: a pineapple.*
*Top, from left: the pattern of the "eyes" of a peacock's tail and the distribution of leaves in a 3/8 phyllotaxis. Fractal spiral for $r_1=0.98$ $r_2=0.15$ $\vartheta=47°$.*
*Left: Rome, the pavement of the Campidoglio from the top of the Capitoline tower. The pavement was executed only in 1936 by Antonio Muñoz, but is pictured in an engraving by Lafrey showing Michelangelo's project for the square. The pavement was inspired by the pattern of sunflower seeds, which the Romans often used for their mosaic pavements.*

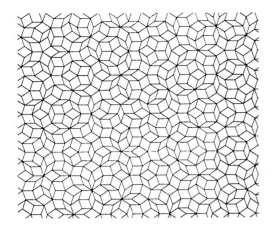

*A tile pattern by Penrose using a pair of rhombi with equal sides. Triangles, squares and hexagons form regular grids that are constantly found – more or less deformed – in nature and in the work of man. Regular pentagons work well in space and form one of Plato's solids (the dodecahedron), symbol of the Universe, but they only work on a plane by giving up their regularity. Even though it was tackled in the 17th century, the problem of the pentagon tile pattern was left unsolved for centuries by architects. Only in 1974 was it solved by the mathematician Roger Penrose; he demonstrated that with only two quadrangular figures, a dart and a kite, it was possible to fill the plane with a non periodical grid containing regular decagons and pentagons. The same thing occurs when two rhombic figures with sides the same length are joined together. The ratio between the two figures always follows the golden rule. In 1984 a crystal of aluminium and manganese was discovered with a fivefold symmetry similar to the one studied by Penrose. This paradoxical discovery, theoretically incompatible with the laws of crystallography, has obliged scientists to invent the category of quasicrystals, still very much a subject of discussion.*

for the floor, regarded as a horizontally built wall. However, the various roles played by the forces of gravity, when the pieces are laid on beaten earth or on mortar instead of standing on top of one another, gave a greater degree of freedom to the composition of floors. This led to a captious research that spread from the minds of the bricklayers to designers, theorists, mathematicians and even philosophers.

Apart from the practical problems of making or decorating a floor or a wall, there was the persistent problem of dividing any given surface into a more or less regular lattice pattern and establishing rules ranging from the simplest to the most complicated. The field in which this option between simplicity and complexity could be put into practice was naturally conditioned by the size of the pieces used to cover a given surface, and this was the reason why mosaics were laid with smaller and smaller tiles, permitting an incredible *escalation* towards freer figurative art and geometric *ecstasy*, later to be pushed beyond perfection by Islamic craftsmen.

Modern mathematics, above all thanks to Roger Penrose, has applied a theoretical rule to the tiling concept by investigating this field far beyond its most elementary solutions based on the mechanical regularity of modular grids.[3] However, the subject had already been studied in great depth by theorists and builders, and during the 17th century, in his *Armonices Mundi*, Kepler had already anticipated some semi-regular patterns based on the repetition of two or three geometric figures.[4]

Even in the classical world, the number of applied geometric combinations are practically endless, giving rise to two main principles that are in some ways connected: *centrality*, which means using very different elements, in extreme cases no two pieces being the same, and *modularity*, based on two-dimensional grids made up of equilateral triangles, squares or hexagons. In ancient times, but above all during the Renaissance, the knowledge and study of Plato's solids and their truncated or stellated editions was exploited to create grids with two or three figures set systematically side by side in order to form a regular fabric that could be extended forever. The most frequently used composite grid was made up of octagons and squares and so fascinated Leonardo da Vinci, Pietro da Cortona and Louis Kahn as to inspire them to design whole buildings based on this model.[5]

The grid with the most important symbolic value is the one made of octagons, hexagons and crosses, first used by the mosaicists who decorated the so-called mausoleum of Santa Costanza in Rome and later by Peruzzi, Serlio and Borromini. The grid of hexagons and triangles in which each hexagon is surrounded by a (single or double) crown of equilateral triangles also caught the attention of F. Lloyd Wright. The other possible combinations include dodecagons, hexagons and squares, or hexagons, triangles and squares or dodecagons and triangles.

In the 16th and 17th centuries, the hexagonal pattern of the hive was systematically used and reinterpreted in terms of chromatic contrast and perspective illusion. Each hexagon was divided into two parts using materials with contrasting hues, normally white and grey marble (*bardiglio*), and rarely were regular hexagon grids used in this context. Generally speaking, the laws governing cutting and execution dictated the use of irregular hexagons with two 45° angles, which allowed the diagonal edges to be aligned. An expert scholar of the *Ars Combinatoria*, Borromini succeeded in using the "vasole" system to create a centralised tiling pattern in the church of Sant'Ivo alla Sapienza.[6]

By arranging the first eight *vasole* in the shape of a cross at the centre of the pattern and by continuing the tiling series in eight different directions, the architect designed an asymmetrical carpet with a remarkable dynamic force. Instead, by slightly modifying the geometric pattern (using two squares and *vasole* of corresponding size) I composed a more complex centralised ensemble in which there is a hierarchy between the four cardinal and four complementary points and I gave this new pattern the name "Almaak," a star of the constellation Andromeda.

For the sheer joy of it, the physicist Roger Penrose began to study tiling and in 1974 succeeded in solving what was considered an unsolvable problem, namely a plane made up of pentagons and another two figures called "darts" and "kites." The elements of this plane are not repeated like those of a hive at regular distances of whole numbers, instead the number that controls the distribution is an irrational number called the "golden ratio" ($1\sqrt{5}/2 = 0.618...$).

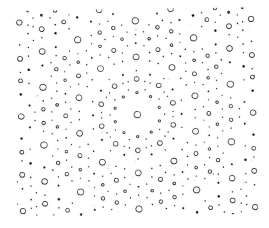

*A diffraction figure with fivefold symmetry.*

*The floor of the church of Sant'Ivo alla Sapienza in Rome seen from inside the clerestory (Francesco Borromini, 1661).*

There are a thousand different ways to use the tiling system invented by Penrose. Sometimes it creates symmetric patterns around an axis, but normally regularity and irregularity are continually intermixed to such an extent that they seem to inspire an unlimited search for an order never totally achieved. Penrose's pentagonal tiling system has been seen to be a sort of labyrinth.[7] In fact, if someone walked around a series of connecting rooms based on the cells of this plane, there would be no way he could find a way out without the help of "Ariadne's thread." Furthermore, the number of "kites" in each of these patterns is always 0.618 times the number of points: this proves how the pentagon governs the pattern and how the golden section recurs in natural and artificial formative processes with mysterious and ironic assiduity.

Penrose also studied other types of tiling systems obtained by combining more than one figure, both on a plane and in space. He did this by creating two rhombohedrons and still he obtained fivefold symmetry. The importance of his work, which might have seemed just a game, only became apparent when a manganese and aluminium crystal with fivefold symmetry was discovered and studied in 1984. This kind of crystallisation, judged to be impossible according to the laws drawn up by crystallographers, is based on the assumption that even nature behaves like a mathematician by using a "quasiperiodic" table that fills in spaces with rhombohedrons that are bound just like two-dimensional tiling. This led to the theory of the "quasicrystals" around which the debate still rages on.

*An example of a floor showing a pentagonal pattern by Penrose (Paolo Portoghesi, exhibition of marble from Verona, 1996).*

New light has, however, been shed on the paradoxes of tiling by an expert named Emil Makovicky[8] who compares the results of Penrose's studies on pentagonal periodicity with a type of tiling used in Iran eight hundred years ago in the Gunbad-i-Quabud blue tomb in Maragha. Apart from a few unimportant differences, with a few changes the two patterns can easily be made to look alike. Their comparison means that new interpretations of Penrose's tiling can be made, interpretations which may prove useful even in the field of crystallography.[9] Makovicky's treatise was published in a collection of texts by various authors compiled by Istvan Hargittai, a professor of chemistry at the University of Budapest and an untiring explorer of symmetry which he considers the unifying link in our comprehension of many natural phenomena.

Up to now, despite its potential, examples of Penrose's tiling applied to the field of architecture are few and far between. The artist Tony Robbin, in his book *En'gineering, a New York Architecture* (Yale University Press, New Haven 1996), singles out as the pioneers of a "quasicrystal" architecture, Haresh Lalvani, Koji Miyazaki, and Steve Baer, as well as himself. This architecture reproduces and exploits the quality of quasicrystals, namely the tridimensional projection of cubes with more than three dimensions. I have started to experiment in this field and have already encountered inescapable difficulties. The tiling specialist who wishes to lay a floor with this design has a difficult task ahead of him, and his experience of executing even very complicated patterns based on matching repetitions is of little avail. If he does not follow a method based on the rigorous repetition of a scale model, his numerous mistakes could oblige him to start all over again since the choice of tile to be laid is not always so obvious. Sometimes there is no choice, but sometimes there are a number of alternatives and an error in the arrangement means it is impossible to proceed without leaving huge gaps in the tiling. The same thing happens when exploring a labyrinth.

*Erice (Italy), square stone paving.*

[1] cf., P. Portoghesi, *La piazza come luogo degli sguardi*, edited by M. Pisani, Gangemi, Rome 1990.

[2] cf., D. Levi, *Antioch Mosaic Pavements*, Princeton University Press, Princeton 1947 and O. Grabar, *The Meditation of Ornament*, Princeton University Press, Princeton 1992 illustrating the mosaics at Khirbat al-Mafiar. These mosaics are extremely interesting in the context of the transition from a Roman and Hellenistic culture to an Arab culture. For the mathematical interpretation of the patterns see D.K. Washburn, D.W. Crowe, *Symmetries of Culture,* University of Washington Press, Seattle-London 1988.

[3] cf., I. Stewart, M. Golubitsky, *Fearful Symmetry*, Blackwell, Oxford 1992, p. 95.

[4] J. Kepler, *Armonices Mundi*, Linz 1619.

[5] cf., C. Baroni, *Leonardo architetto*, in *Leonardo da Vinci*, Istituto italiano di arti grafiche, Novara 1939.

[6] cf., L. Benevolo, "Il tema geometrico di Sant'Ivo alla Sapienza", in *Quaderni dell'Istituto di storia dell'architettura*, no. 3, November 1953, pp. 1-10. Translator's note: a *vasole* is a trapezoidal tile shaped like a flower vase.

[7] cf., I. Peterson, *Il turista matematico*, Rizzoli, Milan 1991, pp. 260-273 (*The Mathematical Tourist*, New York 1988).

[8] cf., I. Hargittai, ed., *Fivefold Symmetry*, World Scientific, Singapore 1992, pp. 67-76.

[9] cf., I. Hargittai, ed., *Symmetry, Unifying Human Understanding*, Pergamon Press, Oxford 1899.

# The Roof, the House, the Tent

*Maison, pan de prairie, Ô lumière du soir
Soudain vous acquérez, presque une face
humaine vous étes près de nous, embrassants,
embrassés.*

Rainer Maria Rilke

*Whoever builds chooses a site, isolating it from
nature through an unnatural act of division and
separation: for this reason it must be explained
and justified. Even during our prenatal stage,
human life is marked by the dual state of
separation and reunification, the driving force
behind the development of civilisation. A site is
divided in order for a house, a city, to be born:
so it is for man who begins life through
division, a separation from his mother. By
rebuilding his nest, his shell, he recomposes an
illusionary unity. It is the symbol of a return to
the maternal womb, a sacred element
permitting the reappropriation of unity.*

Daniela Vigna, M. Silvana Alessandri

"Architecture," wrote Louis Kahn, "is what nature is unable to do. Nature is unable to do what man does. Man takes nature – the means to do – and discriminates between its laws. Nature does not do this, because it works in harmony with these laws and we call this order."[1]

This statement is based on the assumption that man is not part of nature and even if he discovers an undeniable conceptual difference between the natural and artificial worlds, he ploughs an incredibly deep furrow between the two. In practice, man takes only the materials he needs from nature, he applies and interprets only the laws he chooses. In the same way, being himself part of nature, when he decides not to oppose it he lets nature work within him exploiting it to reach his goals. Man does not take from nature the margin of freedom that is based on his conscience, thoughts and language, because it is nature that exercises a secret influence over him, an influence that is not dominated by the mind but operates in his subconscious. Only by acceding to the realm of this secret influence will the relationship between architecture and nature be clearly seen as a dual movement, simultaneously involving both the distancing and the deep acceptance of an influence expressed by images and laws that are not yet scientific "laws of nature," but logical deductions based on specific sensorial impressions with different meanings. This is what we initially called "symbolic imitation."

In this context, the Vitruvian legend of the invention of architecture based on the discovery of fire and language takes on profound meaning. It is worth reading and interpreting once again: "Ergo sum propter ignis inventionem conventus initio apud homini es et concilium et convictus esset natus, et in unum locum plures convenirent habentes ab natura praemium praeter reliqua animalia ut non pronsi sed erecti ambularent mundique et astrorum magnificentiam aspicerent, item manibus et articulis quam vellent rem faciliter tractarent, coeperunt in eo costu alii de fronde facere tecta, alii speluncs fodere sub montibus, nonulli hirundinum nidos et aedificationes earum imitantes de luto et virgulis facere loca, quae subirent, tunc observantes aliena tecta ed adiacentes suis cogitationibus res novas, efficiebant in dies meliora genera casarum, cum essent autem honimines imitabili docilique natura, cotidie inventionibus gloriantes alius alii ostendebant aedificiorum effectus, et ita exercentes ingenia certationibus in dies melioribus iudiciis efficiebantur. primumque furcis erectis et virgulis interpositis luto parietes texerunt, alii luteas glaebas arefacientes struebent parietes, materias eos iugumentantes, vitandoque imbres et aestus tegebant harundinibus et fronde. posteaquam per hibernas tempestates tecta non potuerunt imbres sustinere, fasigia facientes, luto inducto proclinatis tectis, stillicidia deducebant."

Ferri's Italian version remains the most faithful translation. Here translated into English, it reads: "The discovery of fire was hence the reason behind the birth of human society; and so many men gathered in one place, receiving from nature the privilege over other animals to walk upright and not head down, to contemplate the magnificence of the world and the heavens, to easily handle every object they pleased. Thus, in these societies some began to make roofs with branches, others dug caves out of mountains, others, imitating the nests built by swallows, built shelters of mud and sticks. Observing the huts of others, using those improvements or creatively making their own, they began to build better and better dwellings. And since the nature of man is to imitate and learn, rejoicing daily in his own inventions, they showed each other their constructions and thus, by exercising intelligence and emulation, day by day they improved their criteria. And the first thing they did was to stand forked branches upright and put branches in between and so they built mud walls. Others, by drying clay, built walls that they joined together with wood and covered with reeds and leafy branches against the rain and the heat. Having seen that during the winter storms the roofs could not stop the rain, they built pointed roofs, covered in mud, and the pitch of the roof let the rain drain off."[2]

It is true that the creation of the roof and consequently of the house, typically things "that nature is unable to do," are a product of man's intelligence – according to Vitruvius. Not only does man use natural materials, he also picks up on practical examples and stimulating ideas. In fact, as well as being able to handle tools, he is privileged to be able to contemplate the beauty of the world and the heavens and this contemplation (perhaps it would have been better to translate *auspicere* with the verb *to observe*) leads instinctively to imitation, since men reveal themselves to be "*imitabili dolcilique natura*" inclined towards the imitation of and obedience to nature. This means that by observing the world in all its variety man can reunite what is divided and make a whole out of separate parts. Moreover, by pooling his experiences, he can continually improve his inventions and use them to create history.

By doing this, man combines and uses objects and laws that nature had put on the "back burner." One could say that a mind capable of discernment was at work in nature to create from things that were separate – but always "in nature" – that which did not yet exist, or that from the laws man established, based on his observations, he drew up a number of concepts that together created a "corpus" representing architectural knowledge at the nascent state.

Certainly, the branches and trunks of trees, as well as natural caves, functioned as man's first shelter from the elements, above all from the rain, and to some extent this is still so.[3]

In the United States, in the region of the White Mountains, some trees of the *pinus longaeva* species are almost five thousand years old and still survive today. Primitive man was certainly familiar with these millenary trees. Over the course of the years the trunks of some of these species became hollow and these internal spaces offered hospitable abodes that even recently have been used by monks and hermits, thus making these trees famous. In a similar way, in the tropical regions of Africa, the colossal and very soft trunks of the baobab, the bottle tree that seems to have been shaped by an able potter, are hollowed in order to make homes.

In an amusing engraving of his *Lustgarten* executed in 1668, Erasmo Francisi

*A picture of flames. In his treatise, Vitruvius declares the discovery of fire to be the moving force behind the creation of society, as well as the root of language and architecture.*

*The discovery of fire. Xylography of Cesariano's edition of Vitruvius' treatise (Gottardo Da Ponte, Milan 1521).*

*Above, from left: a bird builds his ring-shaped nest by weaving rigid twigs; the hut built by the* Amblyornis inornatus, *one of the eighteen species of bower birds. Note the use of struts to consolidate and anchor the construction which is not used as a nest, but as a place for mating.*
*Right: huts in a village in Dinder (Sudan).*

A primitive hut in an illustration of
Filarete's Treatise.
Left: a cube house without a roof, built by
kneading earth (Omdurman, Sudan).

*A tree house in Indonesia.*
*Above, right: tree dwellers in North America*
*(engraving by Erasmus de Francisi,* Lustgarten,
*1668).*
*Below: an ancient olive tree with a hollow trunk*
*that could be used as a shelter near Tivoli (Italy).*

depicts North American natives perching in trees, intent upon defending themselves by showering stones on indiscreet Europeans who, armed with saws, are trying to destroy their simple abodes by cutting down the trunks. Similarly, it could be said that the olive tree is a plant that lives in symbiosis with man who every spring prunes its branches so that the tree can yield more fruit. Yet when this tree ages its trunk becomes hollow and hospitable, giving shelter to those who enter its enveloping body, an internal space offered with painful abandonment.

Nearly all trees, however, offer shelter from the sun and the rain, and their liveability was convincingly championed by Italo Calvino in his fairy tale entitled *Il Barone Rampante*. This protection against the rain offered by protruding and overlapping branches was noticed and easily exploited by primitive man to shape the pitch of his roofs. The spontaneous gesture of covering one's head with one's hands so that the rain trickles away along one's fingers also contributed to this solution. The relationship between the house and the tree, determined among other things by the tree's symbolic nature considered to be an *axis mundi*, was alive and well even in Homer's time, as illustrated by the description of Ulysses' bedroom in Ithaca:

*Anteroom door of the* Essai sur l'Architecture *by Marc-Antoine Laugier. Laugier sees the birth of architecture, its forms and laws in the imitation of this model in which nature and artifice are well balanced.*

> Inside the court there was a long-leaved olive-tree
> which had grown to full height with a stem as thick
> as a pillar. Round this I built my room of close-set stone-work
> and when that was finished, I roofed it over thoroughly
> and put in a solid, neatly fitted, double door. Next I
> lopped all the twigs off the olive, trimmed the stem from
> the root up, rounded it smoothly and carefully with my adze and
> trued it to the line, to make my bedpost. This I drilled through
> where necessary, and used as a basis for the bed itself, which
> I worked away at till that too was done, when I finished it off with
> an inlay of gold, silver and ivory, and fixed a set of purple
> straps across the frame.[4]

The pages written by Abbey Laugier[5] describing the shift from the observation of the tree to the "invention of the hut" are quite memorable. Based on Vitruvius, Laugier attempts to identify the first architectural model that acted as imitative art: "Let us look at man in his primitive state without any aid or guidance other than his natural instincts. He is in need of a place to rest. On the banks of a quietly flowing brook he notices a stretch of grass; its fresh greenness is pleasing to his eyes, its tender down invites him; he is drawn there and, stretched out at leisure on this sparkling carpet, he thinks of nothing else but enjoying the gift of nature; he lacks nothing, he does not wish for anything. But soon the scorching heat of the sun forces him to look for shelter. A nearby forest draws him to its cooling shade; he runs to find a refuge in its depth, and there he is content. But suddenly mists are rising, swirling round and growing denser, until thick clouds cover the skies; soon,

*Illustration from Filarete's* Treatise *in which the instinctive gesture of sheltering oneself from the rain is considered as being at the heart of the morphology of the roof and pediment.*

torrential rain pours down on this delightful forest. The savage, in his leafy shelter does not know how to protect himself from the uncomfortable damp that penetrates everywhere; he creeps into a nearby cave and, finding it dry, he praises himself for his discovery. But soon the darkness and foul air surrounding him make his stay unbearable again. He leaves and is resolved to make good by his ingenuity the careless neglect of nature. He wants to make himself a dwelling that protects but does not bury him. Some fallen branches in the forest are the right material for his purpose; he chooses four of the strongest, raises them upright and arranges them in a square; across their top he lays four other branches; on these he hoists from two sides yet another row of branches which, inclining towards each other, meet at their highest point. He then covers this kind of roof with leaves so closely packed that neither sun nor rain can penetrate. Thus man is housed. Admittedly, the cold and heat will make him feel uncomfortable in this house which is open on all sides but soon he will fill in the space between two posts and feel secure [...]. All the splendours of architecture ever conceived have been modeled on this little rustic hut I have just described. It is by approaching the simplicity of this first model that fundamental mistakes are avoided and true perfection is achieved. The pieces of wood set upright have given us the idea of the column, the pieces placed horizontally on top of them the idea of the entablature, the inclining pieces forming the roof the idea of the pediment. This is what all masters of art have recognized."

This description is full of the reasonable, soothing tones of the century of Enlightenment still influenced by Rococo tastes. The accompanying illustrations conjure up the hedonism of Boucher and Fragonard rather than the sacred world of primitive man, shipwrecked by the invincible forces of nature against which man tries to defend himself. After all, the scene is witnessed by a personification of architecture which seems to have just come out of a boudoir accompanied by an angelic Bernini-style putto. Three centuries earlier, Filarete, in one illustration of his treatise, shows a man "sheltering" from the rain by using his arms to shape the brim of his hat into a pitched roof.[6] This is similar to the shape made by a young orang-utan hanging a big leaf over his head while ensconced in the hospitable cavity of a tree trunk and photographed by Michel Allaby as part of his book *Animal Artisans*.[7]

The data currently provided by palaeontologists neither confirm nor disprove the theories of Vitruvius and Laugier, but lead to the consideration that it is difficult to trace the birth of the house back to just one genealogy.

If the act of embracing the maternal breast as well as the act of leaving the maternal womb both encompass the principles of dwelling and sheltering, the instinctive gesture of primates who shelter themselves from the sun and the rain with the leaves and bark of trees introduces the concept that hominids and early man needed to improve on this basic shelter to the point of separating it from their bodies. The oldest traces of what can vaguely be called a house with a certain degree of exactitude was found by Mary Leakey in the Olduvai gorge of central Africa and dates back two million years. The hearth is made of a circle of stones and the floor is littered with animal bones and stone tools. The area of the hearth was probably covered with branches and this would explain the circular enclosure.

Fifteen thousand years ago man was already capable of building shelters with branches that joined the ground to a ridge-pole resting on forked posts. When this structure is turned upside down it looks like a boat, highlighting the common origins of the roof and the hull: the skeleton of an animal whose ribs are held together by the spinal "column." In 1957, remains of this kind of hut from the early Palaeolithic period were found in the region of Terra Amata near Nice. Lumley's reconstruction, in which the branches are leafless in order to make the drawing clearer, provides a very precise picture of the elementary nature of the structure and its osteological matrix.[8]

Having conquered this building experience, man turns the hut into the infinitely variable interpretation of a sacred archetype on the basis of the raw materials provided by his surroundings and by the climate that varies from one place to another. This leads to the construction of different types that maintain their identity for thousands of years; some are still used by ethnologically interesting civilisations as well as by more civilised ones, an excellent example being the alpine hut. The archetypal role of the hut refers to houses but also to storehouses for grain (the famous Galician granaries) and other fruits of the earth, as well as to the shelters built by animal species, above all doves, that have become an integral part of the European landscape.

*A gesture similar to the one shown by Filarete in a picture taken in a forest: an orang-utan sheltering from the rain under a big leaf.*

*Drawing of a hut from the early Palaeolithic period.*

A nomad encampment in the desert near Wadi Musa (Jordan), and, below right, a woollen tent built with wooden struts and hemp cords in Hammamet (Tunisia).

A classic example of tepee, the tent of the American Indians. It has an opening above the entrance to let the smoke out and a characteristic ring of poles which acts as a coping. Depending on the seasons and the weather, the tent can be modified to protect the inhabitants from the cold, the heat, the rain and the wind.

100

The evolutionist theories which, despite being clearly unreliable, still influence historical culture, aim at identifying a genealogy of the house that ranges from the cave to the tent to the hut and then to the house. To speak of succession in reference to such closely linked types, whose differences are difficult to distinguish, clearly contributes nothing towards the comprehension of the productive interaction between these different shelters whose contemporary use is often dictated by options which strongly depend on environmental and cultural factors.

The tent's identity depends on its easy assemblage and mobility; but disassembly is just as easy for some kinds of huts and mobility is a feature of certain huts with streamlined structures as well as the house-carts of African and Asian nomads. Similarly, there is ample archaeological evidence that tents and huts were erected inside natural caves.

Apart from presuming to establish verifiable genealogies, the tent can be seen as a transformation of clothing, a second skin protecting us from the rigours of the elements, a gift given to man by animals when the former learnt to cure their skins, stretching them with sticks and chewing them to avoid stiffness. Not only does this stretched skin supply the raw material but, in virtue of the need to maintain its suppleness and elasticity, it also provides the conceptual model of stretching and of pulling (making taut).

This derivation of clothing is particularly suited to the Indian "tepee" which before being assembled looks like a large round cloak with a sort of protruding neck from which ears are cut in order to leave an opening at the top for smoke.[9] Just like the hut, the problem of keeping the roof raised meant that the tent also needed vertical and sloping supports anchored to the ground. However, these light materials had to be held firm and man solved this problem as soon as he learnt how to make ropes by twisting skins or plant fibres. Here nature offers a valuable model for this process of stretching, anchoring and creating a sort of supporting skeleton under the integument of the skins or tissues. The model is the web of the spider, the spider being the architect *par excellence* among animals. To build his house, the spider uses his glands to produce different secretions. This allows him to build a silky supporting structure and a web of sticky threads he uses as a trap to capture insects.[10]

The series of operations that a garden spider has to execute in order to weave his web reveals that his instincts possess a real design strategy. The first thing he does is to build a bridge between two points starting from where he stands. To do this he needs a thread as well as a sort of claw-shaped hook that like a microscopic glider sails on the slightest breeze. The glider leads the silk thread to a landing point and should it not find one the spider then swallows it so nothing goes to waste. Once the bridge is built the spider reaches the centre and from there descends downwards until he finds a third landing point. Before anchoring this new thread, he pulls on the thread so that the bridge is divided into two segments which, together with the new thread, form the axes of a triangle

*From top to bottom: a drawing by Houël of a natural formation of basalt prisms in the Alcantara valley from* Voyage pittoresque en Sicilie; Helicoplacus, *a member of a primitive class of echinoderms now extinct; a stone construction near Bethlehem, Palestine.*

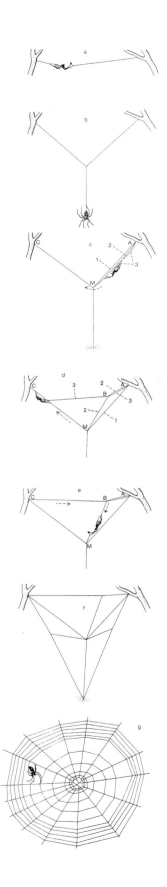

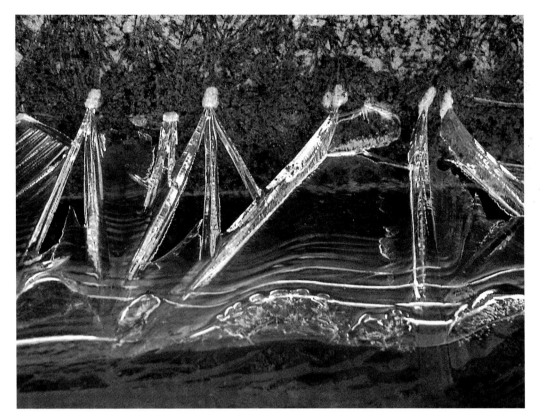

*Ice formation in a fountain in which the water level has gradually subsided.*
*Below: Giovanni Michelucci, project for a multipurpose building.*

*Opposite page, left: the various construction stages of a web. The spider starts by stretching a thread between two branches, the thread acting as a bridge and as the upper part of the construction (a). Then, the spider lets himself fall downwards from the centre of this thread: with a third thread, he hooks onto the structure that has in the meantime become triaxial (b). His third, very clever move, allows him to build another boundary thread as well as one of the radii. When there are enough radii, the spider then moves in a spiral fashion and weaves the web. He does this partly with normal threads and partly with sticky threads to stop the captured insects from getting away. This sticky substance is the secretion with which the threads are made.*
*Right: two similar pictures; the web of a money spider and an experimental structure designed by Frei Otto.*

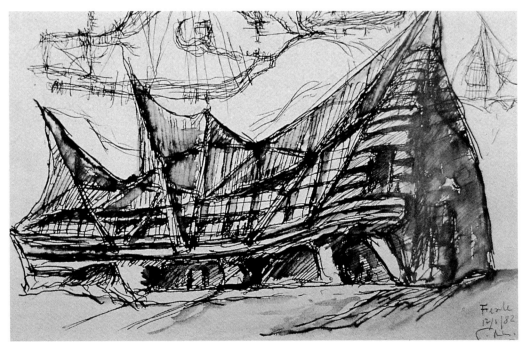

that will be built later on by externally connecting the three landing points using more new threads. The other threads and the central web are then built using crafty solutions, for example doubling or trebling a segment and then dividing the parts in order to make other elements of this ingenious structure which, once finished, is inhabited by the builder who sits in the middle and waits for his prey.

It is true that rather than a tent, the two-dimensional virtuality of a spider's web reminds us more of a tent's layout or a conical cupola and the orthographic projection of its internal structure. However, there are cases in which animal architecture has produced shapes volumetrically similar to the web of the money spider or the net created by the larva of the *Neureclipsis bimaculata*. A tent built 40,000 years ago in Molodova in the Ukraine, covered with skins and supported by the bones and teeth of a mammoth, illustrates how much construction depended on the materials available and how, when Antoni Gaudí used bones for the frame of Casa Batlló, his inspiration actually came from a primordial idea. Wasn't it Gaudí who stated that originality is nothing other than a return to origins?

As the favourite abode of the Mongolian people the tent peaked in complexity and refinement, and back in the Middle Ages European travellers described these taut structures capable of accommodating up to two thousand people. According to Marco Polo, one particular type of tent made of bamboo canes and longitudinally divided into two parts was used as a summer residence: "another large palace, constructed entirely of canes, but with the interior all gilt and decorated with beasts and birds of very skilful workmanship [...]. The roof is also made of canes, so well varnished that it is waterproof [...]. You must know that these canes are more than three palms in girth and from ten to fifteen paces long. They are sliced down through the middle from one knot to the next, thus making two shingles. These shingles are thick and long enough not only for roofing but for every sort of construction [...]. And the Great Khan has had it so designed that it can be moved whenever he fancies; for it is held in place by more than 200 cords of silk."[11]

Marco Polo's description of Kublai's palace was inspired by the bamboo thickets that transformed the tent into a prismatic shell. Instead, the model of the tent is associated with the wind and with sails and the multiple effects of the surface tension of liquids, and in the history of architecture the tent represents an antidote to the obvious simplicity of the right angle and the trilith system. The tent creates catenary curves, slanting surfaces with double curves, lined surfaces; the magical domination of "mathematical forms" is revealed by its unpredictable morphology determined by matter subject to traction. When organising the tent, as well as the house, there is a tendency towards identification with the human body. For example, among Bedouins, the front curtain of the tent is called "face," the rear part "neck," the front corner poles "hands" and the rear ones "legs."[12]

Frank Lloyd Wright was the first architect to free the tent archetype from

*A spider's web on the branches of a boxwood hedge.*

*An open air tepee tent.*
*Left: Paolo Portoghesi, model of an Exhibition Complex in Riyadh, Saudi Arabia (1995).*

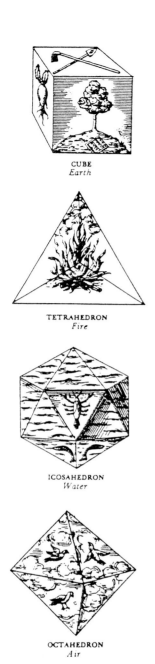

CUBE
*Earth*

TETRAHEDRON
*Fire*

ICOSAHEDRON
*Water*

OCTAHEDRON
*Air*

DODECAHEDRON
*the Universe*

*Plato's five regular solids and their symbols.*

the military and heraldic domination to which European culture had confined it after its Asiatic fortunes by designing his steel cathedral based on the Indian tepee model as well as his fascinating translucent tent in the Beth Shalom synagogue in Chicago. However, it is Frei Otto who lays claim to its applicability. Using the latest modern technologies, he invented a mathematical and glacial landscape that still awaits the poetical interpretation of all its incredible potential. In his institute at the University of Stuttgart, Otto dedicated numerous studies to the similarities between natural and artificial structures. Among these studies, the ones which stand out most are those on radiolarians and diatoms and the book entitled *Architecture of Nature* published in 1974 by the research group "Biologie und Bauen."

A decisive step forward from the pastoral interpretation of the hut, passed on to us by Laugier, is the interpretation provided by Etienne-Louis Boullée.

Boullée's mental project was more important to him than the actual construction of the hut: "What is architecture? Do I consider it, like Vitruvius, the art of construction? Certainly not. This definition contains a glaring mistake. Vitruvius considers its effects as its cause. The concept of the work precedes its execution. Our forefathers built their huts after having created their image. It is this production of the spirit, this creation that constitutes architecture and that consequently we can define as the art of production and refinement of any building."[13]

For Boullée, architecture is not so much a product of the observation of nature but of choosing in nature what is appropriate to man and what is most similar to "our organisation." It is the discovery in nature of something that belongs to us, an aspect of our humanity that leads us to see what is beautiful and then to include it in our building methods. Boullée writes: "When trying to discover in the essence of objects, their traits and similarities with our constitution, I began my research with dark objects [...]. Tired of the mute and sterile image of irregular objects, I began to study regular shaped objects and I immediately saw in them the distinct traits of regularity, symmetry and truth and how these contributed to form and figure. Furthermore, I realised that only regularity could provide man with clear ideas on the shapes of objects and determine their denomination which comes, not only from regularity and symmetry, but also from variety. Composed of a multitude of different faces, the shape of irregular objects, as I mentioned earlier, escapes our understanding. The number of faces and their complexity does not provide us with distinctive criteria: confusion is the image they offer.

"Why do we immediately see the form of regular shaped objects? Because their form is simple, the faces regular and repeated. However, the way we evaluate our impressions when we look at objects, relates to their clarity. What makes us clearly distinguish regular objects is their regularity and their symmetry as images of order and this image is the same as clarity. These observations imply that man did not have any clear idea of the shape of objects until he correlated them with the idea of regularity.

106

"After having established that regularity, symmetry and variety constitute the shape of regular objects, I realised that proportion lies in the ensemble of these traits. In fact, what I mean by the proportion of an object, is the effect that stems from regularity, symmetry and variety. In objects, regularity produces beauty of form; symmetry produces order and overall value. Lastly, variety produces the different faces which make them seem different to us. The union and reciprocal accord of these traits creates the harmony of objects."[14]

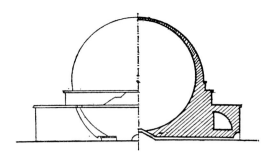

*Etienne-Louis Boullée, view and section of Newton's Mausoleum.*

Reference to regularity is also clearly present in the observations made by William Chambers when he speaks of the hut archetype: "At first," he says, "they most likely retired to caverns, formed by nature in the rock, to hollow trunks of trees, or to holes dug by themselves in the earth. But soon, disgusted with the damp and darkness of these habitations, they began to search after more wholesome and comfortable dwellings. Animal creation pointed out both materials and methods of construction; swallows, rooks, bees and storks were the first builders. Man observed their instinctive operations. He admired, he imitated, and being endowed with reasoning faculties a structure suited to mechanical purposes, he soon outdid his masters in the builders' art.

"Rude and unseemingly, no doubt, were his first attempts; without experience or tools, the builder collected a few boughs of trees, spread them in conic shape, and covering them with rushes, leaves and clay, formed his hut: sufficient to shelter its hardy inhabitant at night or in seasons of bad weather. But in the course of time, men naturally grew more expert; they invented tools to shorten and improve labour; they fell upon neater, more durable modes of construction, and forms better adapted than the cone to the purposes for which their huts were invented [...]. That the primitive hut was of a conic figure is a reasonable conjecture, from its being the simplest of solid forms and most easily constructed. Wherever wood was found they probably built in the manner above described, but as soon as the inhabitants discovered the inconvenience of inclining sides, and the want of upright space in the cone, they changed it for a cube, and as it is supposed, preceded in the following manner."[15]

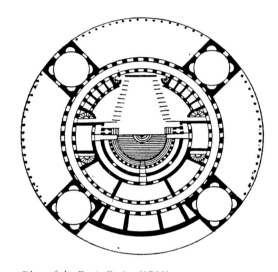

*Plan of the Paris Opéra (1780).*

The theory that the image of a cube is necessary to build a hut, similar to Boullée's reference to regular objects, seems to be a step in the opposite direction from the natural scenario, projecting the genesis of housing onto an abstract and distant horizon. In fact, it means understanding the concept of orthogonality, traditionally considered foreign to the repertoire of natural forms. Certainly there are plants whose smaller branches jet out almost at right angles from the bigger ones; for instance, the flower of the *Ruta graveolens* is characterised by a magnificent cross while cubic mineral crystals such as pyrite and kitchen salt can easily be found in nature, but it is highly improbable that primitive man knew about such rarities and orthogonality seemed to have initially been part of what Kahn defines as "what nature is unable to do."

However, what did exist, and was certainly practised by primitive man, was the cosmic observation of nature which cannot be synchronically condensed in-

*Entrance to houses dug out of the rock near Faleria (Castello di Fogliano), Italy.*
*Above left: a cave used as a house near Soriano al Cimino. Initially, the two cells were separate, but they were later joined together by partially demolishing the rock partition.*
*Below: a cave lit artificially from above, near Tunis.*

*Opposite page: a cave near Sovana. A natural cavity perhaps used as a home and later transformed in tomb and later still into a stall.*

*Branches joined to make a hut near Calcata (Italy). Right: tree in the suburbs of Mogadishu (Somalie).*

*A cubic fluorite crystal.*
*Right: the cubic room of a house in Pyrgos on the island of Santorini (archipelago of the Cyclades).*

110

to fixed images, but expressed by a series of images synthesised and superimposed in man's memory. This kind of observation, which satisfies a need for spatial-temporal knowledge, is memorably expressed by some of the first representations of man's vocation towards architecture, such as the prehistoric cromlech and the renowned complex of Stonehenge.

From its very first construction phase, which archaeologists now calculate to be around 2750 B.C., Stonehenge had all the traits of an enormous solar calendar and perhaps also a lunar calendar. Its circumference was marked by two concentric limestone embankments outlining the sides of a circular ditch. On the inside, the third ring had 56 holes, equal to the number of days in two lunar phases. Four poles marked the four observation points. There were two vertical monoliths at the entrance while on the outside, at a certain distance from the construction, was the Heel stone. On the day of the summer solstice, looking outwards between the two monoliths towards the Heel stone it was possible to see the sun rise.

Similarly, the alignments along the longer sides of the rectangle coincided with the direction in which the full moon rose on the days around the summer solstice. What is most unusual is the fact that Stonehenge is situated on the latitude of the northern hemisphere in which the two alignments are orthogonal. This megalithic monument might therefore have been built by men who had studied the course of the stars for a long time and had found a place whose characteristics were particularly suited to their studies.

The need to consult the stars was, after all, common to many peoples of different origin. Thus architecture, often exploited as a means to amplify this "listening," has long been an instrument of communication and collective celebration of the first great discoveries gleaned from the observation of nature. By observing the heavens and the temporal rotation of the stars, man realised that only one star, the north star, did not move and that all the other stars cast off endless concentric paths of light. Nowadays, this image, showing even the north star moving in a small arc, is easily photographed using a fast film, and has gradually entered into man's memory through the accumulation of repeated experiences. Based on the paths of the seven planets already known in antiquity, this simplification created the cosmic model prevalent in many civilisations: a model made up of seven complanate concentric circles.

The north star thus permitted man to establish both the north, and its opposite the south, as directional points. The observation of the sun's path provided an orthogonal east-west direction, but in a less immediate way. Man had to observe the rising and the setting of the sun for a whole year to realise that the point on the horizon where the sun rose was either nearer or farther from the north depending on a cycle that started at the summer solstice and ended at the winter solstice by way of the two equinoxes.

The idea of orthogonality comes from nature and the questions we ask of it, even if the natural forms mirroring this concept are extremely rare.

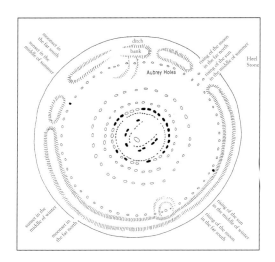

*The prehistoric astronomic observatory at Stonehenge.*
*Below: symmetric cross-shaped flowers with orthogonal axes highlighted by the sepals.*

In the Roman world, the use of orthogonality is rooted in the Etruscan discipline of divination involving the observation of the flight of birds and the entrails of recently killed animals carried out in the *auguraculum* or *auguratorium* of the sacerdotal college of augurs. When explaining the various meanings of the word *templum* in his book *De Lingua Latina*, Varro closely examined that part of the heavens contemplated by the augurs: "Wherever place the eyes *intuiti erant* (gazed on), was originally called a *templum* from *tueri* (to gaze); therefore, the sky where we *attuimur* (gaze at) it, got the name of *templum*. So the verses ran: 'Trembled the mighty temple of Jove who thunders in heaven, that is,' as Naevius says: 'where land's semicircle lies fenced by the azure vault.'

"Of this temple, the four quarters are named this: the left quarter, to the east; the right quarter, to the west; the front quarter, to the south; the back quarter, to the north. On the earth, *templum* is the name given to a place set aside and limited by certain formulaic words for the purpose of augury or the taking of the auspices. The words of the ceremony are not the same everywhere; on the Citadel, they are as follows:[16] 'Temples and wild lands be mine in this manner, up to where I have named them with my tongue in proper fashion. Of whatever kind that truthful tree is, which I consider that I have mentioned, temple and wild land be mine to that point of the left. Of whatever kind that truthful tree is, which I consider that I have mentioned, temple and wild lands be mine to that point on the right. Between these points, temples and wild lands be mine for di-

rect, for viewing and for interpreting and just as I have felt assured that I have mentioned them in proper fashion.'"[17]

The augural *templum* was a quadrangular area whose outer boundaries were marked by trees. It was divided in two by a line ideally extending to infinity and it either faced one of the cardinal points or a particularly significant site. In the case of the Roman *auguraculum* on the Citadel, it furtively faced the *mons Albanus* upon which the sanctuary of Latium Jupiter was situated.

During the foundation rites of a city, the Romans aligned the axis of the *templum* with the cosmic axis marked on one side by the north star and on the other by its corresponding southern point. Consequently, the east-west decuman gate projected the sun's course on the ground crossing the cosmic axis at the point called *groma*. This was the point where the instrument controlling the alignments was placed. "*Ab uno umbilico in quattuor partes omnes centuriarum ordo componitur,*" is written in the *Corpus Agrimensorum Romanorum*. The orthogonal structure of the Roman military camp and later the Roman town, is what makes the latter a terrestrial projection of a cosmic archetype. Similar sacredness may even be found in the *domus*, according to Alberti's theory that a house is a small town, and the town a big house.

The cosmic inspiration of the house is further confirmed by an ancient ritual: the ritual used in China during the Middle Reign (Mi-Tang) for the construction of the "house of the calendar." The geometric design of the house was based on a cross made of five squares; the central square representing the earth was yellow and referred to the in-between seasons; the upward pointing square was red and represented summer and the element fire; the left one was green, represented spring and the element wood; the one on the right was white and represented autumn and the element metal; the one pointing downwards was black and represented winter and the element water; a circular roof, symbol of the sky (the circle and the number three) was placed above the ground (the square and the number two). Thus designed, the house became a cosmic image and represented the "primordial turtle," whose shell bore the inscription of the subdivision and structure of the universe.[18]

The antithesis of the calendar-house, considered the celebration of the cosmic centrality of the Emperor, is the humble watch-house of the Malagasy, the "trano," which was so perfectly orientated that it could act as a sundial. "It is nine o'clock in all Malagasy houses when the sun lights up the eastern wall, midday when it shines down on its roof. At three o'clock it bathes the pestle for the rice, at five the central pillar and at six the sun 'is where the calf is tied.' Inside, the great room is divided into twelve parts, corresponding to the twelve lunar months. The furnishings and the various activities of the house are arranged according to the stars. The rice silo is in the area of the month of Assomboli since this is the time of wealth and health. The great water jar, symbol of continuance, is in the month of Adizawa. Lastly, the phrase spoken to an honoured guest is 'please sit in the north.'"[19]

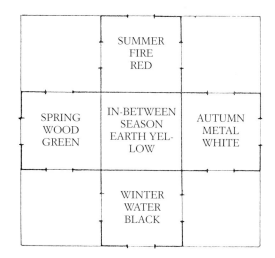

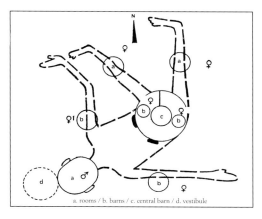

a. rooms / b. barns / c. central barn / d. vestibule

*The design concept of the "calendar house."*
*The Chinese Emperor symbolically opened the doors of the seasons and entered the five sectors of the palace.*
*Below: the anthropomorphic structure of a Fali village (Cameroon).*

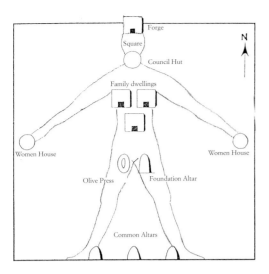

*The layout of a Dogon village.*

Another naturalistic key to the house archetype is its anthropomorphism. Religious traditions in India frequently tend to identify the house with the human body. Manu[20] describes the house as having five elements: the bones correspond to the beams and blood and flesh to mortar; in yoga rituals, the backbone is compared to the cosmic pillar and the body is "a house with a column and nine doors" that obviously are – the eyes, the nostrils, the mouth, the nipples and two orifices – the contact points between the inner and outer parts of the body. But these similarities are negatively used to underline the body's state as a live terrestrial prison: final liberation, nirvana, comes with the destruction of the house. A famous dissertation by Mircea Eliade[21] is dedicated to the comparison between "breaking the roof of the house" and an attempt, on our deathbed, to open a door towards heaven for the soul. This is the reason why this opening is compared to the hole in the sinciput that makes the upper part of our skull discontinuous.

On the other hand, there are no negative connotations in the intentional affinities with the human body of certain villages and some houses of the Dogon tribe. The layout of the village is based on a large square that can be topologically modified, as if it were elastic and the various parts arranged like the limbs of the body. The head corresponds to the village square with the council hut and forge. The houses for the men are situated along the trunk at the level of the chest and abdomen, while the houses for the women are situated to the side, where the hands would be. The olive press (feminine trait) and the foundation altar of the village (phallic shape) correspond to the place of the genital organs. Other altars located to the south of the village coincide with the feet.

The Dogon house often has equally obvious anthropomorphic references, with a few exceptions. In place of the head, the kitchen is situated in a cylindrical room, in place of the trunk there is the main room and in place of the arms there are two longitudinal cupboards. Both legs are replaced by the hall, and the door assumes the role of the sexual organs.[22]

Even modern man does not escape this trend of identifying the house with the Ego, an aspect highlighted by psychoanalytical studies and by Rilke, who seems to interpret this facet of the unconscious when referring to the house, since he defines it:

Oh house, border of the prairies,
light of the evening
suddenly taking on human countenance
next to us
embracing embraced.[23]

For psychoanalysts, dreaming of a house is a way to reveal our Ego and each element has a particular meaning; the roof, the foundations, the attic, the basement, the living-room, the fireplace and the bedroom all correspond to certain levels and conditions of existence. The outside, the façade, can correspond to

The imperial villa in Katsura, Kyoto. The roof is built according to functional and rigid linear criteria.
Left: detail of the roof of an old church in São Paulo, Brazil. The joint between the horizontal pitch and slope of the roof highlights the conflict between the two structures.

The Tea Pavilion of the imperial villa in Katsura, Kyoto. One of the struts of the wooden structure preserves its original shape as a twisted branch. This contrasts with the other supporting elements that have been cut straight using a saw.
Left: Kyoto, this curvilinear roof of Chinese origin appears to express the pressure of the sky upon the earth. It also mirrors the natural structure of conifers with curved branches, struggling between the forces of gravity and the attraction of the light.

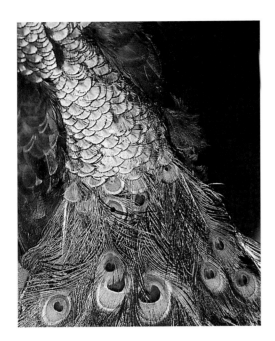

*The overlapping feathers of a peacock's tail that recalls the scale pattern.*

*A roof with curvilinear stone tiles (cupola of the church of Santa Maria in Montesanto, Rome).*

the mask, to the appearances of the dreamer; the roof represents his spirit, his search for unity or his connection with his roots; the lower floors correspond to his instinctual drives, the kitchen is the place of psychic transformation while the discoveries of the dreamer who travels within his own house correspond to the self-images which reveal his unconscious.[24]

There is a famous description by Gustav Jung of a dream in which there was an imaginary house where each floor corresponded to a different period according to the style of the furniture.[25]

In his dream, Jung turns his house into a sort of historical stratification; but the interpretative key offered by Jung himself indicates that the house is the projection of his Ego and intellectual state. Jung writes, "the dream is in fact a short summary of my life, more specifically of the development of my mind. I grew up in a house 200 years old, our furniture consisted mostly of pieces about 300 years old, and mentally my hitherto greatest spiritual adventure had been to study the philosophies of Kant and Schopenhauer. The great news of the day was the work of Charles Darwin. Shortly before this, I had been living with the still medieval concepts of my parents, for whom the world and men were still presided over by divine omnipotence and providence. My Christian faith had become relative through its encounter with Eastern religions and Greek philosophy. It is for this reason that the ground floor was so still, dark, and obviously uninhabited. My then historical interests had developed from an original preoccupation with comparative anatomy and palaeontology while I was working as an assistant at the Anatomical Institute. I was fascinated by the bones of fossil man, particularly by the much discussed *Neanderthalensis*, and the still more controversial skull of Dubois' *Pithecanthropus*."

If the house and our life are – at least in dreams – one and the same, a tale made of moments in which our history unfolds over time and can be reconstructed at will through memory, then it is obvious that this house cannot be reduced to a mere abstract model of functions, of routes, of quantities evaluated according to need. It can be simple like a monk's cell but, in order to help us live, it has to be able to capture and retain something of ourselves, like the sticky walls of a beehive, pieces of life, smells, images, tactile values endowed with "free elements" like chemicals ready to combine with others.

It would be rhetorical to say that in a house the superfluous is as necessary, if not more so, than what is useful, because a clear distinction would have to be made between what is necessary and what is superfluous and this distinction is already burdened by utilitarian overtones. Perhaps it would be right to say that a house becomes a truly inhabited structure when it frees its symbolic potential, when through the house, we also see, listen and feel something more than each of our senses can separately record. *Habitare* in Latin is the frequentative aspect of the verb *habere*, to have; one continually "has" in the house, it accompanies us and defends us like a harbour in which ships anchor to protect themselves from storms and the like.

Whoever designs a house must also design its ability to become receptive, but it would be tactless to program its symbolic potentials without a large dose of ambiguity since a house made solely of "specific places" to do or feel something would be like a tight fitting garment that hinders movement and makes the wearer awkward. Quite rightly, Aldo Rossi distinguishes between the "friendly life" that takes place in a space and its enveloping involucre, which he would like to be neutral and cold, because it is against this backdrop that daily events take place. The architect has the difficult task of not mistaking indifference for discretion and of preparing a terrain in which the imagination of others can freely flourish.

To recognise oneself as being "inside" as well as a part of nature also means: to build houses like landscapes ready to act as backdrops yet poised to impress us at times with the ability that their forms have to mirror our swollen interior, becoming themselves internal spaces, places of the soul.

[1] L. Kahn, *Gli scritti*, edited by C. Norberg-Schulz, Officina, Rome 1981.

[2] Vitruvius, *Architectura (libri I-VII)*, translated by S. Ferri, Palombi, Rome 1960. Translator's note: the version by Ferri has been translated by Erika G. Young.

[3] B. Rudofsky published ancient engravings with illustrations of inhabited trees in his *Architecture Without Architects*, New York 1962.

[4] The reconstruction of Ulysses' bedroom and bed in Homer, *The Odyssey*, Penguin Books, New York, 1946, pp. 345-346.

[5] M.-A. Laugier, *An Essay on Architecture*, Hennessey & Ingalls, Los Angeles 1977, pp. 11-12.

[6] Filarete, *Trattato di architecttura*, edited by L. Grassi, Polifilo, Milan 1969.

[7] cf., M. Allaby, *Animal Artisans*, Knopf, New York 1982, p. 139.

[8] cf., B. Brizzi, *L'Italia nell'età della pietra*, Quasar, Rome 1977, p. 124.

[9] cf., R. and G. Laubin, *Il tipì indiano*, Mursia, Milan 1993 (*The Indian Tipi*, Norman 1977).

[10] For the architecture of the various spider species see R. Preston-Mafham, *The Book of Spiders and Scorpions*, Crescent Books, New York 1991; K. von Frisch, *L'architettura degli animali*, Mondadori, Milan 1975 (*Animal Architecture*, New York 1974) and F. Otto, *L'architettura della natura*, Il Saggiatore, Milan 1983.

[11] Marco Polo, *The Travels*, Penguin Books, London 1958, pp. 108-109.

[12] cf., E. Turri, *Gli uomini delle tende*, Comunità, Milan 1983.

[13] cf., E.-L. Boullée, *Trattato di architettura*, Marsilio, Venice 1967.

[14] Cited in J. Rykwert, *On Adam's House in Paradise*, The Museum of Modern Art, New York 1972, pp. 70-71.

[15] W. Chambers, *A Treatise on the Decorative Part of Civil Architecture*, London 1759, cited in J. Rykwert, *op. cit.*

[16] The Citadel is the area of the Capitoline Hill to the right when looking at the hill from the Forum. The Asylum ditch separates it from the higher hill housing the temple of Jupiter.

[17] cf., Varro, *On the Latin Language*, Harvard University Press, Cambridge (Mass) 1938, pp. 273-274.

[18] cf., J.C. Fabre, *Casa tra terra e cielo*, Arista, Turin 1990, p. 155.

[19] *Ibid.*, p. 142.

[20] cf., Mircea Eliade, *Il sacro e il profano*, Bollati Boringhieri, Turin 1984, p. 110; cf., Idem, *Spezzare il tetto della casa*, Jaca Book, Milan 1988, p. 150.

[21] cf., M. Eliade, *Spezzare il tetto...*, cit., p. 149.

[22] cf., J.C. Fabre, *op cit.*, p. 153.

[23] Cited in G. Bachelard, *La poetica dello spazio*, Dedalo, Bari 1975, p. 36 (*La Poétique de l'espace*, Paris 1967⁵).

[24] cf., O. Marc, *Psychanalyse de la maison*, Seuil, Paris 1972, p. 77.

[25] C.G. Jung, *Man and his Symbols*, Laurel, New York, 1964, p. 42.

# The Pot, the Well, the Cave

*Space around us conquers and interprets things:*
*if you want to guess the existence of a tree,*
*create an internal space, a space whose essence*
*is in you. Surround it with buildings. It is*
*endless and will never become a tree if you do*
*not order it around your renunciation.*

Rainer Maria Rilke[1]

Unless we consider the early influence of craftsmanship on the genesis of forms and architectural types – writes Gottfried Semper – we will never truly understand architecture: "The roots of words preserve their vitality intact, and through subsequent changes and extensions of related concepts always re-emerge in their original form; it is impossible for a new concept to coin an absolutely new term without falling short of its main objective which is to be understood; therefore we can neither neglect nor reject the archaic art types at the origin of this symbolism and choose others instead. As a rule of thumb, the admirers of the work of an architect unconsciously follow this tradition, but the advantages of comparative linguistics and the study of primary relationships between various languages now available to the scholar are also available to the architect; the latter is capable of re-discovering the primordial meaning of ancient architectural symbols and is able to take into account the changes in form and value that have taken place over the centuries, together with the evolution of the art itself."[2]

Although Semper dedicated an entire chapter of his book *Der Stil* to ceramics, he omitted to highlight the crucial role played by man-made liquid holding objects in the genesis of architecture, a point underlined by Frank Lloyd Wright who, together with Baker Brownell, wrote a short book on architecture and modern life that contains interesting historical considerations.[3]

The second chapter of the book reads as follows: "While still dwelling in caves (the) man perhaps learned to make utensils out of wet clay. He burned them hard for use. These utensils he seems to have made with a higher faculty. His instinct became an aesthetic sense of environment. It taught him something of form. He learned from the animals, the serpents, the plants that he knew. Except for this faculty he was no more than any other animal. Still clinging to the cliffs, he made whole caves out of wet clay and let the sun bake the clay hard. He made them just as he had made the vessels that he had previously put into the fire to bake and had used in the cave in the rocks. And so, once upon a time, man moved into his first earth-built house, of *earth*. This large clay cave or pot of the cliff-dwellers, with a lid on it, was among the first man-made houses. The lid was troublesome to him then and has always been so to subsequent builders."

Wright's considerations indirectly refer to the prehistoric settlement of Mesa Verde (built, however, in stone) and certainly reflect a good deal of American patriotism, but his intuition regarding the role of the pot in the genesis of the hut stands on firm ground and, as Neil Levine has recently stated, is vital in order to fully comprehend the architectural philosophy of the great American master.[4]

One could say that for primitive man, the pot was an object of immaterial reality expressed by the word "space." It is easy to imagine that when he first dug for water or made the opening of a spring bigger, man discovered how pliable and soft sandy clay was. Then, when he worked the wet clay with his hands and turned it on the lathe (the archetype of all more complex mechanical tools), man realised that what he shaped could be made to imitate a gesture; he could

118

"freeze" it, impress its image on matter and then turn it into an object. Cupped palms or hands joined together to drink water became a counter-mould, a direct impression of the hand, an embracing and caressing entity that enclosed, protected and separated the "inside" from the "outside." The pot is to the house what the seed is to the plant, since the latter is the source providing the genetic programme for its growth and development.

Wright believed that the circular huts in Mesa Verde had been shaped like giant pots because they were made of clay and that their cylindrical shape came from the use of a technology similar to the one used in ceramics based on a genetic pattern similar to Semper's. However, if one takes this statement one step further, it is undoubtedly true that the architecture that uses independent technology to mix earth does indeed take advantage of the work of the potter and his sensitivity towards plasticity. The rounded corners of architecture in Central Africa and the villages of the Pueblo Indians show similarities in the relationship between the creating hand and the caressed earth, a similarity which initially belonged to the potter.

An African sage once said: "Man builds with his own hands. The hand of man is warm-hearted, he knows not the square; soft clay is tender too: therefore, clay and the hand of man may create nothing but loving forms. Hands do not make sharp corners, no more than clay does. Even rain is friendly. Rain falls. It likes to fall, it is a friendly material that likes to run along friendly forms. The

*The hands of a potter on the lathe and a rivulet in an alpine field in Val Badia (Italy).*

119

*Above: a vase with a concentric pattern; the same pattern on a quince dried by the sun and on the walls of a hut of the Ngwame Bantu tribe.*
*Right: the layout of a some houses in Pueblo Bonito, Chaco Canyon.*

hands of man are made to caress women and clay and rain. This is right, good and beautiful. So why wouldn't a man who caresses his woman not caress his house?"[5]

Neil Levine theorises that, after living for a while in Japan, during the early twenties Wright recognised the archetypal role of the pot. He believes that this was the moment when Wright consciously developed his theory of architecture, substituting the model of imitation of nature that had previously inspired his works, particularly Richard Bock's famous symbolic statue, *Flower in a Crannied Wall*, sculptured for the Dana House, a copy of which the architect had decided to place in the garden of Taliesin East.

In fact, the copy was removed from the garden after the 1914 fire and returning from Japan, Wright decided to place a gigantic blue-glazed earthenware vessel from the Ming dynasty on the hilltop in front of the house.

Levine concludes, "After seeing the idea of making that perfect representation of nature, that Taliesin once was, destroyed and turned into the 'smoking crater of a volcano,' it is as if the great pot on the hill crown above Taliesin was put there by Wright to acknowledge that, in the end, it is naive for any artist to believe he can engage nature directly and form an image of it on his own each time. But if he wants to carry on that monumental tradition of representational architecture, *he must have a model that connects his vision of nature to history*, one that is integral to his culture and derives its meaning from that connection. For Wright, and I hope to have shown, it was the earthenware pot he embodied

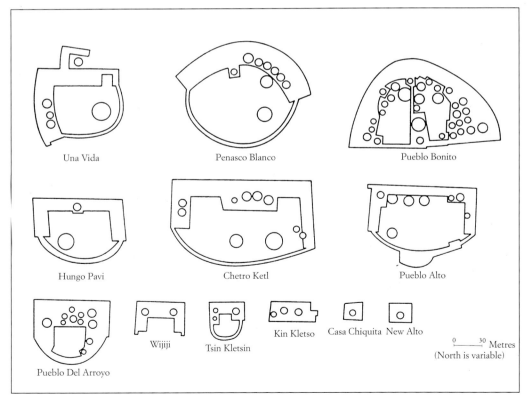

Una Vida

Penasco Blanco

Pueblo Bonito

Hungo Pavi

Chetro Ketl

Pueblo Alto

Pueblo Del Arroyo

Wijiji

Tsin Kletsin

Kin Kletso

Casa Chiquita

New Alto

0   30 Metres
(North is variable)

*This house of the Battamaliba tribe in Koufitoukon, North Togo, is made of earth, just like a pot or an urn. The self-identification of an inhabitant with his house means that architecture has to imitate the gestures and shapes of humans. This tribe considers the house as the involucre of the souls of its inhabitants who do not live in their bodies, but nearby. Another function of the house is to maintain a harmonious balance between body and soul.*

first in his own house for the Mojave Desert that furnished this key to the rest of his work. That model allowed him to ground his revolutionary idea of architecture as space in an ever-expanding series of references to nature and to history, and that gave renewed life in the twentieth century to the classical tradition of architecture as an art of representation."

In the house he built for himself in Death Valley, a small nucleus of enclosed spaces is preceded by an octagonal patio with a circular stretch of water in the centre. This one image unites the pot, the well and the shoot so dear to Sullivan, and perhaps it is not too far a stretch of the imagination to recognise also the matrix of the basket. Even before learning to shape the earth, the Indians of Death Valley had learnt to weave twigs into baskets, a tradition still very much alive when Wright designed his desert refuge. After all, the baskets of the Panamint Indians in the shape of earthenware pots represent (and at one time were perhaps a prophetic anticipation of) the idea of a pot and a hut made of woven branches. This is the point around which the seemingly irreconcilable theories of Laugier and Wright unpredictably converge.

The importance of Wright's intuition regarding the relationship between the pot, the basket and the house has far-reaching consequences since in the genesis of architecture it affirms the primacy of void over solid, internal space over volume, living instead of building, so perhaps it is worth reflecting on the eleventh reflection of the *Tao Te Ching*, dedicated to "Wu Yung," the utility of non-existence:

> Though thirty spokes may form the wheel
> it is the hole within the hub
> which gives the wheel utility.
> It is not the clay the potter throws,
> which gives the pot its usefulness,
> but the space within the shape,
> from which the pot is made.
> Without a door, the room cannot be entered,
> and without windows, it is dark.[6]

At the turn of the century this philosophy played an important role in proposing the topic of internal space as the matrix of every architectural image. For many years the *Raumgestaltung* was central to the productive review of the history of architecture as well as stimulating creative research as shown by the architecture of Art Nouveau and Catalan modernism. F.L. Wright's biography describes his encounter with the words of Lao-Tzu as something of a revelation. It happened quite by chance during the early twenties when the Japanese ambassador in Washington sent him *The Book of Tea* by Kakuzo Okakura.[7] The idea that what counts in a house are not the walls but what they contain (Okakura offers a simplification of the much more complex message of the great Chinese sage) was the perfect verbal expression of what the American master had intuitively felt and incorporated into his prairie houses. The fact that this idea dated back to the 4th century before Christ was initially somewhat disappointing and frustrating for Wright until he convinced himself that the idea "was a deeper, profound something that survived in the world, something probably eternal and therefore universal, something that persisted and will persist for ever" and added, "then I began to feel that I ought to be proud to have perceived it as Lao Tzu had perceived it and to have tried to *build it*!"[8]

In the repertoire of architectural archetypes, the inside of the pot and the hub refer to the inside of the house as well as to the more elementary archetype of the well, a hole dug by the hand of man in the bosom of the earth to extract water or preserve its purity. Liquid elements in nature gush directly from rocks or springs that bubble on the surface of the earth and man very quickly discovered how to bridle these sources, to channel, divert and collect water by creating a specific technique with endless possibilities. But spring water always surfaces through a hole, through a friendly involucre in which space is materialised by clear water in perpetual movement. This natural hole is turned into a well, a pipe or a channel.

Sardinia is an island where landscape and vegetation are the rich expression of nature at its finest. There, the nuraghe civilisation flourished between the 14th and 4th centuries B.C. Most of their sacred buildings that survive today are well temples, built to celebrate the sacred value and secret virtues of water. The stairs, chambers, cylindrical cavities and halls of these temples, built either on plains or along rocky cliffs, all face outwards and along the walls there are ledges for votive offerings.[9] The temples conjure up the compressed spatiality of the nuraghe villages in which the walls seem to create an empty body, the site of many bodies that inside the stone-like involucre act like the marrow of bones, the pulp inside the skin of the fruit.

Even when the well is no longer sacred, the archetype of the "well-head," which is the external continuation of the natural or artificial cavity, still fulfils a number of useful tasks. The well proposes and aesthetically celebrates a process of extraction from the earth, dynamically expressed by combining the cylindrical recipient with the archetypes of the trilith, the aedicula and the primitive forms of wheels and mechanical transmission.

Due to their architectural potential, the archetypes of the well and the pot are linked to that of the fountain, originally used to mark and celebrate the presence of spring water and which, after the invention of hydraulics was later to become one of the great themes of urban culture. The presence of water in the architectural scenario, in canals and fountains, led to a dualism between solids and liquids, immobile and fluid matter; it also offered the architect almost endless scope.

*Water containers made of stone near Castel d'Ischi, Nepi (Italy).*
*Channelled water course in Machu Picchu (Peru).*

The similarities between the area of the spring shaped by the earth, the pot and the interior of the house, all assume a symbolic function if one bears in mind that the house is inhabited by man and the pot is "inhabited" by water or again that the pot is water's outer robe and the house acts as the outer garment of man,

Water shaping the landscape; a small waterfall in
Val Mezdì (Italy).
Below: the small yet famous artificial waterfall in
the garden of the Golden Pagoda (Kinkakuji),
Kyoto. The stone mass that seems to jump out of
the waterfall like a fish trying to swim upstream is
a typical example of abstract symbolic imitation.
In fact, Buddhists believe the carp to be the
symbol of the perseverance necessary to attain
enlightenment.

*The well and the public fountain, two ways for water to enter the city. The water is either hidden, but easily drawn with buckets and pulleys (opposite page: Pienza, well-head by Bernardo Rossellino in the main square, photograph by Alinari, Florence), or else very visible, such as the water in the fountains of Perugia (left) and Palermo (below).*

his projection in space. The house and the pot, and hence the fountain, transform the stream's wild flow into a domestic image, a place of rest and stability for what in nature is unstable and fluid. Goethe and Schubert in the *Spirit Song over the Waters,* have expressed all the poetic value of these similarities reflected in the analogy between pot and abode and in the introduction of running water into the house and city:[10]

> The soul of man
> resembleth water:
> from heaven it cometh
> to heaven it soareth.
> And then again
> to earth descendeth
> changing ever.
> [...]
> Now, in flat channel
> through the meadowland steals it
> and in the polished lake
> each constellation
> joyously peepeth.
> Wind is the loving
> wooer of water;
> wind blends together
> billows all-foaming
> Spirit of man
> Thou art like unto water!
> Fortune of man
> thou art like unto wind!

*A small channel for water or sacrificial blood (the ritual complex of Quenqo near Cuzco).*

*Opposite page: the Fountain of the Four Rivers by Gian Lorenzo Bernini (1648-51). The fountain with its symbolic figures brings natural landscape into the city. An eloquent anecdote alleges that, of all the various parts of the fountain, Bernini sculpted only the rocks, because he believed their naturalness to be a key element in effectively achieving this contrast between nature and artifice.*

[1] cf., *Les Lettres*, IV, m. 14-15-16, p. 13. Cited in French in G. Bachelard, *La poetica dello spazio*, Dedalo, Bari 1975, pp. 221, 275 (*La Poétique de l'espace*, Paris 1967⁵).

[2] G. Semper, *Lo stile*, Laterza, Rome-Bari 1992, p. 45.

[3] cf., B. Brownell, F.L. Wright, *Architecture and Modern life*, Harper's & Brothers, New York 1937, cited in N. Levine, *Frank Lloyd Wright's Own Houses in His Changing Concepts of Presentation*, in *The Nature of Frank Lloyd Wright*, Chicago University Press, Chicago 1984, p. 20.

[4] cf., N. Levine, *Frank Lloyd Wright's own Houses,* cit.

[5] cf., *Edilizia Moderna*, 89-90, number on *Africa*, pp. 78-79.

[6] Lao-Tzu, *Tao Te Ching,* translation by S. Rosenthal, www.clas.ufl.edu.

[7] K. Okakura, *The Book of Tea*, Dover, New York 1964.

[8] cf., N. Levine, *op cit.*

[9] G. Lilliu, *La civiltà dei sardi*, Nuova Eri, Turin 1988.

[10] J.W. Goethe, http://members.aol.com/KatharenaE/private/Pweek/Goethe/goethe.html.

# The Column

"To reflect on the grand event of architecture, when walls were divided and columns appeared [...]. The use of a column should still be considered as a grand event in the creation of space." Louis Kahn was particularly fond of "beginnings"; he believed that beginnings guaranteed prosecution: "Without them," he said, "nothing could or would exist."[1]

Based on Alberti's theory of the colonnade as a "holed wall," one could say that Kahn describes the column, "at the nascent state." After having designed the wall and the door, *homo faber* imagined them as joint elements that obstructed space and diverted the passage of bodies, but at the same time also indicated the possibility of "passing-through."

Its roundness, obtained by freeing its internal matter from its external shell, speaks of an object that has long been touched lightly upon by man and worn down by his passing. It indicates the possibility of passing through surrounding space.

The column personifies the tree trunk, the tree and consequently the forest considered as something that can be penetrated, endowed with its own discontinuous spatiality. A round trunk is something that is born and grows according to the law of "maximum result with minimum effort." To push the foliage of trees to the same height any other form would need much more material substance. The cylindrical shape turns inwards and lets itself be embraced by space like a living body: the column becomes the metaphor and abstract replica of the tree but also of the body. Like the tree and the body, as it grows taller and further away from the ground, its horizontal section may change, becoming thicker or thinner in order to live longer or avoid being weighted down with useless bits and pieces. Yet it is also congenial to imagine that it does so to be pleasing both to the eye and to the touch. In architectural terms this dilatation is called *entasis* from the Greek *téinein*, to make taut, and the outline of the column does in fact resemble the outline of a drawn bow about to shoot an arrow. *Entasis* is the most direct and intimate aspect of the erotic connotation of the column: "In fact," wrote A. Tzonis, L. Lefaivre and D. Bilodeau, "if you lean against a column on a hot summer day you can feel your heart jump, your breathing become deeper and your cheeks redden. However, some people are indifferent to classicism, incapable of distinguishing classical styles and insensible to their complex articulation."[2] It is up to the reader to verify this impassioned statement of the three authors which will be re-examined in the chapter on temples.

The idea behind the column is probably linked to the origin of the menhir, the totem, the central pole of the tent and the hut or even to the column of smoke rising towards the sky from its centre. The cult of the Great Mother often depicts the column as the "column of life." Engraved in stone, it is found in the womb-shaped tombs of Ireland, Brittany and Spain as well as in the temples of Malta. Phallic columns were common in Neolithic constructions in Sardinia, Corsica and Malta and in the Etruria region up to the 5th century B.C. In the so-called "regeneration cathedral" at Gavrinis in Brittany these columns appear to be made of superimposed concentric arches.[3]

128

The column as an offshoot of the trunk mediates the relationship between heaven and earth. The columns of the so-called "Paestum basilica" and a series of sequoia tree trunks: the Parker Group in the Sequoia National Park, California.

*The trunk of a palm tree in the Botanical Gardens in São Paulo, Brazil.*

*The* entasis *of the classic column as the expression of resistance to natural stress.*

The column is institutionalised when it is reproduced in series. Its forked shape either acts as a central support "to receive" other building elements (for example, sloping branches in the conical hut model) or it is repeated on a façade (as in the community huts of the Dogon tribe).[4] It is the first sign of articulation systematically amplified in a law of superimposition. When the column becomes the fulcrum of the architectural order, it is then associated with a law of superimposition which states that the position of the base, shaft and capital cannot be modified.

The syntactic value of the column is validated by repetition and when, according to a law, it grows in number it also acquires necessity and organicity. This value is already present, for example, in the round huts found in the village of Pan-p'o, dating back 4000 years before Christ. This hut can be scientifically reconstructed on the basis of the marks left on the rocky terrain; it had a flat coping and an outline very similar to an upside-down conical pail. The flat part of the roof – like the walls built with a mixture of mud and grass – was supported by a circular architrave held up by six wooden columns; something very similar to what architectural terminology defines as a canopy. In the centre of the canopy there was an opening like a keyhole above the hearth.

This identification between the column and the body was a definite element of Greek architecture and is touchingly described in the verses of the tragedy *Iphigenia in Tauris* by Euripides, when the hero speaks of a dream and then interprets it: "I dreamed that I had left this land to live in Argos and to sleep in the midst of the maidens' rooms; but the earth's back was shaken by a tossing swell. When I escaped and stood outside, I saw the cornice of the house fall, and the whole roof hurled in ruins on the ground, from the highest pillars. One support of my father's house was left, I thought, and it had yellow locks of hair waiving from its capital, and took on human voice. In observance of the art of slaughtering strangers that I practice here, I gave it holy water as if it were about to die, while I wept. This is my interpretation of this dream: Orestes, whom I consecrated by my rites, is dead. For male children are the supports of the house and those whom I purify with holy water die."

The column that turns into Orestes, the blond hair which in the ambiguous oneiric image coincides with the decoration of the capital, are more convincing than any archaeological artefact in trying to make us understand the symbolic and sacral aura of this element of the architectural language of Greek culture. Caryatids and telamones mechanically and naturalistically allude to a symbolic power which is as intense as it is secret, imprisoned in a form which balances abstraction and figuration.

Speaking of the temple of Panionion Apollo, in Book IV of his treatise, Vitruvius explains how the proportional system of the order was established: "Wishing to set up columns in that temple, but not having rules for their symmetry, and being in search of some way by which they could render them fit to bear a load and also of a satisfactory beauty of appearance, they measured the

130

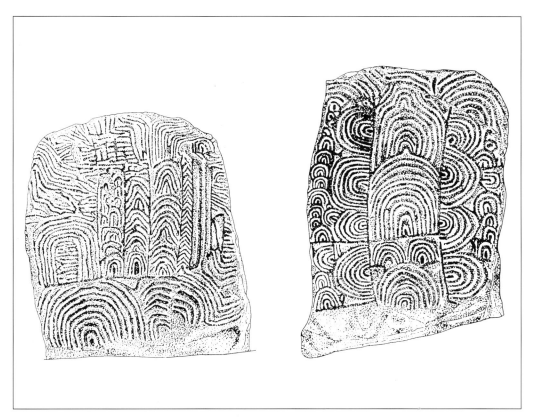

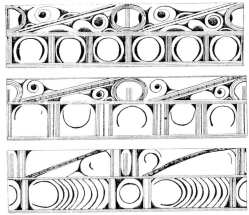

The column of life in primitive societies:
"In ancient Europe, the column of life was considered as the materialisation of a mysterious vital force, a mediator between being and not being; and this vital force was found in the egg, the snake, in water and the womb of the Goddess" (Marija Gimbutas).
Left: two of the orthostats of the Gavrinis sanctuary on a small island (once a peninsula) in the gulf of Morbihan, Brittany.
Above: a sort of temple painted in different ways on three pyriform Cucuteni vases (3900-3700 B.C.).

The caryatid as the humanisation of the column (Rome, church of Santi Vincenzo e Anastasio at Trevi, Martino Longhi Jr., 1644).
Left: forked columns in a Togu-na, the "house of the word" in which the Dogon meet to take important decisions (village of Saredina, Mali Republic). The Togu-na is a sort of portico; once inside, people can only sit down because the ceiling is quite low. Many Dogon believe that the low ceiling was chosen because when people are sitting down this reduces conflict and stimulates reflection.

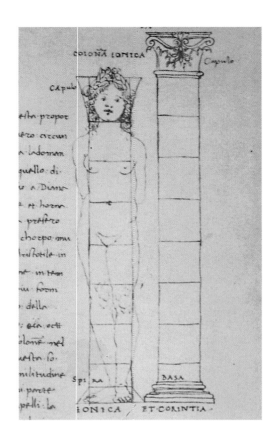

COLOÑA IONICA

Capitello

CAP·lo

CAP·lo

IONICA ET CORINTIA

*The column as metaphor of the human body. A drawing from the* Trattato di Architettura *by Francesco di Giorgio Martini.*
*Below: the genesis of the Corinthian capital based on Vitruvius' tale (from the shortened edition of his treatise by Giovanni Antonio Rusconi, Giolito de' Ferrari, Venice 1790).*

imprint of a man's foot and compared this with his height. On finding that, in a man, the foot was one sixth of the height, they applied the same principle to the column, and reared the shaft, including the capital, to a height six times its thickness at its base. Thus the Doric column, as used in buildings, began to exhibit the proportions, strength, and beauty of the body of a man."[5]

The relationship between the column and the human body appears to be mediated here by its number, but also invoked as a function of the *firmitas* (capable of supporting) and the *venustas* (elegance of the body). In the Ionic order, parts of the column are even more literally identified with female body parts or attire: "Just so afterwards, when they desired to construct a temple to Diana in a new style of beauty, they translated these footprints into terms characteristic of the slenderness of women, and thus first made a column the thickness of which was only one eighth of its height, so that it might have a taller look. At the foot they substituted the base in place of a shoe; in the capital they placed the volutes, hanging down at the right and left like curly ringlets, and ornamented its front with cymatia and with festoons of fruit arranged in place of hair, while they brought the flutes down the whole shaft, falling like the folds in the robes worn by matrons. Thus in the invention of the two different kinds of columns, they borrowed manly beauty, naked and unadorned, for the one, and for the other the delicacy, adornment, and proportions characteristic of women."[6]

If the naturalist elements in the Ionic order increase at the expense of the Doric order's force of abstraction, in the Corinthian order they explode in all their glory. Compared to the shaft the capital plays a role similar to that of the head to the body and this relationship is illustrated perfectly by Francesco di Giorgio in the splendid drawings of his treatise. This reference to the head is implicit in the etymology of the capital that comes from the word *capitulum*, diminutive of *caput*, head, used in Latin to describe a small head. But the Corinthian capital adds another narrative metaphor to this proportional metaphor, a metaphor which admirably mixes nature and human actions: "The third order, called Corinthian, is an imitation of the slenderness of a maiden; for the outline and limbs of maidens, being more slender on account of their tender years, admit of prettier effects in the way of adornment. It is related that the original discovery of this form of capital was as follows. A freeborn maiden of Corinth, just of marriageable age was attacked by an illness and passed away. After her burial, her nurse, collecting a few little things which used to give the girl pleasure while she was alive, put them in a basket, carried it to the tomb, and laid it on top thereof, covering it with a roof-tile so that the things might last longer in the open air. This basket happened to be placed just above the root of an acanthus. This acanthus root, pressed down meanwhile though it was by its weight, when springtime came round put forth leaves and stalks in the middle, and the stalks, growing up through the compulsion of its weight, were forced to bend into volutes at the outer edges. Just then Callimachus, whom the Athenians called *catatechnos* for the refinement and delicacy of his artistic work, passed by this tomb and observed the basket with the tender young leaves growing round it. Delighted with the novel style and form, he built some columns after that pattern for the Corinthians, determined their symmetrical proportions, and established from that time forth the rules to be followed in finished works of the Corinthian order."[7]

This narrated event focuses on a series of facts: the death of the girl from Corinth (the same girl whose measurements were happily used by Valéry's Eupalinos for the proportions of the small circular temple[8] which I will mention later on), the affectionate gesture of the nurse who put the objects the girl loved in a basket, the tile placed over the basket to protect the ornaments, the acanthus growing under the basket and curling under the protruding edges of the tile. One almost feels like an onlooker witnessing the portrayal or rather the intricate spiral of affectionate emotions involving life and death, imbuing this final image with a touching and melancholic message of peace. This repose of form interprets the relationship between man and nature as a filial relationship whose mysterious analogies are governed by fate.

Kahn indicated the origin of the column to be in the discontinuity of the wall and this is indeed a very convincing intuition. Only much later on was the column used as a single element, out of context. From the very beginning it was part of a series, like a tree is part of a forest in which one tree, or particularly significant groups of trees, are always separate from the others. The photograph shown here, taken in a beech wood on the Cimini mountains, portrays a group of seven tree trunks all the same height: these trunks stand out from the rest because they seem to be planted in a circle and bring to mind a circular peripteral temple.

Before ever learning to plant trees in an orderly fashion, man already noticed that in the forest trees grew in rows and groups. Their disconcerting regularity had been created entirely by chance and man immediately applied this concept to both his abstract and his constructive ideas.

Therefore, from the very beginning the concept of the column espouses the concept of the serial repetition of elements. This gives the latter a certain meaning and usefulness and, since nature saw fit to offer such appropriate suggestions, undoubtedly the abstract force of the mind fell on fertile ground, qualified to express the ability to do what – according to Kahn – nature is unable to do.

The problems inherent in the role of the column in the syntax of orders will be examined in the chapter on the architrave, the trabeation and the roof, but the natural analogies of this serial repetition still have to be studied. It is necessary to examine the luminous and luminist value of the column which, due to its roundness, offers the light a constantly changing reflective surface.

The grooves of the flutings control and amplify its luministic effect and hence the balance between the material force of the image and its immaterial traits and abstract design. "I believe" writes Kahn, "that structure determines light. If I choose a structural order that needs a series of columns, one after the other, I obtain a pattern of dark, light, dark, light, dark, light."[9]

*A group of tall beech trees standing alone in a glade in the woods on Monte Fogliano near Vetralla (Italy) brings to mind the concept of the circular temple.*
*Below: the choral monument to Lisicrate (Athens) is a perfect example of a classical building miming the growth of vegetation.*

The side of the Theseion facing the Agora in Athens (4th century B.C.).

The juncture between the Doric column of the Parthenon in Athens and the slightly curvilinear stylobate.

If this serial repetition generates the elementary pattern of alternation, other sequences can underline angles and introduce differentiated natural analogies, from the secular forest to the cane-brake. In Egyptian columns, the phytomorphic analogies are obvious but rarely direct. They often represent the trunks of palm trees or reed bundles decorated with lotus, papyrus or palm leaves transformed into composite stone columns.

"The reed bundles," wrote Joseph Rykwert, "inevitably recall another representation of a mother goddess: the bundle of papyrus called the *Djed* pillar, which represented Hathor pregnant with Osiris in the Egyptian mystery play of the death and resurrection of the god celebrated during the coronation ceremonies, and in which the raising of the pillar represented the resurrection of the dead Pharaoh. The manipulation of the pillar was associated with mock fights, in which the papyrus reed became a ritual weapon."[10] This Djed pillar is an example of symbolic interaction between natural objects, ritual actions and codification of architectural forms.

An interesting theory on the genesis of the fluted column was elaborated by Pietro Imbornone.[11] He believes it comes from the technique called "pisè" (compressed clay) applied to reed moulds held together with rings. Initially created as the negative impression of reed bundles, only later was the Doric column built in stone.

There was a time during the Modern Movement, in particular the international phase of Art Nouveau, when the column experienced a fascinating metamorphosis, a continually osmotic relationship with natural forms. Subsequently it functioned as a mere support, as in Villa Savoye and was used in Euclidean geometry as a simple cylinder. After re-examining the fantastic repertoire of Pompeian paintings proposed by the archaeologist Luigi Canina (author of a novel proposal for the decoration of Paxton's Crystal Palace),[12] Horta and Guimard turned the column into a tree trunk by exploiting its metallic structure while Gaudí used it as a megalith in his chapel of Santa Coloma. In Casa Batlló, Gaudí turned it into a shin-bone for the façade of his house and a vibrant tree trunk in his model of the Sagrada Familia. Expressionism, on the other hand, reinterpreted it in the luminous structure of the glass house.

In 1881 Valéry published *Paradoxe sur l'architecte*, currently considered to be an inspired anticipation of Art Nouveau. In his book Valéry describes the column as a natural image inspired by the musical form of a composition by Wagner: "like a prelude of ensuing rites, the archivolt reveals promises and the slender ribs curve their sweetened gestures while the tender graces of the arches are transposed into the feminine traits of the shafts. Mallow and oblique lilacs cascade from the great glass panels onto marble floors and precious stones pour down in long rain showers. It is the forest of silence [...]. Here, the other flowers of the pillars and pure white columns grow in sumptuous shadows in-between the exquisite paving – blossoming with mysterious flowers that bear those universal magical symbols sculptured under their abacuses, like fruit from the Tree of science."[13]

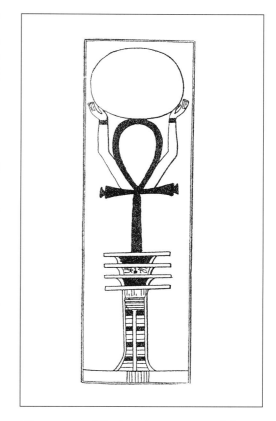

*The tree, especially the palm tree, inspired the Djed pillar. In Egyptian civilisations, it is associated with Osiris, the dying and renascent God of vegetation. As a hieroglyphic it signifies duration and stability.*

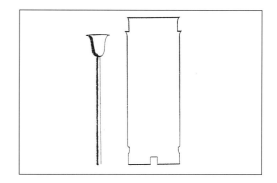

*Profile of the Monadnock Building in Chicago by John Root (1890). Root was well aware of the influence of Egypt in his architecture; this initially led him to include stylistic decorations in his design and later to consolidate reminiscences of bell papyrus in the extremely refined shape of the building.*

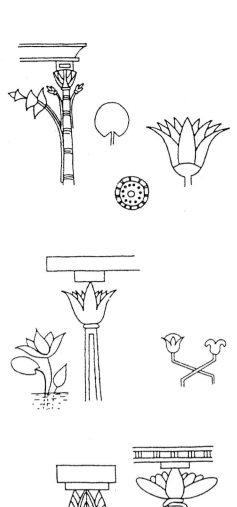

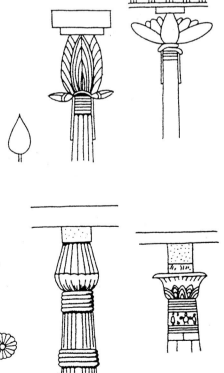

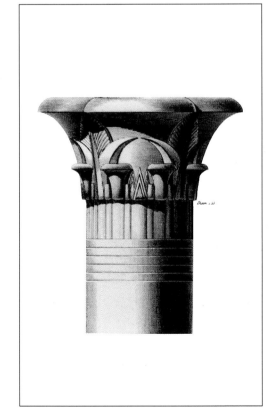

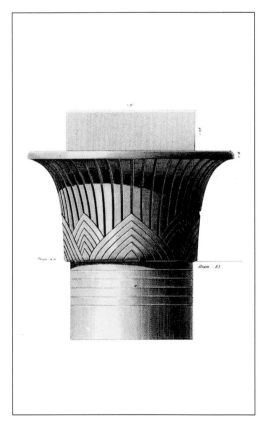

136

Much later, in 1919, Valéry composed the *Cantique des colonnes*[14] with the detachment of a classical intellectual, a detachment that corresponded to the mood of the period:

Nos antiques jeunesses,
Chair mate et belles ombres
Sont fières des finesses
Qui naissent par les nombres!

Filles des nombres d'or,
Fortes des lois du ciel,
Sur nous tombe et s'endort
Un dieu couleur de miel.

Il dort content, le Jour,
Que chaque jour offrons
Sur la table d'amour
Etale sur nos fronts.

Incorruptibles soeurs,
Mi-brûlantes, mi-fraîches,
Nous prîmes pour danseurs
Brises et feuilles sèches,

Et les siècles par dix,
Et les peuples passés,
C'est un profond jadis,
Jadis jamais assez!

*Above and opposite page: Egyptian columns and capitals based on the geometric interpretation of plants (palm, lotus, papyrus) or on the original supports made out of cane bundles or branches, held together with ropes and knots.*

In Eupalinos' dialogue, the column, like every other architectural form, distances itself from nature since it is the "daughter of the golden number," based on a need that Socrates expressed with incredible synthesis: "To impose on stone and communicate to the air intelligible forms, to ask little of natural objects, to imitate as little as possible."[15] These became the rules and conditions that identified the language of architecture and music.

Socrates specified that "these arts that lift our souls to creative heights making them resonant and fecund should instead, through numbers and the relationship between numbers, inflame us not with a fairy-tale but with the hidden power behind all fairy-tales. The soul reacts to the pure and material harmony of these arts with an infinite abundance of clarity and effortlessly animated myths; and to this invincible emotion instilled by calculated forms and correct intervals, it creates infinite imaginary causes which make it flourish with a thousand joint and spirited lives."[16]

For Eupalinos-Valéry asking little of natural objects meant distancing him-

138

self from nature regarded as a repertoire of forms to be imitated blindly, but not to the point of severing a vital bond. A comparison between this "asking little of natural objects," and the identification postulated in *Paradoxe* marks Valéry's indecision between the classicism of the twenties and the symbolism of his youth. Where the latter requires involvement and instinctive harmony with nature, the former calls for skilful balance, a recourse to nature that tends towards numerical abstraction and a sparing use of balance.

In classical poetry the imitation of nature and life is not erased by the creative work of the mind but filtered by numbers. By making Eupalinos speak, Valéry appears to describe something he has experienced: "Bereft of dreams, I conceive as if I were executing, and no longer contemplate, in the formless space of my soul, the imaginary buildings which compared to real ones are like chimaera and gorgons compared to real animals: what I think can be done and what I do is intelligible [...] And [...] listen Phaedrus, [...] if only you knew what the small temple built for Hermes, a few steps away, meant to me. Where the traveller sees only an elegant cella – not much, just four very simply styled columns – I have lain the memory of a happy day of my life. O sweet metamorphosis! That graceful temple, unknown to all, is the mathematical image of a girl of Corinth happily loved. It faithfully reproduces even her most minute proportions. And she lives for me by giving me back what I gave her [...]."[17]

The concept of the small round temple of Eupalinos may also be found in an-

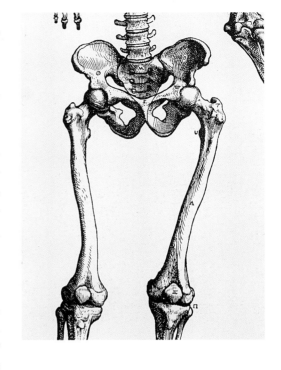

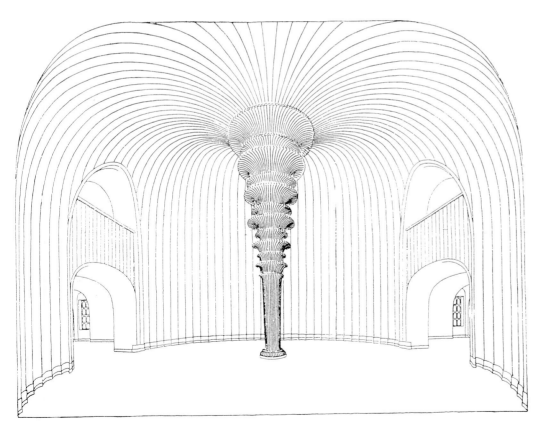

*Biological interpretations of the column. Opposite page: Casa Batlló by Antoni Gaudí (1905-07).*
*From the top down: an engraving by Vesalio illustrating the bone structure of the spine, the pelvis, the thigh-bone, the shin-bone and the fibula; a photograph by Andreas Feininger of the stem of a plant.*
*Left: luminous column in the entrance hall of the Festspielehaus in Berlin by Hans Poelzig (1919).*

other of Valéry's dialogues entitled *L'Ame et la dance* in which Socrates defines dance as: "Dreams, dreams, but imbued with symmetry, all acts and sequences!" and Phaedrus completes this statement with a dazzling image: "How pure and graceful is this small temple, pink and round, that they (the dancers) now fashion revolving slowly like the night! It dissolves in young girls, the tunics flee, and the gods seem to have changed their minds."[18]

In Christian philosophy, the column's role depends on its symbolic power rather than on its aesthetic and structural traits. The fact that it is an *axis mundi* as well as a metaphor of the human body effectively contributes to making a material man-made "church" acceptable; a church not contrasting but closely tied to the real "house of God," to the spiritual life of each believer. It is a well-known fact that the first churches were *domus ecclesiae*, private homes that hosted the ecclesiastical community. In Saint Justin's apology of Christianity sent to the Emperor Antoninus Pius, the meeting place of the community is not named, no-one knows whether it was indoors or outdoors. What counts is the Liturgy of the Eucharist recited in memory of the living God.[19]

However, when the Church came out of hiding, columns began to multiply in the basilicas, the *martyrion* and the baptistries. Between the massive stone structures of the vaults and the delicate structures of the peristyles, the Christians had no doubts. The basilicas were spatially characterised by rows of columns supporting heavy walls that highlighted both their strength and fragility. This effect

*Rome, the house of the Crescenzi family (13th century), detail.*
*A typical example of "fragmentary" architecture. Elements from old buildings are mounted in a new context and with rules that radically change the original compositional syntax. The connective tissue, built in brick, separates the two building "periods," while the chiaroscuro vibrations and plastic style joins them together.*

is intended to recall the procession: gradual initiation and the sense of infinity.

The column already had an important symbolic status in the Old Testament which the New Testament, far from repudiating, simplifies and makes more direct. In Solomon's temple, cedar-wood pillars (symbols of honesty and immortality) held up the roof of the hypostyle hall and two separate bronze pillars stood by the side of the entrance to the temple built by Hiram. The Bible mentions that the two pillars had names: the one on the right was called Jakin, the one on the left Boaz, words which stand for stability and strength and which, together with the symbolic meaning of bronze (alliance between heaven and earth), expressed the power and eternity of the alliance between God and the tribes of Israel (*Kings* 7, 2-22). In the Old Testament, the pillar also symbolises the presence of God among mankind. In fact, a pillar of fire during the night and a pillar of cloud during the day led the Jews across the desert (*Exodus* XIII, 21). Seven pillars form the structure of the house that Wisdom built for herself and in which she laid her table and to which she invited the "poor in spirit to eat her bread and drink her wine." In Christian hermeneutics, the seven pillars later became the seven sacraments (*Proverbs* 9, 1-6).

In his letters to the Galatians, Saint Paul describes James, Cephas (Peter) and John as the "pillars" of Evangelicalism. Remembering how they had given him and Barnabas their right hand, as if to symbolically divide in two the field of action of the Good News (one reserved for Jews and one for pagans), he implic-

*Left: Rome, Santa Sabina (6th century), view of the interior with the original transparent selenite windows. Above from top to bottom: the two columns, Jakin and Boaz, on either side of the entrance to Solomon's temple in Jerusalem (engraving by J.B. Villalpando, in* Ezechielem Explanationes, *Rome 1587); circular temple with seven columns (symbol of the* Domus Sapientiae *and therefore of the church of Christ).*

141

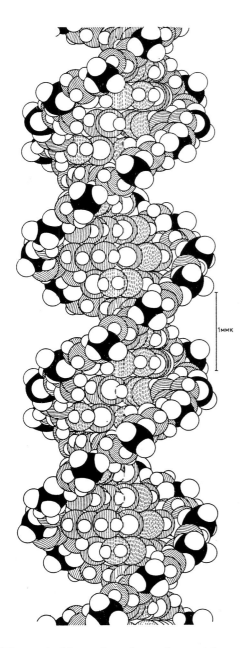

itly defines the task of spreading the Word as a task similar to the temple structure made up of four pillars. In the *Acts of the Apostles*, the temple of Ecclesia begins at Pentecost with the descent of the Holy Spirit: twelve tongues of fire descending from the heavens upon the apostles.

This structure could be considered to be full of architectural references already present in the first constructions built under Constantine. In the Roman basilica dedicated to Saint Peter, a *pergula* supported by twelve spiral columns (that according to legend came from Solomon's temple in Jerusalem) stood over the tomb of the apostle, the first head of the Church and symbol of the Church, built according to the metaphor used by Christ (Matthew 16, 18): "You are Peter and on this rock I will build my Church." The spiral column was already considered by the Greeks and Romans as a symbolic representation of the vine – and therefore of Bacchus and Dionysius – but starting with the *pergula* in Saint Peter's the spiral column began its Christian adventure that culminated in the canopy and continued in an endless series of replica.

In his life of Constantine, Eusebius specifically mentions that the central church built over Christ's tomb in Jerusalem rested on a ring of twelve columns representing the apostles and that the Emperor himself had requested twelve bases around his tomb on the basis of this symbolism, a symbolism he himself had cited during a speech to the Council of Nicaea in which he compared the church to a façade of twelve columns crowned by a pediment.

*The spiral of deoxyribonucleic acid: one of the most popular scientific images, it symbolises the presence of life forms and confirms the intuitive meaning of Solomon's column.*
*Right: the canopy of the main altar in Saint Peter's (Gian Lorenzo Bernini and Francesco Borromini, 1624-32). The reintroduction of the twisted column was inspired by the columns of the altar canopy in Saint Peter's (believed to have come from Solomon's temple in Jerusalem). In the centuries that followed it spread throughout the Catholic world, under the name of "Solomon's column."*

Speaking of the great symbolic and mystical value of the column, John Onians, in his excellent book on orders, cites a text by Saint Paulinus of Nola dating back to the 5th century, in which the concept of the column takes on a precise spiritual connotation: "Christ Himself may erect in us columns and remove the piers which block our souls and that He may thus create wide access to our senses; so that He may Himself walk in them, just as Wisdom was wont to place her healing steps in the five porticoes of Solomon, and so heal our bodies by His touch and our hearts by his teaching."[20]

Quite rightly Onians interprets this excerpt by attributing the comparison between column and pillar to the different degrees to which they absorb light, symbol of the Holy Spirit. The cult of the column basically rests on its symbolic potential and identification with the body, as well as on its role as an excellent intermediary of the many different ways that light is reflected by its cylindrical volume depending on its source and intensity.

Over the centuries, from the monuments of the early Christian era on down to the monuments of Byzantine, Gothic and Islamic architecture, this luminous dynamism that shattered all geometric symmetry became one of the most powerful factors of dematerialisation of architectural elements, along with windows, mosaics, gilding and stained glass.

In Carolingian times, the column was considered as a possible symbolic vector for the memory of Christ as well as a symbol of the apostles. In a book on the life of Abbot Eigil (820-822) there is a description of the crypt of the Abbey in Fulda situated under a chapel in which the eight columns supporting the dome represent the Beatitudes. The keystone of the crypt represents God while the circular plan represents the everlasting "eternal life" that comes from salvation. The column which is often to be found in late Gothic apses has quite rightly been associated with the Christianisation of a mythological figure, the Yggdrasil or Irminsul, the cosmic tree of Nordic and Scandinavian pagan traditions,[21] while the central column, so frequently found in the portals of Gothic cathedrals, represents Christ, simultaneously column and gateway, according to the statements of the Evangelists: "I am the gate of the sheepfold [...]. I am the gate. Anyone who enters through me will be safe; he will go freely in and out and be sure of finding pasture." (John, 10, 6-9)

When Christian culture adopted the architectural order as a principle for stylistic differentiation, it provided added proof of the power of transfiguration of the new religion that affected not only and not so much the field of esoteric theories, but rather the perception of objects.

If architectural order was initially a series of rules that, like the syntax of spoken language, imposed a certain coherence on every tiny decision, fiercely limiting the freedom of the craftsman, for Christian builders what counted most was the plastic characterisation of the capital and in most cases this influenced the choice of materials from pre-existent buildings. The Doric, Ionic, Corinthian and composite capitals mounted on shafts and bases chosen in a haphazard fashion thus

*A double tree. An Etruscan cup (mid 6th century B.C., Louvre Museum) with two trees: on the tree in front of the man there is a bird, on the other, behind his back, a snake is threatening a nest. This image personifies a tradition similar to the one of the two trees of paradise in the Bible.*

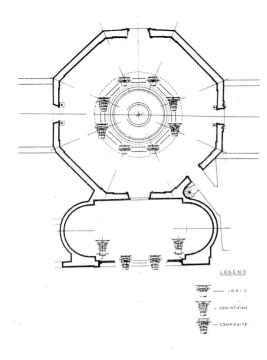

LEGEND

— IONIC

— CORINTHIAN

— COMPOSITE

became the musical tones whose role was to hierarchically differentiate the various parts of a building. A typical example of this is the basilica of San Giovanni in Laterano: two composite capitals mark the exit door of the baptised in the octagonal ring that supports the cupola; two Corinthian capitals mark the entrance to the church, while two pairs of Ionic capitals are situated on the external entry axis; the inscriptions on the architraves provide the key to this subtle hierarchy of openings.[22]

Having established a scale of values, from the simple Doric to the rich and synthetic composite (which took on solemn overtones when used by the Romans in their triumphal arches), medieval architects used it in numerous constructions – the Baptistery in Florence, San Miniato, the Duomo in Pisa – to indicate the most important parts of the buildings and sometimes to create structures similar to a musical "crescendo." In those areas less affected by enduring classical culture, capitals increased their symbolic potential through representation. In Romanesque culture this produced one of the most fertile periods of the marriage between architecture and sculpture, in perennial osmosis with the repertoire of living forms. It was not rare for the world of sounds to forcefully enter the realm of ornament, for example, at Cluny, in the Catalan cloisters of San Cugat and Gerona and the cloister of Santa Maria in Ripoll. This demonstrates how important song was in the configuration of ecclesiastical buildings at that time. It was designed to give continuance and solemnity to sound waves by improving the acoustic quality of those high vaulted ceilings.[23]

*Plan of the church of Santa Maria Novella in Florence and (above) the Lateran Baptistery in Rome indicating the position of the capitals (of various architectural orders): their position indicates an intentional emphasis on the religious meaning of various parts of the building.*

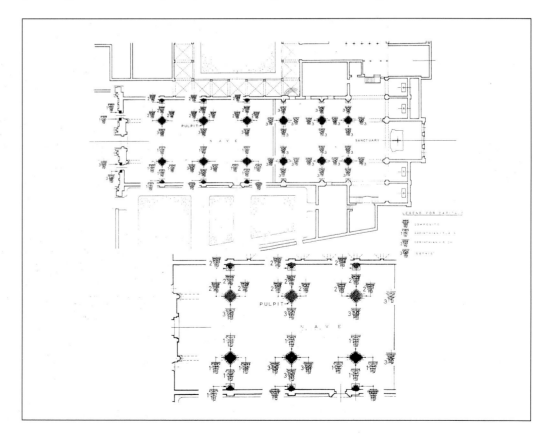

In the Florentine church of Santa Maria Novella, the main nave is flanked by twelve columns dedicated to the apostles. In the presbytery, however, there are sequential classical capitals as well as Gothic capitals whose classical foliage is imbued with a new biomorphic vitality. The fact that this hierarchy tended to progressively shed the legacy of antiquity is of great importance. Before giving way to the humanist revival, the Gothic style was increasingly considered as the only one true Christian architecture, a new and different classicism in which each element was connected to the logic of the orders yet its appearance and its relationship with nature was completely transformed.

When the column entered the symbolic world of Gothic style, it was spiritualised through multiplication. It became a composite bundle of similar elements held together by the common goal of striving upwards and towards the light and it is through this analogy with the plant world that it was revived in a new and convincing manner. This analogy continued to be cultivated during the Renaissance and Baroque periods as a sort of legitimisation of the craftsman, in line with Vitruvius and his critics. Suffice it to recall here the broken branch columns found in the persistent Gothic-like atmosphere of northern European countries, as well as in the world of humanist classicism, the idyllic climate of Arcadia, Rococo and Gothic Revival.

After being compared once again to the trunk and shaft and having suffered algebraic reduction, during the present century the column – as in the 5th and

*A tree trunk in the Botanical Gardens, São Paulo, Brazil (above) and the roof of Amiens cathedral showing one of the four polystyle pillars that support the lantern.*

145

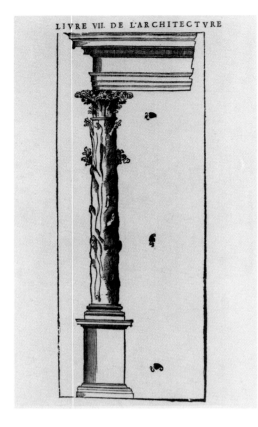

*Above, from left: the column as tree or trunk in a xylograph from the treatise by Philibert Delorme; tree-shaped column in Bechyne castle in Bohemia and a drawing by Karl Friedrich Schinkel for the columns of the Gertraudenkirche in Berlin.*
*Right: a pillar of the Chiesa dell'Autostrada by Giovanni Michelucci (1970) and a photograph of the inside of a human heart. Like the heart, the pillar suggests a two-phase alternation: dilation and contraction, diastole and systole.*

*Opposite page: two drawings by Heinrich Tessenov showing columns inspired by the trunks of birch trees.*

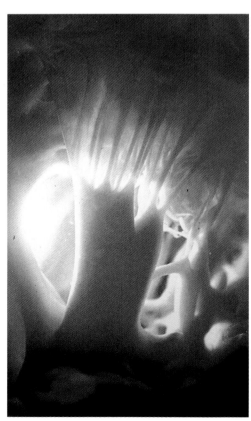

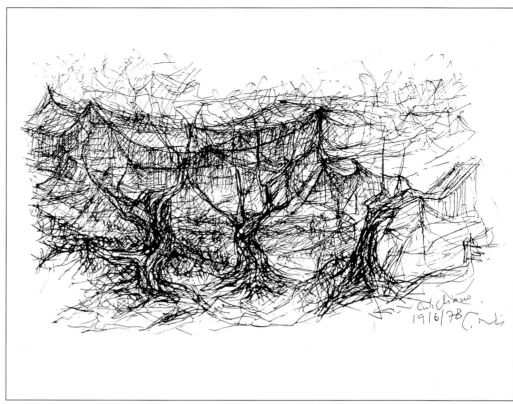

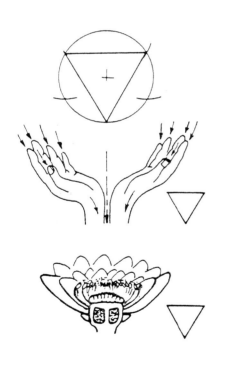

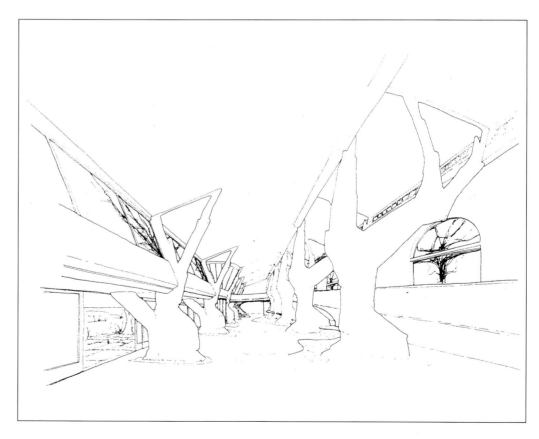

Tree-shaped columns in modern architecture. Opposite page: two drawings by Giovanni Michelucci that architecturally interpret the theme of the olive tree.

Below: a transparent capital of the Rome mosque (P. Portoghesi, V. Gigliotti, S. Mousawi, 1975-95). The capital expresses two metaphors: the palm tree (dracena cordyline) *and hands joined in prayer (see opposite page).*

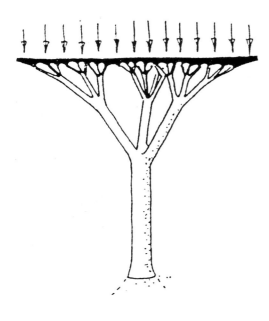

8th centuries A.D. (with the collapse of codes and the technique of fragmentation and parataxis) – has entered a tragic stage, becoming a symbol of confusion but also of renewed hope in the search for a truthful answer from nature.

Only two architects who express all the force behind this tragic trait will be cited here: Henrich Tessenow and Giovanni Michelucci.

Tessenow is a master of simplicity and not, as many would have, of glacial abstraction. He caresses with humble discretion the archetypes of the house, tympanum and colonnade and gives meaning and value to elements submerged by technological rationality, such as the frames of doors and windows, the threshold and the roof. However, at a time of great confusion, confronted with the prevailing external rhetoric of Nazism, Tessenow used the fairy-tale image of the birch wood in his design of Rügen Hall, giving the column proportions of unheard-of lightness. Without dramatising the external form he expresses the tragic condition of confusion as well as the defence of his own area of lucid and free reflection on the nature of things.

Throughout his entire life Michelucci cherished the olive tree, a tree that symbolises the gentleness of the Tuscan landscape, a tree with which man identifies through its "necessary" pruning when the tree grows old and twisted and age forces it into a prone position, facing down towards the earth.

Athena, in her contest with Neptune to see who offered the most beautiful gift to man (Neptune offered a horse), clinched victory by giving the olive tree

*Above: diagram of the tree as a supporting structure. Below: the dendriform structure used in a viaduct (Frei Otto).*
*Right: a photograph of Hamburg airport (Von Gerkan, 1993).*

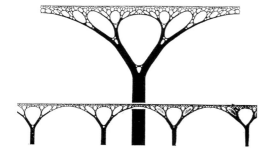

150

to the inhabitants of Attica. The olive tree challenges the passing of time and, after having left many heirs for future generations when it dies, its gnarled trunk still puts forth new shoots. This is the olive tree that Michelucci's body came to resemble, tired yet exalted by almost one hundred years of life. This is the olive tree that in the seventies entered his figurative repertoire (shyly entering the Pinocchio tavern only to triumph in the Chiesa dell'Autostrada, of San Marino and San Casciano and a myriad of other projects).

His last project for the theatre in Olbia, which he had seen only in his dreams, rests on a forest of olive trees. This project can be considered his spiritual legacy because it embodies his search for a state of gentle humility.[24]

And it is Michelucci's legacy that inspired me to impress a "tree" design on the columns of the Mosque in Rome, combining the palm tree and the Roman pine.

*Santiago Calatrava, the support of a wooden structure that conjures up the classical capital and the battering-ram.*

[1] L. Kahn, *Gli scritti*, edited by C. Norberg-Schulz, Officina, Rome 1981.

[2] cf., A. Tzonis, L. Lefaivre, D. Bilodeau, *Le classicisme en architecture. La poétique de l'ordre*, Dumod, Paris 1985, p. 248.

[3] cf., M. Gimbutas, *The Language of the Goddess*, Thames & Hudson, London 1989.

[4] cf., T. Spini, *Togu na*, Electa, Milan 1976. The community hut of the Dogon tribe (togu na) is the communal village house, also called "house of the word." Inside, the occupants must be seated, because this position encourages wise decisions. The forked column confirms the hut's anthropomorphism, with its frontal sculptures representing male and female genital organs.

[5] Vitruvius, *The Ten Books on Architecture*, Harvard University Press, Harvard (Mass.) 1914, p. 103.

[6] *Ibid.*, pp. 103-104.

[7] *Ibid.*, pp. 104-106.

[8] cf. P. Valéry, *Eupalino o dell'architettura*, trans. R. Contu, Carabba, Lanciano 1932 (*Eupalinos; or The architect*, Oxford 1932).

[9] L. Kahn, *Gli scritti*, cit.

[1] cf., J. Rykwert, *On Adam's House in Paradise*, The Museum of Modern Art, New York 1972.

[11] cf., P. Imbornone, "In principio era il dorico", in *Demetra*, no. 3, December 1992, pp. 26-28.

[12] cf., L. Canina, *Particolare genere di architettura domestica etc.*, Bertinelli, Rome 1852.

[13] cf., P. Valéry, "Paradosso sull'architetto", edited by S. Terracina, in *Eupalino*, no. 4, April 1985, pp. 39-41.

[14] cf., P. Valéry, *Oeuvres completes*, Gallimard, Paris 1980, p. 116.

[15] cf., P. Valéry, *Eupalino*, cit., p. 57.

[16] *Ibid.*, pp. 54-55.

[17] *Ibid.*, p. 36.

[18] cf., P. Valéry, *Oeuvres completes*, cit.

[19] cf., *Antologia della patristica*, vol. I, Sei, Turin 1964.

[20] cf., J. Onians, *Bearers of Meaning*, Princeton University Press, Princeton 1988, p. 72.

[21] cf., J. Brosse, *Mitologia degli alberi*, Rizzoli, Milan 1994, p. 9 (*Mythologie des arbres*, Paris 1989).

[22] cf., J. Onians, *Bearers of Meaning*, cit., pp. 62-63.

[23] cf., M. Schneider, *Pietre che cantano*, Guanda, Milan 1980.

[24] cf., G. Michelucci, *Abitare la natura*, Ponte alle Grazie, Florence 1991.

# The Architrave, the Order, the Cantilever

*During the 19th or 20th centuries, the engineer who did his best to design reinforced or suspended beams, found that some of his best ideas had, so to speak, been anticipated long ago by the bone structures of gigantic reptiles and large mammals.*

Wentworth D'Arcy Thompson

*Opposite page: the so-called temple of Neptune (almost certainly dedicated to Hera Argive) in Paestum.*

The column is the arrival point of two genetic processes: the erection of a vertical element, planted on the ground yet reaching skywards (the menhir, the totem, the *axis mundi*) and the hollow wall as defined by Alberti. Rather than cancelling each other out, these two process complement each other and produce different genealogical trees. The column, or pillar, is part of a system or pair of supports joined together by a horizontal element. As Eve was born from Adam's rib, so the portico was born from a transformation of the wall: it is a breathing wall, an open wall, a wall that does not make us deviate or look for an opening, instead it invites us to "penetrate" into a space devoted to the ongoing struggle between light and shadow. The portico either permits entry to a building or runs alongside it: a row of pine trees outlined against a bright sky is like the portico of an unfathomable and mysterious elsewhere. A row of columns united by an architrave, or by an entablature, establishes an "order," not a fixed rule, but a number of flexible rules, so that the architect finds himself facing an "ordered" series of choices.

The system of architectural orders reached its zenith in Greece but is also present in less spectacular forms in all great civilisations and styles, from Ancient Egypt to Japan, from Roman to Gothic to Baroque. It is like a giant tree with endless ramifications, a majestic age-old oak that each season witnesses the birth of new leaves along the strong permanent framework of its branches. Paul Valéry poetically expresses this in his *Cantique des colonnes*: to choose an order means to draw closer to the trunk from which many branches depart at varying heights and by choosing one branch exclude all others.

The choice of the Doric order leads to other dilemmas: the variable distance between the columns (the so-called intercolumniation); the number of flutes or no flutes at all; the shape of the capital; the elements of the cornice; the arrangement of metopes and triglyphs, the form of the cymatium; the slope of the tympanum whose synonym, the "pediment" brings us back to similarities with the human body. Having decided on the type of capital, a choice has to be made regarding the shape of the echinus, and having identified the right triglyph a decision has to be made on the number of guttae and their position. The branches and twigs lead to the petiole to the leaf to the flowers to the fruits of this great tree.

In the Doric order all choices seem to draw on a transparent and incisive rationality and this is similar to what happens in the plant world. Here, there are laws that govern growth and produce forms that are always "necessary" in some way and consequently are also satisfying and harmonious. The design of a Doric temple involves a series of choices. At a certain point the architect is faced with a problem that has no satisfactory solution. He can choose among many, but they are all invalidated by a diminished forcefulness: by a lack of "need." This is the problem inherent in the angular conflict between triglyphs, a conflict that has other hidden problems linked to the wooden archetype of the order "translated" and betrayed by its stone interpretation.

*A reconstruction of the temple to Apollo Epicurius at Bassae.*
*Below: the "American" order decorated with corn cobs to characterise its specificity (Benjamin Henry Lathrobe, 1764-1820).*

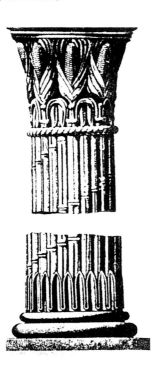

The system of orders adopted by the Greeks and the Romans is a fascinating example of pluralism, of peaceful cohabitation between different stylistic trends. Various ethnic groups determined this differentiation, yet only initially did it appear confrontational, later it led to well thought out choices and even successful associations, for example, the temple of Apollo in Bassae, probably designed by Ictinus for Pericles to celebrate Panhellenic unity after the plague in 429. In Bassae, the exterior is Doric while the cella is surrounded by Ionic columns with the exception of the central column in the rear wall which is Corinthian.

The "five order" system inherited from the ancient world according to the code elaborated by Vitruvius is an extremely rich and varied source. However, over the centuries other forms and other systems were often felt to be necessary, over and above this repertoire. They corresponded to the technical and expressive needs of civilisations radically different from those of the western world; for instance, after the Renaissance, these forms and systems required a more orthodox classical language based on more or less naive nationalistic requirements. A typical example is the French order for which a contest was held in 1672; it was won by Colbert who submitted a mediocre modification of the Corinthian order. A more successful proposal, but again with no staying power, was advanced by Ribart de Chamoust in 1783; his proposal involved both grammar and syntax and required columns to be arranged in groups of three along a hexagonal layout.

Ribart de Chamoust said he had not designed but "discovered" his order when "walking in a shady wood" where he noticed a sort of hexagonal temple spontaneously created by nature; he completed the order by following the laws implicit in nature's model.

Not only did this eclectic attitude make it possible to choose between different regional traditions, bringing them together if this were appropriate, but it also made it possible to codify the sturdiness or elegance of each order and associate their characteristics to male or female beauty, youth, old-age or even to psychological traits, something Blondel did in his *Cours d'architecture* in 1771 by referring to similarities with the human body. By drawing on the symbolic world of numbers and proportions, the imitation of nature, filtered by a need for rational clarity attained through abstraction, reached its zenith accompanied by an agonising mixture of infantile naiveté and judicious tolerance that justified Marx's remark: "The difficulty does not lie in understanding that art and the Greek *epos* are linked to certain forms of social development. The difficulty lies in the fact that they continue to inspire an aesthetic pleasure in mankind and, in some ways, constitute an unattainable norm or model. A man cannot be a child again otherwise he becomes puerile. But doesn't he delight in a child's naiveté and shouldn't he, at a higher level, aspire to reproduce truth? In childish nature, isn't it not true that the traits of each era contain primordial truths? So why shouldn't the historical childishness of humanity, in one of its most incredible moments of development, exert an eternal attraction since it is a period that will never return?"[1]

The architrave and, more in general, the entablature, protect the architectural structure against of deterioration due to the weather, especially rain. There is an ongoing battle against the water that penetrates the cracks between stones, turns into ice, disintegrating joints and jeopardising the very stability of the architectural parts; in this battle the entablature represents a skirmish and an exchange. This situation creates a certain degree of dependency between the imaginary, formidable flow of water and the shape of the cantilevers and contours as well as bringing to mind the relationship between victim and persecutor described by Freud.

Renaissance theorists highlight the fact that the morphology of the mouldings continually reflect similarities with various parts of the human body. This can be seen even in their names, for example nose and corona, or the word "cyma" for the convex-concave shape of the cymatium, or the word pediment for the tympanum. Each layer of the entablature has a name and the various mouldings tend to be grouped together in well defined parts. Above the architrave, often divided into three parts protruding above one another, there is the frieze (often with a horizontally sculpted decoration). Above the frieze there is the bed moulding, which in the Ionic order is made up of eggs and darts, above which juts out a protruding "corona" that acts as a protection for the underlying part of the entablature and at the same time sharply defines the cornice. In fact, above the corona there is only the cymatium which often corresponds to a small drain sticking out from the sloping roof.

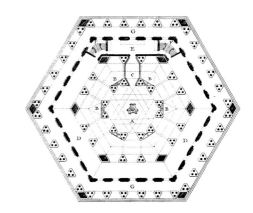

*The French order "found in nature" by M. Ribart de Chamoust (1776). The drawing of the round temple shows the analogy between the columns and trees, while the hexagonal plan (above) is created by arranging the columns in groups of three.*
*Left: Jacques-François Blondel (1705-74), the relationship between the physiognomy and the Tuscan architectural orders based on the Treatises by Scamozzi and Vignola (from the* Cours d'architecture, *Paris 1771).*

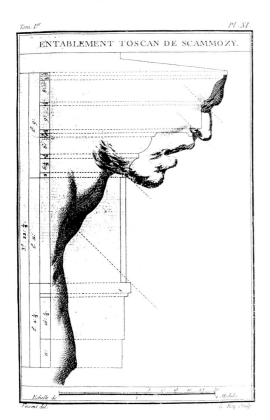

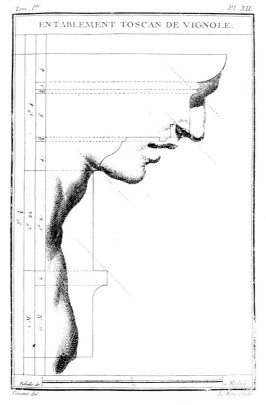

The corona is the whole slab that juts out between the frieze and the cymatium, but the real corona is that small projecting piece whose specific task is to avoid any water on the surface and cymatium from flowing backwards and penetrating the space between the stones.

However, this anti-water logic of the entablature simply interprets the teachings of nature, for example in sedimentary rocks where overhanging cliffs protect the soil below.

The rules of these orders, rules of superimposition and commensurability of conventional parts, may be combined in layouts and elevations, intersections and stratification. On the one hand, this group of rules, considered as the "grammar" or "syntax" of the order, recalls formal logic and therefore the mechanisms of thought. On the other, it is linked to the idea of growth and the ways in which the various parts of a plant combine, detach or divide into a perfect organism. Just as an architect may observe, study and dissect a plant, a botanist can analyse architecture for common laws mysteriously woven into the analogy between growth and construction.

By studying the architrave of the entablature and consequently the trilith or a similar group of horizontal and vertical wooden elements, it is possible to see how the architectural significance of the architrave changes when the latter is longer than the two external rows of lateral columns. If the projection is small and equal on either side, the trilith becomes a portal; the portal can either be a

*Sandro Botticelli,* Pallade doma il Centauro *(1482-83), Florence, Uffizi Galleries. In this painting, as in the later* San Girolamo in penitenza, *Botticelli paints stratified rocks that seem to refer to the close analogy between these rocks and classical architecture with its "orders" and rules.*
*Right: the façade of the castle-palace in Caprarola (Italy) by Jacopo Barozzi da Vignola: the superposition of various architectural orders was an attempt to find a "Caravagesque" chiaroscuro effect.*

functional element permitting entry into an internal space or purely symbolic (as in the Japanese *tor-i* and Indian *torana*) invested with a very precise sacred meaning. If, on the other hand, the projection is pronounced and possibly asymmetric, we are faced with a different archetype: a "cantilevered" or "overhung" archetype found in embryonic form in the cornice. The more pronounced the projection the greater its value and the more it becomes a "type": a family of architecture in which lightness and levitation are exalted until they appear in contrast to the laws of gravity.

In primitive architecture the trilith system certainly fulfilled a ritual role since it is central to every other more complex architectural relationship. The trilith is built in three stages: the erection of each of the two "uprights" and the positioning of an architrave: elements of the same shape and material are often used yet their function is totally different depending on whether they are positioned horizontally or vertically. When man decided to experiment during construction, he began by examining the different roles of the uprights and the architrave and arrived at the conclusion that while the former are homogeneously compressed by the weight above, the stress on the internal fibres of the architrave is not homogeneous. Since the architrave tends to bend downwards, its upper fibres are compressed, while the lower ones are correspondingly tensed. The intermediate layers remain neutral since there is no stress on the fibres. These considerations and their consequences raised the problem of making the massive

*Above: the island of Gozo in the Maltese archipelago, a natural trilith (photo by Maria Ercadi).*
*Below: Giza, temple in the valley of Kefre, a trilith structure without plastic projections.*

*Moscow, reconstruction of a tower and a fragment of boundary walls built with horizontally juxtaposed trunks.*

stone architrave "lighter," due to the fact that, when the empty space below increased, the architrave became so heavy that it was unable to support even its own weight.

The problem was solved by substituting stone with a material that was more stress resistant. Where there was no stress, material was taken away and concentrated where compressive and tension stress existed. The T-bar and W-shape bars (girders) have thus become the archetype of this attention to the internal behaviour of matter, as well as equipping engineers with a first-rate instrument during the course of the 19th century.

The history of architecture is full of examples of forms inspired by the intuitive appreciation of the possibilities inherent in the exploitation of building materials through the subtraction of the superfluous, making them lighter and optimising their yield. Thus there is no doubt that construction theories contributed positively to the repertoire of architectural forms. However, in the interdisciplinary fields of biology, chemistry and physics and in particular in morphological studies, as these successes multiplied, it became apparent that certain rules discovered by science and relating to natural structures had already been applied very rigorously a million or so years ago.

D'Arcy Thompson, the most acute and brilliant scholar of morphology, explains how a Swiss engineer recognised the analogies between bone structure and a large crane he was designing. He writes: "A great engineer, Professor Culmann of Zurich, to whom by the way we owe the whole modern method of 'graphic statics,' happened (in the year 1866) to come into his colleague Meyer's dissecting-room, where the anatomist was contemplating the section of a bone. The engineer, who had been busy designing a new and powerful crane, saw in a moment that the arrangement of the bony trabeculae was nothing more nor less than a diagram of the lines of stress, or direction of tension and compression, in the loaded structure: in short, that Nature was strengthening the bone in precisely the manner and direction in which the strength was required [...].

"In the shaft of the crane, the concave or inner side, overhung by the loaded head, is the 'compression-member'; the outer side is the 'tension-member'; the pressure-lines, starting from the loaded surface, gather themselves together, always in the direction of the resultant pressure, till they form a close bundle running down the compressed side of the shaft: while the tension lines, running upwards along the opposite side of the shaft, spread out through the head, orthogonally to, and linking together, the system of compression-lines. The head of the femur is a little more complicated in form and a little less symmetrical than Culmann's diagrammatic crane, from which it chiefly differs in the fact that the load is divided into two parts, that namely which is borne by the head of the bone, and that smaller portion which is upon the great trochanter; [...] and we have no difficulty in seeing that the anatomical arrangement of the trabeculae follows precisely the mechanical distribution of compressive and tensile stress or, in other words, accords perfectly with the theoretical stress-diagram of the crane. [...] *Mutatis mutandis*, the same phenomenon may be traced in any other bone which carries weight and is liable to flexure; [...].

"It is a simple corollary, confirmed by observation, that the trabeculae have a very different distribution in animals whose actions and attitudes are materially different, as in the aquatic mammals, such as the beaver and the seal. And in much less extreme cases there are lessons to be learned from a study of the same bone in different animals, as the loads alter in direction and magnitude [...].

"In the bird the small bones of the hand, dwarfed as they are in size, have still a deal to do in carrying the long primary flight-feathers, and in forming a rigid axis for the terminal part of the wing. The simple tubular construction, which answers well for the long, slender arm-bones, does not suffice where a still more efficient stiffening is required. In all the mechanical side of anatomy nothing can be more beautiful than the construction of a vulture's metacarpal bone [...]. The engineer sees in it a perfect Warren's truss, just such a one is often used for a main rib in an aeroplane."[2]

The analogy between the Warren truss and the vulture's metacarpal bone introduces the topic of spatial reticular structures that will be examined in the chapter on the cella. However, D'Arcy Thompson's observations are not limited just to bones. The famous naturalist also influences our opinion of the incompleteness and fragility of the animal skeleton as we see it, separate from the rest of the body, in the showcases of natural history museums. He highlights the way

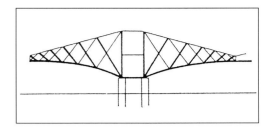

*One of the analogies proposed by W. D'Arcy Thompson: the double truss structure of the bridge over the River Forth near Edinburgh (J. Fowler, B. Baker, 1881-87) and, below, the fossil skeleton of a bison.*
*Below: Pier Luigi Nervi and A. Arcangeli, the ribbed ceiling of the Gatti wool factory in Rome (1953). The arrangement of the ribs corresponds to the isostatics of the main points inside a system subject to stress.*

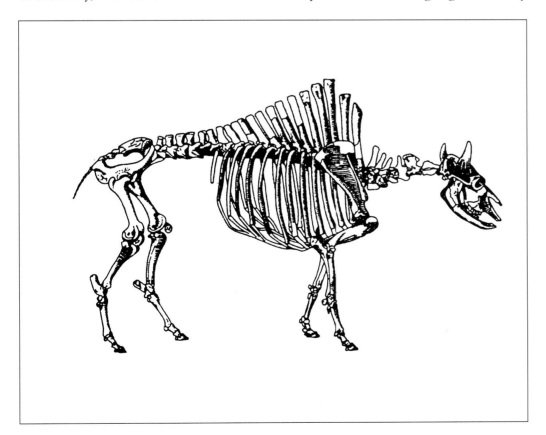

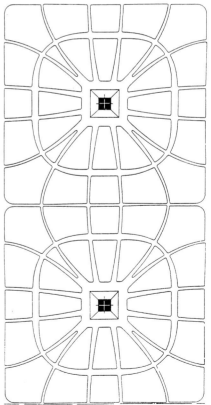

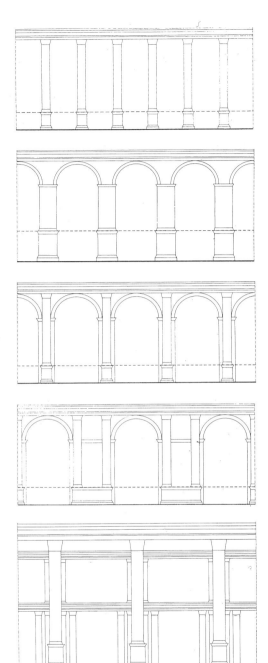

*The laws and operations that characterise the classical architectural order are very similar to those of formal logic. The Greek system is based on superimposition along a vertical axis of defined elements (base, shaft, capital, trabeation) and repetition. The Roman system introduces the superimposition of different orders and the projection of the order onto a series of arches. Michelangelo introduced intersections between orders, therefore a hierarchy between major and minor orders.*

in which it complements the complex system of tendons and muscles which he believes is an integrated system. He also compares the skeleton of a horse to a bridge and considers the beautiful bridge over the Firth of Forth one of the masterpieces of 19th-century engineering, a structural model to which the horse skeleton can be directly compared.

He writes: "Nevertheless, if we try to look, as an engineer would, at the actual design of the animal skeleton and the actual distribution of its load, we find that the one is most admirably adapted to the other, according to the strict principles of engineering construction. The structure is not an arch, nor a tied arch, not a bowstring girder: but it is strictly and beautifully comparable to the main girder of a double-armed cantilever bridge."

"In a typical cantilever bridge," he adds, "such as the Forth Bridge, a certain simplification is introduced. For each pier carries, in this case, its own double-armed cantilever, linked by a short connecting girder to the next, but so jointed to it that no weight is transmitted from one cantilever to another. The bridge in short is *cut* into separate sections, practically independent of one another; at the joints a certain amount of bending is not precluded, but shearing strain is evaded; and each pier carries only its own weight. By this arrangement the engineer finds that design and construction are alike simplified and facilitated. In the horse or the ox, it is obvious that the two piers of the bridge, that is to say the fore-legs and the hind-legs, do not bear (as they do in the Forth Bridge) separate and independent loads, but the whole system forms a continuous structure. In this case, the calculation of the loads will be a little more difficult and the corresponding design of the structure a little more complicated. We shall accordingly simplify our problem very considerably if, to begin with, we look upon the quadrupedal skeleton as constituted of two separate systems, that is to say of two balanced cantilevers, one supported on the fore-legs and the other on the hind; and we may deal afterwards with the fact that these two cantilevers are not independent, but are bound up in one common field of force and plan of construction."[3]

D'Arcy Thompson's book, published in 1917, considerably influenced the debate that unlocked the doors to the architectural rationalism supported by the historical avant-garde between the two world wars. In 1978 Robert Maxwell confirmed this when he presented the works of Robert Venturi.[4]

"Geoffrey Scott's interesting book of 1914," writes Maxwell, "fell on deaf ears, whereas D'Arcy Thompson's book of 1917, *On Growth and Form*, was to have a lasting influence, at least within the English-speaking world. Thompson's book showed very convincingly that the form of organic structures in the natural world were always consistent with a limited set of constructional principles and proportional geometries. Nature seemed to work as if form was the result of function times economy. When these principles were applied to engineering structures like bridges, they were found to work in the same way and produce similar or analogous forms. The discovery, of what amounted to a kind of teleological rationale in nature, seemed to suggest that the general principles of design were common to all construction, whether in nature or at the hands of man, and that there was nothing specifically human in them. It followed that purely human conventions were unnecessary, and might indeed merely offer obstacles to a natural process which could attain evolutionary perfection."

The comparison between the books by Geoffrey Scott and D'Arcy Thompson is particularly interesting because it illustrates the positivistic type of "scientific" support that, at a time crucial to the birth of new architecture, actually endorsed the chance to remove and invalidate all the traditional codes that presided over the communication of symbols, ideas and values.

On the contrary, Scott's conclusions about the "humanist values" of architecture were instrumental in highlighting that it is the way in which we interpret or "transcribe" architecture within ourselves that gives it a semblance of life and organicity, and that this interpretation depends on more or less conscious convictions.

"The whole of architecture is, in fact, unconsciously invested by us with human movement and human moods. Here, then, is a principle complementary to the one just stated. *We transcribe architecture into terms of ourselves.* This is the humanism of architecture. The tendency to project the image of our functions into concrete forms is the basis, for architecture, of creative design. The tendency to recognise, in concrete forms, the image of those functions is the true basis, in its turn, of critical appreciation."[5]

Even clearer is the role of identification between architecture and the human body in an extract on breathing from Scott's book.[6]

"But we possess in ourselves a physical memory of just the movement. For we make it every time we draw breath. Spaces of such a character, therefore, obtain an additional entry to our sense of beauty through this elementary sensation of expansion. Unconscious though the process of breathing habitually is, its vital value is so emphatic that any restriction of the normal function is accompanied by pain, and – beyond a certain point – by a peculiar horror; and the slightest assistance to it – as, for example, is noticed in high air – by delight. The need to expand, felt in all our bodily movements, and most crucially in breathing, is not only profound in every individual, but obviously of infinite antiquity in the race. It is not surprising, then, that it should have become the body's veritable symbol of well-being, and that spaces which satisfy it should appear beautiful, those which offend it ugly."

The differences pointed out by Maxwell between Scott and D'Arcy should be evaluated based on the influence the two books had rather than merely as a difference in theories, since both men never stray from their relative fields as scientist and art historian, and both stubbornly defend their independent "correctness." Both could have subscribed to Scott's conclusions when he maintains that architecture is "a humanised reproduction of the world." He states before: "Nature, it is true, is for science an intelligible system. But the groups which the

*Michelangelo, embedded columns and aedicula in the Repository of the Laurenziana Library in Florence (1523-59) and, below, detail of the plan of the wall that separates the Repository from the Reading Room.*

*An overhanging stratified rock.*

eye, at any one glance, discovers in Nature are not intelligible. They are understood only by successive acts of attention and elimination; and even then, we have to supplement what our vision supplies us by the memory or imagination of things not actually seen. This Order in Nature bears no relation to our act of vision. It is not humanised. It exists, but it continually eludes us. This Order, which in Nature is hidden and implicit, architecture makes patent to the eye. It supplies the perfect correspondence between the act of vision and the act of comprehension."

However it is regrettable that there was no way in which the two points of view, expressed by D'Arcy Thompson and Scott, could be compared and integrated, especially by a culture that was already veering towards separate "specialisms." Fully aware of the difficulties, in his book D'Arcy studies and sustains the advantages of integration between the "two cultures," a fact that could save humanity from the many mistakes caused by a tendency towards rationalism and simplism.

Returning to the "cantilever," it must be said how easy it has been, with the advent of flexible materials, to incorporate it into construction; initially it was experimented in the field of building techniques using wood. However, even in stone constructions it is possible to achieve remarkable projections either by carefully studying the distribution of weights and the thickness of the resisting sections or else by embedding overlapping corbels sufficiently deeply into the wall.

In classical terms, a specific structure is assigned the role of projecting out from the edge of the wall. This is the "console" in the Corinthian cornice underneath the shortened form of the modillion that is, however, still capable of creating particularly beautiful plastic solutions. In some ways the cantilever is a way to move away from the wall towards the building's exterior. As mentioned earlier, it is also an outward projection of the architrave or floor. Its problems are similar to those of the roof which is, on the contrary, a movement that leads inwards from the wall. Nearly all the solutions to the static problem of the cantilever reflect the problems inherent in the division and covering of internal space. So the *tholos* cupola system is represented by overhanging and outward jutting consoles while the vault system is transposed in the vaulted brackets of continuous balconies typical of Roman architecture.

The ideal model for cantilevers is to be found in nature: the horizontal thrust of the branches of conifers, tree trunks bent by the wind, the flight of birds, the rock roofs that break up vertical rock faces, the caps of mushrooms, the way in which certain leaves branch out from their stalk often accompanied by a sort of "winding" that consolidates and strengthens the bond between the vertical and horizontal elements, as for example in the fuller's teasel.

These rounded cantilevers, like disks of varying size clinging to tree trunks, were made of a special fungus and were used by Wright in 1945 as a model for his design of the V.C. Morris House. In Chinese and Japanese architecture, the

*Trees shaped by the wind in Sardinia (Italy).*

*Mushrooms on the trunk of a hazel-nut tree (Treja valley).*

*Frank Lloyd Wright, a drawing for the Play Resort and Sport Club in Huntington Hartford, Hollywood, 1947.*

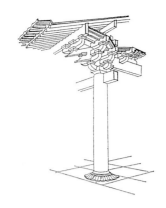

system of "boat-shaped" consoles has permitted roofs to jut out many meters from the vertical structure. The projection is gradual; an upside-down staircase connecting brackets and supports with a sort of transparent frame that looks surprisingly like the system of parallel branches in plants. The equally obvious rationalisation is obtained by "inverting" the profile of a tree (whose lower branches stick out more) and joining the branches together. This creates a structure that filters light and gives the impression that the heavy roofs stretch skywards as if they were being raised by a force pushing upward, shaping the curvilinear contours with elevated corners. Due to this levitation effect, one of the masterpieces of Chinese architecture, in the city of Wanrongxian, is called the "tower of the flying clouds." The building has a base and three pavilions that jut out from the central structure, each with a roof supported by a system of consoles that vary from floor to floor.

The archetype of the cantilever, made technically possible by new materials like iron and reinforced concrete, has represented the *pièce de resistance* of the "heroic period" of "modern" architecture, namely the first few decades of this century. The structural model of the Maison Domino by Le Corbusier, just like the small models draw together with Cor van Eesteren and Theo van Doesburg, as well as Mies' designs in the twenties, are all based on a free façade, on the disassembly and projection into space of the vertical and horizontal sliding panels that appear to be consciously liberated from the laws of gravity.

*The Japanese wooden order has cylindrical columns (at times tapered), light architraves and trusses that tend to multiply in a rigid superposition system (called* masu-gumi *or to-kyô). The extremely protrusive roof exploits this system to gain lightness and character.*
*Above: perspective detail of a column with a truss system and protrusive roof; the corner of a pagoda in the Kijomizu-dera temple in Kyoto.*
*Right: the "phoenix pavilion," an ancient imperial villa that was transformed during the 11th century into the Buddhist temple, Byôdô- in, in the town of Uji (Kyoto). Its name comes from the temple's bird-shaped layout.*

However, it is above all Frank Lloyd Wright in the early years of this century who gave the cantilever strong symbolic significance as an instrument for the destruction of the box-shaped involucre and for the experimentation of a fluent and continuous spatiality. In the prairie houses, the cantilever is the technique which achieves horizontality, the spreading of architectural material parallel to the earth. In Taliesin East, a long balcony juts out from the architect's bedroom like a small boat pointing its prow towards the horizon.

The cantilever as levitation, as the raising of space in space, as a vital movement in the air like the flight of birds. It finds its ideal shape in *Fallingwater* at Bear Run. Here the floating masses are the same size as the stone blocks arranged in layers along the cascade from which they were quarried based on that process of interiorisation that Wright, still very young, called "conventionalisation": "To know a thing, what we can call knowing, a man must first love the thing, sympathise with it. So the Egyptians 'knew' the Lotus and translated the Lotus to the dignified stone forms of their Architecture: this was the Lotus 'conventionalised!' The Greeks 'knew' and idealised the Acanthus in stone translations. This was the Acanthus conventionalised. Of all Art, whatsoever, perhaps Architecture is the Art best fitted to teach this lesson, for in its practices this problem of 'conventionalising' Nature is worked out at its highest and best [...]

"A work of Architecture is a great co-ordination with a distinct and vital organism, but it is in no sense naturalistic – it is the highest, most subjective, con-

*The protrusive terrace of the bedroom in Frank Lloyd Wright's house at Spring Green (1925).*

ventionalisation of Nature known to man, and at the same time it must be organically true to Nature when it is really a work of Art. To go back to the Lotus of the Egyptians (we shall see in this mere detail of Art the whole principle), if Egypt had plucked the flower as it grew and had given us merely an imitation of it in stone, it would have died with the original – but in turning it into stone and fitting it to grace a column capital, the Egyptian artist put it through a rare and difficult process, wherein its natural character was really revealed and intensified in terms of stone, gaining for it an imperishable significance, for the Life principle of the flower is translated to terms of building stone to satisfy the Ideal of a real 'need.' This is Conventionalisation, and it is Poetry. As the Egyptian took the Lotus, the Greek his Acanthus, to idealise the function of the capital, [...] we may take any natural flower or thing."[7]

*Opposite page: Frank Lloyd Wright, the Kaufman House at Bear Run (Fallingwater, 1936). Projection is currently facilitated by new technology. It means that architecture is free from the forces of gravity to such a degree that construction may now be taken to new heights. Wright built his most courageous work in natural settings, thereby avoiding that his research be taken as an exaltation of technology. On the contrary, by using the primary qualities of the landscape and the dialogue between light and shadow, he placed it in the context of what could be called an "unveling".*

[1] cf., K. Marx, *Per la critica dell'economia politica, Introduzione* (1857), Editori Riuniti, Rome 1973, p. 199.
[2] cf., W. D'Arcy Thompson, *On Growth and Form,* Cambridge University Press, London 1961, pp. 232-236.
[3] *Ibid.*
[4] cf., R. Maxwell, *The Venturi Effect*, in *Venturi and Rauch. The Public Buildings*, Academy, London 1978, p. 8.
[5] cf., G. Scott, *The Architecture of Humanism,* Constable & Co., London 1914, p. 213.
[6] cf., *Ibid*, pp. 228-229.
[7] cf., F.L. Wright, *Collected Writings*, vol.1, Rizzoli, New York 1992.

# The Niche, the Apse, the Curve

*[The architect] should consider that nature hates corners; animals are guided by nature and when they change direction they never walk around a corner, but proceed in a curved fashion. In olden days our ancestors always avoided corners and straight lines, especially in temples. Right angles were used in buildings only for comfort's sake in order to find the best arrangement for beds, tables and other necessarily angular objects.*

Francesco Borromini

*According to Le Corbusier, a donkey designed all European cities, including Paris. The donkey avoids all obstacles and large stones so as not to tire. Only man, proud man, knows what he wants: to steer straight towards a well defined objective. But does he have one? Does he really know where he's going? I have more faith in the donkey, the original inventor of organic logic, than in the bards of our deceptive human superiority. And if Le Corbusier declares that the straight line permeates the entire story of humanity, every plan ever elaborated by man, every one of his actions, [...] we can only reply that irregular lines, complicated curves and the enormous variety of European cities also exist. [...] No, it is truly unjust to denigrate the donkey. I am certain that he will influence the town-planning designs of tomorrow. And when re-examining the history of architecture we would do well to consult him every now and then. He is of few words, but is quite level-headed and we have a lot to learn from him. The elementary ideas of mankind and the elementary beauty of architecture have always been expressed, and will always be expressed, through a multitude of forms, since nature too is rich in forms, lines and colours, infinitely different yet harmoniously balanced.*

Erwin Anton Gutkind

Even if the shape of the cylindrical hut is round, the moment it is accessed through an opening, this opening establishes frontality, a trait fully expressed only when shaped objects possess clear orientation, a distinction between "front" and "back." This is characteristic of niches created by hollowing out a wall, but from a conceptual point of view it is merely an abstract operation. The frontal incision in the circular hut creates a spatial involucre to accommodate the human body, almost capturing its essence. The prehistoric temples on the island of Malta present a niche archetype whose form has already been consciously elaborated into an apse recalling the matrix of natural caves in which *inter alia* the primary characteristic was concavity.

Rocks moulded by erosion or by their own volcanic or sedimentary genesis were used by Maltese architects as an excuse for the shape of the excavation which was influenced by the movement of human arms or through the rotation of tools on rock. The ensuing curve also satisfied an inclination to humanise matter, to imitate the typical movements of the human body. In fact, the niche reifies the embrace, the shape of welcoming arms, a gesture of love as well as the sacerdotal gesture of those who wish to act as mediators between the Gods and man.

On the island of Malta, the monumental complexes in Tarxien or the hypogeal tombs in Hal Saflieni elegantly develop the theme of the horseshoe niche-apse. However, they also represent the most radical examples of intentional and generalised curvilinearity in the history of architecture.[1]

It appears that the builders, by refusing to use horizontal and vertical rectilinearity, wanted to adapt the architectural image to human vision that remains focused and accurate only in the centre of the image, corresponding to a visual angle of approximately 43°; around the edges, out of the "corner of one's eyes," our vision becomes blurred and we can only distinguish moving forms. On the other hand, some experts believe that projections on the spherical surface of the retina would create images with spherical aberrations and that the most realistic method of perspective representation would mean projecting a visual pyramid onto a curved surface.

In the Maltese temples, especially in the hypogeum at Hal Saflieni, the way the lines curve does give the impression that the builders of this monument wished to make them "softer" by seconding the tendency of the human eye to deform the edges of images.

To attribute such acute sensibilities to a civilisation so different to ours in terms of the relationship between geometric and visual reality may seem somewhat rash, but in Malta curved lines, as well as the treatment of stone surfaces and the decidedly theatrical morphology of space all point to such a developed level of sensibility or experience as to suggest an "interrupted" civilisation whose conquests appear to have been excluded from the historical evolution of Mediterranean traditions. This civilisation chose a path deemed deviant by history, a "curvilinear" path, a feminine path considered to be in contrast to the "rectilinear" and male choices of classicism, linked to the central Asian cult of concave-convex forms.

On this issue, Hugo Häring's interpretation of Chinese roofs based on remarks by Chen Kuan Li is both pertinent and to the point: "The very essence of the Chinese is immersed in nature, is integrated by it and depends on it and thus comes into contact with the evolution of nature and the cosmic element. The shape of Chinese roofs stems from infinity and floats over the heads of man, enveloping him. It protects man who spends his life observing and meditating on this first great elevation of the terrestrial spirit in the world, immediately ready to descend in order to remain in contact with the world. Over the heads of man, this roof profiles the lie of the land, the mountains and hills of the earth, expressing its cosmic configuration. This shape contains the image of nature and its manifestations."[2]

The refusal of rectilinearity is at the heart of the Chinese philosophy of *feng-shui*, a discipline which establishes the position, shape and layout of buildings, houses or tombs by listening to nature and being in perfect harmony with the universe.[3]

Ancient Chinese sensibilities tend to consider life as something that pervades the entire universe and can be found not only in what we call living beings but also in the wind, in springs, lakes, trees, rocks and the earth. This philosophy is very similar to that of certain American-Indian tribes who refused to cultivate the earth in order not to "wound their own mother." The Chinese revere the landscape and believe that when something new is introduced man has to avoid "sticking a thorn

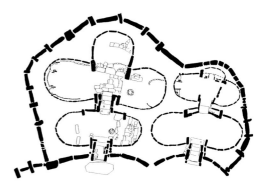

*Maltese temples. Reconstruction of the second and third temples in Tarxien with their original concave façades. The plan, with its five concave apses, could correspond to the fertile and rotund body of the Mother Goddess.*

*Reconstruction by Carlo Ceschi of the interior of the second cella of the first temple in Tarxien and, above, a schematic drawing of the hypogeum in Hal Saflieni, Malta. Note the incredible anticipation of the Italian-style theatre and the curvature of the horizontal and vertical lines (drawing by R. Cantarano).*

*Geomancy specialists (*feng-shui, *literally wind and water) in action in a Chinese engraving. Right: the curved roofs of the Japanese pagoda and temple of Horyu Ji in Nara. Note the dragon, symbol of sexual and cosmic duality, sculpted on the vertical pillar.*

into its flesh." Instead, the designed shape must rumble and flow together with the rhythm of the earth. The cardinal concepts of *feng-shui* are *ch'i* (vital breathe) or *an chien* (secret arrow). The former represents the blood of the earth, the energy running through nature that must be gathered and stored avoiding stagnation, while the latter represents a negative force to be shunned at all costs.

Using the *feng-shui* technique a propitious site should be sheltered from strong winds by a protective row of trees or hills. Its rivers or ditches should flow gently and the site should face southwards and be surrounded on three sides by hills. The horseshoe shape repeatedly present in all Chinese cemeteries is an artificial representation of the ideal protection offered by mountain chains to the rear of the site. The Ming tombs northwest of Peking reflect this ideal configuration and the site was naturally chosen for this reason. This type of house is normally the nucleus of a more complex system of dragons (*lung*) that fan out from the house itself.

In spite of the fact that there are a number of ideal sites in any dragon-configuration, only one will be perfect: the one in which the white tiger of the west and the sky-blue dragon of the east copulate. A number of suitable sites are present in any landscape, but traditionally only one will be the true mating place since only one is infinitely superior to all the others. To live there (or bury one's dead) will ensure a life rich in spiritual and physical well-being. A pearl carved by the dragon is the comparison most often used.

The pragmatic approach inherent in *feng-shui* does take into account the fact that most of us live in houses that are far from perfect and therefore offers a number of suggestions to improve on the house's ability to accumulate *ch'i*.

"The forms and configurations should be looked upon as the body of the dragon; the water and underground springs, the blood and veins of the dragon; th surface of the earth, the skin of the dragon; the foliage upon it, the hair; and dwellings as the clothes, according to the 'Huang-ti Chai-ching' or 'Site Classic'. Along the lines of the ridges, both blown by the wind and carried by the water, as well as through the underground channels, flows the vital *ch'i* which feeds the life on the surface of the earth."[4]

Even this preference for curved lines comes from the latter's ability to facilitate the flow of the "blood of the earth." Stephen Skinner maintains: "As a general rule, which is reflected in the intricacies of Chinese art, the meandering undulating line conducts *ch'i* whilst the straight line, sharp bend or fast watercourse indicates *sha*. In some ways the organic lines are as typical of Chinese civilisation as rectangular Descartian lines are the hallmark of Western civilisation. Basic to the nature of *feng-shui* dragon lines and Chinese civilisation generally is the curve as opposed to the straight line which expresses itself not only in Western architecture, but also in the ley lines which it has often been suggested are the European equivalent of dragon lines. They are in fact diametrically opposed. Straight lines, as we have seen, are anathema in *feng-shui* for they generate *sha ch'i* and 'secret arrows' and let in demons."[5]

A secret thread seems to run between the tombs of Chinese Emperors and one of the most sacred huts of Greek mythology: the laurel wood hut built by Apollo himself.

On the island of Eubea, in a place called Eretria, recent excavations have unearthed the foundations of a hut probably built in laurel wood as well as ropes that presumably held the fragile structure together. Like Romulus' hut on the Palatine Hill, this archaic structure was preserved even after the construction of the nearby temple. The temple was shaped like a "safety-pin" since it was believed to have been built by Apollo. It is similar to the one built and then destroyed during the celebrations of the nine-year festivities. The first temple (7th century B.C.) built at Perachora in the bay of Corinth is very similar to Apollo's hut. It is considered to be the very first Greek temple and became famous when a clay model was made of it. The temple had coupled columns on two sides of the entrance and a convex roof, similar to the roof of a hut. Its convex apse and strong frontality make it look like a frame sculptured around the image of the god. [6]

Frontal concavity was charmingly developed during the Hellenistic period as well as by the Romans rather than the Greeks. The Romans tended to make the rectilinear *nymphaeum* used by the Greeks either concave or mixtilinear and gave it the more exact name of *museum*, a space that Pliny the Elder defined as "*ad immaginem specus arte reddendam*," in other words, that must be built like a

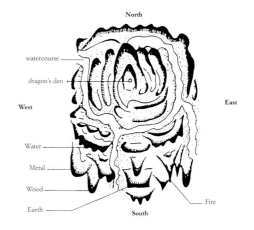

*Chinese map of the "dragon's den"* (hsüeh).

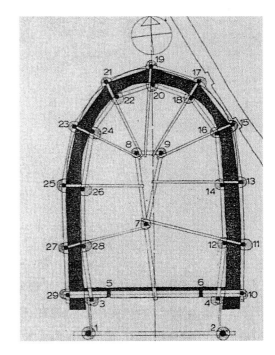

*Reconstruction by Paul Anderson of the Diaphnefhorion: "This is," writes Joseph Rykwert, "a fragile wooden structure held together with ropes and built using a series of double posts placed at both ends of a wall... It is possible that the structure was originally made of laurel"* (from J. Rykwert, On Adam's House in Paradise, Museum of Modern Art, New York 1972).

cave. Roman nymphaea foreshadow the layout of future basilicas; the apses and the rows of columns built so close to the walls reveal a desire to find shelter in the bosom of the earth. In broad daylight, however, the same theme is developed in the exedra situated along the walls of the baths, the great villas or in mountain areas such as the Fortuna Primigenia sanctuary at Praeneste. Trajan's market, the Settizonio and the porticoes of the Imperial Forums, at the heart of the Roman *forma urbis* are littered with congenial niches that were destined to survive and flourish during the Renaissance and Baroque periods, making Rome the curvilinear and "maternal" city *par excellence*.

Christian architecture fully develops spatial concavity. It does so in the catacombs, where it follows the logic of excavation and the measured movements of the pick axe of "grave-diggers," as well as in the basilicas. It is a building type inherited from Roman tradition and expertly transformed, the few meaningful variations dictated by the requirements of the Christian religion. These variations consisted in eliminating the tribunes along the transversal axis and creating a tribune along the longitudinal axis which, as a backdrop to the main nave, underlined the importance of the altar. Having decided to use the nave as the processional path – metaphor of the eschatological path to salvation – a new caesura was placed in front of the apse. Its inclusion in the transept gave the caesura a spatial quality, but it also acted as a wall, since a perforated partition considered as the modified version of the Roman triumphal arch was positioned between the

*Roman* nymphaeum *in a temple in Zaghouan (Tunisia). The relationship between the concavity and the landscape is quite straightforward. Beneath the* nymphaeum *there is a swimming-pool made out of two concavities.*

nave and the transept. The "curved" apse marks the area reserved for the priests. By shedding its original trait of Roman *tribunal,* considered as a place of rest and judgement, it begins to become the final goal, a mirror of infinity, a sacrificial area of the consecration of the Eucharist. The small spherical surface ensconced in the rear wall could now house the figure of the Saviour giving his Blessing, of the *Rex tremendae maiestatis*.[7]

From the point of view of construction, the curve of the apse also demonstrates how resistant matter is dependant on its shape. This typically Roman method was experimented in Hadrian's Villa in Tivoli and in the Horti Liciniani mausoleum in order to absorb the thrust of the vaults. Byzantine architecture inherited and exploited this strategy, fully aware of the mystical value of space that multiplies its lower subdivisions as do certain biological organisms. Like the transparency of jellyfish that creates the illusion of weightless matter, Byzantine spatiality achieves the progressive dematerialisation of the walled involucre, its transformation into pure phenomenon of light, aided by the mosaics and by the incident and reflected light that pours through walls.

Curvilinearity has two qualities that place it in close contact with nature: the absolute preference of other creatures in the world to use curvilinearity when building their shelters and its pervasive presence in the human body and biological forms. We are continually improving our knowledge of animal architecture. We learn how defence against the elements is not the only factor that determines shape and how the animals themselves instinctively create artificial spaces depending on their movements and life styles. This relationship between involucre and movement often determines curvilinearity as well as the incredibly rich repertoire of shapes created by various species.

Birds' nests normally look like upside-down cupola with openings towards the sky, but sometimes they are bag-shaped with just one entrance and exit. This particular solution has the practical elegance of certain shapes studied in advanced geometry. The *Furnarius rufus* normally chooses telegraph poles to build its nest: these nests look like Steiner's Roman surface and are divided into two parts, the smaller one acting as an anteroom.[8] Many animals, including the *Oecophylla* ant and the *Remiz pendulinus*, use the architectural method of bending a surface to make it "cosy" or to make it inhabitable. This type of shelter can be compared to the elegant vaults designed by Nervi and Candela. Bower birds use leaves which they leave on the living stalk and use the cavity to build a soft bed for their young,[9] while the nests of the *Ploceus capensis* are spherical and hang on vertical branches like artificial fruit.

No less curvilinear are the collective nests of the *Philetarius socius,* a Namibian bird that assembles his hanging villages by first building a common roof and then creating interconnected individual cells like village huts. Despite being fairly light, when these settlements grow too large they drop off the supporting branches, obliging the birds to start all over again: an automatically regulated system that stops the inhabitants from exceeding a quantitively defined

*A communal nest of gregarious weaverbirds. This is a group of nests each with its own downward-facing entrance. As in human megalopolis, the abnormal development of the nest can create serious problems, since the supporting branches can break and the structure collapse.*

*A beaver's den with a twig roof: it has one underwater entrance and one aerial opening. The structure resembles Frank Lloyd Wright's orthodox church as well as the openings on the top floor of the Community Center in Marin County (California).*

*The seed of the* Aphelandra squarrosa "Louisae" *with four concave areas compared to the plan of the Greek Orthodox church of the Annunciation in Wauwatosa, Wisconsin (Frank Lloyd Wright, 1955-56).*

limit. Even beavers prefer to use curves during their incessant building activities – and this activity is not limited merely to housing but involves planning, environmental control and exploitation of natural resources. Their sprawling cupola-shaped dens are initially situated underground with underwater entrances and only later, when an environmental balance is necessary, do they continue to dig in order to build their dens above ground, furnishing them with convex roofs made of scrub and cut branches. One of these dens, photographed in the Teton National Park in Wyoming, is structurally similar to the Greek Orthodox church of the Annunciation built by F. Lloyd Wright in Wauwatosa, Wisconsin (1956). The burrow and the heavenly vault seem to mirror one another, joined together like the valves of a shell.

That animal architecture has, so to speak, an "organic" vocation and prefers a repertoire of shapes similar to those of the biological world – for example mole burrows, ant-hills and many other dens – may be explained by the fact that their instinct tells them how to build and this instinct is written in their genes. Beavers born in captivity, unable to learn from adults, have shown themselves capable of cutting down trees and building cupolas. Richard Dawkins has recently introduced into genetics the idea of the "extended phenotype," admitting that hereditary genetics also includes animal behaviour involving actions outside the body. To reflect on this structural link between habitat and biological inheritance could well lead us to attribute greater importance to that part of our genetic heritage

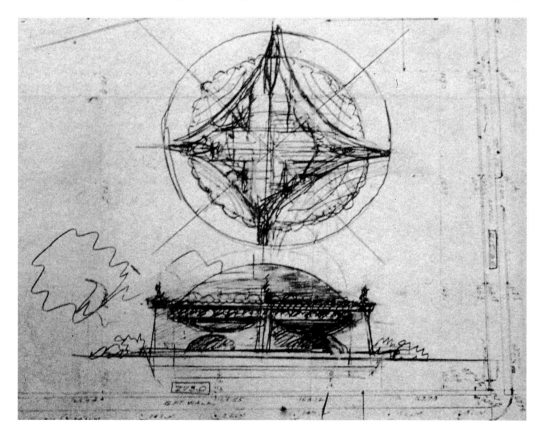

involving spatial configuration and to verify the hypothesis that believes in a progressive diminishment of this heritage due to the acquisition, in pathological terms, of our predisposition to abstraction.

As mentioned earlier, curvilinearity is also consequential to the intentional anthropomorphism of most architecture expressed not only in the field of geometric proportions to which Chapter 19 is dedicated, but also by the symbolic value of our gestures.

The erect position and cross-shaped structure of the human body with outstretched arms determines our idea of orthogonality. Over the centuries it has characterised the planimetric structures of buildings as well as urban organisms.

No less inspiring for architects is the concave position of a body's arms when facing another body to enfold or "embrace" it. The apse, the nymphaeum and the exedra in Roman and Medieval architecture were all inspired by this gesture. During the Renaissance and Baroque periods, this gesture of embrace was achieved in planimetric form by extending the porticoes sideways and joining them to the central body as "arms" or "wings." In *The Four Books of Architecture* Palladio describes numerous villas with curvilinear loggias and explains their metaphoric meaning to the reader. At the end of the second volume when talking about Villa Mocenigo, he describes the four loggias: "following a circumference, like arms to envelop those who approach the house." Speaking of the project for the "Counts of Thieni" Palladio explains that the role of the "two loggias,

*The castle of Chambord on the Loire (16th centurty). Its cylindrical towers are covered with lanterns, chimneys and covered roof terraces that imitate the morphology of plant growth.*

Frank Lloyd Wright, project for the Lake Wolf Amusement Park, Illinois, 1895. The anthropomorphic theme was revised so as to establish a relationship between water and earth.

Le Corbusier, Notre-Dame du Haut at Ronchamp, rear view and detail of the symbolic nave above the entrance (1950-53).

The curvilinear balcony of Maison Solvay in Brussels by Victor Horta (1894-99).

*Above: vortexes produced by the movement of an object. The two alternate series of vortexes generate the so-called "vortex route" initially studied by Theodor von Karman in 1911. Right, from top to bottom: a picture of sea waves and a detail of the model of the Hotel Savoia on the promenade in Rimini (Paolo Portoghesi, 1992-96).*

projecting like arms from the building" is to "connect the owner's house to the farm building."[10] A century later, Borromini echoes Palladio in his *Opus Architectonicum* when, speaking about the Oratorio di San Filippo Neri, he writes: "and when designing this façade I imagined the Human Body with open arms as if to embrace all who enter; as a body with open arms it is divided into five parts, namely the centre chest, the arms divided in two parts by the joints; the middle part of the Façade is the chest and the lateral parts the arms, each divided in two by pillars that stand out in the middle as can be seen in the façade itself." [11]

This analogy with gestures, as well as with the shape of the human body, also applies to the face and hands. If, in the case of the human body, the results voluntarily or involuntarily involve irony and kitsch, for the face and hands the metaphor has produced results of great evocative force. This is especially true in the case of clasped hands or hands stretching upwards in prayer, donation or acceptance, an image often morphologically transposed by architecture. At this point it is appropriate to recall the bronze sculpture modelled by Rodin in 1908 entitled *La cathédrale*;[12] it depicts two hands joined delicately together in prayer. This is the sculptor's way of representing the birth of the ogive and sums up the wonderful work Rodin accomplished in his book, *Les cathédrales de France,* in which he explained the natural genesis of every part of the Gothic organism.[13]

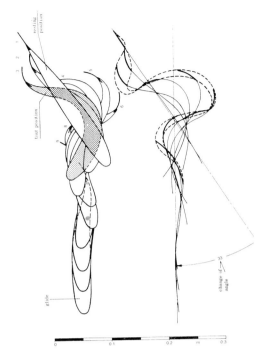

*Graphic study of the movement of a trout in water, in particular the initial thrust.*

[1] cf., C. Ceschi, *I templi megalitici di Malta*, Libreria dello Stato, Rome 1937.

[2] H. Häring, *Il segreto della forma. Storia e teoria del Neue Bauen*, Jaca Book, Milan 1984, pp. 110-117.

[3] cf., S. Skinner, *The Living Earth Manual of Feng-Shui, Chinese Geomancy*, Routledge & Kegan Paul, London 1982; J. Michell, *Lo Spirito della terra*, Red, Como 1988 (*Earth spirit*, London 1975); G. Doczi, *The Power of Limits*, Shambhala, Boston 1981.

[4] Cf., S. Skinner, *The Living Earth*, cit.

[5] *Ibid*.

[6] cf., S. Lloyd, H.W. Muller, R. Martin, *Architettura mediterranea preromana*, Electa, Milan 1972 and J. Rykwert, *On Adam's House in Paradise*, The Museum of Modern Art, New York 1972.

[7] cf., T.F. Mathews, *The Clash of Gods*, Princeton University Press, Princeton 1993.

[8] cf., M. Emmer, *La perfezione visibile. Matematica e arte*, Theoria, Rome-Naples 1991, pp. 177 ff. and L. Sinisgalli, *Furor matematicus*, Edizioni della Cometa, Rome 1982.

[9] Regarding the nests and other animal constructions see K. von Frisch, *L'architettura degli animali*, Mondadori, Milan 1975 (*Animal architecture*, New York 1974); M. Allaby, *Animal Artisans*, Knopf, New York 1982; D. Morris, *Les animaux révélés*, Calman-Lévy, Paris 1990; A. Masi, *Gli uccelli e i loro nidi*, Olimpia, Florence 1986.

[10] cf., A. Palladio, *The Four Books of Architecture*, The MIT Press, Cambridge (Mass.) 1997.

[11] cf., F. Borromini, *Opus architectonicum,* II edition, Edizioni dell'Elefante, Rome 1966, p. 37.

[12] cf., M. Laurent, *Rodin*, Fabbri, Milan 1989, p. 138.

[13] cf., A. Rodin, *Les cathedrales de France*. Colin, Paris 1914.

# The Arch, the Vault, the Bridge

The arch, or the shape of the arch, is visible everywhere in nature: when a gust of wind bends the branches of a tree, or we cup our hands to pick up or handle objects; it is present even in the outline of hills or at the end of a rainbow silhouetted against a cloudy sky. All these geometric images that look like a segment of a circle immediately catch our attention and gratify our minds because this form evokes the feeling of totality.

The arch joins things that are near or far: its outline rises and falls in a more or less accentuated curve. The arch contrasts rectilinearity introducing tension and deviation, estrangement and reconciliation. For instance, the idea of reconciliation is implicit in the mysterious shape of the arch made by the worker termites of the *Macrotermes natalensis* species, the most "artificial" of natural arches.[1] The termites begin by making columns with grains of earth and excrement. In their work, the termites are evidently guided by smell, but perhaps they are influenced by a "field," as theorised by Sheldrake, or else they might be the depositories of a full blown mental project. When the column reaches a certain height the termites begin to bend it towards the neighbouring column until the work of the two worker colonies fuses into a single structure. Louis Kahn uses Alberti's metaphor of the hollow wall as generator of the column, to which the termites add the no less charming metaphor of the arch created by the attraction of two neighbouring columns.

The arch is movement, expansion on the one hand and compression on the other. Its materialisation into such an elementary structure as the bow that permits an arrow to fly into the distance highlights its explosive internal tension. Instead, when talking of rocks, it is rare for an arch to appear in such a simple and complete form, but the potential is internally present in the predisposition of some rocks towards conchoidal fracture. In order to forge the amygdala, the first tool, a number of arches or opposing concavities were superimposed on one another. Cave entrances too are often arched, and the endless series of natural arches or bridges of the great mountain chains anticipate and lay the groundwork for the work of man. They do not necessarily conjure up the image of the arch, but when an object is horizontally supported they express nature's tendency to reduce the contrast between what is supported and what supports, to round corners, to increase matter at the very point in which gravitational forces are strongest and reduce it when those forces are weaker.

To build an arch, the wall had to develop overlapping layers, such as those found in sedimentary deposits. Laying stones side by side only allowed for small openings and corresponded to the space of a missing stone: the architrave, a longer stone spread across the top of the opening, made it possible to create doors and windows even if they were still relatively small. In order to take the weight off the wall above the architrave, two big sloping stones were placed above the opening. In central Italy, the slang used by construction workers for this type of support is "small hood," a term that refers to its elementary shape: two hands joined over one's head resembling the pitches of roofs. The weight on the sloping stones became a diagonal thrust that was released into the structure of the wall. Another way to avoid discharging weight onto the architraves was to place stones on top of one other, taking care that each stone jutted out above the stone below like a corbelled triangle. The less the stones projected, the more solid the structure. This is the reason why Atreus' tomb is pointed like the tip of an arrow and foreshadows the construction system of the internal *tholos* dome.[2]

Even the ancients were well aware of how useless it was to identify the inventor of an idea that had become common knowledge. In Seneca's ninetieth letter to Lucilius, the one in which he states that "happy" was the time when there were no architects, he goes on to explain his scepticism towards the theory of "signature" inventions: Posidonius declares, "Democritus is said to have discovered the arch, resulting in the curving line of stones, which gradually lean toward each other, being bound together by the keystone. I am inclined to pronounce this statement false. For there must have been, before Democritus, bridges and gateways in which the curvature only started towards the top." The thrust of the letter is that it is not the so-called wise men who invent the skills needed in everyday life. Instead, it is the craftsmen, and they could well be uneducated, or even slaves.

Archaeologists have reached similar conclusions and believe that the arch, preceded by structures that partially anticipate its logic, appeared at the same time in various areas of the Mediterranean and gradually grew in importance. We know very little about Democritus of Abdera, a contemporary of Socrates,

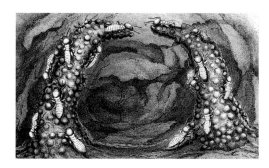

*The arch built by the* Macrothermes natalensis *termites by mixing earth and excrement. When a column reaches a certain height, the termites begin to bend it towards the column nearby. One theory maintains that smell guides the termites when creating the reciprocal convergence of the arches. This has been disproved by the fact that the work continues even if a panel is placed between the two arches.*

*The rainbow, the celestial prototype of every man-made arch or bridge.*

*A parabolic-shaped pseudo-arch in the giant walls in Arpino (Italy), and a vaulted roof in Hadrian's Villa in Tivoli. After numerous intuitions and sectorial experimentation by different civilisations of the ancient world, the arch-building technique reached its peak during the Roman Empire.*

*Right and opposite page, "natural" arches. This series on the island of Santorini was produced by the erosion of volcanic rock; the Rainbow Bridge, Utah (USA); natural arch on the island of Capri; an arch built with twigs by a bower bird near Sydney.*

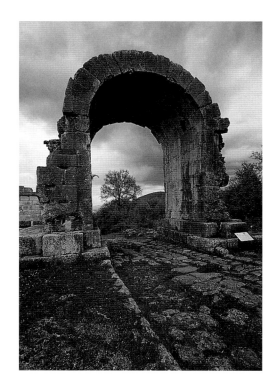

*An arch in the Roman city of Carsulae (Terni); below, the arch in the façade of the Duomo in Civita Castellana (Italy).*

but as arches are well documented long before his birth, if we were to assign the official role of inventor of arches to him, we would have to admit that the invention was left unused by the Greeks for a very long time. On the other hand, the arch system can reasonably be considered an evolution of the projecting corbel system used in *tholos* domes and there are numerous examples of intermediate structures that combine the two techniques, to such an extent that they legitimise the hypothesis of a so-called "spontaneous" birth inspired by observing the static behaviour of the corbels. This behaviour was noticed by the workers who actually hoisted the corbels and were in a position to hypothesise their virtual movements and consequently the fact that they reciprocally supported each other. Apart from other less important examples, such as the Veii Hut Tomb, dating back to the end of the 7th century, the first examples of monumental arches in Italy are the urban doors of Velia and the Etruscan cities. The Pink Door of the Lucanian city of Velia-Elea probably dates to the 4th century, while the Door in Volterra – once dated to the 4th century – is now believed to be from the end of the 3rd century, more or less the same period as those in Cosa and Falerii Novi, the latter being the only ones that can accurately be dated (241 B.C.).[3]

It is very probable that in Rome the first wide-scale use of this building method coincided with the construction of the so-called Servian walls, even if the supporting arches that remain date back no earlier than the 2nd century. In fact, some no longer verifiable historical sources relate that the Porta Trigemina and the Porta Fontinale, both from the middle of the 4th century, had arches and radial ashlars. On the other hand, the small external arch of the tomb of the Scipio family on the Appian Way dates back to 250 B.C. while the older remaining parts of the Cloaca Maxima, once believed to have belonged to the Tarquin era, range between 210 and 179 B.C.

Therefore, if current archaeological theory leaves us in no doubt as to the priorities governing the adoption of the arch in eastern cultures, this does not mean that between the 6th and 4th centuries the arch and the barrel vault did not appear simultaneously in the Etruscan, Greek and Roman worlds. Perhaps this was due to the fact that it was extensively and systematically used in the Servian wall because of the quality of the material employed, mainly tufa, which is not suitable for the construction of big architraves. During recent excavations on the Palatine Hill, under a patrician villa dating to 530-520 B.C., Andrea Carandini has unearthed a vaulted cistern capable of holding 26,000 litres, a discovery that indirectly confirms this hypothesis.[4]

The barrel vault is nothing more than the in-depth extension of the arch, since a two-dimensional arch exists only in geometric abstraction and an arch that is only as thick as its ashlars is, so to speak, a vault *in nuce*; it only has to be extended to cover an area of any length. Therefore natural arches, except for the immaterial rainbow, are always vaults that can be expanded by the imagination, or even rocky caves or arboreal structures made of woven branches that look like hemispherical surfaces.

The bower bird uses straw to build the entrance arch of his small earthly paradise in which to welcome his lover, but its methods change depending on the specific species and the characteristics of the environment.[5]

The Romans used the round arch as well as the depressed arch, whose radii were less than half the span, but it was the Islamic architects who introduced infinite variations often inspired by natural forms. The pointed arch, already known in Sassanide times, forcefully entered the Islamic repertoire in Persia in the 8th century and in Syria and Egypt in the 9th century. Its natural matrices are the woven branches of trees as well as the shapes of leaves and the pointed contours of certain fruits. Nuts and cactus plants might well have been the natural archetype of the horseshoe arch which, when exploited as a rotational surface, is transformed into a bulb cupola with probable phallic overtones. The most typical Islamic arch is in fact a variant of the pointed arch that has two circle segments no higher than the upper part of the span. Often this shape is simplified by joining the two rectilinear segments towards the crown.

Even more closely inspired by nature is the stalactite arch in the Alhambra – the lancet arch similar in shape to the flame and enormously successful in Venice during the 14th and 15th centuries – as well as the foil arch that alludes to organic morphology, in particular the shape of the human ear and the lips of certain shells. The Stuttgart Institute directed by Frei Otto has recently studied the similarities between the Islamic trefoil arch and the spontaneous formation of mixtilinear shapes created by surface tension (soap bubbles).

After having freed the morphology of the arch from static and gravitational forces, Gothic art developed one of the possible options chosen by Islam, in particular the one that rises upwards as if lifted by the wind, or created by a violent vital force like a stalk growing upwards towards the light. From amongst all the other variations, the shape preferred in Tudor England was the "swan" arch, built to correspond to a "rampant" design and obviously associated with a climbing movement, but in fact dictated by the need to contain the thrusts by directing them towards the more massive areas of the construction.

In its attempt to broaden the horizons of the classical codes, the Baroque period typically developed the elliptical arch but even more so the oval arch, composed of numerous circle segments joined together to avoid any visible discontinuity (by aligning the central pair used for the adjacent curves). More than anything else, the oval arch satisfied the need for plastic forms thanks to its variable curvature indicating structural flexibility. Together with the areas around the curvature, the arch became a powerful tool to shape space, like a sculptor using the most pliant and plastic materials possible: clay and hot beeswax. The most commonly used example of this topological adaptability are the massive lateral arches supporting Borromini's cupola in San Carlino which are twisted in order to reconcile the dictates of the plan's orthogonal symmetry and the diagonal symmetry of the pendentives. Nature offers numerous examples of both drop

*A series of superimposed arches in the bell-tower of a church in Messariá (island of Santorini). Below: detail of the arched portico in the Marin County Community Center (California) by Frank Lloyd Wright, 1953-59.*

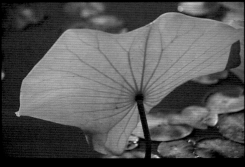

A leaf of the plant, Nelumbo Nucifera (lotus flower); right, a Chinese bridge immersed in the landscape.
Below: the double arch of the feathers of a lyre bird; right, bridge over the Basento river (Italy) designed by Sergio Musmeci, 1957.

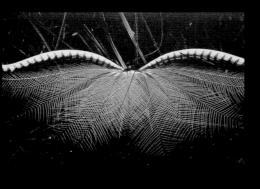

and polycentric arches, such as the branches of trees and the wind-swept trunks often symmetrically situated along the banks of rivers and torrents.

The desire for something new and the inspiration of 19th century research in the field of construction theories brought the parabolic shape of the arch to the fore. However, this shape was already used by the Hittites and the Achaemenids as well as being used in the popular architecture of southern Iraqi populations who gathered bundles of giant canes (*Fragmitus comunis*) from the banks of the Tigris and Euphrates as a building material for their *mudhif*.[6]

Perhaps due to its affinity with the natural openings of grottoes, the parabolic arch found its niche in Renaissance and Baroque architecture. It was often used in gardens and parks, such as the one in Bomarzo, to evoke monstrous mouths ready to swallow the wayfarer. This 19th-century discovery is linked to the study of construction theories that led to the appreciation of the parabolic shape, its correspondence with the curve of compression and its functionality in the design of big bridges.

Due to both its technical qualities and its primordial connotations, for Gaudí the parabolic arch gradually became one of his primary morphological choices. Even in his early works, such as the Güell house and pavilions, the architect used this element to visualise the static behaviour of building materials as well as to highlight elasticity and continuity. Once the shape of the parabolic arch was changed into a rotational surface, this permitted the Catalan master to

*Rampant arches in Strasbourg cathedral; above, the double curve of a swan's neck and the geometric drawings of various types of arches.*

190

revive the external shape of termite mounds and the Adobe mosque in the church of Colonia Güell.[7]

When the arch is turned into a bridge, it inspires movement in two directions: the flowing river below and the racing road above. Two movements that form a cross, two movements that are both possible (even though they seem to cancel each other out) because the raised surface of the road avoids the inevitable cross-road. The bridge replaces the ford, a partial and fleeting victory of man over the obstacle created by water.

This victory is complete when the road becomes a bridge: it overcomes the obstacle and unites the two opposite "banks" creating a visual continuity that conquers the fracture that fades into oblivion. Giorgio de Chirico uses a strong poetic image to attribute the Romans' predilection for the arch to the desire for infinity that man experiences when observing the heavens: "A Rome le sens du présage est quelque chose de plus vaste. Une sensation de grandeur infinie et lointaine, la même sensation que le constructeur romain fixa dans le sentiment de l'arcade reflet du spasme d'infini que la couche célestielle produit quelquefois sur l'homme. Souvent le présage y était terrible comme l'hurlement d'un dieu qui meurt. Des nuages noirs devraient s'approcher jusque sur les tours de la ville."[8]

It is the bridge that reveals the river's mobile nature, its current flowing only in one direction. When a man bends over the bridge to watch the current, his eyes are almost dragged downstream, his imagination racing towards a distant source or river mouth. He feels as if he is stranded in the middle, in the heart of movement, of continuously mutant movement.

After a few minutes the water he is watching is no longer the same water. The bridge is therefore the archetype of the conflict between being and becoming.

Since our bodies can become bridges at any time, the matrix of the bridge is anthropomorphic: for example, crossing a river small enough to be stepped over or shaking hands in a symbolic relationship between two living beings. In ancient Egypt, the vault of heaven was symbolised by a God with an arched body.[9]

The terms used in association with the bridge betray its anthropomorphic origin: the bridge has "shoulders," "brains" and "loins." Each bridge has its own "parapet" allowing us to lean out into space, a wall that is just the right height to stop us from falling: it needs to contact and appease our bodies.

For Hölderlin, Heidelberg is the city of the bridge:

Like a bird flying beyond the peaks
the bridge light and strong busy
with men and carts leaps beyond
the great river glitters alongside.

An enchantment sent by the Gods
enchained me upon crossing the bridge
once and on the mountains
I discerned calls of distance,

*The covered glass tube corridor in the offices of the Johnson Wax company in Racine (Wisconsin) by Frank Lloyd Wright, 1951.*

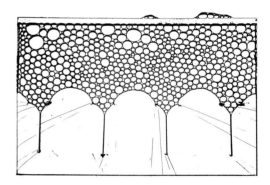

*Experimental model to verify the origin of the trefoil arch (Frei Otto).*

while the young river fled
to the plains, happy in its sadness,
like a heart that in self too beautiful
throws itself loving into the tide of time.[10]

The symbolic attraction of the bridge seduced even Goethe who in *Marchen*, written in 1795, tells the story of a snake that eventually turned into a spectacular bridge: "In all that solemnity, happiness and enthusiasm, no-one noticed that it was now morning and through the open door something completely unexpected caught their attention. A big square surrounded by columns acted as a hallway. At the end of the hallway the numerous arches of a long magnificent bridge spanned the river; on the two sides of the bridge there were rows of beautiful porticoes for travellers who had already gathered in their thousands, walking to and fro. The road running down the middle of the bridge was bustling with herds of sheep and mules, horsemen and carriages flowing like a river, up and down, without getting in each other's way. 'Honour the snake's memory' said the keeper of the lamp, 'you owe him your life, your citizens owe him the bridge, thanks to the bridge these two banks have for the first time been turned into a sole, animated district.' Those shiny floating gems, the remains of its sacrificed body, are the pillars of this miraculous bridge, upon which it has risen of its own accord and of its own accord will remain."[11]

*The bridge in Heidelberg seen from the banks of the Neckar.*

Goethe generally considered the snake a symbol of friendship and dialogue, but the image of the "transparent and luminous" snake that turns into a bridge flanked by porticoes, like the Rialto bridge designed by Palladio, in itself contains the mystical architectural marriage between Palladio and Bernini as well as the anticipation of a profound and mutual analogy. Bridge and snake share linearity, dynamism and the repetition of structure: bridge and dialogue share connection, the dual two-directional movement that makes one out of two. In Goethe's *Fairytale*, the snake coils around the remote, proposing the symbol of eternity, the *ouroburos*, but Goethe also sees something else: "The snake turns into a symbol of eternity, its coils taking the shape of a circle. Instead, I like to consider this an allegory of fortuitous chance. What more can man wish for than being allowed to join the end to the beginning, something that only takes place through lasting affection, trust, love and friendship."[12]

A suspended bridge over the river Apurimac (built using the Inca technique), Peru. Every year, during the celebration of a ritual festivity the bridge is rebuilt using the same type of plant fibres.

[1] cf., E.O. Wilson, *La società degli insetti*, Einaudi, Turin 1976, p. 430, figs. 11, 6, 21 (*Insect Society*, Cambridge (Mass.) 1971). Fig. 4.24 also shows a living bridge made of the bodies of ants hooked together using their tarsal claws. Cf., also in J.L. Gould and C. Grant Gould, *The Animal Mind*, Scientific American Library, New York 1994, fig. on page 117.
[2] cf., A.G.B. Wage, *Mycenae. An Archeological History and Guide*, Princeton University Press, Princeton 1949.
[3] cf., *La Grande Roma dei Tarquini*, catalogue of the exhibition, L'Erma, Rome 1981.
[4] *Ibidem*.
[5] cf., M. Allaby, *Animal Artisans*, Knopf, New York 1982 for the best images and complete history of the gardens of Bower Birds. For the various forms of "furnishings" see H. Cronin, *The Ant and the Peacock: altruism and sexual selection from Darwin to today*, Cambridge University Press, Cambridge-New York 1991 and M. Anderson, *Sexual Selection*, Princeton University Press, Princeton 1994.
[6] cf., B. Rudofsky, *Architecture Without Architects*, The Museum of Modern Art, New York 1965.
[7] cf., Gaudí-Groep Delft, *Gaudí Rationalist*, Delftse Universitaire Press, Delft 1989.
[8] cf., G. de Chirico, *Il meccanismo del pensiero*, Einaudi, Turin 1985, p. 23.
[9] cf., L. Luzzatto, R. Pompas, *Il significato dei colori nelle civiltà antiche*, Rusconi, Milan 1988.
[10] cf., F. Hölderlin, *Le liriche*, Adelphi, Milan 1989, p. 324.
[11] cf., J.W. Goethe, *Favola*, Adelphi, Milan 1990; with an essay by K. Mommsen.
[12] Goethe was referring in particular to his friendship with Schiller; this is the most reliable interpretative key for the book *Favola*, cf., the essay by K. Mommsen, *cit*.

# The Door, the Window, the Light

*The lamp of the body is the eye. It follows that if your eye is sound, your whole body will be filled with light. But if your eye is diseased, your whole body will be all darkness. If then, the light inside is darkness, what darkness that will be.*

Matthew 6, 22-23

Even before man became the builder of artificial spaces, it was the door that demolished barriers. It created openings that permitted access to hospitable territory and the use of the innumerable cavities nature placed at the disposal of primitive man. Man could use them either to flee the "fury of the elements" or – as a projection of the maternal womb – to search for mystery and theophany. Thus having identified the environmental conditions necessary to sustain life, man could use the earth to recreate them whenever they disappeared.

It is very likely that this strong sense of the perception of space did indeed inspire one of the first processes of identification between the human body and the elements of nature. When we walk through a door, there is a fleeting moment in which our bodies actually satisfy their desire. If the opening is too small, either our bodies adapt to the size of the hole by bending down or else we use our hands or tools to make it the right size. Going through a door our feet step across an ideal line that separates what is inside from what is outside. This is the threshold, a concept rather than an object, or perhaps a concept that man turns into an object when he becomes a builder.

Nature had already fashioned many doors before man introduced them into his myths. Natural arches are dotted all over the world's mountain ranges. The Indians named one in particular "Navaho Window." This was a symbolic door leading to the land owned by the tribe, a land that existed long before it was claimed by man. Moreover, the Navaho still worship some rock "monuments" as part of their cultural identity. Now part of Monument Valley, the Navaho called their capital Window Rock. Under this rock stood their Parliament (the Stone Room, lit by an eye similar to that of the Pantheon), the Rainbow Bridge, and the Spider Rock associated with the myth of the spider women.[1] For man the builder, the door comes after the wall. In fact it comes immediately after the wall since its function is to interrupt continuity. The wall is used to restrict and close, while the door is a passageway, a reopening after closure, a way to overcome the limits of what has been built and to access that which divides, that which acts as a limit and a boundary.

In the Roman Forum, one of the most symbolically significant buildings was the temple of Janus, the *Ianus Geminus*, a rectangular sacellum covered in bronze. We know about this building thanks to a schematic image engraved on a coin from the reign of Nero. The two façades were in fact two large doors, temple and doors being therefore one and the same. It is a well known fact that the doors were kept closed during peace time and left open when war raged. For this reason the sacellum was considered the mystical door of Rome, left open during the war to await the return of the warriors.[2] The figure of Janus incarnates the architectural concept of the door and this personification permits the door to take on multiple meanings transcending pure matter. But the Romans needed to reify the god in either a two-faced or four-faced door in order to take possession of a pre-existent architectural model and consecrate it anew. In fact, Rykwert believes that the myth of Janus could possibly contain other Indo-European and

Mediterranean mythologies. "Bridge or door, dawn of the day, month or year, it represents only special or determined cases of the 'beginning' or the passing personified by the god."[3] Initially created as a flaw in walls that surround and separate, the door entered the realm of ideas as pure spatial or temporal transience, and by loosing its specificity combined with a thousand other ideas to become a symbol. This is why we can speak of the door of the heavens, the door of the ocean and the door of folly and wisdom.

In nature, the symbolic potential of the door concept involves numerous perceptive situations: a valley entrance (using toponyms such as "valley closure," "narrowing"), natural mountain passes, the paths caused by natural events, the "cols" typical of mountain ranges, certain areas with forest glades and more in general any place that combines different environmental realities.

The idea of a natural door relates not only to space, but also to time, and some civilisations consider solstices and equinoxes the doors of the seasons. An excellent example is the aforementioned Janus. He is a two-faced god with one head and two faces, one old and one young. The two faces look in opposite directions and will never be able to see each other and are therefore excellent symbols of the past and the future. If in order to fully comprehend the archetype of the door the human body needs to have two divinised faces, it is also true that it possesses a number of "doors" charged with symbolic potential: the mouth as the door of the word, the eyes as the door of what is visible and of light, the ears

*The Navaho window,* Tse bi gha ho dzahi, *Canyon de Chelly National Monument, Arizona. Below: near the Navaho capital, another example of the natural arches the tribe consider sacred.*

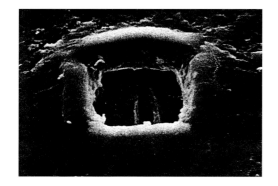

as doors of the universe of sound, as well as the doors of male and female fertility and the door of cleansing and purification. By observing his own body as he observes landscape, man acquires the wisdom of an archetype which he will transfer into the art of construction through its institutionalisation.

Apart from acting as a passageway, glorified in the boundary walls of cities, the door rapidly acquires purely symbolic importance as, for instance, in the Egyptian doors of death. As a boundary between distant and incomparable worlds their multiple frames are like echoes that whisper of an immaterial and fathomless depth. Often these symbolic doors can be found in natural landscapes that evoke immaterial walls invisible to the eye. Examples are the Door of the Sun in Tiahuanaco on Lake Titicaca in Bolivia, or the door to the Sendang Duwar mosque in Java,[4] built to squint through towards the bright sun on certain days and at specific times marking the cycle of the solar calendar and the passing of the seasons. Another type of portal stands on the bigger of the two rocks tied to one another by a long rope in Ise, Japan. The rocks symbolise the male and female concept, myths of the eternal bond between the divine couple. It is at the beach at Futamigenza that the Shinto faithful, on the first day of the new year, wait for the sun to rise, framed by the sacred door considered a universal symbol of immortality. Not far from this spot is the grotto from which Amaterasu, the sun god, rose to illuminate the world with the light of salvation.

*The "Lion's door" in Mycenae and, above, microphotograph of the stoma of the* Aloe magalacantha pubescens. *In botany, the stoma is the opening in the skin that permits gaseous exchanges and transpiration.*

196

There are numerous variations on the theme of the door: open, closed, half-open, seen from the inside or the outside, in darkness or light. It represents one of the most fascinating metaphors of the universe and of life and was quite rightly cast in a masterpiece of figurative art, Bresson's film *Au hasard Balthasar*, in which the door played the feature role. "Balthasar's characters," wrote Michel Cournot, "pass most of their time opening and closing doors, passing through and passing back. If one is even slightly sensitive to transcendence it is easy to realise that a door is not merely an opening in a wall, or just planks of wood rotating on hinges. Open or closed, locked or slamming, without totally changing its nature a door is either present or absent, a reference or a defence, depth or blind plane, innocence or mistake. Take for example a closed door: a person off screen approaches; we just catch sight of his shadow through the door, when he pushes it and disappears: a presence, a split second, an intention, all these are depicted as an understatement, rendered by the camera by using a simple moving surface. In Bresson's mind, universal means ecumenical: and there is no better ecumenical image of the immanence of life than a door that opens and closes: this way, a door can be significant without being decadent."[5]

The door involves a "threshold," a strip of earth that is trodden on when either entering or exiting, quickly materialising as a stone slab. The threshold concept not only sets a limit, but tends to mark more of a pause, an interval, like a moment when the present stands between the past and the future but has its own, almost imperceptible, duration. On the threshold of the cave, man hesitated between dark and light and sensed the two worlds that seemed to caress each other without actually touching.

In the ninth of his *Duino Elegies,* Rilke described the secret meaning of the threshold, indicating that its sacredness lies in the fact that when it is continually crossed an archetypal act is repeated (like sacred time eternally repeated):

*The temple of Janus (Rome) and the image of two-faced Janus on a coin from the reign of Nero.*

> Threshold: what it means
> to two lovers that they too
> should be wearing down an old doorsill
> a bit more after the many
> before them and before
> the many to come ... lightly.[6]

In his book *Der Chinese des Schmerzers*, Peter Handke seriously contemplates the dual concept of the door-threshold: "I am the door. Whoever enters through me will be saved." For most people, therefore, thresholds represent passing from one environment to another. To a certain extent perhaps we are unaware that the threshold is a separate environment, a special place of trial and protection. Isn't the pigsty in which Jacob sat in such miserable conditions a sort of trial threshold? In the past, didn't escapees prostrate themselves on thresholds asking for protection? Doesn't the ancient word *pronaos* describe the threshold as a resting place? Modern science, however, no longer attributes this meaning to the word threshold. The only thresh-

old that remains, according to a master of modern philosophy, is the one between waking and sleeping and even that is hardly perceptible. Only madmen express it clearly, for all to see, in the middle of everyday events, like the fragments of their destroyed temple. The word threshold does not mean boundary at all – since this would spread inwards and outwards – it means area. The word "threshold" contains movement, tides, fords, mountain passes, fences (in the sense of shelters). "A threshold is a source," according to an almost obsolete manner of speech.

This is the context in which Handke examines the relationship between an architectural term and the numerous meanings it has acquired over the years in our civilisation, meanings which clearly show how our language still has profound traces of its natural and pastoral roots. Perhaps one should point out how this linguistic wealth currently lacks a comparable architectural equivalent. How many contemporary architectures have a threshold that is something more than just a stone slab or a prefabricated cement block? Its context and shape make it incapable of transmitting the wealth of its archetype: paraphrasing Heidegger, one could say it is an object that "expresses" nothing, a mute word, a sterile sign, eternally waiting to regain its lost meaning.

In nature, cave openings and certain fissures in rock faces that reveal the blue sky above, prefigure the window as a lookout, as a hole through which light penetrates. A typical example is the window in Monserrat near Barcelona, reproduced by Gaudí at the top of Casa Batlló.

*Mycenae, entrance to the tholos housing Atreus' treasure (13th century B.C.) and, above, entry portal to the Katsura Imperial Villa, Kyoto (17th century).*

The word lookout comes from the identification process between the building and the human body and it is this identification that must be studied in order to discover the natural genesis of the window as the framework of the human figure, a place of outward appearances that does not cross internal limits.

Rilke asks himself in a poem of *Windows:*

Aren't you our geometry,
window, very simple shape
circumscribing our enormous
life painlessly?
A lover's never so beautiful
as when we see her appear
framed by you; because, window,
you make her almost immortal.
All risks are cancelled. Being
stands at love's center,
with this narrow space around,
where we are master.[7]

The idea of the window as a restrictive form, an encapsulating structure that freezes the fleeting moment, can be traced back to the concept of "frame," to whatever in nature encloses the human figure and to what, in virtue of the ensu-

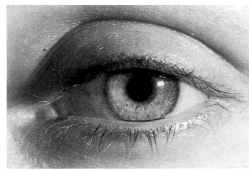

*Rocky opening showing the sky beyond, Capitol Reef, Utah; the human eye as the "door of light."*

ing harmony, separates a specific part from the overall scenario, a sort of "backdrop" or "halo" or "aura" in the literal sense of the word.

To interpret the window as a frame or as a natural casing is the key to underlining the importance of the decorations that were also called window "frames," garlanded frames, aedicules, small temples, miniature architecture or miniature landscapes. In western culture, window frames are the crystallisation of temporary party ornaments: leafs, flowers, festoons and shells live forever in the architectural image, branded with regret for Paradise lost.

The window is but a "daughter" of the door and like all children eventually leaves the maternal nest, duplicating its parent and inheriting certain characteristics. It does, however, find its own identity by developing some of these traits together with any new ones that might emerge. The door permits penetration and passage, but also introduces light and air beyond the barrier in which it has created the opening. On the other hand, even though it is impossible to pass through a window, there is a view, an interrupted passage or a so-called petrified passage that coincides with the magical moment in which we cross the threshold. This is the reason why the window also represents a threshold ready to come into contact with our hands and elbows. It does not require a transient movement but a "staying" movement, it requires observation, illumination and taking "deep breaths" in the open air. The window is the boundary between open-air and closed-air, between light and shadow, inside and out, but, unlike the door, it

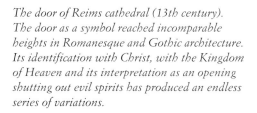

*The door of Reims cathedral (13th century). The door as a symbol reached incomparable heights in Romanesque and Gothic architecture. Its identification with Christ, with the Kingdom of Heaven and its interpretation as an opening shutting out evil spirits has produced an endless series of variations.*

is a limit that cannot be crossed. To jump from a window means to break a spell, violate a norm. What was secondary for the door, illumination and aeration, is vitally important for the window since it represents the chief means of lighting in internal spaces and more importantly, is one of the most significant and valued elements of the architectural image when considered as a work of art.

This lighting criterion is certainly one aspect of typology that is adopted passively, but good architects often tackle it in a novel fashion, demonstrating the enormous importance they attribute to this "subtle" aspect of design.

*The "wedded rocks" in Futami-ga-ura near Ise. The bigger island has a sacred door. According to Shinto tradition, the two little islands symbolise man and woman and for this reason are joined by sacred ropes.*

Among other things, design also – if not always – means to envisage, to understand, in one's own mind and through one's own drawings, what the building will look like and the feelings it will inspire in the onlooker. As far as lighting is concerned, this "forecast" is much more difficult than it is for stability, functionality or acoustics, that remain unaltered all through the day and for which it is easier to establish rules. To forecast the quality of light, albeit in quantitative terms of "illumination technique," not only depends on measurable factors but on complex relationships that can only intuitively and analogically be evaluated.

In every internal space, for example, luminosity depends on the relationship between the incident light we see coming directly from the window and reflected light that follows a much more complex route, for instance, in a room full of mirrors. In fact, the light reflected in a room is the sum total of an infinitely vast number of rays that combine and merge depending on the type of materials used and the colour, tone or inclination of the surfaces.

In prehistoric architecture, as in primitive cultures, no rules governed the window since it was considered similar to a door. However, the window as such first appeared in the temples and model houses of ancient Eastern architecture. Nevertheless, before being turned by Rilke into a place of observation, frame of the human body and element combining the interior and exterior of the house, the window qualified as a source of light, an instrument of differentiation between light and dark in the structure of internal space. In this context, the window allows the architect to incorporate in his work the effects of light on natural surroundings: the blinding force of the sun that penetrates the leaves and tree trunks in a forest, the feeling of unlimited depth that a shaft of light produces in a valley, the contrast between dark and light areas of a cave when light enters from other openings in the vault or rock face in addition to the entrance. The window-frame is a vertical rectangle that "encases" all or part of the image. Its three functions are to provide light, air and a view of the outside world and the remarkable combination of all three has decreed its permanence and extreme variability. Often treated separately, in this century these three functions have caused a proliferation of forms and effects which has led to a certain dispersion, especially in recent years, when the exaggerated tendency towards analysis stripped windows of every and any symbolic connotation.

*The window consecrated to the Virgin Mary in the Monserrat mountains near Barcelona. Antoni Gaudí reproduced this opening in the roof of Casa Batlló in Barcelona.*

The window as a source of light has been used over the centuries as a way to immaterially divide internal spaces into contrasting areas: an illuminated space

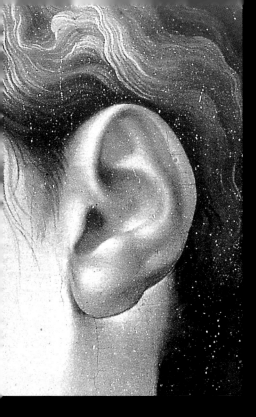

The window and door anthropomorphically interpreted as the house's mouths, ears and eyes. Above, from top to bottom: a woman's ear from a drawing by Sandro Botticelli; a tufa mascaron with a banqueting room inside, located in Vicino Orsini's "Sacred Wood" in Bomarzo (16th century); a window of Palazzo Zuccari in Via Gregoriana, Rome; oculus in the church of Santa Maria al Pian Calcinaio, Cortona (Francesco di Giorgio Martini, 15th century); oculus in the church of San Francesco in Ouro Preto (Alejadino, 18th century).

Opposite page: the weather, personal taste and building materials are all expressed in the window, which in turn characterises the site. A wooden partition wall in a house in Tokyo. The same system dividing internal and external space in São Paulo (Brazil).
Below: a double sliding window in Oslo and a glass window with little curtains in Goslar (Germany).

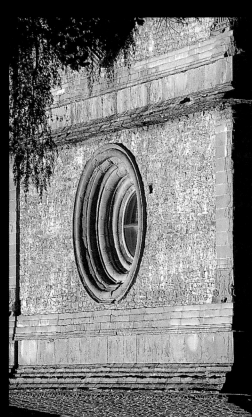

*A window with a decorated wooden frame, a small balcony with a wrought iron railing and lateral supports for an awning, also made of wrought iron. The window thus becomes a projection of internal space towards the road below.*

with clearly defined geometrical boundaries (the luminous cone) and a residual area created by the wall involucre. This contrasts the former like a box within a box or one transparent volume inside another and may be perceived to a greater or lesser degree according to the intensity of the contrast. In theatrical terms this type of lighting is called "bull's eye," a word used for artificial light that provides a truncated conical shaft of light, since the cone of light always intersects with a plane.

These windows were used to obtain a sort of materialisation of the sun's luminous disk and perhaps initially played a role associated with the cult of the sun or else linked to the hours of the day or the seasons.[8] In this context, the *yurta* is an important archetype. Of ancient origin, it is the house of the nomad tribes of central Asia that can be dismantled and transported. The *yurta* has a cylindrical base and a conic roof characterised by a central hole surrounded by a coping, a double ring and a convergent series of thick branches woven in the shape of a square mesh. The central hole functions as a source of light and fresh air, as well as a ventilator for the smoke from the fire below. The size of the cylinder base varies from 5 to 10 meters, the inner space always being organised in such a way as to create dedicated areas in strict observance of a hierarchy in which the guest occupies the place of honour, the "sacred" space. It is easy to recognise the symbolic significance of an opening that allows the sky to be seen from a dark interior, exerting a sort of mysterious attraction on the fire and smoke of the hearth. The ray of light and column of smoke materialise the *axis mundi*, the immaterial tree of life, expression of the central role of the house in the world and therefore of the mystery of a sacred pluricentrality, implicit in the existence of men who believed in the same philosophy or creed.

Emperor Hadrian, who in his lifetime designed at least one building, the temple of Venus in Rome, might have been inspired by the cosmological implications of the *yurta* model when he rebuilt the Pantheon by Agrippa. If this is so, Hadrian anticipated the nostalgic reappropriation of his travel memories that culminated in the construction of his Villa in Tivoli. In this context, the words written by Marguerite Yourcenar in her book, *Memoirs of Hadrian,* are extremely interesting:[9] "In the same day, with graver solemnity, as if muted, a dedicatory ceremony took place inside the Pantheon. I myself had revised its architectural plans, drawn with too little daring by Apollodorus: utilising the arts of Greece only as an ornament, like an added luxury, I had gone back to the basic form of the structure to the primitive fabled times of Rome and to the round temples of ancient Etruria. My intention had been that the sanctuary of All Gods should reproduce the likeness of the terrestrial globe and of the stellar sphere, that globe wherein are enclosed the seeds of eternal fire, and that hollow sphere containing all. Such was also the form of our ancestors' huts where the smoke of man's earliest hearths escaped through an opening at the top. The cupola, constructed of hard yet lightweight volcanic stone, which seemed still to share in the upward movement of flames, revealed the sky through a great hole in the centre,

*The oculus at the top of the Pantheon in Rome (1st century B.C.) and, below, light penetrating down into a natural cave (Gaeta, Località Fontania, the Devil's Well, Italy).*

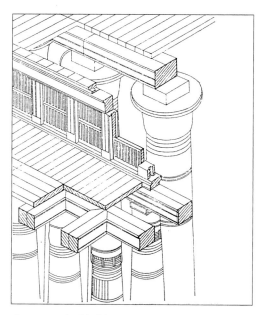

*Openings shielded by screens in the lighting system of the Aniun baths in Karnak (1570-1085 B.C.).*

showing alternately dark and blue. This temple, both open and mysteriously enclosed, was conceived as a solar quadrant. The hours would make their rounds on that caissoned ceiling, so carefully polished by Greek artisans; the disk of daylight would rest suspended there like a shield of gold; rain would form its clear pool on the pavement below; prayers would rise like smoke toward that void where we place the gods. This solemnity formed one of those moments when all things converge. Standing beside me in that well of daylight was my entire administrative staff; these men were the materials which composed my destiny, by then already more than half completed and in its maturity."

A window similar to the one in the Pantheon was designed by Le Corbusier for the church of the convent in Tourette (1952-1960). This is a sundial-window in which the ray of light changes with the seasons and at certain times of the day falls on the priest saying mass. The architect's inspiration for this directional light effect was very probably the oculus of the eastern façade of the Cistercian church in the convent at Le Thoronnet, designated by Father Regamey as the model of Cistercian spirituality.[10]

In Egyptian temples the light was filtered by high grated slits that provided very little illumination. This is in keeping with the temple's magical and evocative functions that considered internal space an interior space, gradually revealed through a process of "penetration" in which height and width gradually diminished until the cella inhabited by God was reached.

During the Middle Kingdom, a series of windows was created in the peripteral pavilion of King Sesostris I, a portico that opened outwards and had no cella. On the other hand, during the New Kingdom, the central nave of the temple was higher than the lateral naves and the lighting from its two-level roof followed an axial route similar to that of Roman basilicas. Subsequently, there was a revival of the system of inserting openings between the ceiling and the walls, showering speckled light on capitals and columns which appeared to emerge from the surrounding darkness as discontinuous apparitions.

Roman civilisation revealed itself to be particularly creative in the field of lighting, not only by doing justice to the complex architectural organisms created by the vault system, but also because it attached much importance to the window as an inspired link between internal spaces and landscape, between architecture and nature. The description by Pliny the Younger of his Laurentian villa contained in his *Letters* (II, 17) illustrates how landscape had become one of the main parameters of the environmental traits of the villa.[11]

"My villa is of a convenient size without being expensive to keep up. The courtyard in front is plain, but not mean, through which you enter porticoes shaped into the form of the letter D, enclosing a small but cheerful area between. These make a capital retreat for bad weather, not only as they are shut in with windows, but particularly as they are sheltered by a projection of the roof. From the middle of these porticoes you pass into a bright pleasant inner court, and out of that into a handsome hall running out towards the sea-shore; so that when there is a south-west breeze, it is gently washed with the waves, which spend themselves at its base. On every side of this hall, there are either folding-doors or windows equally large, by which means you have a view from the front and the two sides of the three different seas, as it were: from the back you see the middle court, the portico and the area; and from another point you look through the portico into the courtyard, and out upon the woods and distant mountains beyond. On the left of this hall, a little farther from the sea, lies a large drawing-room, and beyond that, a second of a smaller size which has one window to the rising and another to the setting sun: this as well has a view of the sea, but more distant and agreeable. The angle formed by the projection of the dining-room of this drawing-room retains and intensifies the warmth of the sun, and this forms our winter quarters and family gymnasium, which is sheltered from all the winds except those which bring on clouds, but the clear sky comes out again before the warmth has gone out of the place, and adjoining this angle is a bed-room forming the segment of a circle, the windows of which are so arranged as to get the sun all through the day [...].

"From thence you go up a sort of turret which has two rooms below, with the same number above, besides a dining-room commanding a very extensive lookout on to the sea, the coast, and the beautiful villas scattered along the shoreline. At the other end is a second turret, containing a room that gets the rising and setting sun. Behind this is a large store-room and granary, and underneath, a spacious dining-room, where only the murmur and break of the sea can be heard, even in a storm: it looks out upon the garden, and the *gestatio* running round the garden [...]. At the upper end of the terrace and portico stands a detached garden building, which I call my *favourite*; my *favourite* indeed, as I put it up myself. It contains a very warm winter-room, one side of which looks down upon the terrace, while the other has a view of the sea and both lie exposed to the sun. The bedroom opens onto the covered portico by means of folding-doors, while its windows look out upon the sea. On that side next the sea, and facing the middle wall, is formed a very elegant little recess, which, by means of transparent windows and a curtain drawn to or aside, can be made part of the adjoining room, or separated from it. It contains a couch and two chairs: as you lie upon the couch, from where your feet are you get a peep of the sea; looking behind you see the neighbouring villas, and from the head you have a view of the woods: these three views may be seen either separately, from so many different windows, or blended together in one."

From a simple opening for air and light the window was transformed into a frame for the surrounding landscape, a link between artificial space and natural scenery: this link was simultaneously static and dynamic, since the landscape can be viewed either from one fixed point, almost like a wall painting or it can be considered a luminous continuum that the various windows either conceal or reveal in what could be called rhythmic perception. This was how peristyles and temple porticoes were transferred to the house, giving them a contemplative dimension.

In the vaulted organisms of Roman architecture, light sources were located near the ceiling; their function was to underline the architectural frame since they were situated below the massive covering arches, a point in which a solid wall would hinder the proper appreciation of this daring structure. This situation led to the creation of the semicircular window apparently inspired by the first light of dawn, focusing on the sun and circumscribed by the earth's horizon.

In the basilicas of Christianity light penetrates discreetly from above the central nave, but in certain 5th-century buildings, such as the Roman church of Santa Sabina, the windows are a little wider than usual and the translucent selenite transforms them into sources of silver, almost lunar light: "*Quoniam apud te*," recites the Psalm (35,10) "*est fons vitae: et in lumine tuo videbimus lumen.*"

Luminous ecstasy, the essential characteristic of so much Late Gothic architecture has two characteristics: it is a spin-off of a building technique used to dematerialise the wall, making it thinner, and it increases the number of light sources. This process can be seen in all its glory in the cathedral of Hagia Sophia in Istanbul. The volume so skilfully created by the "mechanics" Isidorus of Miletus and Anthemius of Tralles, is bathed in light like a large woven basket. At certain times of the day myriad holes transform the wall into a screen pierced by light rays which, in combination with the glow of the nearby windows, create the illusion of a translucent involucre. The cupola itself boldly rests on a continuous shaft of light from a row of small windows that appear to hoist it skywards like a translucent disk. The idea of "fusion" in which light and matter, dust and colour, combine and converge to form a spatial fluid irradiating from a central point personifies the birth of a culture in which the intuitions of Plotinus and Longinus are reified. Beauty, as the expression of transcendence that elevates the spirit towards the divine, initiates a spiritual process ending in ecstasy in which the most spectacular and striking revelations of nature itself are interpreted in terms of transcendence. It is not by chance that this culture initiated "scenography" as a way to teach artists how to ensure that nothing in their work be distorted by distance or height.

In the sixth *Ennead*, Plotinus describes material beauty as the irradiated symmetry of life, a symmetry of movement and in movement, in contrast to absolute symmetry that is absence of life. The centrality of Hagia Sophia is simultaneously affirmed and denied, resolved in the perceptive vibration produced by the dilation and contraction inherent in the role of the walls along the two orthogonal axes. Another example of Byzantine passion for light is the Archbishop's chapel in Ravenna bearing the following inscription: "*Aut lux hic nata est, aut capta hic libera regnat.*"

The negation of mechanical symmetry and the glorification of motivated irregularities is magnificently and fully expressed in certain Croatian architectures of the early Middle Ages, currently being studied by Mladen Pejaković who attributes the cause of these intentional deformations of type to a specific desire to conform the architectural structure to a series of astronomical data in order to

View of the church of Hagia Sophia in Istanbul. The distribution of light sources in the impost of the vaults and the cupola, in the apses and along the walls that laterally compress space, together with the reflecting surfaces of the original mosaics, all contribute to completely dematerialising the wall according to Plotinus' ideals.
In the first part of the Enneads Plotinus writes: "How can the corporate be in accord with what is superior to the body? Tell me how can an architect, after having adapted a house's outer shape to its inner form, call it beautiful? The reason lies in the fact that, apart from the stones themselves, the outer trappings are merely its inner shape, fashioned, yes, into an external material mass, but existent, indivisible, even if contained in multiplicity [...]."
"The beauty of colour is simple; it depends on shape and the triumph of light – incorporate reality, reason, idea – over the darkness of matter. Therefore, more than any other body, it possesses its own beauty, fire; since, compared to all other elements, it is like an idea: in fact, its position is sublime; meek among others; almost to the limits of incorporate nature; it alone does not gather others to itself, while others instead do; in fact, they are warmed by contact with it, while it never cools."

209

*Church of the Holy Cross in Nona (Split). The outer perimeter is positioned according to the direction of the sun's rays on the horizon in the morning, at midday and in the evening. The windows are asymmetrical and rotated to permit the sun's rays to be projected towards certain points inside the building. Here, a regular plan is modified to such an extent that the geographical relationship with a site takes on a particularly profound meaning.*

*Right: the plan of the same church aligned according to the position of the sun on the horizon during the year and rotated based on local geographical and astronomical conditions.*

use the light from specially positioned windows to underline the cyclical value of time during certain sacred and seasonal celebrations.

The beautiful little church of the Holy Cross in Nona, between Pula and Split, is a snow-white cruciform building. Its simple form betrays a complex program that transforms it into a sort of stone calendar. "The linear structure," writes Pejakovič, "of the external plan of the small Holy Cross church is organised according to the spatial and temporal positions of the sun's rays. The plan is encapsulated, so to speak, in the network created by the pattern of the different directions of the sun's rays on each important day of the year. [...] The irregularities depend on the rule, while deviation depends on the inclination. The rule is abandoned only to be revived with greater precision, lost only to be found."[12]

This is also true for the hexalobated church of the Holy Trinity in Poljud, near Split, misshapen in order to adjust to angles of the sun's inclination on the horizon. The apse and its window are built so that the first ray of the sun on the seventh of May, the feast-day of Saint Doimo, is perpendicular to the step of the presbytery (*septum*). The windows of the two lateral apses, rather than being in the centre are carved out of the wall so that sunlight falls vertically to the side of the presbytery step. The position of the front of the step (coinciding with the transversal axis of the basic hexagon) determined the way in which the church was oriented. A number of different lighting details, each one conceived for special days in the liturgical calendar (Christmas, the feast of Saint John), con-

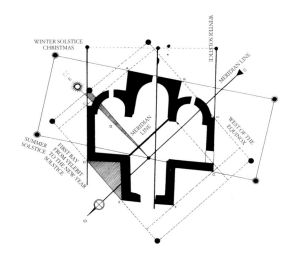

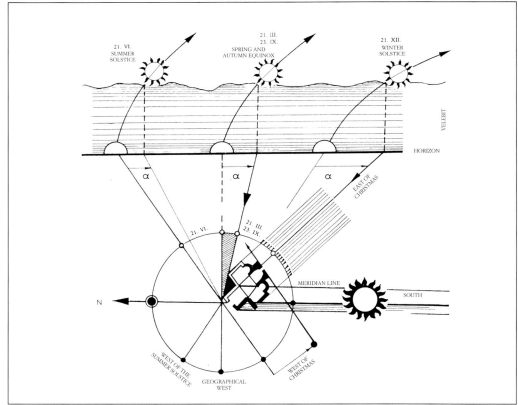

210

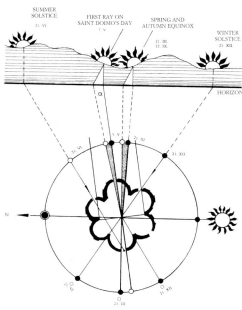

*Above: layout of the centrally-planned church of the Holy Trinity in Poljud. Diagram of the geographical and astronomical conditions of the area. The windows face east towards the first rays of the sun on the feast day of Saint Doimo, May 7th.*

*Above left: windows in the Topkapy Palace, Istanbul. Receptacles with running water replace the windowsills of the lower windows, while light shines dimly through the stained glass windows above.*

*Left: on the saint's feast day light shines on the church in Elrn through a hole in the mountains in the Bernese Alps.*

*Sunlit oculus in the church of the charterhouse in Le Thoronnet (11th century).*

*Light falling on the altar of the church of the La Tourette convent in Éveux, 1957-60. When designing La Tourette, Le Corbusier visited Le Thoronnet with Father Regamey; this visit left a lasting impression on the architect.*

*Opposite page: the point where the transept crosses the main nave in Amiens cathedral (Robert de Luzarches, 13th century).*

tributed to making the faithful feel that the small church was similar to a measuring instrument, gentle and submissive compared to the path of the sun and in tune with the grand rhythm of sacred rites.

The window as an opening through which light penetrates, conquering the encirclement of matter, denouncing its diversity, its immaterial essence, is a frequent occurrence in Romanesque architecture, where contrast reign supreme and *humanitas* is primarily considered inferior to divine perfection. The circular window of the convent church in Le Thoronnet inspired Le Corbusier to design the square slit of the convent church in Tourette. It represents a characteristic ray of divine illumination touching upon man in solitude, dispersing the shadows that surround and besiege him.

On the other hand, Gothic light, caught "at the nascent stage," in the apse of Saint Denis, represents collective illumination, the irruption of sacredness into social life, laically reorganised under the banner of hope.

The builder of the choir of Saint Denis, Abbé Suger, discovered the idea of the centrality of light, in the relationship between God and man, in the writings of Dionysius the Aeropagite, then considered to be Saint Denis himself, apostle from Gaul.

The *De Caelesti Hierarchia* by the pseudo-Dionysius and its critique by Sedulius Scotus gave the abbot of Saint Denis the cue he needed to re-evaluate matter and sensorial reality in the religious experience. "Every creature, visible or invisible, is a light brought into being by the Father of lights [...]. That stone or that piece of wood is a light to me [...]. For I perceive that it is good and beautiful; that it exists according to its proper rules of proportion; that it differs in kind and species from other kinds and species; that it is defined by its number, by virtue of which it is 'one' thing; that it does not transgress its order; that it seeks its place according to its specific gravity. As I perceive such and similar things in this stone they become lights to me, that is to say, they enlighten (*me illuminant*). For I begin to think whence the stone is invested with such properties [...] and soon, under the guidance of reason, I am led through all things to that cause of all things which endows them with place and order, with number, species and kind, with goodness and beauty and essence, and with all other grants and gifts."[13]

If light is the *medium* through which to climb from the nature of pure matter to the experience of the divine, light can also conquer the house of God and triumph over the inertia of the wall.

The window is no longer the opening that breaks the barrier between interior and exterior. Instead, it becomes the supporting structure that interrupts (as little as possible) the continuity of the translucent integument into which light dematerialises and then materialises into images. "Once the rear part is joined to the part in front," Suger writes in his impassioned way, "the church shines with its middle part brightened. For bright is that whence is brightly coupled with the bright, and bright is the noble edifice which is pervaded by the new light." And

212

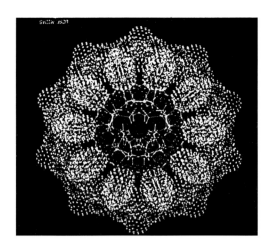

*From the top: the cut-away view of DNA with a stellar decagon; two drawings of Gothic rosettes, one in the north façade of the transept in Chartres, the other in the Sainte Chapelle.*

if the windows of the choir in Saint Denis speak of images and colour, the door is not content to be a symbolic means of communication but is enriched with a verbal caption: "Whoever thou art, if thou seekest to extol the glory of these doors, marvel not at the gold and the expense but at the craftsmanship of the work. Bright is the noble work; but, being nobly bright, the work should brighten the minds so that they travel, through the true lights, to the true light where Christ is the true door. In what manner, it be inherent in this world the golden door defines: the dull mind rises to truth through that which is material. And, in seeing this light, is resurrected from its former submersion."

If the window assumes the role of a transparent wall rising from the ground or from a low base, thereby turning light into the creative root of space, then it is the "rosette," or "wheel" as the builders originally called it, that best expresses the identity of the Gothic window as a place of permanent transformation of light into image, symbol and colour. Placed above façades and entrances, the rosette illuminates and qualifies the entry area like a concise prelude to later developments in naves and apses. Yet for those who enter and exit, it also acts as a point of visual attraction and deployment of meaning like the overlapping layers of a palimpsest: some are obvious and literal, some are identified only after careful and patient interpretation, while others are esoteric requiring true initiation.

The figurative theme of the rosette is therefore like the "opening" of a dissertation. Here the complexity and polyvalence of religious symbolism fans out in many different directions, just like the purely visual plane of kaleidoscopes that at each smallest movement reveal new symmetrical aggregations of elements, established from the beginning, but made unrecognisable by the geometrical forces of the unpredictable compositions that continue to be created. The subject matter of rosettes is linked mainly to the fundamental principles of the Christian faith: the Creation, the life of Christ, the Virgin Mary, Judgement Day and human and divine Wisdom. The symbolic implications are instead both varied and expressive. The first implication is the natural component: the rose as a flower in which centrality and radiality, multiplicity and unity are best identified and expressed; the star with its solar analogy and erupting radiality; ramification as a reference to the tree of life and, during the Late Gothic period, the flame which vibrantly and dynamically represented the geometric structure. No less important was the cosmic symbolism of the combination of the circle and the square, the structure of the wheel and concentric circles, the parallel coils of circular holes and the cruciform or square radials. In Lausanne, the theme of the Creation is combined with the twelve signs of the Zodiac, the four seasons, the four elements and the four rivers of Paradise, thereby enriching the *imago mundi* with a temporal reference between finite and infinite.

John Michell[14] has demonstrated the relationship between the rosette at Chartres and the geometric image of Heavenly Jerusalem as described in the New Testament (*Revelation* 21, 9 ff).

For a long time western culture considered the window to be subservient to

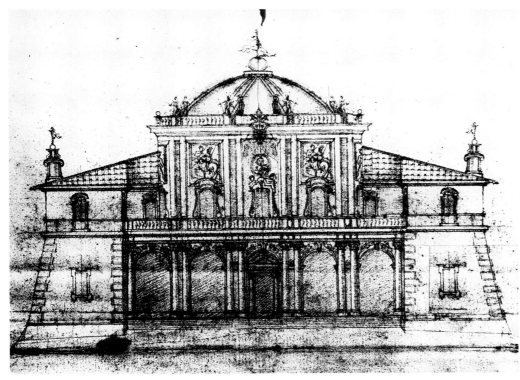

*Design of Villa Pamphili, Rome (Francesco Borromini c. 1645). Borromini considered the building a "study in practical mathematics," closely linked to the geographical and astronomical conditions of the site. It was possible to tell the time according to the shadows cast by the stairs, and every year a ray of sunlight shone through a hole in the roof onto the statue of Innocent X to mark the day and hour of his coronation as Pope.*

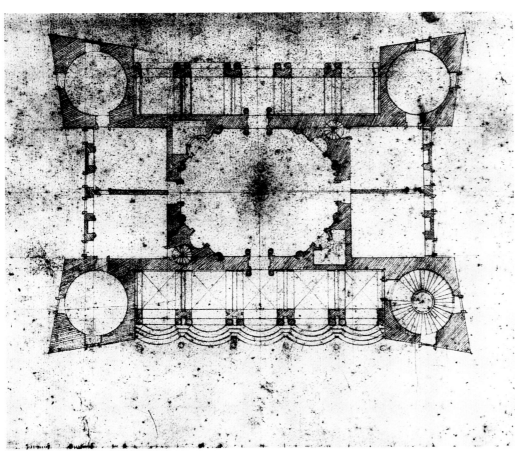

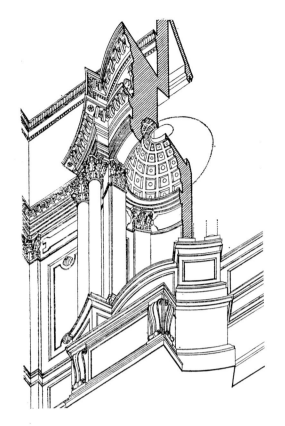

*Axonometric projection of the chapel of Santa Teresa in Santa Maria della Vittoria in Rome (Gianlorenzo Bernini, 1641) and the horizontal window placed by Francesco Borromini in a corridor of the Oratorio di San Filippo Neri in Rome (1637).*
*Right: the parish church in Weingarten, Bavaria. The three-level distribution of light scenographically amplifies the internal space so that the architectural order actually acts as theatre wings.*

the idea of "universal light," an instrument of diffuse and homogeneous light, capable of underlining both plastic and geometric qualities. However, on the basis of theatrical experiences at the beginning of the 17th century, a "Bernini-style" lighting method began to be used. This involved side lighting from a hidden source to illuminate sculptures and architecture. Envisaging "total performance," a sort of forerunner of Wagner's *Gesamtkunstwerk*, Bernini used side light, incident light and reflected light in the See of Saint Peter's and the chapel of Santa Teresa in Santa Maria della Vittoria in Rome. He exploited a subtle psychological trick that turns internal space into "distant space," in which the sacred image is projected into "space for meditated contemplation," in which false observers move into a "light-space": a luminous ray at times real at times materialised that joins these two spaces to the real space of the observer.

At a time when the luminosity *ad organum plenum* investigated by Bernini exalted the spectacular quality and sociality of ritual celebrations, Borromini came up with a totally different theory, aimed at internalising the luminous effect. This is the theory of the ray that is either guided (for example, in the chapel of Sant'Ivo where by using mirrors it strikes a point above the altar) or incessantly reflected in a "light box." Not only is this an impracticable space only partially perceived geometrically, but it also acts as a decompression chamber of the luminous fluid into which light is magically transformed: a light falling from above gently enveloping forms, a light that one could define as fermenting with

216

the shadows. Leonardo's *sfumato* enters architecture covering it in a velvety yet bone-like material, shaped by the mould and by the hand of man in order to exalt its transparency. The issue of guided light as a sign of harmonic correspondence between architecture and nature was also proposed by Francesco Borromini in a letter describing his project for Villa Pamphili.[15]

"My idea would be to erect a building of the size pleasing to your Eminence, where artifices and curiosities would suit both a small and large building whose shape should be massive with four towers, or bulwarks, on the four corners. Preferably the total number of windows along all sides of the building should be 32, namely nine windows for each main façade and seven on each side, totalling the said number 32. If an observer stood in the doorway of some of the rooms (whose size would be calculated accordingly) and looked out through these thirty-two windows, his eyes would be able to discern, on the horizon, the 32 directions from which the wind blows. From the window in the centre of one of the main façades, looking towards the protruding corners of the bulwarks, the observer's gaze would fall on the Tropic of Cancer on the one side and on the Tropic of Capricorn on the other. From the side windows, the observer would be able to see many other things that mathematicians teach us are in the heavens. In fact, the whole building should represent the practical application of mathematical laws: from the shadows made by the steps on the main staircase in front of the façade it should be possible to calculate the days of the month and the hours

*The effect of mirrors and incident light in the charterhouse in Granada (17th century) and the axonometric projection of one of the chapels in the church of Carmine, Turin (Filippo Juvarra, 1732-36).*

of the day, as far as this is feasible. A vault could be built in two circular rooms to the side of a loggia so as to create a heavenly Orbit upon which stars could be drawn, like the night sky. They could perhaps be drawn like the ones Nero drew on the Palatine, so that they rotated. Above all else, the statue of Pope Innocent should be placed so that on September 15 a ray of sunlight kiss the foot of the statue at the very hour of his election to the Papal See; this idea was used by the ancients and recorded by Baronio."

The ray of sunlight that should have kissed the base of the statue of Pope Innocent (Borromini's friend and patron) is influenced by classical precedents as well as by the so-called "astronomic" use of guided light frequently used in Christian architecture as I have already mentioned in relation to the Serbian churches of Nona and Poljud. However, the letter illustrates a building project in which the relationship between architecture and nature is clearly defined as a meeting of laws and unexpectedly gives credence to Alberti's idea of structural imitation. Borromini's light, the light of stars projected into luminous space, of mouldings that play with light to make it triumph in daring constructions of the mind, all echo Suger's thoughts when he admiringly contemplates the precious stones shining on the high altar in Saint Denis: "When – out of my delight in the beauty of the house of God – the loveliness of the many-coloured stones has called me away from external cares, and worthy meditation has induced me to reflect, transferring that which is material to that which is immaterial, on the diversity of the sacred virtues: then it seems to me then that I see myself dwelling, as it were, in some strange region of the universe which neither exists entirely in the slime of the earth and nor entirely in the purity of Heaven [...]."[16]

However, if for Suger the "strange region of the universe" requires the rare splendour of precious stones, on the contrary for Borromini the way to distance himself from the "slime of the earth" seems to be the monochrome vibration of light and the ideal "platonic" quality of its plant decorations, pale and eruptive, like wheat grown in the dark and used to adorn the "Sepulchres" of Holy Week.

If Bernini's legacy is primarily transmitted through the traditions of scenography and total performance (from N. Tomé with his "transparency" in the cathedral in Toledo, to the altars of the Asam brothers), it is Guarini and Bibiena that transmit Borromini's legacy. This legacy influences the pursuit of balance between incident and reflected light typical of J.M. Fischer, of the Dient-zenhofers and of Zimmermann and Neumann who in their complex orchestrations use multiple windows in strategic areas of the structure in order to avoid glare and increase the sense of depth through a calculated alternation of the power of the light fixtures. The distance and concentration of the light is fine-tuned with the dilation and contraction of space and imitates the rhythmic movement of respiration and pulsating circulation of the blood. As a result, in the great naves of the sanctuaries of Southern Germany one can almost perceive the luminous effect of the great alpine valleys when from the union of smaller valleys, light

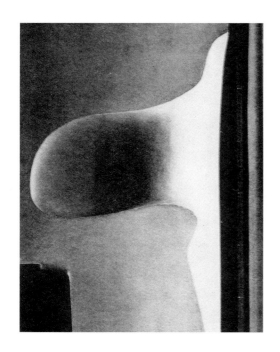

*Light in traditional organic architecture.*
*Above: light "perceived" as a revelation of*
*plasticity in the lateral windows of Villa Mairea*
*(Alvar Aalto, 1936).*
*Right: incident light as a metaphor of the truth*
*revealed in the Unitarian church in Madison*
*(1945-51) and, opposite page, as a "universal*
*light" based on the Pantheon model in the*
*Guggenheim Museum in New York (1943-59) by*
*Frank Lloyd Wright.*

breaks out from behind dark clouds and the sun's rays look very much like reflector beams.

At the dawn of the modern movement, the window was reinvented by its primordial architects, Gaudí, Horta and Hoffmann during his early years; they proposed openings that obeyed the formative impulse of masses and linear interlacement. For the deformed Gothic pediments of his crypt of Santa Coloma, Gaudí drew an organic parallel with the head of a fish. In the four-light windows of the Casa Batlló he substituted the small Gothic columns with bones and joints. In the Sagrada Familia he returned to the archetypal forms of the rosette, giving the impression of sand that generates form, just like the wet sand used by children at the seaside for their sand castles. Horta instead organised the enormous glass openings of the Maison du Peuple like a musical discourse of mixed scales, while during the final years of the last century, before embracing purist poetics, Hoffmann clothed doors and windows with an embracing weave of tentacular ribs.

The avant-garde and rationalism brought back the important theme of "universal light" and the window became a continuous opening or perforation on the

basis of a fixed quantity of incident light, placed in obedience to a detailed behavioural code. Later, it was nullified in the continuous transparent façade into which converged the endeavours of Art Nouveau and the influence of the "crystal architecture" preached by expressionists.

Paul Scheerbart is the literary prophet who inspired Bruno Taut with the mission of transparent architecture translated into the oneiric glass constructions that crown the Alpine peaks, making them shine like gigantic jewels built by man.

Mies van der Rohe briefly embraced expressionist utopia by introducing into the centre of Berlin towers shaped like the crags of glaciers or softly fashioned like crystal flowers. Yet a few years later he preached the architecture-construction equation and renounced the ecstasy of transparency in honour of "beauty as the splendour of truth."

The idea of nature as an ensemble ruled by precise and perfectly balanced laws does, however, remain at the heart of Mies, philosophy even in later years. This is apparent in his interest in Raoul Francé's works[17] as well as in some of his writings in which he rejects Nietzschean pessimism, preaches "the submission of will to knowledge" and proposes "obedience to laws-balance-adaptation" as the trinomial of a style of life.

In his stubborn fight against all formalism, Mies rehabilitates biological analogy (the distinction between the skeleton and the skin of a building) because he redirects the domination of absolute values from the world of aesthetics to the world of life. In the Höchst and Guggenheim buildings, Behrens and Wright designed translucent cupolas in which the lantern is transfigured in an architectural coping, while in the church in Madison, Wright uses light as a blinding shaft crystallised in the surface of the frames. But in the long run the widespread use of the modern meant that creative and qualitative facets of illumination were reduced to quantitative factors that passively adapted to functional requirements.

At the dawn of the third millennium, the task of those who wish to prepare for the changes necessary to combat the threats of self-destruction is apparently to reinvest architecture with the symbolic meaning of its archetypes. Thus the problem of light is essential in order to restore architecture's lost sense of sacredness, without which it runs the risk of remaining a dried fruit of the exasperated individualism that has dominated the twilight years of the last century. To reassume a collective dimension, architecture must acquire new forms of "religious values" in the most universal sense of the word: values expressing the spirit of cohesion that unites men in groups favouring reciprocal comprehension through dialogue.

When recently building a mosque in Rome, I had seriously to tackle the problem of lighting using measuring instruments and models. The mosque's interior is designed to look like a constructed forest in which some light falls directly from the sky through openings in the foliage while more light is reflected by the surfaces of the leaves and grassy lawns that reflect the light skywards.

View of the ceiling of the mosque in Rome (P. Portoghesi, V. Gigliotti, S. Mousawi, 1975-95).

This lighting arrangement with three light sources, from above (the windows of the dome), from below (the ribbon window behind the fascia of the Koranic inscriptions) and from the windows of the Quibla at head height was inspired by one of the sura of the Koran, the sura of Light: "God is the light of Heaven and Earth; his light is like a window in which he is the Lamp and the Lamp is in a Crystal, and the Crystal is like a shining Star and the Lamp burns with oil from a blessed tree, an Olive not from East or West, an oil that could burn without fire even touching it. He is Light upon Light..."

223

The window behind the Koranic inscriptions points the light upwards and has two metaphoric meanings; it is a reference to the way in which man strives towards heaven and the way illumination reaches man through the words of revelation.
Below: the dust in the air materialises the rays that shine through the small dome windows symbolising the spreading of divine mercy.

224

In constructive abstraction, this double direction of the light (upwards and downwards) is achieved by using three types of windows: narrow openings in the steps of the cupola, the façade windows highlighting the *quibla* as an indication of direction, and the continuous window encircling the entire building, letting in only reflected light from behind the fascia overwritten with inscriptions from the Koran. This double flow represents two complementary "tendencies" which, in all religions, are at the very core of the relationship between man and the divine: the tendency for man to rise in prayer and adoration and God's tendency to be merciful towards those who turn to him in prayer. This symbolic design, an architecture that needs no verbal decoding, is joined by the metaphor of the upward release of light which unambiguously represents the source of light, of knowledge, and of the truth of the divine word revealed.

In an effort to exploit the precious legacy of historical traditions – including the modern movement – and in a passionate search for a peaceful solution to the different lines of thought, there is an emergent concept of universality and internationality, quite different from the western ideas that have inspired the utopia of the modern and the eradication of traditions. It represents a different way of thinking and searching, much less certain but also much less presumptuous and aggressive, in line with the new century. However, these gripping problems will have to be tackled by renouncing the arrogance of a "modernity" that has become old and stale. A final solution to these problems will have to be found once and for all.

[1] cf., W. Linding, *Il mondo dei navajo*, Jaca Book, Milan 1993.

[2] cf., F. Coarelli, *Il Foro romano*, Quasar, Rome 1986.

[3] cf., J. Rykwert, *The Idea of a Town*, The MIT Press, Cambridge (Mass.) 1989, p. 139.

[4] cf., *The Sun, Symbol of Power and Life*, compiled by M. Sing, Abrams, New York 1993.

[5] Cited in A. Fenero, *Robert Bresson*, La Nuova Italia, Florence 1979.

[6] R.M. Rilke, *Duino Elegies,* W.W. Norton & Co., New York, 1978.

[7] R.M. Rilke, *The Complete French Poems of Rainer Maria Rilke*, Greywolf Press, Saint Paul 1979.

[8] cf., in the chapter on temples in this book.

[9] M. Yourcenar, *Memoirs of Hadrian*, Penguin Books, London, 1951. It is impossible to attribute the design of the Pantheon to Apollodorus and the reference to the round temples in Etruria is inexact. The latter could perhaps refer to the mound tombs;

however, Marguerite Yourcenar's book contains some inspiring ideas.

[10] cf., F. Cali, *La plus grande adventure du monde: Citeaux*, Artaud, Paris 1956 (preface by Le Corbusier).

[11] Pliny the Younger, *The Letters of Caius Caecilius Secundus*, George Bell & Sons, London 1895.

[12] cf., M. Pejakovič, *Le pietre e il sole*, Jaca Book, Milan 1988.

[13] Cited in E. Panofsky, *Abbot Suger*, Princeton University Press, Princeton 1946.

[14] cf., J. Michell, *The Dimensions of Paradise*, Thames & Hudson, London 1988, p. 37.

[15] P. Portoghesi, *Borromini nella cultura europea*, Laterza, Rome-Bari 1982.

[16] cf., E. Panofsky, *op. cit.*

[17] F. Neumeyer, *The Artless World. Mies van der Rohe on the Building Art*, The MIT Press, Cambridge (Mass.) 1991, pp. 96-109.

# The Temenos, the Altar, the Temple

*Everything is ashes and dust, everything except the Temple within us. It is ours. It is with us until the end of time.*

Vladimir Maximov

*Erect, the building stands on its rock base. The building's repose highlights the rock's obscure support, solid yet unconstructed. Standing there, the building holds its head high against the swirling storm, revealing its violence. The splendour and luminosity of the stones, seemingly a gift from the sun, underline the light of day, the immensity of the sky, darkness of night. Its steadfast silhouette makes the invisible region of the sky visible. The solidity of the object contrasts the surge of the waves, its immutable calm emphasising their impetuous onslaught. Tree and grass, eagle and bull, snake and cricket thus assume their outer form and reveal their true nature.*

Martin Heidegger

The temple as a sacred construction or as the house of the gods is probably the result of repeated attempts by ancient civilisations to establish and visibly render the sites of "theophany" or the explosion of sacredness in nature. In Latin, the word was originally used to signify one of the parts into which the heavens were ideally divided by the augurs. The quadripartite division of the heavens corresponded to the quadripartite division of the *auguraculum*, the area in which the augurs gathered and interpreted omens. Its derivation from the Greek *temenos* (sacred domain, sanctuary) connected *templum* and *temnein* (to cut, to divide) and justified its related meaning of boundary or sacred place until the word became associated with the consecrated building. Before becoming a building the temple was a place, a part of the earth made sacred by the presence of the divine. The appropriation of a natural area was achieved by the religious officiants of numerous civilisations through the use of very elementary tools: the identification of a stone or a tree, not worshipped in themselves but because "they indicated something that was neither stone nor tree, but something sacred, the *ganz andere*."[1] In other cases, identification is a vertical pole or column signifying both the centre of the earth and a shaft towards the sky.

Mountains play a crucial role in identifying sacred places since they are luminous places *par excellence*, especially when they stand alone or rise directly from the plains. Olympus, Parnassus, Etna or Fujiyama are all universally renowned examples, but even hills and rocky outcrops can be sacred mountains, especially when they are used as reference points to get one's bearings or to connect different places. In the Hindu tradition, for instance, the "cosmic mountain" is an ideal model (*meru*) not explicitly identifiable.[2]

The concept of boundary is strictly linked to the field of architecture. In some ways it represents the original moment of appropriation of certain parts of nature. The Sanskrit word *vastu* means architecture, boundary and clothing. The conceptual elements of the boundary are its perimeter, size and orientation. The latter presumes a relationship with the natural environment mediated by reason, the observation of nature and the events that characterise life over a period of time. For primitive man, the horizon was not merely a continuous line but a sort of graduated axis he learnt to use as an instrument to measure the passing of time. In fact, each day of the year is marked by two points on the horizon, the point where the sun rises and the point where it sets. A boundary's orientation (explicitly) identifies not only its position in the world, but also its cyclical position during the year or season.

Sacredness may become manifest even in dreams, but this is not to say that the place in which the dream occurs does not become a sacred and terrible place: in the Bible (*Genesis* 28, 10-16) it is written "Jacob left Beersheba and set out for Haran. When he reached a certain place, he stopped for the night because the sun had set. Taking one of the stones there, he put it under his head and lay down to sleep. He had a dream in which he saw a ladder resting on the earth, with its top reaching to heaven, and the angels of God were ascending and descending on it. There above it stood the Lord, and he said: 'I am the Lord, the God of your father Abraham and the God of Isaac. I will give you and your descendants the land on which you are lying. Your descendants will be like the dust of the earth, and you will spread out to the west and to the east, to the north and to the south. All peoples on earth will be blessed through you and your offspring. I am with you and will watch over you wherever you go, and I will bring you back to this land. I will not leave you until I have done what I have promised you.' When Jacob awoke from his sleep, he thought, 'Surely the Lord is in this place, and I was not aware of it.' He was afraid and said, 'How awesome is this place! This is none other than the house of God; this is the gate of Heaven.'"

In Jacob's dream the concept of a sacred place is enriched with an opening towards the sky, an upward-opening chasm, one of the characteristic elements of the symbolic importance of the temple. This is achieved by using the most eloquent image possible, a ladder upon which angels descend and ascend, intermediaries and heralds of sacredness, invisible beings of light. If in the Bible the place of Jacob's dream represents the spatial dimension of sacredness, the Ark of the Covenant, designed by God himself, may be considered a mobile and relative representation. The tabernacle accompanied the people of Israel and represented the place in which sacredness was revealed as well as a place of welcome

*A wild olive near San Nicola a Luras in the district of Tempio Pausania (Italy). The tree, with a circumference of eleven meters, is thought to be over 2000 years old. The olive stands alone in the fields, surrounded by paths that lead to its welcoming shade. The olive evokes the sacredness attributed by the ancient world to trees as mediators between heaven and earth,* axis mundi, *symbol of elevation, of roots, of balance between opposites.* Le Corbusier (Quand les cathédrales étaient blanches, *Plon, Paris 1937) celebrated the solidarity between tree and man in these verses: "Tree, friend of man! / Symbol of every organic creation / image of all constructions. / Enchanting spectacle / which even in impeccable order / appears before our eyes / with famous arabesques. / Measured mathematical game / of branches that grow / every spring / with a new unfolding hand. /Leaves with veins / perfectly ordered, / roof above our heads / between heaven and earth. / Screen rich in changes / vividly contrasting / the rigid geometry / of our hard constructions. / Presence of nature in cities / witness of our toils and / our pleasures. Tree / millenary companion of mankind."*

227

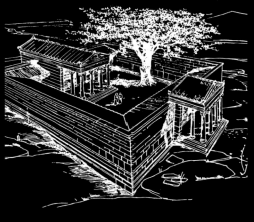

The "numinous" site represents the origin of the temple as a building.
Right: the Loreley cliff on the Rhine, consecrated by German tradition and cited in a poem by Heinrich Heine.
Above: reconstruction of the temple of Jupiter with the oak tree consecrated to Dodona in the front enclosure.

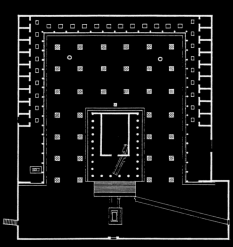

Right: Mount Soratte, sacred to the Faliscan god Soranus and in Roman times sacred to Apollo, Feronia and Juno, as well as to numerous saints after the advent of Christianity. Its impervious isolated mass dominates the Tiber valley, from the Sabina to the Viterbo regions, and, depending from where it is viewed, its shape changes.
Above: plan of the sanctuary of Juno in Gabii. The squares next to and behind the temple represent the seventy sacred trees that were cut down to build the temenos of the temple.

*View and section of the sacred trees in Chôkôkji on the island of Honshu (Japan). The two trunks of dead cedar trees are ritually kept alive every year by covering them with bamboo rings. The upper, freshly-cut rings contrast with those rotting at the bottom of the trunks. The two trees replace the entry portal traditionally situated in front of the sanctuary in Izumo.*
*Below: a group of menhir in Brittany; the stones mark both the path and the sacred enclosure.*

in which people gather, an archetype of the church as an ecclesia: a living community, enclosed and protected.

The tent, the ark, the tabernacle, the altars of sacrifices and incense as well as the external boundary are all symbols of the alliance between God and man, and God himself gave Moses the project to be carried out by Oholiab, "gem-cutter, draftsman and tailor of purple, red and scarlet yarn and fine linen" and by Beszalel, a holy craftsman that the spirit of God "filled with skill, ability and knowledge in all kinds of crafts to make artistic designs for work in gold, silver or bronze, to cut and set stones later, to work in wood, and to engage in all kinds of craftsmanship."

God showed Moses his project on the top of Mount Sinai, a place made sacred by theophany: "On the morning of the third day there was thunder and lightening, with a thick cloud over the mountain, and a very loud trumpet blast. Everyone in the camp trembled." Even before then God had exhorted Moses: "Put limits around the mountain and set it apart as holy."

In the place of theophany, after having announced the commandments and the laws, God showed Moses his project and described the pattern of the sanctuary: "Then have them make a sanctuary for me, and I will dwell among them. Make this tabernacle and all its furnishings exactly like the pattern I will show you" (*Exodus* 25, 8-9).

The description of the tent is extremely detailed and strongly influenced both Jewish and Christian liturgy: "Make the tabernacle with ten curtains of finely twisted linen and blue, purple and scarlet yarn, with cherubim worked into them by a skilled craftsman. All the curtains are to be the same size – twenty-eight cubits long and four cubits wide. Join five of the curtains together, and do the same with the other five. Make loops of blue material along the edge of the end curtain in one set, and do the same with the end curtain in the other set. Make fifty loops on one curtain and fifty loops on the end curtain of the other set, with the loops opposite each other. Then make fifty gold clasps and use them to fasten the curtains together so that the tabernacle is a unit. Make curtains of goat hair for the tent over the tabernacle – eleven altogether. All eleven curtains are to be the same size – thirty cubits long and four cubits wide. Join five of the curtains together into one set and the other six into another set. Fold the sixth curtain double at the front of the tent. Make fifty loops along the edge of the end curtain in one set and also along the edge of the end curtain in the other set. Then make fifty bronze clasps and put them in the loops to fasten the tent together as a unit. As for the additional length of the tent curtains, the half curtain that is left over is to hang down at the rear of the tabernacle. The tent curtains will be a cubit longer on both sides; what is left will hang over the sides of the tabernacle so as to cover it. Make for the tent a covering of ram skins dyed red, and over that a covering of hides of sea cows.

"Make upright frames of acacia wood for the tabernacle. Each frame is to be ten cubits long and a cubit and a half wide, with two projections set parallel to

*The Tent of the Covenant reconstructed according to the detailed description in the* Book of Exodus *(from Bernard Lamy,* De Tabernaculo Foederis de Sancta Civitate Jerusalem, et de Templo eius, *Lyons 1720, p. 89).*

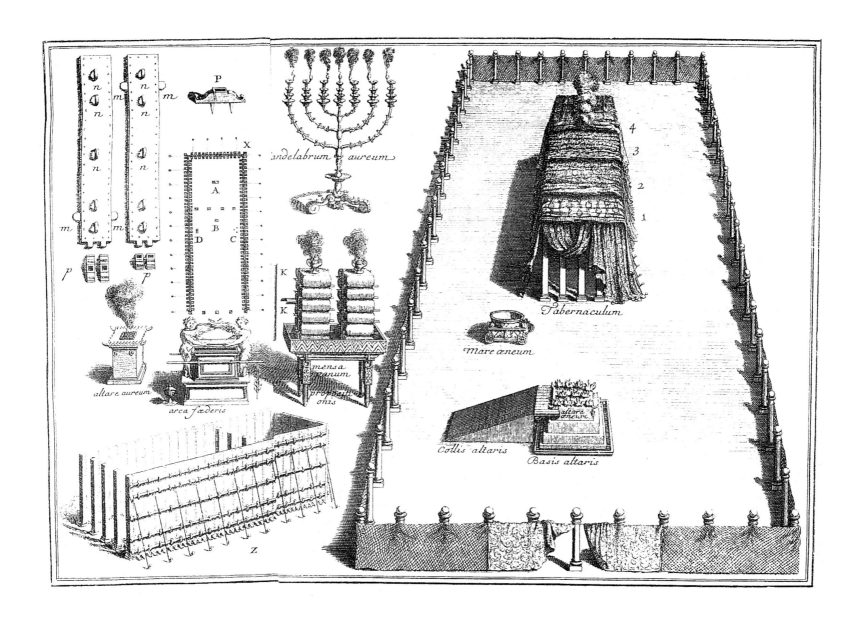

each other. Make all the frames of the tabernacle in this way. Make twenty frames for the south side of the tabernacle and make forty silver bases to go under them – two bases for each frame, one under each projection.

"For the other side, the north side of the tabernacle, make twenty frames and forty silver bases – two under each frame.

"Make six frames for the far end, that is, the west end of the tabernacle, and make two frames for the corners at the far end. At these two corners they must be double from the bottom all the way to the top, and fitted into a single ring; both shall be like that.

"So there will be eight frames and sixteen silver bases – two under each frame.

"Also make crossbars of acacia wood: five for the frames on one side of the tabernacle, five for those on the other side, and five for the frames on the west, at the far end of the tabernacle. The centre crossbar is to extend from end to end at the middle of the frames. Overlay the frames with gold and make gold rings to hold the crossbars. Also overlay the crossbars with gold. Set up the tabernacle according to the plan shown you on the mountain" (*Exodus* 26, 1-30).

In his book, *Vers une architecture,* Le Corbusier inserted a reconstruction of the Tabernacle with a large triangular tent in the middle and called it a "primitive temple."[3]

The ark, the tent and the house of the covenant are located in natural sur-

*Drawing by Le Corbusier showing the ideal reconstruction of Moses' tent (*Vers une Architecture, *Crés, Paris 1923).*

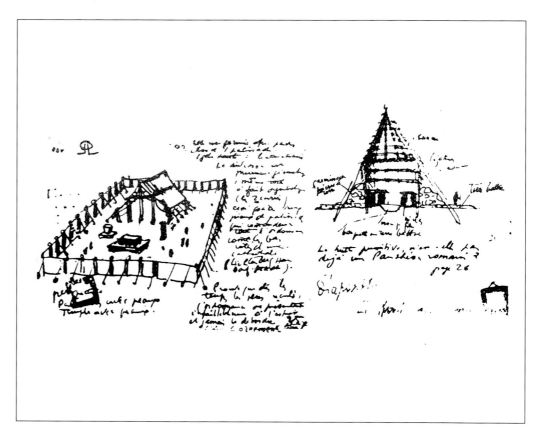

roundings like a divine sign representing the alliance and inseparability of the people of Israel and their God, a tent in the midst of many tents. It is not a sacred place because it is a "non place," not a plant but a seed, not a building but a temporary separation of "another" space travelling with the people of God.

However, as a divine project the tent is, like every other aspect of nature, an integral part of creation, an undertaking dedicated to mankind yet endowed with the same splendour of living organisms, the violent colours, the precious light of noble matter, the organicity of a living being.

In the design of one of the furnishings of the ark, namely the *menorah*, the lampstand with seven branches, the reference to nature is both precise and direct: "They made the lampstand of pure gold and hammered it out, base and shaft; its flowerlike cups, buds and blossoms were of one piece with it. Six branches extended from the sides of the lampstand – three on one side and three on the other. Three cups shaped like almond flowers with buds and blossoms were on one branch, three on the next branch and the same for all six branches" (*Exodus* 37, 17-20). The *menorah* reproduces not so much the shape but the logic of the tree; its branches and flowers become the metaphor of life that passes and is consumed, an object that occupies space but transcends it because it "lives" in time.

To tackle the *vexata quaestio* of the temple of Jerusalem, the conjectural reconstruction of the various building stages and Ezekiel's prophecy, is beyond the scope of this book. Suffice it to recall the structural and decorative elements of the temple of Solomon, closely related to the world of nature through symbolic images, numerical ratios and the materials used during construction. Over the centuries, the story of the building of the temple (*Book of Kings*, 3, 6 ff.), so detailed yet so incomplete, has justified and continues to justify reconstructions which, far from reaching an unattainable historical truth, are the perfect expression of the ever mutant "spirit of the times" and of trends in culture, an omnipresent trait even in the latest extremely well documented proposal contained in a monograph dedicated to none other than "God architect."[4] Apart from the proportions governed by simple numerical ratios (dominated by the eighth part) the description in *Kings* illustrates the building processes and the exclusive use of cedar, olive and pine paneling in the interior. The main hall led to the *sancta sanctorum* whose spectacular decoration included two cherubims 10 cubits high (approximately 4.50 meters) with a wing span of the same length. The two angels formed a sort of transenna in the middle of the room since their wings joined the two walls together. "On the walls all around the temple," says the scribe referring to Solomon and Hiram his architect, "he sculpted with numerous engravings depicting cherubims, palm trees and various figures that seemed to stand out and protrude out from the wall."

Outside and to the side of the temple entrance there were two large columns. The columns were covered with eighty pomegranates, symbol of love

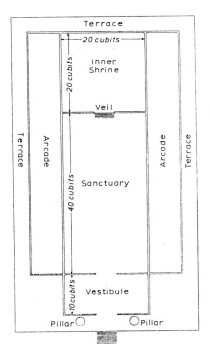

*Reconstruction of the plan of the temple of Solomon.*

*The internal cella of the temple of Solomon in Villalpando's reconstruction (J.B. Villalpando in* Ezechielem Explanationes, *Rome 1594-1605, Book II, pl. VIII).*

233

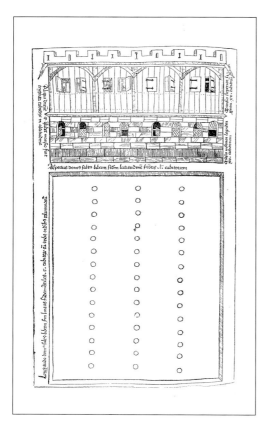

and divine generosity. The capitals, decorated with reticulates and festoons, were crowned with the image of a lily. Of the many structures in Solomon's palace, the one worth mentioning is the "house of the forest of Lebanon"; it had a colonnade with 45 columns forming four naves. This forest of columns was 55 meters long, 25 meters wide and over 16 meters high; a spatial model reproduced many years later in Maghrebian mosques.

Ezekiel's prophecy described the temple as it should have been built after the return of the Jews from their exile in Babylon. The site was no longer the original one (the hill of Zion now home to the Omar mosque) while there are numerous variations that only slightly affected the temple itself. The direct divine inspiration of the prophecy has contributed to creating a feeling of sacredness around this description, admirably interpreted by the Jesuit Villalpando.[5] Many buildings have in some ways laid claim to the legacy of the temple of Jerusalem, in particular the Roman basilicas of Saint Peter and San Giovanni in Laterano. In Saint Peter's, the most tangible element of continuity are the "columns of Solomon" placed by Bernini in the loggia of the aedicula under Michelangelo's cupola and currently unanimously considered to be of Hellenistic origin. In San Giovanni in Laterano, the reference is intentional but mediated by the creative imagination of Francesco Borromini who wanted the pillars to be similar to those in Ezekiel's temple, namely decorated on both sides with palms, cherubs in every nook and cranny, pomegranates in the capitals and above all that "strong"

*A reconstruction of the House of the forest of Lebanon vaguely Gothic in style, in the Koberger edition (1481) of the* Postillae *by Nicolaus de Pyra (1270-1349).*

*Right: the twelve columns of Constantine's pergola later used in the canopy designed by Martino Ferrabosco in the 17th century. Later on, these "columns of Solomon" were placed by Bernini in the four aedicula of the pillars under the cupola. However, the one believed to be the pillar to which Christ was chained during flagellation, was placed in the Cappella of the Pietà.*

*The twisted columns, thought to have come from the temple of Solomon (but dating to the Hellenistic period), became the symbolic element that traditionally linked the Catholic churches, built between the 16th and 18th centuries, with the temple in Jerusalem, and therefore with the traditions of the Old Testament.*

*From the Greeks onwards, the tendril column was part of the traditions of the West. It is based on tree symbolism: the higher it grows, the more it becomes spiral in shape, gradually establishing a relationship with the morphology of the snail and of horns.*

TABVLA 51.

ALIVD ORNAMENTVM MARMOREVM CVM COLVMNIS VITINEIS ANTIQVÆ BASILICÆ

plasticity that "appears to spring out from the wall," described so well in the first *Book of Kings*.

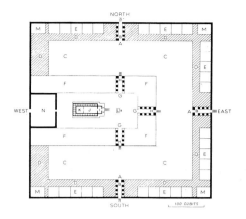

The relationship between architecture and nature, so obvious in the phytomorphism of the Jewish candelabrum, is marvellously balanced in the temples of Egypt which, at a certain point, represented the analogical image of the whole of Egypt or the abstract synthesis of the typical landscape along the Nile. The narrow passage between rows of tall columns corresponded to the Nile flowing between steep rock walls, while the highest point of the temple represented the primordial hill that emerged from the "chaotic swamp of increate matter."[6] The ceilings were always decorated with references to the stellar night sky while around the temple there were trees, bushes and ponds which synthetically and abstractly recalled the image of a swampy landscape.

This iconographic programme is documented only by the unfinished Ptolemaic temple of Khnum in Isna, but the structural analogy with many earlier temples leads one to believe that this was a widespread interpretative key.

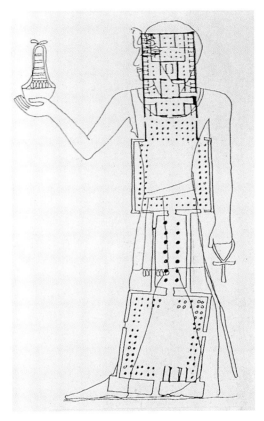

The plan of the great temple in Luxor has major irregularities and asymmetries, but its interpretation by R.A. Schwaller de Lubicz contains some very interesting points.[7] He has discovered that, in various parts of the temple built in different epochs, a coherent effort was made to establish a strict relationship between the proportions of the human body and the role of its various organs. These similarities involve the measurements of the decorative figures as well as the otherwise unexplainable irregularities of the floor which apparently reproduce the cryptic image of a face.

Not only does the temple represent the abstract external form of the human figure, it also reproduces its functional and spiritual essence, its life-giving organs and structure. Familiarity with the temple thus becomes an invitation to recognise in one's own body and spirituality the real temple, the house of God, origin of every element of creation.

The man represented in the figure of the temple relates to the concept of the temple within man, a subject discussed in the Gospel of Saint John and in Saint Paul's First Letter to the Corinthians (3, 16-17): "Don't you know that you yourselves are God's temple and that God's Spirit lives in you? If anyone destroys God's temple, God will destroy him; for God's temple is sacred, and you are that temple."

*The position of the temple on the acropolis in Jerusalem. Layout of the temple as described by Ezekiel. The temple was meant to be built on a mountain and be surrounded by high walls. Below: the temple in Luxor according to R.A. Schwaller de Lubicz. The consecutive construction stages correspond to the various development phases of the human body and its limbs.*

With the advent of the Sumerian civilisation, in the region of Mesopotamia, one type of temple stood out from all the others, the *ziggurat*. It tended to isolate the sacred area from the city of men, placing the religious buildings on top of artificial mountains shaped to obtain the greatest effect of distance and domination through the use of pyramidal shapes and lateral ramps along the front façade. Its sloping sides dominated the stone mass of the *ziggurat* and corresponded directly to the lines of the horizon and surrounding landscape. Apparently these immense platforms were conceived as invitations to the gods who, descending from their remote celestial dwellings, deigned to draw close to life on earth.

The forms and size of the *ziggurat* are surprisingly similar to those of the step pyramids of Pre-Colombian civilisations, principally those with square layouts, but also the circular ones. Luckily the pyramids are sufficiently well preserved and this improves the quality of the architectural interpretation. Even in America, temple buildings rose on gigantic platforms and were normally made out of wood with straw roofs, similar to the huts of the native populations. In Tikal, there are small stone temples crowned with a sort of crest that from below appear to be pierced by the light. Similar forms were very probably used for temples made of perishable materials. The flights of steps, sometimes incredibly steep, clearly illustrate the psychological component which tended to foster in the minds of the observer a sense of vertigo and fear in this progressive detachment from the ground, from all that is human, in order to attain painful ecstasy.

In prehistoric Europe before the advent of Indo-European tribes, the cult of the Earth Mother flourished between 6500 and 2500 B.C. The faithful worshipped nature as the living body of the great female creator, but they also adored all living creatures as participants in her divine nature. Marija Gimbutas wrote: "The Goddess-centered art with its striking absence of images of warfare and male domination, reflects a social order in which women as heads of clans or queen-priestesses played a central part. Old Europe and Anatolia, as well as Minoan Crete, were a 'gylany.' A balanced, non-patriarchal and non-matriarchal social system is reflected by religion, mythology and folklore, by studies of the

*Above: the Intihuatana stone in Machu Picchu (Peru). Below and below right: a drawing and photo of the temples in Tikal (Guatemala).*

social structure of Old European and Minoan cultures and is supported by the continuity of the elements of a matrilineal system in ancient Greece, Etruria, Rome, the Basque and other countries of Europe."[8] In this context, the term "gylany" refers to equality between the sexes and was first introduced by Riana Eisler in her 1987 book, *The Chalice and the Blade*. It is the perfect definition of a different human condition, preceding a long and as yet unfinished period of aggression and dominion of man over man, personified in the cyclical tragic misfortune of war. Based on extensive archaeological documentation, Gimbutas elaborates a fascinating theory regarding a consistent decorative lexicon that was used for a much longer period of time than the one which later characterised Indo-European civilisations. The sources of this lexicon are linked to the cult of the Earth Mother and include dynamic symbols, vortexes, twisted spirals, sinuous snakes, circles and half-moons, horns, seeds and shoots as well as parts of the female body.

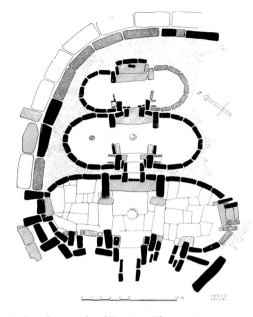

*Malta: the temple of Tarxien. The missing parts were completed by Carlo Ceschi. Compare the temple to the multifoil outline of the Mother Goddess, Karanovo VI, Pazardzik, Bulgaria, mid 5th century B.C.*

A cyclical idea of time dominates the images that allude to perpetual regeneration and the Mother Goddess herself appears both young and old. This religion was born and flourished with the development of agriculture and expressed a sacred respect for nature and nature's creatures. However, only some aspects of this religion, which to a certain extent recalls the beliefs of American Indians, will later filter down to the peasant culture of Europe. This "gylany" has left fewer and more ephemeral traces in architecture than in the field of decoration, visible principally in the temples of Malta, in Catal Hüyük in Anatolia as well as in the Minoan architecture of Crete. I have already mentioned the temples in Malta when speaking of the archetype of the curvature and "column of life."

Instead, the Minoan royal palace is the first construction that bears witness to the relationship nature-temple, nature-sacred space, later to spread to the entire culture of Greece. This is a relationship based on the identification of a spatially defined area in the landscape, in which the altar and the temple represent "catalysts of the perception of the holy."

In the Minoan world there were three types of sacred sites; stone sanctuaries with one or more cella placed on the tops of mountains and hills all over Crete; grottoes with stalactites regarded as "columns of life;" the halls of worship in the great palaces, with canalisations attesting to sacrificial rituals.

The sacrificial essence of temple architecture, recently demonstrated by George Hersey in a brilliant essay, provides a partial but essential key to the comprehension of its structure. However, in order to use this key convincingly it is necessary to conduct a simple review of the ritual sacrifice, according to the description used by Burkert. Having put on the clothes for the ritual, the participants then walked in procession towards the altar, singing as they went. A canephore carrying a basket of wheat on his head preceded the participants, while the sacrificial animal, adorned with garlands and gilded horns, was led on a rope behind the procession. A flautist completed the scene. Having reached the altar, a fire was lit on the sacrificial table. The participants drew a circle

*Drawing by Carlo Ceschi reproducing the first cella in the first temple of Tarxien.*
*Opposite page: the Greek temple in Segesta (Italy) seen from the theatre (5th century B.C.).*

around the altar and stood inside it during the ceremony. Everyone washed their hands; the victim was purified with water and covered with the seeds of wheat taken from the basket while the faithful prayed. From under the wheat in the basket a knife was then drawn. With this knife the priest first cut off a lock of hair from the victim and threw it into the fire; then he slit its throat while the women present let out a scream of surprise that confirmed the presence of the god to whom the victim was being offered. Care was taken that the blood flowed along the altar and into the special grooves dug at its base. The animal's body was then carefully cut to separate the various parts. The heart was placed on the altar while the liver was examined by an expert who then interpreted the message from the God. Some parts were roasted and eaten. The thigh-bones were broken and wrapped in fat, the skin of the animal was placed on the altar and the bones were laid on top in the shape of the animal itself. Finally, everything was burnt.

Hersey believes that the morphology of the temple and the names of its parts are drawn entirely from the sacrificial ritual. On the basis of this hypothesis he compares the volutes of the Ionic capital with the animal's horns, the bulls of the Attic base with the ropes used to lead the victim, the trabeation with the sacrificial table, the Doric triglyphs with the parts of the broken thigh-bone, the consoles with the ears, the dentils with the teeth, the tympanum with the drum and the eagle and so forth. Even if the comparisons between the shape of the parts and the mouldings are not entirely convincing, Hersey corroborates them with a series of tropisms. His comparisons are based on phonetic or conceptual analogies not only between words in Greek or Latin but also between words used in modern languages.[9]

In the more convincing parts of his interpretation of the temple, Hersey confirms the procedure of symbolic imitation and the naturalistic root of the temple. He must also take credit for stressing the function of sacred trees in ancient Greek religion. The basic elements of the Greek landscape, the olive tree, the oak, the laurel and the myrtle were respectively sacred to Athena, Zeus, Apollo and Aphrodite. In Karl Boetticher's reconstruction of classic iconography sacred trees are decorated with garlands or inserted into architectural aedicules.

If this sacrificial theme helps us understand the complex morphology of the various parts of the Greek temple, then to understand its structure it is necessary to examine landscape and history. Lucian relates how the very first temples were rectangular glades made by cutting down trees in the heart of the forest. Indirectly he provides the captivating image of nature, repudiated and re-proposed according to a precise mental order, in the rows of aligned columns that enclose and limit space.

No less fascinating is the genesis of the temple proposed by Vincent Scully, one of the most inspired interpreters of the relationship between architecture and nature. Scully judges the temple to be an allegory of victory and its ordered

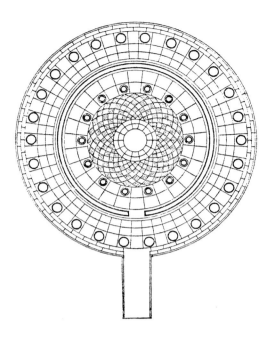

*Layout of the* tholos *in Epidaurus (360-320 B.C.).*

*The columns of the so-called "basilica" in Paestum (6th century VI B.C.). The Greek temple system, culminating in the peripteral temple, is one of the strictest examples of type versus model. There is nothing mechanical about the system's rules which give free rein to the architect in his design of the temple parts and the way in which they fulfil the requirements of the god to which the temple is dedicated. The more general assembly rules remain the same as do those governing the superimposition of the parts. The Greek temple is the logical creation par excellence; it can be built using stones as if they were words in a sentence.*

columns hordes of hoplites, shoulder to shoulder, yielding to the sound of the flute, as depicted on the Chigi vase in the Villa Giulia Museum and described by Tyrtaeus in his onomatopoeic verses:

> Kai poda parpodi theis ep aspidos aspid ereisos.
> En de Lophon te lopho kai kineen kinee
> Kai sternon sterno, peplemenos andri mechesto.

Columns that are joined to form powerful advancing masses are always situated in a natural container.

The landscape in Greece is a fluid mix of mountains and hills surrounding areas called plains or valleys. Often, far away on the horizon, it is possible to catch a glimpse of the sea and all its mutant colours. It almost seems as if an ideal model had decided on the rules governing the endless number of environmental situations that come to be created and in which well-known elements, such as the conical hills and coupled peaks that look like horns, repeatedly re-occur. Scully defined this spatial landscape "natural Megaron" but one might also speak of an ideal enclosure similar to a walled city.

Compared to these environmental conditions, the temple was normally positioned to respect the orientation of the emergent pole of the landscape, while taking into account the view seen by those coming from specific directions as well as the possibility for the observer to simultaneously encompass the view of the temple and this visual pole. Often the main altar was located so that the faithful, gathered for the sacrifice, could see the temple on one side and the hill or double summit on the other. In some cases, there was probably a rest area or lookout near the temple to watch the sun rise in line with the saddle of the double summit on those days of the year in which celebrations were held in honour of the temple god.

A typical example of double summit is Mount Kerata (horned mountain, in Greek) that towers over the Eleusinian acropolis. When wanting to find in Greek temples, or in classical architecture in general, something that contrasts with the nature of its site, an object with a conflictory and antithetic order, it is necessary to ignore the subtle and passionate search for this harmony. For instance, in Palladio's Rotonda, this search stems from a desire to mirror, to join together, to support, in other words, from a desire for a flowing current into which the visible and the invisible converge.

It is not by dissecting landscape to obtain cruel sections nor by placing improbable "macrostructures" upon the earth that we respect nature. Instead, it is by understanding its sacred nature and listening to it that we capture the precious clues it offers on "how to behave," which in fact means "how to improve," "how to avoid wounding" and "how to interiorise" the secret forces of the earth.

In Segesta, as in the sanctuary of Apollo Prous or in Delphi, architecture humbly dialogues with landscape. Where nature forcefully enacts her terrible grandeur, architecture, with infinite delicacy and obvious inferiority of scale, attempts to placate her with filial respect. Herman Melville wisely wrote about Greek architecture:

Not magnitude, not lavishness
But form, the site;
Not innovating Wilfulness
But reverence for the archetype.[10]

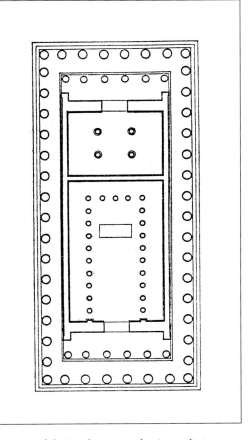

*Layout of the Parthenon on the Acropolis in Athens (447-432 B.C.).*

Temples were not part of Vedic religion.[11] Rites were conducted in the houses of those who carried out the sacrifice or on a lawn next to the house in which the altar was prepared and three fires lit. The first architectural evidence of Hindu religion dates back to the 6th century A.D. and marks the beginning of the growth of Hinduism that lasted until the 16th century, interrupted only by the victory of Islam. In the Hindu religion, the temple is literally the earthly dwelling place of the gods represented by effigies worshipped even by the children who repeatedly wash and dress the sculptured images.

The statues are housed in a place called the *garbha-grha* situated in the middle of the sacred building and characterised by its lack of internal decoration.

The Vedic ritual for the construction of the fire altar (*agnigayna*) conjures up the dismemberment of the universal egg and its division into heaven and earth. Its cosmogonal matrix was incorporated into the Hindu temple, a temple that represents both the world and man and takes its form from the phallic symbol

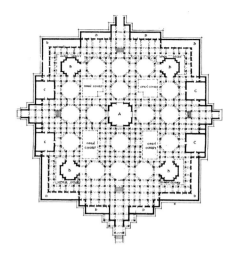

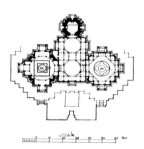

(the *lingham*), the sacred mountain and the reification of the centre considered as the intersection of three axes, the vertical *axis mundi* and the axes that unite the four cardinal points.

Temple typologies vary according to the period and to the region, but there are certain particularly productive and congenial types for the sensibilities of those architects and sculptors who together have created the exceptional flourishing of so-called "medieval" Indian architecture.

The heart of the Hindu temple, the *garbha-grha,* marked the end of an initiation ritual that consisted in a sequential series of rooms that became darker and darker. It was directly connected to the *mandapa,* a prayer hall for the faithful, preceded by a single, sometimes double, portico.

All the buildings were situated inside an enclosure with one or more entrances that gradually became more and more monumental. Initially, the temple was covered by a flat roof and was in some ways reminiscent of the Greek model, while later on the characteristic element became a sort of cupola or spire above the *garbha-grha,* shaped like a pyramid or a sort of parabolic spindle.

When this tower became curvilinear it created the unmistakable outline of the *sikhara,* a word that literally means peak or flame, and more than any other form characterises the identity of the Hindu temple and the "tremendous majesty" of the Vedic pantheon.

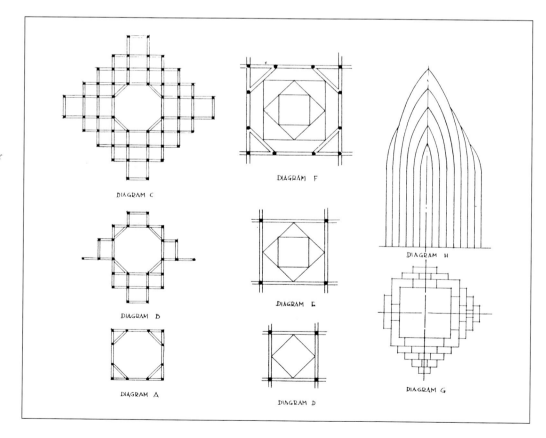

Natural forms are also visible in the remarkable analogy with the young stalk of the *Equisetum hiemale*, with the morphogenetic hypotheses associated with the curvilinear covering of the Indian cart and with the aedicula made out of four bent bamboo canes used as a canopy over the Vedic altar. However, natural forms are above all present in the plastic interpretation of the volume that resembles the phytomorphic growth and geological formation of mountains with horizontal strata of different thickness and the contrasting structural role played by the projecting outcrops. During the foundation ritual, offerings and expiatory sacrifices expressed this respect for "occupied" nature.

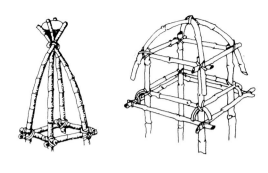

The most elegant *sikhara* models are the temples in Khajuraho built during the Candella dynasty. The parabolic shape of the *chapra,* the vertical body above the base, forms two taut curves like a drawn bow ready to be released and recalls the "ogive" of small spaceships or the explosive fruits of the *Echallium elaterium* that break off from the stalk and violently project their seeds outwards.

The balance between horizontality and verticality is reached through the continued horizontal extension of four vertical poles (*rahnpaga*) whose decoration tapers off like printed patterns on cloth. On the other hand, the convex edges between the poles are decorated in stronger relief highlighting the horizontal stratification (*amla*). This simple model is later made more complex and vibrant by adding, in correspondence to the symmetrical axes, pieces that gradually decrease in size the further away they are from the centre. This represents the precise and proficient application of a principle – self-similarity – whose mathematical aspects have only recently been studied by Benoit Mandelbrot in the framework of fractal mathematics, which will be discussed later on in the chapter on "Numbers."

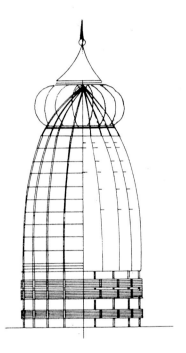

Very few designs – for example Leonardo Da Vinci's design for centrally planned churches[12] – and absolutely no other architectural achievement, have ever given serious consideration to nature's most secret building principles governing the formation of gulfs along the sea coast, the branch structure of trees and the splendid flowers of the now famous (at least among mathematicians) "Romanesque broccoli."

After the *sikhara,* during the 7th century India witnessed the birth of the *vimana*, a square plan temple with a stepped pyramidal roof crowned by a horseshoe-shaped barrel vault. Each step was made of a series of small pavilions in relief symbolising the houses of man clinging to the sacred mountain inhabited by the Gods.

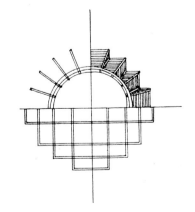

Contrary to the *ziggurat* and pre-Colombian pyramids, the *vimana* cannot be climbed and suggests a purely spiritual ascent. Often there are other rectangular stepped pyramids around it, positioned above the entrances to the temple enclosure. These are the *gopura* that often vie with the *vimana* in the height and complexity of the sculptures. Both types respect the principle of self-similarity reached by making the repeated configuration of each plane smaller and smaller in size. This repetition is called *pancaram*.

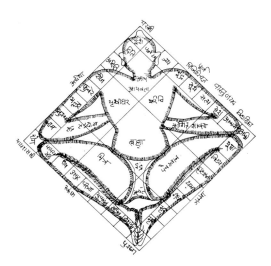

*Mandala used to "calibrate" the guidelines of temple construction* (Vastu-Purusha-Mandala).

In the course of the last centuries and before the Islamic invasion, India was characterised by a number of eclectic trends which ultimately led to stellar temples. These temples represented a sort of fusion between the ogive of the *sikhara* and the stepped pyramid of the *vimana* and resulted in weakening and almost completely nullifying the importance of the cruciform alignment which represented the search for stability as well as a cosmological link. The loss of direction in favour of almost perfect irradiation precipitated a crisis and prepared the way for the turning point that gave excellent local craftsmen the chance to engage in a truly angular reinterpretation of Islamic tradition.

The temples in Madura were more traditional, especially the curvilinear *gopura* that introduced into the structure of the *vimana* the parabolic outline of the *sikhara* by turning the concavity outwards.

The comparison between the strict geometry of the *sikhara* and the *vimana* and the naturalistic complexity of their exterior façades seems to conversely illustrate the gradual process that leads from natural complexity to geometric abstraction. In fact, the basic shape is almost always a square. When based on a certain type of mandala – the *Vastu-Purusha-Mandala* (magical chart of the architecture of supreme man), codified in the theoretical manual of Hindu architects – the division of the square into 64 or 81 squares establishes a regular outline that acts as a frame for the extremely complex contours of the temple layouts.

With regard to the outer configuration of its independent parts with strong biomorphic analogies, insertion into natural surroundings takes place in harmony with the hilly profile of the temple complexes. However, sometimes the architects attempt to make natural and artificial forms dialogue directly with each other, aiming at a sort of reciprocal penetration: this is the case of the temples and palatial buildings in Viajayanagar. Here it is difficult to understand where the work of nature ends and the work of man begins. The chaotic outcrops of the rocks seem gradually to be intensified by an apparently haphazard intermediate order of landscape forms. The presence of an architectural organism offers a logical interpretation almost as if the architect had found in this chaos a precise and secret rule which, once discovered, affects the rest of his work.

The internal spaces of the Hindu temple also bear witness to the inspiration of nature and compared to the buildings coexist quite freely without any relationship whatsoever except in the layout.

In the *Vastshastra*, the most important architectural handbook in India, strict rules govern the construction of temples and the size of each of its parts, but it would be useless to try and read into this a western-style deterministic logic. Basic elements of design such as the layout, the choice of the site, the geological analysis of the terrain and even the thickness of the walls are based on mythological and astronomic considerations rather than technological ones.

So the thickness of a wall or the size of a intercolumniation do not depend on weight calculations or material resistance, albeit intuitively interpreted, but on the day and time that construction begins, the alignment of the temple, the

Sikhara *of a Jaina temple on Mount Girnaz.*
*A trait common to many Indian temples is the*
*similarity between their smaller and bigger parts.*
*Similar forms are repeated in decreasing size, as in*
*vegetation, when gems open to reveal small leaves*
*each at different stages of growth.*
*Self-similarity is a typical characteristic of fractals.*
*Above: an example of self-similarity, the shell of*
*the* Murex Alabaster.

major financier or the position of the stars in the sky. This indeterminate nature of the building rationale is possible because the static building model is also considered natural, as if the latter were hills or stone peaks. *Sikhara* and *vimana* are hyperstatic structures and the internal spaces pose no problems because compared to the volume they are small in size, like grottoes dug out of the rock. The independence of the internal spaces is further underlined by the fact that there are almost no windows immediately below the massive towers. The gods may live in the heavens or on mountain peaks but they meet man in the bowels of the earth or the heart of the sacred mountain, places embodied by the temple building.

As far as Buddhism is concerned, many types of sacred buildings have developed in areas where this religion is present, India, China, Japan, Indonesia, etc.

Initially at least, the *stupa* (meaning top of the roof or tuft of hair) was the tangible sign of the earthly presence of Buddha. Generally speaking it is solid inside and normally marks a site sacred to Buddha and visited by the pilgrim faithful. The original stupa was a hemispheric mass surrounded by a railing that enclosed the ambulatory. On top of the cupola – a symbol of the sky and perhaps a replica of the stone mounds used to mark graves – sits a cubic block on top of which there is a pole with metal disks that decrease in size towards the top.

The *stupa* is the symbol of the body of Buddha and enshrines at least one rel-

*Hindu treatises prescribe that the modularity of temple layouts be either central or bipolar.*

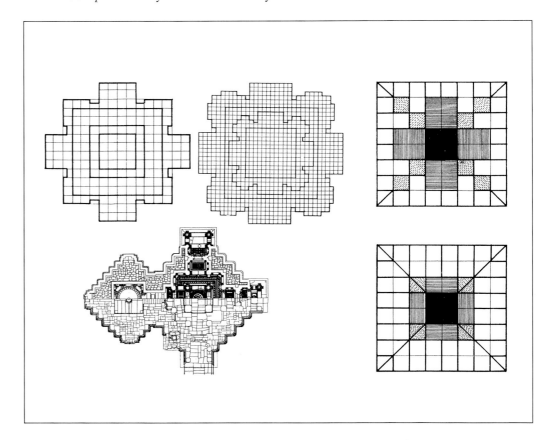

ic. To accentuate its anthropomorphic traits, eyes are often painted on the cube, and each part of the stupa tends to be invested with symbolic meaning. For example, the bell-shaped cupola is linked to the meaning of the word *buddha,* "the awakened one." Sometimes, a smaller *stupa* is also placed in large rooms called *chaitya,* that are often to be found in monastic areas. Certain *chaitya* date back to the 2nd and 1st centuries B.C. Dug out of the rock, some are amazingly beautiful with three naves, a big apse and covered by a sort of barrel vault with parallel ribs.

Another Buddhist archetype is the *torana,* large gateways with two columns that supported superimposed beams positioned at the cardinal points around the big *stupa* leading to the ambulatory.

In China, the *stupa* type tended to become a massive vertical volume with numerous floors that quickly become progressively smaller towards the top, to indicate the concept of elevation and aspiration towards the heavens. This is how the pagoda was born, based on the model of certain plants such as the *Equisetum* or the purple loosestrife (*Lytrum salicaria*) or the comma, in which growth is expressed in self-similarity or in the decreasing length of the shoots.

In Japan, the pagoda assumes a more homogeneous and strictly regulated configuration, becoming the dominant vertical element of Buddhist sanctuaries. Its wooden structure is based on the cantilever whose profile recalls the bodies of certain insects like the wasp or the ant.

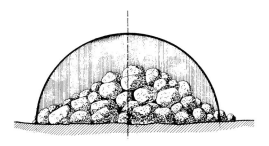

*The Buddhist* stupa *began as a mound of earth (above) to mark the earthly presence of Buddha in places he had inhabited while alive. The rite of circumambulation determines the form of the monumental* stupa *such as the one in Sāñcī (Madhya Pradesh) from the 1st century (below left).*
*Below: the small* stupa *in Swat, 2nd-4th century.*

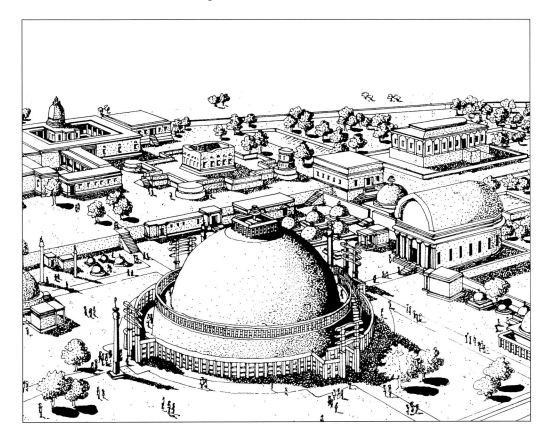

*The Phoenix pavilion (Hôôdô), former imperial villa and, from the 11th century, the Byodo-in temple in Uji.*

*The temple pagoda in Ysakushi-ji in Nara (7th century) and an orchid of the* Gymnadenia Cnopsea *family, photographed in the countryside around Calcata near Viterbo (Italy).*

The central pivot of a Japanese pagoda is made up of a huge powerful trunk, like the mast of a ship; its symbolic function of *axis mundi* combines with its static function as an antidote to the horizontal thrust of earthquakes.

In China and Japan, the characteristics of the Buddhist temple are very similar to those of Greek temples, even if the cellae are normally situated along the longer wall. Rows of wooden columns, sometimes with *entasis*, support a series of superimposed roofs whose curvilinear shape contrast the underlying prismatic volumes. This contrast between curvilinear and rectilinear, space and volume, personifies the contrast between *ying* and *yang*, male and female, heaven and earth.

In no religious tradition is the relationship between the temple type and the house stronger, or more direct, than in the Shinto tradition, especially as far as their common origins and mutual exchange is concerned. The model of the Ise temples, where the sacred mirror of Amaterasu is preserved, is a sublimation of the hut used by Japanese farmers, made of wood and raised off the ground. The ceremony which takes place every twenty years, when the enclosure and the pavilions are rebuilt exactly as they were, is one of the most fascinating examples of man's awareness of the immaterial nature of the architectural form and the fact that buildings, as indeed our bodies, deserve, so to speak, a soul.

More than just a building, the Christian temple is man – he himself House of God – inhabited by the Lord. Following on from its role as a shelter-house or mon-

*A nest of the* Cubitermes *termites with a superimposed roof structure similar to the pagoda. To defend themselves against the tropical rains, termites transform the towers into pagodas. Right: the temple of Kiyomizu-dera in Kyoto (8th-17th century). The main building seems to float in the tree-tops so that it catches the light. The building is supported by a transparent structure of pillars and wooden beams.*

250

ument to the martyrs, the "ecclesia" became the metaphor of a path that leads from the shadows to the light, through a celebration signalling "victory" over death.

If the Christian community is the "mystical body" of Christ, the involucre in which the community gathers may very well resemble a profane place, such as a pagan basilica, so long as the faithful see in this involucre the path to salvation. "Therefore, rid yourselves of all malice and all deceit, hypocrisy, envy, and slander of every kind. Like newborn babies, crave pure spiritual milk, so that by it you may grow up in your salvation, now that you have tasted that the Lord is good. As you come to him, the living Stone – rejected by men but chosen by God and precious to him – you also, like living stones, are being built into a spiritual house to be a holy priesthood, offering spiritual sacrifices acceptable to God through Jesus Christ" (*First Letter of Peter* 2, 1-5).

The swift adoption of the basilica as a Christian church, by rotating its main axis and the ensuing longitudinal vision of space, represents one of the great creative moments in the history of architecture based solely on a profound mutation in the interpretation of space rather than on an outward language change. Indifference to form, inherited from a totally different dominant culture, represents the primacy of the spiritual church over the visible one and the spirit of tolerance that originally inspired the evangelic message. Needless to say, this indifference to language became an extremely important aesthetic factor since it entailed a change in interpretation and in the meaning of form whose permanence is only "material." The rout of the classical code by the so-called "fragmentary" architecture typical of the 8th and 9th centuries highlighted how powerful this "Christian" fracture was, a fracture achieved without using physical force but by applying an unheard-of spiritual violence to the codified forms of classicism.

In his letter to the Ephesians (2, 20-22) Saint Paul writes: "built on the foundation of the apostles and prophets, with Christ Jesus himself as the chief cornerstone. In him the whole building is joined together and rises to become a holy temple in the Lord. And in him you too are being built together to become a dwelling in which God lives by his spirit."

The history of Christian churches continued to develop on the basis of a productive contradiction involving three ways of interpreting the religious building. The first identified the building with the mystical body of Christ on the cross, an image mirrored in the cruciform structure of the basilicas in which the apsidal nave sometimes appears to deviate from the main axis in a conscious reference to the reclining head of Christ after crucifixion. The second saw the building as the mirror of divine perfection, embodied by an absolute organicity based on centrality. The third interpretation envisaged the building as an enormous hut, modestly considered as a prayer space and giving total visibility to the covered space.

*An octagonal temple in Kyoto compared to the fruit of an oriental poppy.*

Islamic worship, instead, takes place in "prayer rooms" which are not really temples. In fact, mosques were never called the house of God, but rather reproduced the archetype of the house of Mohammed in Medina.

251

The Christian church, from longitudinal development to centrality. While the central model descends from the mausoleum and the martirion (*vault of the mausoleum of Santa Costanza in Rome*), the basilica is a more direct interpretation of the processional liturgy and the eschatological theme. It underlines the importance of the path and, by enclosing the space between two walls, sublimes it as a symbol of mystic elevation. In his sculpture, Cathédrale (*shown here with part of the nave in Amiens cathedral, 13th century*), Auguste Rodin wanted to symbolise the transparency and articulated verticality of the ogival system.

Below: plan of a domus ecclesiae, *a private house in which the first believers celebrated Christian rites.*

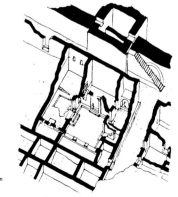

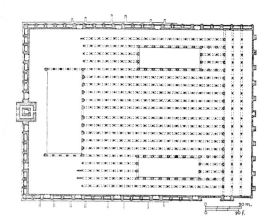

*Plan of the mosque in Rabat (1195).*

*The interlacing arches of the* mirhab *in the mosque in Cordoba.*

*Masjid* in Arab means place of worship and *giami*, a word used to indicate the more important mosques, means "that gathers within." So the mosque is essentially a place to gather the faithful. Its main characteristic is to be "aligned" towards an ideal centre, the *Ka'ba*, and to require all who enter to be "purified." However, it is not only a place of prayer. In fact, even Mohammed is reported to have said "the place where you are at the hour of prayer is a *masjid*." Purification is the only condition necessary for prayer, as well as the act of facing a certain point of the earth: this means that all mosques all over the world, wherever they are, constitute a universal central system. In fact, in order to pray all that is needed is a carpet or a built and aligned stone enclosure, even on the sands of the desert.

The most sacred place of Islam is instead the *Ka'ba*. It is useful to reflect on the fact that, while many mosques seem to be directly inspired by natural forms, especially the palm groves around the oases (the Maghreb model of Cordoba and Kairouan), or by natural caves or termite nests (the mud mosques of central Africa), the *Ka'ba* temple as a point of reference, the centre of the entire Muslim world, is shaped like a cube, the most abstract and cerebral geometric form, as suggested by the Arab word. In the Koran, the *Ka'ba* is often cited as a "sacred mosque."

In the *Sura* verse 5125 (125-128) it is written: "And when we appointed the holy house of Mecca to be the place of resort for mankind, and a place of security; and said, Take the station of Abraham for a place of prayer; and the covenanted with Abraham and Ismael, that they should cleanse my house for those who should compass it, and those who should be devoutly assiduous there and those who should bow down and worship. And when Abraham said: LORD, make this a territory of security, and bounteously bestow fruits on its inhabitants, such as them as believe in GOD and the last day; GOD answered, And whoever believeth not, I will bestow in him little, afterwards I will drive him to the punishment of hell fire; an ill journey shall it be! And when Abraham and Ismael raise the foundations of the house, saying, LORD, accept it from us..." The interpretation of the form and meaning of the *Ka'ba* is one of the favourite subjects of debate for Islamic theologians, especially for the Sufi. The explanation provided by Qazi Sa'id Qonmi in the 17th century and quoted by Henry Corbin[13] is one of the most complete and convincing; however it bases its assumptions on the fact that for the Sufi, apart from the material universe, there is a purely spiritual space in which forms exist in a much more substantial and clear-cut way than ours, they exist in a "pure element of light" very different from the unstable and corruptible elements of our world. In this superior space, in this world of the soul (*makalut*) bodies become thin bodies, "imaginal" bodies made of light.

Going back to the *Ka'ba*, Corbin writes: "While the sociologist sees only a procession of men circling a stone Temple, our theosophists see angels moving in procession from Heaven to Heaven, circling archetypal celestial temples. While we see only a gathering of sages in meditation, the enlightened one sees

254

wagons and knights of fire, in other words the spiritual world that the image represents."[14]

The simple cubic structure of the *Ka'ba*, a sort of tridimensional mandala, induces reflection on two aspects of reality, the material temple and the archetypal spiritual temple. At the same time it glorifies the perfection of the number four that the sage Ikhwan al-Safa describes as follows: "God himself has established that most things in Nature be gathered in groups of four like the four physical natures that are heat, cold, dry and wet; the four elements of fire, water, air and earth; the four humours of blood, phlegm, yellow bile and black bile; the four seasons [...]; the four cardinal points [...]; the four winds [...]; the four directions considered in relationship to the constellations (*awtad*); the four products namely, minerals, plants, animals and man."

An ancient Islamic tradition relates how God himself took a tent from Paradise and placed it on earth when Adam, chased out of Eden, complained of the solitude and wildness of the place. It was the Archangel Gabriel who pitched the tent on the exact spot where the *Ka'ba* was later built. The tent rested on a central support that was the stalk of a red hyacinth; the four poles were golden and the ropes were violet.

Therefore, according to Qazi Sa'id Qonmi, the sage must consider the *Ka'ba* as a celestial archetype, an angelic temple, and give meaning to each of the geometric elements involved. In reconstructing the formation of the cube, he must

*Mohammed visits the heavens on his mare, Buraq.*

*The mosque is a prayer hall and only two elements are required to create it: orientation and a space to kneel. In the desert, rows of stones, or even just a carpet, are quite sufficient since the mosque takes shape like a boundary around the body of a person in prayer.*

start with a square in a circle. The four points where the two figures touch are the four limits of the world of creatures: universal Soul, universal Intelligence, universal Matter and universal Nature. Stretching downwards these four points define the lower horizontal façade of a cube.

The top corners correspond to the four elements: Water, Earth, Air and Fire while below, the corners of the square correspond to the traditional Islamic identification of the corners of the *Ka'ba*: Yemen, Iraq, Syria and the West. These upper corners correspond to four cornerstones that come from the four mountains: Safa, Sinai, Salem and Abu Qobays which, in turn, correspond to the four pickets of the archetypal tent and the four great prophets Abraham, Moses, Jesus and Mohammed. In the Iraqi corner, corresponding to Mohammed, there is the black stone and next to it the entrance and the ritual font (*zamzam*). To fully understand the secret meaning of the *Ka'ba*, the sage must ponder on its symbolic nature as well as on the fact that, as a spiritual centre it is not simply a centre surrounded by infinite points, but must also be that which surrounds. Corbin writes: "Ultimately, the shape of the earthy Temple must therefore accommodate the ambiguity displayed by the centre in its spiritual forms. It is at this point that material form acquires the transparency of spiritual form; the stone temple on earth is transfigured into a spiritual temple of faith. This 'ambiguity' is the driving force behind the dematerialisation process, a typical trait of many Islamic buildings, achieved by using static paradox, geometric decorations and lighting effects."[15]

*Cordoba. The forest-mosque with its arches that rise and double, distancing themselves from the wall. The freedom of the arch culminates in the roof of the mirhab.*
*Above: the arches supporting the dome of the mirhab in the mosque in Cordoba.*

[1] cf., M. Eliade, *Il Sacro e il profano*, Boringhieri, Turin 1967, p. 15.

[2] cf., J. Michell, *Lo spirito della terra*, Red, Como 1988 (*The Earth spirit*, London 1975).

[3] cf., Le Corbusier, *Verso un'architettura*, Longanesi, Milan 1973, pp. 54-55.

[4] J.A. Ramirez et al., *Dios Architecto,* Siruela, Madrid 1991.

[5] cf., H. Rosenau, *Vision of the Temple*, London 1979; C.M. Jones (ed.), *Old Testament Illustrations*, Cambridge University Press, Cambridge 1971, pp. 158 ff.

[6] cf., J. Málek, *Gli Egizi*, De Agostini, Novara 1986; R.H. Wilkinson, *Symbols and Magic in Egyptian Art*, Thames & Hudson, London 1994.

[7] cf., R.A. Schwaller de Lubicz, *Le temple dans l'homme*, Schindler, Cairo 1949.

[8] M. Gimbutas, *The Language of the Goddess*, Thames & Hudson, London 1989.

[9] cf., G. Hersey, *The Lost Meaning of Classical Architecture*. MIT Press, Cambridge (Mass.) 1988.

[10] cf., V. Scully, *The Earth, the Temple and the Gods*, Yale University Press, New Haven 1962; Idem, *Architecture.* Saint Martin Press, New York 1991.

[11] cf., M. Bussagli, *Architettura orientale*, Electa, Milan 1991; P. Brown, *Indian Architecture*, Bombay 1965; S. Grover, *The Architecture of India, Buddhist and Hindu*, Vikas, New Delhi 1980; C. Chao-Kang, W. Blaser, *Architecture de Chine*, Delcourt, Lausanne 1988; M. Gerner, *Architectures de l'Himalaya*, Delcourt, Lausanne 1988.

[12] cf., A. Sartoris, *Léonarde Architecte*, Tallone, Paris 1952.

[13] cf., H. Corbin, *L'immagine del tempio*, Boringhieri, Turin 1983. p. 78 (*Temple and contemplation*, London 1986)

[14] *Ibid.*, p. 76.

[15] *Ibid.*, p. 93.

# The Shell, the Cupola, the Sky

*What man, however hard of heart or jealous, would not praise Filippo the architect when he sees here such an enormous construction towering above the skies, vast enough to cover the entire Tuscan population with its shadow, and done without the aid of beams or elaborate wooden supports? Surely a feat of engineering, if I am not mistaken, that people did not believe possible these days and was probably equally unknown and unimaginable among the ancients.*

Leon Battista Alberti[1]

*It is a universally accepted fact that the cupola obviously represents the sky, thereby turning the domed building into an image of the world. Normally, a cupola rests on four pillars or a square based structure which for the Chinese symbolically signifies the sky that "covers" and the earth that "supports," the round sky and the square earth.*

Pierre Grison

Nature provides us with a wealth of exemplary models that bear an extraordinary resemblance to the tent, with strong frames of taut or compressed elements and membranes securing the frame to the ground; money spiders, for example build traps for insects by stretching their webs between stalks of grass which act as poles as well as ropes. The *Argyroneta acquatica,* on the other hand builds itself a bell-shaped nest which it anchors to the surrounding vegetation by using membranes with furrowed surfaces. The first stages of the building process involve the creation of a round silk membrane, very compact and airtight. Holding its breath, the spider then dives underwater and uses its front legs to trap bubbles of air, placing them under the membrane which gradually swells until it looks like a bell. Once the bell is full of air, the spider enters its cupola-shaped nest which it leaves only to capture its prey or to renew its oxygen supply when it runs low.[2] The web woven by the common spider from branch to branch, or wall to wall, is architecturally just as important. Before becoming a proper "web," an immaterial diaphragm whose linear consistency is visible only when back-lit, it exists simply on a two-dimensional plane, like the plans, elevations and sections that architects draw on paper, or the pentagonal house inhabited by the hero of *Flatland*.[3] This web is the tangible result of a programme contained in the hereditary memory of the spider, often interpreted as the elevation of a central space: a convex orb with meridians and parallels, or an even deeper cavity. In fact, man instinctively considers the sky as an involucre, a roof, and ever since the dawn of time has felt the urge to imitate the sky, to use his own hands to build something similar to the structure shells and snails carry with them. He does this not only to protect himself and his family from the weather on a daily basis, but also to visibly express and effectively portray his "erect" position, his desire to "draw closer" to the sky.

This act of structuring or building corresponds to his desire for elevation and, even though the assembly of heavy objects concretises the force of gravity, it personifies above all man's desire to conquer this force by countering it with a visual idea, a drawing that soars skywards.

We have seen how the work of spiders illustrates just two of the many structural models classified by construction theory: the pneumatic model of the *Argyroneta* and the other based on traction ropes. The tensile membrane structures, that thanks to Frei Otto[4] opened up a whole new world in the field of lightweight roofs, all depend on the analytical studies of natural structures carried out by biologists at the University of Stuttgart. Apart from their similarity with nomads' tents, the morphology of these structures looks astonishingly like wind dunes, the pattern of cusps, the dorsal lines and saddle-shaped surfaces that are visible from higher ground when the desert sands are lit by the horizontal rays of the rising or setting sun. The pliant lightweight membranes of the tensile structures contrast with the rigid supports and the traction-resistant reinforcement elements. Particularly important are the multiple solutions that emerge from the need to strengthen the edges of the membrane which, as in many biological structures, become "lines of force" with an expressive potential in relation to the internal response of matter. It is interesting to note here that along the edges, the auditory nerve's helicoidal surface has a sort of frame that acts very much like the ropes that strengthen the borders of the membranes of tensile structures.

The pneumatic structures recently developed largely to solve the problems involved in the quick assembly of temporary shelters have not yet been convincingly employed in the field of architecture. Nonetheless, in this context they are relevant to my considerations on metaphors and symbolic imitation. Every time man tried to use a resistant involucre as a roof, he had to deal with the forces of gravity. However, in his struggles he always strove to reverse this situation; the end result looked very much like a boat when the wind fills a sail, making it look like a vault and turning it into a precious instrument of propulsion. Nor is it unusual for the wind to blow upwards from the bottom of a rock face and, if necessary, easily fill a tense membrane. When Filippo Brunelleschi built the cupola of Santa Maria del Fiore in Florence (which Alberti states with delighted exaggeration "shades all the peoples of Tuscany with its shadow") he explicitly uses the metaphor of inflation, as noted by G.C. Argan: "A cupola raised on strong supports inserted in the ground would not have been as magnificent or as "inflating" as he would have wished, a present participle that Brunelleschi used in his work program. This clearly indicates that the structure was to be light and not heavy, energised by an expansive thrust."

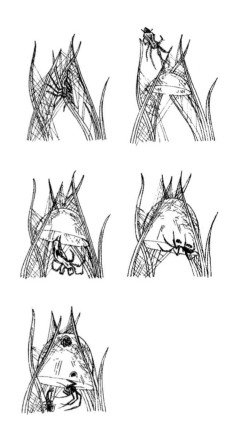

*Five stages in the construction of the underwater nest of the amphibious spider,* Argyroneta aquatica: *an immaterial cupola made of air trapped by using craftily entwined algae.*

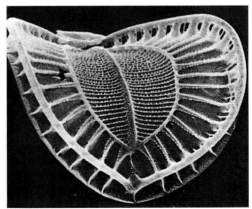

*A tensile structure by Frei Otto compared with the image of a diatom, the* Campylodiscus C, *under an electronic microscope.*

259

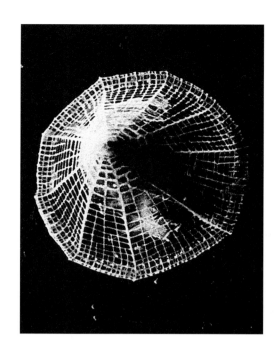

*The skeleton of a radiolarian, the* Litharacnium, *compared with the "rose" pavilion of the Diplomat's Social Club in Riyadh, Saudi Arabia (Jan Liddel Happold Buro, 1975).*

*Design project of the Saitama Arena, Omiya City, Japan (Richard Rogers and partners, 1993).*

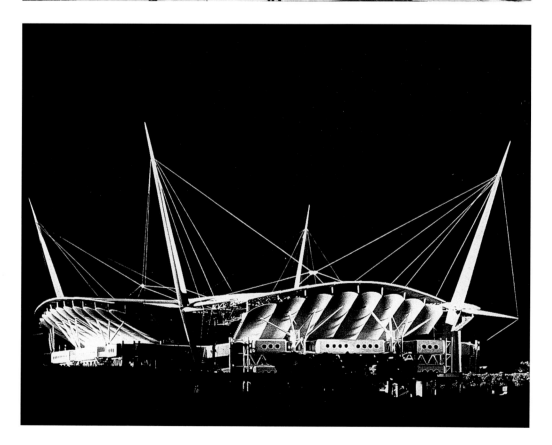

*Central capsule of the skeleton of a radiolarian of the* Didimocyrtis *family, enlarged approximately 4000 times.*

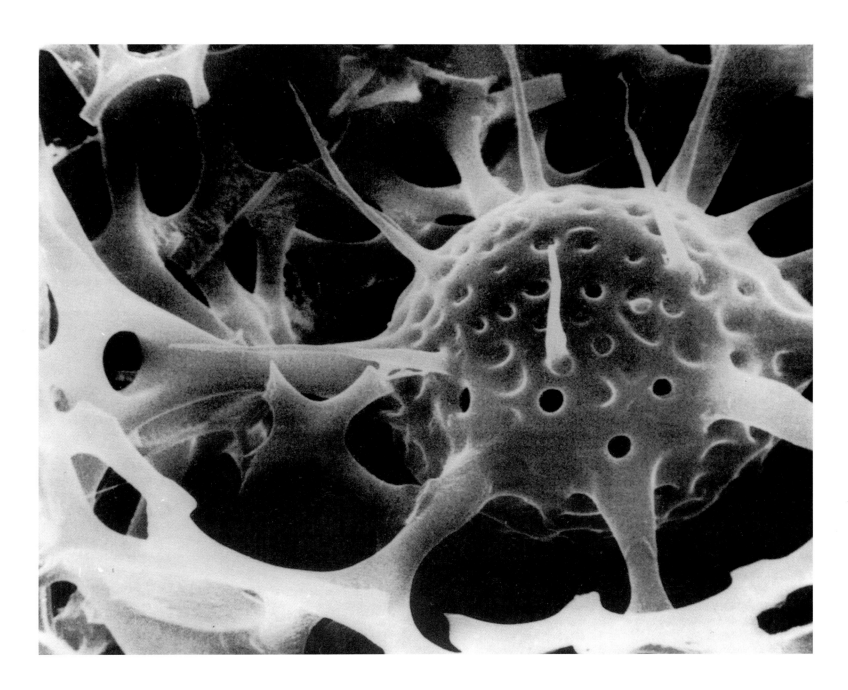

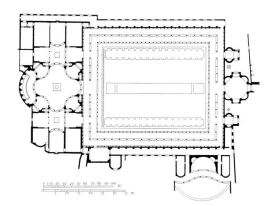

*The Square of Gold in Hadrian's Villa in Tivoli (2nd century): plan and detail.*

In the case of Santa Maria del Fiore, it is quite possible to emphasise how each of the eight segments of the cupola are similar to sails. The cupola patented by the engineer, Mr. Bini, looks like a series of inflated balls that rest on the ground to act as the ribs of a hemispherical roof. A framework is then placed over the ribs and covered by a thin layer of cement. Hermetically sealed plastic membranes are also used in roofs in which the involucre is supported by mechanically compressed air.

Roofs that use cables normally need a primary supporting structure, be it natural or artificial, on which to hang a second "supported" structure using filiform elements. This second structure fulfils the function for which the building was designed. What immediately springs to mind is how similar it is to living creatures with external skeletons, such as snails and shells, but in this case, the similarity is only theoretical and has no morphological correspondence. Such similarities can be found in foraminifers and other aquatic organisms. Construction cables can be compared to the thousands of pseudopodia that stick out of the skeleton pores of aquatic organisms and billow in the water. This particular filiform structure is set in motion not by gravity, but by an irradiating centrifugal force very similar to sunlight.

But the most obvious similarities are those mentioned earlier: spider webs that exploit the law that states that resistance is inversely proportional to the thickness of the thread. In fact, the secretion from the spinneret of spiders weighing 1.1 g/sq.cm is 30 kg/mm and its breaking point is 27 km. The cement harp built by Calatrava in Seville to support the bridge over the river Guadalquivir is just as bewitching as one of those webs which, when entering a cave filled with just one ray of sunlight, seem to capture the light and suggest imminent sound.

Whatever its supporting structure, the roof of a circular hut is in itself a small cupola. Since it covers an internal space and is shaped like a shell, it tends to fulfil the symbolic role of an artificial sky. In some primitive societies, the roofs of their huts are built separately and then lowered over the cylindrical basement that will anchor them to the ground. A detailed description of the construction of a cupola-hut, regarded as a microcosm, has been handed down to us by the old Indian witch-doctor, Black Moose, who belonged to the North American Sioux tribe, Ogdala. He writes that one of the ceremonies of the tribe held during its sacred year involved building a pavilion dedicated to the dance of the sun. Together with his assistants the first thing the witch-doctor did was to choose a cotton tree as the central support of the conical roof and, having found it, mark it with sage. The next day he offered his pipe to the tree and warned it that, in accordance with the sacred rites, it had been chosen to be the central pillar of the pavilion to be erected at the intersection of the four sacred routes representing the great powers of the universe. After having offered his pipe to the sky and the earth, the witch-doctor touched the tree-trunk at the four cardinal points. After the chief had danced a victory dance around the tree, a man "of impeccable character" was chosen to cut it down while another man, "of calm and solemn" manners, was chosen to strike the final blow. Great care was taken to ensure that the trunk never touched the ground. The cotton tree was chosen for its microcosmic nature because the sectioned tree trunk has a five-pointed star which the Ogdala Sioux believed indicated the presence of the Great Spirit. After another sacred dance, the trunk of the cotton tree was re-erected on a base and then surrounded by twenty-eight forked pillars corresponding to the twenty-eight days of the lunar calendar. At the same time, a symbolic conical vault was created by connecting the central pillar to the peripheral ones by means of an equal number of poles, each symbolising one particular aspect of creation.

The clearest expression of the celestial symbolism of the cupola may be seen in Nero's Domus Aurea, with its large spherical roof "quite versatile, in which the celestial spheres revolved and the planets were all plain to see."[5] It is not certain, but it is very probable, that this roof covered the *coenatio* that still exists today: the rotating mechanism "like the engine of the world" could therefore be seen from the room's central oculus.

Less obvious, but no less direct, is the relationship between the image of the sky and the cupola of Hadrian's Pantheon. On this subject a 3rd-century writer, Dio Cassius, wrote: "Perhaps its name comes from its many ornamental statues of gods, including Mars and Venus; but I believe instead that it depends on the fact that the cupola of the Pantheon looks like the vault of heaven."[6]

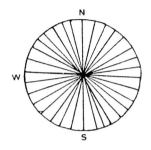

*The tent of the Sun Dance of the Ogdala Sioux.*

*Section of Hadrian's Pantheon in Rome highlighting the visual angles from three observation points (drawing by Otto Schubert).*

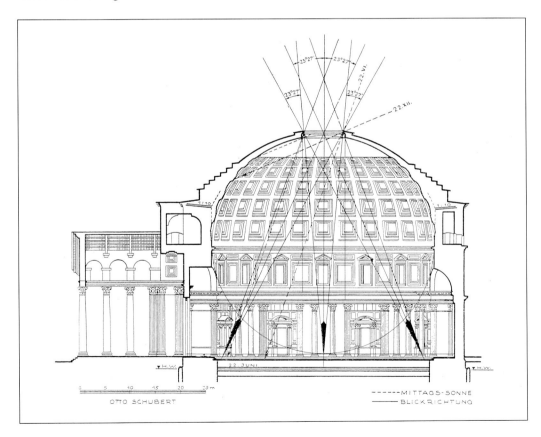

*Photograph of a melon (*Cucurbita melo*) and, below, the cupola of a small orthodox church at Messarià (island of Santorini). An intrados with crests and sails is frequent in Hadrian's architecture, while it is much rarer in the extrados of the cupola of this type of geometric structure.*

Emperor Hadrian was probably the inspirational force if not the actual architect of this great building. He studied the model of the *yurta*, but more than anything else he wished the Pantheon to be the image of a universe reunited, exemplified through the supremacy of one city and one man over the world. The cylindrical base, symbolising the earth, is divided into layers that appear to rotate perhaps due to the vertical non-alignment of the superimposed orders, while the central oculus that lets in the light is an eloquent solar image. If one reflects on the fact that Hadrian, during his Roman sojourns, used to administer justice inside the temple, it isn't difficult to agree with Henry Stierlin's statement that the Pantheon was Hadrian's *aula regia* as well as a temple to himself.

If the naturalistic inspiration of the Pantheon is typically structural in nature, in the sense that the building is a microcosm that reflects the macrocosm in contracted form, Hadrian's career as an architect is also influenced by another, even more naturalistic type of inspiration that earned him the venomous comments of his contemporaries, namely the umbrella vaults used in his Villa in Tivoli and in a pavilion of the Horti Sallustiani whose resemblance to a pumpkin was a matter of ironic censure. It is worth rereading the whole story written by Dio Cassius on the conflict between the Emperor and Apollodorus of Damascus: "but [Hadrian] first exiled Apollodorus and later did him to death. Apollodorus was the architect of many of Trajan's creations in Rome, the Forum, the Odeon, and the Baths. The reason cited was that he had committed a number of murders; but the real reason lay elsewhere. While answering Trajan who had consulted him on certain aspects of construction, Hadrian had interrupted him so he had answered: 'Be off and draw [his] gourds.' For it so chanced, continues this narrator, that Hadrian at this time was priding himself on his painting. He never forgot nor forgave the insult, when Emperor."[7]

After Hadrian, the pumpkin or melon-shaped form dividing the cupola into segments was inserted in the intrados of canopies in Syria and Palestine. It is also associated with Indian archetypes inspired by the lotus flower, considered a cosmic symbol.[8]

In Hadrian's Villa, the way in which the buildings' organic complexity adapts to the complex lie of the land illustrates how classical language can dialogue with nature, how structural imitation and the harmonious relationship between natural and architectural spatiality can co-operate so well as to create a dynamic whole, thereby enriching the relationship between the parts.

According to the latest expert theories, the mysterious maritime theatre, situated in an important area of the Villa, has even closer ties with the Pantheon, since the theatre repeats in a more articulate and subtle way the Pantheon's cosmological conception as well as its overall size. The theatre consisted of a circular island surrounded by a ring canal perhaps symbolising the primordial ocean from which the earth emerged. In the middle of the theatre there was a baldachin with a lightweight roof, perhaps a transparent aviary like the one made famous by Varro. In this very private *aula regia* Hadrian probably consulted the

*Left: the* Echinocactus grusonii *(also called "golden barrel" by the English and "mother-in-law's chair" by the Italians).*
*Above: the* Astrophytum myriostigma *cactus and an Islamic cupola in Samarkand.*

The Astrophytum ornatum *cactus and the great ribbed cupola of the Shir Dar Madrasah in Samarkand (Abdul Djabbar, 1619-32). Below: interior view of the cupola of the Ambassador's Hall in the Alhambra in Granada that may be interpreted as the counter-form of a fully flowered* Mammillaria marnieriana.

*Opposite page, the cupola of Sant'Ivo alla Sapienza in Rome (Francesco Borromini, 1645-55) compared with a shell (the* Turritella terebra) *and a Brazilian cactus.*

*The cupola with crests and sails in the new sacristy of San Lorenzo in Florence (Filippo Brunelleschi, 1421) and, below, the cupola of the chapel of the Holy Sindon in the Duomo in Turin (Guarino Guarini, 1668). The system of superimposed arches looks like the structure of fish scales and peacock feathers.*

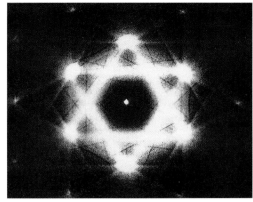

*The cupola of the church of San Lorenzo in Turin (Guarino Guarini, 1666-80) compared with a diffusion diagram of a silicon crystal.*

*The cupola of Sant'Andrea al Quirinale in Rome (Gianlorenzo Bernini, 1676). The beehive coffers with hexagonal cells, adapted to centrality by reducing their size towards the centre, is comparable to the crown of a hornet's nest.*

Spherical aggregates of azurite crystals and the church of the Sanctuary of Mary at Lomec (author unknown, 1692-1702). The church is located in the centre of a pattern of tree-lined avenues that form a sort of leafy basilica.

A roof terrace covered in lead in Palazzo Rocca on the Grand Canal in Venice and, right, a building made of branch bundles and plastic sheets in Langenthal Switzerland (Marcel Kalberer, architect, 1988). This is a modern interpretation of the "mudhif," a type of roof believed to be 7000 years old and still used in Iraq in the region between the Tigris and the Euphrates, where it is built by women who use canes of the Fragmitus comunis species, and only knives and billhooks as tools.

*The dried skin of the calyx of a winter cherry* (Physalis alkekengii) *and, below, detail of the church of Saint Basil in Moscow (16th century).*

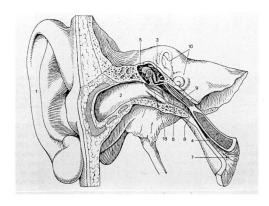

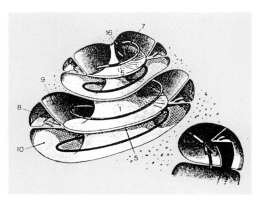

*Two drawings of the human ear and the auditory duct and the project by Frank Lloyd Wright for the Crescent Opera, Civic Auditorium, Garden of Eden in Baghdad, 1957.*
*Right: the greenhouse designed for the Natural History Museum in Taiwan (Bryan Irwin and Ian Tyndal, architects; Bruce Denzinger and Ove Arup Ass., structuralists). A cupola that uses the spider's technique as well as phyllotaxis.*

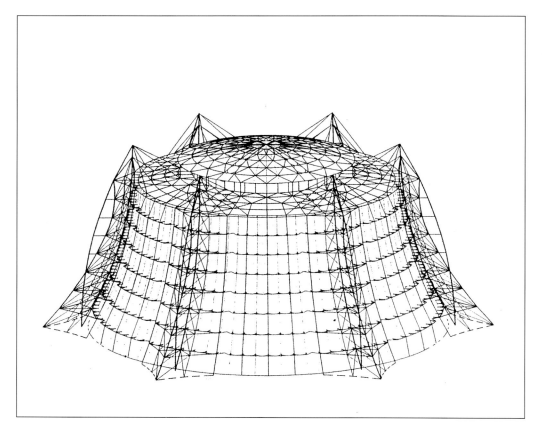

stars to draw up his horoscope and ritualised his public appearances, his escape from the responsibilities of command, his hours of solitude and meditation.

The dome of the Pantheon, with its low and compressed external profile, corresponded to the needs of its internal spatiality. Initially only barely visible from the square in front, it was Early Christian architecture that laid the ground work for the invention of the cupola as a vertical volume crowning a building by highlighting the central walls. Later, the cupola gained importance in Byzantine architecture by obeying the logic of internal space. In order to achieve the model of the emergent volume with sufficient verticality to create a sense of movement towards the sky, it was necessary to separate the internal space and the volume obtained by superimposing wooden structures on the cupola, as in Saint Mark's basilica in Venice. These wooden structures rose upwards to make an otherwise incommunicable reality visible from the exterior. After the important preparatory experiments of the great Armenian lanterns, the theme of the cupola exploded in the Islamic world because it had become necessary to clearly identify the buildings destined to be used as sepulchres. Thus the Islamic world resorted once again to nature by shaping convex volumes as phallic symbols, as pointed fruits, as cactus lined with parallel or helicoidal ribs.

In Russian architecture, on the other hand, other natural structures such as the onion are translated into wood and stone using overlapping patterns, a mixture of arches and horizontal beams and a plastic effect that recalls the rhythmic layers of growth (Saint Basil in Moscow, 1554) or the growth of vegetable bulbs when they come into contact with the earth (church of the Transfiguration in Kizi, 1714).

[1] cf., C. Grayson, *Leon Battista Alberti, On Painting and Sculpture*, Phaidon Press Ltd., London 1972, p. 33.

[2] cf., R. Preston Mafham, *Spiders and Scorpions*, Crescent Books, New York 1991, p. 99.

[3] cf., E.A. Abbott, *Flatlandia*, Adelphi, Milan 1992 (*Flatland*, New York 1998).

[4] cf., F. Otto *L'architettura della natura*, Il Saggiatore, Milan 1986.

[5] cf., P. Portoghesi, *Borromini nella cultura europea*, Laterza, Rome-Bari 1982, p. 29 ff.

[6] cf., W.L. Macdonald, *Hadrian's Villa and Its Legacy*, Yale University Press, New Haven 1995; H. Stierlin, *Adrien et l'architecture romaine*, Payot, Paris 1984.

[7] cf., B.W. Henderson, *The Life and Principate of the Emperor Hadrian*, Methuen & Co., London 1923.

[8] cf., E. Baldwin Smith, *The Dome*, Princeton University Press, Princeton 1950.

# Ribs, the Venation, Vaults

*Harmony, unity.*
*Amongst all our trees, the linden is one of the most noble.*
*Its balanced ramification may be found in the veins of leaves.*
*Unity.*

François de Pierrefeu and Le Corbusier

In architecture the term "ribs," clearly borrowed from anatomy, indicates a membrane that either crosses a structural expanse, in particular a vaulted surface, or juts out from it and in this case is synonymous with the term ribbed vault. In certain primitive walls built with mud, branches or canes, it is sometimes possible to see these ribs since they protrude slightly from the layer of mud used to cover them. The rib may be used either as a reinforcement or as an element that generates a contrast of light and shadow, like the fluting of columns. In olden days in the East, a wall with pilaster strips and cornice, such as the one in the temple of Sakhara, fulfilled three functions: it provided geometric clarity, was visible from a distance and had a visual "hold." As far as the structure of the hut is concerned, the rib is either a support that "innervates" a surface made of leafy branches or animal skins or, when the leaves of the branches are thick enough to guarantee isolation and impermeability, it is a unique and independent building element. In the architecture of animal "primates," who are close to man in their intelligence and ability to make tools, but so very distant in their architectural ambitions, the rib is used by the gorillas of the Virunga mountains; they either bend branches to fashion ingenious tree nests, or break them off to weave nocturnal shelters on the ground, at times with intuitive geometric precision. This is the case of the nests illustrated by George B. Schaller where one can see interesting examples of intersecting ribs built by coupling branches and planting just one end in the ground.[1] This architectural theme is best represented by the complex and poetic cupola of the Mirhab in the mosque in Cordoba. As far as wooden structures are concerned, the rib corresponds to the beam, the supports and the balloon frames of the walls. This is the osteological model that grows endemically and together with the nervous system and the network of tendons which permits movement, contributes to stability in a living body by balancing the force of gravity. To this organic comparison one must add the "constructive" experience of weaving and the art of the basket-maker that reveals the "case model" vocation of human intelligence that never tires of experimenting diversity.

Between the 10th and 16th centuries the *Fachswerkbauten* technique developed differently from one European country to another. The remarkable effects of this development demonstrate the successful interpenetration of organic inspiration and geometric abstraction and allow the relationship between structure and decoration to be expressed as freely as possible. These interpretations, alternately either rigorously univalent or ambiguous and imaginative, bordered on the limits of expressionism.

The pattern created by the skeleton frame of the wooden structures, so different in France, England and Germany, seems to reflect the quality of the materials and the landscape as well as certain aspects of each countries' different collective sensibilities. These patterns also recall the dappled coats of the animals that inspired Blake with the expression "fearful symmetry."[2]

As a synonym of the human rib, the architectural rib confirms its bonds with biological forms that develop longitudinally under the surface of the skin. It began to take root in Roman architecture when brick arches were inserted into the large vaulted roofs made of concrete. These arches were either built at the groins of a transept or, as in the Horti Liciniani mausoleum, used to divide the hemispheric cupola into panels, discharging the weight onto the groins in order to insert large windows. In Roman cupola, instead, the rib does not normally protrude from the intrados. However, in the coffered ceiling of the cupola in the Pantheon and the apsidal bowl-shaped vault of the Temple of Venus in Rome dating back to the Servian period, excavation of the laquears revealed a "ribbed" structure along the meridians and parallels of the spherical surface, and in the temple of Venus in Rome the rib is portrayed as a diagonal weave very similar to that of baskets.

On the other hand, the system that unites arch and entablature, eclectically superimposing the various orders, creates a plastic projection of the wall that gradually increases towards the top and could be considered a sort of evaginated nervous system. In this context, Hellenistic and Roman architecture paves the way for the linear and plastic interpretation of the forces that subtend to the brick surfaces.

But it is during the 8th century, in the chapel of Acphat in Armenia, that for the first time the rib as an arch breaks free of the wall and stands alone with a certain degree of independence. This single act sparked the Islamic system of in-

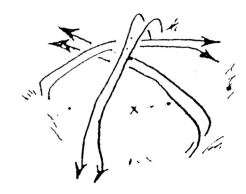

A gorilla's nest in the Virunga mountains (Kabara). The drawing illustrates the criteria with which the grass bundles and branches are bent to form a pattern of intersecting ribs.
Below: the nervous system of the human body (A. Vesalius, De Humani Corporis Fabrica, Basel 1553, pl. 82).
Left: Moreton Hall Castle with its wooden structure (16th century). The contrast between the wooden and plastered parts form a vibrant linear fabric.

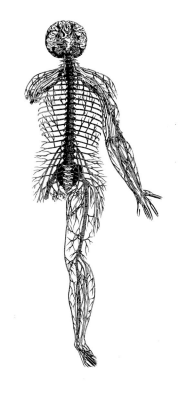

terlacing arches that quickly spread to Spain and India under the reign of the Moguls, only to return to Romanesque and Gothic Europe in the form of ribs used to highlight the groins and to fuse polystyle pillars and vaults into a unitary system ultimately leading to the invention of the "ogival" system.[3]

In the Late Gothic architecture of Northern Europe and England, the ribbing system that had simplified building techniques by taking the weight off the centering system now acquired distinct expressive traits, and the infinite variety of the different patterns became the central theme of compositional research for almost two centuries. In the heyday of the Gothic period, the historical evolution of the great French cathedrals appears to bear witness to the progressive refinement of an established system based on a series of spans covered by cross vaults, but in Late Gothic architecture the intersection of the ribs seems to follow a "case model" method that experiments with increasingly complicated and paradoxical systems. It almost seems as if this architecture wished to imitate the entire array of natural forms, the inexhaustible creative skills that nature uses every spring to fill fields and forests with infinite varieties of blooming flowers. The use of words such as "impoverishment" and "decadence" in relation to this culture comes from a censorious partisan attitude which should be overcome in order to bring one of the most interesting pages of 15th- and 16th-century architecture back into the spotlight.[4]

The geometrical design of the intersection of the ribs fans out from the diagonal pattern of the transept, enriching it in a number of complementary direc-

*The main nave of Nôtre-Dame cathedral in Laon (1174-1205). The ribs of the ogive generate a series of small cylindrical columns against the wall, but remain completely rounded.*

*The centrally planned entry portico of the church of Saint Mary Redcliffe in Bristol (1280). Ribs spring from the groins and open at the top like branches to support the central hexagon.*
*Below: ceiling of Amiens cathedral seen from the chorus below.*

*Internal structure of a passion-flower of the* Quadrangolaris *variety and, below, internal view of the bell involucre of the datura flower. Opposite page: the fan vaults of King's College chapel in Cambridge. This type of vault, particularly loved by the Tudor King Henry VIII, probably had a symbolic meaning since it was based on the repeated theme of the circle and the wheel. The sundial, which was even paraded during the welcoming ceremony to honour the arrival of Catherine of Aragon in England, was used in the chapel to evoke "celestial space," while the circle perhaps alluded to the heavenly vault and divine perfection.*

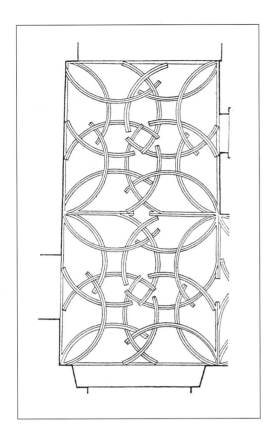

*The geometric pattern of two spans of the vault over the Horsemen's staircase in the Castle in Prague (Benedikt Ried, 1493-1502).*
*Right: the ribbed ceiling of the former dining room in the Hotel Villa Igea in Palermo (Ernesto Basile, 1898).*

tions. While maintaining its encapsulation within a rectangular cell, the first step is to elaborate increasingly complicated stellar variations of the transept. In the opposite direction, the modular units of the transept tend to join together, creating either ribbed barrel vaults or stellar vaults that spring from the supporting pillars through the use of corbels and consoles. A totally different morphology results from the use of curvilinear or mixtilinear ribs that extend beyond the boundaries between the transepts, introducing fan or "mushroom" vaults characterised by stellar or flower-shaped patterns; this pattern was used mainly in England. These symbolic and naturalistic implications are confirmed in yet another area of study: the symmetric grids and interrupted ribs that imitate the growth and intertwinement of rambling plants.[5] In some cases, the ribs break loose from the surface of the vaults and meet in space, resting on suspended keystones that, like virtuosi, express the way in which the wall gradually frees itself from the forces of gravity. The most bewitching examples of this type of "staccato" technique are to be found in the Wladislao room and adjoining corridor of the Castle in Prague designed by Benedikt Ried,[6] an expressionist *ante litteram* whose dramatically intense images are comparable to the tragic realism of Roger van der Weyden. This phytomorphic analogy culminates in the parish church of Weistrach in Austria in which the curvilinear ribs are wound together and overlap like large transparent lobate leaves. This structure gives the onlooker the impression of being in a forest, not a Nordic forest, but a forest of luscious tropical

280

plants or else in a magical forest full of flowers, the exact vision seen by a bee when buzzing around under the corolla.

The Gothic interpretation of ribs as living membranes, as suggestive as it is arbitrary, is based on the careful imitation of a wood and the natural convergence of branches whose intersecting pattern resembles a series of ogives. In an exceptionally poetic passage of his book *Aesthetics*, Hegel expresses some reservations regarding this interpretation: "Penetrating into a medieval cathedral, one's mind grapples not so much with the solidity and mechanical functionality of the supporting pillars and the vault above, but with the images of an arched woodland, in which rows and rows of trees bend their branches towards one another until they touch. A cross-beam needs a fixed point of support and a horizontal plane; but in Gothic buildings the walls independently and freely rise upwards, as do the pillars which at the top branch out in various directions and almost haphazardly intertwine. In other words, the fact that they support the vault, even if the latter does in fact rest on pillars, is neither obvious nor a given fact [*für sich hingestelt*]. It's almost as if they [the columns] do not support it, just like the branches of a tree are not supported by the trunk, on the contrary, their slightly bent shape seems to be a continuation of the trunk itself. These branches, together with the branches of other trees, create a leafy roof [...]. This is not to say, however, that the Gothic architect took trees and woods as a model for his forms."[7]

This ability to discern between analogy and conscious imitation was not a trait that belonged to the Scottish geologist Sir James Hall who, to demonstrate his belief in the systematic traits of analogy, attempted a personal experiment ironically illustrated by Rykwert in his marvellous book *On Adam's House in Paradise*: "Hall was struck by the beauty and stylistic coherence of many French Gothic buildings, and familiar as he was with the theory of the origin of the orders, he thought that 'some rustic buildings, differing widely from the Grecian original, might have suggested the Gothic forms.' He decided to investigate the matter, when he, too, came upon a happy accident. His journey through that part of France happened to be just after vintage time. The peasants were 'collecting and carrying home the long rods or poles which they make use of to support their vines, or to split into hoops; and these were to be seen in every village, standing in bundles, or waving, partly loose, upon carts. It occurred to me that a rustic dwelling might be constructed from such rods... bearing a resemblance to works of Gothic architecture.'

"The discovery involved Hall in an experiment, which, as he points out, is true *histoire raisonnée*, since he is verifying a hypothesis about the past by re-enacting it and hopes that his researches will lead to literary or archaeological discoveries which may either confirm or refute it. The system is simple. A row of equidistant poles of more or less the same height is fixed in the ground, as in various accounts of the origin of orders. But to each of these 'Gothic poles', a surround of pliant willow rods is applied and fixed. When the opposite willow rods

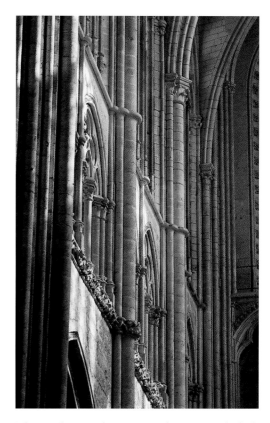

*The windows in the transept of Amiens cathedral (Robert de Luzarches, 13th century).*
*Below: plan of the roof in the Ludwig wing of the Chancery in Prague (Benedikt Ried, 1505).*

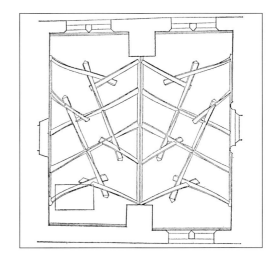

*Vault of the church of Saint Barbara in Kuttenberg (Benedikt Ried, 1512-48) and, right, intersecting ribs in Wells cathedral (14th century).*
*Below: vault of the inner portico of the church of Saint George in Nordlingen (16th century).*

are brought together and tied, the resulting form is something like a groined vault, strong enough to carry a thatched roof, say. Small variations in the joining of the willow rods provide the models for varieties in arching and vaulting. Hall assumes the complexity to have been progressive: so the pointed arch, the clustered column, the branching roof, 'the three leading characteristics of Gothic architecture,' have been accounted for.

"The sides of the building are filled with upright rods on which in-and-out split willow rods are plaited horizontally, and probably caked with clay where that is available. Where windows are required, the matting is omitted, and this means that the windows are inevitably mullioned. Indeed, the upright rods, which are not rigid, may be tied together in various ways where they are free. And so another feature, tracery, is explained. The experimental verification had to be made. 'Finding that all the essential parts of Gothic architecture could thus be explained [...]. I was desirious of submitting the theory to a kind of experimental test... With the help of a very ingenious country workman [John White, cooper, in the village of Cockburnspath in Berwickshire], I began this in Spring 1792, and completed it in the course of the winter following.'

"Hall is convinced that the method is so simple that it could be executed anywhere, with the help of almost any sharp instrument: 'A set of posts of ash, about three inches in diameter, were placed in two rows, four feet asunder [...] then a number of slender and tapering willow rods, ten feet in length, were ap-

*A flower of the* Butumus umbrellatus *variety and the ribs of a chapel in the Frauenkirche in Ingolstadt (1509-24).*

plied to the posts [...] and formed into a frame which, being covered with thatch, produced a very substantial roof, under which a person may walk with ease [...]. In the course of spring and summer, 1793, a great number of the rods struck root and throve well. Those of the door, in particular, produced tufts of leaves along the bent part, exactly where they occur in stone-work [...]. I have likewise had the satisfaction in the course of last autumn (1796) of finding one entire cusp formed by the bark in a state of decay, in a place corresponding exactly to those we see in executed Gothic works.'

"Although the foliation was not quite as abundant as Hall had hoped, he had justified, to his own and his friends' satisfaction, the timber origin of most Gothic forms."[8]

The use of ribs was experimented internally by Filippo Brunelleschi who used the "crest and sail" model in the sacristy of San Lorenzo and the Pazzi chapel in Florence. This same artist, the heretical heir of Gothic culture filtered by the plasticity of Italian taste, was the first to use ribs in the external structure of Santa Maria del Fiore. These ribs acted as a link between the external vault made of real sails and the internal vault woven like a basket to keep it as light as possible. This model was later used in the cupola of Saint Peter's by Michelangelo who also inserted ribs into the intrados, thus establishing the fruit-shaped model of Baroque cupola, divided into segments and positioned in such a way as to graft these characteristic vertical projections onto the city's skyline.[9]

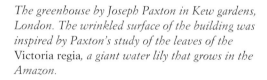

*The greenhouse by Joseph Paxton in Kew gardens, London. The wrinkled surface of the building was inspired by Paxton's study of the leaves of the* Victoria regia, *a giant water lily that grows in the Amazon.*

In modern architecture, ribbed surfaces gradually become increasingly important and this naturalistic inspiration often turns into quite a conscious choice. This is the case of Paxton's spatial structure, Crystal Palace, based on the *Victoria Regia*, a tropical water lily whose leaves (with raised edges like small boats) can bear the weight of a man.[10] Although gifted with very different sensibilities, Alessandro Antonelli and Antoni Gaudí both creatively tackled this ribbing theme. Antonelli elaborated bold structures in the filigree of his most daring buildings, raising masonry techniques to unheard-of virtuoso levels: the cupola of San Gaudenzio in Novara and the Mole Antonelliana in Turin. In both cases, the frames that connect the vaults are used to lighten them, to free them from the inert mass and develop classic naturalistic themes with laconic elegance. Gaudí picks up on the legacy left by Gothic and Islamic architecture and similarly innervates surfaces in order to leave them as translucent as skin. The crowning structure of Casa Milá, the roofs of the village of Bellesguard, and the crypt of Santa Coloma in Park Güell are all excellent examples of a technology that unites artisan simplicity with a deft technique rooted in a profound knowledge of the achievements of construction theory. However, in the main church of Park Güell and in the Sagrada Familia, naturalistic inspiration goes well beyond surface ribbing. It is the columns, multiplying in ever more minute branches, that become trees and find their "treeness,"[11] and it is the cupola, growing out of one another in a gemmation process in which certain elements of the mineral

*The leaf of a* Victoria regia.

285

*Detail of the underside of the leaf of the* Victoria regia: *the ribs of the leaf are easily seen.*

*A wing of a dragonfly.*

world mix with others, that confirm the architect's organic vision. In the model and plans for Park Güell, space is like an ensemble of adjacent cells and the involucre is furrowed by a continuous web of frames plastically representing the network of the lines of force. Introduced by Gaudí, based on the teachings of the Gothic and Islamic worlds and the intuitions of Viollet-Le-Duc, the column-tree officially entered modern repertoire. On the one hand, it was destined to be adored by the creators of those metallic structures used to cover large spaces, such as the Machine Gallery at the Universal Exhibition in Paris (F. Dutert and H.J. Coutamin, 1889) and on the other, it was lovingly used in expressionist research and the work of Giovanni Michelucci.

Ribbing also caught the attention of the masters of reinforced concrete. Anatole de Baudot,[12] Perret, Maillart, Nervi, Torroja, Candela, Morandi and recently Calatrava, have all interpreted it individually according to their own sensibilities, taking into account the "resistance of form" that requires the use of inflected or bent surfaces. By so doing they modified the role of ribs, from a mere element added to strengthen a frame, to an intrinsic characteristic of the membrane itself which, when bent, is capable of playing the role of both skin and bone. In this case too, nature has been plentiful in supplying models, permeated by a tendency to fully exploit the resistance of the various forms. Take for instance the wing of the dragonfly, the natural example that most morphology scholars use due to its complexity and the remarkably efficient output of its slender structure. The wing of the dragonfly, a transparent membrane stretched over a delicately ribbed fabric, possesses three different resistance strategies, intelligently combined in order to function perfectly. The wing's main ribs are parallel to its upper edge, joined together by small orthogonal ribs. On the edge opposite the main ribs, the membrane is innervated by a network with approximately one hundred polygons with three, four, five, six and seven sides. These polygons demonstrate how the functional response of all biological forms is associated with a need for self-presentation.[13] To achieve this greater resistance, dictated by the incredible speed of the dragonfly's wing beat, the wing's design presents another astute invention: the membrane between the parallel ribs of the upper edges is situated on a zigzag slope created by introducing special transversal reinforcement frames.

The feeling one gets from an exhaustive knowledge of certain natural structures is that research in this field has only just begun and in time could become a remarkable driving force, not only in aeronautical engineering and other specific fields of technology, but also in an uncompromising review of architecture. However, from a communications point of view, one must not forget that in this case, symbolic analogy, indissolubly linked to the role of the archetype, works alongside structural analogy.

How important it would be for acoustics to discover the mechanism that permits the wings of owls, with their special hook-shaped feathers, to open and close so silently that the bird can snatch his unsuspecting prey at night. Even in the field of botany, this structural viewpoint has forged new horizons in interdisciplinary dialogue.

The research by Adrian D. Bell from the School of Biological Sciences of the University of North Wales includes a chapter on the architecture of trees: his work may easily be transposed into the field of design.[14]

Bell's idea of "treeness" as a law that determines ramifications and articulations throughout the plant world, unites the column and the rib in a single plastic unit. During structural analysis, this structure highlights the contrast between the open form of the branch system and the closed form of the leaves based on the model of a rigid irrigation system rather than that of a river basin. If the ribbing of leaves has a main system that is either forked or parallel-nerved, often a secondary system exists as an offshoot of the first and functions as a feeder membrane through the smaller network of the veins.

[1] cf., G.B. Schaller, *The Mountain Gorilla. Ecology and Behavior*, Chicago University Press, Chicago 1963.

[2] Blake uses this expression when referring to the coat of the tiger. Cf., I. Tewart, M. Golubitsky, *Fearful Symmetry*, Blackwell, Oxford 1992.

[3] cf., K.H. Clausen, *Deutsche Gevölbe der Spätgotik*, Heuschel, Berlin 1958.

[4] cf., P. Portoghesi, *Le inibizioni dell'architettura moderna*, Laterza, Rome-Bari 1974.

[5] cf., K.H. Clausen, *op. cit.*

[6] cf., G. Fehr, *Benedikt Ried*, Calway, Munich 1961.

[7] cf., G.W.F. Hegel, *Estetica*, Feltrinelli, Milan 1966 (*Ästhetik*, Frankfurt a.M. 1966).

[8] Cited in J. Rykwert, *On Adam's House in Paradise*, The Museum of Modern Art, New York 1972.

[9] The ribs of the cupola are very similar to the membrane of cacti as well as the protruding ribs of many shells. This is visible in the photographs taken by Feininger in A. Feininger, *Nature and Art*, Dover, New York 1983.

[10] The first time Paxton used the *Victoria regia* model was in the greenhouse he built in Kew Gardens to accommodate one of these plants.

[11] The word stand for the Japanese word "Edaburi," which Wright translates as "the formative arrangement of the branches of a tree" see F.L. Wright, *In the Cause of Architecture*, Collected Writings, vol. 1, Rizzoli, New York 1992.

[12] cf., A. de Baudot, *L'architecture, le passé, le présent*, vol. 1, Renouard, Paris 1916; Rizzoli, New York 1992.

[13] cf. Chapter one of this book.

[14] A.D. Bell. *Plant Form*, Oxford University Press, Oxford 1991.

# The Tower, the Obelisk, the Castle

*Now the whole world had one language and a common speech. As men moved eastwards, they found a plain in Shinar and settled there. They said to each other, "Come, let's make bricks and bake them thoroughly." They used brick instead of stone, and tar for mortar. Then they said, "Come, let us build ourselves a city, with a tower that reaches to the heavens, so that we may make a name for ourselves and not be scattered over the face of the earth."*

Genesis, 11.1-4

*In the middle of the sacred enclosure of Babel there is a huge tower whose base is one stadium long and one stadium wide. On top of this tower there is another one and then another and so on, in all eight towers on top of one another. External steps curl around each of the towers: half way up there is a landing with seats upon which the climbers may rest. In the highest tower there is a great temple, with a golden bed and richly decorated blankets as well as a bedside table , it too made of gold. Here there are no statues of the god. No mortal can sleep there, except for one woman from the town, chosen by the god from amongst them all, at least this is what the Caldei, the priests of the God Zeus Belo, affirm. Again it is the Caldei – but I don't believe this – that say that the divinity comes in person to the temple to sleep on the bed.*

Herodotus

The tower represents the way in which architecture frees itself from its desire for balance based on its relationship of similarity and identification with the human body. If the hut is associated with the earth, like the wall and the tent, the tower "rises"; it stands out against the sky, uniting earth and sky to the advantage of the latter. The fact that it is visible from a distance is one of the tower's characteristic elements. If the house battles the elements and protects our bodies, the tower fights against distance and separation, against the tendency of manmade objects to disappear, engulfed by the forces of the landscape and the curve of the earth. A tower's presence imposes artificiality much more than any other building, but it too owes much to the language of nature, to mountains and rocky peaks, to the great tree trunks that in winter loose their leaves and stand stark against the sky and last, but not least, to the erect body of man.

The genesis of the tower is intimately linked to that of the spire, the *menhir* and the *totem*. Before becoming an inhabitable space, the tower was a vertical anthropomorphic sign, a solid volume erected to remember those no longer present. Loos speaks of a mound of earth that, in remembrance of a person departed, becomes architecture, *monumentum* in the sense of recollection (from *monere*, to recall). Similarly, we can say that the tower signifies the act of moving beyond its sheltering function, investing architecture with a symbolic function. When attention is focused on an image from a distance (in this sense architecture and sculpture are coherent) this activates the mechanism of duration and continuance as well as the horizon of conveyance and memory which is thus entrusted to a sign to combat its own immaterial and transient nature.

The *menhir* (a word in Breton dialect composed of *men*, stone, and *hir*, long) is a roughly hewn stone erected either singly or in aligned and concentric groups. It is the original and truly ancient expression of man's desire to remember through construction. Certainly, one of its symbolic functions was the glorification of virility, later associated with the small phallic symbols so frequently found in burial grounds.[1]

From the point of view of recollection, the totem poles of the Haida Indians in the centre of the façades of their splendid wooden huts play a sacred role, besides being an immediate reference to nature. These poles were the characteristic traits of houses built according to established typologies, their animal symbols and human figures representing family tradition, just like our coats-of-arms. The pictures of certain Haida villages such as Skidgate and Masset Ninstints, taken by photographers at the end of the 19th century, when the villages were still inhabited by fur traders, are particularly fascinating.[2] The sculpted poles that stick out from the houses, and those that stand alone in remembrance of the souls of the dead, bring to mind those fields that in springtime are carpeted with tall flowered stalks.

The tower becomes a space looming over the heads of humans mainly as a defensive structure. Together with the wall, it becomes the cornerstone of military architecture. Certain locations are naturally "fortified" because they are in a dominant position and men settle there when they want to be safe from aggression and attack. The transition from natural fortresses to man-made fortresses characterises man's tendency to take possession of the strategies and forms of nature. Those who are familiar with the mountainous landscape of Sardinia, with its projecting conical peaks, consider the nuraghes dotted all over the island as the amplification and repetition of a theme already present in the silhouettes of the isolated peaks that stand out against the sky's bright background.

Walls and towers have the power to turn settlements without any natural fortifications, merely because they are situated on flat land, into safe havens. Solitary towers can warn of danger by using the system described by Polybius (*Stories*, X): torches at night and smoke during the day.

Walls and towers form a ring around the city, like the shores of a lake. Their powerful rhythm is either constant or variable and it is this variability that unites the city to its site, an *ad hoc* bond that is continually renewed since it corresponds to the vocation of the landscape. Whoever travels between Siena and Florence and looks upwards at the walls of the city of Monteriggioni feels he is facing a natural metaphor, since the work of man fades into the hillside like a sacred forest, highlighting its forms as well as exalting them in song. After all, wasn't it Amfion with his lyre who lifted the walls of Thebes out of the ground? By proposing this similarity between music and architecture in the construction of city walls and towers, the Greek myth underlines its importance in those cities considered complete organisms, such as walled cities.

*Nuraghe Sant'Antine in the countryside near Gennargentu in Sardinia (Italy). The countryside in Sardinia is frequently dotted with conical plateaux that seem to prefigure the nuraghe, an artificial element that defensively interprets the geomorphological characteristics of the landscape. Below: a house with a totem pole rebuilt in Ketchikan (Alaska).*

289

If the towers along the walls create a peaceful and reassuring pattern, when they are near the city portals they resonate with *anakrousis*, the explosion of sound that marked the start of Greek plays. Like sentinels placed at the entrance to the city, the "coupled towers" similar to church steeples and the twin minarets of mosques, create a magnetic field just like the two ends of a magnet. They carry our imagination back to the forms of living nature: two, like our hands and arms, like jaws that close and grind, like the tusks of the elephant and the horns of the deer, so that in its uniqueness the door can become a mouth, a spring or a river estuary.

The Tower of Babel encompasses all the archetypes of the tower and the ladder. Western iconography is overwhelmingly dominated by the model of the spiral staircase and this is perhaps due to the influence of the helicoidal minarets of Samarra. Apart from shells and snails, this spiral image can also be found in the cochlea of our inner ear.

In his *Duino Elegies*, Rilke includes certain architectural archetypes among the things that mark the presence of man on earth: "Are we on this earth to say: House / Bridge, Fountain, Jug, Gate, Fruit tree, Window / at best: Column, Tower [...] but to *say* these words / you understand with an intensity the things themselves never dreamed they'd express."[3]

Together with the bridge, the gate, the window and the column, this familiar picture includes the cosmic image of the earth. For an architect, building a tow-

*An aerial view of Cittadella near Padua.*

er ultimately means using the sky as a background, as the paper on which to draw; because, by definition, the tower is something that rises above the magma of the city and the countryside to play a role that is simultaneously a superior observation point and a protruding site, clearly visible from a distance. This is why the tower exalts the optical values of architecture. It is the symbol not only of elevation, but also of solitude and challenge; a place of ascension above the mundane city, but also a place of danger and doom. Ibsen's story of the builder, Sollness, summarises the perverse attraction of an archetype. Clearly, it is one of the easiest to which anthropomorphic and psychomorphic significance can be attributed, so much so that it enters our everyday language thanks to its metaphoric meanings and not because it represents an innocent building type.

Built to see and be seen, the tower has always inspired the architect to express the simplicity and purity of a construction that rises up from the ground while remaining invariant from its foundations to its crown, like an extruded section. On the other hand, it also offers its architect the opportunity to shape his construction and perhaps rediscover, in the superimposed parts, the rules inherent in the idea of projecting the forms and proportions of the human body into a building. Thus the tower becomes a "person" considered by city dwellers with the same attention and trust they accord a familiar face. Why, what would Italian cities be without the towers that interpret their most secret identity? Siena without the Torre del Mangia, Rome without the Torre Capitolina, Bologna without

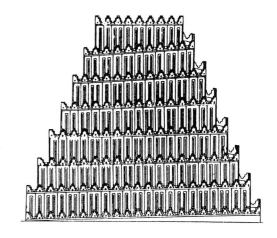

*The ziggurat in Kujundschik (reconstruction by Victor Place).*

*Pieter van der Borcht,* The Tower of Babel, *a brass engraving.*

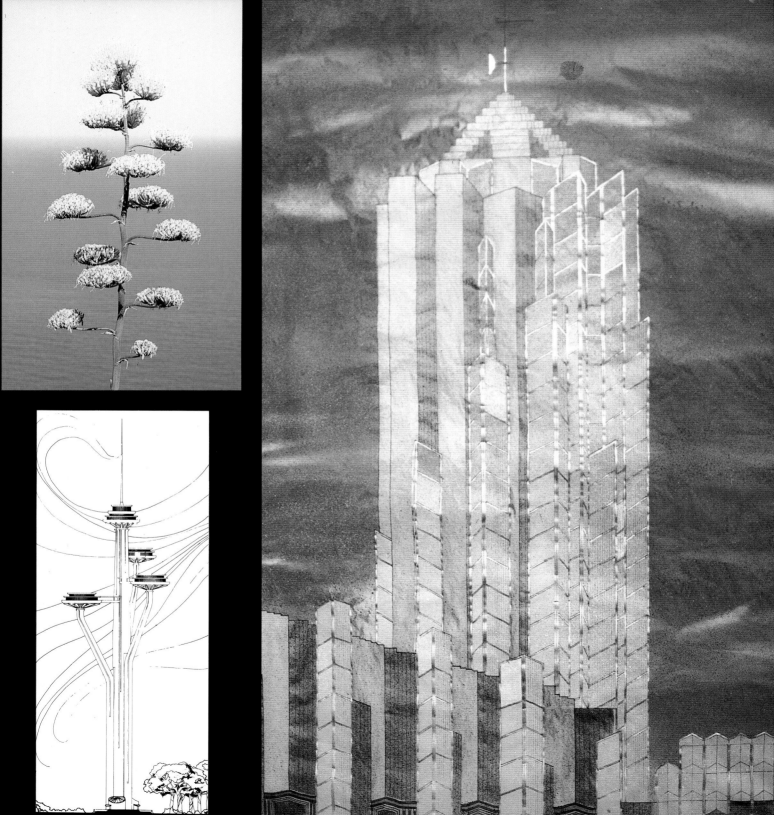

*Opposite page: the flower of the agave and two drawings by Paolo Portoghesi: a panoramic tower in Khartoum (with V. Gigliotti) and a residential tower for* A Style for the Year 2001 *(1985).*

*Below: the picture of an ear of corn that inspired the project illustrated in the drawing.*

*Rock towers in Monument Valley, Arizona.*

*The skyline of the town of San Gimignano, near Siena.*

her divergent twin towers, Pisa without her leaning bell-tower and so on. If any of these symbols suddenly crashed to the ground, it would be so inconceivable that the towers would be reconstructed notwithstanding any rational philological scruple.

But the theme of the tower offers the architect another possibility: to give a volumetric block, anchored to the ground by its weight and horizontality a new dimension, making it bloom, so to speak, with pinnacles profiled against the sky. Whether the towers are gigantic or microscopic like chimneys, they suddenly give the geometric block zoomorphic traits. Towers are like eyes, ears and arms lifted above one's head, they are like a splendid head-dress that allows architecture to rise above its true dimension and impose itself at a distance, letting space tell of its extension and history.

By the nature of their profession, painters tend to define the relationship between the environment and the tell-tale signs of human presence. They are inclined to consider the tower as an abrupt accident which modifies the continuous "line of the sky," giving it character and meaning. In imaginary landscapes there are often many towers because their verticality balances the horizontality of the signs of the earth, of agriculture and orography. The tower emerges as a unique occurrence, as a paraphrase of individuality as well as an element of crystalline gemmation and therefore of "different repetition." For example, solitary towers are represented by the Tower of Babel, the *Castello del Limbo* in the *Codice urbinate*, Sassetta's *Carità di San Francesco,* Rubens' *Shipwreck of Enea* or the surrealist iconography of the lighthouse. More frequently, the tower resembles an initial elevation that is repeated like a mirrored image, like an endemic tendency of building materials to oppose the forces of gravity with their own anti-gravitational force. Like crystalline aggregations, towers repeat and multiply, forming spontaneous aggregates that express the idea of "castle." These are not normally copies of real castles that obey a constructive and orographic logic like defensive constructions based on a strategic military plan, but imaginary castles that obey only a purely visual logic: castles that evoke concrete reality to the extent that this helps to "dream" of something universal, almost mythical, namely, the ideal world of architectural archetypes.

The tower would not have been quite so significant in painting if it were not somehow linked to the biblical story of the Tower of Babel and if this had not represented its most productive and ambiguous exemplification. It is true that Zeus' throne stood on a column and that in Greek mythology Danae received the fertile golden rain in the bronze tower which held her captive, but rarely has painting touched on these mythological cues. Instead, it has dedicated to the Tower of Babel a host of passionate iconographic images that express not only, and not so much, the search for a lost image reconstructed through literary sources, but the different ways in which every age has imagined its past and made it come to life, filtered by its own aesthetic sensibilities, its own interpretation and dreams.[4]

*A termite mound in Australia and, below, the Asinelli tower in Bologna.*

295

*The vertical inflorescence of the mullein and the model of the entry tower of the church in the Smol'nyj monastery in Moscow (Bartolomeo Rastrelli, 1748-54).*
*Opposite page: two minarets in Cairo near the El Hamra mosque.*

*A quartz crystal and the skyscraper of the Bell Telephone Company in New York (Voorhees, Gmelin and Walker, 1927).*

In the 20th century, by far and wide the most impressive towers ever portrayed on canvas are by Giorgio de Chirico. These towers appear by the dozen in the works of his metaphysical period, and decades later, influenced and induced architecture to bestow renewed prestige and honour on the grand forces of archetypes.

*"Sur les places carées les ombres s'allongent dans leur énigme mathématique,"* writes de Chirico in his Parisian manuscripts, *"derrière les murs les tours insensées apparaissent couvertes de petits drapeaux aux mille couleurs, et immutables comme ses racines, partout c'est l'infini et partout c'est le mystère."*[5] The "absurd towers," crowned by the small, ever-present flags that billow gently in the wind, are one of the main ingredients of metaphysical cuisine. In his book *Noi Metafisici*, he writes: "The atelier of the visionary philosopher is something of an astronomic observatory, a revenue office, a harbour-master's cabin. Any futility is removed; instead certain objects that universal stupidity has relegated among futilities stand there in triumph. A few odds and ends. Those small paintings and laths needed by the expert craftsman to create perfection."[6] The towers are among those "odds and ends." They are treated in an extremely simplified way as living archetypes: familiar objects never before seen in that light and from that particular angle, immersed in that unique and enigmatic atmosphere. De Chirico's first tower is probably the one drawn on the horizon between the undulating tops of Tuscan cypresses in his 1909 painting entitled *Serenata*. However, it is still only a descriptive element, while the tower in *Arianna*, once property of Jean Paulhan and dated 1913, is already a metaphysical object, one of the "odds and ends" that make up the painting, creating that enquiring expectation which the author described as something of an "omen." The tower is shaped like a lime-kiln or a coastal watch-tower. It strongly resembles the iconography of the *athanor*, the alchemist's furnace in which matter is transformed and which is often shaped like a tower to assert the fact that transmutation is always an elevation, a passage from a lower to a higher state. Without necessarily wanting to establish a connection between alchemists' symbols and the ingredients of a metaphysical landscape, it is worth noting how the painter tends to highlight the hierarchical "rank" of his vision.

De Chirico writes: "Early populations unconsciously exploited the metaphysical power of objects by isolating them, by creating insurmountable magical barriers around them: the fetish, the sacred image, the *xoamon* of the ancient Greeks are real accumulators, real concentrates of metaphysics. Everything depends on how they are grouped and isolated. Primitive man does this unconsciously following a sort of vague mystical instinct; modern architects, on the other hand, do this consciously, even increasing, altering or shrewdly exploiting the metaphysical nature of objects. The objects that possess this metaphysical nature have a distinguishing trait determining their level. This means that intrinsically, the graduated object is worth as much as a non-graduated object. Thus, amongst the mass of polymorphic or monomorphic volumes that clutter up our

*Basalt columns in the Alcantara valley (Italy) and, below, a drawing by Hugh Ferris for an hypothetical skyscraper that fulfils the building regulations of the city of New York.*

299

*A photograph of fossil shells and a skyscraper on Madison Avenue, New York (Philip Johnson, J. Burgee, 1987).*

planet, decorated or gallooned objects take on special meaning or value. It must also be said that the patented metaphysical object should be viewed in a certain way and from a certain angle in order to appreciate its true value, like a captain, a colonel or a general in camouflage who should be looked at square in the face, or from the side, with his beret on, because if you looked at him from behind and without his beret, he could well be taken for a simple army soldier. And, like a careful and competent commander who will only rank a talented, wise and able soldier capable of doing his duty to the full, the metaphysical painter will only 'metaphysicalise' those objects that represent the best possible contribution to the creative value of his work."[7]

In the language of metaphysics, the tower indicates the ascensional elevation often contrasted by the horizontal movement of a train and the wind that makes the multicoloured flags flutter in the wind. In *Pomeriggio di Arianna*, there is a truncated cone mass with a convex base, contrasted by a second tower: a prism built with superimposed reddish blocks. The blocks have slightly rounded corners and four small banners continue the vibrant lines of the corners. The towers converse, while a buttressed wall hides the point where they rise out of the ground. Perhaps this is the same contraposition that marks the life of Ariadne, loved by Apollo and then by Dionysius who set her free saying: "I am your Labyrinth."

The only building type invented in our time to have conquered full independence is the office building, eloquently and originally expressed in the vertical rise of the skyscraper. By turning into a tower, the office building affirms the additive character of bureaucratic organisation and the capitalistic tendency towards limitless accumulation. In some big American cities, the height of office towers corresponds exactly to a block graph of site costs. Perhaps this is why the New York skyline, with its concentration of buildings in the centre and at the end of the island of Manhattan, can still be compared to the natural image of a grassy field with two springs around which the vegetation grows taller and greener.

More artificial than any other construction, the skyscraper does, however, aspire to distance itself from the human dimension in a well-defined and uncompromising way, so much so, that prompted by the vision of a mountain or a precipice, it often stirs up a sense of giddy contrast with our real dimension.

Perhaps the reason why the skyscraper is incorporated into literature is due to the optimistic amazement it inspires, just like a natural phenomenon. This statement is confirmed by Dos Passos when he writes about the Woolworth Building soon after it was finished: "Jobless, Jimmy Herf came out of the Pulitzer Building. He stood beside a pile of pink newspapers on the curb, taking deep breaths, looking up the glistening shaft of the Woolworth. It was a sunny day, the sky was a robin's egg blue. He turned north and began to walk uptown. As he got away from it the Woolworth pulled out like a telescope. He walked north through the city of shiny windows, through the city of scrambled alphabets,

*Towers in the Canyon de Chelly National Monument, Arizona.*

*The Twin Towers of the International Trade Centre in New York (Minoru Yamasaki, 1969).*

*A picture of the* Equisetum hyemale.
*The Kuala Lumpur City Centre (Cesar Pelli, 1993-96).*

*The stalactite-stalagmite towers 38 meters high in the grotto of Ispinigoli near Dorgali (Italy).*

*Rocks shaped by the wind and the rain in the Sassolungo mountain range (western Dolomites).*

*The bell tower of Strasbourg cathedral. The walls are divided again and again by frames, slits, avant-corps and recesses.*

through the city of gilt letter signs. Spring rich in gluten [...] Chockful of golden richness, delight in every bite."[8]

The telescopic structure of the Woolworth so vividly and graphically described by Dos Passos brings to mind the rapid growth of a stalk, the vertical division of canes, the open and incompressible verticality of living forms. This is in complete contrast to the skyscraper model studied by Louis Sullivan who, despite his love of vegetation, perspectively defined his volumes and drew their proportions like those of a human body, taking into consideration another aspect of organicity: the completed form, a form that grows only internally. In his project for the Chicago Tribune Tower, Adolf Loos later adopted this completed form, the column, verbatim.

The instant comparison between the image of skyscrapers, enveloped by clouds, and the rocky peaks so dear to photographers in the thirties, is perhaps an embryonic attempt to reconcile a model with nature. A model that, with the all-embracing and conclusive experience of Mies' prisms, had been transformed into a purely geometrical event, that could only be superficially modified by windows, thus turning its skin into scales like those of a snake.

In the seventies, influenced by the figurative provocations of the "Site" and the "Superstudio," Roger Ferri, a young American architect who died at a very early age, designed a series of towers in which reconciliation with nature became the paradoxical objective of a project that was anything but utopian. The first

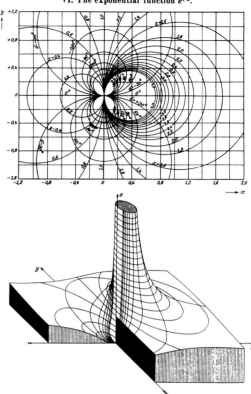

*Cylindrical tower in Kitzbühel along the Romantischer Strasse and, above, graphic diagram of an exponential function.*

305

proposal of this kind dates back to 1978 and involved a skyscraper designed for a corporation in Times Square and Madison Square. The prismatic volume was covered in a fantastic scenario of rocks and trees inspired by the real landscape found in granite quarries. These natural elements shattered its geometric integrity like a sort of leprosy that corrodes or swells the smooth crystal volumes and turned the building into a sort of giant ruin in which nature rapidly got the upper hand, as in Angkor Vat. Ferri wrote: "The skyscraper is considered a dynamic civic monument, capable of integrating a corporations objectives of power and influence with the aspirations of the community to participate in recreational activities as well as to fulfil the needs of each individual, namely that the urban environment foster and satisfy his own sensorial adventures. An environment that encourages creativity through silent inner listening... The tower creates a wall eleven storeys high next to the road. Then it recedes, giving way to the golden tower on the north side of the square. When seen from the square the spire also enters into the compositions. The wide ledges contain a mountain landscape carved from the rocks above New York City, thereby grafting and indigenous landscape, with all its flora and fauna, onto the Manhattan skyline. This is complemented by deep cement basins arranged along the ascending diagonal line that groups together the mountain fragments of the original site. Small lakes, mountains, hillsides, lawns, woody gorges and waterfalls all come together on a plateau shaped much like a pinnacle that acts as a small clearing of wild nature accessible from all sides. On the first ledge there is a restaurant offering the public a pleasant, relaxing area, both indoors and out. On each intermediate floor, the work areas face a square are giving constant access to this vision of the dense metropolis and wild nature, while the staff may enter directly from outside."[9]

The crude contrast between nature and artifice was no longer part of Ferri's sensibility when, a few years later, he proposed a similar project in a competition for the skyscrapers in Times Square and the 1986 Spiral Tower. The design experience of *Pedestrian City*, with its explosion of fairytale naturalism schematising the phytomorphic structures to such a degree that they became part of a rigorous language, led Ferri to integrate his trees and ramblers with a much more complex biomorphic architecture (spirals, sheaves of vertical elements, growth structures).

*The model of a skyscraper by Roger Ferri in New York (1985).*
*Opposite page: the crystal forest on the top of the skyscraper.*

[1] cf., K. McNally, *Standing Stones*, Appletree Press, Belfast 1984; M. Cippolloni Sampò, *Dolmen*, De Luca, Rome 1990.
[2] A. Jonaitis, *From the Land of the Totem Poles*, New York - London 1988; P. Nabokov, R. Easton, *Native American Architecture*, Oxford University Press, Oxford 1989.
[3] cf., R.M. Rilke, *Duino Elegies*, W.W. Norton & Co., New York 1978, p. 80.
[4] cf., "Turris Babel", edited by M. Scolari, *Rassegna*, no. 16, Electa, Milan 1983.
[5] G. de Chirico, *Il meccanismo del pensiero*, edited by M. Fagiolo, Einaudi, Turin 1985, p. 24.
[6] cf., Z'ev bem Shimon Halevi, *Kabbalah*, Thames & Hudson, London 1979.
[7] G. de Chirico, *Il meccanismo del pensiero*, cit.
[8] J. Dos Passos, *Manhattan Transfer*, Houghton Mifflin Co., Boston 1925, p. 351.
[9] This excerpt was written by Roger Ferri in Italian for Paolo Portoghesi.

# The Stairs, the Step, the Terrace

The possibility of moving upwards, not only by adapting one's footstep to the gradient, but by shaping the surface of the earth to assist the rhythm of our gait, is such an obvious discovery that all architectural organisms have different levels showing the boundaries between quantitatively different spaces.

The step and the threshold are often called to mark this separation, this fracture between inside and out (in Latin *porta*, *janua*, *ostium* and *fores* have more or less the same meaning), between the sacred site of theophany and the chaos of the profane. In Peter Handke's novel, *Der Chinese des Schmerzes* the main character, who professes to be an expert on thresholds, says: "When I was chased by some older children brandishing sticks, I ran inside and waited for them on the threshold. They waved to me and acted as if nothing had happened. Some thresholds were very high and to cross them you had to bend your knees and hit your head. Sitting on the doorstep meant: 'Here the door cannot be closed!'"

Threshold and step both have the same sacredness, the same symbolic importance, but the step is also characterised by repetition, by its transformation into a stair.

The natural model of stairs is the cascade, when water leaps gently from level to level, breaking its fall, and the total height is divided into shorter distances; a rhythm with different beats which tend to vary and in turn give rise to a melody. Contemplating cascades, like the contemplation of fire, is an instinctive act of observation of nature. The archetype of the stairs, closely related to the archetype of agricultural terracing that reconciles natural and artificial order, may be found *in nuce* in sedimentary rocks. Often the horizontal layers of these rocks are separated by thin layers of loose material that highlight the detachable nature of the slabs used in construction. On the other hand, the ladder, a transformed tree trunk with no branches, originates from the energies of primitive architects and all through history accompanies architecture as one of the most fundamental objects on the construction site.

A by-product of quarrying stone slabs are flights of steps which often become quite scenic and monumental. This occurrence highlights another genetic path of architectural archetypes, namely the path created when parts of the earth's surface are appropriated for construction. Whoever has seen the Apuane caves, or the caves in Siracusa and Matera, is well aware to what extent the work of man has modified space and volume and, "by taking away," has created a "potential" architecture that represents a never ending source of inspiration for architects.

Even in the structure of crystals, staircases with steps of equal height appear to be the result of a "separate strata" growth model. In his treatise written in 1802, Haüy studied fluorite crystals. He used fascinating axonometric projections to demonstrate how this aggregation process (that chooses where to place new cubic elements in order to guarantee contact with the greatest number of sides) generated an ideal solid resembling the intersection of fourteen orthogonally arranged staircases: it was a sort of abstract model of the "stair's nature" and recalls the structural and decorative use of the step.

The morphology of stairs develops in close symbiosis with the interpretation of the landscape and its transformation for practical and ritual purposes. When a path is trodden over and over again, steps are often built to make walking a little easier, but only small changes are made so as not to alter the path's gradient. The winding path that accesses the Acropolis in Athens is an example of man's desire not to mediate the contrast between architecture and landscape, but to exploit it in order to maintain the feeling of sacredness inspired by the difficult ascent and by the sudden unexpected view that extends beyond the portico of the Propylaea to the rocky plateau on which the Parthenon, the Erechtheoin and the temple of Nike Apteros all stand.

If a staircase with rectilinear or broken flights follows the logic of visual continuity used in the construction of roads, for staircases that run parallel to a wall it is quite another matter. Visual continuity is no longer maintained: on the contrary, it is interrupted by introducing an irrational and contradictory element. The shortest route is discarded *a priori* in favour of advantages that depend on a complex ratio system between the various parts of the building and the landscape.

The symmetrical repetition of staircases parallel to the two levels to be joined overcomes this contradiction and shifts the interpretation of the organism onto another plane. This is a different way of emphasising the axis of penetration of the building along which a third, wider flight of steps will be placed to receive

*Multiple cascade near Campo Tures (Italy).*

*Stepped erosion of calcareous rock near Vieste (Italy) and terrace formations in Yosemite park.*

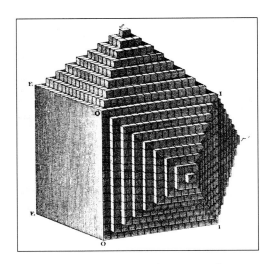

*Illustration from Haüy's book (1803) explaining his theories on the nature of crystals and their aggregation.*

the unified flow of the two lower flights. The temple of Fortune in Palestrina clearly shows the nascent system of a double-return staircase that seems to be inspired by racemed inflorescences, by the forked branches of a tree trunk or the structure of the iris flower with alternatively ascending and descending petals. The chapter on centrality will examine a hexagonal staircase designed by Bernardo Vittone in the 18th century in which the artist captures the essence of the splendid spatial structure of this fascinating flower that the city of Florence had chosen as its emblem.

Evident signs of its biomorphic nature are inherent in the archetype of the spiral staircase, also called "snail," based on the radial arrangement of the steps and the element that Theodore A. Cook called the "curve of life." He maintained that the beauty of the spiral staircase as a visual concept was its form, a form that continued to grow, never occupying the same space, consequently, not only was it an explanation of the past but a prophecy of the future.

By observing the structure of aquatic or terrestrial animals that use an external skeleton similar to what we would call a house, man has learnt that a flight of steps can curl around itself, occupying a minimum amount of space and creating a sort of channel, as entwined as entrails, in which the human body can move like the liquid in Archimedes' screw.

The theme of the elliptical staircase is sensationally expressed in spiral columns and through all sorts of virtuoso achievements implemented during the Middle Ages. During the Renaissance and Baroque period, it reached the pinnacle of its glory: Bramante's staircase in the Vatican; the castle of Chambord in Caprarola; the oval staircase in Rome's Palazzo Barberini; the staircase without steps in Palazzo Carpegna that could be used by horses (the last two designed by Francesco Borromini). In the *ziggurat*, as in the stepped pyramids or in the archetype of the Tower of Babel, the staircase is transformed into a cosmic symbol, a desperate attempt to bring the sky closer to earth. The influence of this plastic interpretation of the staircase stretching externally around a walled nucleus is clearly visible in the minarets of Samarra, the lantern of Sant'Ivo alla Sapienza in Rome and Frank Lloyd Wright's Guggenheim Museum in Manhattan.

The fact that the inspiration behind the spiral staircase of Sant'Ivo is organic and biomorphic as well as symbolic, is obvious from the relationship between its form and decoration. A very singular historical piece of evidence confirms this fact, the list of objects found in Borromini's house immediately after his tragic suicide: "Two snail shells, one with a ovate brass pedestal, the other without." This is a clear sign of Borromini's interest in natural images, also evident in his *Opus Architectonicum* where he invoked the authority of nature to justify his originality and unconventional linguistic choices: "Observe," he writes in Chapter VI of the *Opus*, "that these niches recall the architects of the past rather than the present since their openings are narrower than the space inside. Neither do I hide the fact that I have designed the balustrades to be triangular, placing them one up one down. This has been done because otherwise the Cardinals who will

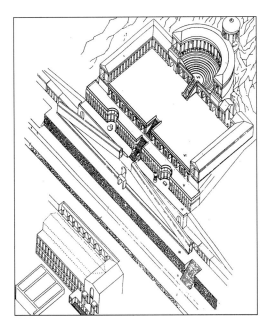

*Reconstructed axonometric projection of the temple of Fortune in Palestrina near Rome (2nd century B.C.), one of the best examples of the architectural interpretation of a natural slope based on the use of staircases and steps.*

310

*Alabanuel, design by Piero Portaluppi.*

*A free-well staircase in one of the "small towers" of Palazzo Ducale in Urbino (photo Maria Ercadi). Axial view of the shell of the* Galeodea echinophora *species.*

*The elliptical staircase in Chambord castle on the Loire (16th century).*

*The grand staircase of the fortress-palace in Caprarola, Italy (Giacomo Barozzi, called Il Vignola, 1562).*

*As the fruit of the banana tree gradually drop from the pine-shaped seed nucleus they form a sort of spiral staircase (Acireale, Italy).*

*A spiral root on the Nuvolau plateau near Cortina d'Ampezzo (Italy).*

sit behind these six balustrades (if designed as is the custom) with their small pedestal or low bulbous column in a row, will not be able to see through the balustrade where the bulbous shapes of the columns join. Instead, the shape I have designed, placing the outline of the columns parallel to one another, provides the same view from top to bottom. The fact they are triangular recalls the hole through which cannons fire; the openings are such that everything may be seen. Therefore, those who are seated can easily see the events below, as if they had before them a paper with holes; instead, if in front of the viewer the bulb was square or round this would not happen. To comprehend more clearly, consult plate 43. It is well known that many of those incapable of inventing or creating, believed this to be a truly capricious and unruly act since part of these balustrades are wider at the top than at the bottom; they do not realise that nature (that we must imitate) creates trees larger at the bottom than at the top, so too does it create man larger at the top than the bottom."[1]

In medieval architecture, the stepped motif appears in the multiple frames that surround the great church portals, creating a perspective repetition reminiscent of the natural phenomenon that goes by the name of echo. This motif was extensively employed, both horizontally and vertically, in pre-Columbian architecture, above all by the Maya, the Aztecs and the Incas who studded their ceremonial cities with stepped pyramids which they considered sacred mountains. With incomparable skill, they exploited these different heights by turning

*The platform surrounding the Moon Square in Teotihuacan (Mexico).*
*Above: reconstruction of the second temple in Tikal (Guatemala).*

*The double dog-legged staircase in the charterhouse in Padula near Salerno (Italy), 18th century.*

314

Machu Picchu, the stepped pyramid where the Intiwatana stone is located. Intiwatana means "where the sun sets" and the sculptured stone was used as a ceremonial place, an astronomical observatory and a centre for communication.

them into complex patterns of intersecting steps, for instance, in the splendid acropolis of Comalcalco. In modern times, Louis Sullivan was probably the first to discover and experiment with the expressive potential of this theme, adopting it on a grand scale for the roof of the Chicago Auditorium (1887-90) and for the gold door used in the Colombian Art Exhibition.

In Art Nouveau, the volumetric step theme dissolves into linear references that pick up on the growth process of a plant's seed and the way in which leaves fan out in successive "waves." Wagner, and to a lesser degree Mackintosh, recover the rectilinear matrix of this theme. During the early years of the 20th century, Wagner and his school used it as a recurrent theme to set themselves apart from the traditional classical repertoire, while at the same time highlighting their decision not to forgo these "glimmerings" of light, these vibrations of the moulding. As early as 1905, Hoffmann used steps to substitute the niche's mellow hazy shadows with the crystal-clear echo of a stepped frame. In 1921, Loos used it symbolically to finish the funerary cube he dedicated to Max Dvorák, the great maestro of the *Kunstgeschichte als Geistgeschichte*. He used it again in 1923 in his project for the Grand Hotel Babylon, a charming interpretation of a big hotel as the new theatre of confusion of languages.[2] But at this point, the pattern had been taken over by fashion, industrial design and mass culture: this motif was transferred from the tomb to perfume bottle and, thanks to Sonia Delaunay, to a delightful pink and brown overcoat. Akem Weber, an outstanding American de-

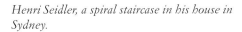

*Henri Seidler, a spiral staircase in his house in Sydney.*

signer, decided to transpose steps into everyday objects, while Raymond Templier used them to design lovely pieces of jewellery: a swallow, a snail, a sort of hourglass studded with diamonds. After a significant anticipation in 1915, Frank Lloyd Wright creatively interpreted the theme in his Californian houses. He used it intrepidly during the thirties and, in a brilliant albeit discontinuous way, continued to do so right up until his death.[3]

We owe the most systematic and coherent results from experimentation on steps to the New York school, and in particular to Voorhees, Gmelin & Walker. The elegant coating of the walls of the Salvation Army Building gives the entrance to the temple of worship the contradictory charm of a naturalistic form created by erosion and the continual dripping of water. Its precise geometric form is governed by a strict and simple law. This juxtaposition of contrasting materials in different structures demonstrates the subtle sensibilities of this unjustly forgotten group of architects who gave us the most architecturally successful skyscraper in New York, the Irving Trust Building, with its fluted walls, its telescopic display of volumes wedged inside one another, its magical roof flaking like a crystalline gemmation and windows that reveal the large salon inside.[4]

It would be difficult to find a more daring and unpredictable way of using the stepped motif than the one Van Alen invented, after much soul-searching, for the Chrysler Building. Here too one gets the impression of a gushing spring, of a rising disk (the disk of the sun?) frozen by a stroboscopic flash during the

*A palm leaf in the botanical gardens in Sydney.*

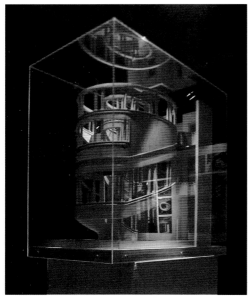

*Right: the staircase in Palazzo Corrodi in Rome (Paolo Portoghesi, 1987). The stairs hang from the ceiling with steel cables that pass through the centre of the columns.*
*Above: model of the staircase in Palazzo Corrodi, and, top, a sea snail,* Papuina multicolor.

various stages of its ascent. In fact, the top of the building has a series of super-imposed and intersecting coved vaults. In order to compensate for the inevitable flattening that occurs when seen from the street, each vault is designed differently, with a curve that is initially circular and then elliptical, gradually becoming taller until it slowly dissolves into the antenna of the spire pointing skywards like the sting of a bee.

However, the most sensational spire invented by New York architects was the one designed by Voorhees, Gmelin & Walker: the Genesee Walley Trust Company Building in Rochester. Instead of a closed spire, the obligatory metaphor of the Renaissance, Walker imagined four metallic blocks completely separate from one another and shaped like complex mathematical surfaces, in some ways similar to the wings of an insect rising from below like petrified jets of water. Mediation between these elements and the prismatic block of the building beneath was achieved by employing four stripped radial frames with their hallmark stepped motif subtly used both vertically and horizontally.[5]

Perhaps the most complex stepped motif was exploited during the twenties. Wenzel Hablik proposed a design that looks more like a free geometric exercise than a fully fledged project: his steps generate independent groups that twist like spirals on different surfaces, projecting the concept of the labyrinth into space.[6] But it was Frank Lloyd Wright in Fallingwater (1936) who exalted this motif which was seemingly condemned to being a mere decorative element: he projected it in a vortex of superimposed open planes skimming over the void, like the twisted layers of a bismuth crystal.

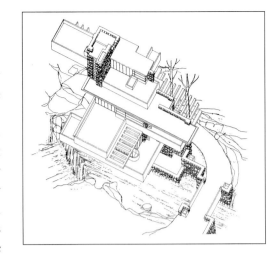

*Axonometric projection of Fallingwater in Bear Run (Frank Lloyd Wright, 1936).*

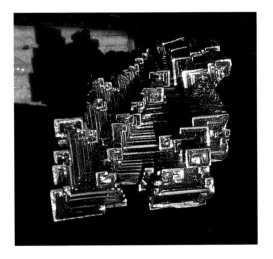

*Artificial bismuth crystals with their characteristic stepped structure.*

[1] cf., F. Borromini *Opus Architectonicum* II, L'Elefante, Rome 1964, p. 37.
[2] cf., B Gravagnuolo, *Adolf Loos*, Idea Books, Florence 1981.
[3] cf., G. Massobrio, P. Portoghesi, *Album degli anni Venti*, Laterza, Rome-Bari 1976.
[4] *Ibid.*
[5] There are no thorough studies on the work of R. Walker and his studio. Many of the decorative motifs of the Irving Trust building are based on the compo-sitional ideas of C. Bragdon during his untiring work, crucial for the so-called American Art Deco. Cf., L. Darlymple Henderson, *The Fourth Dimension*, Princeton University Press, Princeton 1983, pp. 186 ff.
[6] For stair types see J. Templer, *The Staircase*, MIT Press, Cambridge (Mass.) 1992; C. Baldon, I. Melchior, J. Schulman, *Steps and Stairways*, Rizzoli, New York 1989; C. Gambardella, *L'architettura delle scale*, Sagep, Genoa 1993.

# The Room, the Chamber, the Cell

*Rooms are* unspecified *spaces, empty stages for human action, where we perform the rituals and improvisations of living. They provide generalized opportunities for things to happen, and they allow us to do and be what we will. When we understand rooms in these ways, we can address freely their qualities which are hardly ever mentioned in the real estate ads, the essential qualities which give them a memorable sense of being special places to inhabit.*

*The empty stage of a room is fixed in space by boundaries, it is animated by light, organized by focus, and then liberated by outlook.*

Charles Moore

The archetype of a room, *stanza*, does not only refer to the concept of a segregated space surrounded by walls, but instead signifies a whole that can be divided into distinct parts. In fact, in literary terms the word *stanza* has long been used to define a group of verses that constitute the metrics of songs. For a room to exist, in other words, for a place "to be," a place in which to linger, there must be other rooms nearby so that there is a choice. Differential and relative, the term's synonym is "chamber," a word that comes from the Greek *kamara* meaning vaulted room, a room surrounded not only by walls, but also by a ceiling.

All the rooms together form the building, the house or simply the apartment. The rooms either follow on from one another, joined together by doors, or else they are arranged in a discontinuous sequence united by a hallway, a corridor or another larger room with smaller ones around it.

A thousand different forms that look like rooms can be found in the animal and plant worlds: living cells, soap bubbles, the combs of beehives, the chambers of certain hollow stalks like the cane, the structure of inflorescences such as spikes, spadix, racemes, corymbs, umbels or panicles. If the spike resembles the cells of a convent joined by a corridor and the panicle conjures up images of the catacomb labyrinths, the compound umbel recalls the chapels of cathedrals at the top of the apse or Roman nymphaea with niches and smaller rooms arranged in a semicircle.

The hexagonal pattern of so many "organic" architectural projects is based on the hexagonal combs of the hive, true symbols of architecture. This fact led Karl Marx to reflect on the differences between the work of bees and the work of architects. According to Marx, these involved prefigured designs, perhaps not for animals, but certainly typical of the human mind.[1]

The externally accessible combs of beehives may prompt the mind to think of niches rather than rooms, but many animals build their nests with a series of differentiated spaces that look like the interior of a building.

Some unicellular protozoa feel the need to hide inside an involucre, a protective shelter that artificially defines their body. The *Difflugia piriformis* achieves this by covering itself with grains of sand, while the foraminifers commonly found in beach sand and similar in appearance to microscopic shells, extract the calcium carbonate contained in sea water and build a "niche." They then build onto this first niche by constructing others of the same shape, but larger in size, until they form a spiral with rooms that communicate through a series of holes, a characteristic that gives the species its name.

A similar growth mechanism can be found in certain shells, among which the incredible *Nautilus*, the archetype of staged growth and the visual equivalent of a musical "crescendo." On the other hand, a different type of spatial composition characterises the radiolarians, a unicellular animal lazily floating among the plankton perpetually caressed by the warm waves of the south seas.[2] In order to sustain and protect the protoplasm in their bodies, the radiolarians extract silicic dioxide from the water precipitating it in microscopic crystals which they use to create the most incredible skeletons whose central and radial structures are exploited with inexhaustible geometric imagination. This imagination is highlighted by the poet-biologist, Ernst Haeckel, in his famous book *Kunstformen der Natur*, published in 1899, at the height of the Art Nouveau period. His book placed a pleasant repertoire at the disposal of those who intended to develop a style based on the beauty of nature.

The spatiality of the radiolarians creates "rooms," but not separate independent spaces to be added together or joined in series. Instead, their spaces are transparent, permeable to water and light and often fit inside one another like Chinese boxes: spaces within spaces, obeying a common law, held together by paper-thin bonds made of silica (the main component of glass), a material that makes them barely visible.

While exploring these curvilinear spaces, one's gaze is caught in astonishment and contemplation, captivated by the visual effects of involucres positioned in such a way as to amplify, beyond one's wildest imagination, the perception of depth as something that reflects the swell of the waves in its repetition of consecutive stimuli. Thus our memory, lost like *flâneurs* in this oneiric city, conjures up awesome similarities: the iconostasis of the early basilicas and their orthodox tradition of filtering vision in order to reveal the "most sacred" through multiple spirals; the medieval canopies that characterise a place without enclosing it or the Palladian spatiality that culminates in the church of the Redentore in Venice, in which light and matter become allies to hurl us into a world of transparency and repeated echoes.

*The pierced ceiling of the church of Santa Chiara in Bra, Italy (Bernardo Vittone 1734).*

No less pertinent is their similarity with the increasing number of involucres used in the Baroque roofs of halls and churches, the superimposed and pierced cupolas by Gherardi, the multiple communicating spherical vaults designed by Guarini for the church of San Lorenzo, the Holy Shroud, or San Gaetano in Vicenza, the pierced vaults executed by Bibbiena in Parma or Revere, the Vittone-style cupolas by Vallinotto and the church of Santa Chiara in Bra.

And then again – after Haeckel's book – the cupola and reticular domes by Buckminster Fuller and Frei Otto: involucres often with a double structure to strengthen the fragile kaleidoscopic structural adventures of those master glassmakers engaged in the construction of their skeletons that are, in essence, radiolarians and diatoms.[3]

The internal space of shells is sometimes shaped like a helicoidal funnel in which the mollusc can retreat until it reaches the most intimate and original part of its home: the space existent before existence. In other cases, space is shaped like a container with several rooms, arranged according to a "historical" order, leaving the mollusc only the last and biggest room. Be this as it may, the helix is reified history, a cyclical sediment of the seasons like the concentric circles of the operculum or those of trees, a corneal mass created by the shell's inhabitants to shut and lock their natural front "door."

Other families of shells build rooms that can be accessed through an open-

*Soap bubbles tend to unite with implacable logic, combining bubbles of all different shapes and sizes.*

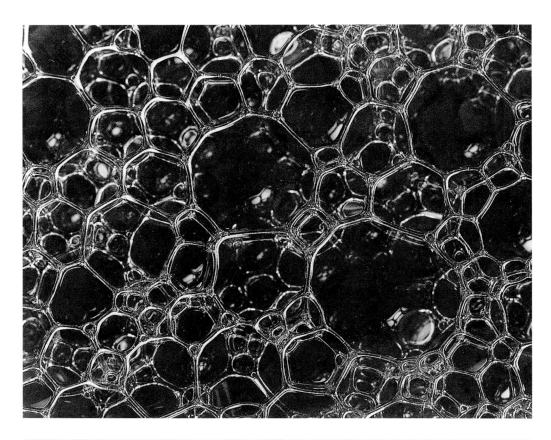

*The bee, like the spider or the beaver, is one of those animals with a pronounced architectural flair. The cells of the comb represent the archetype of the room as an isolated space.*

ing that either hides them or reveals them to the world: rooms that can be disassembled, held together by a retractile body; ribbed involucres such as the *Pectenscallop* that, like other similar forms of nature, have inspired man with radiality; the fan, the zip, the concept of resistance based on form and frontality.

From a symbolic point of view, all shell varieties are associated with the moon, the female sex and the fertility of eternal life and regeneration. Architecture, instead, has drawn from the shell the archetype of the theatre and the spiral staircase as well as one of the most beloved forms of its decorative repertoire.

Men have always admired the construction skills of bees and wasps, but we know much less about the architecture built during the social life of solitary insects. For example, when the mason bee lays its eggs, it creates a series of bags that it ties firmly to a clay involucre used to protect them. For the same reason, the "potter" wasp uses earthenware pots so smooth as to appear turned on a lathe, while the hornet's nest looks like a series of large rooms one on top of the other. The various parallel floors of the combs are held up by little columns, so without this opaque involucre it would look like a sort of Colosseum with superimposed orders. The difference lies in the fact that instead of starting from the bottom up, the hornet works from the top down, so the floors hang from one another and the little columns are subject to tensile rather than compressive stress, just like architectural designs that envisage one main structure and another suspended one.[4] Examples of this type of suspended structure are the Mondadori Headquarters in Milan by Oscar Niemeyer, the Enpas Building in Rome by Luigi Moretti and the staircase of Palazzo Corrodi by the author.[5]

The three different species that attest to the spectacular examples of the architectural skills of animals are: termites, beavers and bower birds.

Termites, like men, have more than one architectural culture. Each species has a different morphological repertoire and, according to the weather conditions of the region they live in, families of the same species have different repertoires. The most elementary termitaries have simple underground tunnels, with rooms that act as homes, specialised kitchen gardens and storerooms. However, since the species is intolerant of heat and sometimes light, when weather conditions become particularly severe they create termitaries with a complicated aeriation system which, according to the criteria adopted, is very similar to an air-conditioning system.

The *Macrothemes bellicosus*, for example, builds a mound that looks like an ogival arch with extremely protuberant ribs. At the bottom of the mound there is an empty room joined to the external ribs and packed with small pipes. Above the underground room there is a sort of thick ceiling-floor held up by *pilotis*, on top of which the living area of the termite mound is positioned. This is a labyrinth of tunnels and small rooms, including the royal suite which, during their lifetime, will act as home to the king and queen, prisoners of the community. The network of rooms and tunnels is interrupted by the mushroom beds, home-made "agricultural" crops that give off heat during fermentation, thereby

*The shell of a* Cryptopecten pallium.

*The coralline skeleton of a colony of* Tubipora musica. *With its horizontally linked little pipes, the* Tubipora *looks like an organ as well as a series of hypostyle rooms one on top of the other. Minuscule sage-green polyps live inside the small red brick pipes.*

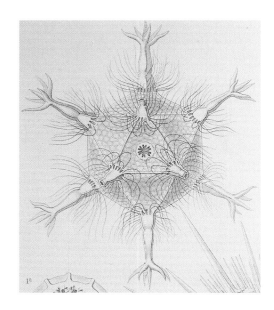

Radiolarian skeletons (from E. Haeckel, Art forms in Nature, *New York 1974*).
*The* Ophiothrix capillaris, *its ventral side enlarged three times. Other sea urchins around the* Ophiothrix *(pl. 10, p. 7); right,* Circogonia icosahedra, *protozoa of the* Radiolaria *order and the legion of the* Feodarie. *(pl. 1, fig. 1); below,* Pediastrum elegans, *a protophyte of the subclass of the small Algae and the class of the* Meletallie, *disk-shaped fresh water algae. The disk of the* Pediastrum *has 32 cells: one central and three rings of five, ten and sixteen cells respectively. The picture shows the alga giving birth to other disks (pl. 34, fig. 8).*

initiating the heating and cooling mechanism. In fact, when the hot air rises, the pressure in the upper chamber increases and this speeds up the circulation inside the pipes situated in the ribs. Since they are porous, the ribs expel carbon dioxide and absorb oxygen from the outside. Returning to the lower chamber or cellar, the air is cooled and ready to be pumped into the upper chamber through a series of chimneys that run between the two rooms.[6] To protect themselves from the rain, the constructive genius of the termites invented the system of overlapping mouldings, while to recycle air they fabricated the oriented towers (the "compass" termite earned this name because of its skill in establishing the cardinal points). This activity kindled much naive admiration in the natives of the Ivory Coast who imitated this form when building their mosques of kneaded earth, symbols of matter rising like leaven bread. This is a theme that must have fascinated Gaudí in his later years when he searched for a religious impulse in the profound structures of nature. The Spanish architect used the outline of a termitary for his towers in the Sagrada Familia and used it as an even more direct reference in his design of the church in Park Güell.[7]

When talking about beavers, on the other hand, one should remember the strategy they use to protect their nests, a strategy that includes underwater entrances. They also have a passion for isolated houses which bring to mind the Aviary by Varro and the house of meditation in Hadrian's Villa in Tivoli just outside Rome. Beavers exploit an extremely ingenious hydraulic system to build the

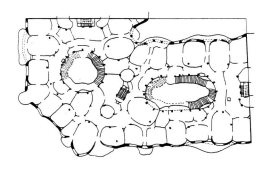

*The plan of Casa Milá by Antoni Gaudí. Its similarity with the section of cellular tissue is both visual and structural.*

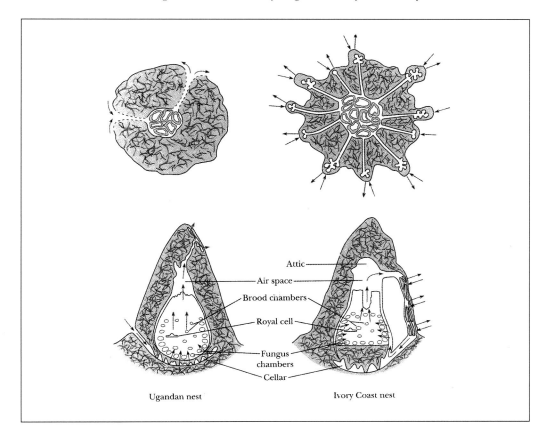

Attic
Air space
Brood chambers
Royal cell
Fungus chambers
Cellar

Ugandan nest          Ivory Coast nest

*Plans and sections of termitaries in Uganda and the Ivory Coast. In the latter, the cellar is used to cool the air. When the air circulates in the external pipes it effectively creates an air conditioning system.*

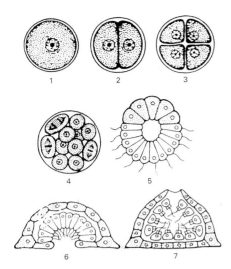

*Initial development and metamorphosis of a sponge: 1) the fertilised egg; 2) the two-cell stage; 3) the four-cell stage; 4) further division of the cells produces a sort of bundle of cells; 5) the larva determines the flagellate terminations; 6) the flagellate cells turn inwards; 7) the young sponge with its coat of collar cells; an opening is then created in its upper part.*

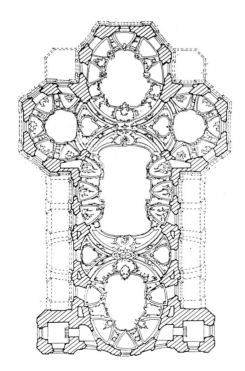

*Plan of the sanctuary of the Fourteen Saints (Balthasar Neumann, 1743-72). An example of cellular aggregation in which centrality and frontality are combined.*

little lakes they use as protection from the swirling currents of the river: their house has two main rooms, one just above the water level, with a sort of internal beach used as a dining room, and another at the top of the "castle" used as a bedroom.

As mentioned earlier, bower birds are by far the most original and ambitious nest builders. Rather than emulating the technical skills of architects, they emulate the latter's inclination towards decoration and the joy of embellishing one's very own shelter. In the tropical forests of New Guinea, the *Amblyornis subalaris* builds a nuptial nest with two doors joined by an annular corridor. The column between the two entrances is normally covered with musk and decorated with iridescent sky-blue coleoptera, a garland of small yellow flowers with pieces of shell in the middle. In front of the nest, a hedge made of woven branches with flowers and fruit marks the edge of the garden.

The "satin" bird (*Ptilonorhynchidus violaceus*), belonging to the family of the *Ptilonorhynchidae*, carefully cleans an area roughly one square meter in size and circles it with a path along which it places small twigs and branches approximately 30 centimetres high. At the southern end of the path it builds a sort of ballroom. Having prepared its *garconnière* it begins to travel in search of anything that might make this walkway attractive and inviting. Not only does it gather the leaves, berries, flowers and parrot feathers offered by nature, but when it lives near a town it picks up and places in its arbour and garden the brightest and most multicoloured objects it can find, just so long as they correspond to its favourite colours and match the fine livery of which it is so proud. The Bible says: "See how the lilies of the field grow. They do not labour or spin. Yet I tell you that not even Solomon in all his splendour was dressed like one of these."[8]

Amongst all these builders of rooms and gardens, man was dangerously close to making a bad impression, at least as far as the talents received and exploited were concerned, if it hadn't been for the genius of a few masterful builders, eternally dissatisfied with their designs of the ever changing sequences of spaces. The spaces they designed were hinged together like episodes in a book in which contraction and expansion reflected the rise and fall of breathing, transforming them into a grandiose representation of unfathomable desire. It was the Romans who excelled in this art of joining and juxtapositioning space. Based on Roman design, Andrea Palladio studied and codified certain rules which he published in 1570 in his book *I Quattro Libri*. Not only did Palladio indicate the best proportions between width and length of a room, but he completed the ratios he described in his drawings with the respective heights as well as taking into consideration the ratios between rooms that are part of a sequence.[9]

A number of shapes are recommended for rooms: the circle, the square, the rectangle in which the ratio between the sides is the same as the one between the side and the diagonal of the square; the rectangle with sides that have a 3:4 ratio and ones in which this ratio is 2:3; 3:5; 1:2.

As far as the respective heights are concerned, Palladio (I, 23, 53) provides a geometrical method: a 6 × 12 room requires a height of 9 while a 4 × 9 room requires a height of 6. Using a different method, the same 6 × 12 room may also require a height of 8. These three ratios correspond to the arithmetic, geometric and harmonic mean. Just like Francesco Giorgi, who advised Sansovino on the proportional system of Sant'Andrea della Vigna in Venice, Palladio was convinced that: "voice tones are our ears' harmony, so measurements are our eyes' harmony and obey a gentle, felicitous custom, known only to those who study the reasons for such matters."

In Villa Malcontenta on the banks of the River Brenta, this proportional mechanism reached an admirable degree of organicity and is described by Rudolf Wittkower in one of his most enlightened pages of analytical exegesis: "The smallest room on either side of the cross-shaped hall measures 12 × 16 feet, the next one 16 × 16 and the largest 16 × 24, while the width of the hall is 32 feet. Thus the harmonic series 12, 16, 24, 32 is the keynote to the building. As if in an ouverture the first and last members of this series appear in the ratio 12:32 of the portico, which is a diapason and diatessaron (for 12:24:32). The inter-columniation of the centre (6 feet) is related to the depth of the portico (12) as 1:2. The smaller inter-columniations are 4 $^1/_2$ feet; they are related to the central one as 3:4 which, incidentally, is the ratio of the smallest rooms. Finally, the diameter of the columns, 2 feet, represents the smallest unit, the module, and by a process of multiplication beginning with two all the ratios of the building can be derived."

In such an organism built up with the *regola homogenea*, there is no room for incommensurable quantities; however, the application of the module does not necessarily mean that the ratios throughout a whole building must be harmonic. But the systematic linking of one room to the other by harmonic proportions was the fundamental novelty of Palladio's architecture, and we believe that his wish to demonstrate this innovation had a bearing on the choice and character of the plates and the inscription of measurements. Those proportional relationships which other architects had harnessed for the two dimensions of a façade or the three dimensions of a single room were employed by him to integrate a whole structure.

The demand that 'parts should correspond to the whole and to each other' was generally adhered to in churches, for the relation of nave, aisles and chapels, and here the Renaissance could build on mediaeval traditions. But for domestic buildings the decisive step was taken by Palladio. He formulated his views on this point in one very important sentence which will add weight to the analysis of the two buildings which we have given: "But the large rooms ought to be so related (*compartite*) to the middle ones, and these to the small, that, as I have said elsewhere, one part of the building may correspond with the other, so that the whole body of the edifice may have in itself a certain harmony (*convenienza*) of members which may make it entirely beautiful and graceful."

No less complex and fascinating are the proportions used in Villa Barbaro in

*A diamond structure shown as the sequence of three layers: "In layer A, the lowest, carbon atoms with an upward-facing fourth orbital combine with the atoms in layer B whose fourth orbital faces downwards. In the same way, layer C fixes onto B, then a new layer A joins to C and so on. Overall, the structure is formed by successive layers of ABCABCA....".*

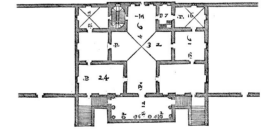

*Plan and elevation of Villa Foscari on the River Brenta (from A. Palladio,* I Quattro Libri dell'Architettura, *De Franceschi, Venice 1570, II, XIV, p. 50).*

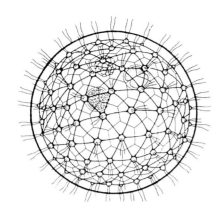

The structure of a Volvox, a small green sphere one or two millimetres in diameter. There are thousands of flagellate cells on the surface of its gelatinous cell. The Volvox has often been considered a colony of independent cells rather than a multicellular organism. Despite its spherical morphology, the Volvox has a frontality that stems from its behaviour. In fact, when advancing it keeps its body in the same position and its cells assume different functions: the front ones do not reproduce while the rear ones do. There is an obvious analogy with geodesic domes.

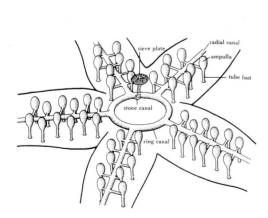

The vascular system of a starfish and the transversal section of one of its arms.

Maser, built by Palladio for one of those persons "who studies to understand the nature of things." Among other things, this client wrote one of the most humanistic critiques of Vitruvius to date, as well as publishing the most simple and elegant edition of the Vitruvian text to which Palladio contributed exceptionally beautiful illustrations.

It is easy to understand what "correspondence of loving senses" infused the relationship between the client and the architect during the design of the villa. Instead of triumphing over the landscape, the villa seems to be quietly immersed in the vast natural countryside, to the point that it almost seems to consciously and gently drown in it.

"The long wings behind the main building," writes Wittkower, "contain three groups of three rooms each – two of these groups are repeated at each side of the third central one – the widths of which are inscribed as 16, 12, 16; 20, 10, 20; 9, 18, 9. It is obvious that the ratios in each set of rooms are consonant (4:3:4; 2:1:2; 1:2:1). But one can go a step further. In the front of the main building are three rooms – of which the middle one is part of the cruciform hall – all 12 feet wide (together 36); in the corresponding part of the wing the three rooms reappear with the different orchestration 9, 18, 9 (together 36). The 12 is the harmonic mean between 9 and 18 and divides the octave into fourth and fifth; the two inscribed figures 12 and 18, one above the other, are indicative of Palladio's intentions. We find the figure 12 again in the outside group of rooms of the wing,

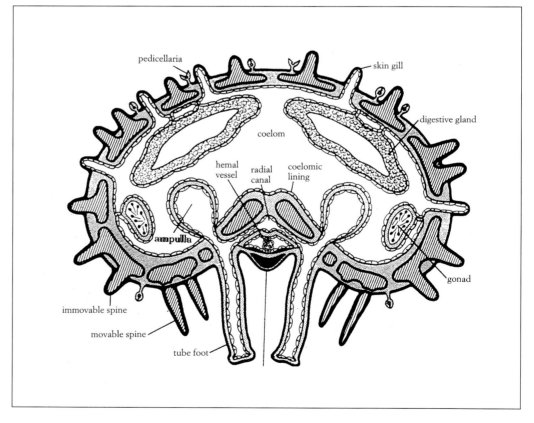

while the depth of the front rooms, 20, is repeated in the width and depth of the middle group of the wings. In other words, the three groups of rooms of the long wing repeat and develop the theme of the main building. At the same time, the figures inscribed in the three groups of the wings are interrelated, the smaller class of rooms as 9:10:12 (minor tone and minor third), the larger class of rooms as 16:18:20 (major tone and minor tone). The relation between the lengths of rooms, 20 and 32 (farthest group) is 5:8 (minor sixth, or minor third and fourth – 20:24:32). The stables, the courtyard, the colonnade all form part of this symphony. 12, the basic term of the building, returns in the width of the fountain in the main axis at the farthest end of the yard and also in the width of the colonnade. This figure is further divided and appears as 6 in the smallest room of the house and as 3 and 4 in the niches and the passage of the exedra leading to the fountain. The width of the courtyard, 32, corresponds to the length of the farthest group of rooms, and the width of the exedra, 60, is a fivefold proportion of 12 or a triple proportion of the equally important term 20. As the ratios of this building are evolutions of one and the same harmonic pattern, the proportional affinities could be stated in still greater detail."[19]

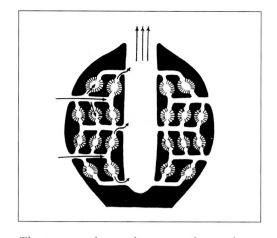

*The structure of a complex sponge: the corridor and rooms guarantee a simple distributive hierarchy.*

The concept of room held by the modern movement was violently disputed by F. Lloyd Wright, van Doesburg and Schwitters only to be rehabilitated by the philosophy of Kahn and Charles Moore. Wright seriously questioned the concept of the architectural box: a prismatic space, permanently enclosed on six sides, condemned to spatial inertia.[11] Whereas, by disassembling the sides using a sliding mechanism, space becomes fluid, passing from the inside out and from the outside in, without violent interruption, like water that flows in the riverbed between gorges and meanders. The poetics of spatial continuity is diametrically opposed to the model of bourgeois apartments with rooms to either side of a "corridor" protecting private space. Initially perceived as a liberating experience it gradually turned into individualistic isolation. Van de Welde designed his Biyenkorf so that from the corner of the room in which he worked he could see the rituals of everyday life all through the day. In his residential houses, Wright assigned the role of unifying element to the fireplace and in post-modern architecture the sequence of specialised spaces is again of interest to architects. This is the repeated cycle of acceptance and refusal of the same archetype: a permanent sign of the need for the art world never to give ideas or archetypes exclusive rights for a long period of time. "Art disrupts life," wrote Karl Kraus in an aphorism and followed it up with another, no less incisive: "only in the voluptuousness of linguistic creation does chaos become a world."

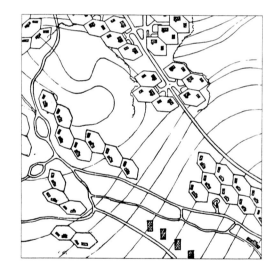

*Organic allotments in Tapiola (Alvar Aalto, 1936).*

Apart from the problem of the room as the basic element of domestic space, for the modern movement the important issues involve the minimum spatial units and their process of aggregation and disaggregation, disassembly and re-assembly, construction and deconstruction. It is in this field of study and reflection that the scientific studies of natural structures are particularly inspiring. Biology and chemistry, for example, provide architectural theory with

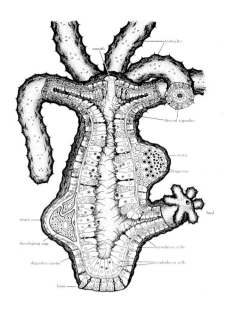

*The section of a* Hydra*, a minuscule fresh water coelenterate with long tentacles, well known for its impressive ability to regenerate parts of its body. Its internal cavity, with an endodermis of epithelial cells, recalls the structure of villages in which one-family houses are grouped together around a central space and its access routes.*

*The schematic plan of the village of Bawômataluo on the island of Nias, Indonesia.*

various structural concepts that complete and qualify the principles of geometry.[12]

The aggregation of spheres and polygons had already been summarily examined by Kepler. In his treatise *De Nive Sexangula*, published in 1611, he attempts to explain the macroscopic symmetry of snow crystals by examining the way in which they form a system.

The various crystals, assimilated to spheres, can in fact form an aggregation by positioning themselves in a square (in this case each sphere touches the ones around it in four points) or a hexagon (each sphere touches six adjoining spheres to form a network of lines that cross at 60° and 120°). The hexagonal system, whose use in agriculture was praised even by Virgil, saves space and permits even more restrictive compactness. In the same book, Kepler tackles a similar problem involving the seeds of a pomegranate and discovers how, in this case, nature uses a polyhedron, the rhombus-dodecahedron, a cube with square-based pyramids on its faces. Kepler explains this type of compactness by theorising that the seeds are originally spherical and that when they grow they adapt and form as tight an aggregation as possible through an "adaptation" process that is important even in architecture.[13] Given the experience of minimum surfaces and soap bubbles, the problem of the aggregation of spherical and polygonal cells was fundamental in the architecture of the second half of this century. It involved the research carried out by architects who came from extremely different backgrounds

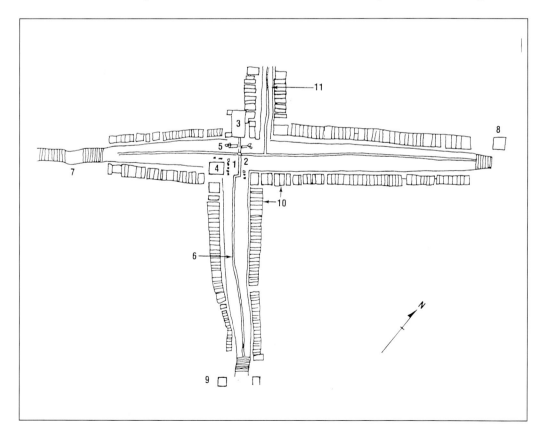

330

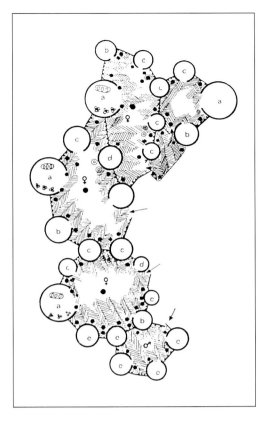

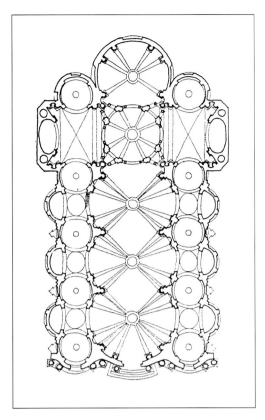

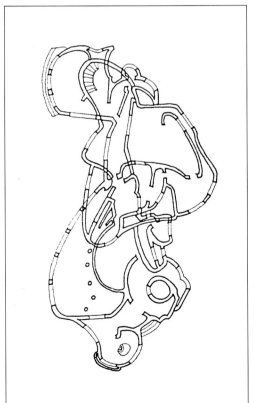

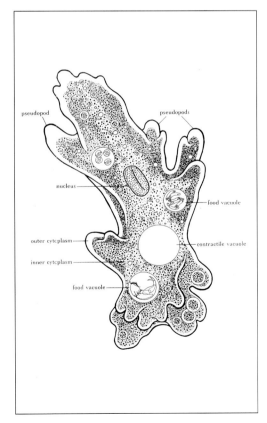

*Cellular designs in architecture: Fali (Cameroon), the house of a patriarch; the plan of a church by Guarino Guarini, taken from pl. 33 in the appendix of* Architettura civile, *Mairese, Turin 1737; the plan of a house made of ice. The spatial units are igloos, made of blocks that form an elicoidal shape.*

*An "amoebic" plan designed by Herman Firnsterlin and the section of an amoeba showing its main parts, arranged in an undefined and haphazard manner.*

*The inside of a pomegranate exposing the compact
structure of the fleshy seed capsules.*

and sensibilities, from Kahn to Tange to Moshe Safdije to Zwi Hecker and theorists such as Konrad Wachsmann, Robert Le Ricolais, Buckminster Fuller, Robert Williams and Peter Rice who, even recently, have continued to provide remarkable contributions in this field.

Fuller's "geodesic dome," patented in 1953, is not substantially very different from the iron-cement cupola built in 1922 in Jena for the first projector system (called "Planetary") that allowed the movement of the stars and planets to be simulated on a hemispherical surface.[14] But Fuller's patent managed to capture the imagination of the community, making the "geodesic dome" not only a light and economical structure, but also a redeeming myth. In this, Fuller imitated the pioneer spirit of Alexander Graham Bell who, by maniacally exploiting a tetrahedral structure, succeeded in making a man fly on a kite. Fuller's philosophy is a "cosmic" philosophy. He believes that man and the universe are not separate entities but part of a single structural process. Man becomes conscious of nature depending on the partial elements it offers. His universe is a "limited accumulation of human experiences consciously acquired or transmitted." In his experiments, all aimed mainly at creating structures useful to man, Fuller is inspired by the more general principles of scientific laws and stresses the types of energy accumulation that can be obtained, based on the principles of cosmic organisation. Fuller comments that nature is made of trees, human beings, birds, fish, butterflies, etc., and not simply of structures that absorb as yet indeterminate tension, but also of catalysers of an energy that they themselves use in an impredictable and subtle way to ensure the survival of the species through the chemical structures and principles of locomotion inherent in external forces.

The real problem is to discover the general principles of natural structures which normally occur at microcosmic level. Even if the structures that emerge from all this research do not correspond to the real structures present in nature, they are very similar. "The structure of a geodesic dome is very similar to that of radiolarians or a fly's eye, even if they are fundamentally different in nature."

Without Fuller's prophetic tone and media ability the theme of the cupola, as a microcosm in synergy with the macrocosm, would never have been so popular, especially among the youths of the sixties. It symbolised their desire to rediscover the original meaning of "inhabiting the earth." In fact, in 1967, hippies built Drop-City near Trinidad, Colorado, a city made only of cupolas.[15]

The experience and studies of Graham Bell, Fuller, Wachsmann and Le Ricolais, always in close association with organic and inorganic morphology, have crystallised the concept of spatial or cellular structure and have extended the model of grid and network to the third dimension. They employed both the cubic and orthogonal system of hives, concentrating their attention on the way in which the components are joined together. Architectural experimentation now involves a new field of the most varied types of cellular aggregation. It is extremely interesting to compare the work of the structuralists – who took natural elements and abstractly developed them in order to apply them practically in the

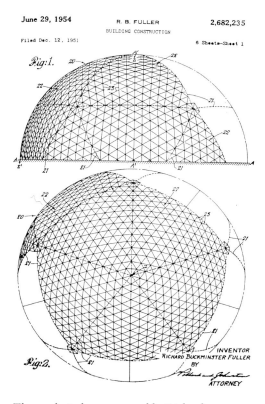

*The geodesic dome patented by Richard Buckminster Fuller.*

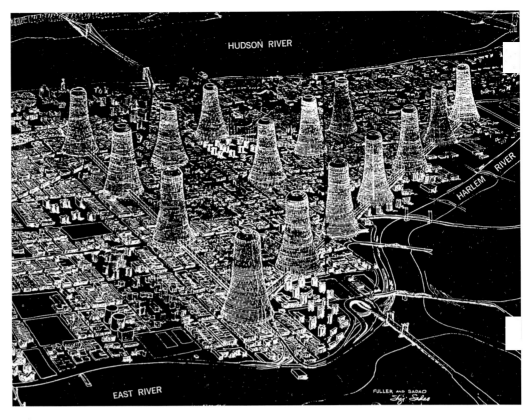

*Richard Buckminster Fuller, Harlem Highrise
Project, New York, 1964.*

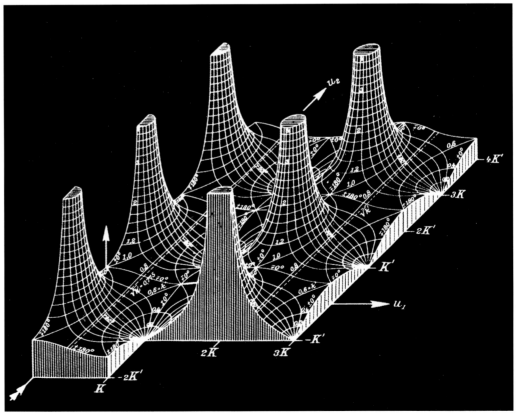

*Survey of the double periodic elliptical
function for k=0.8.
Section of the Harlem Highrise (Richard
Buckminster Fuller, Soji Sadao, 1964).*

334

field of construction – to the work of scientists who were, at that time, expanding the horizons of knowledge on the morphology of living beings and inorganic matter. These two worlds often cross over and overlap, demonstrating how nature is paradoxically able to exemplify many of those abstractions that seemed inevitably linked to the work of the human mind.

Like the two-dimensional module before it, the reticular spatial structure has provided architects with the chance to trust in the *esprit de système* and imagine a continuous reticular universe in which to insert inhabitable cells, like drawers in a cupboard; cells that are free in space and bear no relationship to the earth and the archetype of the house.

The second generation of researchers in this field abandoned the ambitious idea of building a world based on a systematic hypothesis and followed the road opened by Louis Kahn with his tower in Philadelphia in 1957.

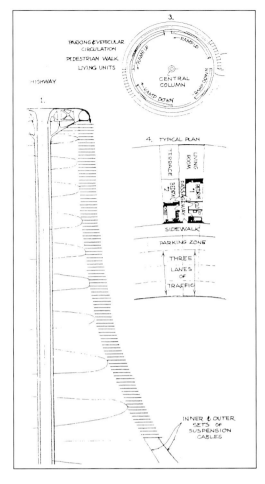

*Section of the Harlem Highrise (Richard Buckminster Fuller, Soji Sadao, 1964).*

[1] F. Ruttner, *Naturgeschichte der Höninghienen*, Ehrenwirt, Munich 1992.

[2] J. Gerhard Helmke and K. Bach, *Radiolarien*, Institut für Leichte Flächentragwerke, Stuttgart 1990.

[3] cf., F.E. Round et al., *The Diatoms*, Cambridge University Press, 1992.

[4] cf., K. von Frisch, *L'architettura degli animali*, Mondadori, Milan 1974 (*Animal Architecture*, New York 1974); M. Allaby, *Animal Artisans*, Knopf, New York 1982; D. Morris, *Les Animaux révélés*, Calmann Levy, Paris 1990; J. Gould, C. Grant Gould, *The Animal Mind*, Scientific American Library, New York 1994.

[5] cf., *Architettura e Natura*, catalogue of the exhibition on the Rome mosque and other recent works by P. Portoghesi, Fabbri, Milan 1994.

[6] cf., K. von Frisch, *op.cit.*, and A. Anderson, P. Jacklyn, *Termites of the Top End*, Csiro, Australia 1993.

[7] Gaudí-Groep Delft, *Gaudí Rationalist*, Delfte Universitaire Press, Delft 1989.

[8] Matthew 6, 29-30.

[9] cf., R. Wittkower, *Architectural Principles in the Age of Humanism*, The Warburg Institute, University of London 1949.

[10] *Ibid*.

[11] cf., F. Lloyd Wright, the battle of the box did not stop Wright as an architect from "designing" exceptional boxes, such as the Winslow House or the A.D. German Warehouse.

[12] See the chapter on numbers.

[13] cf., P. Portoghesi, *Borromini, architettura come linguaggio*, Electa, Milan 1967, pp. 386-400.

[14] Z.S. Makowski, *Räumliche Tragwerke aus Stahl*, Stahleisen, Dusseldorf 1963, p. 110.

[15] cf., A.V. Shelter, *Shelter Publications*, Bolinas Cal., 1973.

# Centrality

According to legend, Buddha gave a sermon without saying one word. This is the description of that sermon from a text narrating his life based on the most reliable sources available.[1] "That day the Buddha's Dharma talk was most special. He waited for the children to be seated quietly, and then he slowly stood up. He picked up one of the lotus flowers and held it up before the community. He did not say anything. Everyone sat perfectly still. The Buddha continued to hold up the flower without saying anything for a long time. People were perplexed and wondered what he meant by doing that. Then the Buddha looked out over the community and smiled. He said, 'I have the eyes of true Dharma, the treasure of wondrous insight, and I have just transmitted it to Makakassapa'.

"Everyone turned to look at Venerable Kassapa and saw that he was smiling. His eyes had not wavered from the Buddha and the lotus he held. When the people looked back at the Buddha, they saw that he too was looking at the lotus and smiling.

"Though Svasti felt perplexed, he knew that the most important thing was to maintain mindfulness. He began to observe his breath as he looked at the Buddha. The white lotus in the Buddha's hand had newly blossomed. The Buddha held it in a most gentle, noble gesture. His thumb and forefinger held the stem of the flower which trailed the shape of his hand. His hand was as beautiful as the lotus itself, pure and wondrous. Suddenly, Svasti saw the pure and noble beauty of the flower. There was nothing to think about. Quite naturally, a smile arose on his face.

"The Buddha began to speak. 'Friends, this flower is a wondrous reality. As I hold the flower before you, you all have a chance to experience it. Making contact with a flower is to make contact with a wondrous reality. It is making contact with life itself.

"'Mapakassapa smiled before anyone else because he was able to make contact with the flower. As long as obstacles remain in your minds, you will not be able to make contact with the flower. Some of you asked yourselves, 'Why is Gautama holding that flower up? What is the meaning of his gesture?' If your minds are occupied with such thoughts, you cannot truly experience the flower.

"'Friends, being lost in thoughts is one of the things that prevents us from making true contact with life. If you are ruled by worry, frustration, anxiety, anger, or jealousy, you will loose the chance to make real contact with all the wonders of life.

"'Friends, the lotus in my hand is only real to those of you who dwell mindfully in the present moment. If you do not return to the present moment, the flower does not truly exist. There are people who can pass through a forest of sandal-wood trees without ever really seeing one tree. Life is filled with suffering, but it also contains many wonders. Be aware in order to see both the suffering and the wonders in life.

"'Being in touch with suffering does not mean to become lost in it. Being in touch with the wonders of life does not mean to lose ourselves in them either. Be-

*A lotus flower* (Nelumbo nucifera). *Buddha gave a sermon to his followers which consisted in showing them a single lotus flower to contemplate: "Friends, this flower is wonderfully real. Holding it up in front of you, you can all experience it. To enter into contact with a flower is to enter into contact with something wonderfully real, to enter into contact with life itself."*
*Architecture owes to the observation of flowers, fruits and crystals the concept of centrality: a law consistently applied by all civilisations.*

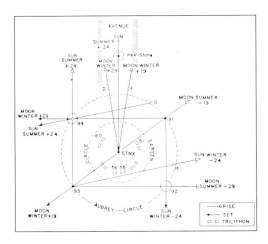

*Diagram drawn by Gerald Hawkins showing the lines of visibility of the sun and the moon from the oldest parts of Stonehenge.*

*A bird's eye view of Stonehenge showing a reconstruction of its fourth stage of growth.*

ing in touch is to truly encounter life, to see it deeply. If we directly encounter life, we will understand its interdependent and impermanent nature. Thanks to that, we will no longer lose ourselves in desire, anger , and craving. We will dwell in freedom and liberation.'"

Architecture owes many of its laws to the observation of flowers, fruits and plant forms. These laws are unwritten but can be gleaned from the corpus of architecture's concrete achievements and theories. Axiality and centrality are exemplified in flowers and fruits, as they are in micro-organisms and certain animals, yet up to now man has exploited only an infinitesimal part of this abundant treasure. In particular, with regard to centrality, nature provides examples of all forms of rotatory symmetry. There are flowers with four, five, six or seven petals and so on. In many cases either the petals are different or have alternative forms, or else they alternate and intertwine with the sepals or small leaves to form complex images.[2]

Zero degrees in centrality is the circle that defines the relationship of man with nature as being total visibility. Round is the eye of man and circular is the line of the horizon when viewing the plain or desert. What could have been considered a straight line, the straight line *par excellence*, became a continuous and complete circle when eyes panned over the horizon. Along this line, indirectly perceptible even when slopes hid it from view, man began to discern the cyclical laws of nature, directions established by watching the orbit of the sun, the planets and the stars.

The megalithic complex at Stonehenge is a magnificent example of the structural imitation of nature made possible by impressive creative abstraction. Here, architecture makes it possible for man and the universe to simultaneously initiate a process of listening, inquiry and knowledge and to confirm the theories mentally formulated by memories of the past, by reflection and the repetition of direct experience accrued over time.

The flower originally entered architecture through the hut type. However, even in Chinese culture and classical antiquity there were centrally-designed buildings that interpreted its compositional logic in a more complex form. In its development from pure circularity to complex rotatory symmetries, the idea of centrality was personified by the cross with equal arms, later to be called "Greek cross": the first sign that implicates orientation and the definition of an unambiguous relationship with the earth. The matrix of the cross, and therefore orthogonality, is rooted in the relationship between the horizon and the erect position of the human body, but ever since the beginning of time, the mind tends to project the cross onto a horizontal plane in order to pinpoint its "cardinal points."

Together with the centre, the circle and the square, the fundamental symbols of unity, the cross is the most all-inclusive element, since it establishes a system of dynamic relations between all the others. In fact, it transforms the centre by pointing it outwards. It fits into the circle which it divides into segments: by draw-

The cross as a natural structure, as the symbol of anthropisation of the landscape and the geometric nucleus of a centrally-planned city.

Left, from the top: the "medicine wheel" in Sedona (Arizona), an ancient site sacred to American Indians; Koy-Krylgan Kale, Khwarizin (Asia Minor), centrally planned settlement inspired by astronomy dating to the 2nd century B.C. At that time, a civilisation influenced by the Han dynasty in China and by the Greek-Bactrian culture that flourished around the river Oxus.

Below: the Lethoptera dodecaptera, a protozoon of the class of the radiolarians, subclass of the rhizopods, legion of the Actipilates, order of the Acanthometers.

ing a line between its points, the cross creates both the square, symbol of the earth, and the triangle, symbol of the sky. In nature, it is present mainly in micro-organisms, crystals and flowers. Apart from being the cosmic symbol *par excellence*, the geometric equivalent of a man with raised arms and a bird in flight, the cross is also the symbol of intermediation, of communication between different places, spaces and times, an open and radiant crossroad pointing in four directions. Centrifugal and centripetal at the same time, the cross expresses diffusion, emanation, reunion, recapitulation. It also integrates the opposition of the parts, transforming them into equilibrium and therefore revealing the mysterious and ambivalent aspects of the centre. Quite apart from the fact that for Christianity the cross is the supreme symbol of salvation and the matrix of the church, architecture has always used it as a precept for order and as a geometric pattern since it permits space to dilate in four directions. When the cross has several parallel arms, like the cross of Lorraine, it also enables the theme of the crossroads to be repeated more than once along a longitudinal line, as for example in Hindu temples. In so doing, it opens up to spatial models which, in contrast to the main body, reveal arms, legs and "wings," just like those of living beings.

In his *Apologia* (1,55), Saint Justin lists the *cruces dissimulate* such as the anchor, the trident, the helm, the pulley, etc., images frequently found in the iconography of architecture and in the decoration of Christian churches. For the Romans, the sacred enclosure or *templum* was shaped like a quadrangle because

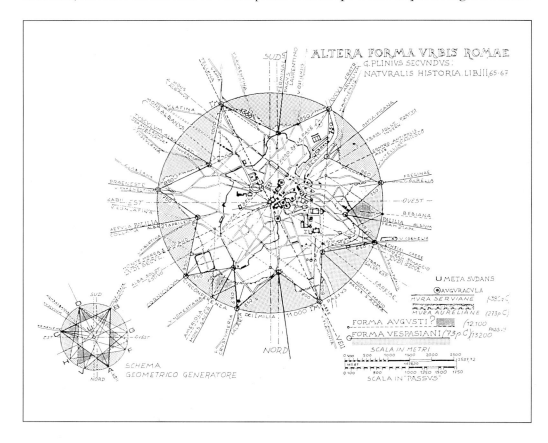

*The cruciform structure of a* Astrophytum myriostigma quadricostatum.

*The nest of a nightjar (*Caprimulgus europaeus). *The spherical nest is made of a mixture of earth, straw and excrements similar to the pisé used in manmade buildings in various regions of the world.*
*The nest of the nightjar is divided into two "rooms" by a thin wall made of the same material.*

*Geometric patterns of settlements found in medieval treatises of Indian architecture (Manasara; Mayamata-Silparatha; Samarangana). From the top: the orthogonal city in the form of a lotus flower (central* Nadyavarta) *and two types of* Padmaka *respectively based on a orthogonal grid and on a spike-shaped system that branches out in four directions. This image looks very much like a tree seen from above.*

it was directional, and even though the *mundus*, the image of the sky, was circular, it too was divided into quadrants by a cross in order to obtain the same result. The *mundus*, seed and navel of the city, is a ditch dug to hold the fruits of the earth. It is sacred to the chthonic gods and those who guarantee the fertility of the earth. A child used to be lowered inside this ditch in order to vaticinate the outcome of the harvest.

Many flowers have a cruciform structure, for instance those with four petals such as poppies, jasmine, veronica, capers or the fragrant daphne. The orthogonal axes in these flowers are marked by the empty spaces between the petals, while the other components adapt to this symmetry, revealing examples of geometric order and compositional logic. When the sepals are rotated with respect to the petals, this suggests the "binary growth" of two separate structures that develop in harmony, but interpret this common law in different ways.

The fact that flowers open upwards and towards the light must have been an important stimulus in planimetry. Traces of this particular form of abstraction have been found as far back as ancient Egypt and China. Even before this projection process was clearly identified, rough planimetries were used to turn the design concept into ideograms; the latter were not only related logically to the flower, but also reflected its compositional logic determined by a complex and harmonic attraction between the centre and the borders.

The symbolism of the centre and therefore of the circle is a matter of interest to all civilisations. Together with its infinite elaborations and variations, it has certain common elements that are of great importance in architecture. The most intuitive and immediate aspects of its circular and spherical symbolism is illustrated in an excerpt from the book *Black Elk speaks* in which the author states that everything produced by the Force of the World finds its perfection in the circle, since the circle is round and, he has heard, so is the earth, as round as a ball, and so too the stars. He goes on to explain that this is due to the great force of the wind which creates vortexes. Birds build round nests, since they share the same faith as mankind. The sun rises and sets in a circle. As does the moon. Both are round. Even the seasons in their passing form a circle only to return again. The life of man is like a circle from infancy to infancy, and this is because everything is moved by a force. The author goes on to point out that all their tepees were round like birds' nests and arranged in a circle, the ring of their peoples – a nest made of many nests in which, according to the will of the Great Spirit, their children were born, raised and protected.[3]

It is through circularity that the house, the temple and the city acquire a direct relationship with the universe and their foundation eternally reproposes cosmogony. The model of circular subdivision is based on the flower, in particular the Indian lotus (*Nelumbo nucifera*), the Egyptian lotus (blue waterlily) and the rose, symmetric organisms that unite heaven and earth in a symbolic union. Apart from its use in sacred architecture, the combination of the circle, the cross and the square is present in all graphic representations used to favour religious meditation. A typical example is the Indian mandala, a geometric projection of the world "paradigm of the evolution and involution of the universe"[4] made to recover the unity of a "meditative and attentive" conscience, and to discover the ideal principle of things. The mandala can be a painting or a small coloured drawing, but originally it was a big drawing dug in the earth, in a specially chosen place, usually near a river. The designated ground was weeded and levelled and before admitting the initiate, the teacher prepared its basic structure with two ropes: a white one to mark the boundaries of the mandala and another one with five twisted threads of different colours to represent the deities. A north-south axis was established with the dual function of indicating the cardinal points and the *axis mundi*, while the other axis was oriented in an east-west direction. Five vases full of precious and perfumed substances were then placed at strategic points. The blindfolded neophyte was admitted to the mandala after a series of purification and elevation exercises: by walking across it he passed through several levels of awareness in his conscience until he reached the centre where he experienced "mandalic catharsis" and the transposition of the mandala into his own body.

Mircea Eliade writes in her book: "The first thing a neophyte conquers during meditation is the act of *gathering*, *reunion*, concentration, unification of conscience states. The mandala anchors them in reality, just like the Indian building ritual 'anchors' the snake's head and defends the house from earthquakes. By concentrating on a mandala, the neophyte is protected against the external chaos that tries to draw him away, to break his concentration and scatter his energy by deceiving him with illusion and futile entreaties. The mandala is a centre and by meditating on it, the neophyte is able to avoid drowning in the ocean of mental, psychological and subliminal life (illusory for him) and anchor himself to the centre of reality. Salvation (which for Indians means liberation from illusion and pain) is attained only through understanding (for Christians) and participation in final reality. The mandala's function is to lead and anchor the soul in the heart of reality thereby illuminating the path to salvation."[5]

Even when the untrained eye of a westerner observes the mutant characteristics of the mandala, he notices that it reflects a series of geometric elements that make it seem familiar: the presence of cardinal axes, the rhythmic pattern of its components, the feeling of balance and the exaltation of centrality, all these traits recall the form of utopian cities or the natural structures of certain micro-organisms such as the radiolarians or the diatoms. When looking upwards at buildings such as the church of Santa Maria della Consolazione in Todi, the Madonna di San Biagio in Montepulciano, Sant'Ivo alla Sapienza in Rome or Saint John Nepomuk church in Zdar (Bohemia), the impression one gets is that the regularity of the forms seen by the viewer corresponds to a logical comprehension of the relationship linking our ego to the harmony of the universe. This is the same process of identification with the mandalic structure that a person feels when climbing Borobudur or observing the stupa and pagoda of the East. What is

The mandala of Sricakra *(lotus of a thousand petals). Inside the circular frame that contains the flower petals there are nine isosceles triangles, five with their vertices turned downwards and four with the vertices turned upwards. The former symbolise Shiva or the stage of return; the others represent the Sakti, a divine power and driving force of the universe in accordance to which God reveals himself and is manifest in objects. The triangles' intersection and progressive size represent the way in which the divinity spreads throughout the universe. The city of Bhaktapur in Nepal corresponds in every iconographic detail to a mandala based on the Sricakra, even if its organic and mixtilinear plan is based on the need to adapt to the orography of the site.*
*This correspondence is topological and not geometric. In Patan, instead, a series of monuments correspond precisely to the vertices of two equilateral triangles that overlap.*

344

even more surprising is that something similar occurs when, quite by chance, one unconsciously scribbles symmetrical doodles on a piece of paper during a boring conference or while waiting for a person for a long time. In his essay, *The Mystery of the Golden Flower*, G.C. Jung wrote that with no knowledge of eastern techniques, some of his patients built mandalas to recover from illnesses or to protect themselves from evil.[6]

One of the most sensational examples of centrality in architecture is Palladio's Rotonda that inspired the poet, von Hofmannsthal, with a similar feeling of "becoming whole again," of completeness, a fact that refers us back to the psychological power of the *imago mundi*.

"Here the builder climbed and saw that the top of this gentle hill crowned the landscape. So he crowned the hill with his sweetest dream. On the hill Palladio built the Rotonda. Not a house, not a temple, yet both. It is a vast round room covered by a dome, four doors lead to four halls supported by columns each in turn opening onto an external flight of steps. Everything is overshadowed by the magnificence of this Rotonda: the rooms of the house fit between the pillars, between the arches that bear that large pure circle: hidden rooms surround the façade of the Rotonda and burst out under the dome of the high room; rooms reach far under the four staircases and stare out from barred windows, as dark as slaves on whose shoulders the weight of such magnificence rests [...]. Immense emphasis is required by these four large staircases that face the

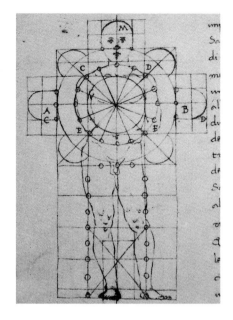

Andrea Palladio's Villa Capra in Vicenza is the prototype of centrality that was the rule applied to houses in order to bestow on them a certain sacredness. The building is a prismatic volume covered by a roof, pertaining to all houses. But the cupola and the four loggias on each façade are elements that are characteristic of temples and give the house another dimension expressed by the vertical axis (axis mundi) and by the four symmetry axes that initially divide the block into four and then (with the two diagonal axes) into eight. This cruciform centrality has anthropomorphic roots shown in the drawing by Francesco di Giorgio Martini (above), and is linked to the pattern of the mandala (left). The relationship with nature is expressed here in the cosmic reference to the cardinal points, to the vault of the sky and to the principles of equality, orthogonality, diagonal lines, symmetry and unity. The holistic principle according to which the "whole is more than the sum of the parts" is sensationally celebrated here. In his Dictionnaire, A.C. Quatremère de Quincy defines with great exactitude how this "imitation" of nature takes place: "it is nature itself, in its abstract essence that it (architecture) takes as a model. It is the order par excellence of nature that becomes its archetype and genius [...]. And so this art that, more than any other, appears to have become a tributary of matter, has, in this case, become more ideal than the others, in other words, more apt to exercise the intellectual part of our soul. In fact, nature only provides analogies and intellectual relationships to be imitated by matter."

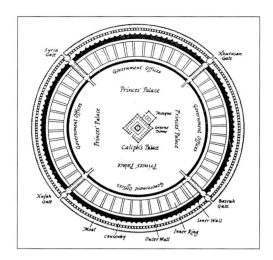

Baghdad. Plan of the circular city of al-Mansur (hypothetical reconstruction by Hitti). Proclaimed Caliph in 754, al-Mansur built Madinat as-Salaam, "the city of peace," according to the model of certain centrally-planned Hittite, Assyrian, Parse and Sassanide cities. Around the mosque and the palace compound there was a circular ring two kilometres wide and each sector of this ring corresponded to a district. The shape of the solar wheel accentuates its characteristic as a cosmological symbol and as the centre of the world, and is perhaps comparable to paradise on earth.

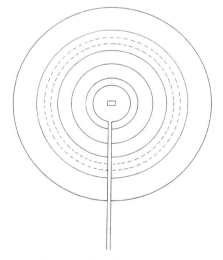

The city of Atlantis, described by Plato (in the first part of the Timeus and the Critias) in a graphic interpretation by John Michell. In the centre, the island with the temple of Poseidon surrounded by the first city ring, the internal canal, the external canal and the canal that marks the city limits. A straight road crosses the canals, linking the various areas of the city.

mountains, the sea, the plains and the city [...]. Crowning the hill of Vicenza is neither house nor temple, it is more than either. An immortal dream, a miraculously shaped symbol which seems to beckon the impetus of the distant mountains, the impetus of gushing waters, which finally reach it, surround it and, placated, gently lap the foot of each of the four staircases, delivered and liberated from its symbolic essence [...]."[7]

It is von Hofmannsthal, rather than many critics and art historians, who seems to exquisitely capture both the aesthetic and structural qualities of Palladio's building as well as the intentions of the architect, his passion for simple forms and obvious hierarchies. In the second chapter of his book *Quarto Libro dell'Architettura*, Palladio wrote: "Therefore, to maintain decorum in the shapes of our temples, we too, who have no false gods, should choose the most perfect and excellent one; and because the round form would be just that, as it alone amongst all the plans is simple, uniform, equal, strong, and capacious, let us build temples round; this form is far and away the most appropriate for them, because it is enclosed by only one boundary in which the beginning and end, which are indistinguishable, cannot be found, and since its parts are identical to each other, all of them contributing to the figure as a whole, and finally, since at every point the outer edge is equidistant from the center, it is perfectly adapted to demonstrate the unity, the infinite existence, the consistency, and the justice of God."[8]

If the circle is empowered with divine perfection, Palladio also believed it reflected cosmic harmony. In the Preface of his fourth book, he wrote: "Indeed, if we consider what a wondrous creation [*machina*] the world is, the marvellous embellishments with which it is filled, and how the heavens change the seasons of the world by their continuous revolutions according to the demands of nature, and how they maintain themselves by the sweetest harmony of their measured movements, we cannot doubt that, since these small temples which we build must be similar to this vast one which He, with boundless generosity, perfected with but a word of command, we are bound to include in them all the embellishments we can, and build them is such a way and with such proportions that together all the parts convey to the eyes of onlookers a sweet harmony and each church fulfils properly the use for which it was intended."[9]

Palladio was well aware of the cosmic harmony he impressed on the Rotonda. From the very start, western civilisation dreamed of setting the same all-inclusive seal on the city which it considered an organism. As for the mandala, it aims at confining chaos beyond the circle of the walls and at organising the urban fabric in a series of clearly identifiable parts that communicate yet remain separate.

In real cities, a difficult and infrequent balance is sometimes reached after blow-to-blow battles between order and chaos, almost as if a sudden earthquake had subverted the ordered geometric structures, leaving them topologically transformed yet perfectly functional (the planimetries of Siena, Rome or Algiers are perfect examples). In dream cities, some of which have been partially built (ancient Baghdad, the Roman *castra*, the City of the Sun, Thomas Moore's Utopia, Palmanova, etc.), the cosmological model seems to act as an element of contemplation as well as a behavioural model.

It is Plato who theorises the city in this way, describing in his *Laws* an ideal Magnesia to be built on the island of Crete and in *Critias* and *Timeus*, the destruction and construction of the legendary city of Atlantis.[10]

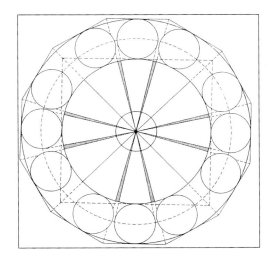

*The ideal plan of Plato's Magnesia, interpreted by John Michell in analogy with the Heavenly Jerusalem described in the book of* Revelations. *Plato dedicated his dialogue in his* Laws *to Magnesia. He envisaged a city-state built in a sparsely populated area of the island of Crete. The inhabitants were to number 5040.*

Magnesia was a recipe for salvation since Plato was convinced that "a state could be happy only if the designer used a divine model." His attempt to put his convictions into practice at the court of Dionysius, the tyrant of Syracuse, was so unsuccessful that in the end the courtiers accused him of plotting against Dionysius' son – Plato was his tutor – and drove him out of the city, selling him as a slave.

The ambiguous structure of Magnesia can be interpreted in two different ways. Either it is a series of concentric circles with four radial roads that converge on the acropolis or it is an orthogonal plan with four intersecting main roads and a square area in the centre for the acropolis.[11]

Plato indicates that this cruciform structure, corresponding exactly to the pre-Colombian Mexican village, Mexcaltitán, was built in the shape of a single house. It is easy to see how this statement inspired the double comparison used by Alberti, Palladio and Louis Kahn, of the house as a small city and the city as a large house.[12] The inhabitants of Mexcaltitán, who still practise the ancient cult of the Moon, consider the plan of their village a symbol of the quadripartition of the sky as well as a representation of its position at the centre of the earth.

The description of Atlantis highlights its cosmological roots, its analogy with the shape of the egg and its mandalic links: the city of Atlantis was shaped like a perfect circle. In the centre stood the temple of Poseidon and three annular canals, all connected to the sea by a straight canal. High walls rose along the canals. The outer wall was covered in bronze, the middle one in tin and the inner one in copper.

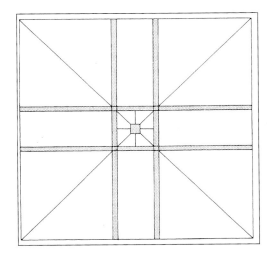

*The ideal plan of Magnesia in another reconstruction by John Michell. Four tribes were to inhabit the area between the strips that intersect in the centre; another eight tribes would have lived in the triangles created by the external squares and one of the eight trapezia of the intermediate squares.*

The central sanctuary was surrounded by golden walls and the buildings were made of red, white and black bricks mixed together to give an accentuated decorative effect. If the metals of the city walls recalled the skies of the planets, it was cosmic harmony that inspired the complex numerical machinery that determined the ratio between each part, a ratio similar to that of Heavenly Jerusalem described in the book of Revelations.

Centrality as a structural rule and at the same time as a frame that sustains and directs the unravelling of a story, is an architectural quality that is sometimes transferred into literature. In Dante's *Divine Comedy*, centrality is expressed by the three stages of his journey. Hell is described as an enormous well, with steps and rings that become narrower towards the centre; Purgatory is the counterform of Hell: a sort of mountain with seven terraces along its sides. On the top of the mountain a crown of fire surrounds Eden.[13]

Paradise, instead, has a discontinuous and dynamic structure although it maintains the pattern of concentric circles overlapping along an axis.

*simplest example of a wave expanding in concentric circles, a pattern used in cosmology to represent the heavens.*

*A pattern of concentric waves, with celestial implications, in the church of the Sacra Famiglia in Salerno, Italy (P. Portoghesi, V. Gigliotti, 1968) and, below, the cupola of the Rome mosque (P. Portoghesi, V. Gigliotti, S. Mousawi, 1975-95). Below right: part of the external membrane of an* Euplectella aspergillum (Oweri), *a siliceous sponge of the order of transparent hexaradial sponges.*

The first seven circles are made of matter, even if they are composed of incorruptible and interpenetrating substances. Beyond the eighth circle lies the domain of the immaterial, beyond space and time. Higher still, after the first mobile ring, lies Heaven, the immaterial circle of fire from which the rose of a thousand petals sends forth a stream of light.

> A Light is there above which makes
> the Creator visible to every creature
> that has his peace only in Beholding Him.
> It spreads so wide a circle
> that the circumference would be
> too large a girdle for the sun.
> Its whole expanse is made by a ray
> reflected from the summit of the Primum Mobile,
> which therefrom takes its life and potency;
> and as a hillside mirrors itself in water
> at its base, as if to look upon its own adornment
> when it is rich in grasses and in flowers,
> so above the light round and round about
> in more than a thousand tiers I saw
> all that of us have won return up there.
> And if the lowest rank encloses within itself
> so great a light, how vast is the spread
> of this rose in its outermost leaves!
> (*Paradise*, XXX, 100-117)

In this excerpt, Dante describes an incredible architectural model comparing matter and non-matter, sacred time and profane time. In some ways, the model is a perfect machine that executes harmonious and balanced movements, a cosmic clock that ticks like a human heart. But the rigidity of the machine continually dissolves into the "indescribable." The absence of matter and the eclipse of space create in man's mind something that words and vision cannot render. Unconsciously, Dante anticipates that view into the deep made possible by non-Euclidean geometry through the description of the multiple dimensions of spaces drawn up by Lobacevsky and Rieman.

Just like initiates who travel the mandala to try and improve their knowledge of sacredness, in his image of Heaven Dante uses all kinds of metaphor for the divine, for example the metaphor that alludes to the mystery of the Trinity.

> Within the profound and shining subsistence
> of the lofty Light appeared to me three circles
> of three colours and one magnitude;
> and one seemed reflected by the other,
> as rainbow by rainbow, and the third seemed fire

breathed forth equally from the one and the other.
(*Paradise*, XXXIII, 115-120)

To convince himself of the presence of the image of man in the second circle, Dante uses the mathematical paradox of the quadrature of the circle.

> As is the geometer who wholly applies himself
> to measure the circle, and finds not
> in pondering, the principle of which he is in need,
> such was I at that new sight.
> I wished to see how the image
> conformed to the circle
> and how it has its place therein;
> (*Paradise*, XXXIII, 133-138)

In buildings dug out of the rock, it is often possible to see forms shaped like lobes or petals that combine with the frontality created by excavation. Towards the end of the Great Age, centrally-planned buildings began to be constructed: there were rooms along their circular perimeters, joined in such a way that their profile became a multiconcave shape, for example in the temple of Venus in Baalbeck.

Traces of flowers are also visible in Christian churches based on the *martyrion* and later in Gothic lanterns often influenced by the crystalline geometry of Islamic culture. Starting with the Renaissance, from the Rotonda degli Angeli by Brunelleschi to studies by Leonardo, centrality was a way to imbue religious buildings with a sense of perfection and the absolute. Leonardo, who researched biological reality with "obstinate, pre-meditated rigour," examined the full potential of the rules of irradiation governing the structure of flowers, even if he was often attracted by the morphology of crystals.

Late Gothic and Renaissance cultures also explored another floral family: the family with ternary and hexagonal symmetry. The symmetrical *tricora,* built during the Romanesque period,[14] seems to be a simplified reproduction of the structure of the castor-oil plant, the snowdrop or the arrow-head; so too is the observatory by Tycho Brahe, or Francesco Contini's country house ("Casino") in Palestrina designed for the Barberini family. In F. Lloyd Wright's synagogue in Philadelphia, the triangular structure with its translucent integument is reminiscent of certain micro-organisms and diatoms.

One example of planimetric forms cited by Serlio in his treatise is a six-sided polygon actually built in the 16th century in Parma. However, it was Baroque culture that did justice to the hexagon – comb of the hive, symbol of fertility and integration of opposites – in its role as the matrix of new architectural adventures, the finest example being the church of Sant'Ivo[15], image of the bee, and the biblical Domus Sapientiae. The alternation of concave and convex vaulted cells in the Domus Sapientiae is a direct imitation of the structure of the *Iris ger-*

*...spherical fruit compared to the cupola of the ...arish church in Gibellina, Italy (Ludovico ...Quaroni, 1970) and to a nuraghe.*

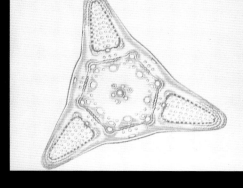

The cupola of Sant'Ivo alla Sapienza in Rome (Francesco Borromini, 1660) compared to the photograph of an Iris germanica. In both cases, the compositional law is based on two groups of three equiangular symmetry axes rotated by 30°.

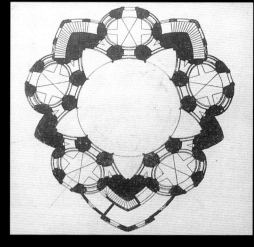

The flower of the Nigella damascena *species, showing its pentagonal symmetry, compared to the plan of the chapel of Saint John Nepomuk on the Green Mountain in Zdar, Bohemia (J. Santini Aichel, 1719-22) and the heptagonal symmetry of a pomegranate fruit compared to Bruno Taut's Haus des Himmels.*

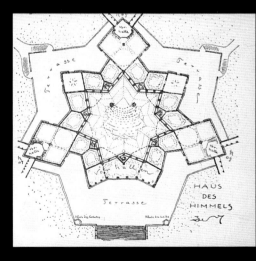

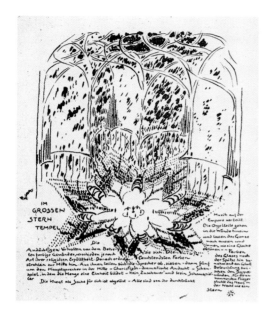

In the great temple of the sun, *a plate of the* Die Auflosung der Stadt *by Bruno Taut (1920):* *"Music sounding above. The organ pipes in the walls make the whole building resonate, inside and out, like a bell. The colours of the glass are more intense towards the ceiling; illumination between the double walls. Arriving by plane the house shines like a star. Before entering the temple the faithful receive coloured clothes according to their religiousness. Dramatic choral devotion. The crowd is like one sole unit in this show – there are no actors or spectators. Art as reality unto itself is ended – everyone is imbued."*

*manica.* This is perhaps the most architectural flower that exists because of the magic of its internal spaces illuminated by the empty spaces between its petals and the iridescent transparencies of the petals themselves. In the 18th century, this spatial model in which upward and downward facing petals alternate, inspired Bernardo Vittone to draw a staircase illustrated in plates LXII and LXIII of his book, *Istruzioni diverse.*

However, the most widespread polygon in the configuration of flowers, is neither the quadrangle nor the hexagon, but the pentagon. Rarely exploited in the field of architecture, it was skilfully and effectively used in Palazzo Farnese in Caprarola or in the Saint John Nepomuk in Zdar (Bohemia) in which the inorganic geometric theme of the star and the organic theme of the flower come together in perfect harmony, almost like a premonition of that profound unity between various morphological worlds illustrated by Lima-de-Faria.[16] Pythagoreans were already well aware of the practical impossibility of dividing a circumference into seven parts. They justified this fact by asserting that the number seven was the symbol of virginity. Despite the inherent practical and theoretical difficulties, even heptagonal symmetry has its own secret space in architecture: the Romanesque pillar in the church of Saint Remi-de-Reims is heptagonal and in Nôtre-Dame there is a rosette with the same geometric pattern. The Old Testament (*Proverbs*, 9) describes the luxurious and hospitable house of Wisdom: "Wisdom has built her house; she has hewn out its seven pillars. She has prepared her meat and mixed her wine; she has also set her table."

Two examples of heptagonal temples – the Sabean temples of Harran – are described by the 10th-century Islamic historian Mas'udi. It would be futile to look for any archaeological remains, but Mas'udi has left an accurate and inspiring description.[17]

The first temple had seven doors, one on each side, and a roof with seven floors and a precious stone at the top. Whoever tried to approach fell to the ground struck by lightening, while the arrows shot against its walls bounced back against the archer. Inside there was a heptagonal well with an inscription around the well-head: "No-one may enter or draw on these treasures except for those who equal us in knowledge, power and wisdom." Inside the well was the "book treasure," custodian of the science of the Earth and the Heavens, of the chronology of times past and times to come. The temple was near the Chinese border on a rock jutting out of the earth.

The other temple was divided into seven oratories lit by seven windows. In front of the windows there were seven images of seven different stars: the five planets and the two major stars. Near the temple stood an incredibly deep well.

The first to grasp the architectural virtuality of the heptagon was Francesco Colonna, author of the *Hypnerotomachia Poliphili*, who described a small temple of this shape in the centre of a garden-theatre.[18] In his first designs for the chapel of Sant'Ivo alla Sapienza, Borromini had envisaged an apse with seven columns, referring specifically to the verses of the Bible (*Proverbs*, 9, 1-6) cited in one of his drawings for the State Archives in Rome.[19] A temple with seven columns also appears on the title-page of the third volume of *Apparatus urbis et templi hierosolymitani* (1606). The next architect to propose the heptagon as the basic form of a building was Bruno Taut who used it in one of his most symbolically charged glass building: the Haus des Himmels.[20]

Since Taut was never able to build any of his heptagonal buildings, to do justice to the passion he shared with Borromini I would like to dedicate what is the only, albeit ephemeral, concretisation of his heretical dream: the "House of Wisdom" built in Modena on behalf of the Gallery of Modern Art and re-assembled in 1986 in Rome in the courtyard of Palazzo Falconieri enlarged by Francesco Borromini.

Bruno Taut was undoubtedly the architect who exploited the archetype of centrality as coherently and explicitly as possible, taking his cue from two natural models, the star and the flower. He was the most intense and enigmatic figure among the masters of the modern movement (the generation born between 1880 and 1890).

Naturally, the seeds of his passion for central forms were sown during his early years, but they continued to bloom even after 1924 and re-emerged in his final project: the house he built for himself on the banks of the Bosphorus. His is an aesthetic and iconographic predilection, because Taut, from the very beginning of his career, was fascinated by the symbolic force of forms and colour. In 1904, at the age of twenty-four, he wrote an essay entitled, *Natur und Baukunst* – the unpublished manuscript still exists today – and in a few delicate pastel drawings of the same period he reproposed the analogy between the Gothic nave of the Stifskirche in Stuttgart and a forest of conifers. The manuscript talks of an "extremely subtle sensibility for the construction of space that only nature can demonstrate in the most diverse ways" and, with regard to the pastel drawings, states that "the details are radically different, but the basic configuration of space remains the same."[21]

Taut is interested in the star because it is persistently present in various forms of nature: at microcosmic level in the radiolarians and diatoms illustrated by Haeckel and at macrocosmic level in so far as the star becomes an immaterial irradiation of light. The symbolic connotations of the star generically embrace the idea of totality, of the synthesis between matter and spirit and of open centrality. However, if one bears in mind the fact that Taut's stellar buildings were almost always built using a system of seven axes, this more than clarifies their metaphorical meaning.

As mentioned earlier, the seven-pointed star contains the magical symbol of the figure 7, the perfect number *par excellence*, even if this number is excluded from architecture due to a sort of geometric curse, or else indirectly interpreted as the sum of 6+1 and consequently applied to hexagonal plans with the addition of the vertical axis.

As the sum of 3 and 4, 7 unites the sky (3) and the earth (4), the elements of masculinity and femininity.

The great flower, *another plate of the* Die Auflosung der Stadt. *"Techniques are now completely different to those associated with the early history of factories with chimneys. A sanctuary to absorb solar energy with glass panels, lens and burning glass heaped together as beacons for planes. Man is so transformed that all he does is joy. This would be impossible to impose. Man is no longer a dog. Primordial wisdom revived: absolute frankness – the overcoming of instincts through instincts – phallus and rosette - newly reinstated sacred symbols, indecency is impossible without subterfuge and silence. The concept of possession has disappeared – therefore matrimony too. Everything is borrowed talent – pleasure and pure joy."*

*Illustration by Botticelli for the* Paradiso (*canto XXV*) *by Dante. Berlin, Reading Room of drawings and prints.*

Saint Augustine indicates the number 7 as the number of cyclical perfection, of eternal return. The seventh day is the day God claims for himself after the cosmogony. Not only does it symbolise totality and completion, but it continually re-emerges in the prophecy of Celestial Jerusalem certainly cited in Taut's utopia.

Apart from the Haus des Himmels mentioned earlier, this septenary symmetry appears in the great stellar temple illustrated in the *Die Auflosung der Stadt* described as follows by its author: "Before entering the temple the faithful receive coloured clothes according to their religiousness. After which they form a line. The more brilliant colours towards the centre. Seven – then five – preachers stand apart, near the head preacher. Dramatic choral devotion. Music all over the women's gallery. The organ doors fit into the walls and make everything ring, inside and out, like a bell [...]. The colour of the glass is more intense towards the top. Lighting between the double walls. For arriving aviators the house shines like a star in the night."

Apart from the stars, a number of town-planning designs and buildings inspired by the shape of flowers also appear in the books *Alpine Architektur* and *Die Auflosung der Stadt*. First of all the "Tals als Bluthe," a valley like a flower, plate 48 of *Alpine Architektur*, seems to correspond to the unbridled cosmic hedonism veined with irony that initially coloured Taut's utopia in 1919.

"Below, a lake with floral ornaments of stained glass," explains the caption, "that shine like the walls, the crystal points embedded on the summits lit up during the night. A flower-shaped valley. Walls built along the stained glass slopewalls. The transient light is the source of the successful lighting effects for both valley dwellers and astronauts. The view from the top will greatly affect architecture and architects."

Emblematic is the use of flowers to celebrate the sacred symbols of Phallus and Rosette: "The great flower. Technique nowadays is a far cry from the age of factory chimneys. A sanctuary to harness solar energy with sheets of glass, concave lenses and mirrors, heaped together luminous beacons for planes. Man is so different that he need not work without joy. Constriction is impossible. Man has lost his 'dog' characteristic. Ancient wisdom is new born: true openness in sexual matters. The ego overcomes instinct. Phallus and Rosette are again sacred symbols, indecency is impossible without subterfuge and silence [...]. The concept of possession has disappeared, so too the concept of matrimony. Every thing is 'borrowed talent.' Only pleasure is joy."

To the concept and compositional procedures of centrality it may be useful to associate the growth processes of crystals, especially "gemination." Often, a number of crystals simultaneously grow together. This usually happens because, when the crystals grow in a compressed space, they end up by intersecting each other. Gemination occurs when in this type of double growth the crystals present a regularity governed by a given orientation. This gemination can either be simple or multiple according to whether two or more crystals are involved.

A typical example of simple gemination in architecture are the double intersecting structures found in many of Michelangelo's constructions: the Palazzo dei Conservatori on the Campidoglio in Rome, in which the gigantic order is sectioned by a minor order, and the Biblioteca Laurenziana in Florence and Porta Pia in Rome. Gemination as a central radial structure is often found in buildings by Frank Lloyd Wright, and before that, with regard to cruciform patterns, in the "panoptic" and "windmill" structures exemplified by Serlio in his treatise. During the Baroque period these structures inspired Juvarra with the design of the saltire cross pattern in the hunting lodge he designed in Stupinigi.

Even if these vortex systems refer more to a rotatory symmetry that has nothing to do with pure centrality, they should be studied here for reasons of affinity. These systems can be compared to the "spiral" or "screw" growth processes of crystals such as paraffin. Rotatory symmetry excludes bilateral specular symmetry but is implicit in what is called "chilarity."[22]

The spiral growth model "envisages the growth of a crystal according to growth spirals generated by the presence of screw patterns on the surface of the crystal. This model no longer has to create new layers. Each component is positioned in an opening in the screw pattern and, based on its order, follows the helicoidal trend of the layer that delimits the pile, generating new openings that shift around the outline of the screw pattern. Lastly, the crystal does not grow because the components are piled in layers; it grows because it develops a layer that twists in a spiral around the profile of the screw pattern." This vortex system is created because the marginal elements are tangentally linked to the central nucleus, like the paddle-wheel of a turbine. This system is quite frequent in plant structures (for example in periwinkles, cyclamens and thorn apples) and due to its implicit dynamism became one of the favourite themes of Art Nouveau culture.[23]

*Bio-energy spa in Canino; the application of a vortex pattern to the design of a building that runs on a passive, solar energy system (P. Portoghesi; builders, Coop. Cobase, 1975).*

[1] Thic Nhat Hanh, *Old Paths, White Clouds*, Parallex Press, Berkeley (Ca.) 1991.

[2] cf., B. Gibbons, *The Secret Life of Flowers*, Blandford, London 1990; A.D. Bell, *Plant Form*, Oxford University Press, Oxford 1991.

[3] Text taken from the anthology *Sai che gli alberi parlano?*, Il punto d'Incontro ed., Vicenza 1992, p. 75.

[4] cf., G. Tucci, *Teoria e pratica del mandala*, Ubaldini, Rome 1969.

[5] cf., M. Eliade, *I riti del costruire*, Jaca Book, Milan 1990, p. 67.

[6] cf., *Ibidem*, p. 69.

[7] cf., R. Assunto, *La città di Anfione e la città di Prometeo*, Jaca Book, Milan 1983, p. 102 ff.

[8] cf., A. Palladio, *The Four Books of Architecture*, The MIT Press, Cambridge (Mass.) 1959.

[9] cf., *Ibid*.

[10] cf., J. Michell, *The Dimensions of Paradise*, Thames and Hudson, London 1988.

[11] cf., Plato, *The Laws*, 745.

[12] cf., Leon Battista Alberti, *L'architettura*, Il Polifilo, Milan 1966. The Mexican village is reproduced in J. Michell, *Lo spirito della terra*, Red, Como 1988, p. 9 (*The Earth spirit*, London 1975).

[13] cf., B. Cerchio, *L'ermetismo di Dante*, Mediterranee, Rome 1988.

[14] cf., G. Caronia, *La chiesa*, Palermo 1965.

[15] cf., P. Portoghesi, *Francesco Borromini*, Electa, Milan 1990, pp. 151-184.

[16] cf., Lima-de-Faria, *Evolution without Selection*, Elsevier, Amsterdam 1988 and X. Galmiche, *Santini, architecte gothico-baroque en Bohême*, Damas, Paris 1989.

[17] cf., H. Corbin, *L'immagine del tempio*, Boringheri, Turin 1983, p. 52 (*Temple and contemplation*, London-New-York 1986).

[18] cf., F. Colonna, *Hypnerotomachia Poliphili*, Venice, apud Aldum Manutium, 1499 and the critique by G. Pozzi and L. Giapponi, Antenore, Padua 1964.

[19] cf., P. Portoghesi, *Borromini nella cultura europea*, Officina, Rome 1964, fig. 58.

[20] cf., *Fruhlicht*, no. 7, 1920, pp. 109-112.

[21] cf., *Daidalos*, no. 32, 1990.

[22] cf., M.P. Verneuil, *Étude de la plante*, Librairie Centrale des Beaux Arts, Paris, no date.

[23] cf., *Ibid*.

# Frontality, Axiality,
the Theatre

*When giving form to this façade I imagined the Human Body with open arms, as if embracing all who entered; the body with open arms has five parts; namely the chest in the middle, and arms articulated in two parts; but in the Facade the central part is shaped like the chest, and the lateral parts like the arms, each distinctly divided in two by two pillars that stand out in the centre of each.*

Francesco Borromini

The concept of frontality originates in man's tendency to identify with what he builds, as if his body virtually enters the space of the constructed object. The word, to interpenetrate, clearly describes this psychological process. If it is true, as the supreme theorist of the *Einfuhlung*[1] maintains, that to delight in something aesthetically is to delight in ourselves reflected in a sensory object different to us, then frontality is at the heart of aesthetic delight.

Already implicit in the door, frontality presides over the identification of the building as an organism and the hierarchy of its component parts. This gives rise to the tendency to pick out a "façade" from amongst the various parts that enclose a system of spaces. Like a human face, the façadeof a building tends to summarise and represent its traits in a plastic synthesis that recalls the concept of depth. In the same way, Filarete[2] writes: "it is the head of man, or rather his face, which *is its principal beauty, through which each person is recognised; so all the parts of a building should be in conformity with the façade, even if the beauty of some men lies in their face while other parts are counterfeit* and crooked, or even lacking entirely. People avoid looking at them because they are not beautiful, the same applies to buildings." The concept of frontality applied to living beings characterises the more complex and diverse forms of life, while symmetry around a vertical axis is a trait of those primitive organisms more suited to aimlessly travel the seas rather than walk on the earth. In Plato's *Symposium*,[3] Aristophanes gives his first-born spherical form. It was Zeus who cut man in half to humble his arrogance and power and ordered Apollo to transform his face and genitals.

"For our original nature was by no means the same as it is now [...] the form of each person was round all over, with back and sides encompassing it every way; each had four arms, and legs to match these, and two faces perfectly alike on a cylindrical neck. There was one head to the two faces, which looked opposite ways; there were four ears, two privy members, and all the other parts, as may be imagined."

The fact is, that men in that form felt so strong and so proud that they tried to climb to the heavens and violently attack the gods.

"Thereat Zeus and the other gods debated what they should do... Then Zeus, putting all his wits together, spake at length and said: 'Methinks I can contrive that men, without ceasing to exist, shall give over their iniquity through a lessening of their strength. I propose now to slice every one of them in two, so that while making them weaker we shall find them more useful by reason of their multiplication; and they shall walk erect upon two legs. If they continue turbulent and do not choose to keep quiet, I will do it again,' said he; 'I will slice every person in two, and then they must go their ways on one leg hopping.' So saying, he sliced each human being in two."

When the façade is ripe with architectural meaning, not only does it explicitly indicate access, but it anticipates in contracted form the feeling of progression and the spatial experience of depth. Long before perspective was studied as a way to represent the third dimension, architecture had experimented with architectural

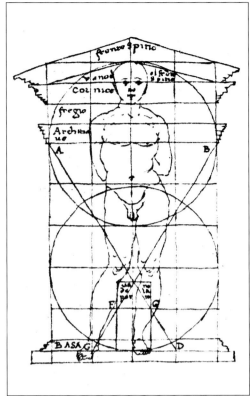

*Roman sculpture, 1st century B.C. (Berlin, Antikensammlungen).*
*Architectural frontality corresponds to the tendency of the viewer to identify with the building by projecting onto it certain characteristics of his own body.*
*Two drawings of the treatise by Francesco di Giorgio Martini from the* Codice magliabechiano *II 1.141: f. 38 v. and f. 33 v.*

361

*Façade of the Cappella del Presepe in Fonte Colombo near Rieti (Italy).*

orders so as to represent depth abstractly. This was done by using a series of silhouettes and multiple lighting effects that took their cue from certain landscapes in which the outline of hills and mountains stood out against one another. This differentiated repetition of wavy lines evoked the feeling of fathomless distance.

A stunning glorification of frontality is experienced when arriving in Petra through the narrow rocky gorge of the Siq: the observer's entire field of vision is filled with the El Chasne temple dug out of the fire-red rock. What emerges in this enigmatic monument is the artist's intention to model the façade, to come to terms with the natural scenery, rather than with the simple bare cell accessed by the façade.

Exalting the façade and its historical phenomenology is one way to connect the building to the city and not, as mistakenly affirmed by certain "modernist" historiographers, to privilege one part of the brick block thus preventing the interpretation of the spatial organism that lies behind it. Therefore this is not the "involution" of a model, but the original intuition of a need to visually express orientation. Long before architecture elaborated its constitution of artificial works, the façade was the expression of man's appropriation of the cave and the grotto.

Evidence of this "mental," rather than material, birth of the façade is clearly visible on the island of Santorini, in the archipelago of the Cyclades. Here one can see the gradual shift from natural caves, still present in the landscape, to in-

*Façade of the church of the Santo Rosario in Ouro Preto, Brazil (1785).*
*Façade and plan of the temple in Tarxien on the island of Malta (2nd millennium B.C.).*

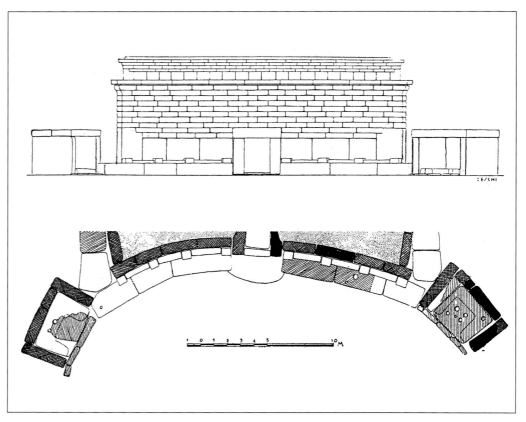

habited caves and the construction of organisms with barrel vaults in which the internal configuration was exactly the same as the cave, so much so that these houses resembled the evagination of an internal space faithfully covered with a brick counter-form.

An intermediate lull in this process of metamorphosis from nature to a "type" governed by precise laws, involved the creation of a "natural" façade. This was achieved either by geomitrising the entry to the cave (for instance, the gypsy houses in Cadiz, Spain), an operation still visible in certain areas, or by simply painting the rock face white. On the island of Santorini this process of abstraction from the cave to this volume type is particularly evident. The horseshoe façade, with a door flanked by two small windows (and often by another three windows on the axis of the lower floors) is again repeated when two buildings are placed next to each other, like the carriages of a train. Having studied the environment of Santorini in depth, the architect Warlamis illustrated this growth system in his surveys.[4]

Frontality transposes into architecture one aspect of the spatial experience of living beings, while maintaining the duplicity (and ambiguity) inherent in the fact that this "forehead" or "front" can either be one's own, or belong to any other living creature, or even metaphorically refer to a specific object such as a house or temple. A painter and poet living in Rome in the thirties, Gino Bonichi known as Scipio, believed "the forehead of Rome" to be the Acqua Paola fountain on

*An example of natural frontality in the Ciudad Encantada near Cuenca (Madrid).*

*Right: Petra (Jordan), façade chiselled in the rock called El Chasne, the treasure.*

*Above: the so-called "emperor's tomb" in Machu Picchu (Peru) below the temple of the Sun. If in Petra the façade lies on the Siq axis, the narrow gorge accessing the urban area, the Inca tomb obeys no rules of frontality and interprets the natural characteristics of the site without imposing a mental order.*

*Below: Varano near Parma (Italy), the Zermani house (Paolo Zermani 1996).*

*Below right: a large rock weathered by the wind and the rain on the island of Santorini (Cyclades). The arched cave seems to prefigure the typical underground houses of the island with rooms all the same size arranged in an axial sequence. The rooms built above ground, or in front of the subterranean ones, are the same shape (a prism covered by a semicylinder) and this seems to suggest a process involving ideal transference and direct interaction between nature and architecture.*

A panorama of the houses in Ja on the island of Santorini (Cyclades). The façades of the vaulted rooms all have the same characteristic groups of holes.

Below left: a settlement of gypsies in Guadix, Spain. Like metaphysical objects, the façade and chimneys of every underground house protrude from the grass or the rock.

Below: the façade of an underground house on the island of Santorini (Cyclades).

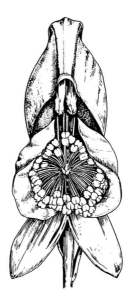

*Not always do flowers appear as figures that rotate around a vertical axis, inspiring centrality. Influenced by the forces of gravity, or based on relational strategies with pollinating insects, some flowers have a decidedly frontal structure, like this Aconitum napellus.*

*The façade of the cathedral in Laon. In the façades of Gothic cathedrals certain elements such as the portals, the rosettes and the bell-towers are there to exalt frontality and therefore orientation. The phytomorphic nature of the rosettes is quite literal, while the series of decorative and symbolic patterns in the portals conjures up images of sea waves and the concentric circles that ripple the surface when a stone is thrown into the water.*

top of the Janiculum Hill, one of the highest spots in the city. The fountain's marble slab below its large concave "front" was so big that it resembled the high forehead of a philosopher.

In certain cases, the frontality of a building involves the enrichment of its most visible parts. If the building is symmetrical, this determines a privileged axis to be used both as a means of access and as an element of order influencing a more or less large area. Even in living beings frontality implies adaptation to the forces of gravity accomplished by distinguishing between high and low as well as by the presence of only one vertical axis of symmetry. Most flowers and fruits obey vertical axiality as do the less complex organisms of the animal world (radiolarians, jellyfish, etc.), but there is no lack of anisotrophy and consequently of frontality, defined by biologists as zygomorphism. In the case of orchids, as in architecture, frontality seems to correspond to an ambiguous need to provoke a process of identification in the viewer. It is a well-known fact that the orchids of the *Ophrys* species are unable to exploit anemophilous pollination, so in order to reproduce they need the collaboration of certain insects, at times almost exclusively, to carry the sticky pollen from one flower to another.

The flower of the *Ophrys* orchid is equipped with a flabellum whose pattern attracts insects. It also acts as a landing pad. The colour and shape of this visual attraction is similar to the female insect of the species targeted by the orchid to become the pollinator in its fertilisation process. Apart from this, the flower also exploits its olfactory appeal by emanating pheromones. This substance is similar to the secretion used by the female to lure the male of the same species. Having landed, the male is persuaded to remain by the tactile similarity between the down on the flower and the down on the back of the female.[5] Even the system of adhesion to the pollinating insect reveals a perfect "welcoming strategy." Given the pincer-like position of the pollen tubes, when an insect penetrates a flower it is obliged to brush past these tubes: as these tubes are very sticky, they remain attached. Since the sticky liquid involved in this operation has variable drying times depending on the orchid species, the ones with the faster drying liquid will produce less pollen. The insect's visit lasts long enough to guarantee this difficult fertilisation process.

The proposed analogy between the strategy of the orchid and the strategy of the façades and fountains of churches, at least as far as the plastic density of many Romanesque, Gothic and Baroque buildings is concerned, does in no way seem disrespectful. The strategy of attraction and identification is similar, even if it is not sex but rather a common religious creed that in this case attracts the matchmaker. The great portals, often surrounded by statues and sometimes by monsters, possess an immediately appealing plastic synthesis. The portals propose the imminence of theophany. Inside, this will explode in all its splendour, imbued with perfumed incense and lit by sunlight streaming through the multicoloured windows. Not content to attract from afar, the Baroque façade bends or curves forward, miming both the shape of our bodies with arms outstretched

*An orchid of the* Odontonia *species.*
*The strategy of attracting pollinating insects due to similarity with other members of the same species, but of the opposite sex, is very similar to the strategy of certain buildings that expressly manifest a function they are able to perform only metaphorically.*
*Inspired by nature, Erich Mendelsohn drew this sketch that elaborates the theme of frontality.*

367

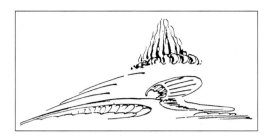

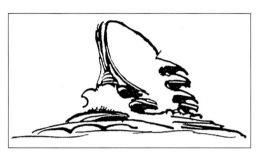

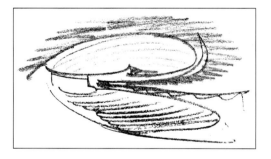

in welcome and the procession and movement of those who enter and exit. The pictures included here show the upper edge of the median sepal of an orchid that towards the top is shaped like a mixtilinear tympanum. Once again, nature and architecture mount a united search to strike a magical balance between external and internal space, between the outline of a form and its luminous background.

Apart from the façade model, the concept of frontality is also associated with the optimal view, since the latter is the best way to present a tridimensional structure. The European countryside is full of toponyms like *bellavista*, belvedere and balcony that create a complementary relationship between the point of observation and the surrounding landscape. The same thing occurs in architecture that does not always consider frontal elevations optimal and at times prefers more or less angled views, highlighting the volumetric structure rather than one or other of the façades.

Frontality is also expressed by the concept of a compositional "axis" that determines the visual connection between a number of architectural or urban elements, thereby orienting the viewer in a certain direction. The common definition of axis in large-scale architectural projects is governed by the hierarchical value attributed to planimetric designs. This is a mistake, because in architecture, tridimensional objects and spatial voids involve planes rather than two-dimensional axes of symmetry. When a monumental building is placed at the end

*Four sketches by Erich Mendelsohn in which frontal symmetry combines with dynamic spatiality and a sense of inward attraction. The first three date from around 1920 and refer to a hunting lodge and garden pavilions at Luckenwalde, while the fourth depicts the Universum in Berlin (1926-28). The picture of an* Iris germanica *showing the internal space created to accommodate pollinating insects.*

of a street or a tree-lined avenue, the term "telescope" or "perspective telescope" is used. This is because the street acts as a cylinder, like a telescope that by uniting two lenses, permits a specifically "identified" object to be brought closer and into focus. The fact of drawing an object closer by using frontal vision is not a matter of size but a matter of psychology. This does not mean it is any less efficient, as proven by many classically inspired town-plans that position architectural organisms, such as cities, according to backgrounds, views and special objects that define and exalt distance. In Domenico Fontana's plan of Rome for Sixtus V, this role is played by obelisks. These elements mirror frontal vision while behind them rise the more complex silhouettes of the buildings outlined against the background. Furthermore, they are generally positioned obliquely compared to the perspective framework suggested by the rectilinear roads.

Axiality cannot be identified with symmetry, frontality or orientation, although to a certain extent it is the synthesis of these three elements. Its natural roots are to be sought in the mechanisms of perception, in the practicality and ritualism of the straight line and in the orderly will of the mind that attributes an almost magical value of long-distance appropriation to the act of looking at a site from a specific viewpoint.

In the primitive world, the fire-screen alignment that coincided with the direction from which the main winds blew, was projected into the structure of the hut where it marked a sacred path from the entrance to the hearth. Later on, it was to characterise the axial route governing such great religious structures, as the ones at Teotihuacán and Angkor Vat, as well as Caesar's forum and the Champs Elysées.

In Christian basilicas, the naves reflect the processional route, while the parallel alignment of the columns metaphorically mime the faithful taking part in the procession. So the axis becomes a void, a longitudinal space that during the liturgy creates a remarkable dynamic balance between the community and the architectural space.

In natural morphology, the axis is reified in the animal world, in the backbone and in the planes of symmetry of invertebrates, while in botany it corresponds to the tree-trunk, the branch, the stalk, the rachis and the main venation of the lamina of a leaf: it is the basic element of a structure that has acted as a model primarily for structures used in town-planning.[6] Unfortunately, orthogonality almost always takes over.

The place where frontality is expressed in its most complete and convincing form is the theatre.

In ancient Greece, the word theatre (from *téaomai*, I look, I contemplate) was originally used to describe a group of people who sat together to watch a play. Later on, perhaps influenced by agricultural terracing, it defined the hillside cut into steps for the spectators to sit on, and still later it came to signify the theatre as a whole. This gradual evolution of meaning clarifies a no less "natural" genesis. In this case, it was a behavioural model before it ever became an ar-

*A public fountain in Ouro Preto, Brazil (attributed to Antonio Francesco Lisboa, known as the Alejadinho).*

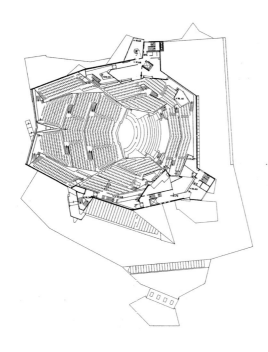

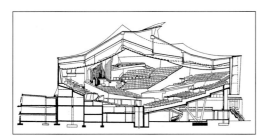

*Plan and section of the Philharmonic in Berlin (Hans Scharoun, 1954-57).*

*Opposite page: the theatre of Dionysius in Athens, seen from the Acropolis.*

chitectural one. A crowd spontaneously assembles, "faces," "huddles together" when someone feels the need to express himself with words, gestures or sounds. The way in which the group congregates is either a circle, when the action entails gestures, or a semicircle when it is important to listen to two opposing factions. In the West, the history of theatrical architecture began in 543 B.C. when Pisistratus, tyrant of Athens, introduced the dramatic agon into the famous Dionysia and a permanent theatre initially called Thespis was established in the city, later known as the Theatre of Dionysius, a theatre that was periodically rebuilt.

The widespread participation of citizens in theatrical plays, which in Greece lasted from sunrise to sunset, meant that the place chosen to stage a play had to be a large hollow at the foot of a hill. This hollow was shaped like a shell or, in geometric terms, like an upside-down truncated cone with the narrowest part at the bottom. The shape made it easier for the spectators to hear the voices and musical instruments and created a certain aura around the play. At the base of the cone, a semicircular flat surface acted as a stage. An alternative arrangement, involving two right-angled steps that originated in the theatres of the Palace courts in Crete, was described by Homer in Book VIII of the *Iliad* (v. 256-264).[7]

Greek theatre assumed its codified form after the Persian wars and its archetypes date back to the second theatre of Dionysius in Athens and the theatre in Syracuse. A permanent architectural stage to enact the dramas of the ancient courts of Greece was introduced only at the end of the 5th century, during the third season of the theatre of Dionysius.

Before Greek theatre was architecturally defined, other similar constructions or religious buildings did exist: the *telesterion* in Eleusis, the first example of a sacred Greek building (dedicated to Demeter) open to large groups of initiates (7th century), the *bouleuterion* and the *ecclesiasterion* that also doubled as meeting places.[8]

The *ecclesiasteria* in Paestum and Agregentum, with circular concentric steps, probably inspired the first Roman *comitium* in front of the Senate which, according to legend, was built by King Tullo Ostilio.

However, it is in Roman times that the theatre leaves its natural setting to become a free-standing building with a monumental stage set. Plays mainly involving physical action, such as gladiator fights, were held in the elliptical amphitheatre which, like the circular *comitia*, saw the crowds seated in concentric circles around the sides of a sort of crater, completely separate from the rest of the world. The hidden entrances through the vomitoria were almost completely concealed by continuous flights of steps, giving this type of building an unprecedented organicity and absoluteness that even religious buildings had never attained.

Leonardo da Vinci realised this immediately, so even though he developed the amphitheatre model, he also designed the spherical "preaching theatre" in which the preacher stood like a stylite on a pillar in the centre of the sphere surrounded by steps and balconies. The external form of this building with its trun-

cated cone profile transformed spatial absoluteness in volumetric absoluteness, incorporating a level of abstraction later reached only by Boullée in his mausoleum dedicated to Newton. This mausoleum admirably transforms the cosmic model into an involucre of absolute unity, bringing together heaven and earth in an attempt to draw them closer and define them according to a mystical interpretation of the Enlightenment, true expression of the appropriation of the mystery of nature, through its introjection and reduction in size.

The Renaissance used Palladio's Olympic theatre to repropose the old model of a semicircular *cavea*. However, since the stage was set apart and turned into a perspective space, this tended to separate the theatrical representation from the real space experienced by the viewer. This is how the proscenium and the stage were created and became institutionalised: the so-called glass wall introducing the realm of theatrical make-believe. Again, the example of the landscape is nature's way of providing a model for this magical separation that often occurs when an object in the forefront blocks the sun and its horizontal rays light a "backdrop" which then appears remote and unreachable, a sort of paradise lost.

The classical shape of open theatres involves a large number of natural images that range from the geological charm of concave space with good acoustics to the morphology of microorganisms. The concave banks of steps are mirrored by the shape of a bivalve shell, the *venerids*. Many species of these shells are almost semicircular in shape and have convex chisel marks on the outer side of their shield. By pressing a valve on the sand, the mark left looks like a concavity with concentric steps very similar to the auditorium of a theatre.

On the other hand, the elliptical amphitheatre can be compared to certain types of limpets and to the *Nacemila deaurata*. The coastal limpet seems to have inspired the planimetric configuration of Scharoun's designs for the Berlin Philharmonic, even if it is a well known fact that the terraced vineyards along the convergent slopes of the Rhine and Moselle valleys were the real inspirational model of this incredible musical theatre.

*A reconstruction of the Globe Theatre in London.*

[1] cf., A. Plebe, *L'estetica tedesca del 900*, in *Momenti e problemi di storia dell'estetica*, III, p. 1186; *Empathy, Form and Space*, The Getty Center Publication Programs, 1994.

[2] cf., Filarete, *Trattato di architettura*, Polifilo, Milan 1967, p. 25.

[3] cf., Plato, *The Symposium*, 190, 1-4.

[4] cf., E. Warlamis, "Die Herkunft der Architektur aus der Höhle," in *Daidalos*, no. 12, 1984, pp. 14-31.

[5] cf., A. Lima-de-Faria, *Evolution without Selection*, Elsevier, Amsterdam 1988.

[6] cf., M. Morini, *Atlante di storia dell'urbanistica*. Hoepli, Milan 1963.

[7] cf., *Le lieu théâtral à la Renaissance*, Editions du Centre nationale de la recherche scientifique, Paris 1964.

[8] cf., G.C. Izenour, *Roofed Theatres of Classical Antiquity*, Yale University Press, New Haven-London 1992.

# Numbers

It is said that those who first uncovered the secret of the incommensurable were shipwrecked and perished. Because the inexpressible, the inform should remain secret. And those who touched and discovered this image of life were instantly destroyed and will remain forever exposed to the eternal wash of the waves.

Proclus

"All that has by nature with systematic method been arranged in the universe" wrote Nicomachus of Gerasa, "seems both in part and as a whole to have been determined and ordered in accordance with number, by the forethought and the mind of Him that created all things; for the pattern was fixed, like a preliminary sketch, by the domination of number preexistent in the mind of the world-creating God, number conceptual only and immaterial in every way, but at the same time the true and the eternal essence, so that with reference to it, as to an artistic plan, should be created all these things, time, motion, the heavens, the stars, all sorts of revolutions," Nicomachus wrote his book, *Introduction to Arithmetic* in the 3rd century.[1] In it he illustrates the theories of Pythagoras and Plato and summarises the Greek's concept of the pervasive nature of numbers with practised competence.

The tendency to interpret nature in quantitative terms is closely linked to the development of architecture as a theory and as a specialist aspect of the work of man. When walls are built of square ashlars or wooden elements of established size, then space is enclosed according to individual or collective needs. Having decided on a "unit of measure," often named after a part of the human body (arm, foot, palm, thumb), it is necessary to take measurements and then translate them into numbers. In his role as a site manager, the language an architect uses basically involves quantities and often his approach towards nature, as a provider of materials and models for his constructions, is also numerical. But in the Greek world, a number is not simply a quantitative notion. This is clearly stated by Nicomachus: a number is a sort of vestige of divine thought, a memory of creation hidden at the very heart of things and our minds delight in its retrieval. Numbers are translated into form and symbol in the so-called Platonic solids that provided and continue to provide architecture with some of its purest images.

In the *Timeus*, an excerpt relates: "Now we must declare what are the four fairest bodies that could be created, unlike one another, but capable, some of them, of being generated out of each other by their dissolution: for if we succeed in this, we have come at the truth concerning earth and fire and the intermediate proportions. For we will concede to no one that there exist any visible bodies fairer than these, each after its own kind."[2] In truth, Platonic solids possess a "finite" beauty, radically different to the wondrous and infinite horizons so typical of mathematics. In fact, like numbers, regular polygons are infinite, but there are only five regular polyhedrons. And it is this uniqueness and numerableness that creates their metaphysical charisma.

*Timeus* also lauds the sphere as an image of the universe: "So the universal design of the ever-living God, that he planned for the God that was some time to be, made its surface smooth and even, everywhere equally distant from the centre, a body whole and perfect our of perfect bodies. And God set soul in the midst thereof and spread her through all its body and even wrapped the body about with her from without, and he made it a sphere in a circle revolv-

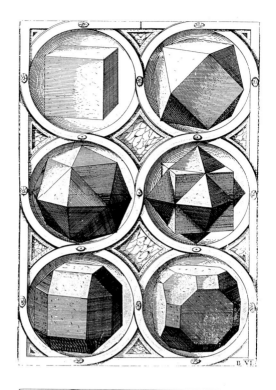

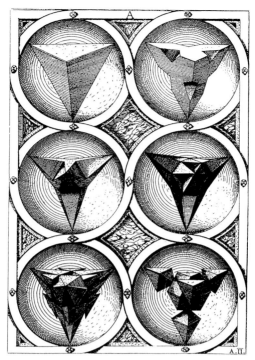

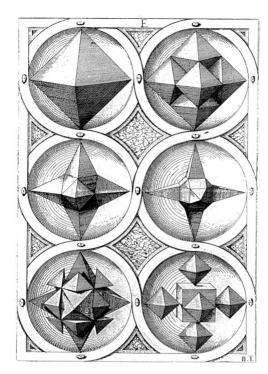

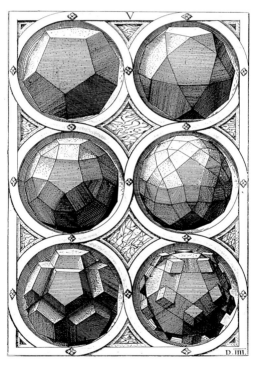

*The five regular polyhedrons or platonic solids in five plates of the book* Perspectiva corporum regularium, *by Wentzel Jamnitzer, printed in Nuremberg in 1568.*
*Various ways to make the structure more complex using elementary geometric operations are shown next to the platonic polyhedrons.*

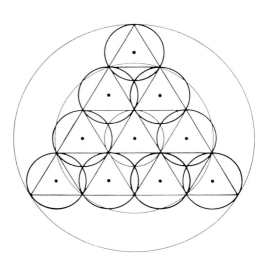

ing, a universe one and alone; but for its excellence it was able to be company to itself and needed no other, being sufficient for itself as acquaintance and friend."[3]

In 1784, when designing Newton's cenotaph, Etienne-Louis Boullée translated into architecture the platonic emotion of the simplest and most perfect form conceived by the human mind. By placing the entrance in the lowest part of the building corresponding to its centre of gravity, he imagined the viewpoint of the observer as being the moment in which he perceived the idea-form of the hollow sphere. During the day, pierced by a myriad of small windows, the sphere was to reproduce the shape of the night sky while during the night, flooded with artificial light the concave surface was to resemble the solar system moving within the universe. Like the sphere, the other "cosmic figures," the cube, the pyramid, the octahedron and the icosahedron are explained in symbolic terms in *Timeus*: "let us assign the figures that have come into being in our theory to fire and earth and water and air. To earth let us give the cubical form; for earth is least mobile of the four and most plastic of bodies: and that substance must possess this nature in the highest degree which has its bases most stable [...]. Therefore in assigning this to earth we preserve the probability of our account; and also in giving to water the least mobile and to fire the most mobile of those which remain; while to air we give that which is intermediate. Again we shall assign the smallest figure to fire, and the largest to water and the intermediate to air: and the keenest to fire, the next to air, and the third to water [...]. Let it be determined then, according to the right account and the probable, that the solid body which has taken the form of the pyramid is the element and seed of fire; and the second in order of generation let us say to be that of air, and the third that of water."[4]

From a structural point of view, Plato describes polyhedrons in terms of generation and regeneration. The tetrahedron, the symbol of fire, is made up of four equilateral triangles joined together to form a solid angle for every three convergent straight angles. Eight united equilateral triangles form the octahedron symbolising air, while "one hundred and twenty solid triangles joined together [...] and twelve solid angles" make up the icosahedron, symbol of water, with twenty triangular faces. Instead, the right-angled isosceles triangle is the figure that creates the cube, symbol of the earth. "A fifth combination remained," adds Plato, "and God used it to decorate the universe." This is the dodecahedron, the cosmic symbol par excellence, made of twelve pentagonal faces. During the Renaissance, Piero della Francesca dedicated a treatise to the cult of the polyhedrons[5] that inspired Luca Pacioli to write *De Divina Proportione*, a study that includes the field of "stellar" polyhedrons and semiregular polyhedrons.[6]

In the course of history, the cube, the tetrahedron and the sphere have been part of architecture's compositional repertoire for centuries. The icosahedron, used by Borromini in the Filomarino altar in Naples, as well as the dodecahedron, would both have to wait until the present century to tiptoe surreptitiously into design, above all thanks to Richard Buckminster Fuller and the expressionist architects.

Numbers define quantity and ratios as well as quality: they permeate language and determine its logical structure. "One" is necessary to identify the singularity of an object, but it is also a fundamental concept that permits comprehension of the nature of its inner structure in which multiplicity becomes unity. "Two" is necessary to highlight a couple of apples, but it is also duality, another concept indispensable to knowledge and reason. And so from three comes the triad, from four the *tetrakis,* that in Pythagorean catechism is synonymous with "pure harmony" (the harmony of sirens). From five comes the pentagram and the tenth, the most perfect of the groups, typical of living forms and the human body in particular. The conceptual aspect of numbers is essential to architecture as a discipline, because it permits the architect indirectly to control the quality of his work through the rules of ratio and proportion.

For Nicomachus, proportion is the combination of two or more ratios, since the ratio is the relationship between two terms that can be expressed algebraically by the fraction a/b. To talk of proportion three terms are necessary, since the two terms may have a term in common (in this case, proportion can be expressed by two fractions a/b = b/c). According to this theory, it is easy to see how the famous golden section is the most simple possible proportion; it only needs two terms since the third is a sum of the other two. In fact it can be expressed in algebra as : a = b/a = a/b or, in verbal terms, as the ratio between the sum of two quantities when one of them (the biggest) is equal to the ratio between the two.

Simple ratios and privileged proportions are the tools used by an architect to connect his work to the rules of order governing the universe, to the secret law of creation, the same law that presides over musical harmonies. By drawing on a source of inexhaustible riches, an architect can imitate the visible and invisible structures of nature.

The Pythagorean theory of musical harmony is a mathematical theory based on proportions, since the length of musical strings, inversely proportional to the number of vibrations, permits sounds and linear measurements to be combined.

As Plato wrote in his book *The Republic*, "Beauty is accord and harmony of parts in relation to the whole to which they are linked, based on number, delimitation and place, as required by the concinnitas, the basic and most exact law in nature."

On the other hand, these musical ratios theorised by Pythagoras and Plato and described by Vitruvius, had been perceived by the Greeks as being present in the human body. Therefore, by adopting them in buildings, they created a double system of correspondence within the laws of nature, namely be-

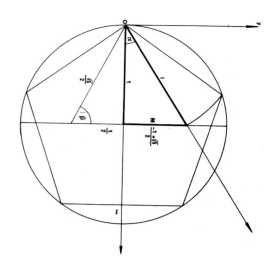

*Starting from a regular pentagon, a diagram showing the construction of a triangle with sides of 3, 4 and 5 and the golden section.*

377

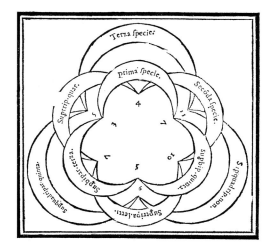

tween sonorous and architectural proportions and between architectural proportions and the proportions of the human body.

In Renaissance treatises, triple correspondence is fundamental to basic terms. For instance, Alberti talks about it immediately after having illustrated his concept of "Agreement of Sounds (*concinnitas*)." "Beauty is agreement and harmony of parts in relation to the whole to which they are bound by number, limitation and position, as required by the 'agreement of sounds,' namely the most exact and fundamental law of nature." A little further on in the fifth chapter of *Book IV*, Alberti introduces the concept of number and its projection in the world of sounds: "By the Finishing I understand a certain mutual Correspondence of those several Lines, by which the Proportions are measured, whereof one is the Length, the other the Breadth, and the other the Height. The Rule of these Proportions is best gathered from those Things in which we find Nature herself to be most compleat and admirable; and indeed I am every Day more and more convinced of the truth of Pythagoras' Saying, that Nature is sure to act consistently, and with a constant Analogy in all her Operations: From whence I conclude that the same Numbers, by means of which the Agreement of Sounds (*concinnitas*) affects our Ears with Delight, are the very same which please our Eyes and Mind. We shall therefore borrow all our Rules for the finishing our Proportions, from the Musicians, who are the greatest Masters of this Sort of Numbers, and from those particular Things wherein Nature shews herself most excellent and compleat: Not that I shall

*Two illustrations from the treatise* Le Istituzionni Harmoniche *by M. Gioseffo Zarlino, Francesco Senese, Venice 1562. A graphic pattern called* "Superpartiente" *and, right,* Syntony diatonic tetrachord *by Ptolemy.*

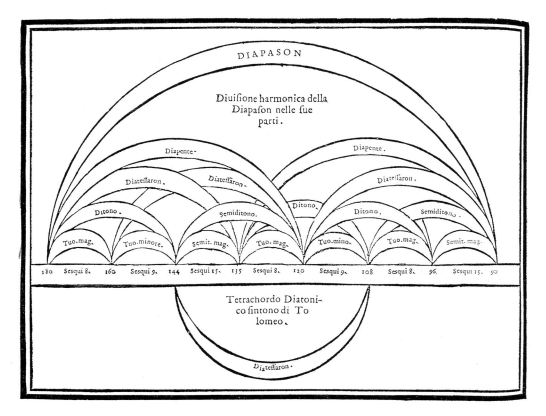

look any further into these Matters than is necessary for the Purpose of the Architect. We shall not therefore pretend to say any thing of Modulation, or the particular Rules of any Instrument; but only speak of those points which are immediately to our Subject, which are these. We have already observed that harmony is an Agreement of several Tones, delightful to the Ears. Of Tones, some are deep, some more acute. The deeper Tones proceed from a longer String; and the more acute, from a shorter: And from the mutual Connection of these Tones arises all the Variety of Harmony. This Harmony the Ancients gathered from interchangeable Concords of the Tones, by means of certain determinate Numbers; the Names of the Concords are as follows: *Diapente*, of the Fifth, which is also called *Sesquialtera* ('one and a half'): *Diatessaron*, or the Fourth, called also *Sesquitertia* ('one and a third'): *Diapason*, or the Eight, also called the double tone; *Diapason Diapente*, the twelfth or triple Tone, and *Disdiapason*, the fifteenth or *Quadruple*. To these were added the *Tonus*, which was also called the *Sesquioctave*. These several Concords, compared with the Strings themselves, bore the following Proportions. The *Sesquialtera* was so called, because the String which produced it bore the same Proportion to that to which it is compared, as one and an half does to one; which was the Meaning of the Word *Sesqui*, among the Ancients. In the sesquialtera therefore the longer String must be allowed three, and the shorter, two. [...] The *Sesquitertia* is where the longest String contains the shorter one and one third more: The longer therefore must be as four, and the shorter as three [...]. But in that Concord which was called *Diapason*, the Numbers answer to one another in a double Proportion, as two to one, or the Whole to the Half: And in the *Triple*, they answer as three to one, or as the Whole to one third of itself [...]. In the *Quadruple* the Proportions are as four to one, or as the Whole to its fourth Part. [...] Lastly, all these musical Numbers are as follows: One, two, three, four and the Tone before-mentioned, wherein the long String compared to the shorter, exceeds it one eighth Part of that shorter String.

"Of all these Numbers, the Architects made very convenient Use, taking them sometimes two by two, as in planning their Squares and open Areas, wherein only two Proportions were to be considered, namely, Length and Breadth; and sometimes taking them three by three, as in publick Halls, Council-chambers, and the like; wherein as the Length was to beat a Proportion to the Breadth, so they made the height in a certain harmonious Proportion to them both."[7]

The musical intervals cited by Alberti are the natural fifth (2:3); the fourth (3:4); the eighth (1:2); the twelfth and the fifteenth as well as the tone or interval equivalent to the difference between the fifth and the fourth (8:9). The similarities between musical ratio and the proportions of the human body were highlighted with inspired eloquence by Daniele Barbaro in his comments on Vitruvius in 1556: "Mother nature teaches us how to apply the measurements and proportions of buildings consecrated to gods, and from none other she

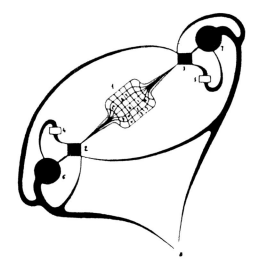

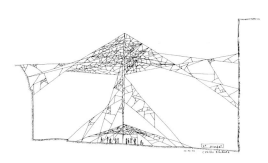

*Iannis Xenakis,* Stratégie, *a musical scherzo for two directors and two orchestras (1965). Organisational chart of the actions and reactions between the orchestras, the directors and the public. Below,* Politopo *for the inauguration of the Centre Pompidou in Paris (1974). Two examples of Xenakis' organic inspiration that may also be found in the Philips pavilion, built together with Le Corbusier in 1957, whose planimetric form looked like a stomach.*

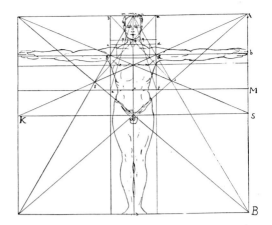

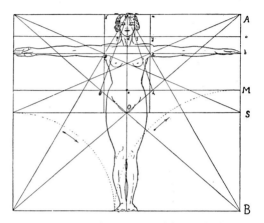

*The proportions of the male and female body according to M. Ghyka, from his book* Essai sur le rythme, *Gallimard, Paris 1938, pp. 21, 22. A "magic" star, since the sum of its numbers is always the same. In this case, there are nine types of lines, characterised by their thickness and the dotted lines that connect them. Every straight line gives a different result.*

wishes we learn the rules of Symmetry, rules we should use in Churches, like man, the Sacred temple made in the image and likeness of God, in whom all other marvels of nature are contained, which with good foresight the ancients gleaned every rule in the measurement of the human body [...]."

During the Mannerist period, the triple correspondence was so important that it inspired Lomazzo with the concept of a "minor world" with regard to the human body: "The human body, being a perfect and beauteous achievement created by God in His likeness, has rightly been called a minor world. Since within itself it contains in perfect composition and certain harmony all numbers, measurements, weights, movements and elements. So mainly from this body, and from no other work that the hand and members of God fashioned, came the rule and model to shape Temples, Theatres and all buildings with all their parts such as columns, capitals, canals and the like; channels, machines and every sort of artifice."

Like orthogonality that comes from the observation of the horizon from a standing position and permits the architect to set his work against the natural scenery, so numbers and proportion, even if an offspring of nature's search for order, give him the tools to unambiguously take possession of the scope, breadth and depth of his design images. Quite rightly, however, Valéry underlines the risks inherent in the temptation to consider proportion as the basic parameter of architectural theory and Apollinaire echoes his thoughts when he

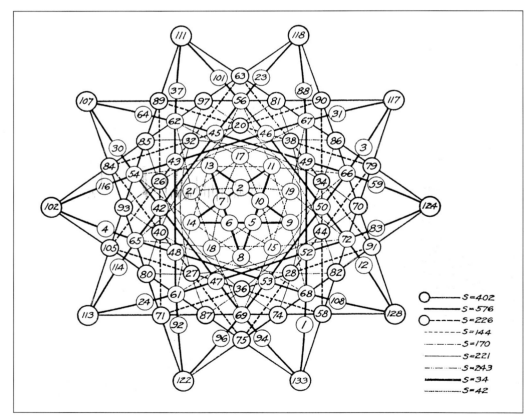

says: "C'est de souffrance et de bonté/Que serait fait la beauté/tout parfaite que n'était celle/Qui venait des proportions."

Establishing the right ratio between the parts and between the parts and the whole can, in fact, create the illusion that the problems regarding materials, the site and the real size of the architectural object are secondary. But here again nature steals the scene as a master player, because nature itself is a "whole": all its parts are proportional and it assigns well-defined, individual roles to the big and to the small.

The fact remains that over the centuries man has chosen different solutions when it comes to architectural proportions. By dedicating more, or less, attention to the problem, he has expressed the spirit of his period, at times concentrating on rendering the tactile merits of matter, at times striving to idealise and dematerialise the built images.

One particular aspect of proportion, and an alternative to the concept of compositional unity as a supreme law, is the archetype of repetition, as ancient as architecture from a practical point of view, but supremely present when architecture abdicates its ambition to unity and hierarchy. Repetition is the most elementary form of rhythm as far as order in movement is concerned. In music, rhythm is determined by the relationship between the length of sound based on certain units of time. Repetition is linked to the musical concept of rhythm, while in architecture it marks the connection between several units, or

*Francesco Borromini, a portal with a magic square at Rome's La Sapienza university (F. Borromini,* Opera architettonica, *Giannini, Rome 1725, pl. XLIV).*

*Left: a photograph of a backbone.*

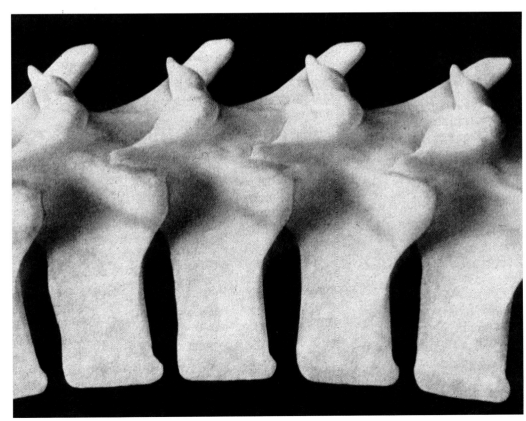

381

between several identical or similar elements. A façade with lots of identical windows, or better still a road with a row of houses, all identical or all the same type, are classical examples of repetition. In the world of nature in which nothing is perfectly identical, the concept of repetition and analogy is an intrinsic part of life. Repetition is manifest in the day and night cycle, the act of love, the form of inflorescences, in crystalline ensembles and osteological structures such as the thorax and the backbone, and in general in the modular structure of a great many animals, just as it is in the spontaneous grouping of living beings, in "queues" and "huddles."

The charm of serial repetition is particularly evident in music and architecture. What would a column be if it wasn't able to multiply to form an aedicula, a portico or a colonnade? What would become of music if it didn't include repetition and the introduction of variations on a theme? What would happen to a building if every window was different? Identity and analogy permit groupings and consequently intervals, silences and spaces. The axis presides over the type of repetition we call specular symmetry which can either be purely immaterial or become incarnate in a predominantly vertical series of elements that may be emphasised by using variable orientation.[8]

Repetition is also central to other types of symmetry, such as rotatory and translational symmetry. As in music so in architecture, repetition does not necessarily imply that all elements are equal. It becomes particularly important,

*Panorama of the district of Rhonda in Andalusia.*

*Quartz crystals and a row of houses in Amsterdam with façades that repeat a theme with slight variations.*

*Aerial view of Danzig, Poland. In this case too,
the varied repetition of a theme creates the*
concordia discors, *the order and complexity that,
according to Francesco Milizia, turns the urban
fabric into the metaphor of a forest.
Above: the linear repetition of the seeds in a corn
cob, with variations and shifts,.*

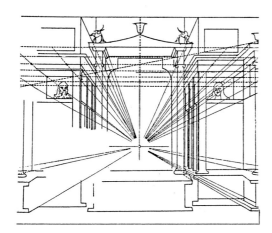

*A fresco in the villa of Augustus on the Palatine hill where the fugues converge to a point. Frequently in Roman frescoes, especially in Pompeii, there were many fugues of parallel lines aligned along a vertical axis. Panofsky's theory is based on this particular trait.*

however, when certain traits are varied while the more universal ones remain unaltered. This is what happens when more than one façade of similar width, but corresponding to the different modes of expression of one building type, are aligned along a road. It is like looking simultaneously at more than one face with similar traits: an amazing aesthetic pleasure, similar to the feelings transmitted by a novel, comes from comparing and appreciating both analogies and differences. Only a few things other than variety housed in a unitary ensemble satisfy our desire not only to softly caress the image with our eyes but also to penetrate it with the power of our minds, letting ourselves be drawn by its solid structure as we would by the currents flowing in a river.

While the first chapters of this book examined the archetypes that initiated the development of the building and linguistic elements of architecture involving numbers, repetition and geometry, this chapter deals with the conceptual source of archetypes.

Geometry and mathematics have provided the architect with a profusion of knowledge, concepts, rules and abstract procedures without which the moment of design, the moment of prefiguration of the architectural object, would never have been able to develop and come into its own. Construction would probably have remained the domain of a repetitive and conservative discipline, unable to exploit *forward-looking theories* as an instrument of experimentation and cognitive achievement. Mathematics and geometry have let architecture freely develop its mental and imaginary potential, anticipating through representation the final outcome of construction previously programmed in the domain of the immaterial. Apart from this process of liberation, by becoming part of geography and history, mathematics and geometry have contributed to differentiating the cognitive wealth of architecture in relation to a variety of human civilisations and their continually different stages of growth.

For example, the problem of portrayal. Euclid systematically eliminates it from the treatises illustrated in his *Geometry* and places it in the field of optics. His ideas of visual perception focus on the concept of "visual angle" and he imagines that the eye emits rectilinear rays. The upper angle, created at eye level by connecting its summit to two points of a given object, forms the visual angle which is in proportion to the distance of the eye from the object.

Following the logic of the visual angle, Euclid establishes that "parallel lines when observed at a certain distance, do not appear to be equally distant," thus putting the fifth postulate of his book *Elements* in a critical position since the latter states: "Only one line may be drawn through a given point parallel to a given line." Centuries of meditation and experimentation were necessary before the problem of perception and representation managed to show how convincing non-Euclidean geometry could be.

The problem of representation presents an ample and established variety of options relating to different eras and civilisations. By systematically studying these options, Margaret Hagen attempts to draw up a convincing list.[9]

384

First of all, Hagen distinguishes between the options: "metrical," "based on the concept of geometrical affinity" and "projective." For each of the above, one or more point sets may be chosen. The metrical option, typical of ancient Egypt and Mayan civilisations, roughly coincides with the method of orthographic projection and privileges frontal vision or profiles. The affinity option involves maintaining the alignment of three points with the parallel lines; early traces of pictured objects, drawn as if seen from above or in axonometric projection, can be found in Chinese and Japanese paintings. In this case too, there can be either one or more point sets, allowing the designer either to "tell" various episodes of a story or to highlight different aspects of an object, as in Greek vases or late medieval paintings.

In Roman wall paintings, which in many ways are similar to the depth effect of central perspective, parallel lines only rarely converge to a point and more often then not they do so on a vertical line. The analysis of this method has enabled Panofsky to clarify the various objectives pursued by painters in antiquity and during the Renaissance: "Classical art, the pure art of buildings, considered everything visible and tangible as being part of artistic reality; it did not pictorially combine each single materially tridimensional element in a spatial unit [...] instead, it tectonically or plastically fused them into a number of groups."[10] For this reason in the ancient world, "the whole world remains basically discontinuous." Panofsky associates the conquest of "perspective" with a gradual process that begins in Byzantine art, and through Gothic and Romanic culture, leads to a systematic vision of space as a measurable extension.

The problems inherent in portraying nature, bodies and visible objects influence architecture not only because drawings are the basic instrument of design, but also because their style is a function of how one perceives and imagines space which, in turn, is deeply affected by the method of representation. In classical architecture, for example, when Brunelleschi, with incredible propaganda-like flair, orchestrated his experiment involving painted panels, his main aim was to demonstrate how portrayed space could join and merge with natural space. The subject portrayed – as meticulously related by his anonymous biographer – was the Baptistery of Saint John and its surrounding urban fabric, as seen from the point sets of the portal of Santa Maria del Fiore. With one hand the viewer held the panel to his forehead so that he could look through the hole, and with the other he held a mirror parallel to and at a certain distance from the panel. He could then see how the lines of the painting continued beyond the mirror. Brunelleschi's choice of a typically architectural set of points and landscape was his way of affirming the unity between visual arts and architecture in the linear and geometric reduction of forms. This is why the area of sky painted on the panel was filled by shiny surfaces so that, if clouds went by, they appeared as an integral part of the landscape, evidently affirming the art-nature relationship as well as the relationship between represented space and real space.

*Plans of the church of San Carlo alle Quattro Fontane in Rome (Francesco Borromini, 1634-40). Opposite page: the planimetric solution, based on an oval, prompted Borromini to topologically deform the large arches that encompass the bowl-shaped vaults of the side chapels that appear to have been twisted (drawings by Enzo di Grazia).*

Brunelleschi's discovery strongly influenced the evolution of Renaissance and Baroque architecture. However, the roots of this discovery lie in the treatises on optics written during the last years of antiquity and in the Middle Ages, while it made its first timid appearance in the paintings of Giotto and Simone Martini as well as Romanesque and Gothic architecture. The relationship between art and science and between architecture and geometry is only rarely a cause and effect relationship. Instead it is more like a continuous mixture of reciprocal influences. The modern vision of continuous and universal space gradually flourished and the evolution of architecture provided an experimental support as well as a precious testing ground and opportunity for abstract representation.

Like Euclid's *Optics*, the essays by Ptolemy and the triumph of medieval perspective by Robert Grosseteste, Roger Bacon and Vitellione were milestones in the attainment of the syntheses reached by Brunelleschi, Piero della Francesca and Alberti. The successful progress these artists achieved in the field of practical representation paved the way for the foundation of projective geometry elaborated by Desargues, Guidobaldo del Monte, Pascal and Descartes.

"Projective geometry," wrote Giuseppe Archidiacono, "studies the priorities of geometric figures from a more general point of view than that of elementary geometry, and establishes the priorities applicable to a whole range of geometric figures (for example, cones) which were previously considered to be totally different."[11]

The theory of perspective representation prompted Renaissance architecture to employ new tools to study ways in which tridimensionality could be rendered by using the classical system of orders. Instead, the virtuoso investigation of perspective techniques and the ensuing development of perspective provided the architects of the 17th and 18th centuries with the possibility of "staging" a complex, multidirectional and diagonal spatiality. Moreover, the possibility of representing irregular and complex polygonal forms gave new impulse to "stereotomy," the art of cutting stone ashlars, as well as tackling the difficult problems relating to very complex geometric vaults. If perspective deeply affects how we think and imagine architecture, the many ways in which it is applied to architecture during the conceptual and design stages makes it an integral part of the structure. Apart from the sculpture technique, Bramante was the first person to employ perspective in the third dimension in the apse of Santa Maria near San Satiro. Here he used the typically sculptural technique of so-called "stiacciato" (a sort of bas-relief) already used by Donatello.

Perspective embrasures that connect the entrance-gallery of Palazzo Farnese with the arches of the courtyard are another novel way of applying perspective technique, since they join rooms of different size and height, making space seem flexible and adaptable. This joining technique was to fascinate the

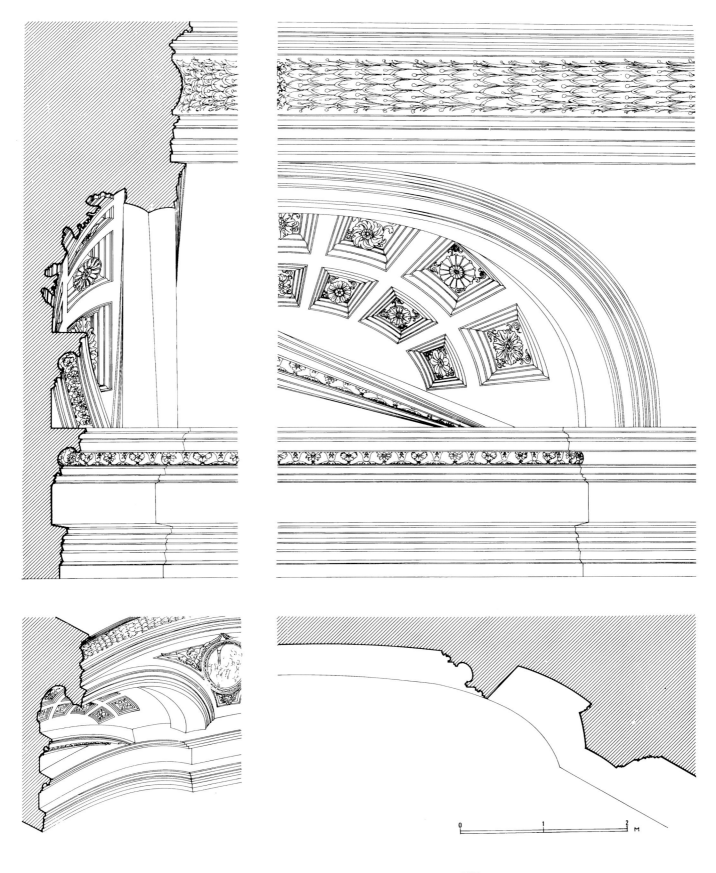

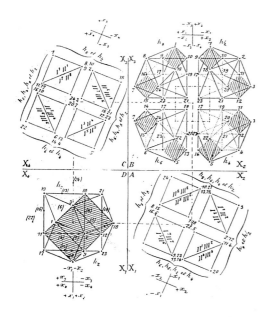

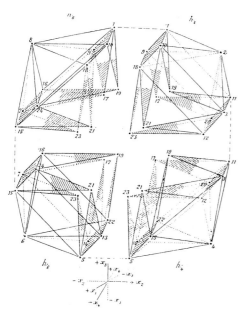

*Drawings from the* Traité élémentaire de géometrie à quatre dimensions *by E. Jouffret, Paris 1903. These images certainly influenced cubist painters and avant-garde culture.*

architect and theorist, Philibert de l'Orme, who employed an irregular and twisted biomorphic form when designing the squinch that supported a small tower in Diana de Poitiers' castle in Anet. The technique also influenced Spanish architecture, especially in Andalusia, where it is possible to see embrasures and lined surfaces shaped liked lacunars; the impression is that the whole masonry involucre has been twisted.

Due to this perspective expedient, the architect appropriates another field of biological analogy, contracting and dilating space as if space could "grow" or become finite. Borromini is the most profound poetical interpreter of this new biological essence of architecture. In San Carlino, he tests the elasticity of space by twisting the lateral arches that support the cupola and designing a perspective lacunar on the bowl-shaped vaults of the apse.

During the two centuries that followed, the grand theme of the ribbed cupola, born from Michelangelo's unpredictable fusion between the Pantheon and Santa Maria del Fiore, was exploited from the point of view of its cosmological context: a space that perspectively represents infinity through the convergence of its lines and its progressive contraction in size ending in the circle of the lantern, the triumph of light and symbol of perfection.

In the perspective of Palazzo Spada in Rome, this decreasing perspective leaves the tridimensionality of the columns intact while their contraction simulates a path that looks twice the size of the real one. Here, Borromini furthers the captious game begun by Brunelleschi by intervening with mirrors and freezing the virtual images on their surface.

But while Brunelleschi tended to stress the reasons for transferring reality onto these panels, Borromini seems to be more interested in showing the relativity of every partial certainty and the illusive nature of every grandeur. He does this by bringing together and mixing geometric reality and perceptive reality, truth and illusion.

The Latin epigram written to illustrate the secret meaning of the Galleria Spada leaves no doubts as to its allegory.

Within its slender structure, ponder an immense loggia
And in a small space perceive a long walkway,
The longer the walkway, the greater appear
the forms small in their natural seat.
Splendid artifice, figure of a deceptive world
That in its own way reveals great things,
Great only in appearances; close up they become small
Illusory larva here on earth is greatness.

If the rules of perspective provide architecture and scenography with a ticket to travel in endless imaginary worlds in which space dilates as if beaten by a hammer and attracted by a magnet, non-Euclidean geometries (perspective being their forefather) have generated a radical way to escape from real tridimensional space towards multidimensional space, unperceived by our senses, yet stimulating our minds that race through them by making a deliberate effort of abstraction.

The exploration of non-Euclidean geometry began with Gauss, who was persuaded to publish nothing on the subject so as not to trouble the dreams of the orthodox mathematicians of that period.

Between 1830 and 1850, Lobacevskij and Bolyai established the basis of non-Euclidean geometry. Emmer quotes a tell-tale letter in which Bolyai's father, a professor of mathematics, tries to convince him not to go against Euclid: "For Heaven's sake, I pray you to give this up. The problem of parallels is a thing to be feared and avoided no less than the passion of the senses, since it too can rob you of all your time and damage your health, serenity, spirit and happiness." In 1854, Riemann takes a similar view and proposes to think of geometry in even greater and more inspiring terms, based on any number of dimensions.

The representation of multidimensional geometric figures was initially tackled by Ludwig Schaefli, but his work was largely ignored. W.I. Stringham had more luck and in 1880 published an article on the subject in the "Journal of Mathematics." Another treatise written in 1903 by E. Jouffret contained impressive illustrations which supposedly had a direct influence on cubist painters and architects. Figures with four or more dimensions, based on flat projections or tridimensional models, have only recently become truly influential due to computer animation and cinematographic language, as shown by Michele Emmer in his film *Hypersphere*.

We owe the first fascinating popular illustrations of the achievements of Gauss, Lobaceveskij and Riemann to the priest, pedagogue and Shakespearean scholar, Edwin Abbott, author of *Flatland, a Romance of Many Dimensions*, published anonymously in 1882.[12]

The hero of *Flatland* is a Square who lives in a two-dimensional world organised like our tridimensional one (Spaceland) but in which the inhabitants see themselves as more or less pointed segments. So in order to recognise their social class (workers and soldiers are triangles, professionals are either squares or pentagons, noblemen are polygons from the hexagon upwards and priests are circular) they have to use colours. At a certain point in his life the hero receives the visit of an inhabitant of Spaceland who teaches him the mysteries of the third dimension, making him understand that as a "solid" he can access the surfaces of Flatland from above or below, without crossing its borders, and can, for instance, enter a house without going through the door.

The book's hidden message is to make the reader think about the relativity of Flatland and Spaceland and the possible existence of universes with more than three dimensions in which man would have the same difficulties the Square had from his "two-dimensional" point of view.

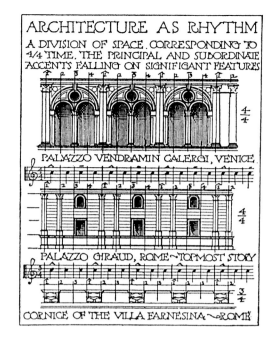

*Claude Bragdon, the musical transposition of certain architectural scores.*

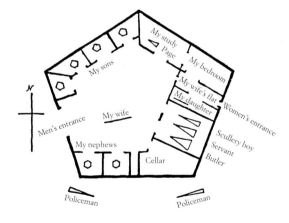

*Plan of the pentagonal house of the hero of Flatland.*

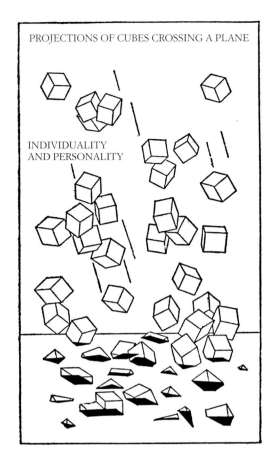

PROJECTIONS OF CUBES CROSSING A PLANE

INDIVIDUALITY
AND PERSONALITY

*Inspired by Abbott, Claude Bragdon drew this sketch to illustrate the shift from a three dimensional to a two-dimensional world.*

It is well worth citing at least parts of the conversation between the hero of the novel and the most perfect figure of Spaceland. The Square addresses the Sphere respectfully, saying: "My Lord, your own wisdom has taught me to aspire to One even more great, more beautiful, and more closely approximate to Perfection than yourself. As you yourself, superior to all Flatland forms, combine many Circles in One, so doubtless there is One above you who combines many Spheres in One Supreme Existence, surpassing even the Solids of Spaceland. And even as we, who are now in Space, look down on Flatland and see the insides of all things, so of a certainty there is yet above us some higher, purer region, whither thou dost surely purpose to lead me – O Thou Whom I shall always call, everywhere and in all dimensions, my Priest, Philosopher, and Friend – some yet more spacious Space, some more dimensionable Dimensionality, from the vantage-ground of which we shall look down together upon the revealed insides of Solid things, and where thine own intestines, and those of thy kindred Spheres, will lie exposed to the view of the poor wandering exile from Flatland, to whom so much has already been vouchsafed."

Sphere replied: "Pooh! Stuff! Enough of this trifling! The time is short, and much remains to be done before you are fit to proclaim the Gospel of Three Dimensions to your blind benighted countrymen in Flatland."

The Square doesn't give up and when the Sphere tells him that a four-dimensional world is quite impossible, he answers: "Not inconceivable, my Lord, to me, and therefore still less inconceivable to my Master. Nay I despair not that, even here, in this region of Three Dimensions, your Lordship's art may make the Fourth Dimension visible to me; just as in the Land of Two Dimensions my Teacher's skill would fain have opened the eyes of his blind servant to the invisible presence of a third Dimension, though I saw it not.

"Let me recall the past. Was I not taught below that when I saw a Line and inferred a Plane, I in reality saw a third unrecognized Dimension, not the same as brightness, called 'height'? And does it not now follow that, in this region, when I see a Plane and infer a Solid, I really see a Fourth unrecognized Dimension, not the same as colour, but existent, though infinitesimal and incapable of measurement?"

The conversation culminates in the oneiric and exalted vision of the Square: "There, before my ravished eye, a Cube, moving in some altogether new direction, but strictly according to Analogy, so as to make every particle of his interior pass through a new kind of Space, with a wake of its own – shall create a still more perfect perfection than himself, with sixteen terminal Extrasolid angles, and Eight solid Cubes for his Perimeter. And once there, shall we stay our upward course? In that blessed region of Four Dimensions, shall we linger on the threshold of the Fifth, and not enter therein? Ah, no! Let us rather resolve that our ambition soar with our corporal ascent. Then yielding to our intellectual onset, the gates of the Sixth Dimension shall fly open; and after that a Seventh, and then an Eighth – ."

In 1920, *Flatland* was again placed in the limelight of our century by a letter sent to "Nature," interpreting it as a prophecy of Einstein's theory of relativity. The letter stated that Dr. Edwin Abbott had composed a "jeu d'esprit" about thirty years earlier and that at the time of publication, the book had not received all the attention it deserved. The author of the letter explained that Dr. Abbott had depicted intelligent beings whose experience was confined to a single plane, or two-dimensional space. These beings were unable to conceive of anything outside that space and had no way to exit from the surface on which they lived. Dr. Abbott then went on to ask the reader, who could imagine the third dimension, to imagine a sphere landing on the plains of Flatland and crossing through it. What would the inhabitants of Flatland think of such an event? They would not see the sphere getting closer and would have no idea of its consistency. They would only see a circle cross through their plane. At first this circle would be a point, then it would gradually increase in size, pushing back the inhabitants of Flatland with its circumference. This process would continue until half of the sphere crossed through the plane. Then the circle would diminish slowly until it became a point and finally disappear, leaving the inhabitants of Flatland as the indisputable masters of their country. The author goes on to say that their experience would be of a circular obstacle growing or expanding by degrees, only to contract again and the inhabitants would attribute this to a "growth in time," an event that an external three-dimensional observer would attribute to three-dimensional movement. The author points out that Dr. Abbott would like the reader to transfer this analogy to a four-dimensional movement in a three-dimensional space, to believe that the past and future of the universe are depicted in four-dimensional space and visible to anyone who has knowledge of the fourth dimension. Furthermore, he cites Dr. Abbott's theory that if there is movement of our three-dimension-

*Claude Bragdon, another drawing from* Square and Cube *illustrating the multiple intersections of a cube with a plane.*
*Left: a drawing by Bragdon illustrating the usefulness of polygonal models made with iron wire in studies on the fourth dimension.*

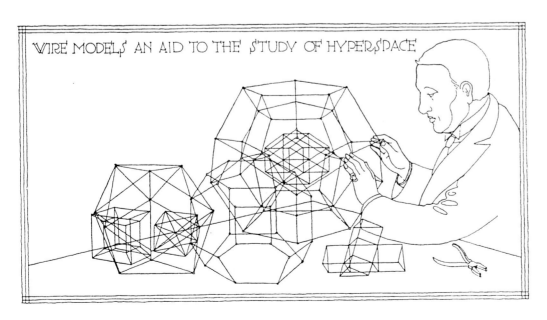

391

SINBAD PUSHES ASUNDER THE TESSERACT CUBES TRYING TO FIND THE FOURTH DIMENSION

*Claude Bragdon, drawing from* The Frozen Fountain. *The hero, Sinbad, in the middle of the cubes that generate the* tesseract, *the four-dimensional cube.*

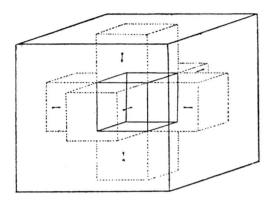

*The* tesseract, *shown by using the cubes that represent its faces* (De Stijl, *the magazine edited by Theo van Doesburg, 1924).*

al space in relation to the fourth dimension, then all the changes we experience and attribute to the passing of time will all be caused very simply by this, since the future and the past will always exist in the fourth dimension.

Reverend Abbott had come to realise the disquieting aspects of non-Euclidean geometry and even to sense how, to a certain extent, time could also be considered a further dimension. However, many decades passed before artistic and architectural culture hooked – even slightly – onto this discovery. From Cézanne to Picasso, from Kandinsky to van Doesburg, the progressive negation of perspective depth, expressed according to the rules of projective geometry, went hand in hand with a simultaneous search for a mentally perceived depth rendered by a pulsating and dynamic space, though eternally tempted by the two-dimensional reduction that Mondrian strove to achieve.

Naturally, what captured the imagination of architects most was the theory of hyperspace, especially four-dimensional space, since it promised to be a first decisive step away from nature as well as a way into an immaterial world not perceived by the senses, but represented through tridimensional projection.

The hypercube, a geometric figure defined by eight cubes – as the cube is defined by eight faces – whetted the imagination of many architects and scholars among whom it is worth remembering Matila Ghika, M. Borissalievitch and Claude Bragdon, one of the most passionate interpreters of the relationship between nature and architecture and architecture and geometry, inspired by an avowed theosophical approach. Bragdon was unsuccessful as an architect (he built just a few buildings in Rochester and Genesee), but his work as critic and theorist should be completely reappraised. It is incredible that architectural culture in America, so attentive at the time to European events, almost totally ignored such an original thinker. Among other things, he was one of the first to recognise the genius of Louis Sullivan and in 1901 published Sullivan's *Kindergarten Chats.*

Bragdon's intense publishing activity was accompanied by a series of images which exhaustively illustrate his imaginative decorations. His compositional method is similar to Sullivan's. He concentrates on well-defined areas of the spatial volume and proposes unusual forms based on a novel approach towards classical decorations as well as daring incursions into the field of non-Euclidean geometry.

In a series of articles tackling the theme, *Ornament from Mathematics*, written before and during the First World War and published in "The Architectural Review," "The Architectural Forum" and "The American Architect," Bragdon illustrates the flat representation of four-dimensional hyperpolyhedrons and elaborates decorative solutions by elegantly interpreting their graphic potential. He later revisited this theme in 1932 in his famous book *The Frozen Fountains*,[13] an enthralling and ironical volume that best depicts the intellectual atmosphere that generated that season of American architecture mistakenly baptised "Art Déco," even if it was quite independent from its European namesake inspired by the 1925 Exhibition of Decorative Arts in Paris. Suffice it to cite just one example of this type of masterpiece: the Irving Trust Building by Ralph Walker on Wall Street in which the role of decoration, totally in harmony with Bragdon's proposals, paved a completely new, extremely qualitative way forward. Bragdon did not view incursions into hyperspace as a way to abandon nature and its secrets and advance towards an abstract, purely cerebral world. On the contrary, it seems as if his images wish to imprison fantasy and imagination in nature, interpreting hyperspaces as Platonic solids multiplied by the ideal transparency of their faces exposed to the reflections of light. However, the path of abstraction would later be exploited to the full in the framework of avant-garde and post avant-garde culture, from cubism to constructivism to neo-plasticism to recent deconstructivism.

Hypersolids re-emerged as decorations in the Czechoslovakian architectural cubism of Jofan, albeit in forms that were a little more indefinite than those of Bragdon. In his 1924 house in Hannover, Kurt Schwitters seems to capture from these reflections on hyperspace a sense of disaggregation and centrifugation of natural space: the results are similar to the plastic disaggregation of the figure carried out by Boccioni.

The models elaborated by van Doesburg and van Eesteren between 1920 and 1923 aim at finding the fourth dimension by confronting the viewer with an aggregation-disaggregation process reflecting the regular yet chaotic logic of mineral crystals. Form is the result of a period of time that the viewer has to reinstate in order to understand compositional laws and the contemplative result. Other fields of mathematical research, especially topology, appear to have inspired the expressionist Finsterlin and, a few decades later in 1954, Frederick Kiesler, author of the "house without limits." The plastically distorted forms of the internal spaces designed by both architects partially reflect Klein's bottle, one of the paradoxes of topology also known as the "geometry of the rubber leaf," since it no longer deals with the lengths, areas and volumes of geometric figures but only studies the "qualitative priorities" that remain the same throughout the transformation processes.

The term "topology" was coined by K.B. Listing in 1847. But this new branch of geometry was actually elaborated in the famous book *Analysis Situs* by Poincaré, published in 1895.[14]

Klein's bottle, discovered by F. Klein in 1882, is the spatial analogy of Moebius' ribbon (a surface with one face that can continue to infinity). To build it, all you need is a rubber tube that narrows at one end like the neck of a bottle while, at the other end, the bottom is bent backwards. A circular hole is cut in the bottom: the neck is bent so as to pass along the side of the vessel and then welded to the holed bottom. There is neither an outer or inner surface to this vessel. Depending on how you look at it, the surface is either all external or all internal. Inevitably, this fantastic form aroused great enthusiasm in the archi-

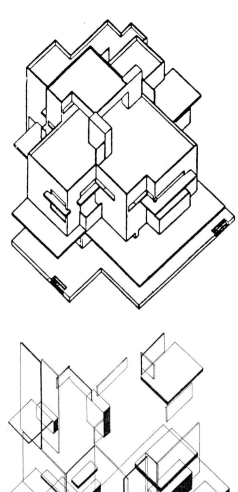

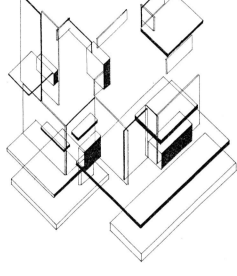

*Cor van Eestern and Theo van Doesburg, the axonometric projection of a house and the pattern of its prismatic slabs. Their obvious intention is to picture the fourth dimension by using projections of the* tesseract.

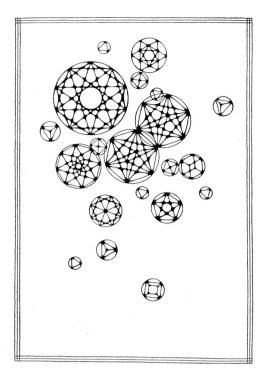

*The fourth dimension interpreted as a decoration by Claude Bragdon.*

tects of the period since both theorists and critics focused on internal space as a specific element of architecture. Schmarsow's theories (illustrated by Zevi half a century later in his *Saper vedere l'architettura*) found in Klein's bottle a sort of paradigm, while other exponents of expressionist and organicist conviction treated it as a model similar to certain biological forms such as blood vessels, the vascular tissue of plants, the structure of flowers and the digestive system.

Finsterlin models the internal spaces of his houses on digestive systems, while in his "house without limits" Kiesler plastically shapes space, twisting it like a mass of clay depending on the form of the involucre. Le Corbusier, on the other hand, bases his design for the Philips pavilion on the shape of a stomach, a fact recorded by Xenakis in his book *Musique et Architecture*.

From the point of view of its possible revolutionary impact on architecture the greatest achievement of modern mathematics is so recent that a definite evaluation cannot be made. I am speaking here of fractal mathematics, codified by Benoit Mandelbrot in his book published in 1977. The development of fractal mathematics continued at incredible speed resulting in the discovery in 1980 of the so-called "set of Mandelbrot," one of the most complex and fascinating geometric forms that science has ever produced and similar in so many ways to a product of nature.

Born in 1924, when he was twenty Mandelbrot enrolled in the Ecole Normale in Paris only to leave a year later to choose a more congenial place of study, the Ecole Polytechnique. Born with a true vocation for mathematics, he did not, however, share the abstract approach advocated by a group of mathematicians who hid behind the pseudonym of Nicolas Bourbaki: the latter opposed any type of graphic application.

During the fifties, when together with Leonardo Sinisgalli we were setting up an exhibition of mathematical forms in Turin for the 1961 Italian Expo, I too personally experienced the effects of this "antigraphic" prejudice that was still very strong in Italy.

Fascinated by the plastic models of the surfaces of the fourth order which at the turn of the century had totally captured the attention of mathematicians, we turned to professors and clerks to find the ones Sinisgalli had seen as a very young boy in Via Panisperna. After overcoming enormous difficulties, we managed to find a few pieces in a wooden box in the cellar of the Institute of Matematics of the University of Rome. Among the pieces that had been saved we found the famous "Roman surface" by Steiner (Sinisgalli describes it in his *Furor mathematicus* as "a tuber as big as a stone with three navels," topologically transformed by American scholars using a computer into what was later baptised "topological Venus") that I used to crown a chimney in Casa Baldi, my first personal project designed in 1959. The beds and some railings in Casa Baldi were based on the graphic representation of certain equation systems taken from a book by Le Lionnais.[15]

"The fact that on principle Bourbaki did not include any figures," wrote

Mandelbrot, "was for me a sort of amputation; it's like presenting a body without arms." Not a surprising statement from a mathematician whose discoveries forcefully put mathematical forms back into the collective imagination and who had a special way of expressing himself and communicating his experiences so that even people who were not experts in this field were able to grasp the concepts.

If Mandelbrot succeeded in a few short years to redirect certain areas of mathematical research towards the domain of what is visible, he owes it to computers, especially the last generation of computers that are capable of showing on a screen extremely complicated operations impossible to execute manually. This new instrument allowed him to pick up the baton and run with the many reflections left by a group of mathematicians. Almost a century earlier, they had foreseen and studied forms that they themselves judged to be monstrous and undrawable. Mandelbrot, instead, was able to transform these mental concepts – so daring that it was necessary to have a strong feeling for abstraction to imagine them – into graphic equivalents whose beauty has thrilled even those who know absolutely nothing of mathematics. Fractal objects have not only contributed to a better understanding of certain "secrets" of the universe, but they also possess an undeniable aesthetic beauty and look uncannily like natural images, even if in nature they seem to be, so to speak, "truncated" when compared to the infinite developments implicit in their theoretical enunciation.[16]

Let us take for example the rocky shores of an island. The fractal model postulates that the infinite subdivision of the profile of every gulf into a series of smaller gulfs is repeated *ad infinitum*, while in fact this "scaling" process stops when, having reached the smallest possible cove, the splitting of "selfsimilar" forms also stops and we are left with sand and sea water.

The notion of "self-similarity," in which the part resembles the whole, is one of the typical qualities of fractals and, as we will see later, is also the one that turns them into a close relative of architecture and urban form. On the subject Jonathan Swift has written a short verse:

So, Na'tralist observe, a flea
Has smaller fleas that on him prey,
And these have smaller fleas to bite'em,
And so proceed ad infinitum.[17]

Lewis Fry Richardson, amongst other things a student of weather forecasts, paraphrased Swift in another verse on vortexes:

Big whorls have little whorls,
Which feed on their velocity;
And little whorls have lesser whorls,
and so on to viscosity
(in the molecular sense).[18]

*Casa Baldi in Rome (1959-61) and the chimney-pot crowned by Steiner's Roman surface (Paolo Portoghesi, 1959-61).*

*Frank Lloyd Wright, community centre, Marin County, near San Francisco. The rhythm of the overlapping windows brings to mind the Pont du Gard and the rods of Cantor.*
*Cantor dust graphically represented by Benoit Mandelbrot.*

In the history of architecture, self-similarity, "cascading" structures, scaling, and geometric fragmentation are all "tools of the trade," compositional procedures used to attain unity in multiplicity and often recognised as being the key to beauty.

Let's take the Cantor set (also called "Cantor dust" because so thin and slender as to be invisible), one of the mathematical "monsters" Mandelbrot placed at the basis of fractal geometry. Looking at a rough graphic representation, the one called "Cantor rod" it is possible to recognise a similar rule in the structure of the Town Hall designed by Frank Lloyd Wright in Marin County, near San Francisco. Previous examples in classical works include the portico once attributed to the Balbi crypt in the archaeological centre of Rome, the courtyard of Palazzo Borso d'Este in Ferrara designed by Biagio Rossetti, or the Gothic-Romanesque model of the mullioned windows with several lights, in which several arches separated by columns are framed by a bigger arch. The concept of scaling is present in architecture in the West and in the East and characterises towers, bell-towers and pagodas, but it is above all in Hindu temples that perhaps the most convincing prefiguration of fractal self-similarity may be found.

In the classical world, an ensemble made of two columns joined by an architrave and a pediment (the aedicula) may be found in temples and churches in increasingly smaller sizes – like Russian dolls and Chinese boxes – as one moves away from the façade towards the portal, the windows of the ciborium,

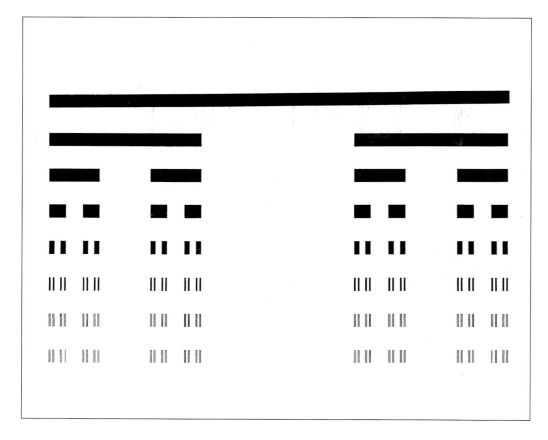

the altar and the tabernacle. This self-similarity between the parts and the whole is even more obvious in Hindu and Jaina temples, in which the "shikhara" appears to be made of a multitude of small "shikharas" decreasing in size.

Another of the "monsters" tamed by Mandelbrot is the "snowflake" or "Koch island." The name comes from the Swedish mathematician Helge von Koch who in 1906 wrote an article on the "discovery" of a special curve based on a line divided into three equal parts. Substituting the intermediate part with two segments of similar length that unite in a point creates an angular profile made of four segments that form two angles. Repeating the whole operation for each of the four segments will result in a profile with sixteen sides. In turn, each one can be substituted by the quadripartite profile, and so on. If one starts from a triangle instead of a tripartite line, working in the same way on each of the sides instead of the original line, the result will be the famous snowflake or Koch island, a figure whose perimeter tends towards infinity while the area remains finite. The Koch island is a close relative of many centrally-planned buildings in which the encompassing walls are, so to speak, curved or hollowed out by increasingly smaller cavities. The most important examples of this kind are Saint Peter's by Bramante, Sant'Ivo by Borromini, or ancient buildings like San Vitale and Santa Sofia in which the walls shape space, giving it an almost *res extensa* consistency. The dialectic between external and internal space that takes place on the wall, creating a compactness or

*An example of Roman broccoli and, above, the sanctuary of Lodurva in the Thur desert near Jaisalmer (India), a shikhara of a Jaina temple based on the repetition of self-similar parts.*

A Menger "sponge," a fractal ensemble whose size is log.20/log. 3=2.7268.
An engraving by Franco Purini.
Right: detail of the shikhara in the sacred village of Palitana, a group of 863 Jaina temples, most of which date to the 11th century.

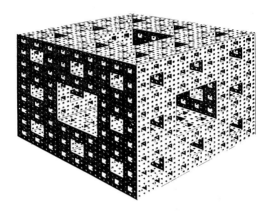

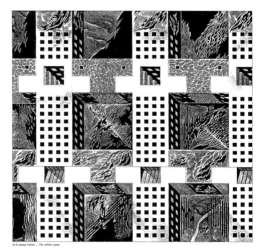

398

a subdivision or pulverisation of space, is efficiently represented by the graphic transformations of the Julia system.

The repetition of a pattern within a pattern that recalls a process that could go on indefinitely is a psychological truth that certainly influenced the adoption of serial models or scaling procedures in the field of art. These choices might be motivated by what could be called "nostalgia of infinity," an emotion that justifies the enthusiasm of many artists for fractal mathematics in which infinity is just around the corner. At this point, one wonders whether fractals – apart from their presence *ante litteram* in the history of architecture – have had any influence on recent architectural research. Notwithstanding brief encounters between the two fields, real contact is still to come and all the indicators point to the fact that it will be both important and fruitful.

In the case of the architect Franco Purini, it is quite possible to talk of perfect agreement since his geometrical research concentrates on the division of square surfaces and cubic volumes with such rigorous logic that it conjures up another of the monsters tamed by Mandelbrot: the "Sierpinski-Menger sponge," a cube whose faces are "Sierpinski carpets," squares pierced *ad infinitum* by small square windows that end up having no area, while the perimeter of the holes becomes infinite. By employing a similar and equally rigorous compositional process, Purini theorises transparent structures, creators of shadows that envelop space and "divide it up rigidly, alarmingly."

In the sixties I tried to create a geometry that made it possible to use natural forms, especially living forms, in my designs, and starting with Casa Baldi, this led me to experiment with structures based on self-similarity that prefigured the world of images later revealed by fractal mathematics. Recently, the Company Headquarters built in Pietralata marks a renewal in my research.

In his fantastic and ironic manner of speech that brings to mind Calvino's *Invisible Cities* or Borges' *Library of Babel*, Benoit Mandelbrot often uses metaphors and his discoveries, like those of his predecessors, always have charming names. An explicit use of architectural metaphor may be found for the fractal illustrated in plate 146 of his book *The Fractal Geometry of Nature*, called the "split snowflake halls": "Long ago and far away, the Great Ruler and his retinue had sat their power in the splendid Snowflake Halls. A schism occurs, a war follows, ending in stalemate, and finally Wise Elders draw a line to divide the Halls between the contenders from the North and the South. Riddles of the Maze. Who controls the Great Hall, and how is it reached from outside? Why do some Halls fail to be oriented toward either of the cardinal points?" Mandelbrot's solution can be found in another of his metaphorical constructions: the "monkey tree," illustrated on page 31 of his book.

Apart from its political background, the metaphor of the hall has something passionate about it. In fact, the centre hall is like a small cathedral with a nave, an apse divided into four chapels and an articulated and pulsating space almost totally symmetrical except for some minor details. The other

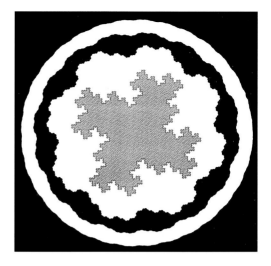

*Koch island and lakes in a complex elaboration (the size of the coast line ranges from 1 to D=log. 3/log. √1.3652).*
*Like a Russian doll, the island is situated in the middle of a lake which is in the middle of an island which, in turn, is in the middle of a lake.*

*Partial view of the tridimensional section of a Julia ensemble in four-dimensional space and, below, the Tersigni house in Castel Gandolfo (P. Portoghesi, V. Gigliotti, 1970).*

*F. Purini,* Trees Retreat after the Arrival of the Hut, *an engraving.*

400

Paolo Portoghesi, design of a commercial centre in Pietralata (Rome), 1996. The geometric form and the shape of the garden faithfully reproduce part of the Mandelbrot ensemble. All the floors in the towers are the same height, but each one is rotated at a slightly different angle (collaborators: B. Castagna, G.C. Mencerella, R. Palombi, G.C. Priori).

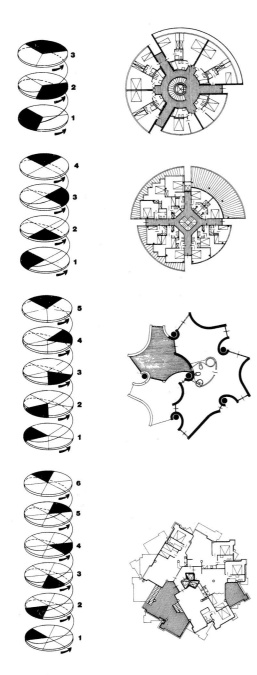

*Tower houses built by superimposing floors of the same height but rotated by 120, 90, 72 and 60 degrees respectively (P. Portoghesi, V. Gigliotti 1962-65).*

halls of the building are a little less symmetrical and the fact that they are arranged differently means they obey a mysterious rule. Of all the labyrinths created by architects from Theseus on, few can lay claim to the complexity and enigmatic character of this one which I would like to call "the castle of heresies"; "castle" for its likeness to the one built as a hunting-lodge by Frederick II in Castel del Monte, "of heresies" because it is the symbolic place of a tendency so typical of the human soul to split hairs, to make distinctions and to spread itself thin.

No less interesting are the tangencies between fractal figures and architectural decoration, above all lattice structures which are based on removal and repetition, but which often tend towards self-similarity, as well as possessing a so-called fractal nature. Besides, the most natural lattice, that of the hive, is one of the possible forms of the Koch curve when a given line is chosen as an initiator and the three bisectors of the equilateral triangle with sides equal to the line is chosen as a generator. The most amazing anticipation of fractal logic in the field of decoration was provided by E. Lauweriks in a number of his projects and in the front cover of the magazine "Wendingen."

The "Sierpinski triangle" also has a noble architectural history. It appears as a recurrent motif in the decoration of the Cosmati school. Numerous equilateral or rectangular versions can be found in the floors of many Roman basilicas such as San Giovanni in Laterano and Santa Maria Maggiore, and a version adapted to a circular outline also appears in Westminster Abbey in London.

A totally different picture emerges when speaking of the analogy between the more complex visual fractals, like the set of Mandelbrot and of Julia, and the classical wavy embellishments in which the spiral motif is regarded as the section of a sea-horse, or, better still, the fantastic and periodic incrustations of the *rocailles* typical of late Baroque decorations. The *rocaille* is based on the different repetitions of a concave mark, always accompanied by a frothy corona that recalls the turbulent movement of water, one of the most congenial subjects studied by fractal mathematics.

At this point, it is worth saying a few words on centralised geometric divisions in which certain motifs tend to endlessly contract. Normally, there is no division around a circle in order to avoid the practical difficulties of tackling the infinitesimal, but Roman floors often have motifs that start from punctiform patterns that represent what cannot be designed in practice. The lacunars on the ceiling of the Pantheon solve this problem by inserting a silent ring in which the divisions end and the circular window triumphs: a sole source of light that acts as a gnomon revealing the movement of the earth from sunrise to sunset.

Fractal mathematics provides no less amazing interpretative keys with regard to the history of the city and its structures. First of all, it must be said that the field in which new geometry was first applied scientifically was town-planning, through the study of vehicular traffic and demography. In the field we

402

are most interested in, that of structural analogies, the tree-shaped model with its implacable logic (one divides into two) characterises many urban areas, especially in Islamic cities and many medieval cities, leaving limited fractals the task of bringing to mind the logic of the ideal city. In one particular case, Mandelbrot's research on fractals led him to use an urban metaphor, namely the "city of the aleatory roads" illustrated in his first book published in 1975. This metaphor is created by haphazardly drawing lines that get smaller and smaller. If this procedure continues on to infinity the space between the roads, where the houses should be, tends to be cancelled out. Mandelbrot asks himself, would we have to build never-ending towers?

This excursus on "fractal architecture" was not meant to distract the reader from the main theme of this book. On the contrary, it was meant to take him by the hand and lead him down a path to the heart of a problem that appears to have been solved: the question of finding new links between nature and intellectual research, new keys to unlock the hidden mystery of beauty. Mandelbrot entitled his most famous book *The Fractal Geometry of Nature* and with condescending irony underlined the fact that those branches of mathematics that seemed to be the most abstract and distant from nature – so much so that they were considered dead branches in so far as they generated self-contained "monsters" – were ultimately fundamental in improving man's knowledge of the laws that govern natural forms.

In 1626, Galileo Galilei wrote in his book *Il Saggiatore*: "Philosophy continues to be written in this large volume open in front of us (I say the universe), but it is incomprehensible unless we learn to understand its language and letters. It is written in a mathematical language, its letters are triangles, circles and other geometric shapes. Without them it would be impossible to humanely understand a single word: without these, it would be like wandering aimlessly in a dark labyrinth."

One century later, Pascal expressed a less confident thought: "Imagination will tire of inventing sooner than nature of revealing." Mandelbrot quite rightly agrees with Pascal and not with Galileo, having dared to wander around a labyrinth, not "aimlessly," but, on the contrary, gathering extremely useful tools accrued during his courageous journey. These tools are neither triangles nor circles, but they are nonetheless geometric figures straddling order and disorder, and if left uncomprehended many aspects of nature, especially the unexpected and the irregular, will remain mysterious. Even if we can calculate the exact orbit of a planet and its speed, we also realise how difficult it is to predict the journey of the clouds and spells of bad weather, even for short periods. When faced with turbulence, even the smallest changes in the environment can have enormous repercussions: the beat of a butterfly's wings can cause a hurricane.

Fractal mathematics is not consolatory like traditional science; it does not promise us "magnificent progressive destinies" but invites us into a labyrinth

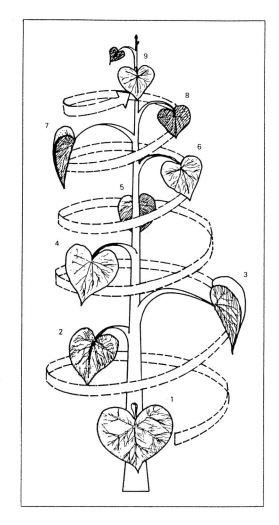

*Top, vegetal phyllotaxis, used as a model for the towers on the opposite page, was also applied to the profile of Solomon's columns.*
*Detail of the design of the commercial centre in Pietralata (Rome).*

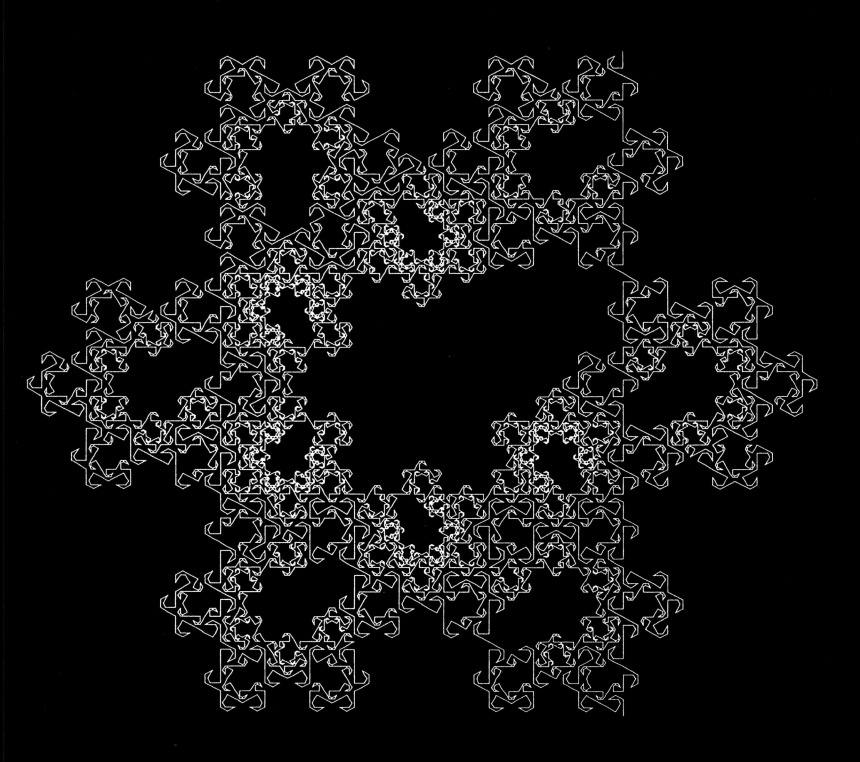

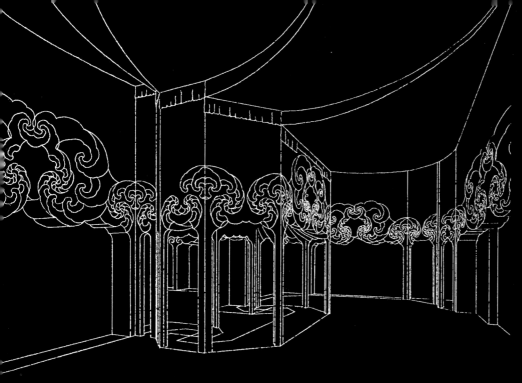

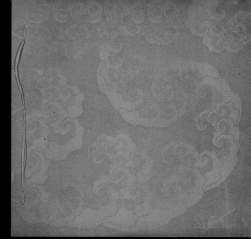

*Opposite page: Mandelbrot's "Rooms": a fractal that evokes an extravagant itinerary inside a building. Even Mandelbrot commented this ensemble with Italo Calvino's irony: "Long ago and far away, the Great Ruler and his retinue had sat their power in the splendid Snowflake Halls. A schism occured, a war followed ending in stalemate, and finally Wise Elders drew a line to divide the Halls between the contenders from the North and the South. Riddles of the maze. Who controls the Great Hall, and how is it reached from outside? Why do some Halls fail to be oriented toward either of the cardinal points?" Mandelbrot provides the answer by having another fractal, called the "monkey tree," speak.*

*From top left: the inside of a room and the cover of the magazine Wendingen. Based on the theories of August Tiersch, who believed in the repetition of a basic form and its division as a factor of compositional harmony, Lauwericks drew up a decorative system which fully corresponded to the fractal logic of self-similarity.*
*Partial enlargement of Mandelbrot's system.*

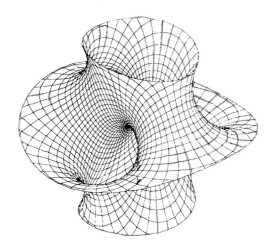

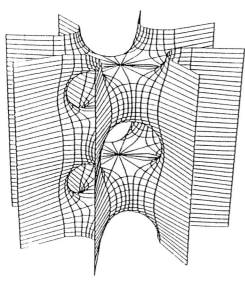

*Two examples of minimum surfaces with obvious architectural potential.*
*The minimum surface discovered by the mathematicians Hoffman and Meeks is the first complete and compact surface discovered two centuries after the catenoid and helicoid; the second is taken from* The 18th Book *of the Research Institute of Stuttgart University run by Frei Otto, 1987 (p. 319).*

that looks very much like a downward spiral accessing numerous smaller self-similar labyrinths. As a reward for this dubious and light-hearted progress it offers a world of beauty to be explored with the help of computers. This instrument initially showed us cold, monotonous images in a particularly simplistic language. In the field of design it was merely a static instrument of representation that depended on traditional academic methods. With difficulty it conquered realism, like certain ugly tempera perspectives drawn by mercenaries of perspective architectural design. Suddenly, fractals prompted computers to reveal their hidden virtues and they became the furnace of the imagination, a place of fascinating metamorphoses in which fractals revealed their soul through enlargements and changes in the spectrum of conventional colours. After being taught by man to pretend to be a good designer, finally the computer was given a task worthy of its capabilities: to represent what the mind of man had conceived but which his hands could not transform into form because of the excessively complicated operations involved.

In yet another field, the computer is a primary tool in the study of spatial involucres with new properties and complex regularity: the field of minimum surfaces. Once upon a time, this was the undisputed domain of models that exploited the surface tension of liquids, an extension of the domain of soap bubbles. Today the computer is able to represent even those minimal surfaces that cannot be created with models, since the soapy film would close up the holes.

By incorporating in their studies the work of the mathematician Costa, in 1984 David Hoffman and William Meeks managed to prove that apart from the plane, the catenoid and the helicoid, there was at least another complete and immersed minimum surface. This surface, like others shown at the world-wide exhibition, "Getting to the Surface," is clearly architectural in essence giving us the impression that if built to size, it could actually be a complex space with exceptional qualities. To wander inside this space would be like walking inside a flower, an *Ophris* orchid or an *Iris germanica*.

If what I have been trying to prove in this book is true, namely that a return to nature is the way out of a severe identity crisis, will architecture be capable of using the new geometry of nature as it did in the past with the achievements of geometricians and mathematicians such as Euclid, Brunelleschi and Monge?

For some decades now architecture has laid claim to independence, and this isolation has in some ways helped it to avoid abuse and licence, but now independence is used only to justify the supreme indifference of architects for anything that is not "in" the discipline, a discipline that – with a few exceptions – is increasingly removed from the problems of those who inhabit the earth and would like to lead a better life with less risk for both the earth and its inhabitants. At this point, the fence around this branch of learning, a fence that looks increasingly like the barbed wire of concentration camps, will have to be torn down without delay, and a clean getaway made of the one-way street of "architecture for architects."

If architecture takes this step it will enter a labyrinth: the labyrinth that is one of its most ancient symbols. Perhaps at the threshold of the third millennium it is the return of the labyrinth that we are awaiting, the Ariadne-Mandelbrot thread that stands guard over his tamed animals.

*Frank Lloyd Wright uses his hands to demonstrate two principles that inspired his work: upward tension (veneration and aspiration) and the resistance of tension through weaving which is at the heart of "tenuity," the principle behind tensile structures.*

[1] cf., Nicomachus of Gerasa, *Introduction to Arithmetic*, The Macmillan Co., London 1926.

[2] cf., R.D. Archer-Hind, *The Timeus of Plato*, Macmillan & Co., London 1888.

[3] *Ibid.*

[4] *Ibid.*

[5] cf., Piero della Francesca, *De quinque corporibus regolaribus*, written between 1482 and 1492.

[6] cf., L. Pacioli, *De Divina Proportione*, Venice 1494 and P. Portoghesi, "Luca Pacioli", in *Civiltà delle macchine*, 1956.

[7] cf., L.B. Alberti, *Ten Books on Architecture*, Alec Tiranti Ltd., London 1955.

[8] cf., Palladio's indications commented by R. Wittkower, in *Principi architettonici nell'età dell'umanesimo*, Einaudi, Turin 1964.

[9] cf., M.A. Hagen, *Varieties of Realism*, Cambridge University Press, Cambridge 1986.

[10] cf., E. Panofsky, *La prospettiva come forma simbolica*, Feltrinelli, Milan 1973.

[11] cf., G. Archidiacono, *Spazio, iperspazi, frattali*, Di Renzo, Rome 1993.

[12] cf., the preface by M. d'Amico to E. Abbott, *Flatlandia*, Adelphi, Milan, p. 15.

[13] Bragdon was certainly influenced by the book, *Geometry of Four Dimensions* by H. Parker Morning, published in 1914. Cf., also L. Dalrymple Henderson, *The Fourth Dimension*, Princeton University Press, Princeton 1983.

[14] H. Poincaré, "Analysis Situs," in *Journal d'Ecole Polytechnique*, no. 2, 1985, p. 1.

[15] F. Le Lionnais, *Le grands courants de la pensée mathématique*, Blanchard, Paris 1962.

[16] For Mandelbrot and fractal mathematics see: B.B. Mandelbrot, *The Fractal Geometry of Nature*, Freeman, New York 1977; idem, *La Geometria della Natura*, Theoria, Naples-Rome 1989; idem, *Gli oggetti frattali*, Einaudi, Turin 1987; M. Otto Peitgen, H. Jurgens, D. Saupe, *Chaos and Fractals*, Springer, New York 1993; G.A. Edgar, *Classic on Fractals*, Addison-Weley, Reading (Mass.) 1993; J. Briggs, *L'estetica del caos*, Red, Como 1993 (*Fractals: the patterns of chaos*, New York 1992); H.O. Peitgen, P.H. Richter, *La bellezza dei frattali*, Bollati-Boringhieri, Turin 1987 (*The beauty of fractals*, New York 1986); M. Field, M. Golubitsky, *Symmetry in Chaos*, Oxford University Press, Oxford 1992; M. McGuire, *An Eye for Fractals*, Addison Welsey, Redwood City (Ca.) 1991.

[17] J. Swift, *On Poetry and Rhapsody*, 1773.

[18] L.F. Richardson, *Weather Prediction*, 1922.

# The Garden, Paradise

The English word "garden," and the equivalent words in nearly all European languages, all come from the French *gard*, probably an abbreviation of the Latin *hortus gardinus*, a cultivated enclosed area. The notion of limitation and closure lies at the very heart of the concept of garden, in turn indissolubly linked to the idea of paradise, a word that comes from the Persian *paridaeza* meaning enclosed orchard, from which originates the Jewish word *pardes* translated by the Septuagint as *paradeisos*.

Originally, the garden was a part of the earth surrounded by a fence, but it is also memory and the portrayal of something primitive, lost but not forgotten, something that can partly be regained or at least re-evoked.

If the relationship between architecture and nature is normally filtered by symbolic imitation, in the case of the garden archetype this relationship is exemplary. Every time man asks nature to become a garden, to renounce its mysterious universality, to redefine itself on a human scale in a meaningful ensemble, it conjures up a primitive past, a state of lost happiness, of which the garden is a symbol.

Marius Schneider wrote: "In symbolic thought, numerous existential forms may be considered similar, so long as they are governed by the same rhythm, at least temporarily."[1] Perhaps it is possible to say that the garden grows out of a desire to reinstate the rhythms of nature as they were in the beginning.

The "importance" of this link with paradise is naturally particularly strong in western gardens, especially those influenced by Jewish and Christian traditions, but it is present in nearly all religious traditions and its roots are even more ancient perhaps than those of the Bible. One of the first literary records of the garden archetype is a Babylonian tablet bearing the inscription of a 278 line poem dedicated to the Sumerian myth of paradise. Dilmun is described as a "pure, bright and dazzling" place where its fortunate inhabitants knew neither illness, violence nor old age. Initially there was no water in Dilmun, but then the god Enki ordered Ytu, god of the Sun, to create a divine garden in which water welled up from below so that fruit trees and green grass could grow.[2]

In prehistoric ceramics, archaeologists have frequently found traces of sacred trees – the trees of life linked to the myth of the garden-paradise. Thus, it seems almost as if this nostalgia for a non-conflictory relationship with nature be as ancient as the first forms of civilisation itself.

In fact, the idea of fencing in vegetation is associated with the birth of agriculture, when man realised that taking care of the earth meant guaranteeing a "harvest," otherwise entrusted to the good fortunes of the nomad who searched for his nourishment during his travels.

The declarations of many American Indians explain why man hesitated so long before he began to artificially transform the landscape. The fact is they considered the earth their mother.

Their truly filial attitude is illustrated in an extraordinary passage in the writings of Smohalla, the "dreamer prophet" who at the end of the last century, a pe-

A fresco in the tomb of a senior officer in Thebes, 15th century B.C.
The plants are placed geometrically; the practical aspects of agriculture and animal husbandry are combined with the aesthetic aspects of contemplation.

*Front cover of the book* Paradisi in Sole, Paradisus Terrestris, *by John Parkinson, London 1629.*

riod in which *ghost dances* were starting to become fashionable among the Pinte Indians,[3] announced the restitution of the land to the Indians and the ejection of the white conquerors.

In a text of collected essays, Smohalla is reported to have answered a journalist who had asked him why he didn't want to plough the land whether he should use a knife and plunge it into the breast of his mother. As far as he was concerned if he did that, his body would not be embraced by the earth upon his death, and if he cut hay, as did the white man, he would be cutting his mother's hair. Against the white man who at the time was invading the land belonging to the Indians, Smohalla launched a challenge in which he called for his people to remain there with him. His ancestors would come back to life and their spirits would become reincarnate. Why? Because this was the land of their fathers, because this was the place to wait to meet them again, in the bosom of their earthmother. [4]

If for some populations this hesitation over the "right" to wound the earthmother was insurmountable, it was quickly solved by others who transformed it into a sort of pact, an alliance that respected the integrity of the earth from a religious viewpoint and permitted the elaboration of landscaping projects such as irrigation ditches, the adoption of geometric grids for plantations, the transformation of steep hills into terraces and the channelling of water through the use of artificial dams in order to make rice cultivation possible. Architecture and agriculture are closely related techniques and disciplines and some of the breathtaking manmade landscapes along the Chianti hills, or the moraines that descend the Valle d'Aosta (with its lovely Carema pergolas supported by stone columns) or the mosaic fields of central China, have earned the right to be considered examples of an architecture in which the landscape is translated, so to speak, from its original language into a new language, with stricter and more elementary rules than those nature chooses to follow in her steadfast complexity.

The oldest historical image of a garden is perhaps the wooden model of a small house with a garden surrounded by walls found in the tomb of Meketre (eleventh Theban dynasty). Instead, a less laconic document comes from the New Kingdom. In his tomb in Thebes, a soldier wanted to portray his symmetrical garden which contained, however, certain exceptions to the strict geometric order. Apart from the orderly rows of trees, stretches of water and small constructions, in the middle of the rectangular lot there was a large area probably planted with vines. In Egypt, luxurious vegetation only existed around the springs and cultivated fields along the Nile. This meant that the garden of Thebes was comparable to an oasis in the middle of the desert or to a strip of agricultural land along the banks of the Nile, criss-crossed by a geometric pattern of small canals.[5] Certainly in Egypt during the New Kingdom, pergolas supported by columns were quite commonplace.

*Genesis* (2, 8-14) recites: "Now the Lord God had planted a garden in the east, in Eden; and there he put the man he had formed. And the Lord God made all kinds of trees grow out of the ground – trees that were pleasing to the eye and good for food. In the middle of the garden were the tree of life and the tree of knowledge of good and evil. A river watering the garden flowed from Eden; from there it was separated into four headwaters. The name of the first is the Pishon; it winds through the entire land of Havilah, where there is gold. (The gold of that land is good; aromatic resin and onyx are also there.) The name of the second river is the Gihon; it winds through he entire land of Cush. The name of the third river is Tigris; it runs along the east side of Asshur. And the fourth river is the Euphrates."

Every age has imagined and portrayed Eden differently, and the debate still wears on. Those who imagined it as a sort of tidy garden were probably influenced by the fact that in the Bible, Paradise on earth had a centre (geometric concept) and had been "prepared" by God for man, to make his life easier. It was totally different to the one experienced by man, characterised by suffering and toil. If nature as we see it here on earth corresponds to this kind of human condition, considered by certain 17th-century theologians as a "land of ruin,"[6] then it seems logical to suppose that if a different human condition existed, a condition of pure happiness, it would correspond to a different kind of nature, a kind of nature ready to satisfy every desire and yearning and therefore arranged in a strict rational order.

In the Bible, however, the precarious scenario of Paradise on earth, invented

*A clearing in an acorn wood at the foot of the Gennargentu hills in Sardinia (Italy). Often the landscape has such harmonious and gentle traits that it seems to be the careful work of a gardener intent at pruning hedges, cutting lawns, planting flowers and rare bushes in strategic positions, in accordance with the rules laid down by William Robinson in his book,* The Wild Garden *(1881).*

to test mankind, prefigures another garden, a celestial garden, placed at the end of time and corresponding in the book of *Revelations* to Heavenly Jerusalem, a walled city with twelve gates whose walls were made of precious stones such as those described by Saint Augustine in his *Civitas Dei*. Traditionally, the garden archetype is tinged with the colours of nostalgia and expectation, an ongoing exchange between the plant and human world aimed at the attainment of justice, peace and contemplation.

In this context, the famous verses of the *Song of Songs* (4, 12-15) provide the key for a mystical interpretation of Paradise later to be embroidered with endless nuances by Christian philosophy:

> You are the garden locked up, my sister, my bride;
> you are a spring enclosed, a sealed fountain.
> Your plants are an orchard of pomegranates
> with choice fruits,
> with henna and nard,
> nard and saffron,
> calamus and cinnamon,
> with every kind of incense tree,
> with myrrah and aloes
> and all the finest spices.
> You are a garden fountain,
> a well of flowing water
> streaming down from Lebanon.

The equation garden = paradise, garden = universe re-emerges in the classical world together with the myth of the golden age, described by Hesiod as an age of well-being in which men lived as gods, their heart free from all care and safe from pain and misery.

"[...] no miserable old age came their way; their hands, their feet, did not alter. They took their pleasure in festivals, and lived without troubles. When they died, it was as if they fell asleep. [...] And there they have their dwelling place, and hearts free of sorrow in the islands of the blessed by the deep-swirling stream of the ocean, prospering heroes, on whom in every year three times over the fruitful grainland bestows its sweet yield."[7]

Similarly, in his book *The Republic*, Plato describes the kingdom of Cronus. This kingdom had no constitution or laws, men lived naked outdoors in a temperate, balanced climate and used soft grassy fields as beds.

In Book IV of the *Odyssey*, Proteus announces to Menelaus that the gods will take him beyond the ends of the earth, to the Elysian plains, where man partakes of the "easy life." Instead, in the twelfth *Olympian Ode* Pindar sings of the happy islands: "There shine flowers of gold, some in the earth on branches of beauteous trees, others nourished by the waters."[8]

*Other examples illustrating the way in which nature seems to imitate or, better still, teach artifice. Partial view of a valley near Calcata (Italy) and a group of evergreen shrubs near Sopramonte di Orgosolo (Italy).*

*Bomarzo (near Rome), grotesque mask in the Sacred Wood by Vicino Orsini (16th century).*

*Nine different types of nuptial gardens prepared by as many species of bowerbirds.*

In his *Theogony*, Hesiod also describes the orchard of the Hesperides, where the nymphs, daughters of night, used to cultivate lovely golden apples. In this garden, the ideal model of so many Renaissance gardens, Zeus and Hera were married.

The golden age described by Virgil inspires nostalgia but also hope: hope in an eternal return to the age of innocence and peacefulness. Again, it is a garden, considered a sublimation of agriculture, that inspires this sentiment.

The relationship between garden and nature is one of the most circuitous imaginable, especially considering how docile the human mind is towards nature and man's tendency to imitate it. It is a game of mirrors that simultaneously destroys and exalts "distance." The construction materials of a designed garden are not "natural" materials but living matter. However much you control, educate and force them into geometric straight-jackets, they possess a vitality and interior freedom that is difficult to restrain. A garden is partly the assembly of previously witnessed images taken from nature and artistically reassembled, and partly a distorted, oneiric image, a secret violence carried out on the natural landscape by man's imagination and enacted according to a strategy involving space and time, seasonal rhythms and cycles. The stolen fragments, put together by a demiurge gardener, that might even be a tender sparrow, are clearly recognisable and often coincide with the places and moments in which nature appears to be guided by a hidden hand that is fully aware of the goal to be achieved. It is above

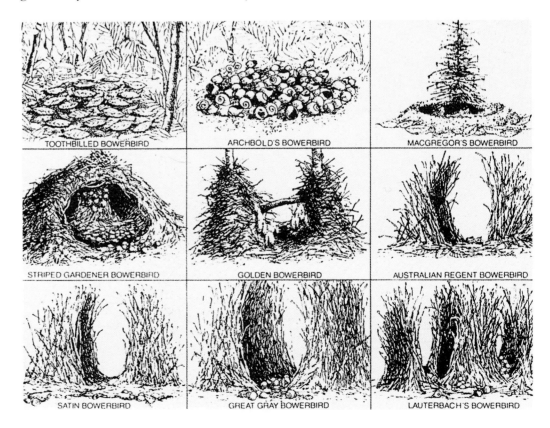

TOOTHBILLED BOWERBIRD — ARCHBOLD'S BOWERBIRD — MACGREGOR'S BOWERBIRD — STRIPED GARDENER BOWERBIRD — GOLDEN BOWERBIRD — AUSTRALIAN REGENT BOWERBIRD — SATIN BOWERBIRD — GREAT GRAY BOWERBIRD — LAUTERBACH'S BOWERBIRD

all in those places and those moments that the equation garden = paradise becomes tangible reality: when a plant of boxwood, myrtle or privet in the border of a flower bed seems to be artistically pruned and the matching colours of the leaves and flowers seem to be dictated by the sensitivity of a landscape painter. Equally beautiful, in the sense of Paradise lost, are the images of abandoned gardens in which nature reigns supreme again, inflicting foreseeable defeats on those who dared to challenge her. This is exactly what happened in Bomarzo before excavations and restorations tried, in a truly incompetent way, to reinstate the former order designed by Vicino Orsini. This is the risk run by other gardens (some of which are truly beautiful) situated to the north of Rome in the region that goes by the name of "Tuscia." Here, gardens live in harmony with Etruscan necropolises and are quite rightly defined as "the gardens of the dead." Behind this threat by a crafty and sly nature to reconquer its lost chaos lie the materials used for the walls, beds, fountains and paths scattered around the countryside: tufa and peperino, soft water-loving stones that during the rainy season become covered in multicoloured musk and lichens, thereby losing much of their artificial air almost as if they had undergone an ironic deformation, a partial cancellation or a calibrated "clouding-over." Rarely has man been so successful – not always unwittingly I believe – in turning nature and its different methods of procedure and creation into a valuable collaborator.

In Persia, the garden is a geometric oasis and a place of running waters, a

*The main fountain of the villa in Bagnaia (Italy) belonging to Cardinal Gambara (16th century) and, above, detail of the Papacqua fountain near Palazzo Albani in Soriano (Italy), built by Cardinal Cristoforo Madruzzo (16th century).*

piece of land from whose centre four rivers (cited in the Koran) depart. These rivers are woven into the world-famous Persian carpets, between palm trees and flowered borders. On the other hand, in India, these springs are often substituted by a symbolic sacred mountain.[9]

In Chinese tradition, nature is imitated much more faithfully. Efforts are made to try and find a hidden order appropriate to the contemplation of each of the parts that narratively compose the unity of the garden, a unity transmitted during movement, walking or meditation. One of the most typical cosmogonies in Chinese culture narrates how the world was born from a primordial egg, hatched by a god who lived for eighteen thousand years. After he died his head burst open and turned into the sun and the moon, his blood generated the sea and the rivers, his hair the plants, his limbs the mountains, his voice thunder, his sweat rain, his breath wind, his fleas the forefathers of man.[10]

This type of tale reveals the sense of humour and humility of the Chinese, their respect for nature as well as their tendency to consider the entire universe as a *human subspecies*, based on a relationship between man and nature founded on familiarity, reciprocal understanding and trust.

The Chinese garden does not flaunt its balanced artificiality. It is the poetic interpretation of a place that already existed, in which the landscape is seconded and enhanced, the result of obedience to the structural laws of nature that have no need to be enunciated in abstract terms but intuitively followed as one does the current when swimming in the sea.

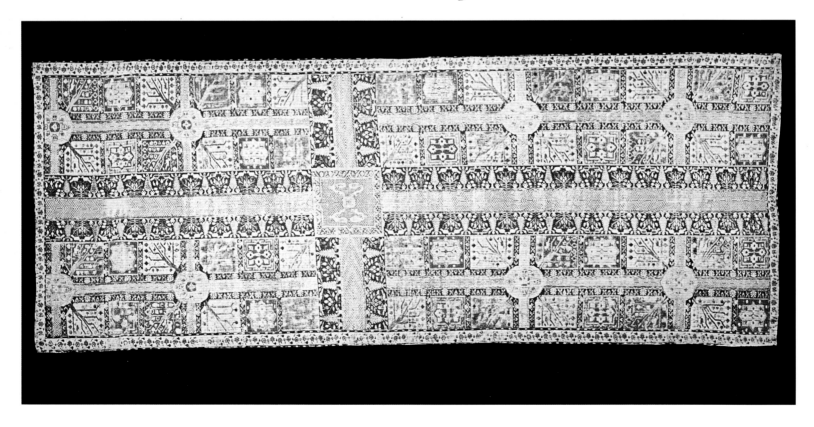

درختهای انار بهم بست کردا کرد حوض تمام سه برگ زار

Nature described, or nature re-evoked in a garden is not necessarily the uncontaminated and wild nature that existed before the arrival of man. Even if there are places and moments in Chinese gardens that conjure up the dismay felt when faced with scenes rich in incredibly strong contrasts, everything seems to have in some way been humanised and interiorised. It is memory that works this magic and the force of the imagination that makes certain forms comparable and equivalent despite their true size. In fact, in Chinese gardens nature is miniaturised or, perhaps we should say, it is partially miniaturised so that our imagination is obliged to follow the continuous scale "changes," to seek out and – mentally – reconcile what is said and what is suggested, what appears and what is imagined.

It is not surprising that Chinese poets and scholars once identified the garden with their symbolic space, a projection of their ego, protected from the miseries of life and the alternate fortunes of consensus.

Chinese men of letters, initially steeped in Taoist sensitivity and later in Buddhism, considered the garden as a place of evasion from the confines of their time, a place in which writing enabled them to converse freely with their predecessors, a place of waiting and a place to heal the wounds of wrongs suffered while preparing for justice to be rendered later by future generations. In this sense the garden, quite apart from its material consistency, incarnates the Tao itself, regarded as absolute totality, as the sum of the past and the future in a state of continuous metamorphosis.

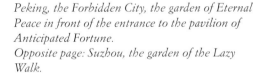

*Peking, the Forbidden City, the garden of Eternal Peace in front of the entrance to the pavilion of Anticipated Fortune.*
*Opposite page: Suzhou, the garden of the Lazy Walk.*

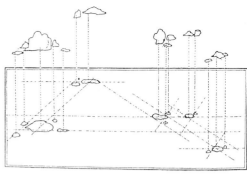

A graph showing the position of the stones in groups of five, three and two. The fifteen elements form an harmonious whole based on mathematical laws as well as on an extremely acute visual sensitivity: they take into account the multiple observation points situated along one of the longer sides of the rectangle. The garden is the famous Ryoan-ji temple in Kyoto, built during the 15th century.

Left from top: the zen garden in the Daitoku-ji temple in Kyoto. From an elevated position, the garden looks like an archipelago in the middle of a sea made of pebbles, raked in such a way as to imitate sea waves.
In this case, the interpenetration between the islands and the sea, obtained by mixing the grass and moss with pebbles, is a winning solution.
Another garden running alongside the monk's area in the Daitoku-ji temple, designed to be viewed from close quarters.
Opposite page: Sozhou, the garden in the Wood of the Lion.

"Without an old tree and a beautiful garden / I know not how the house can donate / the daily joys of life," wrote Ch'en Hao-tsu, the hermit of the flower, as he was wont to define himself.[11] By strategically arranging stones, some of which are quite large and are transported with great difficulty from far-off places, Chinese gardens are furnished with mountains, albeit miniature ones. Based on the complex and unusual shapes created by the erosive action of wind and water, the stones focus on two specific themes: the isolated peak and the pierced rock. Placing them in the garden satisfies man's need to reproduce the feelings that mountains and rocks inspire. It presumes that the viewer has a special perceptive ability requiring a sort of initiation or at least a gradual comprehension of the narrative logic implicit in its composition.

The most intense and passionate creation of a stone garden was the Ken-yu mountain garden built at the request of Emperor Hui-Tsung. To transport gigantic fragments of rocks from all over China, the Emperor not only dissipated a fortune, but neglected his duties to such an extent that his capital was sacked and the garden destroyed. He himself died in prison, a victim of his "stone mania." The Ken-yu monoliths were placed along the garden paths confronting the visitor with a series of surprise apparitions since the shape of the stones was very similar to certain places, animals, trees or persons.

In Japanese gardens, the role of stones is no less important. Normally, it avoids unusual and excessive complexities and gambles on their similarities with miniaturised mountains and islands. To build a garden presumes a complex mas-

*Yuan Ming Yuan, the Summer Palace near Peking in an 18th-century watercolour. Behind the main pavilion, along the entry axis, there is a group of vertical stones erected in order to draw closer and anticipate the circle of distant mountains beyond the artificial lake.*

ter plan handed down from generation to generation in writings that, in order to be understood, need a sort of initiation or careful apprenticeship based on verbal communication but even more importantly, on direct experience. All this is learnt through practice: nature should not only be visually built and observed, but drawings should continually be made of what is observed, thus involving body movements in this knowledge.[12]

There are many conventional archetypes on which the theory of the Japanese garden is based, reflecting the periods and reigns to which they belong. One of the most famous is the dry garden (*karesansui*). This garden involves a landscape with rivers and lakes, islands and land (with or without vegetation), hills and mountains of all shapes and sizes. All these elements are portrayed without the use of water, while gravel is used to imitate the surface of the waves. Sometimes in this landscape there is a *karetaki*, a waterfall created by mixing areas of gravel and stones. Normally surrounded by high walls, the dry garden is viewed from above, sitting on benches or steps. Only the people charged with its exacting maintenance are allowed to step on it.

The imagination of the viewer is stimulated by the lack of any and every realistic reference point, by this extreme abstraction, stressing the analogies more as metaphors than as figures. For instance, the most captivating element of the famous "zen" garden by Ryoan-ji in Kyoto is the void emphasised by the gravel and the particular elegance used to evoke the beach around the islands as well as the transparency of its water achieved by mixing gravel and moss. Other *topoi* of the Japanese garden are associated with the tea ceremony, such as the basin dug between the stones (*chozubachi*), the stone vessel for water (*tsu-kubai*) and the room of echoes that amplifies and softens the noise of the water that runs away after the basin has been used (*suikinkutsu*).

The subtle exchange that takes place between viewing nature as a living landscape, built without forcing its "naturalness," and viewing certain areas of the garden as the smaller or simplified, and therefore illusionary, images of other remote natural landscapes, is perhaps at its best when the two "scales" are not juxtaposed, but mix and overlap. This happens in some of the moss gardens, such as the one in the temple in Kyoto.

If it is true that western culture strongly supports the idea of the geometric garden as emended nature or as a mirror of the golden age, it is also true that it possesses a contradictory vein of aversion to artifice and of appreciation for irregularity, asymmetry and harmony, which cannot be reduced to numbers as well as a sense of non-compliance to rules. In the Roman world, literary sources do in fact hint at this counter-melody, and figurative sources often portray landscapes in which natural rhythms seem to dominate artificial ones, or at the very least blend them together. They offset the garden with sacred woods (called *luci* or *nemores*) such as those that characterised the seven hills of early Rome named according to their endemic tree species. In the sanctuary to Juno in the town of Gabii, the sacred oaks were planted in a strict orthogonal grid pattern, whereas

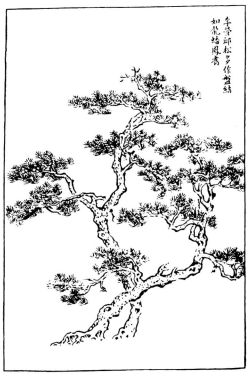

*Two engravings of a "cloud-shaped" stone and a twisted pine tree whose form incorporates the three vital forces: horizontal, vertical and diagonal.*

423

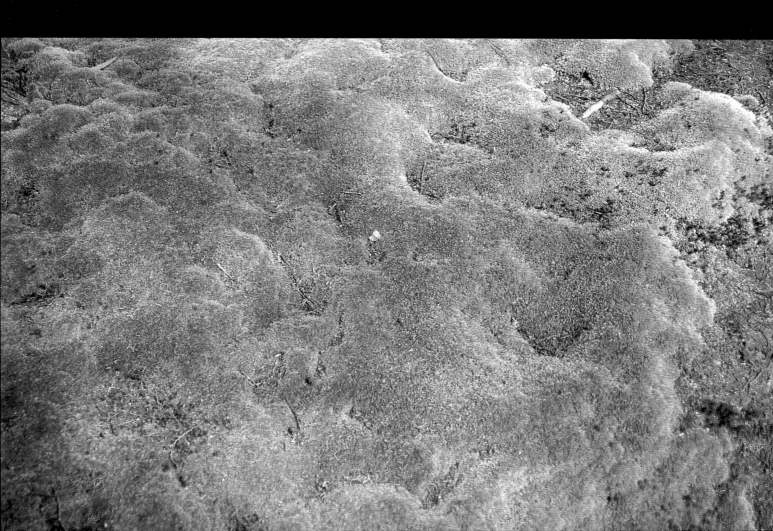

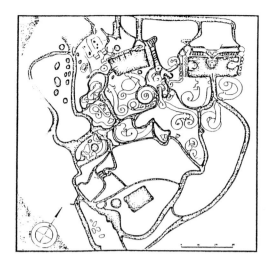

*Pre-Colombian aquatic labyrinth called "Lavapatas" (leg wash), in San Augustin (Colombia). The stream is diverted into a network of channels. On the islands created by this network are many representations of animals, including snakes, snails, lizards, salamanders and animals associated with fertility.*

*The garden of the House of Pleasure, in the grounds of Palazzo Farnese in Caprarola, Italy (Jacopo del Duca, Girolamo Rainaldi, 1584-1625).*

in Nemi, as in the temple of Zeus in Dodona, only one tree grew in the sacred enclosure, a tree that played a decisive role in the succession of the *rex nemorensis*.

Pliny the Younger when describing his villa in Tuscany speaks of a garden that is very similar to the model later called "Italian garden": "There is a garden in front of the portico. The garden is divided up by hedges made of box tree, cut variously. On a slope further down there is a lawn where the box tree has been shaped to look like animals facing one another. Even further down the flat land is covered in soft, and I would venture to say, perfumed acanthus. It is surrounded by a small path lined with low shrubs, each pruned differently. From this point an avenue begins, along which one can stroll in one's litter. The circular avenue runs around multiform box tree plants and miniature trees, pruned to keep them that way."[13]

However, it seems reasonable to believe that inside Villa Laurentina there were areas in which the vegetation took the form of a wood where it was possible to walk in the shade. The fact that the Romans did not really appreciate excessive rigidity seems to seep from between the lines of an epigram by Martial:

Our friend Faustinus's Baian farm, Bassus,
does not occupy an ungrateful expanse
of broad land, laid out with useless myrtle groves,
sterile plane-trees, and clipped box-rows,
but rejoices in a real unsophisticated country scene.[14]

This opposition between geometric garden and parkland was solved during the Renaissance and Baroque period by having the two types coexist, but the argument was re-ignited by the Anglo-Saxon controversy over what they considered to be the intransigent artificial traits of Italian and French gardens.[15] Into this controversy crept ideological and political considerations, expressed by the poet James Thomson who wrote about the gardens in Versailles as follows:

Detested forms that on the mind impress
Corrupt, confound and barbarize an age...

In a much less argumentative fashion, Joseph Addison proclaimed a poetics of the natural garden that became the cornerstone of the contribution that English culture donated to Europe during the 18th century. In his essay Addison maintains that there is more courage and excellence in the negligently unfinished shapes of nature than in the brush strokes and embellishments of art. Addison believes that even the beauty of a garden or a building is confined to a narrow space while our imagination is boundless and requires something more to be satisfied. Lost in vast rolling landscapes, the eye roams undisturbed and feeds on an unending illuminated variety of images. This is the reason, continues Addison, why poets are always in love with country life in which nature appears in all its glory, clothed in all those visions which delight and excite the imagination. He af-

*The entrance to the nuptial garden of the silk bird, one of the bowerbirds that live in Australia and New Zealand. Sydney, botanical gardens.*

*Garden in Calcata, Italy (Paolo Portoghesi, Giovanna Massobrio 1993).*

*Detail of the fountain of the torches in the villa belonging to Cardinal Gambara (later Villa Lante) in Bagnaia (Italy).*

firms that many of these wild visions are more pleasing than any other landscape and that mankind considers the creations of nature, many of which look like works of art, much more interesting. In this case, Addison maintains that our pleasure has a double root, the delight of looking at objects and their similarity with other objects. This is why we love looking at a beautiful landscape of fields and pastures, woods and rivers, at the haphazard panorama of trees, clouds and towns that may be discerned in the veins of marble, in the peculiar erosion of rocks and grottoes and, in a single word, in what we would call a work of chance and not in any object whose variety and regularity appears to stem from a well-thought-out project.[16]

Perhaps the English garden should not have been compared to everything French culture had produced. In the 17th century, for instance, in his *Bosquet de Louvenciennes* in Marly, Le Notre had juxtaposed one of his typical geometric gardens with an informal park very similar to the landscape designs of the century that was to follow. However, its novelty lay in his *a priori* refusal of the geometric order and the juxtaposition of orderly disorder. His idea was to stop using symbolism, the concept of paradise on earth or of happy isles to imitate nature and instead use the painted landscapes that had shaped the taste and sensibilities of a whole generation.

For two centuries, the efforts involved in being inspired by nature gave rise to endless disputes and a sort of escalation towards "naturalness." Landscaped

gardens, still judged to be very artificial, were set against the picturesque garden championed by Claudius Loudon. Prince Pükler-Muskau, a German aristocrat and friend of Heine, wrote a treatise full of practical common sense that can be considered the most convincing conclusion of this logomachy. Moreover, it also cites all the possible alternatives to avoid planting trees in an unnatural and affected way.[17]

During the rise and fall of the modern movement, the garden has always swung between maximum abstraction (reducing gardens to abstract paintings created with natural materials in the style of Burle-Marx, or wooden or cement trees by Balla and Mallet-Stevens) and the exaltation of wild nature as a background to enhance the geometrical purity of architecture through contrast (Le Corbusier, Aalto).

The hanging vegetation that like cascading liquid flows over the projecting volumes of Frank Lloyd Wright's buildings almost as if oozing vital nourishment, stages an architecture that surrenders to nature, not like ruins that speak of death, but like an element absorbing and transmitting the *élan vital* that wells up from the earth.

*Design of a garden in Vienna (F. Lebisch), from* Moderne Bauformen, *1908, p. 403.*

[1] cf., M. Schneider, *Il significato della musica*, Rusconi, Milan 1970, p. 93.

[2] cf., E.B. Moynihan, *Paradise as a Garden*, Scholar Press, London 1980. For Sumerian texts cf., S.N. Kramer, *Rom the Tablets of Sumer*, Indian Hills, Colorado 1956, p. 172.

[3] cf., E. Braschi, *Il popolo del Grande Spirito*, Mursia, Milan 1986, p. 270.

[4] cf., V. Lanternari, *Movimenti religiosi di libertà e di salvezza dei popoli oppressi*, Feltrinelli, Milan 1970.

[5] cf., A. Badawy, *A History of Egyptian Architecture*, University of California Press, Berkeley 1996, p. 235.

[6] cf., H. Capel, *La fisica sagrada*, Ediciones del Serbal, Barcelona 1985. This important research compares optimistic concepts of nature and in Chapters 3-6 examines the theory of progressive and relentless deterioration of the earth's surface.

[7] cf., Hesiod, *The Works and Days*, University of Michigan Press, 1959.

[8] cf., Pindar, *Odi*, Rizzoli, Milan 1974.

[9] cf., J. Lehrman, *Earthly Paradise*, Thames and Hudson, London 1980; E.B. Moynihan, *op.cit.*

[10] M. Keswick, *The Chinese Garden*, Rizzoli, New York 1978; P & S. Rambach, *Jardins de longevité*, Skira, Paris 1987.

[11] cf., M. Keswick, *op.cit.*; C. Chao-Kong, W. Blaser, *Architecture de Chine*, Delcourt, Lausanne 1988.

[12] I. Yoshikawa, *Elements of Japanese Garden*, Graphic-sha Publishing Co. Ltd., Tokyo 1990; D.A. Slawson, *Secret Teachings in the Art of Japanese Garden*, Kodanshe, Tokyo 1991.

[13] Pliny the Younger, *Lettere ai familiari*, Rizzoli, Milan 1986.

[14] Martial, *The Epigrams*, George Bell & Sons, London 1897.

[15] cf., *De Folie en Folies*, introduction by François Cruze, text and images by M. Saudlan and S. Saudan-Skira, La Bibliotèque des Arts, Geneva 1987.

[16] J. Addison, in *The Spectator*, London, June-July 1712, ns. 411-412.

[17] cf., H. Fürst von Pükler-Muskau, *Giardino e paesaggio*, Rizzoli, Milan 1984; W. Robinson, *Il giardino naturale*, Muzzio, Padua 1990.

# Growth and Metamorphosis

*In the acacia thicket a shiver ran
harshly twisting the branches.
Churning in the calm sea, livid
with delight, were currents earlier rebels.*

*On the water all wefts and tracks
struck the flood gust,
and the quivering heap was embedded
with conchs, countless sweet conchs.
It was the sea like those exalted
if spoken of a spirit persuasive of escape;
but mutilated the breath, soon every wrinkle
vanished
the plant of untouched asphalt returned.*

*Nature are these unexpressed questions
no-one answers:
from mountain tops to earthly fissures,
listen, if you can, to the spreading clamour.
And finally here perhaps destiny,
on paper where restless numbers gather
syllables; and the earth juices which at times
understand, is supreme goodness, for those.*

Eugenio Montale

In 1827 Goethe created a discipline he himself defined as morphology to study the forms of living organisms and the relationship between growth and form. Goethe maintained that all plants descended from an *Urpflänze*, a primitive plant with an axial structure (the stalk and trunk) and lateral appendices (the leaves). He considered the growth of this primitive plant as a reiteration of sequential parts during which the inevitable metamorphosis of the leaf culminated in the creation of a flower.[1]

Even if Goethe's theory was criticised as being "formalist" because it did not highlight the functional aspects of plant structure, it was to constitute the basis of *Naturphilosophie* and greatly influence modern biology. Nevertheless, in the field of morphology, Goethe tented to carry out sectorial studies rather than systematic research.

It is curious to note that the coeval images of the *Urpflänze* give the impression that Goethe had tried to find in nature a sort of stylistic coherence, a programmed search for unity in complexity very similar to the compositional process of an artist. The petals that act as leaves and the obedience of the parts to an abstract rule unconsciously repropose the myth of nature imitating art described by Ovid.[2]

At first the idea of growth, so typical of biology, seems a far cry from a discipline like architecture that deals with objects made of inert material that can degenerate but certainly not grow in a literal sense. However, it is also true that architecture is not merely a mass of connected objects, but a sort of language; it inhabits manmade buildings as well as our memory and minds in its immaterial form. It aspires to participate in the organic form of living beings declared by D'Arcy Thompson always to be a "function of time," so that growth and metamorphosis be considered "events in time and space."

What is defined elsewhere as the "hidden face of architecture"[3] is no less important than the visible face that forms the "exact and magnificent game of volumes in the light" as defined by Le Corbusier. When architecture is merely thought and language it can temporally grow and materialise in our minds and memory so that once freed from our minds and materialised in concrete objects, it grows and reproduces as a series of experiences, ideas, designs and types that spread out and change, like plants born from the union of male and female principles joined by proximity, insects and the wind. As a design project, architecture is created by a mental process that draws on memory, the perception of the environment and construction materials.

It could be said that the concept of house, for example, is born from a centre, a privileged space, "the heart of the house," as Leon Battista Alberti defines it in his treatise.[4] In primitive homes, as in Wright's Prairie Houses, this centre is the hearth, enveloped by a protective involucre around which the less important rooms cluster. In religious buildings, the centre may be the statue of the god, the sacrificial altar or in ancient times, the sacrificial act itself. In monotheistic religions, the *ecclesia* as a community of rites and prayer is at the heart of the configuration of sacred space regarded as an involucre. So, since in the Christian church the old liturgy obliged the faithful to move in procession, the idea of advancing forward influenced the metamorphosis of Roman basilicas and their endless interpretations.

In central buildings, the architectural structure is often doubled and the parallel growth of the two parts produces the phenomenon of concrescence. In fact, between the development and articulation of the parts (the cupola and the canopy, the transept and the lantern) it is possible for a shift to occur, at times even a rotation, a movement of the axis that brings with it a process of transference, or rotation, often caused by a need for orientation. This is the case of the Parliament in Dhaka by Louis Kahn, where in order to face Mecca the mosque is rotated with respect to the primary axes of the building. On the other hand, symbolic requirements often dictate the rotation of medieval churches in which the top part of the cross is inclined, like the head of Christ on the cross. Francesco di Giorgio Martini uses this rotation for his fortress in Sassocorvaro, shaped like a turtle with its head (a tower) out of line with the axis.

One aspect of biological growth is expressed in dynamic forms that involve a temporal process. The temporisation of spatial models is manifest in the sequence of sunflower seeds or the scales of pine cones covering its seeds. Observed from above, the mass of sunflower seeds seen on a plane reveals a sort of torsion highlighted by the surrounding spirals. The intersecting spirals rotate in two directions that generally conform to the two adjacent numbers in the series 1, 1, 2, 3, 5, 8, 13, 21..., the so-called Fibonacci series in which each number is equal to the sum of the previous two.[5]

In the apical bud of plants, in which the embryos of leaves develop, the points where the leaves are attached are transversally crossed by a helix. Their geometric centres are supported by two spirals that rotate in opposite directions, as established by the Fibonacci series. This geometric leaf arrangement is called phyllotaxis and the use of computers has contributed enormously to the mathematical studies of this growth model.

In 1968 Astrid Lindenmayer fine-tuned the so-called L-system used to study the development of simple multicellular organisms. Today this system enables complex plant organisms to be studied and makes it possible to realistically simulate any plant species.

In 1990 Przemyslaw Prusinkiewicz posthumously published Lindenmayer's book, *The Algorithmic Beauty of Plants*, illustrating extremely interesting models of growth and metamorphosis that have enormous potential in the field of design. Apart from the studies on ramified patterns and phyllotaxis, Ned Greene's simulation of the growth of a rambler on a centrally-planned wooden structure should be mentioned here.[6]

In the history of architecture, the spiral and the helix, so congenial to the structure of stairs, have been used in countless decorations, from the engraved blocks in the temples of Malta to the Ionic capitals and volutes typical of the plastic repertoire of the Baroque. They have also been used in more abstract

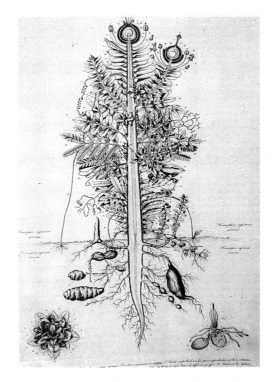

The Urpflänze, *the first plant according to Goethe's theories. For Goethe, every element of a plant's structure came from successive transformations of the leaf.*

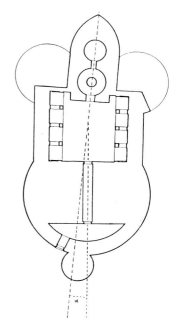

*Plan of the fortress of Sassocorvaro (Italy), highlighting the rotation of the biconvex tower and smaller tower.*

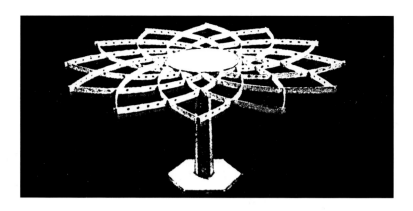

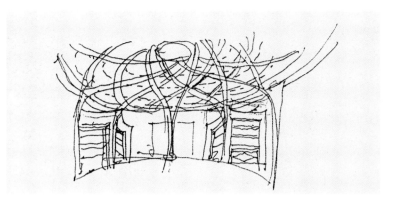

The sunflower is a typical example of geometric growth processes. The seed pattern follows the Fibonacci series involving a series of numbers; each number is equal to the sum of the two preceding ones.

Above from left: study of a mushroom column in the Bionic Laboratory of the University of Moscow; Paolo Portoghesi, drawing for a library in laminated wood, Rome, 1987.

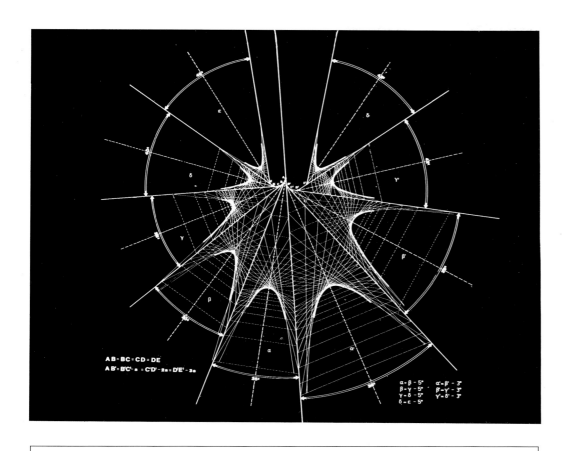

AB = BC = CD = DE
AB' = B'C'- a = C'D'-2a = D'E'-3a

α - β - 5°     α'- β' - 3°
β - γ - 5°     β'- γ' - 3°
γ - δ - 5°     γ'- δ' - 3°
δ - ε - 5°

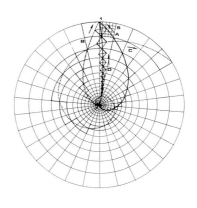

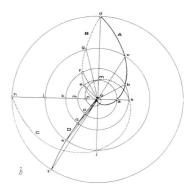

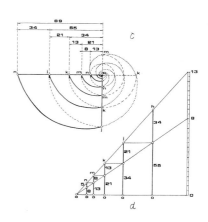

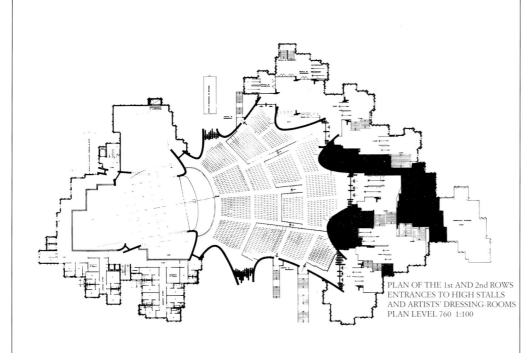

PLAN OF THE 1st AND 2nd ROWS
ENTRANCES TO HIGH STALLS
AND ARTISTS' DRESSING-ROOMS
PLAN LEVEL 760  1:100

*Left: geometric drawing and plan of the theatre in Cagliari, Italy (P. Portoghesi, with P. Marconi, V. Gigliotti, N. Zedda, 1966). The drawing illustrates the genesis of the shape used for the hall with nine hyperbolas whose asymptotes have angles that increase from the stage towards the back of the hall. The area housing the other rooms obeys a modular law producing simple ratios. Above: four graphs illustrating the sunflower seed pattern. The rule is a Fibonacci series (in which each number is equal to the sum of the two preceding ones). This series proposes a ratio very similar to the golden rule.*

*Enlarged photograph of a tree trunk showing its concentric rings. Each ring corresponds to a year's growth.*

forms in the regulatory geometric outlines that govern planimetric designs and determine the relationships and proportions between architectural parts.

I too have experimented in this field, using in my designs helicoidal models and structures similar to those of leaves. The structures I used were the symmetrical pattern of the sycamore and the extremely asymmetric pattern of the elm and the begonia.

While in architecture the concept of growth focuses mainly on the design process and the historical development of forms, in cities this similarity with the organism focuses on its synchronous image in which the diachronic process of growth is impressed and frozen, legible in diachrony. In fact, the original architectural unit rarely grows over time (in this case the terms wings, arms, avant-corps, raised floor, immediately conjure up an organic concept), but town planning, instead, studies and programs urban growth and, over the centuries, has developed models similar to those of human beings. Take for example the expanding "amoeba" model of urban growth or the consecutive ring model. This phenomenon is very similar to what botanists call secondary growth (for example, the progressive thickening of a tree trunk). Dendrochronologists, the scientists who carry out historical studies based on the growth rings of trees, are able to tally samples of living and dead wood. This enables them to put together a continuous series of rings that starts roughly 8200 years ago (the oldest living specimen of *Pinus longeva* is almost 5000 years old). This research has made it possible to calculate changes in the earth's weather, in particular in the region of the White Mountains in California.[7]

Whoever studies the history of cities will recognise the similarities between the growth of the urban nucleus and the growth of a tree trunk. Even linear and radial growth, so frequent in the history of cities, has a phytological counterpart in the logic that governs primary growth. I will attempt to illustrate this process so that the reader is able to recognise the infinite analogies and differences that exist in an "area of the city," a road with houses and public buildings, serviced by systems and vehicles that supply the houses with water and food, a road with forks and crossroads that, to a greater or lesser extent, either slow down or accelerate these growth processes.

Unlike animals who move about, and can therefore search for what they need to survive, plants have to establish an alliance with their earthly home, an alliance that will provide them with the constant supply of light, water and mineral salts they need to grow. The role of the roots is to gather water, while the leaves are assigned the process of photosynthesis that exploits a chemical reaction to transform the bright solar energy captured by the leaves into chemical energy.[8]

A continuous stream of water penetrates the root hairs, peripheral ramifications of the roots, and flows along the roots and up the stem until it reaches the leaves. The leaves are covered in small mouths (the stomas) which open and close as necessary to absorb carbon dioxide and oxygen. In Goethe's *Urpflanze*, the leaf was considered the primary element from which the stem and the roots were created through differentiation. Nowadays, biologists attribute this role to the stem that carries water and nourishment through its two vascular systems: the

A boat used by native inhabitants on Lake Titicaca (Peru).
Left: leaves often develop from a cuspidate nucleus containing a lamina that twists around itself. The leaves of a Philodendron Pertusum (Monstera deliciosa) *and of a* Nelumbo nucifera *stretching outwards in the sun to carry out their chlorophyllous function to the full.*

*The glass and crystal scenery created for the play*
**Festa a corte** *held in Mantua, Piazza Sordello, in*
*1988 (P. Portoghesi with M. Checchi,*
*P. Bernitsa).*

*The inflorescence of a mullein, also called "king's chandelier."*

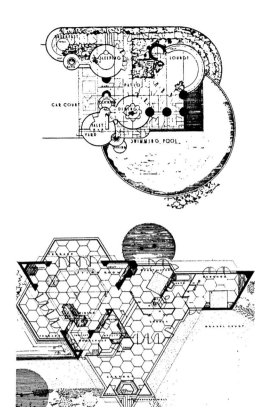

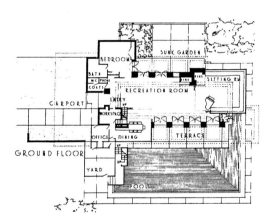

*The memorial garden in the cemetery in Lund, Sweden (Sigurd Lewerentz) and, above, three plans of houses by Frank Lloyd Wright: the 1938 Life House; the Ralph Jester House built in the same year; the 1941 Vigo Sundt House. The morphology of the houses is very different, yet they all have the same distribution plan that can be portrayed using a mathematical graph.*

*xylem* for water and the *phloem* to distribute the substances produced by the leaves to the whole plant.[9]

The growth of the plant depends on the work of certain small tissue areas that always remain in an embryonic state. These areas dedicated to growth are concentrated in what are called meristems, clustered mainly at the tips of stems and roots. On the one hand, the plant uses these courageous hunters to move towards the light and the sky and, on the other, towards darkness and the bowels of the earth. This linear dilation in two directions (that could be defined as "foundation" and "elevation," two words taken from the language of construction), is one of the most eloquent symbols of life. The vascular system in the stem is divided into nodes and internodes. The node is the part where one or more leaves are attached. The gems normally form at the axils where the leaves branch out from the stem: another strategic position of the meristems.

Far from imprisoning the reader's imagination by denying him the joy of discovering the Baudelaire-type "correspondences" between urban growth, the technical systems involved in the functioning of a building, its windows and stairs, and the primary growth of the plant world, the illustrations presented in this Chapter and an attentive study of this explanation should be sufficient to stimulate free-ranging analogical thought. Suffice it here to include another catalyst of metaphors and analogies: Valerio Magrelli's poetic description of the house, a house that is both a microcosm and a small city:

Imagine
the shape of a house
is its religion
and thus needs
liturgical images.
As though the whole habitation
lived within
a single belief
being only the decor.

[...]
In one room
the fountain
where water
flows forever.
Cloistered source
cold dwelling-place
lacustrine
northern seat.

Never had pantry
a better name.

*Leonardo da Vinci, design of a centrally-planned church based on self-similarity. The central nucleus is surrounded by eight peripheral ones with five projecting niches similar in shape.*
*Left: a* Mammillaria *with the same growth laws as Leonardo's building.*

A Stenocereus *photographed in the gardens of the Perego family in Sanremo (Italy).*

*Opposite page, from top to bottom: a termitary in Australia and a dirt earth mosque in Bourkina Faso; rocky peaks in Monument Valley; the design of the chapel of Santa Coloma in Park Güell near Barcelona (Antoni Gaudí, 1898-1914).*

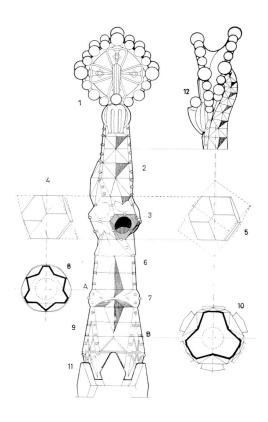

*The top of a cusp in the church of the Sagrada Familia in Barcelona (Antoni Gaudí, 1891-1926).*

Heart of food placed
in the heart of the house
like the still engine
of cosmologies.
Tabernacle place
of food and secrecy.

The kitchen full of objects
could easily seem a wood.
Every plant in its place
rises where planted
with infinite patience rests.
Think of things
the metallic
flora of cutlery.

Fluorescent lamp
the light that in the country
precedes the storm
and heralds it.
Afternoon light
abolishing morning
establishing day in rotation
steady on the wire like a jumper.

If waiting could
be transfigured
it would resemble a chair.
A town waiting
to be inhabited
the house's only animal.

[...]
Water waiting in pipes
still like a beast in its lair.
The house within the house
is this house of water.
All around near and still
suspended storm.[10]

Metamorphosis, illustrated by D'Arcy Thompson[11] in the chapter of his book dedicated to biological morphology, is just as inspirational as the key to growth. The topological relationship or relationship of regular deformation that links

442

various animal species, especially fish, leaves and the osteological structures of vertebrates, is the same relationship that groups buildings or parts of buildings into typological, stylistic and geographical families. If architectural morphology had been more advanced it would never have neglected a field of comparative study that the advent of computers has made so much easier.

Metamorphosis in architecture is intentionally cited when comparisons are made between similar forms.; for example, when studying buildings and decorations with different versions of the same image: columns that become figures, tympanums that break, inflect or double, always inspiring in the viewer the archetype and its transformation. Excellent examples include the herma and the caryatid, figures caught at the fleeting moment of transformation (otherwise why is there a capital on the head of the caryatids?); the ovolo of classical cornices transformed into cherubims in a plate by Villalpando showing the temple of Jerusalem in Ezekiel's prophecy;[12] the cornice of Borromini's lantern in Sant'Ivo alla Sapienza and the two embracing doors designed by Michelangelo for the inner door of the reading room of the Biblioteca Laurenziana in Florence.

Even the law of the superposition of orders is a metaphoric rule. When it is interpreted vertically, it bears witness to a stylistic variation while still allowing the relative law of superposition to remain. Whatever the order, this law identifies the more generalised coded elements: the base, the shaft, the capital, the trabeation. In the case of Bramante's stairway in the Belvedere courtyard of the Vatican, it is possible to speak of an "ongoing metamorphosis" in which the Tuscan columns gradually and uninterruptedly become Doric, Ionic, Corinthian and composite. Only if seen from below does metamorphosis seem to coincide with traditional superposition, leading the viewer to believe that discontinuity and obedience to the rules are reconciled. Instead they have merely been avoided or outwitted by a precocious example of architectural *agudeza*.[13]

*Two columns transformed into caryatids and telamones. A square in Poggioreale near Trapani Italy (P. Portoghesi with S. Lonardo, 1987).*

[1] O. Krätz, *Goethe und die Naturwissenschaften*, Callwey, Munich 1992, pp. 92-105 and A. Bettex, *La filosofia della natura*, Longanesi, Milan 1965, pp. 146-197.

[2] cf., Ovid, *Metamorphosis*, III, V, 157.

[3] cf., G. Ciucci (ed.), *L'architettura italiana oggi*, Laterza, Rome-Bari 1989, p. 182.

[4] L.B. Alberti, *L'architettura*, Il Polifilo, Milan 1966.

[5] cf., W. D'Arcy Thompson, *On Growth and Form* (1917), Cambridge University Press, Cambridge 1961; H. Weyl, *La simmetria*, Feltrinelli, Milan 1962 (*Symmetry*, Princeton University Press, Princeton 1952); P.S. Stevens, *Patterns in Nature*, Brown, New York, 1977; A.D. Bell, *La forma delle piante*, Zanichelli, Bologna 1993 (*Plant form*, Oxford-New York 1991) A. Lima-de-Faria, *Evolution without Selection*, Elsevier, Amsterdam 1986, pp. 173-174; R. Lawlor, *Sacred Geometry*, Thames and Hudson, London 1982; P. Prusinkiewicz, A. Lin-

denmayer, *The Algorithmic Beauty of Plants*, Springer, Berlin 1990.

[6] cf., N. Greene, "Voxel Space Entomata: Modelling with Stochastic Growth Processes in Voxel Space, Proceedings of Siggraph '89," in *Computer Graphics*, August 1989, pp. 175-184.

[7] cf., E. Stresburger, *Trattato di Botanica*, edited by A. Pirola, Delfino, Rome 1991, p. 166.

[8] *Ibid.*, p. 124.

[9] cf., O. Krätz, *op.cit.*, p. 204 ff.

[10] cf., V. Magrelli, "La forma della casa," in *Eupalino*, no. 2, Spring 1984, pp. 14-15.

[11] cf., W. D'Arcy Thompson, *op.cit*.

[12] cf., J.B. Villalpando, *In Ezechielem explanationes*, Rome 1596.

[13] cf., P. Portoghesi, *Bernardo Vittone*, Edizioni dell'Elefante, Rome 1966, pp. 14-17.

# Architectural Decoration

*"Such as the life is, so is the form." Can the Ethiopian change his skin or the leopard change his spots? Or the turtle be without the pattern of his shell? Expression of the constitution of nature is emphasized, unified, clarified, identified by what we call Ornament? True architectural form has innate significance of character expressed and enhanced by the creative architect's organic uses of organic ornament. As melody is in music ornament is in architecture revelation of the poetic principle, with character and significance. Ornament is as natural to architecture of the genus Man as the turtle's shell is to the genus Turtle. Inevitable as plumage to the bird: natural as the form of any seashell; appropriate as scales of the fish or leaves of the tree or the blossom of a blooming plant.*
*So every living thing bears innate witness to the need for love, expressing the poetic principle by what we call "pattern": visible in all organism. Creation as eye-music is no less expressive than ear-music because it too is heart-music, appealing too, to human life at the very core. Both melody and ornament reach us by way of the soul of all Creation and as we are made we respond.*

Frank Lloyd Wright

"In their rich and very precise language the Greeks use the same word to describe three different things: the ornaments we use as jewellery, the objects we cherish and the highest degree of conformity to the laws of nature and cosmic order." Gottfried Semper once opened a conference[1] with this sentence in which he ironically called the women present "natural past-masters" well versed from birth in the art of making themselves as impressive and attractive as possible by wearing ornaments.

Semper's theory is illustrated analytically in his book, *Der Stil*. He states that cosmetic art lies at the origin of architectural decoration. It is an art achieved through the tattoos, clothes or objects created to embellish the various parts of our bodies.

The fact that the decorative repertoire of architecture was plucked from the world of nature and that the various techniques greatly influenced primitive man are two cornerstones of Semper's theory. He believed that nature is *die grosse Urbildnerin*, the great shaper and muse of art since an artist "can only create a form by following the teachings of nature." But what inspires and conditions artistic production is not so much "natural" inspiration, as the ability to listen to the laws of nature and meekly surrender to them.

In his treatise[2] Vitruvius spoke about *homines imitabili docilique natura*, and Semper clarifies: "Like nature that has its own evolutionary history in which old themes resurface in each new creation, art too has just a few regular forms and types that descend from long lost traditions. These infinitely variable themes and types constantly reappear and, like nature, have their own history." This art-nature analogy is not merely the product of a passive relationship, but ensues from the naturalness of the human mind that obeys laws common to nature itself and is part of the process of creation and evolution. Semper was a truly classical scholar, and he believed that these few *Grundformen* (fundamental forms) guaranteed a creative method not based on individualistic originality, but on creative repetition which, at the same time, also respected a model and the fact it could be improved: "The new is so tied to the old but is not a copy; it is freed from the influence of empty fashion."[3]

The privileged role Semper assigned to the techniques exploited to compile a comprehensive classification of the motifs used in architectural decoration led him to write a complicated and confused presentation. However, it also allowed him to clarify the way in which the various fields are connected (textile art, ceramics, metallurgy, woodwork, stone cutting and wall painting) and the way in which decoration develops in the framework of this endless and amazing interaction. When forty years later Alios Riegl studied these problems from a totally different viewpoint, privileging the independence of artistic creation based on a "desire for art" (*Kunstwollen*), he was obliged to acknowledge the importance of Semper's analytical work and the far-reaching vision which often led Semper to admit that his insufficient technical motivations did not satisfactorily explain the development of decorative art.

*Greek frieze with palmettes, volutes, and birds.*
*Real acanthus leaves.*

*The genesis of the Corinthian capital according to Vitruvius.*

*A Corinthian capital from the monument to Lisicrate in Athens.*

Riegl believed that decoration was above all the expression of the artistic intentions of populations or ethnic groups that in turn walk the stage of history, rather than just the single individual. Compared to these purely aesthetic goals, symbolic and technological motivations are almost like chains that shackle the freedom of expression and ongoing development of a certain form. Indeed, naturalistic inspiration became a limitation and obligation that Riegl considered disparagingly, ironically commenting on the anecdote about Callimachus that Vitruvius introduced into his treatise.[4]

Totally useless as an explanation for the development of Greek art, Riegl, however, believed that the imitation of plant forms was important in Egyptian art since it fulfilled symbolic and religious functions. In fact, both the decorative lotus motif and the shape of columns were emblems of the Egyptian cult of the sun. Riegl also attributed to the shape of Egyptian flowers, the "papyrus" and the "honeysuckle" patterns created by stylising to the point of exaggeration the sepals and petals. For Riegl, even the rosette was nothing more than the aerial interpretation of the lotus flower, a viewpoint underlining its apparent analogy with the radiant sun and therefore its symbolic and religious essence. Compared to Semper's theory, the importance attributed to the observation of nature is strongly reappraised. For the Viennese historian, recourse to nature merely involved the initial impulse upon which a vast repertoire of forms are based and develop independently, in line with an abstraction that affiliates geometry, rhythms, symbols and metaphors in a process that moves further and further away from nature. Riegl's thesis regarding the genesis of the Corinthian capital is of particular interest here. Riegl maintains: "All that narrative seems like a fairy tale – admittedly a fairy tale full of grace – so I don't think there are any scholars who would seriously admit it corresponds to reality... no-one that I know of has yet dared to doubt that the characteristic plant motif of the trimmings around the Corinthian capital are anything but an imitation of the *Acanthus spinosa*, as stated by Vitruvius. The unfortunate result of all this is that certain texts illustrating the already unclear history of the initial development of the acanthus are completely lacking."[5]

Even if he does not tackle the problem philologically, Riegl does try to demonstrate that the pattern similar to acanthus leaves that appears in Greek art is not a direct imitation of the natural model, but a "simple process of the artistic and historical development of the ornate." He believes that "in the beginning there was the Egyptian honeysuckle with its sheaves of leaves growing in a radial pattern. The development of this motif, which reached its zenith in the frieze of the Ionic capital of the Erechtheum, would have led to an abstract leaf model in which the vertical elements of the sheaves are not detached like the honeysuckle leaves, but united at the base and fan-shaped at the top. The main difference between these leaves and those of the *Acanthus spinosa* is that instead of a sheaf grouping the nervations at the base, there is a central nervation from which the others branch out."

Regarding the moral of his "story," Riegl wrote: "Strangely enough, it has not crossed anyone's mind how improbable it is that the first weed discovered by chance be elevated to the rank of artistic inspiration." This is a so-called "fairy tale" because, even if it were based on the *Kunstwollen* (so important in the field of art history), Riegl's theory was not, and could not, be considered a confirmation. It is merely a series of considerations steered towards a hurried conclusion to free the field from other partial truths considered pure and simple prejudices. But it was not easy to put to rest the debate over the acanthus. Generalised contributions include those by Wörringer, Gombrich and recently the little book written by G. Hersey on the lost meaning of form in classical architecture.[6]

In his book published in 1908, Wörringer subscribes to Riegl's critique of Vitruvius and underlines not only his artistic aspirations, but also the dual concept of empathy-abstraction examined in his studies.[7] Writing about the book, *De Architectura*, Wörringer says: "The only thing this superficial interpretation proves is that now, as in the days of Vitruvius, there is no sensitivity for the truly productive processes of a creative and artistic spirit. Banal and contrived attempts are made to explain and unravel the mystery of artistic creation in Greece." Despite this severe reprimand, Wörringer unwittingly contributes to the reappraisal of Vitruvius' story when he states that, inspired by plant patterns, man does not directly transfer the image of the plant organism, but its "structural law." So, when Callimachus observed the leaves curled around the urn-basket of the "girl from Corinth," he could well have used this to re-elaborate the concept of the "weed" he discovered and then turn it into a law. It is of no consequence – I would like to add – that the law did not mechanically correspond to the structure of the acanthus leaf since this law is present in other leaves (for example, the colewort and in particular the *Brassica campestris pekinensis*) and can be attributed to the acanthus if the foliage is viewed from above. No less important, from the point of view of sculptural representation, is the comparison with certain types of *Cereus*, a succulent plant with extraordinary plastic qualities.

Returning to the subject in 1979, Gombrich attributes war honours to Vitruvius, calls his story "moving" and ironically highlights the captiousness of Riegl's exposition.[8] Riegl, on the other hand, carefully selects the Corinthian capitals he includes in his dissertation on the basis of his declared objective, namely the glorification of the "continuity" of development inherent in decorative motifs and the fact that they change when tastes change.

The reason for such a long methodological digression on the theme of architectural decoration is to underline a pluralistic and open-minded approach to the problem, much like Gombrich's. To explain the forms and role of architectural decoration a one-sided attitude is not enough. It would be useless to assert the decisive role of naturalistic "inspiration" (obviously not to be confused with imitation) if this aspect of morphology were not considered to-

*The leaves of a Peking cabbage. Note the obvious similarities with the acanthus as depicted in Corinthian capitals.*

Cactus browningia, Hertlingiana monstruosa.

*Friezes on* Cucuteni *vases with snake and egg motifs. The serpentine pattern and the wave pattern unite in the undulated frieze (Romania, 4th millennium B.C.).*

*Ornate decoration on the handle of a Greek amphora.*

gether with others. These other aspects include morphology's symbolic and religious meaning, the pattern's relatively independent continuous development and the all-important structural imitation filtered by geometry and mathematics. From this point of view, even if Vitruvius' story were not the chronicle of an actual event, it still exudes great humanity because it stresses a series of elements that have no recognisable hierarchy: empathy, abstraction, narrative, direct and structural imitation, the description of feelings, the compositional requirements activated through repetition and different types of symmetry.

Academic classification divides the ornate into two large families: geometric decoration and biomorphic and naturalistic decoration. This classification has no meaning when studying the origins of patterns, later defined as geometric or biomorphic, since it is easy to forget that geometry involves measuring the earth and for centuries the earth was considered a living being. This concept has surfaced again recently in the holistic outlook of many ecologists, particularly in the inspirational proposals of Jim Lovelock,[9] later elaborated by Rupert Sheldrake.[10]

According to research carried out by anthropologists who have gathered an enormous amount of convergent data, it is not the geometric "taste" of primitive man that is at the basis of decoration, but an explicit desire for signs and symbols. In particular, Marija Gimbutas' book, dedicated to the cult of the mother goddess in Neolithic Europe, rigorously illustrates the theory according to which the geometrical forms used for many thousands of years in Europe, are simply signs that refer to a religious cult based on natural elements.[11]

This fascinating book illustrates certain basic archetypes of architectural decoration used in ceramics and metal objects. A "zigzag" pattern, for example, was found on a tool used 40,000 years ago by Neanderthal man. More recently, it was one of the evocative signs of femininity and water in the cult of the earth mother. An important endemic pattern used by this cult was the "pubic" triangle, whose connotation – again derided by Wörringer – is corroborated by a number of sign-associations that would otherwise be difficult to explain. The serial vertical repetition of the letter "V," a simplified version of the triangle, is the basis for the *chevron* pattern employed both horizontally and vertically. Instead, when the mother goddess takes the shape of a bird goddess, other well-identified patterns are used, such as the comb, a chain of superimposed rhombi, the meandering flight of the butterfly and the spiral, all symbols associated with the myth of regeneration. All the patterns representing water and waves are also connected to the idea of femininity and generation: the zigzag pattern, the letters "S" and "M," as well as the parallel, straight and curved lines that are often inserted in boxes. Mingled with these abstract forms are more realistic representations of breasts, eyes, ram's horns (the animal sacred to the goddess) and lenticular shapes that refer either to the vulva or to fish. In some cases, the pubic triangle is interpreted as the final sprout of a twig with numerous branches, almost as if to capture the coincidence between human and plant fertility.

The decorations in this repertoire contain the most abstract themes of duplicity and triplicity, in the form of repeated lines, coupled balls and eggs grouped or joined by a serpentine line. Even if they contradict the theory of clear-cut contrast between geometric and naturalistic patterns, the conclusions of this anthropological research do not affect the thesis of continuity and the relatively independent development of decorative language. In fact, many of the motifs and patterns associated with the cult of the mother goddess "continue" in later cultures which confirm, change and lose sight of the original system, but rarely do they misplace syntactic discoveries and fundamental acquisitions relating to composition. The "history" of the great "discordant" civilisations fosters an amazing series of "non-synchronic" phases between forms and their meaning, making the work of the historian both difficult and deceptive unless he takes into account the fact that none of the critics' models are one hundred percent foolproof. So, in order not to work in vain, he will have to compromise and draw only partial, temporary conclusions.

The first decorative repertoire that questioned the development of mathematics belongs to the Egyptian civilisation. Determined by symbolic and religious requirements, naturalist inspiration dictated the choice of forms. However, the structural links, elaboration and combination between these forms swiftly took the upper hand and began to privilege experiences and culture based on geometric abstraction. When A. Speiser presented a brief history of this theory in 1927, he stated that the origins of advanced mathematics, then considered to date back to the 4th century B.C., should be pushed back 1000 years to the time when the Egyptians began to use one-dimensional or two-dimensional decorative patterns based on complex systems of symmetry invested with profound mathematical meaning.[12]

A characteristic of the Egyptians was their passion for endlessly extendible decorative graphic patterns in which a basic pattern was repeated in different spatial situations and formed a continuous network. On the contrary, Greek culture preferred simpler solutions based, like scripture, on the linear concatenation of forms or the rhythmic repetition of closed or half-closed forms.

I have already mentioned how Hersey associated most of the decorative elements of the Greek temple system to sacrificial rites and to the objects used during celebrations.[13] The temple as a "path running between rows of sacred trees" (turned into columns) in which garlands, eggs, necklaces, bones, bucranes, horns and curled tails (in the attic base) conjured up the original temple, when the "temple" did not yet exist but was prefigured by the *temenos*, a place believed to be sacred. This image is extremely effective since it gives decoration a structural role in the communicative programme of architecture.

In order to highlight some of the most important aspects of this grand communicative programme, I will attempt to describe some of the decorative

*Egyptian decorative motif.*

*A* Cucuteni *lid with the snake pattern transformed into divine eyes.*

450

motifs that apparently come from the observation of nature or from man's efforts to understand the laws governing morphology, laws which, in most cases, provide further examples of the structural analogy between nature and artificiality.

*Stratification*

Building a wall, like weaving cloth, involves the overlapping of various layers. This permits materials that are different in colour and structure to be placed on top of one another. This possibility engenders the pseudo-isodomic apparatus of Greek architecture in which the distinction between the layers is determined only by the greater or lesser height of the stones used. Greater differentiation between the courses has led to the alternate superimposition of materials of different colours. Probably dictated by technical requirements, it was certainly consolidated for aesthetic reasons.

In nature there are thousands of different examples of the law of differentiated superimposition: the geological sedimentation that can be seen after excavation, the livery of animals or of birds whose plumage shines with horizontal or vertical stripes (one typical example are the striped Maraus chickens) and certain types of shells that use their alternate stripes either as a way to underscore their visibility or camouflage themselves in the environment.

The task assigned by architecture to stratification is either to highlight tem-

*Opposite page: the capital of the Erechtheum on the Acropolis in Athens (4th century B.C.). The horns of a ram and a girgentana sheep. In Greek civilisation the horns are considered sacred. Spirals and helixes were already part of architectural terminology in Greece.*

451

*A shell of the* Cancellaria reticulata Linneo *family. The horizontal stripes, so typical of architecture involving superimposed layers of stones or bricks, are mirrored in both inorganic and organic nature.*
*Above: a picture of the mountains of the Pollino massif (Italy); detail of a* Passiflora quadrangulari.

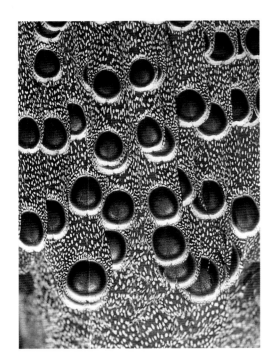

*Feathers of a pheasant of the* Polyplectron bicalcaratum *species.*

*A shell of the* Comus nobilis Linneo *family.*

poral succession or to stress the visual effects of a volume or surface, projecting onto the object artificial characteristics that come from the interpretation of natural forms.

*Alignment*

The linear repetition of a geometric or naturalistic element, whether along a straight line or a curve, produces an alignment. If this pattern is bordered by two margins, then it creates a band or ribbon pattern, one of the primary resources of architectural decorations. In fact, it is often used to frame a hole, circling it entirely, but it can also divide a walled surface into superimposed parts or layers, enunciating both a system of proportions and a rhythm. When a band along the walls of a fortress marks the point in which the sloping surface of the ramparts mellows into the vertical surface of the upper walls, it acts like a belt at the "waist" of the fortress, emphasising the dividing line between the "trunk" and the "hips," with evident anthropomorphic connotations.

On the subject of alignment, Semper introduced the theme of the garland or leafy crown that the ancients placed around a person's head. He believed that the garland marked the beginning of decoration and liberation from tattoos.

Even if alignment is obviously connected to the artificial act of weaving and braiding, there are many examples in the world of nature that could have inspired man with the construction of cyclical and rhythmic images evoking the passing of time and ordered movement.

Corn cobs, pomegranate seeds, the backbone and ribs of the human body, the alignment of leaves and thorns, the scales of reptiles, the feathers of birds' wings and the barbs of a feather are all examples of extremely regular parallel braids. On the other hand, rhythmic repetition is visible in the ribbed structure of shells such as the *Tonna melonostoma* and in the feathers of birds such as peacocks, pheasants and lyres.

*Concatenation*

When the repeated elements in the band are joined together by sinusoidal or spiral lines, it is possible to talk of concatenation. One effect of concatenation is the intensification of the dynamic element and the introduction of a "direction" in the decorative pattern, a fact that contrasts the rule of specular symmetry and non-oriented repetition. The "wave band" belongs to the family of concatenated motifs, otherwise known as "running dog." This motif, already present in the decorative repertoire of the Egyptians, was passed down to the Aegean, Greek and Roman civilisations and later became the preferred motif of Italian architects in the early 16th century. This motif is a fabulous abstraction of the outline of sea waves and the growth of vine-shoots, while at the same time it is free to develop like a bunch of knotted spirals.

The wave band contains a highly conventional form of the spiral that is known as the "curve of life" due to its pervasive presence in the organic world. In architectural decorations, this form, together with its tridimensional counterpart, the helix, was sown in fertile ground suitable to growth. Ever since the beginning of time, man has felt the urge to transform the surface of stones by using a system of symbolic signs. The most prominent of these was the spiral which stands out for its ability to join in space and to suggest the intimate vitality of matter. It is not by chance that stones painted with spirals and concentric circles – the conventional way of portraying electric fields – are amazingly similar to the corrugated surface skin of a withered fruit hanging on a tree. Biological and morphological studies have shown that spiral and vortex configurations are present on the most intimate fibres of living beings, from the structure of the heart to that of the ear. Furthermore, these structures are always involved in growth processes, for example in the phyllotaxis that determines the position of meristems on the stalk of a plant and consequently the exact point where the leaves will sprout. This fact has created a sort of sacred aura around this type of curve, an aura similar to the one around the golden section to which it is closely related. Indeed, the logarithmic spiral can roughly be created by combining the quarters of a circle obtained by pointing the compass on the vertex of a rectangle whose sides have a golden section.[14]

One of the decorative forms that had found its niche in the plastic development of the spiral and the helix is the "corbel," characteristic of the Corinthian

*Dorsal feathers of a guinea fowl.*

*A frieze on a* Cucuteni *vase showing the joint wave pattern.*
*A wave frieze in Palazzo Cicciaporci, Rome (attributed to Raphael).*
*Left: a section of rock showing the vortex shape of lava.*

*An example of radiation in the crest of a crowned crane.*

order and particularly developed in 16th-century Italy. During this period it was traditionally employed in cornices and doors as an independent plastic element, as well as being used "upside down" as a base for window sills. In the repository of the Biblioteca Laurenziana, Michelangelo designed such a personal version that it appeared "tragic," the expression of matter so compact as to contrast a stress. From the corbel spring the "volutes," joining planes of different widths in Renaissance facades. This permitted the structural arrangement of basilicas with naves of different heights to be well interpreted from a classical point of view. Recently, Antonio Giuliano has declared that there is a link between the spirals (plant volutes) of the acanthus, the *apotheosis* of the Dionysiac cults and the triumphal traits of the Ara Pacis Augustae.[15] Rome lent this theme to the Christian faith which used it as an allegory of the triumph of Christ in heaven.

The fact that the volute is inseparable from the criteria of concatenation is demonstrated by the typical tendency of wrought iron to create a continuous frame that gains structural consistency from its elasticity. One of the curvilinear frames in which plastic material tends to coagulate into a volute is the *rocaille* inspired by the action of water. Unlike the wave band, this is not achieved by turning it into a simple structural diagram, but by trying to mime the tendency of the froth of the waves in order to create a network to be distributed to the borders of the curvilinear fields. In recent decades, fractal mathematics has provided analogical models of this concatenated fragmentation such as gulfs that have become smaller and smaller due to the turbulent erosive action of waves upon the sea coast.

The way in which volutes are considered and interpreted by Art Nouveau culture is linked to their tendency to twist around themselves (the favourite form is the stalk). Art Nouveau pursues concrescence rather than concatenation, the former being the parallel vertical dilation of lines which, without touching, unite in obedience to a "palpable" visual law.

*Radiation*

Although linked to the idea of centrality, radiation is a separate concept in so far as it does not involve completeness. Lines radiating from a point or a body with a real dimension do not necessarily spread in all directions: it is sufficient for multiple directions to have one or more points in common. The palmette is probably the paradigmatic example of this radiating pattern, its natural origins confirmed by the name of the plant at the root of this inspiration, later "transformed" into a model.

In architectural decorations, the radiating poles may either be bundled together in a process of repetitive transference or placed alone: in this case they assist the vertical tension of a specific architectural motif, for example, the acroteria of Greek and Etruscan temples. Instead, the fan pattern in which the radial elements are inserted in the profile of a semi-circumference is well suited to the planes of semicircular windows and the terminations of barrel vaults and lunettes.

At the end of the nineteenth century, perhaps due to the way in which glass

*Examples of radiation on the roof of the Chrysler Building in New York (William van Alen, 1928-30).*

tends to break, the radial pattern was re-discovered and interpreted by Drexler as a rigid geometry. This lighted the spark that led to the explosion of Art Déco, a decorative repertoire that proved how strong the need for new decorative forms still was, even after the nihilistic prophecies of Adolf Loos. Art Déco countered the linear fluidity of Art Nouveau with geometric rigidity, its decorative patterns winking at futurism and cubism by irreverently translating the dramatic seriousness of the avant-garde into "lightness" and symbolic fatuity.

Radiation in the inorganic world may be considered the result of the multiple germination of crystals that in gemmology are called "asterisms,"[16] such as the stellar sapphires of mesolite, auricalcite and erythrite.

In botany, radiation is inherent in umbel inflorescences and the nervation of palmate leaves,[17] while in the animal world it can be seen in claws, birds' tails and the crests of cranes. Its most spectacular and full-bodied expression is the peacock's tail, an indirect and direct influence on decoration in general. Together with the splendid "parade" adornment of what has been defined as an "arena bird," the peacock bears witness to the fact that an aesthetic sensibility very similar to that of mankind exists and operates in the animal world.[18]

*Borders and Crenellation*
Decoration is often used in architectural composition to identify the specific parts of an organic whole or to signal its boundaries. The cornice is an ele-

*Examples of radiation in nature: a group of quartz crystals in a stone and a palm leaf in the botanical gardens in Sydney.*

457

*Detail of a diatom of the* Aulacoseira crenulata *species.*
*Battlements of the Ca' d'Oro in Venice (14th century) and, below, Arab battlements called reciprocation battlements since their profile mirrors the empty spaces in between.*

ment codified in the architectural order that often acts as a border, and by so doing confirms its dual nature as both a structural and decorative element. The door and the window – to which I have dedicated a whole chapter of this book – mirror this ambiguity: thresholds, frames and crownings are structural elements as well as being what we could call in biological terms, "meristematic" moments, particularly suited to the "growth" of decoration regarded as a symbolic enrichment and interpretation. Classical mouldings, for example, give weight and body to the concept of cornice when it has no figurative covering yet still plays a vital role in the definition of form. Calling it an ornament would be a mistake: it revels in the capture of light, alternating light and dark to reveal the full range of intermediate shades. Classical mouldings make the building react to the light and highlight atmospheric changes between day and night, winter and summer, good weather and bad. However, when figurative elements are added, the cornice, and even the moulding, enhance their structural values with those of ornament and symbol. The tendency to highlight the edges of an object is typically used in clothing, which often has strongly decorative borders or stitching. Nowadays, modern clothes, but more in particular the woollen jackets and pullovers produced in Austria, are characterised by decorated borders: the contrast between the border and the material is so characteristic that, even if it has become an international item, it has not lost its local flavour. It is possible that this simple pattern influenced Joseph Hoffman when he designed Maison Stoclet in Brussels, as it did indeed many other projects of the early 20th century. In Maison Stoclet, every surface used to define the building is edged with a bronze frieze that doubles at the corners. The architectural effect of this omnipresent border accentuates and disassembles the building volumes, reducing them to a mere sum of orthogonal surfaces that, like the diaphanous panes nearby, reveal the spatial reality of the interior.

The rusticated angle irons used by Sangallo had a different, largely plastic role. These systematic borders were used in ancient architecture, for example in the lighthouse in Ostia depicted in the mosaics that still exist today, but above all they were exploited by Islamic architecture.

Islamic (and pre-Islamic) culture decorated the battlements built for functional purposes on the top of fortresses and city walls. Later, this decoration migrated to the tops of buildings, where it shed its defensive role and maintained only its visual effect. The osmotic relationship between wall and sky is all the more intense and subtle the more the shape of the battlement loses its *raison d'être* in order to develop freely, gradually becoming lighter until it assumes the immaterial value of the flame. What kind of archers can one imagine behind the merlons of Palazzo Ducale, the Blue Mosque or the Ca' d'Oro? The desire to establish a sense of belonging between the building and its sky-blue background is the reason why the Islamic world, and later Venice, decided to transform the merlon series into a weightless and immaterial open pattern that vanished in the afternoon light only to regain substance and form when framed against the fading light of evening. In nature, borders and crenellation are quite usual and express precise, obvious morphological laws.

Many leaves and flowers have borders, but the decorative effect reached in the crests and feathers of many birds, such as peacocks, pheasants from the Far East and Sebright hens, or the underside of starfishes, is something of extreme beauty.

There are significant similarities between crenellation and the suture of skull bones, the crests of birds, the manes of many animals and the jagged outline of certain rocky peaks that jut out against the sky.

*Detail of Maison Stoclet in Brussels (Joseph Hoffman, 1905-07).*

### Geometric arabesque

The geometric *games* associated with the concept of tessellation were mentioned when examining the archetype of the floor. But the arabesque – the geometric *furor* that fills every available space enveloping not only floors, but ceilings, vaults and walls – is one of the most rigorous expressions of decorative desire and may not be ignored here. Geometric ornaments are as old as ornamentation itself and, based on contemporary architectural remains, geometric ceramics bear witness to its development in years gone by. As mentioned earlier, in the Egyptian world the ornament expressed advanced mathematical knowledge otherwise impossible to demonstrate. In the Hellenic world, geometry invaded the Greek key design and the exquisitely elegant repetitive friezes of the architectural orders, but it was in the Roman world that it began to be studied and later developed by Islamic civilisations. Extensive comparative studies still need to be carried out on the development of geometric patterns in Roman times, but some mosaic floors in Rome, Pompeii and Hadrian's Villa in Tivoli as well as in various towns in North Africa, demonstrate that the legacy appropriated by the Islamic world was much more than a mere prefiguration. In particular, in Room 9 of the Hall of the Cubicles in Hadrian's Villa, three areas, each with a repeated vortex pattern that turns clockwise and then anticlockwise, run along three sides of a square decorated with a pattern similar to the annular vault of Santa Costanza in Rome. These areas could almost be a model for the one in the Ambassador's Hall

*Meteorite showing the Widmanstätten figures. On the surface, the tetrahedral structure of the holosiderite creates a minute geometric pattern similar to the one used in Islamic decorations. Top, a cerussite crystal.*

in the Alhambra in Granada in which the darker tiles of the mosaic, veering from sky-blue to tawny, seem to play "tag" with one another as if blown about by the wind. In Room 2 of the same building, a circular pattern is surrounded by three areas decorated with the framed fylfots that are so characteristic of Islamic culture. A mosaic recently discovered among the remains of a Roman villa in Luxembourg has a pattern of intertwining bands on an octagonal base. This pattern prefigures the three-dimensional development of the intersecting nervation of the Mirhab in the mosque in Cordoba.

It is difficult to deny that to a certain extent this furious development of the geometric pattern, so typical of Islamic countries from the 10th century onwards, was one way to express their desire to glorify the divine, since iconoclasm forbade it to be portrayed. However, teeming with references to the wonders of architecture, Islamic literature is almost completely silent regarding the possible symbolic meanings of geometric patterns, which it appears to consider as garments to bejewel architectural elements that may be poetically identified with parts of the human body. For example, the poet Hasan ibn Hissan when commenting on a building in Cordoba speaks of "arches similar to the thick curls of a virgin's hair," or "columns that shine with the water of their ornaments upon which the eyes rest."[19] Ibn al-Gayyab describes a pavilion facing the Alhambra mosque in Granada as follows: "Like a bride that takes her place / overshadowing the beauty of the young virgins. / Eyes are imprisoned and one's gaze / becomes ecstatic. All the jewels adorning female beauties / turn pale in comparison to what you have created. / A garden in which the rain has embroidered drawings of wondrous hues [...]." These scholarly descriptions, full of flattering words, attribute a sort of female grace to ornaments, a grace later extended to all architectural forms. There are arches "like a young girls' brows" and a bride's eyes "wet with tears," a direct reference to the expanse of water in the Lion's Court. The lack of literary references to the symbolic meaning of this geometric *furor* could depend on an instinctive and purely visual approach typical of the relationship between literature and the visual arts. However, this silence rings out even in theoretical texts on construction such as the treatise by Al-Kashiç, *Miftah al-Hisab* (the key to arithmetic).

In an essay dated 1989 entitled, *In the Tower of Babel*, W.K. Chorbachi seriously tackles the problem of geometric arabesques by examining a number of extremely precious manuscripts. In particular he examines two sources: a manuscript treatise for artisans about geometrical problems, by Abdul-I Wafa al-Buzjani, who lived in the 10th century, and the commentary on geometrical problems, written three centuries later by Kamal al-Din Yuniss bin Man'a, one of the most important exponents of Sufi philosophy. Chorbachi found the text in an anonymous Persian manuscript dedicated to the "connection of similar or congruent figures" and housed in the Bibliothèque Nationale in Paris. Chorbachi has begun to interpret these manuscripts in mathematical terms, adopting the criteria elaborated by Edith Müller who in 1944 studied the mosaic of the Al-

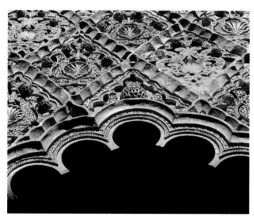

*Capitals in the Lion's Court in the Alhambra, Granada; the Patio de la Doucelles in the Alcazar, Seville; the octagonal cupola in the Ambassador's Hall in the Alhambra, Granada.*

461

A *butterfly of the* Idea lynceus *species belonging to the* Nymphalidae *family.*

hambra based on the conventions established in the *International Tables of Crystallography*. Chorbachi, however, is trying to use more suitable references.

This syntactic research carried out with more appropriate mathematical tools will certainly permit Chorbachi to improve our knowledge of the design methods of the Islamic masters. This is evident from Chorbachi's initial in-depth examination of the problems inherent in the Parisian manuscript which he illustrated in his first essay and in a second published at a later date together with Arthur L. Loeb, entitled *An Islamic Pentagonal Seal*.[20]

However, the sarcastic vehemence with which the scholar attacks those who have used other methodologies to try and interpret Islamic geometry is somewhat disconcerting. The fact that the work of Abul-I Wafa and the Parisian manuscript do not attribute any symbolic meaning whatsoever to these geometric patterns is not sufficient to disavow the fact that their creators may have intended them as symbols. Likewise, it would be wrong to deny the symbolic value of some of the paintings in Christian catacombs if by chance all the literary texts explaining their true meaning had been lost. Chorbachi has found and utilised a number of manuscripts that have lain dormant for years in libraries and therefore has been able to scientifically explain the syntactic aspect of geometric decoration and its design methods. It is quite possible that in the future a scholar in another field might be able to find equally precious and unused sources that illustrate the semantic aspects of these decorations.

In the meantime, iconology and morphological analysis should operate sep-

*Old Moreton Hall (Cheshire), 1559, typical example of a wooden structure exploited for its decorative properties.*

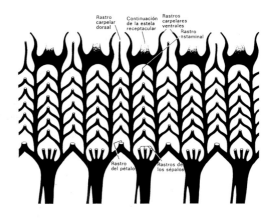

*From top: diagram of the stalk of an open* Aquilegia *on a flat plane.*
*A flower of the* Aquilegia.
*Wrought iron railings in the ground floor windows of the Casa dei Filippini, Rome (Francesco Borromini, 1637-42).*

arately, recognising each other's legitimate working hypotheses. Even when these hypotheses are not verifiable, if they are correctly formulated, they do contain important proposals. One should also remember that the tradition of geometric decoration is still very much alive in the Islamic world, especially Persia and Morocco, so it would be useful to study the expertise of the artisans who verbally pass on their skills from one generation to the next.

The texts Chorbachi derides for their mystical approach have contributed enormously to our knowledge of the Islamic world, even if they contain non-verifiable statements. On the other hand, it is difficult to avoid being dogmatic, even when one does apply scientific rigour, since the latter is nonetheless a product of time and space and does not protect the scholar from trends or errors.[21]

According to Critchlow, the key to understanding the orientation of Islamic research in the field of geometry lies in Islam's need to celebrate unity (*tawid*) and the glory of God by using non-verbal methods with the same meaning. In fact, mosques almost always have inscriptions from the verses of the Koran, and these verses normally extol unity and the uniqueness of God. The physical superimposition of this calligraphic decoration, linked by a univocal code to abstract geometric decoration, may well lead one to believe that the latter is connected to a more complex, decipherable code. These two elements come together here, like prayer and song, and the observer is struck in two ways: by the words and, on an instinctive and emotional level, by the kaleidoscopic splendour of the multicoloured geometric pattern.

Critchlow examines the main families of geometric patterns, highlighting the fact that they are normally created by composing overlapping grids, each linked to one type of symmetry. The grid of squares and the grid of hexagons are regular grids with closed links, while the grid of pentagons needs to be mixed with other polygons. Placing two of these grids on top of one another is like uniting two inharmonious systems. It results in a single whole in which unity and multiplicity are combined, strengthening one another. The links and polygons of this whole are connected to the system of meanings based on numbers and their combinations according to Pythagorean theories, theories that are very much appreciated in the cultural traditions of Islam, and to cosmology. The symbolic value of numbers charges these geometric patterns with meanings and allusions.

Pythagoras' *tetraktis* (an aggregate of four consecutive numbers whose sum is ten) may be represented as a triangle divided up into sixteen triangles each the same size. This representation is at the core of numerous geometric patterns in Islamic decoration, including the incredible motif made up of pieces of equal size and similar to the one in the already cited Hall of the Ambassadors in the Alhambra in which hexagonal stars are inserted in the centre of curvilinear triangular fields. Another geometric pattern, characterised by the rhythmic repetition of a geometric flower with ten petals, which Critchlow calls "much revered," is found all over India, Egypt, Morocco, Turkey and Persia. The connecting structures are tremendously complicated. Even if based on strict internal laws of inversion, this polymorphic grid contains intricately intertwined rhombi, hexagonal pentagons that lead to furious multiplicity which makes the attainment of geometric unity almost an act of pure magic.

To ask whether the process of unifying what is multiple, so close to the Islamic *tawid* concept, is, or is not, the message transmitted by the "much revered" geometric pattern cited by Critchlow leads nowhere. Nor can one exclude the possibility that in its lifetime this pattern was created, and perhaps even used, semantically. The fact remains that the Moroccan artisans who currently use it, consider it to be merely an exceptionally complex geometric pattern whose elegance makes it particularly suitable to highlight the importance of a room.

In this context, the experience of some *maallems* is extremely useful. *Maallems* are the artisans who prepare the geometric decorations. They have inherited these ancient skills, traditionally handed down by word of mouth, and often possess manuals and drawings dating back to the last century. The stories[22] told by the *maallems* bear witness to a decline in the esoteric aspect of geometry in favour of a structural type of decoration that judges the legacy of these concepts to be a series of experiences whose complexity may be increased indefinitely with the passing of the years.

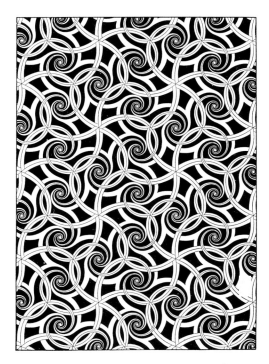

*A decorative illustration from the book* Dynamarhythmic Design *by Edward B. Edwards, The Century Company, New York 1932, pl. VII.*

The *maallems* are extremely at home with the different geometric forms and their syntactic meanings. They have a specific name for each form or tile in a ceramic mosaic, even if there are 358 different types in their repertoire. In turn, the patterns they create all have a name which either refers to the visible characteristics of the decoration (for example, "fluttering" or "winged") or has an allusive or metaphorical meaning (such as "fig leaves," "heifer's eyes," "black eyes facing sideways," "painted eyes," "sectioned tears," "spider's web," "small cone"). The whimsical name, "sandal with a wooden sole," is both technical and imaginative. It involves the vibrant mix of small central motifs made up of paired footsteps, all the same colour and equidistant from one another. On the basis of these allusive figurative fragments there is no point in studying a system of lost meanings. Instead, confronted with this "game" that encompasses the experiences of so many generations, it is worth acknowledging its analogical potential. This potential is neither classified nor classifiable and may be associated with the multicoloured "fluttering" that makes a repertoire so attractive, a repertoire created to inspire meditation and contemplation, like the vibrant shape of the flames that burn in the hearth.

*The ENEL Building, Tarquinia (Paolo Portoghesi, 1986).*

One of these Moroccan *maallems*, Moullay Hafid. describes his work as follows: "The day will come when, observing our work, man will understand that every sign is an image, a falling star, a bunch of flowers, a fairy tale telling another fairy tale. If this is so, abstraction is a word with no meaning, my profession, the mosaic, is an ongoing party."[23]

No less precise and complete – at least as far as Moroccan craftsmanship is concerned – is the terminology relating to the *muqarnas*, those stalactite frames considered one of the most typical elements of Islamic architecture. The *muqar-*

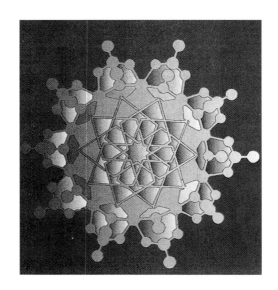

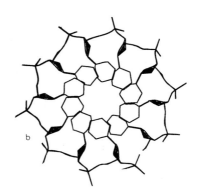

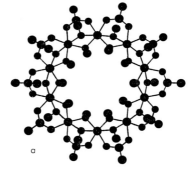

*A ferric wheel by K.L. Taft and S.J. Lippard and, below, the structure of one of the layers of the double DNA spiral.*
*Right: grids activated by photoelectric cells to control light in the Centre of Islamic Culture in Paris (Jean Nouvel, Architecture Studio, 1987).*

*nas* are normally used to join adjacent architectural elements. Through the plastic contraction and dilation of architectural stalactites, arches of varying sizes, cupolas and polygonal brick involucres that would need complex surfaces to be joined together are able to come together convincingly, so that any impression of heaviness is lost, giving way to a feeling of levitation and vibrant light.

Built either in stone, plaster or wood, the *muqarnas* of the various national schools correspond to a different geometric logic, based on a single original source. In Morocco, eight pieces make up the alphabet, or rather the musical scale, of this strict compositional system capable of producing infinite variations depending on their combination. The outward appearance of each piece cannot be used to create intuitive combinations. Like a game of chess or bridge, an exceptional memory is required. But the *maallems* put the pieces together instinctively and those who comment on their speed and accuracy are told that "each piece entices and calls to its friend."

The similarities between the mathematical logic of the arabesque and natural forms may only be discovered by shedding all prejudices and false certainties. But everything changes if we move from the morphologies of living nature to crystallography and the hidden structures that in the intimate recesses of matter avoid visibility and representation. In the world of crystals, modular grids, intersections and the complex laws of symmetry govern the processes of aggregation and growth, as they do in geometric decoration. When geologists

and chemists have to draw complex structures (such as diamonds or lons-daleite) their graphs either end up looking like these arabesques or evoking the formative processes mediated by the geometric plan. These sensations are similar to the ones experienced when looking at the more complex examples of geometric ornaments, sensations described by Thomas Mann in *The Magic Mountain* when the hero Castorp watches snowflakes blowing about in a blizzard: "Among the myriad of tiny magical stars, in their secret minuscule magnificence, not made for human contemplation, no two were the same. A boundless inventive pleasure was involved in the creation, variation and extremely detailed elaboration of the same basic theme, the regular hexagon; but each one of those cold objects was perfectly symmetrical, icily regular, and this was the frightening element, anti-organic and hostile to life. These small stars were too regular, in life these substances never obeyed such order, life shrunk from exactitude, believed it to be as lethal as the mystery of death itself and Hans Castrop began to understand why the ancient builders of cathedrals had secretly but intentionally modified the symmetry of the column order ever so slightly."

Involuntary challenges to divine perfection are also present in Islamic culture, but the most sensational "voluntary mistakes" are clearly visible in the splendid Romanesque monuments of Florence: the Baptistery, San Miniato and the façade of the Badia Fiesolana. Here this "mock" logic is rife with

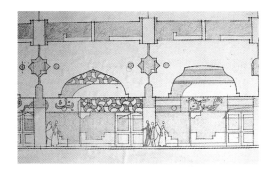

*Robert Venturi, Denise Scott Brown, design for the Baghdad mosque, 1988.*
*Roger Ferri, the Americana restaurant in Fort Worth, Texas.*

*Two plates from the book by L.F. Day,* Anatomy of Pattern, *London 1890.*

467

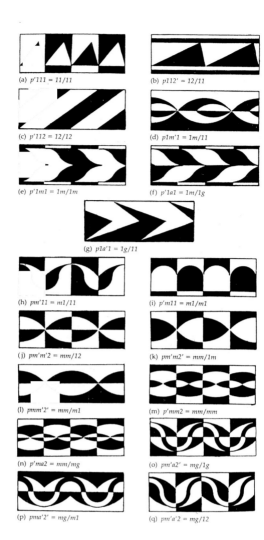

(a) $p'111 = 11/11$

(b) $p112' = 12/11$

(c) $p'112 = 12/12$

(d) $p1m'1 = 1m/11$

(e) $p'1m1 = 1m/1m$

(f) $p'1a1 = 1m/1g$

(g) $p1a'1 = 1g/11$

(h) $pm'11 = m1/11$

(i) $p'm11 = m1/m1$

(j) $pm'm'2 = mm/12$

(k) $pm'm2' = mm/1m$

(l) $pmm'2' = mm/m1$

(m) $p'mm2 = mm/mm$

(n) $p'ma2' = mm/mg$

(o) $pm'a2' = mg/1g$

(p) $pma'2' = mg/m1$

(q) $pm'a'2 = mg/12$

*The seventeen one-dimensional dichromatic motifs created by Belov in 1964.*

internal contradictions, deviations and metamorphoses which break down the rigidity of the geometric design: this is an ironic and exciting game similar to the complexities of the most subtle and refined games played out in literature.

The presence of a structural order that the eye perceives without immediately understanding the rules governing its creation, means that the decorative order seems to be a sort of second nature to which our senses succumb. While enjoying the mellow feeling of this surrender, the mental pleasure of this structural study and its semantic decoding unite with the whimsical roaming of the eye, a fact that could be interpreted as being the one true reason behind ornamentation. On this issue, Grabar believes that the architectural ornament is a "go-between"[24] that facilitates the comprehension of the visual message contained in the structure, creating what could be called a friendly and complicitous relationship between the user and the structure.

However, none of these three aspects has escaped that sort of revived interest in decoration that has taken place over the past few decades, from either a critical, historiographical or creative point of view, a revival pioneered by architects such as Robert Venturi and Sandro Mendini.

[1] The conference, reported as an essay, was published for the first time in *Monatschrift des wissenschaftlichen Vereins* in 1856 with the title "Über die formelle Gesetzmassigkeit des Schmuckes und dessen Bedeutung als Kunstsymbol," cf., N. Squicciarino, *Arte e ornamento in Gottfried Semper*, Il Cardo, Venice 1994.

[2] Vitruvius, *De Architectura*, II, 1.10.

[3] cf., G. Semper, *Lo stile*, Laterza, Rome-Bari 1992, p.16.

[4] cf., A. Riegl, *Problemi di stile*, Feltrinelli, Milan 1963 (*Stilfragen*, Berlin 1893).

[5] cf., *Ibid.*, p. 212 ff.

[6] cf., G. Hersey, *The Lost Meaning of Classical Architecture*, MIT Press, Cambridge (Mass.) 1988.

[7] cf., W. Wörringer, *Astrazione e empatia*, Einaudi, Turin 1975 (*Abstraction and Empathy*, Chicago 1967).

[8] cf., E.H. Gombrich, *Il senso dell'ordine*, Einaudi, Turin 1984, pp. 300-308 (*The sense of order*, London 1984).

[9] cf., J.E. Lovelock, *Gaia*, Boringhieri, Turin 1980 and by the same author, *Le nuove età di Gaia*, Boringhieri, Turin 1991.

[10] cf., R. Sheldrake, *The Rebirth of Nature*, Bantham Books, New York 1991.

[11] cf., M. Gimbutas, *The Language of the Goddess*, Thames & Hudson, London 1989.

[12] cf., A. Speiser, *Theorie der Gruppen von edlicher Ordnung*, Springer, Berlin 1927.

[13] cf., A. Hersey, *op.cit.*

[14] The bibliography on spirals is extensive and expands steadily. I will cite here only the more interesting and specific studies, omitting those dedicated to more general subjects and cited elsewhere in the book (such as the works of W. D'Arcy Thompson, M. Ghyka, P.S. Stevens etc.). Cf., T.A. Cook, *The Curves of Life*, Dover, New York 1979; T. Schwen, *Il Caos sensibile*, Arcobaleno, Oriago di Mira 1992; I. Hargittai, A. Pickover, *Spiral Symmetry*, World Scientific, Singapore 1992; F. Manna, *Le chiavi magiche dell'universo*, Liguori, Naples 1988.

[15] cf., A. Giuliano, *Vitruvio e l'acanto*, in "Palladio," n.14, July-December, 1994, p. 29.

[16] cf., M. Gramaccioli, *Il meraviglioso mondo dei cristalli*, Calderini, Bologna 1984, p. 163 and G.W. Robinson, *Minerals*, Nicholson, London 1994.

[17] cf., A.D. Bell, *La forma delle piante*, Zanichelli, Bologna 1993 (*Plant form*, Oxford-New York 1991).

[18] In recent years there have been an increased number of very interesting studies on the question of animal beauty, the nuptial parades of birds and the gardens built by bowerbirds, among which A.F. Skutch, *Origins of Nature Beauty*, University of Texas Press, Austin 1992; P.A. Johnsgard, *Arena Birds*, Smithsonian Institution Press, Washington,-London 1994; H.

Cronin, *The Art and the Peacock*, Cambridge University Press, Cambridge 1991.

[19] These and other literary citations are from M.J. Rubiera y Mata, *L'immaginario e l'architettura nella letteratura araba medievale*, Marietti, Genova 1990; for the inscription of the Lion's Court see instead O. Grabar, *Alhambra*, London 1978.

[20] cf., also M. Frishman, Hasan-udin Khan, *The Mosque*, Thames and Hudson, London 1994, and in particular the essay *Applications of geometry* by Mohammad Al-Asad, pp. 55-75.

[21] The texts to which Chorbachi refers are largely inspired by Seyyed Hossein Nasr, who deserves credit for having rekindled the tradition of Sufi philosophy. In 1973 he prefaced the book, *The Sense of Unity* by Nadar Ardalan and Laleh Bakhtiar. In 1976 Bakhtiar published *Sufi, Expressions of the Mystic Quest*, Thames and Hudson, London and *Islamic Science*, World of Islamic Festival Publishing Company, Westerham. The following studies examine geometric decoration more specifically: K. Critchlow, *Islamic Patterns, an Analytical and Cosmological Approach*, Thames and Hudson, London 1976 (with a preface by Hossein Nasr); Issam el-Sayd, Ayse Parman, *Geometric Conceptions in Islamic Art*, World of Islam Festival, London 1976.

[22] cf., A. Paccard, *Le Maroc et l'artisanat traditionnel islamique dans l'architecture*, Editions Atelier 74, Annecy 1983.

[23] *Ibid*. vol.1, p. 441.

[24] O. Grabar, *Meditation of Ornament*, Princeton University Press, Princeton 1992.

*Six examples of dichromatic tessellation.*

# The City

In its specific role as a human landscape, the city seems to be the opposite of nature, "what nature cannot do," according to Louis Kahn. And yet, when a theorist of the Enlightenment such as Francesco Milizia, one of the most vehement critics of Baroque naturalism, describes the traits of a city, he surprisingly uses a certain number of metaphors that come straight from nature: "The city is like a *forest* [...], a picture modified by infinite accidents; extreme order in details; confusion, uproar and turmoil all together... in which the layout of a city is like a *park*. It needs squares, crossings, lots of roads, wide and straight. This is not enough; the layout has to be designed tastefully and with verve so that it amalgamates order and eccentricity, harmony of proportions and variety: in one place the roads should irradiate like a *star*, in others like a *duck's foot*, in some places like a *spike* in others like a *fan*. Then there should be long parallel roads and everywhere triple and quadruple cross-roads facing in different directions, together with a multitude of differently designed squares of various sizes and decoration. In this composition, the more choice, abundance and contrast there is, *even to the point of a certain disorder*, the more it will be picturesque and display humorous and charming beauty."[1]

It is plain to see how the infinite variety of nature's landscapes often prefigure spatial forms applicable to an urban context.

On the Tassili plateau of the Aijer in Algeria, erosion has shaped the rocks into separate blocks, creating a sort of enchanted city. Ever since the Neolithic Age, man has walked along these highways and engraved numerous graffiti on the rock walls. This has prompted Pietro Laureano to use the metaphor of an "art gallery" created by nature. The paintings are not positioned haphazardly, but exploit the concavities and convexities of the rock, almost as if they represented the artificial decoration of a natural architecture. In the Sefar complex, the blocks of rock are irregularly positioned based on an orthogonal pattern. The size of the rocks and the spaces between them varies, simulating a sort of functional hierarchy, just like cities in which houses, buildings, temples, squares, avenues, streets and alleys all correspond.[2]

The Dolomite mountains, for example the Sella or Rosengarten, also recall the prefiguration of urban spaces. Here their grandiose scale conjures up the image of a city inhabited by giants with roads flanked by cathedral spires, surrounded by unassailable bastions.

Using charming place names, popular imagination has often recognised the affinity between internal spaces in mountain chains and the concept of city. In Spain, near Madrid, it is possible to admire the "ciudad encantada." In Brazil, in the Perana, the term "Vila Velha" was used for centuries to describe a rocky formation fashioned by the wind and the rain that dated back to the Palaeozoic Age. In the countryside around Petra the remarkably effective identification between rocky landscapes and the city is still clearly visible in the caravan city of the Nabataeans hidden between the mountains of Wadi Musa accessed through the Siq gorge. Passing through this natural bottleneck that looks very similar to a crevasse in a glacier, the presence of an aqueduct and a series of anthropic rocky niches measure the wild landscape. They herald the event that is revealed upon reaching the urban area, introduced not by a city gate but by an exceptionally beautiful architectural backdrop: the facade hewn out of the Al-Khazneh rock, the "treasure" that perhaps acted as a warehouse or a meeting place. The walled city was situated where the mountains fade into the distance forming a sort of basin, while an ensemble of facades of different sizes reflected the shape of the city on the surrounding rock walls. Some of these facades were man-size and were probably used as tombs, other were monumental and many different theories exist as to their use.

A mirrored city in which the human figure and the environment established (and still establishes today) a sort of mysterious dialogue that recalls the journey of Alice in Wonderland. Instead of turning inwards, the city projects itself into the environment which it absorbs into its image. At the same time, since the new structures are built in pink sandstone, the environment influences the city like a parent does a child. Unfortunately, one vital element is now missing: the open-air aqueduct that ran along a rocky bed in the area of Wadi-al-Mataha, creating a spectacular waterfall next to the so-called tomb-palaces that prefigure in such an extraordinary way Michelangelo's model of the repository of the Laurenziana and the apse of Saint Peter's.[3]

*Left: an orographic situation prefiguring an urban space in all its complexity and volumetric differentiation.*
*Top: the orography of an area of the plateau of the Tassili of the Aijer in Algeria (drawing by G. Canterano). Above: a picture of the main square in Montalcino near Siena.*

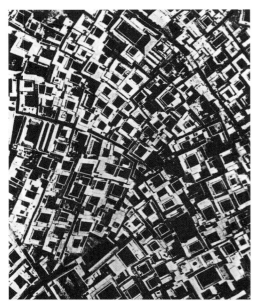

*The fissured surface of a gelatinous substance.*
*The urban fabric of Marrakech, Morocco.*

*Right: the Siq gorge leading to the city of Petra.*
*An architectural detail is partially visible in the*
*background.*

The comparison and oneiric exchange between the urban and natural images is repeated in other monumental complexes such as the tombs of the Achaemenids in Naqs-i Rustaw, Iran, dating back to the 5th and 6th centuries B.C., the Myra necropolises in Turkey (5th, 6th centuries B.C.), the tombs of Pantalica (13th century B.C.) and the Etruscan tombs in Norchia and San Giuliano, the "Sassi" in Matera in Italy and the temples of Ellora and Ajanta in India.[4] Instead, the "sub rock" settlements of the Anasazi should be included among the cities of the living; they are dug out of rock and have mimetic and geomorphic characteristics. In Mesa Verde (Colorado) as in White House Ruin and Betatakin (Arizona), the city is situated in a recess created by erosion under a gigantic depressed arch that looks something like a bridge. The cylindrical or prismatic elements are joined together under a single natural "roof" which also acts as the boundary wall of the settlement. The harmony of the city's relationship with nature is clearly visible in the affinity between the shape of the buildings and the rocks above, especially in Betatakin.[5]

This geomorphism is even more obvious in Machu Picchu in Peru where the profile of the mountain that overshadows the urban area, the Huayna Picchu, seems to have inspired the shape of the tympanums and the roofs of the houses that are even more pointed than those in Cuzco or other Inca cities. In this sacred centre, probably dedicated to the cult of the sun and the mountains, the va-

*The San Giuliano necropolis near Barbarano Romano, (Italy). The Etruscans designed the city of the dead to look like the city of the living. They used the house as a model for their tombs which were not built but "dug" in the soft tufa rock present in the region.*
*Above: Machu Picchu (Peru). In the forefront, one of the typical constructions closed on three sides. Note the similarity between the slope of the straw roof and the outline of the mountain in the background.*

*Machu Picchu, the sacred city of the Incas, built on a plateau 2500 meters above sea level. The Incas' respect for nature and their incredibly refined building skills makes Machu Picchu one of the best examples of harmony between nature and architecture.*

riety of ornaments that decorate the structures around the squares, and the way in which the buildings are linked to the parallel stepped terracing of crops, represent one of the most amazing examples of man's ability to listen to the forms and forces of the landscape.[6]

Yet another kind of city-nature relationship comes from the Cappadocia region of Turkey. The Hittites lived in this region in which persecuted Christian communities later took refuge and where thousands of people still live in grottoes and subterranean houses. The landscape in the region of Göreme (once Göremi, meaning "you" cannot see) easily confirms Ovid's theory that nature does sometimes seem to imitate man. The volcanic landscape appears to be dominated by a recurrent geological structure: cones of tufa that stand next to each other like the huts or tents of a never ending encampment. The "fairy chimneys," as these cones are called, represent the work of the wind, rain and snow on the uneven tufa mass; they constitute a monumental version of the more widespread system of needle-shaped deposits so typical of areas of eroded land. These cones present complex and stratified morphologies that sometimes look like coupled spires, Antoni Gaudí's chimneys or crystal gemmations.[7] The landscape in Göreme is dotted with numerous chimneys that have reached various phases of their geological evolution and their appropriation by man. This helps us to understand the intuition that led the first inhabitants to exploit the architectural and urban vocation of this landscape, transforming

*Houses dug out of the rock face on the Göreme plateau in Cappadocia (Turkey) and, above, the landscape of the so-called "chimneys of the fairies" untouched by man. The hut-shaped rocks inspired the Byzantine population in Derinkuyu to take refuge in this mysterious place when faced with the advancing Arab armies.*

*Two pictures of valley floors that look like roads.*

the complexity of the natural elements, inhabiting and interpreting it, in order to defend and protect themselves.

During the sixties, an underground settlement was discovered in the city of Derinkuyu, a short distance from Göreme. It had eight underground floors with wide roads, houses, shops and meeting areas. Perhaps the inhabitants of Göreme who came from Derinkuyu took over the fairy chimneys after their experience in an subterranean habitat, without sunlight and fresh air. This lifestyle was certainly suited to meditation and ascetic life, but it lacked the metaphysical dimension of a natural scenery so terse and spare that it resembled a space for ideas and concepts similar to Plato's Hyperouranious beyond the Heavens.

Rudolf Schwarz wrote: "We speak of scenic spaces and think of landscape as if it were a house. We consider mountains as walls, the valley bed a floor, the rivers roads, seashores thresholds, and where the mountain is lowest we consider this a door."[8] Schwarz's theory could easily work the other way around, since man recognised in his house the tree, the cave or the nest: the road was a river, the square a clearing or a lake and the temple a path winding between the majestic trees of the woods. The identification with a river is one of the more pertinent and spontaneous, because the road is shaped as a throughway, as a direction, while the river is a pondered and relentless movement that shapes the earth with its passing. Those who know Rome, its terri-

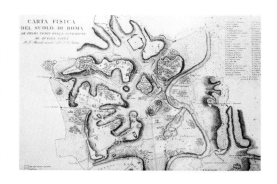

*An aerial view of the late Medieval town of Campagnano (Rome). The houses completely cover the rocky ridge between two parallel gorges with ditches that reunite at the end of the spur. Above: the orographic structure of the Roman landscape before the construction of the city.*

*An Etruscan gorge near Civita Castellana in the Fantibassi district and, below, Via dei Banchi Nuovi in Rome, near the Ponte district. The facades along the road encompass space like a canal or a ditch, to such an extent that it seems as if the volcanic landscape around the city influenced its spatial model. Rome was one of the first cities to develop vertically, using the* insulae *model.*

tory and its history, will be able to fully appreciate the importance of this identification.

Before the land on which Rome was to be founded became the focal point of a gigantic cosmic event during the Quaternary, an event that created the largest volcanic area in Europe, there was a gulf in the region between Monte Amiata to the north and the Lepini mountains to the south. The estuary of the Tiber faced the island of Cetona and the seven hills were merely sea beds.[9]

A colossal bradyseism marked the beginning of a new era dominated by terrestrial vulcanism. An inclined platform rose out of the sea. This created a longitudinal fissure that effectively established the direction of what was later to be the Tiber valley. After this geological catastrophe the sea withdrew from the area of the valley now situated to the right of the Tiber, but remained on the left side, later to become the birthplace of the city.

The oldest volcanic formations emerged during or a little before the Pliocene: the mountains of Tolfa, Volsini (Lake Bolsena now fills one of its craters), Cimini (Lake Vico) and Sabatini (Lake Bracciano). The Albani mountains are the most visible remnants of the volcanoes of the southern range that date back to the Neozoic Age and their eruptions and transformations probably continued up until the early years of recorded history.

The two volcanic systems that emerged from the sea, the lava flows, the rain full of dust and debris, the bradyseisms, the quakes, were all events that took place to the north and to the south. The land on which Rome was to rise was the scene of a violent and spectacular cosmic upheaval. And when the flow of lava from the north was slowly stopped by the advancing waters, more lava flowed down from the south almost as if to establish a balance between the opposing forces and create a dividing line that more or less coincided with the bed of the Tiber, a bed that the eruptions had often forced to change course.

However, if these eruptions shaped the outline of the Roman landscape, it was the waters that shaped its characteristic forms by eroding the tender tufa rock to the point that they uncovered its underlying sedimentary base. These rock were hollowed by water, creating narrow valleys like canals in the rock face and earthy cliffs. This favoured the growth of wild plants and the famous "gorges" and "ditches" that like veins and capillaries still feed the Roman countryside.

Found mainly in southern Etruria, these gorges have always been used as paths, and their rock walls and ramifications conjure up an enchanted city, inhabited by divine chthonic gods.[10]

Imitating their morphology, the Etruscans built mysterious open air passages near these gorges. The passages were up to 20 meters high yet scarcely wide enough for a cart to pass through. Apart from the practical aspect of making it possible to cross torrents and ditches without having to build bridges, it is very likely that these "channels" had a sacred meaning: to draw closer to the bowels of the earth, regarded as places of the supernatural. At least this is the idea that springs to mind when considering the series of channels that converge on the rock face near Pitigliano or those around Viterbo.[11] These shadowy areas built by the hand of man and inspired by his natural surroundings anticipate the traits of roads and alleys in ancient Rome such as the Argiletum or the Suburra along which the *insulae* were built. The *insulae* were six floors high and were almost always built in brick. The powerful similarities between the valleys, the Etruscan channels and these winding roads are certainly very inspiring. Vestiges of these similarities remain in those areas of the city which between the Middle Ages and the 19th century were rebuilt according to the "hinged wall" design.[12]

The analogy between river and road is mainly a visual one and its seeds may have been sown in the minds of man at the dawn of civilisation. On the other hand, the analogy of the urban fabric with natural forms should be considered from a structural point of view against the logic of "permanence," of "flow," of growth and the aggregation of living organisms.

The typologies that group settlements according to their shape and relationship to the earth facilitate the identification of the structural similarities between city and nature. Born as a sum of huts, houses or intermediate spaces, in primitive societies the village was organised according to rules established by the community, and Alberti's metaphor of the city as a big house is a perfect fit for this new and more complex order. Tangential aggregation along a road was the simplest solution, but for reasons of security and to respect the coral needs of the community, settlements with a single entrance to an enclosed area, or aggregations around a square where people met and exchanged views, were also common. Centrality and frontality, lattice or spiral patterns, were present even in extremely ancient settlements. They more or less consciously come from observing the position of certain parts of living organisms as well as the structure of the landscape, rocks, dances and religious rites. The lattice pattern was used earlier on in settlements on stilts and in Egyptian civilisations and was to become the "Hippodameus rule." This rule is based on the regularity of the woven fabric whose structure may be found in the orthogonality of the yarn and warp. Depending on the homogeneity of the thread the loom can produce more or less regular fabrics: this is exactly what happens during the construction of a city. It is worth noting that, on a larger scale, the Hippodameus city and the *castrum* simply repeat the genetic program of an algae called "tetrapaedia." The two varieties of this species both present cruciform segmentation.[13] Cities that have partly grown spontaneously and cities that have been designed possess different characteristics: the latter are more regular and the boundary, be it or not a wall, is fundamental in establishing the rules that govern its growth and form. In the case of spontaneous cities, their analogy lies in natural forms found outdoors, such as trees that spread and ramify when they grow, while in designed cities the anal-

*A primitive example of weaving. Orthogonality and repetition were introduced into manual weaving. These two concepts are at the basis of what is incorrectly called* Hippodameus *town-planning.*

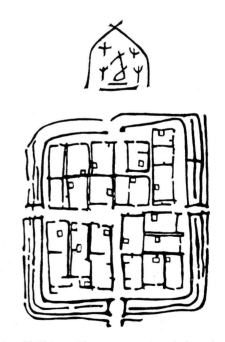

*An old Chinese ideogram meaning shelter; the plan of the prehistoric village of Karanovo in Bulgaria, 3500-3000 B.C.*

479

*The reconstruction of the sixth level of Hacilar (6th millenium B.C.).*

*Below and at the bottom of the opposite page: four stages of a "pearl ring" elaborated by a computer.*

ogy refers to animals whose outer form remains almost exactly the same throughout their entire growth period.

The similarity between the most elementary covered area and a living cell is important because it demonstrates evolution's ability to use differentiation and multiplication to create complex organisms with billions of cells.

Cellular aggregation is probably the oldest and most instinctive model consisting of three separate phases depending on the different relationship between internal and external space. The first phase involves the aggregation of completely isolated units, each in its own territory, with or without a boundary. The second mainly involves the tangential aggregation of rectangular cells with more or less rounded edges. The third phase is the one with the most potential and involves the aggregation of coupled cells, one open and one closed. Bill Hillier and Julienne Hanson, two English scholars, have recently dedicated a scientific study to the social logic of space.[14] They concluded that one of the most basic building systems, endowed with an important psychological quality that encouraged inhabitants to meet and exchange points of view, is what they call "beady ring". They discovered this system while studying a small agglomeration of houses in the Vaucluse region of Southern France and then experimented abstractly with its combinatorial logic and sociological implications.

From an analytical standpoint, the beady ring may be traced back to an aggregate of just two elements: the closed cell with an opening on one side to per-

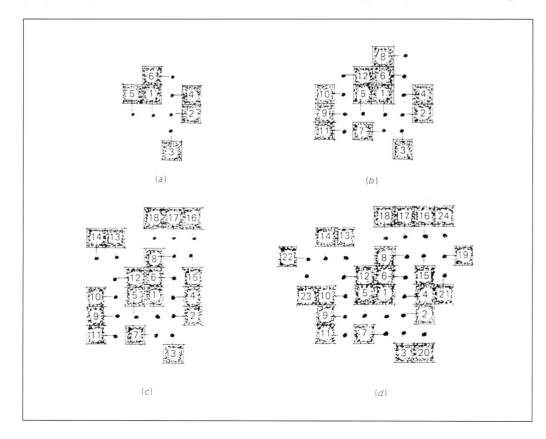

480

mit entry and the open cell, linked to the first by a door. Faced with this absolutely casual aggregation there is only one obligation: each new pair of elements must join with the others so that the adjacent open cells face one another. Hillier and Hanson state: "Other important formal properties seemed to be implicit in the beady ring generative process. All that happened, formally speaking, in that process was that each cell (with its attached open space) had been made a continuous neighbour of one other cell. Now the relation of neighbour has the formal property that if A is a neighbour of B, then B is a neighbour of A – the property that mathematicians call symmetry [...]." Hillier and Hanson call this process "distributed", since the global structure was defined by virtue of the positioning of a collection of similar yet single cells, rather than by the superimposition of a cell of a higher order vis-à-vis all the others.

The name, beady ring, corresponds perfectly to one of the first examples of the elaboration of urban culture: Hacilar's sixth strata dating back to the 6th millenium B.C. This definition may also be used for the traditional corridor road, the labyrinthine layout of Muslim cities and neighbouring districts in cities built during the Middle Ages. The sociological characteristic of this urban fabric that induced the greatest possible number of meetings between the inhabitants persuaded Hillier and Hanson to update the system by carefully projecting it into a possible future that is in some way linked to the dream of Dikaia, the good city

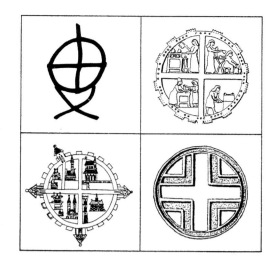

*Four very old drawings of the concept of city linked to the cross and orthogonality. A Chinese ideogram meaning "village"; an Assyrian bas-relief with city scenes (1600 B.C.); an Egyptian hieroglyphic meaning "city" and an Icelandic drawing of Celestial Jerusalem described in the* Book of Revelation.

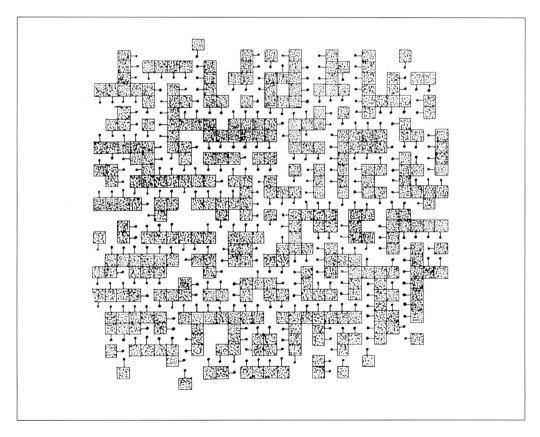

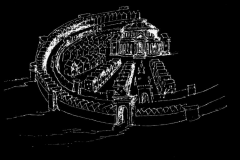

Fra Giocondo's ideal city (16th century) and a crown of pistils in a wild rose.
Right: a schematic drawing of the arrangement of the pips and stomatal lamina in chloroplasts (organelles containing chlorophyll typical of the plant parts exposed to light).

Opposite page: four examples of fortified hilltop towns drawn by Francesco di Giorgio Martini in his treatise.
Below: a panorama of Canberra (Australia).

Laminillas estromáticas (conexiones)
Grana
1

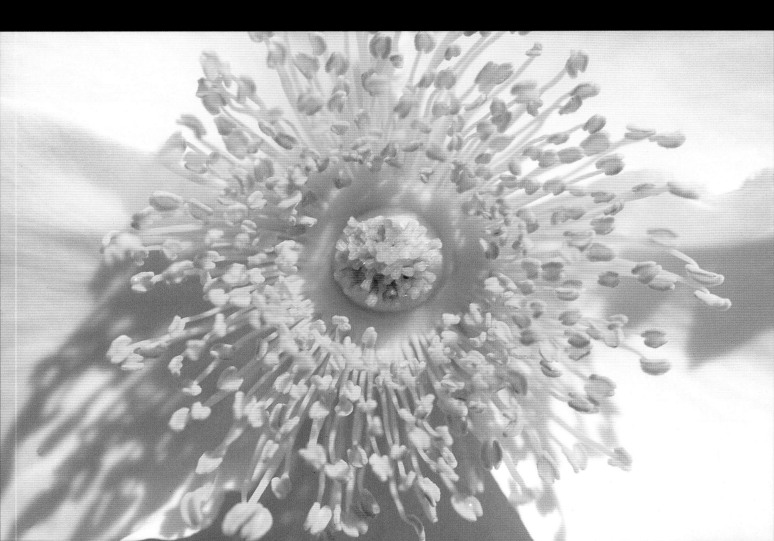

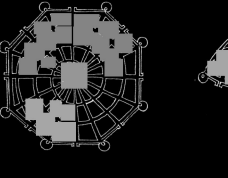

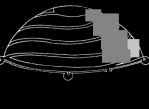

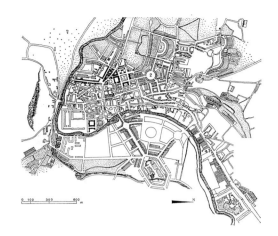

*An example of polycentrism: the plan of the village of Kunzstof in Russia (1780).*

*A view of the Royal Crescent in Bath (John Wood Jr., 1767). During the 18th-century reconstruction of Bath, polycentrism triumphed in geometrically defined independent residential homes.*

that is able to offer its citizens the joys of communication without spatial or psychological barriers.

The distributive quality, in other words the participation of each cell in the rules that govern the whole, is no longer valid when a superior cell contains all the other aggregate cells. This type of composition within a boundary is typical of urban organisms based on centrality. This subject was examined in the chapter on centrality, but it also involves town-planning and architecture. At this point, it is necessary to stress a couple of concepts regarding the specificity of urban centrality and multiple centres.

Even in the construction of cities the first sign of centrality is the cross. The Egyptian hieroglyphic for a city is a cross inside a circle and is extremely similar to the Chinese ideogram for a village. One thousand six hundred years before Christ, an Assyrian bas-relief similarly synthesised urban life by inserting four scenes into the quadrants of a circle.[15]

Rotating the cross generates more complex symmetries. The sketched drawing of a city by Fra Giocondo looks like the slices of a dissected fruit or the receptacle of a flower. Instead the most innovative design of a fortified town by Francesco di Giorgio Martini was inspired by a shell that generated the helicoidal curves of a road climbing up a hillside. The design of cities and fortifications between the 14th and 18th centuries swung between a fascination for crystalline or stellar structures and a similar attraction for biological organisms.

Polycentrality is a characteristic of the urban fabric in which either the orography or the plurality of meaningful parts has emerged vis-à-vis the overall fabric in areas of increasing functional or visual interest. For the nobleman de Chantelou, Gian Lorenzo Bernini's description of Rome is a truly effective illustration of this theatrical polycentrism: "The gentleman pointed out that from where we stood Paris appeared to be just a mass of chimneys, giving us the impression of a comb. He added that Rome was another matter, because it is possible to see Saint Peter's on one side, the Campidoglio on another and Palazzo Farnese on yet another, as well as Monte Cavallo, Palazzo San Marco, the Colosseum, the Chancellery, Palazzo Colonna and so on, all situated here and there and all so grandiose, magnificent and superb in appearance."

Polycentrism is either the result of a free and contradictory process or a sort of organically developed genetic program. If the first hypothesis fits Rome like a glove, the second is well suited to the Apulian area of the *trulli*, Alberobello, the farms in the Idra valley near Martina Franca as well as the urban district of Denbidolo in Wollega, Ethiopia.[16] The circular huts in this Abyssinian settlement play a key role in determining how the lots should be arranged. They created a polycentric pattern that to a large extent remained unaltered over the years despite transformations and market influences. On the other hand, the industrial village of Kunzstof (1780) and the town plan of Canberra by Walter Burley Griffin are intentionally polycentric; here each of the centres fulfils a different function. Despite the strict separation of function reflecting a rationalist approach *ante litteram*, the Canberra town plan integrates the urban structure and the natural landscape, partially counterbalancing its analytical severity. The outcome reached two centuries earlier in Bath is very different. Here is a city in which the Baroque legacy regarding the curvilinear shaping of space and the relationship with its natural surroundings was exploited more successfully. The Royal Crescent by John Wood the Younger juxtaposed the orderly front facade with the free volumetric design of the rear, an attempt to satisfy the different requirements of the owners. However, there is an ambiguous balance between the natural and artificial elements that interpenetrate and blend in the calculated contrast between the artificiality of the lawn and the colonnade and the natural landscape in the distance.

Natural polycentric models may always be found when matter is organised in a complex manner, especially, for instance, in crystalline aggregates.[17]

In primitive civilisations, the layout of the various areas of the village, as well as of the house, often corresponds to an anthropomorphic model that determines the orderly distribution of those parts which fulfil functional and psychological requirements. This is the case of the Fali settlements of the already cited houses of the Dogon tribe, the Todo villages in Indonesia and the village of Togo on the island of Manggarrai West Flores in Indonesia. This anthropomorphic interpretation often extends to the entire territory as on the island of Ponape in Mi-

*An example of polycentrality in nature: the inflorescence of the* Ferula comunis, *a herbaceous plant of the Umbrellifers.*

*The city suggested by Dinocrates to Alexander the Great in an imaginative reconstruction by Johann Bernhard Fischer von Erlach (*Entwurf einer Historischen Architectur, *Vienna 1721).*

485

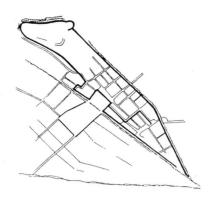

cronesia. According to legend, the island embodies its original builder, Mautok. His body, stretching from east to west, corresponds to the various areas of the island: his head to the east (district of Matoleim), his arms to the north (district of Not), his body to the northwest (district of Tsokes) and his legs to the south-west (district of Kiti).[18]

Vitruvius and Herodotus tell the story of Dinocritus who suggested to Alexander the Great that Mount Athos become an enormous open-air representation of the conqueror himself, portrayed with a city in one hand and a spring in the other. This is probably the most sensational case so far of anthropomorphism and urban megalomania: however, it got no further than the design phase. Instead, a clear case of zoomorphism is Brasilia by Lucio Costa. When Kubischek tasked him with this project, Costa chose the symbolic profile of a bird in flight.

More ancient examples of intentional zoomorphism include the Inca capital of Cuzco, shaped like a puma,[19] and the city of Musumba, capital of Mwata Yamvu, shaped like a turtle, perhaps due to the defensive characteristics of its shell. In a less direct way, these zoomorphic traits are also present in certain projects of fortified cities by Francesco di Giorgio Martini, as well as the fortress of Sassocorvaro.

Apart from consciously choosing zoomorphism for symbolic reasons, in certain settlements biomorphism is often an unconscious choice. This type of bio-

*Examples of zoomorphism in the design of cities: Cuzco during the Inca period with its characteristic profile of a puma, an animal they considered sacred. The fortress (or temple) of Sacsahuaman acted as the puma's head.*
*The Indian village of Nodwell near Lake Huron with houses along the inside of the fence.*
*Below: a photograph of a microbic culture.*
*Right: the plan of Brasilia (Lucio Costa, 1958) with the cross structure that resembles the profile of a big bird (Lucio Costa, 1960).*

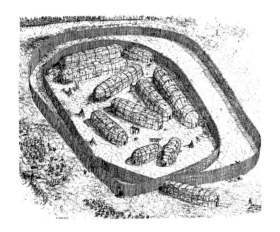

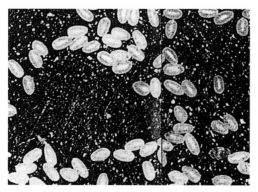

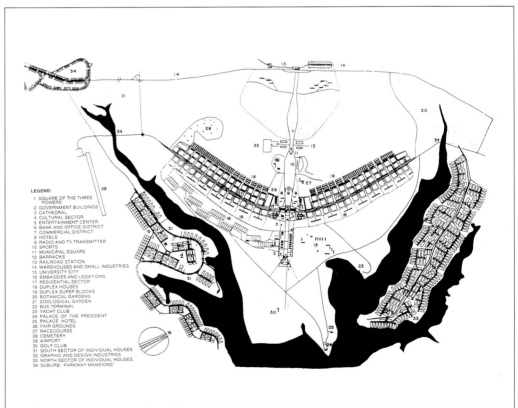

LEGEND:
1 SQUARE OF THE THREE POWERS
2 GOVERNMENT BUILDINGS
3 CATHEDRAL
4 CULTURAL SECTOR
5 ENTERTAINMENT CENTER
6 BANK AND OFFICE DISTRICT
7 COMMERCIAL DISTRICT
8 HOTELS
9 RADIO AND TV TRANSMITTER
10 SPORTS
11 MUNICIPAL SQUARE
12 BARRACKS
13 RAILROAD STATION
14 WAREHOUSES AND SMALL INDUSTRIES
15 UNIVERSITY CITY
16 EMBASSIES AND LEGATIONS
17 RESIDENTIAL SECTOR
18 DUPLEX HOUSES
19 DUPLEX SUPER BLOCKS
20 BOTANICAL GARDENS
21 ZOOLOGICAL GARDEN
22 BUS TERMINAL
23 YACHT CLUB
24 PALACE OF THE PRESIDENT
25 PALACE HOTEL
26 FAIR GROUNDS
27 RACECOURSE
28 CEMETERY
29 AIRPORT
30 GOLF CLUB
31 SOUTH SECTOR OF INDIVIDUAL HOUSES
32 GRAPHIC AND DESIGN INDUSTRIES
33 NORTH SECTOR OF INDIVIDUAL HOUSES
34 SUBURB "PARKWAY MANSIONS"

morphism is visible in the similarities between the vascular system and the urban fabric from the point of view of mobility, its wide and narrow roads, its open areas, its squares. A milestone article by Christopher Alexander in 1965[20], persuasively states that the city cannot be reduced to just a seamless system of ramifications, like some sort of tree. It has to be full of intersections and superimpositions and assume the shape of a "semi-lattice." Alexander maintains that for the human mind, the tree is the best instrument to control complex thoughts. But the city is not a tree, not should it be. The city is the receptacle of life. But a dendromorphic city is the type of receptacle that severs every superimposition, every inference of vital elements. Like a box internally lined with razor sharp blades ready to cut up anything placed inside, life itself would be cut to shreds inside this receptacle. If we design tree-shaped cities, this is what will happen to our lives.

Thirty years after Alexander's criticism of the artificial city championed by the Modern Movement had been universally accepted, perhaps it is now possible to ransom the tree from the sins of the analytical city by stating that, even though branches maintain their independence, leaves do brush one other and intersect exactly as Alexander had said they should in a natural city, namely through the intense and multiple relationships between people and objects that are generated by the city's complex spatial structure.

Notwithstanding the sociological implications, it is difficult to deny that the most common growth process in human settlements is linked to ramification, despite the fact that in our modern cities – so indifferent to orographic faults yet faithful to Hippodameus' model – ramification is normally characterised by the rigidity that marks the "dendridical" growth of mineral crystals.[21]

Generally speaking, dendrite development occurs when there is rapid growth (excessive cooling of molten metal and, in general, excessive saturation in a solution) or a chemically and physically non-homogeneous environment (little diffusion and convection of matter and thermal gradients). The model examines a crystallisation nucleus that begins to grow by adding atoms or groups of atoms in specific directions, depending on the arrangement of the atoms in the various levels of the nucleus and the chemical and physical characteristics of the environment around those specific directions. As soon as each group of atoms enters the crystallisation nucleus it releases a certain amount of latent heat that causes the temperature immediately surrounding the point of contact to rise. When the temperature around the developing branch of a dendrite reaches the melting point of that metal, growth in that direction stops momentarily and begins in other crystallographic points initially less favourable. During this process, some dendrite arms can melt and provide new centres of enucleation that tend to continue to develop as dendrites. The speed of growth of the various dendrite arms therefore depends on how quickly this latent crystallisation heat is removed.

"Repeating this process in different directions will create 'dendrite arms,' and may thus be considered as a single crystal characterised by just one crystal-

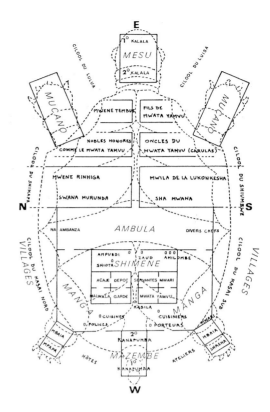

*The city of Musumba, capital of the Empire of Balunda (Zaire). A typical example of African capitals that changed location every time there was a new monarch (19th century).*

487

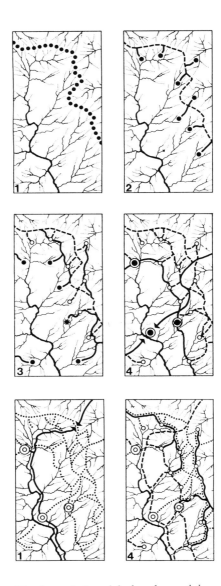

lographic orientation that has grown in a disorderly fashion from a sole crystallisation nucleus."[22]

A dendritic analogy closer to the plant world is visible in those settlements in which the main road has a series of side roads that branch off in a pattern that, depending on the angle, looks like a fish bone, a hazel leaf or a spike. When two streets are parallel they can be compared to the leaf of the *Clidemia hirta*. Instead, when many transversal nervations are joined only by a ring-road, the closest biological model is the *Mallomones*.

This similarity with leaf venation also applies to the tissue of the veins that vascularise the tissue of the areola contained in the nervation. This labyrinthine tissue in which the veins ramify in a *cul de sac* fashion is amazingly similar to the structure of Islamic cities as well as many cities in Spain and Southern Italy. As I pointed out in the chapter on metamorphosis, the ring morphology so typical of hilltop town is similar to the growth of tree trunks which acquire a new ring every year, while the amphitheatre or half-moon pattern recalls the curve of ribs and inspired Soria y Mata to invent the Ciudad Lineal.

Adaptation to the site is one of the more tangible results of this alliance with the earth and is normally expressed through the settlement's docile obedience to the lie of the land. This consists in placing the building units along the same contour lines. By so doing, this artificial operation reproduces the shape of the sedimentary rocks turned into terraces by the erosion of wind and water. There are

*The theoretical model of road growth based on the orographic lie of the land. Initially, only the ridge route along the valley existed. Then transversal roads leading to hilltop sites chosen for the settlements branched off this route. The third phase involved counter-ridge roads, settlements on low headlands and elementary urban nuclei.*
*In the fourth phase these counter-ridge roads became continuous; urban nuclei at the beginning or half way up the valley gradually began to be built along the river bed.*
*The last two phases involved the construction of roads along the valley floors and the solution to the problem of mountain passes, and lastly, when the territory seemed to be completely structured, the counter-ridge roads became more important.*

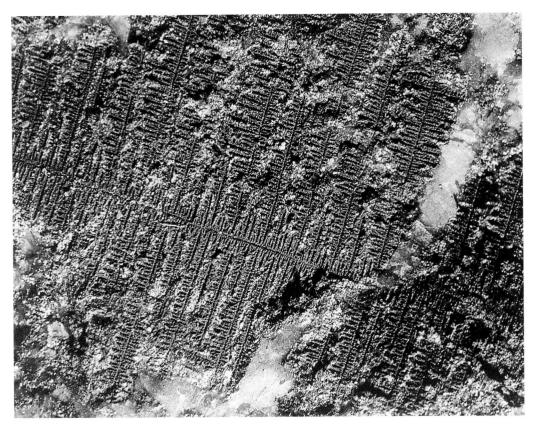

488

An aerial view of an agricultural settlement in the
Xinjiang province in China.

489

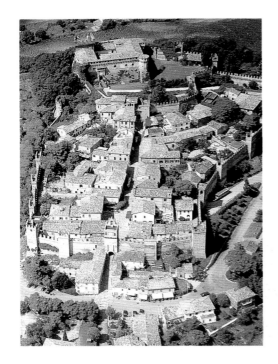

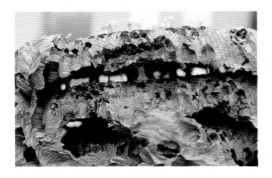

*Top: the medieval town of Gradara in Romagna (Italy) next to the structure of a leaf; above: a termite mound photographed in Sydney and a hornet's nest photographed in Abano (Italy).*

*An aerial photograph of Palombara Sabina near Rome (Italy), a typical example of a central settlement with concentric rings.*

A spider's web and an aerial photograph of a Chinese city on the tropical delta of the River of Pearls near Guangzhou.

Opposite page: various types of leaf venation:
a) Clidemia hirta; b) Ficus religiosa; c) Plantago lanceaolata, parallel venation; d) Plantago major; e) Smilax aspera, reticular venation;
f) characteristic configuration of the areola with terminal veins; g) variations in a constant type of secondary venation; Dt: guttation apex.
Below: an aerial view of Martina Franca (Italy), a labyrinthine plan with curvilinear roads that spread out in all directions.

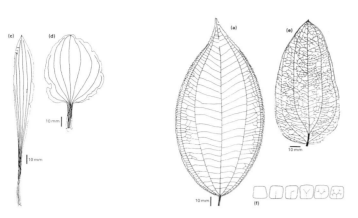

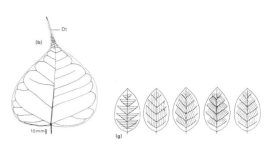

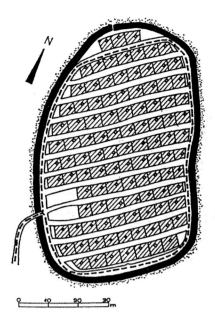

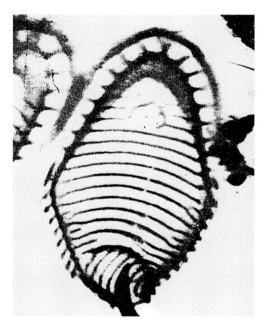

*From top: a plan by Morini; the image of a diatom.*
*Right: the labyrinthine pattern of the veins of a leaf.*

desert regions in China where the wind and water have formed regular-shaped terracing, anticipating the rice fields built by man. The concept of terracing reveals the intense relationship between architecture and agriculture, a relationship solemnly and indelibly impressed in the colonnades that support the pergola of the Carema vineyards in Piedmont.[23] Agricultural terracing is also responsible for having created complex shelters for the characteristic citrus orchards of the Sorrento coastline. On a broader scale, settlements nestling on hillsides the world over bear witness to a common inclination to listen humbly to nature. This inclination has given rise to the more typical settlements such as those along a ridge or a headland, "like the acropolis spindle," winding around a generating nucleus or shaped like a bell, an octopus or an amphitheatre.

When favourable conditions are created by pathways and the way in which they are linked, the patterns inspired by orography are also developed on flat land. Often over the centuries, curvilinear squares and roads have revealed man's appreciation for the visual virtues of curved structures in the urban fabric due to the variety of lighting effects and the element of surprise they produce; they let symbolic or architectural objects be discovered gradually and create a feeling of enveloping space. After three centuries in which big straight roads became the preferred solution since they allowed popular uprisings to be tackled with crossbows and firearms, even Leon Battista Alberti in his *De Re Aedificatoria*[24] had to praise the attractive charm of curvilinearity.

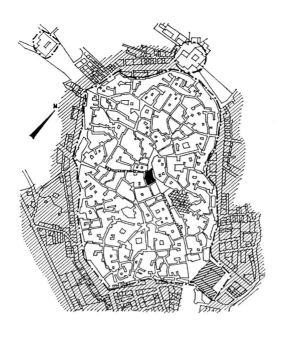

*The plan of Martina Franca (Italy) and, below, the structure of the city of Edo in Japan (Akira Naito). Left: natural terracing in a desert area in China.*

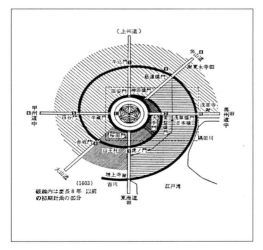

*Pergola and terraces for grape growing in Carema (Italy).*

*An Apennine settlement on a hillside.*

*Left, from top: the boundary walls of fields near Ragusa and cane brakes to protect fruit trees from the cold (Sorrento). By fencing and defending the crops, agriculture anticipates or transcribes the language of architecture.*
*Above: an aerial view of Vignanello near Viterbo (Italy) with the castle belonging to the Ruspoli family; the trunk of an olive tree whose curvilinear branches seem to have been used as a model for the roads of late Medieval towns.*

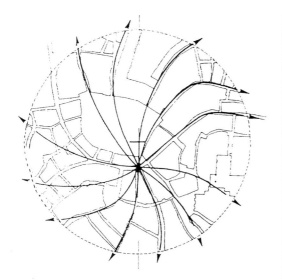

An aerial view of the centre of Siena, and a schematic drawing of the curvilinear roads that lead to Piazza del Campo.

Siena is one of the cities in which this curvilinear concept triumphs in an un-equalled masterpiece of town-planning on a human scale. The Piazza del Campo (its fan-shape recalls the cloak of the Virgin Mary in the iconography of "Maestà") is surrounded by a spiral of roads whose curvilinear pattern is only partially justified by the lie of the land. Instead, the pattern seems to be both a question of taste as well as a homage to natural morphology, leaf venation and the ring of petals around a flower's receptacle.

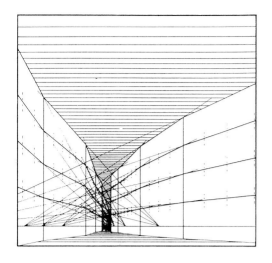

A significant variation on the curvilinear model, often due to the changes that take place over the years in the alignment of buildings along a road, is what I have called the "hinged wall" model.[25] In this case the curves are substituted with disjointed segments (sometimes with a number of curvilinear traits) which correspond to the roadside lot. Extremely frequent in the Renaissance district of Rome, this model constantly modifies the spatial value of the road, giving each facade the privilege of being the one to act as a backdrop to the perspective.

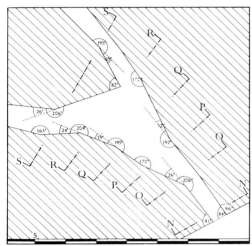

Apart from its development, the city represents the most extensive and violent act of man as an agent of change upon the face of the earth. However, it is also the phenomenon which, in certain places and during certain periods in the history of mankind, has intensely and poetically illustrated his ability to obey the *genius loci*, interpreting a sort of hidden vocation of the landscape and at times succeeding in convincingly "continuing" the work of creation.

In those areas in which nature has drawn welcoming forms, made to envelop, contain and embrace, such as gulfs, hollows, hilltops and rocky peaks, the work of man has been added to the landscape as a "preordained" event, necessary and expected. In these cases, the events that take place during the birth of a city are similar to crystals falling into a liquid or the transformation of water into snowflakes due to a drop in temperature: a change in condition, an internal reaction within mother earth, a non-violent transformation, as if matter possessed a secret desire to interpret its own latent laws governing composition. The naturalness surrounding this event is all the more forceful the more explicit the feeling that a place, a defined portion of space, has been "measured" and enclosed, to wait, like a flower awaiting the fertile pollen, for the advent of Amfion's lyre capable of lifting stones and transporting them to their proper and definite resting place. This has happened in Orvieto, Machu Picchu, Calcata and Scicli. Here, where the morphology of nature reverberates in the houses of man built in the same material as the underlying rock, the everyday repetition of a sacred temple, is Celestial Jerusalem incarnate.

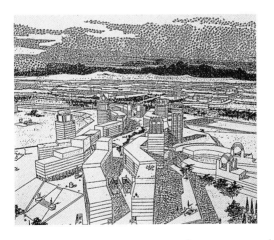

*The theme of the "hinged walls;" the study of part of the urban fabric of Rome included in the project for an office complex in the Prenestino district (L. Passarelli, P. Portoghesi, E. Salzano, P.L. Spadolini, 1990).*

Like a large living organism, the city contains organs and systems that have a certain degree of independence yet carry out specific functions in conjunction with one another. The overall picture of urban mobility corresponds to both the nervous and circulatory systems. It is the mould, so to speak, of the built volumes that make up the material structures of the city and constitute the immaterial *continuum* that makes the city inhabitable. Mobility is made of roads,

*Pictures of Calcata, Scicli and Orvieto: three Italian examples of the perfect balance between the natural landscape and the city.*

*Opposite page: "The city is not a tree," wrote Christopher Alexander, but a complete relational system. Nor may we say that a city is like a leaf in which all the veins lead to a sole canal; but this analogy helps us to understand the difference and continues even when the leaf has withered and crumbled. Then its shape evokes the city cancelled by time and discovered anew by the hand of man in the form of fragments, fragile remains menaced by time.*

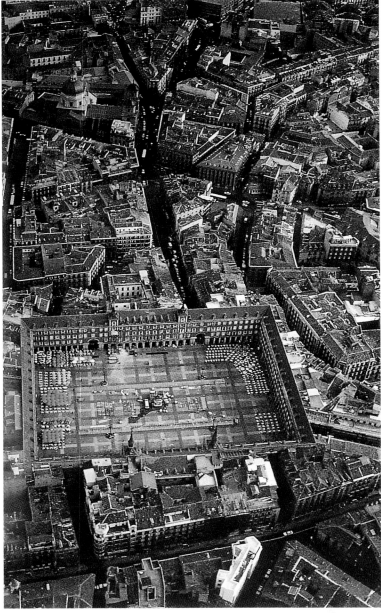

*Aerial views of Bath with the Royal Circus and the Royal Crescent, and of the Plaza Major in Madrid.*

squares and all those intermediate and complementary intersections such as junctions with two or even three roads, squares, gardens, terraces, open or semi-open spaces in which to sit or walk, meet, be together, exchange goods and glances, carry out rites or battles. In brief, everything man does in everyday life is executed and sediments; it acquires new value for the simple reason it is contained in an involucre in which the past and the future confront each other.

After having been simple walkways slowly taking possession of nature, roads enter the city. Upon entering they become internal space, the corridor of everyone's house. To each side "walls" rise up, separating yet at the same time creating a link through doors and windows. What was a walkway, a frail sign left to the incessant action of the elements, is turned into a protected space, a conquered space, ratified by being given a toponym, by being destined to generate true dialogue between different generations separated by physical time but reunited by the sacred time of the city.

Crossroads, intersections and junctions represent the ramification of this walkway, the reification of possible choices. They give the road a history that blends past events with the prefiguration of the unknown. On the other hand, the square, a point of arrival and respite, a place of convergence and ramification, is also absorbed by the city structure as a contemplative exception. It is a rose between the thorns of the streets, a symbolic site of exchange and encounter, a "place of glances," in which events dig deep roots, a place of collective memory. It demands to be noticed and introjected, a symbolic place of comparison, confrontation or structure of civilian, religious, governmental and dynastic powers. The "heart" metaphor has often been used to define the role played by the square in the city. Nostalgia clouds the fact that in most modern cities this role has been substituted by the assault of motor vehicles. In the fifth of this *Duino Elegies*, Rilke talks of the square. Instead of using a stale metaphor, he highlights how this archetype of *living together* with places on earth has been internalised:

*Piazza Santa Maria della Pace in Rome compared to a gorge near Calcata (Italy).*

*Brazil, a steep road in Ouro Preto (Brazil).*

503

*A picture of the "organ towers" in Zion Canyon (Utah).*

Angel: suppose there's a place we don't know of and there
on an indescribable carpet lovers could show the feats
they aren't able to show here
the daring high figures of the heart's leap
their towers of ecstasy their ladders long since
propped against each other where there was never any ground
trembling and they *could* before the surrounding spectators,
the hushed innumerable dead:
wouldn't those dead throw them then their forever hoarded
and hidden unknown to us but eternally current coins of happiness
at the feet of the pair whose smile was finally
truthful there on that fulfilled carpet?[26]

*Project by Hans Poelzig for a big building in Berlin. Encircled by the railway like a river, the building rises like a rocky peak and adds a dramatic flavour to the urban scene, considered a tangled mass of conflicting forces.*

[1] cf., F. Milizia, *Principi di Architettura Civile*, Remondini, Bassano 1813, t. II, p. 27.

[2] cf., P: Laureano, *Sahara, giardino sconosciuto*, Giunti, Florence 1988 and *La piramide rovesciata*, Bollati Boringhieri, Turin 1995.

[3] cf., J.-P. Maurer, G. Maurer, *Petra Frühe Felsarhitektur in Jordanien*, Turistbuach, Hannover 1985.

[4] cf., M. Bussagli, *Architettura orientale*, Electa, Milan 1981; P. Portoghesi, B. Zevi, *Michelangelo architetto*, Einaudi, Turin 1964.

[5] cf., J.J. Brody, *Anasazi*, Jaca book, Milan 1990.

[6] cf., G. Gasparini, Margolies L., *Inca Architecture*, Indiana University Press, Bloomington 1980, pp. 160 foll.

[7] cf., Ö. Demir, *Cappadocia*, Demir, Ankara 1990.

[8] R. Schwarz, *Von Bau der Kirche*, Werkbundverlag, Würzburg 1938; cf., also R. Schwarz, *Kirchenbau, Welt vor der Schwelle*, Kerle, Heidelberg 1960.

[9] cf., P. Portoghesi, *Le inibizioni dell'architettura moderna*, Laterza, Bari 1979, p. 44.

[10] cf., *Roma interrotta*, catalogue of the Exhibition held in the Mercati di Traiano, Officina, Rome 1977.

[11] cf. for this interesting hypothesis on the religious meaning of the channels: G. Feo, *Dei della terra*, ECIG, Genoa 1991.

[12] cf., P. Portoghesi, *La piazza come luogo degli sguardi*, edited by M. Pisani, Gangemi, Rome 1990, p. 109.

[13] cf., J. Antonio Martinez Perez, M. Elias Gutiérrez, *Introduction a la protozoología*, Trillas, Mexico 1985.

[14] cf., B. Hillier, J. Hanson, *The Social Logic of Space*, Cambridge University Press, Cambridge 1994.

[15] cf., N. Crowe, *Nature and the Idea of a Manmade World*, The MIT Press, Cambridge (Mass.) 1995, p. 52.

[16] cf., P. Maretto, *Nell'architettura*, Teorema, Florence 1973, p. 209: "The analysis of the current lie of the land makes it possible to study the traces of primitive tribal headland settlements, circular in shape from the point of view of the estate, the buildings and the architecture (zariba ghebì tucul); the basic layout remained even after transition to a barter economy."

[17] cf., C.S. Hurlbut Jr., *Il mondo dei minerali*, Garzanti, Milan 1968 (*Minerals and man*, New York 1968).

[18] cf., P. Olivier, *Shelter, Sign and Symbol*, Barrie & Jenkins, London 1975; R. Pettazzoni, *Miti e leggende*, Einaudi, Turin 1963, v. II, p. 517.

[19] cf., G. Gasparini, L. Margolies, *op.cit.*, p. 48.

[20] C. Alexander, "The City Is Not a Tree," *The Architectural Forum*, April-May 1965. The Italian translation is in the Appendix in: idem, *Note sulle sintesi della forma*, Il Saggiatore, Milan 1967, p. 194.

[21] cf., G. Tanelli, *Conoscere i minerali*, Longanesi, Milan 1988.

[22] cf., G. Tanelli, *op.cit.*, pp. 97-99.

[23] cf., A. Cavallari Murat, *Tra Serra Orco e Po*, Turin 1976.

[24] cf., Leon Battista Alberti, *L'Architettura*, translation by G. Orlandi, Il Polifilo, Milan 1989, Book IV, chap. V, p. 162.

[25] cf., P. Portoghesi, "Roma Amor: Difference and repetition", in *VIA, The Journal of the graduate school of Fine Arts*, University of Pennsylvania, no. 5, The MIT Press, Cambridge and London 1982, p. 37.

[26] R. M. Rilke, *Duino Elegies*, W.W. Norton & Co., New York 1978, p. 56.

# Bibliography

The term of the bibliography is 1995, consignement date of the manuscript.

**A**

Abas Syed Jan, Amer Shaker Salman, *Symmetries of Islamic Geometrical Patterns*, World Scientific Publishing Co., Singapore 1995.

Ackermann Jennifer G. (ed.), *The Curious Naturalist*, National Geographic Society, Washington 1991.

Adams William Howard, *Nature Perfected. Gardens Through History*, Abbeville Press, New York 1991.

Ageitos de Castellanos Zulma J., Lopretto Estela C., *Los invertebrados. Tomo II*, Libreria Agropecuaria, Buenos Aires 1990.

Agostino Aurelio, *Ordine, musica, bellezza*, Rusconi, Milan 1992.

*Ai tempi della Bibbia*, Mondadori, Milan 1989.

Albera Giovanni, Monti Nicolas, *Mediterranean Houses Italy*, Editorial Gustavo Gili, Barcelona 1992.

Albrecht Benno, Benevolo Leonardo, *I confini del paesaggio umano*, Laterza, Rome-Bari 1994.

Allaby Michael, *Animal Artisans*, Alfred A. Knopf, New York 1982.

Alleau René, *La scienza dei simboli*, Sansoni, Florence 1985.

Amariu Costantin, *L'uovo*, Edizioni Mediterranee, Rome 1988.

Andersson Malte, *Sexual Selection*, Princeton University Press, Princeton 1994.

Andrews George F., *Maya Cities. Placemaking and Urbanization*, University of Oklahoma Press, Oklahoma City 1975.

Andrews W.S., *Magic Squares and Cubes*, Dover Publications, New York 1960.

Angela Piero, *La macchina meravigliosa. Alla scoperta del corpo umano*, Istituto Geografico De Agostini, Novara 1990.

Anderson Donald M., *Elements of Design*, Holt, Rinehart and Winston, New York 1961.

Antoniades Anthony C., *Poetics of Architecture. Theory of Design,* Van Nostrand Reinhold, New York 1992.

*Antropologia della casa*, Carabba, Lanciano 1981.

Appleton Jay, *The Simbolism of Habitat. An Interpretation of Landscape in the Arts*, University of Washington Press, Seattle-London 1990.

Arcidiacono Giuseppe, *Spazio, iperspazi, frattali. Il magico mondo della geometria*, Di Renzo, Rome 1993.

Ardalan Nader, Bakhtiar Laleh, *The Sense of Unity. The Sufi Tradition in Persian Architecture*, University of Chicago Press, Chicago-London 1973.

Aristotele, *Breviario*, Rusconi, Milan 1995.

Aristotele, *Poetica*, Laterza, Bari 1946.

Aristotele, *Retorica*, Laterza, Rome-Bari 1961.

Arnheim Rudolf, *La dinamica della forma architettonica*, Feltrinelli, Milan 1981.

Arnheim Rudolf, *The Dynamics of Architectural Form*, University of California Press, Berkeley-Los Angeles 1977.

Arnol'd Vladimir I., *Teoria delle catastrofi*, Bollati Boringhieri, Turin 1990.

Artemidoro, *Il libro dei sogni*, Adelphi, Milan 1975.

Ashe Geoffrey, *Atlantis*, Thames and Hudson, London 1992.

Assunto Rosario, *Il paesaggio e l'estetica*, Giannini Editore, Naples 1973.

Assunto Rosario, *La città di Anfione e la città di Prometeo. Idea e poetiche della città*, Jaca Book, Milan 1984.

Assunto Rosario, *La critica d'arte nel pensiero medievale*, Il Saggiatore, Milan 1961.

Assunto Rosario, *La natura, le arti, la storia*, Guerini e Associati, Milan 1990.

Atkinson R.J.C., *Stonehenge*, Pelican Books, Harmondsworth 1960.

Attenborough David, *A vida na terra*, Martins Fontes Editora, São Paulo 1990.

Attenborough David, *La vita sulla terra*, Rizzoli, Milan 1986.

Augé Marc, *Non luoghi. Introduzione a una antropologia della surmodernità*, Elèuthera, Milan 1993.

**B**

Bach Klaus, Graefe Rainer (eds.), *Form. Il 22*, Institut für Leichte Flächentragwerke, Stuttgart 1990.

Bach Klaus (ed.), *Radiolarien. Il 33*, Institut für Leichte Flächentragwerke, Stuttgart 1990.

Bachelard Gaston, *La poetica dello spazio*, Dedalo Libri, Bari 1975 (*La Poétique de l'espace*, Paris 1967[5]).

Bachelard Gaston, *La Terra e le forze. Le immagini della volontà*, Red, Como 1989.

Bachelard Gaston, *Psicanalisi delle acque. Purificazione, morte e rinascita*, Red, Como 1992.

Badawy Alexander, *A History of Egyptian Architecture*, University of California Press, Berkeley-Los Angeles 1966.

Baicchi Elio, Degli Esposti Umberto, Habert Isacco, *Di luogo in luogo*, Pitagora, Bologna 1989.

Bain George, *Celtic Art. The Methods of Construction*, Constable, London 1977.

Bairati Cesare, *La simmetria dinamica, scienza ed arte nell'architettura classica*, Libreria Editrice Politecnica Tamburini, Milan 1952.

Baker Geoffrey, Gubler Jacques (eds.), *Le Corbusier. Early Works by Charles-Edouard Jeanneret-Gris*, Academy Editions, London 1987.

Bakhtiar Laleh, *Sufi. Expressions of the Mystic Quest*, Thames and Hudson, London 1976.

Baldon Cleo, Ib Melchior, with Julius Shulman*, Steps & Stairways*, Rizzoli International, New York 1989.

Ballard Robert D., *Alla scoperta del pianeta terra*, Touring Club Italiano, Milan 1988.

Bamford Christopher (ed.), *Homage to Pythagoras*, Lindisfarne Association, Hudson (N.Y.) 1982.

Banchoff Thomas F., *Oltre la terza dimensione*, Zanichelli, Bologna 1995.

Bancroft Peter, *Le pietre più belle del mondo*, Muzzio, Padua 1990.

Barlow Connie (ed.), *Evolution Extended. Biological Debates on the Meaning of Life*, MIT Press, Cambridge (Mass.) 1994.

Baroni Eugenio, Guzzanti Vincenzo, *Elementi di biologia. Vol. I - Botanica*, Cappelli, Bologna 1937.

Gregory Bateson, *Mente e natura*, Adelphi, Milan 1984.

Batty Michael, Longley Paul, *Fractal Cities*, Academic Press, London 1994.

Beaumont de Gérard, *Guide des vertébrés fossiles*, Delachaux et Niestlé, Neuchâtel 1973.

Bechmann Roland, *Le radici delle cattedrali. L'architettura gotica espressione delle condizioni dell'ambiente*, Marietti, Casale Monferrato 1984.

Bell Adrian D., *La forma delle piante. Guida illustrata al-*

*la morfologia delle angiosperme*, Zanichelli, Bologna 1993 (*Plant form*, Oxford-New York 1991).

*Bellezze del mondo invisibile*, Istituto Geografico De Agostini, Novara 1960.

Belli Gabriella, Rella Franco (eds.), *La città e le forme*, Mazzotta, Milan 1987.

Belotti Gabriella (ed.), *Del virtuale*, Editrice il Rostro, Milan 1993.

Benjamin Walter, *L'opera d'arte nell'epoca della sua riproducibilità tecnica*, Einaudi, Turin 1966.

Bentley W.A., Humphreys W.J., *Snow Crystals*, Dover Publications, New York 1962.

Bernbaum Edwin, *Le montagne sacre del mondo*, Leonardo, Milan 1990.

Bettex Albert, *La filosofia della natura. Enciclopedia universale illustrata delle scoperte dell'uomo*, Longanesi, Milan 1965.

Betto Frei, *A Obra do Artista. Uma visão holística do Universo*, Editora Ática, São Paulo 1995.

Bevilacqua Francesco, *Calabria. Immagini della natura*, Abramo Editore, Catanzaro 1992.

Biedermann Hans, *Dictionary of Symbolism*, Meridian Book, New York 1994.

Bierhorst John, *Miti pellerossa*, Longanesi, Milan 1984.

Biraghi Marco, *Porta multifrons*, Sellerio, Palermo 1992.

Blackwell William, *Geometry in Architecture*, Wiley-Interscience Publication, New York 1984.

Bloch Ernst, *Spirito dell'utopia*, La Nuova Italia, Scandicci 1992.

Blossfeldt Karl, *Fotografie*, Cantz Verlag, Ostfildern 1994.

Blossfeldt Karl, *Urformen der Kunst Wundergarten der Natur*, Schirmer-Mosel, Munich-Paris-London 1994.

Bodanis David, *The Secret House*, Simon & Schuster, New York 1988.

Bolon Carol R., Nelson Robert S., Seidel Linda, *The Nature of Frank Lloyd Wright*, University of Chicago Press, Chicago-London 1988.

Boncompagni Solas, *Il mondo dei simboli. Numeri, lettere e figure geometriche*, Edizioni Mediterranee, Rome 1990.

Bonet Correa Antonio, *Figuras, modelos e imágenes en los tratadistas españoles*, Alianza Editorial, Madrid 1993.

Bonner John Tyler, *Morphogenesis*, Atheneum, New York 1963.

Bonucci Andrea, *Guida alla speleologia*, Editori Riuniti, Rome 1983.

Bony Jean, *French Cathedrals*, Thames and Hudson, London 1954.

Borissavliévitch M., *Les théories de l'architecture*, Payot, Paris 1951.

Borissavliévitch M., *Traité d'estétique scientifique de l'architecture*, Paris 1954.

Borsi Franco, König Giovanni K., *Architettura dell'espressionismo*, Vitali e Ghianda, Genoa 1966.

Bortolotti Lucio, Pierantoni Maria Assunta, *I boschi d'Italia*, Edizioni Abete, Rome 1992.

*Botanica. Photographies des végétaux aux XIX et XX siècles*, Centre National de la Photographie, Paris 1987.

Botkin Daniel B., *Armonias discordantes. Una ecologia para el siglo XXI*, Acento Editorial, Madrid 1993.

Boudon Philippe, *Sur l'espace architectural*, Dunod, Paris 1971.

Boulay Roger, *La Maison Kanak*, Editions Parenthèses, Marseilles 1990.

Bourgeois Jean-Louis, Pelos Carollee, *Spectacular Vernacular. The Adobe Tradition*, Aperture Foundation, New York 1989.

Bourne Samuel, *Images of India*, The Friends of Photography, Carmel 1983.

Boys Charles V., *Le bolle di sapone e le forze che le modellano*, Zanichelli, Bologna 1982.

Bragdon Claude, *Architecture and Democracy*, Alfred A. Knopf, New York 1918.

Bragdon Claude, *The Beautiful Necessity. Architecture as "Frozen Music"*, Theosophical Publishing House, Wheaton 1978.

Bragdon Claude, *The Frozen Fountain*, Books for Libraries Press, Freeport, New York 1970.

Bragdon Claude, *Projective Ornament*, Dover Publications, New York 1992.

Braschi Enzo, *Il popolo del Grande Spirito. Le tradizioni, la cultura e i riti religiosi degli indiani d'America*, Mursia, Milan 1986.

Breeden Stanley, Wright Belinda, *Kakadu. Australia*, Steve Parish Publishing, Fortitude Valley, Queensland 1995.

Breger Dee, *Journey in Microspace. The Art of the Scanning Electron Microscope*, Columbia University Press, New York 1995.

Briggs John, *L'estetica del Caos. Avventure nel mondo dei frattali: scienza, arte e natura*, Red, Como 1993 (*Fractals: the Patterns of Chaos*, New York 1992).

Briggs J., Peat F.D., *Espejo y reflejo: del caos al orden*, Editorial Gedisa, Barcelona 1994.

Brizzi Bruno, *L'Italia nell'età della pietra*, Edizioni Quasar, Rome 1977.

Broadbent Geoffrey, *Design in Architecture*, David Fulton Publishers, London 1988.

Brockman John, *La terza cultura*, Garzanti, Milan 1995.

Brodatz Phil, *Land, Sea & Sky*, Dover Publications, New York 1976.

Brody Jerry J., *Anasazi. La civiltà degli antichi indiani Pueblo*, Jaca Book, Milan 1990.

Brosse Jacques, *Mitologia degli alberi. Dal giardino dell'Eden al legno della Croce*, Rizzoli, Milan 1994.

Brosse Jacques, *Storie e leggende degli alberi*, Studio Tesi, Pordenone 1991.

Bryan James, Sauer Rolf (eds.), *Structures Implicit and Explicit*, Graduate School of Fine Arts, University of Pennsylvania, Philadelphia 1973.

Buchsbaum Ralph, Buchsbaum Mildred, Pearse John, Pearse Vicki, *Animals Without Backbones*, University of Chicago, Chicago-London 1987.

Beuno Mariano, *Vivir en casa sana*, Ediciones Martínez Roca, Barcelona 1988.

Buisson Dominique, *L'architecture sacrée au Japon*, ACR Edition, Courbevoie 1989.

Burckhardt Titus, *L'art de l'Islam. Langage et signification*, Editions Sindbad, Paris 1985.

Burckhardt Titus, *Moorish Culture in Spain*, George Allen & Unwin, London 1972.

Burger Edmund, *Geormophic Architecture*, Van Nostrand Reinhold, New York 1986.

Burgess Jeremy, Marten Michael, Taylor Rosemary, *Microscopie. Explorer l'invisible*, Larousse, Paris 1991.

Bussagli Mario, *Architettura orientale*, Electa, Milan 1988.

**C**

Caglioti Giuseppe, *Simmetrie infrante nella scienza e nell'arte*, Clup, Milan 1983.

Caillois Roger, *L'écriture des pierres*, Editions d'Art Albert Skira, Geneva 1970.

Calasso Roberto, *Le nozze di Cadmo e Armonia*, Adelphi, Milan 1988.

*Calatrava Santiago 1883-1993*, Exhibition's catalogue, Valencia, 1993, El Croquis Editorial, Madrid 1993.

Calderon Gérald (ed.), *La vita segreta degli insetti*, Istituto Geografico De Agostini, Novara 1975.

Cali François, *La plus grande adventure du monde*, Citeaux, B. Arthaud, Paris 1956.

Cali François, *L'ordre flamboyant et son temps*, B. Arthaud, Paris 1967.

Campbell Joseph, *The Mythic Image*, Princeton University Press, Princeton 1981.

Campedelli Luigi, *Esercitazioni complementari di geometria*, CEDAM, Padua 1962.

Canter David, *The Psychology of Place*, Architectural Press, London 1977.

Capasso Aldo (ed.), *Le tensostrutture a membrana per l'architettura*, Maggioli, Rimini 1993.

Capel Horacio, *La física sagrada. Creencias religiosas y teorías científicas en los orígenes de la geomorfología española*, Ediciones del Serbal, Barcelona 1985.

Casati Giulio (ed.), *Il Caos. Le leggi del disordine*, Le Scienze, Milan 1990.

Cassigoli Renzo (ed.), *Giovanni Michelucci. Abitare la natura*, GEF, Florence 1991.

Castelli Enrico (ed.), *Il simbolismo del tempo*, Istituto di studi filosofici, Rome 1973.

Castiglioni Piero, Mosconi Davide, Munari Bruno (eds.), *Uno spettacolo di luce. Sorgenti luminose usate per il loro colore*, Zanichelli, Bologna 1987.

Cauvin Jacques, *Naissance des divinités. Naissance de l'agriculture. La révolution des symboles au néolithique*, CNRS Éditions, Paris 1994.

Cavallari Murat Augusto, *Tra Serra d'Ivrea Orco e Po*, Istituto Bancario San Paolo, Turin 1976.

Pierre Caye, *Le savoir de Palladio. Architecture, métaphysique et politique dans la Venise du Cinquecento*, Klincksiek, 1995.

Cazzato Vincenzo, Fagiolo Maurizio, Giusti M. Adriana, *Teatri di verzura in Italia. La scena del giardino dal Barocco al Novecento*, Edifir, Florence 1993.

Cellini Francesco, D'Amato Claudio, Valeriani Enrico (cat., eds.), *Le architetture di Ridolfi e Frankl,* Terni, Palazzo Mazzancolli, De Luca Editore, Rome 1979.

Cerchio Bruno, *L'ermetismo di Dante*, Edizioni Mediterranee, Rome 1988.

Cerulli Sergio, Santini Giovanni, *Rappresentazione di una solidarietà fra tradizione gotica e innovazione barocca*, Carucci, Rome 1988.

Ceschi Carlo, *Architettura dei templi megalitici di Malta*, Fratelli Palombi, Rome 1939.

Chaloupka George, *Journey in Time. The World's Longest Continuing Art Tradition. The 50,000-Year Story of the Australian Aboriginal Rock Art of Arnhem Land*, REED, Chatswood 1993.

Champdor Albert, *Les ruines de Pétra*, Albert Guillot, Lyons 1972.

Champeaux de Gérard, Sterckx Dom Sébastien, *Introduction au monde des symboles*, Zodiaque, Paris 1966.

Chang Amos Ih Tiao, *The Tao of Architecture*, Princeton University Press, Princeton 1981.

Chao-Kang Chang, Blaser Werner, *Architectures de Chine*, Editions André Delcourt, Lausanne 1988.

Chauvet Gilbert, *La vie dans la matière. Le rôle de l'espace en biologie*, Flammarion, Paris 1995.

Chevalier Jean (ed.), *Dictionnaire des Symboles*, Editions Robert Laffont, Paris 1969.

Ciarla Roberto (ed.), *La civiltà del Fiume Giallo. I tesori dello Shanxi dalla preistoria all'epoca Ming*, De Luca Editore, Rome 1992.

Cicerone Marco Tullio, *Dell'Oratore*, Rizzoli, Milan 1994.

Cipolloni Sampò Mirella, *Dolmen. Architetture preistoriche in Europa*, De Luca Editore, Rome 1990.

Clark Roger H., Pause Michael, *Precedents in Architecture*, Van Nostrand Reinhold, New York 1985.

Clasen Karl Heinz, *Deutsche Gewölbe der Spätgotik*, Henschelverlag, Berlin 1958.

Clément Pierre, Clément-Charpentier Sophie, Goldblum Charles (eds.), *Cités d'Asie*, Editions Parenthèses, Marseilles 1995.

Coaldrake William H., *The Way of the Carpenter. Tools and Japanese Achitecture*, Weatherhill, New York-Tokyo 1990.

Coarelli Filippo, *I santuari del Lazio in età repubblicana*, Nuova Italia Scientifica, Rome 1987.

Codino Fausto (ed.), *Miti greci e romani*, Laterza, Rome-Bari 1971.

Coineau Yves, Kresling Biruta, *Le invenzioni della natura e la bionica*, Edizioni Paoline, Cinisello Balsamo 1989.

Colerus Egmond, *Piccola storia della matematica. Da Pitagora a Hilbert*, Einaudi, Turin 1941.

Collins George R., Bassegoda Nonell Juan, *The Designs and Drawings of Antonio Gaudí*, Princeton University Press, Princeton 1983.

Collins Peter, *I mutevoli ideali dell'architettura moderna*, Il Saggiatore, Milan 1973.

*Comportement des animaux (Le)*, Pour La Science, Paris 1994.

Conrads Ulrich, Sperlich Hans G., *Fantastic Architecture*, The Architectural Press, London 1963.

Consiglieri Victor, *A morfologia da arquitectura 1920-1970*, vols. I - II, Editorial Estampa, Lisbon 1994.

Cook Roger, *L'arbre de vie*, Editions du Seuil, Paris 1975.

Cook Theodore Andrea, *The Curves of Life*, Dover Publications, New York 1979.

Coppola Pignatelli Paola et al. (eds.), *Tempo e architettura*, Gangemi Editore, Rome 1987.

Cowen Painton, *Rose Windows*, Thames and Hudson, London 1979.

Cramer Friedrich, *Chaos and Order. The Complex Structure of Living Systems*, VCH Verlagsgesellschaft, Weinheim 1993.

Cristofani Mauro (ed.), *Gli Etruschi. Una nuova immagine*, Giunti, Florence 1984.

Critchlow Keith, *Islamic Patterns. An Analytical and Cosmological Approach*, Thames and Hudson, London 1989.

Cronin Helena, *The Ant and the Peacock*, Cambridge University Press, Cambridge 1994.

Crosbie Michael J., *Green Architecture*, Rockport Publishers, Rockport 1994.

Cundy H. Martyn, Rollett A.P., *Mathematical Models*, Oxford University Press, Oxford 1989.

Cuneo Paolo, *Storia dell'urbanistica. Il mondo islamico*, Laterza, Rome-Bari 1986.

Curtis Helena, Barnes N. Sue, *Invito alla biologia*, Zanichelli, Bologna 1991.

**D**

*Dalla natura all'arte*, Centro internazionale delle arti e del costume, Palazzo Grassi, Venice 1960.

Dalrymple Henderson Linda, *The Fourth Dimension and Non-Euclidean Geometry in Modern Art*, Princeton University Press, Princeton 1983.

Damisch Hubert, *L'origine de la perspective*, Flammarion, Paris 1993.

Dance S. Peter, *Conchiglie*, Fabbri, Milan 1993.

Dani Filiberto (ed.), *Il libro delle case*, SARIN, Pomezia 1989.

Daniel Glyn, *The Megalith Builders of Western Europe*, Pelican Books, Baltimora 1963.

Danielli Lina, *Giardini della poesia*, Edagricole, Bologna 1993.

Day Christopher, *La casa come luogo dell'anima*, Red, Como 1993.

Dawkins Richard, *Il fenotipo esteso*, Zanichelli, Bologna 1986.

Dawson Barry, Gillow John, *The Traditional Architecture of Indonesia*, Thames and Hudson, London 1994.

De Albertiis Emidio, *La casa dei romani*, Longanesi, Milan 1990.

De Biasi Mario, *Il terzo occhio sulla natura*, Edizioni FotoSelex, Veniano 1979.

De Cesaris Alessandra, *Tendenza all'astrazione e progressiva denaturalizzazione dell'edificio*, Gangemi Editore, Rome 1993.

Del Boca Bernardino, *La Quarta Dimensione. L'evoluzione della coscienza*, Casa Editrice L'età del-l'Acquario, Grignasco 1993.

Della Porta Patrizia, *Fotografia e architettura trasfigurazioni*, Fotografis, Bologna 1980.

Del Prete Carlo, Tosi Giuseppe, *Orchidee spontanee d'Italia*, Mursia, Milan 1988.

Demir Ömer, *Cappadocia culla della storia*, Ömer Demir, Ankara 1990.

Déribéré M., Scaioni E., *Minerali*, Istituto Geografico De Agostini, Novara 1956.

Devereux Paul, Steele John, Kubrin David, *Gaia: la Terra intelligente*, Ediciones Martínez Roca, Barcelona 1991.

Devereux Paul, *Symbolic Landscapes. The Dreamtime Earth and Avebury's Open Secrets*, Gothic Image Publications, Glastonbury 1992.

Divorne Françoise (ed.), *Ville forme symbolique pouvoir projets*, Pierre Mardaga Éditeur, Liegi-Brussels 1986.

Doczi György, *The Power of Limits. Proportional Harmonies in Nature, Art & Architecture*, Shambhala Publications, Boston-London 1981.

Donadoni Roveri Anna Maria (eds.), *Civiltà degli Egizi. La vita quotidiana*, Istituto Bancario San Paolo, Turin 1987.

Dorfles Gillo, *Artificio e natura*, Einaudi, Turin 1968.

Dorlot Jean-Marie, Baïlon Jean Paul, Masounave Jacques, *Des matériaux*, Éditions de l'École Polythechnique de Montréal, Montréal 1986.

Doubilet David, *Colori nascosti. Le meraviglie del mondo subacqueo*, Rizzoli, Milan 1990.

Doumas Christos, *The Wall-Paintings of Thera*, The Thera Foundation, Athens 1992.

Doumenc Dominique, Lenicque Pierre-Marie, *La morphogenèse. Développement et diversité des formes vivantes*, Masson, Paris 1995.

Drabkin David L., *Fundamental Structure: Nature's Architecture*, University of Pennsylvania Press, Philadelphia 1975.

Dubbini Renzo, *Geografie dello sguardo. Visione e paesaggio in età moderna*, Einaudi, Turin 1994.

Duneau Michel, Janot Christian, *La magie des matériaux*, Editions Odile Jacob, Paris 1996.

Duly Colin, *The Houses of Mankind*, Thames and Hudson, London 1979.

**E**

Eck van Caroline, *Organicism in Nineteenth-Century Architecture*, Architectura & Natura Press, Amsterdam 1994.

Edgar Gerald A. (ed.), *Classics on Fractals*, Addison-Wesley Publishing Company, Reading 1993.

Edwards Edward B., *Pattern and Design with Dynamic Symmetry*, Dover Publications, New York 1967.

Egli Ernst, *Sinan der Baumeister Osmanischer Glanzzeit*, Verlag für Architektur A.G., Zurich 1954.

Eibl-Eibesfeldt Irenäus, *Etologia umana. Le basi biologiche e culturali del comportamento*, Bollati Boringhieri, Turin 1993.

Eisler Riane, *El caliz y la espada. Nuestra historia, nuestro futuro*, Editorial Cuatro Vientos, Santiago 1993.

Eliade Mircea, *Storia delle credenze e delle idee religiose*, vol. I, Sansoni, Florence 1979.

Emerson Ralph Waldo, *Nature and Other Writings*, Shambhala Publication, Boston-London 1994.

Emmer Michele, *Bolle di sapone. Un viaggio tra arte, scienza e fantasia*, La nuova Italia, Scandicci 1991.

Emmer Michele, *La perfezione visibile. Matematica e arte*, Theoria, Rome-Naples 1991.

*Empathy, Form and Space. Problems in German Aesthetics, 1873-1893*, Getty Center for the History, Santa Monica 1994.

*Enciclopedia*, vol. III: *Città-Cosmologie*, Einaudi, Turin 1978.

Engel Heinrich, *Sistemas de estructuras*, H. Blume Ediciones, Madrid 1979.

Engel Leonard, *Il mare*, Mondadori, Milan 1974.

Esiodo, *Le opere e i giorni*, Rizzoli, Milan 1994.

**F**

Fagiolo Marcello, "L'umanesimo, Raffaello e la 'storia dell'architettura'", in *QUASAR*, nos. 6-7, 1992.

Fagiolo Marcello, *Rome antica*, Capone Editore, Cavallino di Lecce 1991.

Fahn A., *Anatomia vegetal*, Ediciones Pirámide, Madrid 1985.

Faïk-Nzuji Clémentine M., *La puissance du sacré. L'homme, la nature et l'art en Afrique noire*, La Renaissance du Livre, Brussels 1993.

Farb Peter, *The Insect*, Time-Life International, Amsterdam 1969.

Fanfani Alberto, *Orchidee*, Mondadori, Milan 1988.

Farrelly David, *The Book of Bamboo*, Sierra Club Books, San Francisco 1984.

Fathy Hassan, *Natural Energy and Vernacular Architecture*, University of Chicago Press, Chicago 1986.

Feininger Andreas, *Leaves*, Dover Publications, New York 1984.

Feininger Andreas, *Nature and Art*, Dover Publications, New York 1983.

Feininger Andreas, *Nature in Miniature*, Rizzoli International, New York 1989.

Feininger Andreas, *Shells. Forms and Designs of the Sea*, Dover Publications, New York 1983.

Feininger Andreas, *Stone and Man*, Dover Publications, New York 1979.

Feininger Andreas, *Trees*, Thames and Hudson, London 1968.

Feo Giovanni, *Dei della terra. Il mondo sotterraneo degli etruschi*, ECIG, Genoa 1991.

Ferrari Andrea e Antonella, *Natura protetta. Venezuela nel regno del giaguaro*, Bolis, Bergamo 1990.

Ferri Sergio, *L'ufficio del futuro*, Sarin, Marsilio, Venice 1983.

Ficino Marsilio, *Sopra Lo Amore ovvero Convito di Platone*, Carabba Editore, Lanciano 1934.

Field Michael, Golubitsky Martin, *Simmetry in Chaos. A Search for Pattern in Mathematics, Art and Nature*, Oxford University Press, Oxford 1992.

Figuier Guillaume Louis, *Storia delle piante*, Messaggerie Pontremolesi, Milan 1989.

Fiori de' Mario, Morello Carlo, *Il ballo*, Salani, Florence 1899.

Firket Henri, *La cellula vivente*, Newton Compton, Rome 1994.

Focillon Henri, *Vita delle forme*, Alessandro Minuziano Editore, Milan 1945.

*Fonti francescane*, Edizioni francescane, Assisi 1986.

Forest J., *Meraviglie dei fondi marini*, Istituto Geografico De Agostini, Novara 1958.

Forti Leone Carlo, *John Ruskin: un profeta per l'architettura*, Compagnia dei Librai, Genoa 1983.

François Yvonne, *Le Togo*, Éditions Karthala, Paris 1993.

Frank Edward, *Pensiero organico e architettura wrightiana*, Dedalo Libri, Bari 1978.

Frank Ellen Eve, *Literary Architecture. Essays Toward a Tradition. Walter Pater, Gerard Manley Hopkins, Marcel Proust, Henry James*, University of California Press, Berkeley 1983.

Frederic Louis, *Il loto*, Edizioni Mediterranee, Rome 1988.

Freguglia Paolo, *Fondamenti storici della geometria*, Feltrinelli, Milan 1982.

Frisch von Karl, *L'architettura degli animali*, Mondadori, Milan 1975 (*Animal Architecture*, New York 1974).

Fumagalli Giuseppina (ed.), *Leonardo omo sanza lettere*, Sansoni, Florence 1939.

Futagawa Yukio, Bruce Brooks Pfeiffer, *Frank Lloyd Wright, Monograph 1924-1936*, A.D.A. Edita, Tokyo 1991.

**G**

Gablik Suzi, *Has Modernism Failed?*, Thames and Hudson, London 1988.

Gambardella Cherubino, *L'architettura delle scale*, Sagep Editrice, Genoa 1993.

Garisto Leslie, *From Bauhaus to Birdhouse*, Harper Collins, New York 1992.

Gasparini Graziano, Margolies Luise, *Inca Architecture*, Indiana University Press, Bloomington 1980.

*Gaudí Antoni, Idee per l'architettura. Scritti e pensieri raccolti dagli allievi*, Jaca Book, Milan 1995.

Gauquelin Michel, *Il dossier delle influenze cosmiche*, Astrolabio, Rome 1975.

Gazzola Luigi (ed.), "Cina: architetture e città," in *Bollettino della biblioteca della facoltà di Architettura dell'Università degli studi di Roma "La Sapienza"*, no. 52, Gangemi Editore, Rome 1995.

Gennaro Paola (ed.), *Architettura e spazio sacro nella modernità*. Exhibition's catalogue, Biennale of Venice, December 1992, Editrice Abitare Segesta, Milan 1992.

Gensini Stefano, *Il naturale e il simbolico. Saggio su Leibniz*, Bulzoni, Rome 1991.

Gerner Manfred, *Architectures de l'Himalaya*, Editions André Delcourt, Lausanne 1988.

Gerster Georg, *Grand Design. The Earth from Above*, The Knapp Press, Los Angeles 1988.

Ghyka Matila C., *Essai sur le rythme*, Librairie Gallimard, Paris 1938.

Ghyka Matila C., *Esthétique des proportions dans la nature et dans les arts*, Gallimard, Paris 1927.

Ghyka Matila C., *Le nombre d'or. I: Les rythmes*, Gallimard, Paris 1931.

Giavarini Ida, *Le razze dei polli*, Edagricole, Bologna 1983.

Gibbons Bob, *The Secret Life of Flowers*, Blandford, London 1990.

Gilardi Mario (ed.), *Ritmi e simmetrie. Strutture algebriche e reticoli modulari dagli arabi al computer*, Zanichelli, Bologna 1990.

Gilson Etienne, *Matières et formes. Poétiques particulières des arts majeurs*, Librairie Philosophique J. Vrin, Paris 1964.

Gimbutas Marija, *The Language of the Goddess*, Thames and Hudson, London 1989.

*God's Wonderful World*, Autumn House Publications, Grantham 1992.

Godwin Joscelyn, *Athanasius Kircher. A Renaissance Man and the Quest for Lost Knowledge*, Thames and Hudson, London 1979.

Goethe Johann Wolfgang, *Baukunst. Dal Gotico al Classico negli scritti sull'architettura*, Medina, Palermo 1994.

Goethe Johann Wolfgang, *Favola*, Adelphi, Milan 1990.

Gombrich Ernst H., *Arte e illusione. Studio sulla psicologia della rappresentazione pittorica*, Einaudi, Turin 1965.

Gottardi Glauco, *I minerali*, Boringhieri, Turin 1986.

Gould James L., Gould Carol Grant, *The Animal Mind*, Scientific American Library, New York 1994.

Gramaccioli Carlo M., *Il meraviglioso mondo dei cristalli*, Calderini, Bologna 1986.

Grimal Pierre, *I giardini di Roma antica*, Garzanti, Milan 1990.

Grimaldi Roberto, *R. Buckminster Fuller 1895-1983*, Officina Edizioni, Rome 1990.

Greco Carlo, Greco Stefano, *Natura ai raggi X*, Gilardoni, Milan 1986.

Grover Satish, *The Architecture of India. Buddhist and Hindu*, Vikas Publishing House, New Delhi 1980.

Guénon René, *L'esoterismo di Dante*, Editrice Atanòr, Rome 1976.

Guénon René, *Simboli della scienza sacra*, Adelphi, Milan 1990.

Guidoni Enrico, *Architettura primitiva*, Electa, Milan 1989.

Guidoni Enrico, *L'architettura popolare italiana*, Laterza, Rome-Bari 1980.

Guidoni Enrico, *La città europea*, Electa, Milan 1978.

Guidoni Enrico, *Storia dell'urbanistica. Il Duecento*, Laterza, Rome-Bari 1989.

Guidoni Enrico, *Storia dell'urbanistica. Il Medioevo. Secoli VI-XII*, Laterza, Rome-Bari 1991.

Guillerme Jacques, *La figurazione in architettura*, Franco Angeli, Milan 1982.

Gutkind E.N., *Architettura e società*, Edizioni di Comunità, Milan 1958.

**H**

Haeckel Ernst, *Art Forms in Nature*, Dover Publications, New York 1974.

Hale Jonathan, *The Old Way of Seeing*. A Richard Todd Book, Houghton Mifflin Company, Boston, New York 1994.

Halevi Zev ben Shimon, *Kabbalah. Tradition of Hidden Knowledge*, Thames and Hudson, London 1988.

Hall Nina (ed.), *Caos. Una scienza per il mondo reale*, Muzzio, Padua 1992.

Hanks David A., *The Decorative Design of Frank Lloyd Wright*, E.P. Dutton, New York 1979.

Hargittai István (ed.), *Simmetry 2. Unifying Human Understanding*, Pergamon Press, Oxford 1989.

Hargittai István, Pickover Clifford A. (eds.), *Spiral Symmetry*, World Scientific, Singapore 1992.

Harlow William M., *Art Forms from Plant Life*, Dover Publications, New York 1976.

Harpur James (ed.), *Ai tempi della Bibbia. Popoli, luoghi, storia ed eventi del mondo biblico*, Mondadori, Milan 1989.

Harpur James, Westwood Jennifer, *Atlante dei luoghi leggendari*, Istituto Geografico De Agostini, Novara 1990.

Harvey Virginia I., *The Techniques of Basketry*, University of Washington Press, Seattle-London 1986.

Headstrom Richard, *All about Lobsters, Crabs, Shrimps and Their Relatives*, Dover Publications, New York 1985.

Heidegger Martin, *Saggi e discorsi*, Mursia, Milan 1985.

Heilbronner Edgar, Dunitz Jack D., *Reflections on Symmetry*, Verlag Helvetica Chimica Acta, Bâle 1993.

Hensel Wolfgang, *Pflanzen in Aktion. Krümmen Klappen Schleudern*, Spektrum Akademischer Verlag, Heidelberg 1993.

Henze Anton, *La Tourette. The Le Corbusier Monastery*, Lund Humphries & Co., London 1966.

Hersey George, *The Lost Meaning of Classical Architecture*, MIT, Cambridge (Mass.) 1988.

Hertzberger Herman, *Lessons for Students in Architecture*, Uitgeverij 010 Publishers, Rotterdam 1991.

Hildebrandt Stefan, Tromba Anthony, *Mathématiques et formes optimales, L'explication des structures naturelles*, Pour la Science, Paris 1986.

Hillier Bill, Hanson Julienne, *The Social Logic of Space*, Cambridge University Press, Cambridge 1990.

Hirsch Charles, *L'albero*, Edizioni Mediterranee, Rome 1988.

Hoffmann Anita, *El maravilloso mundo de los arácnidos*, La ciencia, México 1993.

Hoffmann Roald, *The Same and Not the Same*, Columbia University Press, New York 1995.

Höhn Reinhardt, *Curiosities of the Plant Kingdom*, Cassell, London 1980.

Holden Alan, *The Nature of Solids*, Dover Publications, New York 1992.

Hölderlin Friedrich, *Le liriche*, Adelphi, Milan 1977.

Howell Alice O., *The Web in the Sea. Jung, Sophia, and the Geometry of the Soul*. Wheaton, Madras-London 1993.

Huet Jean-Christophe, *Villages perchés des Dogon du Mali. Habitat, espace et société*, Editions L'Harmattan, Paris 1994.

Huntley H.E., *The Divine Proportion. A Study in Mathematical beauty*, Dover Publications, New York 1970.

Hurlbut Jr. Cornelius S., *Il mondo dei minerali*, Garzanti, Milan 1968 (*Minerals and Man*, New York 1968).

Hutton Edward, *The Cosmati*, Routledge and Kegan Paul, London 1950.

Huyghe René, *Formes et forces, de l'atome à Rembrandt*, Flammarion, Paris 1971.

**I**

Illich Ivan, *Nello specchio del passato*, Red, Como 1992.

Ingvar David H., Nordfeldt Stig, Pettersson Rune, Nilsson Lennart, *Questo è l'uomo. Viaggio fotografico dentro il corpo umano*, Edizioni Paoline, Cinisello Balsamo 1977.

Innes Clive, Glass Charles (eds.), Enciclopedia delle cactacee, Zanichelli, Bologna 1992.

**J**

Jacquod Jean (ed.), *Le lieu théâtral à la Renaissance*, Editions du Centre National de la Recherche Scientifique, Paris 1964.

Jahnke Eugene, Emde Fritz, *Tables of Functions. With Formulae and Curves*, Dover Publications, New York 1945.

Jahns Hans Martin, *Felci, muschi, licheni d'Europa*, Muzzio, Padua 1992.

Jamnitzer Wentzel, *Perspectiva corporum regularium*, Ediciones Siruela, Madrid 1993.

Janus Horst, *Baumeister Natur*, Verlag "Die Schönen Bucher", Stuttgart 1953.

Jencks Charles, *The Architecture of the Jumping Universe*, Academy Editions, London 1995.

John Brian, *L'evoluzione del paesaggio*, Istituto Geografico De Agostini, Novara 1981.

Johnsgard Paul A., *Arena Birds. Sexual Selection and Behavior*, Smithsonian Institution Press, Washington-London, 1994.

Johnson Paul-Alan, *The Theory of Architecture*, Van Nostrand Reinhold, New York 1994.

Jonaitis Aldona, *From the Land of the Totem Poles. The Northwest Coast Indian Art Collection at the American Museum of Natural History*, American Museum of Natural History, New York 1988.

Jones Clifford M. (ed.), *Old Testament Illustrations*, Cambridge University Press, Cambridge 1984.

Jones Owen, *The Grammar of Ornament. The Victorian Masterpiece on Oriental, Primitive, Classical, Mediaeval and Renaissance Design and Decorative Art*, Portland House, New York 1986.

Jucker Giacomo, *Alberi ornamentali in Italia*, Istituto Italiano d'Arti Grafiche, Bergamo 1958.

Jung Carl G., *Gli archetipi dell'inconscio collettivo*, Boringhieri, Turin 1977.

**K**

Kappraff Jay, *Connections. The Geometric Bridge between Art and Science*, McGraw-Hill, New York 1991.

Kaufmann Edgar (ed.), *An American Architecture. Frank Lloyd Wright*, Horizon Press, New York 1955.

Kawashima Chuji, *Minka, Traditional Houses of Rural Japan*, Kodansha International, Tokyo-New York 1990.

Kearton Michel, *Il tempio magico. Invocazioni, tecniche e rituali*, Hermes Edizioni, Rome 1984.

Kemp Martin, *The Science of Art*, Yale University Press, New Haven-London 1990.

Kendrick Sue, Kendrick Brian, *Australia. Beneath the Southern Cross*, Lightstorm Publishing, Nowra 1994.

Kepes Gyorgy, *The New Landscape in Art and Science*, Paul Theobald and Co., Chicago 1963.

Kern Hermann, *Labirinti. Forme e interpretazioni. 5000 anni di presenza di un archetipo*, Feltrinelli, Milan 1981.

Knapp Bettina L., *Archetype, Architecture, and the Writer*, Indiana University Press, Bloomington 1986.

Koepf Hans, *Stadtbaukunst in Österreich*, Residenz Verlag, Salzburg 1972.

Komonen Markku (ed.), *Finland: Nature, Design, Architecture*, Museum of Finnish Architecture, Finnish Society of Crafts and Design, Helsinki, no date.

Konstantinidis Aris, *Elements for Self-knowledge*, Athens 1975.

Krätz Otto, *Goethe und die Naturwissenschaften*, Callwey Verlag, Munich 1992.

Kremser Engelbert, *BauKunst 1967-1987*, Nicolaische Verlagsbuchhandlung, Berlin 1986.

Kretzulesco-Quaranta Emanuela, *Les jardins du songe. "Poliphile" et la mystique de la Reinassance*, Editrice Magma, Rome 1976.

Krier Leon, *Atlantis*, Exhibition's catalogue, Galerie der Stadt, Stuttgart, February 1988.

Krueger Myron W., *Realtà artificiale*, Addison-Wesley Italia Editoriale, Milan 1992.

**L**

Lalvani Haresh, *Structures on Hyper-structures*, Promotion Services, New York 1982.

*Language of Pattern (The)*, Thames and Hudson, London 1974.

Lao-Tse, *Il Tao-Te-King*, Laterza, Rome-Bari 1989.

La Pietra Ugo (ed.), *Il concetto di classico*, Grafis Edizioni, Bologna 1987.

Laseau Paul, Tice James, *Frank Lloyd Wright. Between Principle and Form*, Van Nostrand Reinhold, New York 1992.

Laubin Gladys, Laubin Reginald, *Il tipì indiano. Storia, costruzione, uso*, Mursia, Milan 1993 (*The Indian Tipì*, Norman 1977).

Laureano Pietro, *La piramide rovesciata. Il modello dell'oasi per il pianeta terra*, Bollati Boringhieri, Turin 1995.

Laureano Pietro, *Sahara giardino sconosciuto*, Giunti Barbèra, Florence 1988.

Lawlor Anthony, *The Temple in the House. Finding the Sacred in Everyday Architecture*, G.P. Putnam's Sons, New York 1994.

Lawlor Robert, *Sacred Geometry. Philosophy and Practice*, Thames and Hudson, London 1992.

Le Corbusier, *Précisions sur un état présent de l'architecture et de l'urbanisme*, Éditions Vincent, Fréal & C., Paris 1960.

Leedy Walter C. Jr., *Fan Vaulting: A Study of Form, Technology, and Meaning*, Scolar Press, London 1980.

Lehrman Jonas, *Earthly Paradise. Garden and Courtyard in Islam*, Thames and Hudson, London 1980.

Leoncini Marco-Leone, *Natura in primo piano*, Edizioni Paoline, Cinisello Balsamo 1991.

Leti Messina Vittorio, *L'Architettura della Libertà. Studi sul pensiero architettonico di Rudolf Steiner*, Japadre, L'Aquila 1976.

Lima-de-Faria A., *Evolution without Selection*, Elsevier Science Publishers, Amsterdam 1988.

Lovelock James, *Le nuove età di Gaia*, Bollati Boringhieri, Turin 1991.

Lovelock Jim E., *Gaia. Nuove idee sull'ecologia*, Bollati Boringhieri, Turin 1990.

Loyola di Ignazio, *Esercizi spirituali*, Edizioni Paoline, Cinisello Balsamo 1988.

Luciano Alessandra, *Il segreto delle spirali e le loro magiche energie*, Edizioni Horus, Turin 1993.

Lucrezio Caro Tito, *La natura*, Rizzoli, Milan 1953.

**M**

McClung William Alexander, *The Architecture of Paradise. Survivals of Eden and Jerusalem*, University of California Press, Berkeley 1983.

MacDonald William L., Pinto John A., *Hadrian's Villa and Its Legacy*, Yale University Press, New Haven-London 1995.

MacDonald William L., *The Pantheon*, Harvard University Press, Cambridge 1976.

McGuire Michael, *An Eye for Fractals*, Addison-Wesley Publishing Company, Redwood City 1991.

McHarg Ian L., *Design with Nature*, John Wiley & Sons, New York 1992.

McHarg Ian L., *Progettare con la natura*, Muzzio, Padua 1989.

McNally Kenneth, *Standing Stones and other Monuments of Early Ireland*, Appletree Press, Belfast 1984.

Maki Fumihiko et al. (eds.), *A Style for the Year 2001*, Shinkenchiku, Tokyo 1985.

Makowski Z.S., *Räumliche Tragwerke aus Stahl*, Verlag Stahleisen, Düsseldorf 1963.

Málek Jaromir, Forman Werner, *Gli Egizi. Splendori e civiltà dell'Antico regno*, Istituto Geografico De Agostini, Novara 1986.

Mandelbrot Benoît B., *Gli oggetti frattali*, Einaudi, Turin 1987.

Mandelbrot Benoît B., *La geometria della natura. Sulla teoria dei frattali*, Theoria, Rome-Naples 1989.

Mandelbrot Benoît B., *The Fractal Geometry of Nature*, W.H. Freeman and Company, New York 1983.

Maniglio Calcagno Annalisa, *Architettura del paesaggio. Evoluzione storica*, Calderini, Bologna 1983.

Mann A.T., *Sacred Architecture*, Element Books, Shaftesbury-Rockport-Brisbane 1993.

Manna Filippo, *Le chiavi magiche dell'universo*, Liguori, Naples 1988.

Marc Olivier, *Psychanalyse de la maison*, Éditions du Seuil, Paris 1972.

Marchianò Grazia, *La religione della Terra*, Red, Como 1991.

Maretto Paolo, *Nell'architettura*, Teorema Edizioni, Florence 1973.

Marten Michael, May John, Taylor Rosemary, *Weird & Wonderful Wildlife*, Chronicle Books, San Francisco 1983.

Martinez Pérez José Antonio, Gutierrez Manuel Elias, *Introduccion a la protozoologia*, Editorial Trillas, México 1985.

Marziale, *Epigrammi*, Einaudi, Turin 1964.

Mathews Thomas F., *The Clash of Gods. A Reinterpretation of Early Christian Art*, Princeton University Press, Princeton 1993.

Mattheck Claus, *Design in der Natur. Der Baum als Lehrmeister*, Rombach GmbH Druck, Freiburg 1993.

Mattheus Rupert O., *Atlante delle meraviglie naturali*, Istituto Geografico De Agostini, Novara 1989.

Mazzeo Donatella, Silvi Antonini Chiara, *Civiltà khmer*, Mondadori, Milan 1972.

Meinhardt Hans, *The Algorithmic Beauty of Sea Shells*, Springer Verlag, Berlin-Heidelberg 1995.

Meiss von Pierre, *Dalla forma al luogo*, Hoepli, Milan 1992.

Menocal Narciso G., *Architecture as Nature. The Transcendentalist Idea of Louis Sullivan*, University of Wisconsin Press, Madison 1981.

Merisio Pepi, Turri Eugenio, *Il volto di una terra. L'Italia*, Amilcare Pizzi, Cinisello Balsamo 1985 (for the Italian Esso).

Messina Giuseppe L., *Dizionario di mitologia classica*, Angelo Signorelli, Rome, no date.

Micara Ludovico, *Architetture e spazi dell'Islam*, Carucci, Rome 1985.

Michell John, *A Little History of Astro-Archaelogy*, Thames and Hudson, London 1989.

Michell John, *The Dimensions of Paradise. The Proportions and Symbolic Numbers of Ancient Cosmology*, Thames and Hudson, London 1988.

Michell John, *Lo spirito della Terra. L'energia del mistero vivente*, Red, Como 1988 (*The Earth Spirit*, London 1975).

Mitscherlich Alexander, "La città materna," in *Eupolis*, no. 6, Nov.-Dec. 1991.

Moholy-Nagy Sibyl, *Matrix of Man*, Pall Mall Press, London 1968.

Moles Abraham, *Il Kitsch. L'arte della felicità*, Officina Edizioni, Rome 1979.

*Momenti e problemi di storia dell'estetica*, Marzorati, Milan 1961.

Monetta Alfredo, Mordo Carlos, *Ischigualasto Talampaya*, Manrique Zago, Buenos Aires 1995.

Monod-Herzen Edouard, *Principes de morphologie générale*, vols. I - II, Gauthier-Villars Editeur, Paris 1956-57.

Monteiro Salvador, Kaz Leonel, *Amazonia Flora Fauna*, Ediçóes Alumbramento, Rio de Janeiro 1993-94.

Monteiro Salvador, Kaz Leonel, *CaaTinga. Sertão Sertanejos*, Ediçóes Alumbramento, Rio de Janeiro 1994-95.

Monteiro Salvador, Kaz Leonel, *Floresta atlantica*, Ediçóes Alumbramento, Rio de Janeiro 1991-92.

Moreno Paolo, *Pittura greca*, Mondadori, Milan 1987.

Morini Mario, *Atlante di storia dell'urbanistica*, Hoepli, Milan 1963.

Morolli Gabriele, *L'architettura di Vitruvio*, Alinea Editrice, Florence 1988.

Morris Desmond, *Les animaux révélés*, Calmann-Lévy, Paris 1990.

Morris Jan, *Europa dal cielo*, Rizzoli, Milan 1992.

Moscovici Serge, *La società contro natura*, Ubaldini, Rome 1973.

Mossa Vico, *Architettura domestica in Sardegna*, Carlo Delfino, Sassari 1992.

Mosser Monique, Teyssot Georges (eds.), *Histoire des jardins de la Reinassance à nos jours*, Flammarion, Paris 1991.

Moynihan Elizabeth B., *Paradise as a Garden, In Persia and Mughal India*, Scolar Press, London 1982.

Muller-Karpe Hermann, *Storia dell'età della pietra*, Mondadori, Milan 1992.

Muratore Giorgio, *La città rinascimentale. Tipi e modelli attraverso i trattati*, Mazzotta, Milan 1975.

Muratore Giorgio (ed.), *L'architettura nella città contemporanea*, Consorzio provinciale pubblica lettura, Bologna 1979.

Murchie Guy, *Music of the Spheres. The Material Universe from Atom to Quasar, Simply Explained*, vol. I, Dover Publications, New York 1967.

Murphy Pat, Neill William, *By Nature's Design*, Chronicle Books, San Francisco 1993.

**N**

Nabokov Peter, Easton Robert, *Native American Architecture*, Oxford University Press, New York-Oxford 1989.

Nardi Guido, *Le nuove radici antiche*, Franco Angeli, Milan 1994.

Nasr Seyyed Hossein, Michaud Roland, *Islamic Science. An Illustrated Study*, World of Islam Festival Publishing Company, London 1976.

Natzmer von Gert, *Nel segreto del mondo vivente*, Aldo Martello Editore, Milan 1954.

Neill William, *Patterns in Nature. The 1993 Exploratorium Calendar for Curious People*, Golden Turtle Press, Richmond 1992.

Neri Gianfranco, Zoffoli Paolo, *L'architettura dell'immateriale*, Edizioni Clear, Rome 1992.

Nicolas Adolphe, *Principes de tectonique*, Masson, Paris 1989.

Nicoletti Manfredi, *L'architettura delle caverne*, Laterza, Rome-Bari 1980.

Nivola Costantino, *Ho bussato alle porte di questa città meravigliosa*, Arte Duchamp, Cagliari 1993.

Norberg-Schulz Christian, *Genius Loci. Paesaggio ambiente architettura*, Electa, Milan 1979.

Norberg-Schulz Christian, *Intenzioni in architettura*, Officina Edizioni, Rome 1977.

**O**

O'Brien Joanne, Man Ho Kwok, *The Elements of Feng Shui*, Element Book, Longmead 1991.

Oelschlaeger Max, *Caring for Creation. An Ecumenical Approach to the Environmental Crisis*, Yale University Press, New Haven-London 1994.

Oliver Paul (ed.), *Shelter, Sign & Symbol*, Barrie & Jenkins, London 1975.

Omero, *Odissea*, Garzanti, Milan 1968.

Omodeo Salé Serena (ed.), *Architettura & natura*, Exhibition's catalogue, Turin, April 1994, Mazzotta, Milan 1994.

Onians John, *Bearers of Meaning. The Classical Orders in Antiquity, the Middle Ages, and the Reinassance*, Princeton University Press, Princeton 1990.

Orunesu Gianfranco, Passi Lucio, Tiezzi Enzo (eds.), *Antologia verde. Letture scientifiche, filosofiche e letterarie per una coscienza ecologica*, Giunti Marzocco, Florence 1987.

Ottaviano Carmelo, *La legge della bellezza come legge universale della natura*, CEDAM, Padua 1970.

Otto Frei, "Ausblick auf eine heitere Kulturlandschaft," in *Daidalos*, no. 21, 1986.

Otto Frei, *L'architettura della natura*, Il Saggiatore, Milan 1985.

Ovidio, *Metamorfosi*, Einaudi, Turin 1994.

**P**

Paccard André, *Le Maroc et l'artisanat traditionnel islamique dans l'architecture*, vols. I - II, Editions Atelier, Annecy 1983.

Palladio Andrea, *The Four Books of Architecture*, The MIT Press, Cambridge (Mass.) 1997.

Paltrinieri Marisa (ed.), *Meraviglie e misteri della natura intorno a noi*, Selezione del Reader's Digest, Milan 1973.

Papanek Victor, *The Green Imperative. Ecology and Ethics in Design and Architecture*, Thames and Hudson, London 1995.

Parmenide, *Poema sulla natura*, Rusconi, Milan 1991.

Parodi Bent, *Architettura e mito*, Pungitopo Editrice, Marina di Patti 1988.

*Parte del tutto. Saggi sull'olismo (La)*, Casamassima, Udine 1992.

Patzelt Otto, *Wachsen und Bauen. Konstruktionen in Natur und Technik*, Verlag fur Bauwesen, Berlin 1972.

Pearce Peter, *Structure in Nature is a Strategy for Design*, MIT Press, Cambridge (Mass.) 1990.

Pearson David, *Earth to Spirit. In Search of Natural Architecture*, Gaia Books Limited, London 1994.

Pedoe Dan, *Geometry and the Visual Arts*, Dover Publications, New York 1983.

Pehnt Wolfgang, *Expressionist Architecture*, Thames and Hudson, London 1973.

Peitgen Heinz-Otto, Jurgens Hartmut, Saupe Dietmar, *Chaos and Fractals. New Frontiers of Science*, Springer-Verlag, New York 1993.

Peitgen Heinz-Otto, Jurgens Hartmut, Saupe Dietmar, *Fractals for the Classroom. Part Two. Complex Systems and Mandelbrot Set*, Springer-Verlag, New York 1992.

Peitgen Heinz-Otto, Richter Peter H., *La bellezza dei frattali*, Bollati Boringhieri, Turin 1991 (*The Beauty of Fractals*, New York 1986).

Pejaković Mladen, *Le pietre e il sole. Architettura e astronomia nell'alto medioevo*, Jaca Book, Milan 1988.

Pellerin Pierre, *Nature insolite en France*, Éditions Nathan, Paris 1993.

Pennick Nigel, *The Ancient Science of Geomancy. Man in Harmony with the Earth*, Thames and Hudson, London 1979.

Pepper Elizabeth, Wilcock John, *Terre e città di magia in Europa*, Garzanti, Milan 1991.

Pérez-Gomez Alberto, Parcell Stephen (eds.), *Chora 1: Intervals in the Philosophy of Architecture*, McGill-Queen's University Press, Montreal 1994.

Périgord Monique, *L'esthétique de Teilhard*, Editions Universitaires, Paris 1965.

Pesando Fabrizio, *La casa dei greci*, Longanesi, Milan 1989.

Peterson Ivars, *Il turista matematico*, Rizzoli, Milan 1991 (*The Mathematical Tourist*, New York 1988).

Peterson Ivars, *Islands of Truth. A Mathematical Mistery Cruise*, W.H. Freeman and Company, New York 1990.

Petit Jean (ed.), *Un couvent de Le Corbusier*, Les Cahiers Forces Vives-Editec, Paris 1961.

Petruccioli Attilio, *Dar al Islam. Architetture del territorio nei paesi islamici*, Carucci, Rome 1985.

Pfeiffer Bruce Brooks, *Frank Lloyd Wright Drawings*, Harry N. Abrams, Publishers, New York 1990.

Philippides Dimitri, *Santorini*, Melissa Publishing House, Athens 1987.

Pickover Clifford A., *Keys to Infinity*, John Wiley & Sons, New York 1995.

Pierantoni Ruggero, *Forma Fluens*, Boringhieri, Turin 1986.

Pirenne Maurice H., *Percezione visiva*, Muzzio, Padua 1991.

Plebe Armando (ed.), *Estetica*, Sansoni, Florence 1965.

Portmann Adolf, *Anfruch der Lebensforschung*, Zürich 1965.

Potter Timothy W., *Storia del paesaggio dell'Etruria meridionale*, Nuova Italia Scientifica, Rome 1985.

Prescott Lansing M., Harley John P., Klein Donald A., *Microbiologia*, Zanichelli, Bologna 1995.

Preston-Mafham Rod, *The Book of Spiders and Scorpions*, Crescent Books, New York 1991.

Preston-Mafham Rod & Ken, *Spiders of the World*, Blandford Press, London 1984.

Prigogine Ilya, Stengers Isabelle, *La nuova alleanza. Metamorfosi della scienza*, Einaudi, Turin 1993.

Prusinkiewicz Przemyslaw, Lindenmayer Aristid, *The Algorithmic Beauty of Plants*, Springer-Verlag, New York 1990.

Pückler-Muskau Hermann, Fürst von, *Giardino e paesaggio. Le idee sul giardino di un grande architetto dell'Ottocento*, Rizzoli, Milan 1984.

Purini Franco, *Dal progetto. Scritti teorici 1966-1991*, Edizioni Kappa, Rome 1992.

**Q**

Quantrill Malcom, *Reima Pietilä. Architecture, Context and Modernism*, Rizzoli International, New York 1985.

Quilici Lorenzo, *Le strade. Viabilità tra Rome e Lazio*, Edizioni Quasar, Rome 1990.

**R**

Rainero Enrico, *Giardini labirinti paradisi*, Studio Enrico Rainero, Florence 1985.

Rainero Enrico, *L'albero memoria di civiltà*, Studio Enrico Rainero, Florence 1989.

Rambach Pierre, Rambach Susanne, *Jardins de longévité. Chine Japon*, Albert Skira, Geneva 1987.

Ramirez Juan Antonio, *Edificios y suenos. Estudios sobre arquitectura y utopia*, Editorial Nerea, Madrid 1991.

Ramirez Juan Antonio, Taylor René, Corboz André, Pelt van Jan Robert, Ripoll Antonio Martinez, *Dios arquitecto. J.B. Villalpando y el templo de Salomón*, Ediciones Siruela, Madrid 1991.

Ramorino Felice, *Mitologia classica illustrata*, Hoepli, Milan 1981.

Recheis K., Bydlinski G. (ed.), *Amicizia con la terra. La via degli indiani d'America*, Edizioni Il Punto d'Incontro, Vicenza 1994.

Recheis K., Bydlinski G., *Sai che gli alberi parlano? La saggezza degli indiani d'America*, Edizioni Il Punto d'Incontro, Vicenza 1992.

Reeves Hubert, *Polvere di stelle*, Ulisse Edizioni, Turin 1989.

Renan Ernest, *Preghiera sull'acropoli. Souvenirs*, Edizioni Novecento, Palermo 1992.

Rheingold Howard, *La realtà virtuale*, Baskerville, Bologna 1993.

Rhodes Robin Francis, *Architecture and Meaning on the Athenian Acropolis*, Cambridge University Press, Cambridge 1995.

Rice Peter, *An Engineer Imagines*, Artemis, London 1994.

Richards Sim Bruce, *Nature in Architecture*, Exhibition's catalogue. San Diego Natural History Museum, April 1984.

Rigillo Marina, Paris Tonino, *Miralles/Pinós*, Gangemi Editore, Rome 1994.

Riley Terence, Reed Peter (eds.), *Frank Lloyd Wright Architect*, The Museum of Modern Art, New York 1994.

Rilke Rainer Maria, *Duino Elegies*, W.W. Norton & Co., New York 1978.

Robert D., Catesson A.M., *Biologie végétale*, vol. 2: *Organisation végétative*, Doin Editeurs, Paris 1990.

Robin Christelle (ed.), *Architectures et Cultures*, Editions Parenthèses, Marseilles 1992.

Robinson George W., Scovil Jeffrey A., *Minerals*, Weidenfeld and Nicolson, London 1994.

Rogers Raymond A., *Nature and the Crisis of Modernity*, Black Rose Books, Montreal 1994.

Roggero Egisto, *La vita nel mondo delle piante*, Unione Tipografico-Editrice Torinese, Turin 1931.

Roland Jean-Claude, Szollosi Annette, Szollosi Daniel, Callen Jean-Claude, *Atlas de biologie cellulaire*, Masson, Paris 1993.

Roland Jean-Claude, Vian Brigitte, *Atlas de biologie végétale*, vol. I: *Organisation des plantes sans fleurs*, Masson, Paris 1992.

Roland Jean-Claude, Roland Françoise, *Atlas de biologie végétale*, vol. 2: *Organisation des plantes a fleurs*, Masson, Paris 1995.

Romeno Elisa, *La capanna e il tempio: Vitruvio o dell'Architettura*, Palumbo, Palermo 1987.

Rosenau Helen (ed.), *Boullée's Treatise on Architecture*, Alec Tiranti, London 1953.

Rosenau Helen, *Vision of the Temple. The Image of the Temple of Jerusalem in Judaism and Christianity*, Oresko Boosk, London 1979.

Rossbach Sarah, Yun Lin, *Living Color*, Kodansha International, New York-Tokyo-London 1994.

Round F.E., Crawford R.M., Mann D.G., *The Diatoms. Biology & morphology of the Genera*, Cambridge University Press, Cambridge 1992.

Rowan-Robinson Michael, *L'universo*, Zanichelli, Bologna 1992.

Rowe Colin, *La matematica della villa ideale e altri scritti*, Zanichelli, Bologna 1993.

Rubiera y Mata María Jesús, *L'immaginario e l'architettura nella letteratura araba medievale*, Marietti, Genoa 1990.

Rudofsky Bernard, *Architecture without Architects*, The Museum of Modern Art, New York 1965.

Rudofsky Bernard, *Le meraviglie dell'architettura spontanea*, Laterza, Rome-Bari 1979.

Rudofsky Bernard, *The Prodigious Builders*, Secker & Warburg, London 1977.

Ruiu Domenico, Brotzu Renato, *Il monte Ortobene*, Amministrazione comunale, Nuoro 1993.

Ruttner Friedrich, *Naturgeschichte der Honigbienen*, Ehrenwirth Verlag GmbH, Munich 1992.

Ruyer Raymond, *La genesi delle forme viventi*, Bompiani, Milan 1966.

Rybczynski Witold, *La casa. Historia de una idea*, Emecé Editores, Buenos Aires 1993.

Rykwert Joseph, *On Adam's House in Paradise*, The Museum of Modern Art, New York 1972.

Rykwert Joseph, *The Idea of a Town. The Anthropology of Urban Form in Rome, Italy and the Ancient World*, Princeton University Press, Princeton 1988.

Rymer Jones Thomas, F.R.S., *The Natural History of Animals*, vol. II, John van Voorst, London 1852.

**S**

Saarinen Eliel, *The Search for Form in Art and Architecture*, Dover Publications, New York 1985.

Sale Kirkpatrick, *Le regioni della natura. La proposta bioregionalista*, Elèuthera, Milan 1991.

Saliga Pauline, Woolever Mary (eds.), *The Architecture of Bruce Goff, 1904-1982*, Prestel and The Art Institute of Chicago, Munich-New York 1995.

Sallis John, *Stone*, Indiana University Press, Bloomington 1994.

Salvadori Mario, Heller Robert, *Le strutture in architettura*, Etas Kompass, Milan 1964.

*Santini architecte gothico-baroque en Bohème (1677-1723)*, Jacques Damase Editeur, Paris 1989.

Satolli Alberto, *Il Pozzo della rocca in Orvieto volgarmente detto di San Patrizio*, Ambrosini, Bolsena 1991.

Satz Mario, *El arte de la naturaleza*, monograph of the review *Integral*, no. 18, Barcelona 1988.

Saudan Michel, Saudan-Skira Sylvia, *De folie en folies. La découverte du monde des jardins*, La Bibliotheque des Arts, Geneva 1987.

Saunders J.B. de C. M., O'Malley Charles D., *The Illustrations from the Works of Andreas Vesalius of Brussels*, Dover Publications, New York 1973.

Scagel R.F., Bandoni R.J., Rouse G.E., Schofield W.B., Stein J.R., Taylor T.M.C., *El reino vegetal*, Ediciones Omega, Barcelona 1983.

Scapino Michele, *Casa dolce casa*, Edizioni Horus, Turin 1993.

Scarano Rolando, *Processi di generazione della configurazione architettonica*, Fratelli Fiorentino, Naples 1988.

Schaller George B., *The Mountain Gorilla. Ecology and Behaviour*, University of Chicago Press, Chicago 1963.

Schama Simon, *Landscape and Memory*, A.A. Knopf, New York 1995.

Schelling Friedrich, *Le arti figurative e la natura*, Aesthetica Edizioni, Palermo 1989.

Scerrato Umberto, *Islam*, Mondadori, Milan 1973.

Schiefenhovel Wulf, Uher Johanna, Krell Renate, *Eibl-Eibesfeldt*, Verlag Langen Müller, Munich.

Schneider Marius, *Il significato della musica*, Rusconi, Milan 1970.

Schneider Marius, *Pietre che cantano. Studi sul ritmo di tre chiostri catalani di stile romanico*, Guanda, Milan 1980.

Schopenhauer Arthur, *Metafisica della natura*, Laterza, Rome-Bari 1993.

Scully Vincent, *Architecture: the Natural and the Man-made*, St. Martin's Press, New York 1991.

Scully Vincent, *The Earth, the Temple, and the Gods, Greek Sacred Architecture*, Yale University Press, New Haven-London 1962.

Schwaller de Lubicz R.A., *Le temple dans l'homme*, Imprimerie Schindler, Cairo 1949.

Schwenk Theodor, *Il caos sensibile*, Edizione Arcobaleno, Oriago di Mira 1992.

Sedlmayr Hans, *Perdita del centro*, Borla, Rome 1983.

Semper Gottfried, *Lo stile*, Laterza, Rome-Bari 1992.

Servier Jean, *L'uomo e l'invisibile*, Borla, Turin 1967.

Sheehy Terence J., *An Irish Moment*, John Hinde Product, Dublin 1989.

Sheldrake Rupert, *A New Science of Life*, Paladin Grafton Books, London 1987.

Sheldrake Rupert, *The Rebirth of Nature*, Bantham Books, New York 1991.

Sheldrake Rupert, *The Presence of the Past*, Harper Collins Publishers, Glasgow 1989.

Sica Paolo, *Storia dell'urbanistica. Il Settecento*, Laterza, Rome-Bari 1976.

Silvester Hans W., *Tauben*, Albert Müller Verlag, Rüschlikon-Zurich 1990.

Sinclair Kevin, *Cina dall'alto*, Giorgio Mondadori, Milan 1988.

Sinisgalli Rocco, *La prospettiva di Federico Commandino*, Edizioni Cadmo, Florence 1993.

Skutch Alexander F., *Origins of Nature's Beauty*, University of Texas Press, Austin 1992.

Slack Adrian, Gate Jane, *Carnivorous Plants*, Alphabooks, A & C Black, London 1988.

Slawson David A., *Secret Teachings in the Art of Japanese Gardens*, Kodansha International, Tokyo-New York 1991.

Small James, *A Textbook of Botany*, J. & A. Churchill Ltd., London 1937.

Smith Peter F., *Architecture and the Principle of Harmony*, Riba Publications Limited, London 1987.

Smith Peter F., *Architecture and the Human Dimension*, George Godwin Ltd., London 1979.

Snijders C.J., *La sezione aurea. Arte, natura, matematica, architettura e musica*, Muzzio, Padua 1993.

Spini Tito, Spini Sandro, *Togu Na. Casa della parola. Struttura di socializzazione della comunità Dogon*, Electa, Milan 1976.

Soldern von Schubert, *Stilisieren der Naturformen*, Verlag Art Institute Orell Füssll, Zurich-Leipzig 1989.

Soper Kate, *What is Nature?*, Blackwell Publishers, Oxford 1995.

Sordi Marta, *I cristiani e l'impero romano*, Jaca Book, Milan 1986.

Squicciarino Nicola, *Arte e ornamento in Gottfried Semper*, Il Cardo Editore, Venice 1994.

Starker Leopold A., *Il deserto*, Mondadori, Milan 1974.

Steadman Philip, *Arquitectura y naturaleza*, H. Blume Ediciones, Madrid 1982.

Steiner Rudolf, *L'edificio di Dornach*, Edizioni Arcobaleno, Oriago di Mira 1989.

Steiner Rudolf, *Verso un nuovo stile architettonico*, Editrice Antroposofica, Milan 1979.

Stevens Garry, *The Reasoning Architect. Mathematics and Science in Design*, McGraw-Hill, New York 1990.

Stevens Peter S., *Les formes dans la nature*, Editions du Seuil, Paris 1978.

Stewart Ian, Golubitsky Martin, *Fearful Symmetry. Is God a Geometer?*, Blackwell Publishers, Oxford 1992.

Stewart Ian, *Does God Play Dice?*, Penguin Books, London 1990.

Stewart R.J., *The Elements of Creation Mith*, Element, Rockport 1991.

Stierlin Henri, *The Cultural History of India*, Aurum Press Ltd., London 1983.

Strappa Giuseppe, *Unità dell'organismo architettonico*, Dedalo, Bari 1995.

Strasburger Eduard, *Trattato di botanica. Parte generale*, Antonio Delfino Editore, Rome 1991.

Strasburger Eduard, *Trattato di botanica. Parte sistematica*, Antonio Delfino Editore, Rome 1995.

Suagher Françoise, Parisot Jean-Paul, *Jeux de Lumière. Les phénomènes lumineux du ciel*, Éditions Cêtre, Besançon 1995.

Sullivan Louis H., *Autobiografia di un'idea e altri scritti di architettura*, Officina Edizioni, Rome 1970.

Sweeney James Johnson, Sert Josep Lluís, *Antoni Gaudí*, Verlag Gerd Hatje, Stuttgart 1960.

**T**

Tagliolini Alessandro, Venturi Ferriolo Massimo (eds.), *Il giardino. Idea natura realtà*, Guerini e Associati, Milan 1987.

Tagliolini Alessandro, *Storia del giardino italiano. Gli artisti, l'invenzione, le forme dall'antichità al XIX secolo*, GEF, Florence 1988.

Tanelli Giuseppe, *Conoscere i minerali*, Longanesi, Milan 1988.

Taut Bruno, *Frühlicht*, Der Zirkel Architekturverlag, Berlin 1920.

Teiwes Helga, Lindig Wolfgang, *Il mondo dei Navajo*, Jaca Book, Milan 1993.

Templer John, *The Staircase*, MIT Press, Cambridge (Mass.) 1992.

Theurillat Jacqueline, *Les mystères de Bomarzo et des jardins symboliques de la Renaissance. Le trois anneaux*, Geneva 1973.

Thiis-Evensen Thomas, *Archetypes in Architecture*, Norwegian University Press, Oslo 1987.

Thom René, *Structural Stability and Morphogenesis*, Addison-Wesley Publishing Company, Redwood City 1989.

Thomas Jacques, *La divine proportion & l'art de la géométrie. Etudes de symbolique chrétienne*, La Nef de Salomon et Archè Edidit, Dieulefit 1993.

Thompson D'Arcy W., *Crescita e forma*, Bollati Boringhieri, Turin 1992.

Thomsen Christian W., *Visionary Architecture. From Babylon to Virtual Reality*, Prestel-Verlag, Munich-New York 1994.

Tood Nancy Jack, Tood John, *Progettare secondo natura*, Elèuthera, Milan 1989.

Tornatore Giuseppe, *Gole e valli dell'Alcantara*, Kina Italia, Milan 1991.

Torroja Eduardo, *La concezione strutturale*, Città Studi Edizioni, Milan 1995.

Tosco Uberto, *Il mondo delle piante e degli animali*, Istituto Geografico De Agostini, Novara 1970.

Tuan Yi-Fu, *Topophilia. A Study of Environmental Perception, Attitudes, and Values*, Columbia University Press, New York 1990.

Tucci Giuseppe, *Teoria e pratica del Mandala*, Ubaldini Rome 1969.

Turri Eugenio, *L'Italia vista dal cielo*, Vallardi Industrie Grafiche, Lainate 1990.

Twohig Elizabeth Shee, *Irish Megalithic Tombs*, Shire Publications Ltd., Princes Risborough 1990.

Tzonis A., Lefaivre L., Bilodeau D., *Le classicisme en architecture. La poétique de l'ordre*, Dunod, Paris 1985.

**U**

Uher Johanna, Krell Renate, *Eibl-Eibesfeldt. Sein Schlüssel zur Verhaltensforschung*, Langen Müller, Munich 1993.

Uhlig Helmut, *I sumeri*, Garzanti, Milan 1981.

Uribe Diego, *Fractal Cuts*, Tarquin Publications, Norfolk 1993.

**V**

Valéry Paul, *Il mio Faust*, SE, Milan 1992.

Vandenbeld John, *Nature of Australia*, BBC Book, London 1988.

Vercelloni Virgilio, *Atlante storico dell'idea del giardino europeo*, Jaca Book, Milan 1990.

Verneuil M.P., *Etude de le plante. Son application aux industries d'art*, Librairie Centrale des Beaux-Arts, Paris, no date.

Virgilio, *Tutte le opere*, Sansoni, Florence 1989.

Vitruvio, *The Ten Books on Architecture*, Harvard University Press, Harvard (Mass.) 1914.

Volpicelli Ignazio, *A. Schopenhauer. La natura vivente e le sue forme*, Marzorati, Settimo Milanese 1988.

**W**

Wachsmann Konrad, *Una svolta nelle costruzioni*, Il Saggiatore, Milan 1960.

Wade David, *Crystal & Dragon. The Cosmic Two-Step*, Green Books, Ford House, Bideford 1991.

Waller Mary Désirée, *Chladni Figures. A Study in Symmetry*, G. Bell and Sons LTD., London 1961.

Washburn Dorothy K., Crowe Donald W., *Symmetries of Culture. Theory and Practice of Plane Pattern Analysis*, University of Washington Press, Seattle-London 1988.

Waterson Roxana, *The Living House. An Anthropology of Architecture in South-East Asia*, Oxford University Press, Singapore 1991.

Wechsler Judith, *L'estetica nella scienza*, Editori Riuniti, Rome 1982.

Wells David, *The Penguin Dictionary of Curious and Interesting Geometry*, Penguin Books, London 1991.

Wells Malcom, *Gentle Architecture*, McGraw-Hill, New York 1982.

Weston Richard, *Alvar Aalto*, Phaidon Press, 1995.

Westwood Jennifer (ed.), *Atlante dei luoghi misteriosi*, Istituto Geografico De Agostini, Novara 1988.

Whitfield Philip, *From so Simple a Beginning. The Book of Evolution*, Macmillan Publishing Company, New York 1993.

Whyte Lancelot Law (ed.), *Aspects of Form*, Indiana University Press, Bloomington 1961.

Wilkinson Richard H., *Symbol & Magic in Egyptian Art*, Thames and Hudson, London 1994.

514

Williams Robert, *The Geometrical Foundation of Natural Structure*, Dover Publications, New York 1979.

Wilson Edward O., *Le società degli insetti*, vols. I-II, Einaudi, Turin 1976 (*Insect Society*, Cambridge, Mass. 1971).

Wine Humphrey, *Claude. The Poetic Landscape*, National Gallery Publications, London 1994.

Wines James (ed.), *Site*, Verlag Gerd Hatje, Stuttgart 1989.

Wood Elizabeth A., *Crystals and Light*, Dover Publication, New York 1977.

Wright Frank Lloyd, *Testamento*, Einaudi, Turin 1963.

Wright Olgivanna Lloyd, *Frank Lloyd Wright. His Life. His Work. His Words*, Horizon Press, New York 1966.

## X

Xenakis Iannis, *Musica architettura*, Spirali Edizioni, Milan 1982.

## Y

Yates Frances A., *L'arte della memoria*, Einaudi, Turin 1972.

Yoshikawa Isao, *Elements of Japanese Gardens*, Toppan Printing Co., Tokyo 1990.

## Z

Zarlino M. Gioseffo, *Le Istitutioni Harmoniche*, Francesco Senefe, Venice 1562.

Zolla Elémire, *Archetipi*, Marsilio, Venice 1988.

**Periodicals**

*Architectural Design*, special issue "Tensile Structures", vol. 65 nos. 9/10, September-October 1995; *Bollettino della Biblioteca della Facoltà di Architettura dell'Università degli studi di Roma "La Sapienza"*, special issue "Cina: architettura e città", no. 52, Gangemi, 1995; *50 rue de Varenne*, special issue on the square and the city, December 1995; *Daidalos*, "Inventionen: Sonnen-Schaufel und Licht-Filter", no. 27, 1988; *Daidalos*, "Widewolke", no. 29, 1988; *Quaderni di Synaxis*, "La terra e l'uomo: l'ambiente e le scelte della ragione", Galatea Editrice, Catania 1992; *Rassegna*, special issue "I sensi del decoro", no. 41, March 1990; *Rassegna*, special issue "Turris babel", no. 16, December 1983; *Rivista di Estetica*, special issue on the ornament, December 1982.

# Index

# Index of Place Names

525